HEALTH POLICIES
AND
BLACK AMERICANS

Second Printing 1994

Copyright © 1989 by Transaction Publishers,
New Brunswick, New Jersey 08903.

Library of Congress Catalog Number: 88-8633
ISBN: 0-88738-249-5
Printed in the United States of America

Library of Congress Cataloging-in-Publication Data

Currents of health policy–impacts on Black Americans.
    Health policies and Black Americans.

    Has also been published as: The Milbank quarterly, v. 65, suppl. 1,
1987, with title: Currents of health policy–impacts on Black Americans.
    1. Afro-Americans–Health and hygiene.   2. Medical policy–United
States. I. Willis, David P. II. Title. [DNLM: 1. Blacks–United States. 2.
Health Policy–United States. WA 300 C976]
RA448.5N4C87 1988   362.1'08996073   88-8633
ISBN 0-88738-249-5

CONTENTS

Introduction

DAVID P. WILLIS

POLICIES ARE GENERALLY BASED UPON SOME NOR-
mative assumptions that have been shaped by perceptions of
how, why, when, and where people and their needs are distributed
around those norms. In a heterogeneous society, many of these assumptions are strained: policies based upon them will be imperfect,
at best, and may even entrench maldistributions. In a changing society,
this process is likely to be increasingly divisive.

These supplements are intended to examine the relation between
policy and the distribution of needs and effects in a general way.
None of the currents of policy is explored as a specific legislative
program.

This focus on the policy impacts on black Americans is meant to
serve two purposes. First, and with due regard for the caveats that
follow, this is a relatively identifiable subpopulation against which
the normative assumptions can be measured. Second, and with further
caveats, black Americans are often assumed to be the portion of the
population least benefited by past and current policies.

The politics of enumeration—who are counted, how they are categorized, and for what purposes—is an integral part of the recorded
history of all nations. Two hundred years ago, the new American
republic inscribed the process in Article I of its Constitution. Rep-
resentational apportionment in the House of Representatives was to
be based on "the whole Number of free Persons . . . [and] . . . three
fifths of all other Persons." The status of the white population, almost
all of European birth or ancestry, was unambiguously that of whole
persons. (Native American Indians were variably whole or nonexistent,
depending on whether they lived in the general population or on

I

reservations.) The relatively few free blacks, concentrated in the nonrural North, were whole persons. But without ambiguity, race was made to count—perversely, to "discount"—differently for more than 90 percent of America's black population.

Our purpose here is not to root out the injustices and contradictions inherent in this political (and, ineluctably, economic and social) apportionment of meaning and worth by race. Rather, it is to underscore that the way we classify people—and the ascriptive terms (they are rarely precisely descriptive) used to do so—most often reflects a specific set of purposes. As the purposes change, so do the classifications and the terminology.

The story of the rise of "ethnicity" in our cultural life and national record keeping postdates that of "race," and, indeed, has served different purposes. It is also a more nettlesome and plastic taxonomic construct. One need only consider the use of the term "Hispanic" to gauge the problems of definition. The still more recent term "minority" is equally troublesome and obfuscating for analytic purposes; for purposes of advocacy it may have its uses.

We have chosen to organize these supplements around race because, after sex and age, it has probably been the most consistently gathered and reliably reported involuntary attribute of variation measured within the American population. But even here, consistency and reliability over time, and accuracy at any point, must be accepted with great caution, even with a measure of skepticism.

Race, like any dichotomous variable, masks extraordinary heterogeneity and generates dysfunctional stereotypes, either negative or positive. Paradoxically, the last national census before Emancipation reported more race-specific variables pertinent (or presumed to be so) to blacks than did the census of 1980. Sex, age, residence, and other enumerated items were tabulated separately for free Negroes, mulattoes, and West Indians. Of course, some of the attributes ascribed to these classifications were patently wrong, and are more precisely captured by direct measurements today. Nevertheless, we still lack ways to summarize the heterogeneity of biology, ethnicity, and culture of race. The "black condition" is no more homogeneous than is the "white condition." But the distribution of persons along the *range* of conditions is likely to be different between the black and the white populations. Thus, comparison between the respective *medians*—or norms—will be misleading and often futile.

The decision to impose *black* over *Black* as the basic racial descriptor throughout was made by the editor, and is symmetrical with the use of *white*. Such usage has become common and standard in the scientific and scholarly literature. Several contributors demurred and argued forcefully for other choices. In the end, they graciously consented— in this instance—to allow the data and the analyses to make the points rather than risk the reader's distraction by variant capitalization.

These two supplements are organized into seven thematic sections: three in part 1 and four in part 2. Even while highlighting special aspects of *Currents of Health Policy: Impacts on Black Americans,* each section—indeed, each article—has elements in common with others. The ambiguity of race is pervasive, as is attention to heterogeneity. Many also caution about the limitations imposed by cross-sectional data as a guide to our understanding of change. There are, as well, the inevitable calls for more research and for better longitudinal data. These are balanced by counsel to improve our critical understanding and interpretation of the data we already have, upon which many public policies are now being based.

I. Who Are Black Americans?

This portrait of black Americans raises fundamental questions for any scheme of depiction: Who will be included? Is it to be a snapshot or a moving picture? How many dimensions will be included?

Reynolds Farley begins by suggesting that phenomena at any one time are best understood in relation to what has preceded them. Here, change is seen in light of the promise and the expectations of the mid-1960s, through a variety of indicators. William O'Hare focuses on other demographic measurements of portraiture, largely those of spatial distribution. Residential patterns, while themselves the product of other political, social, and economic phenomena, also effectively produce color-coded access to services and opportunities. Finally, Doris Wilkinson and Gary King raise profound and abiding questions about *any* racial portraiture: Just what is being portrayed, and for what purposes? Policy responses will differ according to whether the depiction is implicitly genetic or is an indicator of socioeconomic status. There are times (cf. Savage, McGee, and Osten on hypertension) when both may be involved, making the explication of meaning even more essential.

II. Mortality and Morbidity of Black Americans

The purposes of health policy—to address public and private resources to health needs in effective ways—are shaped, in large measure, by how we perceive need. This section elucidates some of the implications of using the grossest measurements of death and sickness.

Ronald Andersen and his coauthors begin with attention to the most fundamental methodological issues, especially as they relate to measuring sickness and wellness as a numerator. But the denominator—who we count—is cause for equal concern. Problems of sampling (cf. Gibson and Jackson) and observational bias (cf. Friedman et al.) can lead to profound distortions. Perhaps the most objective and uniform measure—albeit an imperfect one—of relative differential need is death. Douglas Ewbank's historical reconstruction of black mortality is importantly descriptive and suggestive. Public health improvements, such as clean water supplies, have been more colorblind in their impact than have specific medical care interventions. Kenneth Manton and his colleagues attempt to describe need through measuring excessive and premature deaths among black Americans. Whether the rates for whites are the best measure of progress and well-being for blacks is a contentious question (cf. Savage, McGee, and Osten; Baquet and Ringen; Miller) but reducing the preventable relative disadvantage of blacks is an attainable—but difficult—goal.

III. From Universal Entitlements to Employment-based Entitlements

Public health services in the United States are generally distributed across populations in an undifferentiated way, i.e., without regard for individual needs, preferences, and descriptive or ascriptive categories. Not so with personal health care services, to which individuals must seek access and for which providers seek payment. "Entitlement" describes the basis upon which access is granted and paid for. Traditionally, for some *classes* of people—e.g., Indians, veterans, presidents—entitlement was universal and publicly paid for. Medicare was widely regarded (expectantly by some, ruefully by others) as "a foot in the door" for a policy of universal entitlement for entire populaions. Today, a host of public decisions, even including provisions of the

Tax Reform Act of 1986, indicate a redirection of public policy. More and more do we look to the private employer as the guarantor of goods and services. In the past, employers in large national industries (those most likely to have strong trade union representation) provided the most generous benefits. As the overall economy shifts—the highest employment gains are in the less organized and lower-paying service sectors—this depth and breadth of insurance is likely to change. The impact of such structural change in employment opportunities will be most marked on the black labor force.

Stephen Long's synoptic review of employment-related insurance for health care services codifies the results of these trends. Measured by the increase in number of the uninsured, current policies are highly imperfect. For complex reasons, employment-related insurance, even if mandated, cannot singularly correct deeper problems in the structure of employment or social arrangements.

Karen Davis and her coauthors critically examine the complementary role of public insurance and service programs. They attribute to these procedures much of the absolute and relative health gains made by black Americans. Public programs, carrying public sanctions, have effectively lowered racial as well as economic barriers (cf. Schlesinger). Even though politically vulnerable, these programs are essential—a safety net for some, a foundation for others.

IV. Implications of Selected Policy Directions

American approaches to national health policy are only infrequently and inconsistently characterized by the usual political "isms." Pluralism, incrementalism, and a certain pragmatism do constrain the often ambiguous *processes* of reaching goals, but they do not describe the *content* of the end result very precisely. (The World Health Organization's "Primary Care for All by the Year 2000," specific of goal, but devoid of process, is non-American.) One process-cum-direction of current health policies is "making the system more efficient"—i.e., reducing expenditures for ineffective use of services by constraining their supply and raising their price. Three separate and independent policy clusters moving in this direction are reviewed in the five articles in this section. Each is seen to have special implications for black Americans.

Ruth Hanft and Catherine White examine a set of responses to the presumed "surplus" of physicians, the putative agents of excessive use and explosive costs. Retrenchment in federal support to medical education has particularly disadvantaged young black aspirants to medical practice. The promise of relieving a physician *shortage* in major areas will be negated (cf. Schlesinger; Davis et al.). Mark Schlesinger reviews the widening promulgation of the ethos and and economics of competition in the health care system. In both publicly and privately funded markets, institutional responsiveness to local community needs will be diminished. The least advantaged—disproportionately black—will be at greatest risk.

The next three articles examine a parallel but older set of issues only recently revived under an economic/efficiency rubric. These deal with "prevention," i.e., earlier case-finding and more efficient intervention.

Daniel Savage and colleagues note that a uniform national approach to hypertension control has had marked success, especially among blacks. In examining the program's sociocultural adaptations and community acceptance that promoted this achievement, the authors caution that more biologically strategic targeting for blacks may be needed to sustain progress in the future. Claudia Baquet and Knut Ringen, on the other hand, find that approaches to control of cervical cancer disproportionately have benefited white women. Differences in racial biology cannot account for the discrepancy that the authors attribute to mutually dysfunctional behaviors between providers and black women. Harold Neighbors takes a less clinical and more social-structural view of preventing psychological malfunctioning and distress. Strategies will have to begin earlier, last longer, and be invoked at more critical points if mental health is to become a positive enablement, as well as an end in itself.

V. Groups at Special Risk

Although the United States has no coherent and cohesive policy directed to or covering most groups per se, special group interests and needs are not entirely neglected. Sometimes, as with adolescents, the attention is directed to localized and miniscule efforts to cope with the unintended fallout from the disarray of more massive policies and programs. In the case of workers in high-risk jobs, the seeming consensus among policies and agencies of 15 years ago now appears as a conflict of competing rights. Once again, the least advantaged are the most vulnerable. In contrast, the "aged" were singled out by a policy for the most comprehensive universal health insurance, but essentially without differentiation by needs or resources of members of the group.

Frank Furstenberg, Jr. carefully analyzes how teenage sexuality has been cloaked in myth and misperception, thereby stigmatizing a group and obscuring the real problems. Without a more penetrating understanding of the cross-sectoral nature of the issues—education, employment, welfare—limited health policies are not likely to have an impact. James Robinson notes both cross-sectoral and intra-sectoral shortfalls in the *implementation* of policies that need not be in conflict. Racial equity in employment opportunities can be achieved along with increased safety in all jobs. Rose Gibson and James Jackson discuss the black elderly, the beneficiaries of a universal policy based on assumptions of a "normal" and linear process of aging. They find it impossible to isolate a "norm" in the heterogeneity of functional status and need; indeed, key measures may indicate that the aging process among blacks occurs in different ways and at different points in the life cycle. In common with others (cf. O'Hare; Neighbors; Furstenberg, Jr.), Gibson and Jackson call attention to the need to incorporate cohort effects in future projections. Black elderly of the next few generations may be increasingly middle class, but still larger numbers will have fewer traditional family supports and a lifetime of greater poverty.

VI. Racial Dimensions of AIDS: Attitudes and Policies

If policy is broadly construed as the product of a political and administrative consensus at an effective operational level, then nowhere in the nation do we find an AIDS policy. The course of the epidemic reveals how rigid attitudinizing—both within and without the communities at risk—may deflect attention from policies needed to protect the public.

Samuel Friedman and his nine coauthors find it helpful to reveal their own racial and ethnic diversity as they deal with the disproportionate toll of AIDS among blacks and Hispanics. In their agglutinative approach to the cultural variables surrounding various modes of transmission, they elucidate the cultural constraints to effective action within each "community at risk." Myths and stereotypes impede rational policy making at all levels.

VII. Conclusion

Health policy—as a whole and in its parts—is ultimately a part of broader public policy. S. M. Miller, in summarizing the evidence of preceding articles, argues that differentials in health mirror differentials in other dimensions of life. Traditional frameworks of analysis of need and approaches to entitlement may not serve well in the future if they are perceived as opposing equity against efficiency. The national interest compels attention to both.

Acknowledgments: More people were helpful in preparing these supplements—through advice, counsel, and precept—than can be properly acknowledged. Because their names are not otherwise recorded, I wish especially to thank Thomas Chapman, Robert Hill, Jacquelyn Jackson, Tom Joe, William Petersen, Frances Fox Piven, Sara Rosenbaum, Eric Springer, and Robin Williams. They are absolved from my personal failure to follow their lead.

The Quality of Life for Black Americans Twenty Years after the Civil Rights Revolution

REYNOLDS FARLEY

RECENT RAND CORPORATION REPORT CONCERNING racial differences generated a new controversy about the status of blacks. The authors, James Smith and Finis Welch, focused on men who worked at least one-half time during the year before the censuses of 1940 to 1980, and concluded that the economic position of blacks improved greatly because racial differences in earnings declined drastically. Indeed, black wages as a percentage of white increased from 44 percent in 1940 to 73 percent in 1980 (Smith and Welch 1986).

Arguing that the report gave an erroneously optimistic picture of progress, civil rights organizations and other analysts noted that for more than a decade there has been little reduction in the poverty rate among blacks, that the ratio of black to white median family income has stagnated, and that, since the mid-1950s, the unemployment rate of blacks has been double that of whites (Jacob 1986; Swinton 1986). Despite substantial increases in federal funding, the infant death rate of blacks remains double that of whites, and the life span of blacks in the 1980s is about seven years shorter than that of whites. In the words of Senator Moynihan, "The decade of the 1970s was the first in which, as a group, black Americans, with respect to white Americans, were better off at the beginning than at the end" (Moynihan 1986).

This controversy reflects the problems that arise when analysts measure racial progress. We have an extensive statistical system that generates hundreds of indicators of the health and economic status of blacks. Improved statistical models help us assess the net effects of race on vital rates, earnings, occupational achievement, and poverty. In addition to indexes from the federal agencies, there are measures of the attitudes of blacks such as their beliefs about racial change, their feelings of alienation, and their perceptions of white support for or opposition to equal opportunity programs (Schuman, Steeh, and Bobo 1985).

There is, however, no consensus about which are the most important measures or how different indicators should be weighted to reach a judgment about whether racial gaps are narrowing or growing larger. This dilemma comes about because there are two fundamentally different models of this nation's social structure.

America as a Melting Pot

Many social science theories and empirical investigations stress the assimilation process that incorporated Europeans, Asians, and Latin-American immigrants. Presumably these groups entered the United States in an impoverished status, were concentrated in urban slums, and were the targets of discrimination. In the course of several generations, they took advantage of opportunities—especially educational opportunities—and prospered.

An elaboration of this model stresses that blacks were once singled out for unusually harsh treatment but places greater weight upon the removal of those barriers that formerly excluded them from white society. Court decisions in the post-World War II era, encompassing civil rights laws, and the sustained growth of the economy permitted blacks to compete equitably. Advocates of this model will point to those many measures that show rapid declines in black-white differences.

America as a Polarized Society

A different model sees this country as riven by racial, ethnic, and economic class issues. Gains for any one group are made at the expense of another. Powerful groups seek to retain their economic advantage and pass it on to their offspring. Hostility and discrimination have been useful for this purpose and the nation has a history both of legislation which favors one group over another and of conflicts over who controls jobs and neighborhoods.

From the earliest days of the colonial era, common customs and laws mandated special treatment for blacks because of their supposed racial inferiority and their unique economic niche. Advocates of this model doubt that great change occurred after World War II and are skeptical about the removal of those barriers that kept blacks out of the economic mainstream. They emphasize indicators which show little racial change.

Under either or both models, blacks have clearly not fared as well as other ethnic groups. The controversy over the degree of black progress is largely due to the fact that it is impossible to gauge the status of blacks by examining just one indicator, even such an important measure as the life span or the earnings of men. To understand the extent of racial change, it is necessary to analyze the aims, accomplishments, and failures of the civil rights movement. Its aims include equity in health care, housing, educational opportunities, employment, and citizenship rights.

Voting Rights and Equal Access to Public Places

Racial barriers have been effectively removed in two important areas by civil rights legislation of the 1960s: voting rights and equal access to public accommodations. The Fourteenth and Fifteenth Amendments seemingly guaranteed blacks their voting privileges, but for a seven-decade span these rights were denied in southern states. The Voting Rights Act of 1965 as designed to ensure blacks the opportunity to influence the electoral process in the same manner as whites. Since the early 1960s, the proportion of southern blacks casting ballots has increased sharply (U. S. Bureau of the Census 1985a, table A). Differences in voting remain large, even after the effects of factors influencing turnout such as education and place of residence are taken into account (Abramson and Claggett 1986, 418), but no one contends that this results primarily from the systematic abridgements of voting rights.

Although outlawed by the Civil Rights Act of 1875, racial segregation in public transportation, parks, and most other public places was called for by Jim Crow laws in southern states, and in the North by common customs and policies of local governments. Sit-ins, protests, marches, and strikes designed to end this segregation led to enactment of Title II of the Civil Rights Act of 1964 which proscribed such racial practices (McAdam 1982; Morris 1984). Although a few cases arise each year where a black is denied service in a restaurant, a hotel, or a barber shop, the blatantly discriminatory policies of the Jim Crow era have ended. By the late 1960s, blacks in all regions could use the same public accommodations as whites.

Residential Segregation and the Quality of Housing for Blacks

In most metropolitan areas, de facto racial segregation persisted long after the laws were changed. As a result, shopping areas, parks, hospitals, restaurants, and transit lines are thoroughly coded by color. This racial residential segregation is a development of the late nineteenth and early twentieth centuries (Taeuber and Taeuber 1965, chap. 3; Spear 1967, chaps. 1 and 2). When blacks first came to live in cities in large numbers, municipal authorities passed laws to guarantee that whites would not live next to blacks. Courts overturned such ordinances on the grounds that they infringed upon property rights, but private practices, such as restrictive covenants and government policies, segregated blacks from whites (Vose 1967, chap. 1). Supreme Court decisions and local open-housing ordinances supported the right of blacks to live where they could afford, but the major change was the Fair Housing Act of 1968, which outlawed racial discrimination in the sale or rental of most housing units.

Its proponents believed that this law would reduce the traditional geographic isolation of blacks in American metropolises. Although there were some declines in residential isolation, the separation of blacks from whites did not end in the 1970s (Taeuber 1983; Logan and Schneider 1984). In areas that have large black populations, there are many central city neighborhoods and a few suburban neighborhoods that are either all-black or well along to becoming exclusively black enclaves; most other neighborhoods have no more than token black populations. Studies of residential patterns in 1980 reveal that blacks are very different from other minority or ethnic groups in this respect. In particular, they are much more residentially segregated from whites than are two more newly arrived groups: Asians and Hispanics (Langberg and Farley 1985, 75).

Other studies demonstrate that not only poor blacks but blacks at *all* economic statuses are highly segregated from whites of the identical economic level (Taeuber 1968; Massey 1979, 1015; Farley and Allen 1987, table 5.10). It is apparent that the Fair Housing Act of 1968 produced much less change in the status of black Americans than did the Voting Rights Act of 1965. In the nation's large metropolitan areas, blacks are still as residentially segregated from whites as they were four decades ago.

A major effort of civil rights organizations has been the upgrading of housing quality for blacks. In the recent past, many blacks lived in dilapidated rural housing or in urban slums, often units that lacked the basic plumbing and kitchen facilities we take for granted; for example, almost one-half of the housing units occupied by blacks in 1950 lacked an indoor flush toilet (U. S. Bureau of the Census 1950a, table 8). The movement of blacks to cities, urban renewal projects of the 1950s and 1960s, new federal housing programs, and improvements in the economic status of blacks led to great changes in the quality of housing. By 1980, only 6 percent of the homes and apartments occupied by blacks lacked complete plumbing facilities (U. S. Bureau of the Census, 1980, table 84). Unlike the modest changes in residential segregation, racial differences in housing quality have been greatly reduced.

Educational Attainment

Throughout this century, civil rights leaders have continued their efforts to bring about equal educational opportunities (Kluger 1976). One set of efforts sought equal facilities for black students and equal pay for black teachers. Another sought racial parity in amounts of education. Finally, a major aim of the civil rights movement was the actual integration of public schools, an achievement which would seem to guarantee that black and white children receive identical educations. In terms of measurable aspects of school facilities such as age of the building, presence of libraries or laboratories, extracurricular activities, degrees of teachers and their salaries, changes occurred in the post-World War II era and black students approached parity with whites in the 1960s (Coleman, Kelly, and Moore 1966, section 2.0).

There is no evidence that black children now attend public schools that are less-well-equipped or have less-well-paid teachers than white children in the same area.

In addition, we are nearing a time when the years of schooling completed by blacks and whites will be the same. Figure 1 shows the average years completed by black and white men and women when they reached ages 25 to 29. In 1940, young blacks averaged about three fewer years of attainment than whites. By the 1970s, racial differences in enrollment rates through the teen years were eliminated and, despite claims to the contrary, the long-term trends suggest a racial convergence in college enrollment (U. S. Bureau of the Census, 1981a, table A-1). We have not yet reached educational parity but, unless there is a reversal of established trends, young blacks and whites will differ little in the number of years they attend school.

Racial differences in scores on tests of intellectual skills and learning, however, have been large. For twenty years, innovative programs such as Head Start sought to improve the educational achievements of children and reduce racial differences. The National Assessment of Educational Progress, which measures the skills of national samples of students, found that there were modest declines in black-white differences on tests of reading, writing, mathematics, science, and social studies (Burton and Jones 1982; Grant and Snyder 1983, tables 15–19). Although differences remain large, the 1970s were years in which there was some convergence, not only of the enrollment rates of blacks and whites, but also of their test scores.

The goal of racial integration in the schools, which many think is essential if we are to achieve equal educational outcomes, is not being reached. In small and medium-sized cities throughout the country, public schools are generally integrated. The gains in the South have been impressive largely because federal courts in that region ordered a thorough mixing of students and teachers (Orfield 1983, chap. 1). The situation in the largest metropolitan areas is very different. Thirty years ago schools in southern cities were segregated because of state laws and in the North, because of residential segregation. School districts, however, enrolled both blacks and whites so integration could be accomplished by transferring students within the districts. Today, public schools are segregated primarily because blacks and whites live in separate districts; in most large central cities, the public

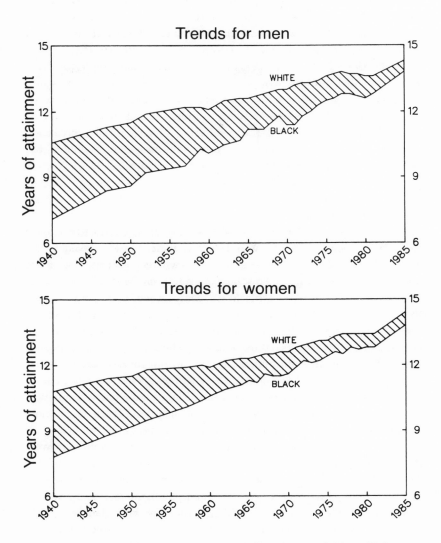

FIG. 1.   Average educational attainment of persons aged 25 to 29 by race and sex, 1940 to 1985.

schools enroll few whites but many blacks and Hispanics. In 1980, three-quarters of the nation's public school students were non-Hispanic whites (U. S. Bureau of the Census 1981b, table 6), but in Washington, D.C., only 4 percent were non-Hispanic whites; in Atlanta, 8 percent; in New Orleans, Detroit, and San Antonio, 12 percent (Orfield 1983, chap. 1). Only 3 of the 25 largest central city school districts had a majority white enrollment in 1980. Within these metropolises, white students are in the suburban ring or attend private or parochial schools. Unless policies that separate city and suburban students into different school districts are altered, the persistence of residential segregation will combine with demographic trends to produce public schools that are almost as segregated as those permitted before 1954.

Trends in Employment, Occupations, and Earnings

We would expect that racial differences on economic indicators would contract in the post-World War II years. First, blacks moved to the North where wage rates were higher and where, perhaps, they faced less prejudice. Second, the educational attainment of blacks increased, presumably allowing more blacks to compete for good jobs. Third, the activities of civil rights groups and changing employer attitudes opened opportunities for blacks. Finally, the 1965 law banned discrimination in all aspects of employment. The actual trends are mixed, with clear gains on some indicators but no improvements on others.

Unemployment and Labor Force Participation. The monthly unemployment rate—that is, the percentage of labor force participants who look for work but cannot find it—is the most widely cited gauge of economic status (U. S. Bureau of Labor Statistics 1976, chap. 1). This rate, of course, varies inversely with the rate of economic growth. Among adult black men, it fell to a low of 3 percent during the late 1960s and reached a post-Depression high of 13 percent at the start of the 1980s. Thirty years ago, the unemployment rate of black men first attained a level twice that of white men and there has been little change in that ratio since then (Killingsworth 1968, table 1; Levitan, Johnson, and Taggart 1975, fig. 3–3; Farley 1984, fig. 2.4). The upper panel of figure 2 shows the proportion of male labor force participants aged 25 to 54 who were unemployed. We see that the unemployment rates of blacks and whites have moved in a parallel manner, implying that the racial difference has not diminished.

TABLE 1

Percentage Unemployed in 1985, Percentage Who Did Not Work in 1984, and Percentage out of Labor Force in 1985, for Black and White Men Classified by Age, Place of Residence, and Educational Attainment.

Classification	Percentage unemployed in March 1985		Percentage out of labor force in 1985		Percentage who did not work in 1984	
	Black	White	Black	White	Black	White
Age						
15–24	32%	13%	47%	33%	49%	24%
25–34	15	6	14	5	18	6
35–44	13	5	13	5	17	6
45–54	10	5	16	8	17	9
55–64	10	4	46	31	41	25
65+	9	4	85	83	81	78
Place of residence (men 15 and older)						
*North and West**						
City of large SMSA	21	8	40	31	40	29
Suburbs of large SMSA	15	6	36	23	33	19
Other SMSA	20	8	38	25	39	21
Non-metropolitan	19	9	38	28	45	22
*South**						
City of large SMSA	8	6	33	23	35	21
Suburbs of large SMSA	14	3	20	22	19	18
Other SMSA	14	5	32	26	32	23
Non-metropolitan	16	6	38	30	33	26

1960 (Mare and Winship 1984, 49; Levitan, Johnson, and Taggart 1975, fig. 3.3; Murray 1984, fig. 5.4; Cave 1985). Whites are now much more likely than blacks to hold jobs while they attend school or when they move from the completion of high school into their twenties.

Among both races, there has been a steady rise in the employment of women. The recent increases, however, have been greater for whites. Traditionally, a higher proportion of black than white women held jobs but, by the early 1980s, white women caught up with and then surpassed black women in terms of employment (Bianchi and Spain 1986, chap. 5; U. S. Bureau of Labor Statistics 1985, table 8).

Occupational Achievement.   Unlike the indicators of employment itself, there is unambiguous evidence that the occupational distribution of employed blacks has been upgraded and is gradually becoming similar to that of whites. At the end of World War II, blacks were concentrated in a narrow range of unskilled occupations: 69 percent of the black men in 1950 worked on farms or as laborers or machine operators; 50 percent of black women were domestic servants or farm laborers (U. S. Bureau of the Census 1950b, table 9). As blacks moved into cities and their educational attainments rose, they obtained better jobs.

Figure 3 indicates this by showing the proportion of employed workers who held professional or managerial jobs from 1950 to 1982. The occupational distribution of whites improved as the focus of the economy shifted from blue collar jobs to white collar and service jobs. The changes, however, were greater among blacks. The percentage of white men, for example, with these jobs at the top of the occupational ladder went up from 20 to 32 percent; for black men, from 6 to 20 percent.

Numerous investigators analyzed racial differences across the entire occupational distribution, and their findings demonstrate that employed blacks moved into better jobs more rapidly than whites and that upgrading continued throughout the 1970s and into the 1980s (Beller 1984; Freeman 1976). Studies of occupational mobility also report a declining net effect of race, suggesting that the process is becoming more egalitarian (Hout 1984; Featherman and Hauser 1976, 1978, chap. 6). Nevertheless, large occupational differences remain. In 1982 the proportion of black men with professional or managerial jobs was equal to what it was among white men three decades earlier. Among

The lower panel of figure 2 reports the proportion of adult black and white men, aged 25 to 54, who were neither at work nor looking for a job—that is, they were not participating in the labor force. At these ages, only a small fraction are out of the labor force because they are full-time students or retirees. Among black men, there has been a persistent rise in nonparticipation since 1960, a trend that was hardly influenced by year-to-year changes in economic conditions. By the early 1980s, 1 black man out of 8 had dropped out of the labor force; among whites, about 1 in 20.

Some explanations for this phenomenon contend that many black men lack the skills to be employed or have personal habits and criminal records which make them unacceptable to employers (Anderson 1979, 1985). Others believe that the expansion of federal welfare programs offers attractive alternatives to men who have limited earnings potential (Anderson 1978, p. 47; Gilder 1981, chap. 11; Murray 1984, chap. 5). Another view stresses that blacks are concentrated within cities while the growth of employment is occurring in suburbs, often in areas far from central city ghettoes (Kain 1968). There is no single convincing explanation for the sharp increase in the proportion of black men who are neither working nor looking for employment. High unemployment rates and low rates of labor force participation are not restricted to young black men, to those in central cities, or to those who dropped out of school. Table 1, based upon data from the Census Bureau's (March 1985) Current Population Survey, classifies men by age, residence, and attainment, and it indicates the unemployment rate, the proportion out of the labor force, and the proportion of men who did not work at all in 1984. For almost all groups—including those in the suburbs and those with five years of college—the unemployment rate for blacks was double that of comparable white men, and the proportion who were out of the labor force or who did not work during 1984 was much higher.

When age groups other than 25 to 54 are considered, we find some trends that are similar and others that are different. Among those aged over 54, labor force participation has declined because of improved Social Security benefits, better private pensions, and the greater availability of Supplemental Security Income. At the other end of the age scale, there has been an increase in the employment of white youths but not of black. Indeed, all indicators report that the employment situation of young blacks vis-à-vis that of whites has deteriorated since

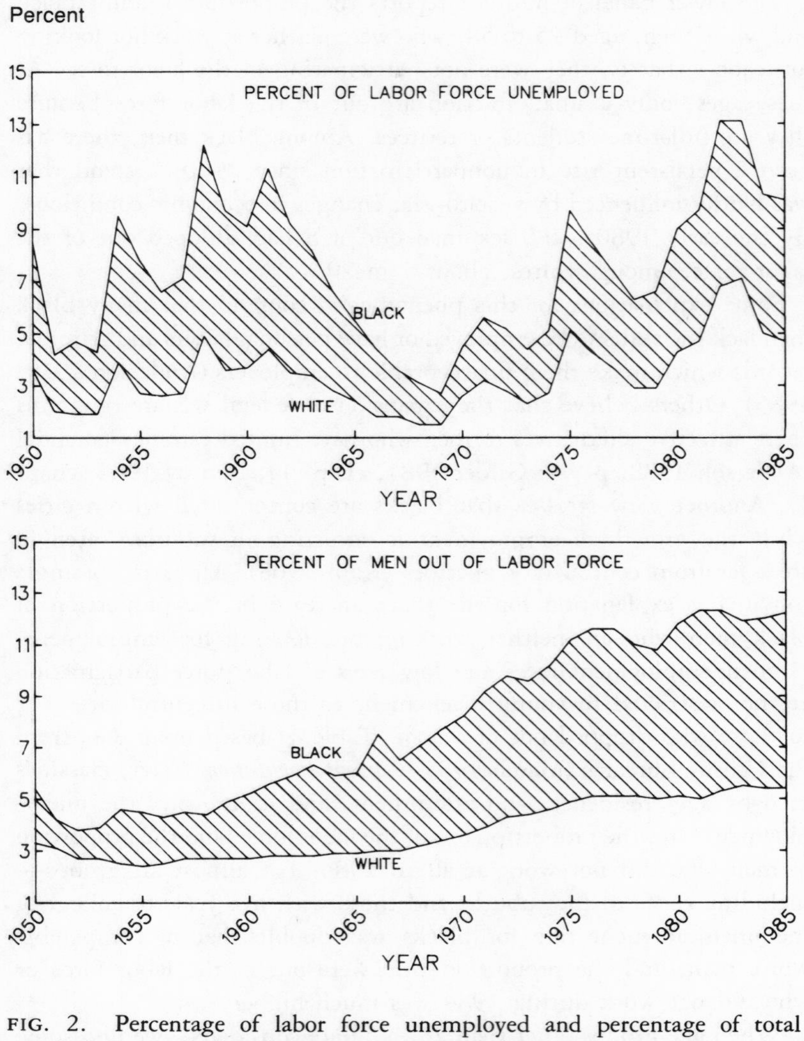

Percent

FIG. 2.   Percentage of labor force unemployed and percentage of total population out of labor force for men 25 to 54, 1950 to 1985.*

*These data are the annual averages which are developed from the monthly estimates. They have been standardized for age to remove the confounding effects of changes in age structure. Data refer to whites and nonwhites in all years.

Sources: U.S. Bureau of Labor Statistics, *Handbook of Labor Statistics: 1978,* Bulletin 2000 (January, 1979), table 4; *Handbook of Labor Statistics,* Bulletin 2217 (June, 1985), table 5; *Labor Force Statistics Derived from the Current Population Survey: A Databook* (September, 1982), Vol. 2, table B-8; *Employment and Earnings,* Vol. 32, No. 1 (January, 1985), tables 3 and 4; Vol. 33, No. 1 (January, 1986), tables 3 and 4.

Educational attainment
(men 25 and older)

Elementary	14	10	59	55	58	53
High School, 1–3	16	10	30	32	31	31
High School, 4	14	6	18	19	20	18
College, 1–3	11	4	13	15	17	14
College, 4	8	3	10	11	13	11
College, 5+	5	2	18	11	13	10

* These data pertain to the ten largest metropolises in each region. Central cities are distinguished from suburban rings.
Source: U.S. Bureau of the Census, *Current Population Survey*, March, 1985 (Tape File).

Percent

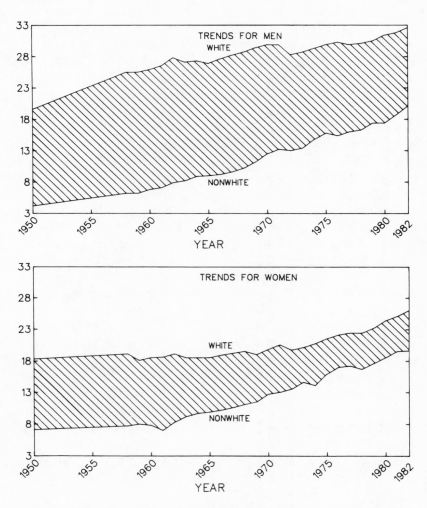

FIG. 3.   Percentage of employed workers holding professional or managerial jobs by race and sex, 1950 to 1982.*

*The time series reported in this figure cannot be extended to more recent dates because a new system for classifying occupations was introduced in the Census of 1980 and Current Population Survey in 1983 and the new occupational categories are not comparable to the old.
Sources: U.S. Bureau of the Census, *Census of Population: 1950,* P-C1, table 128; U.S. Bureau of Labor Statistics, *Handbook of Labor Statistics: 1978* (June, 1979), table 18; *Employment and Earnings,* Vol. 26, No. 1; Vol. 27, No. 1; Vol. 28, No. 1; Vol. 29, No. 1; Vol. 30, No. 1, table 22 in each publication.

women, the corresponding lag was two decades. Several more decades will be required before the occupational distributions of employed blacks and whites are similar.

Earnings of Employed Workers. Findings from many studies show that blacks once earned much less than similar whites, but this racial difference has declined among men and has just about disappeared among women (Smith and Welch 1977, 1986; Hirschman and Wong 1984, 584; Datcher 1980). This is often accepted as evidence that racial discrimination in pay rates has been substantially reduced, and perhaps even eliminated among women.

The decennial enumerations and the Census Bureau's March surveys ask national samples about their earnings, hours of employment, and educational attainment. These data may be used to fit models that relate the wages of workers to those factors that influence earnings. The analysis reported here is based upon data from the census of 1960 and surveys conducted in March of 1970, 1980, and 1985. All non-institutionalized persons aged 25 to 64 who reported cash earnings during the previous year were included.

Trends in the relative earnings of blacks are described in table 2 which shows the average *hourly* and *annual earnings* of blacks as a percentage of those of whites. Then, using a model which sees hourly earnings as a function of education, place of residence, and years elapsed since completion of school—i.e., years of potential labor market experience—estimates were derived for blacks and whites with specific characteristics such as college education or southern residence.

In 1960 black men had 61 percent of the hourly earnings of white men, and in the next two decades this increased to 74 percent. Black men—on an annual basis—do less well because they experience much more unemployment. Nevertheless, the annual earnings of black men, as a percentage of those of whites, increased from 52 percent in 1960 to 66 percent in 1980.

When men are classified by region, education, and years of experience, we find that racial differences in relative earnings were much smaller in the North than in the South. Racial differences, however, varied little by educational level or by years of experience. Regardless of how long they spent in school, black men earned about 60 percent as much as white men in 1960; 75 percent as much in 1980.

The 1960s and 1970s were decades of improvements in the relative earnings of black men, but there has been stagnation in the 1980s.

TABLE 2
Earnings of Employed Blacks as a Percentage of Those of Whites, Persons
25 to 64, 1960 to 1985 (amounts shown in 1984 dollars)*

Earnings and Classification	1960	1970	1980	1985
Hourly earnings of men	61%	68%	74%	74%
Annual earnings of men	52	59	66	65
Annual earnings for men with specific characteristics				
Place of residence				
North and West	67	68	71	66
South	48	56	64	65
Educational attainment				
9 Years	60	68	73	69
12 Years	57	63	74	70
16 Years	60	60	78	76
Years of labor force experience				
5 Years	54	61	73	68
15 Years	53	59	65	66
25 Years	53	58	62	62
35 Years	53	57	64	66
Hourly earnings of women	61%	75%	98%	101%
Annual earnings of women	55	74	103	107
Annual earnings for women with specific characteristics				
Place of residence				
North and West	72	88	113	117
South	59	67	98	103
Educational attainment				
9 Years	74	76	106	111
12 Years	74	98	107	111
16 Years	97	103	117	118
Years of labor force experience				
5 Years	54	87	101	98
15 Years	56	91	104	106
25 Years	56	71	104	111
35 Years	54	69	102	113

* Based on data for persons who reported that their race was black or white and
that they worked in the year prior to the census or survey and had wage, salary, or
self-employment earnings of $1 or more. This model uses the log of the hourly wage
rate as its dependent variable, regressed upon years of elementary and secondary
education, years of college education, years elapsed since estimated completion of
schooling, the square of that variable, and a dichotomous variable indicating southern
residence.
Source: U.S. Bureau of the Census, *Census of Population and Housing: 1960,* Public
Use Sample (Tape File); *Current Population Survey,* March 1970, March 1980, and
March 1985, Public Use Samples (Tape Files).

An examination of annual data shows that the earnings of blacks rose more rapidly than those of whites until the recession of 1973-1975. Following that, the earnings of men—in constant dollars—generally fell, with the rates of decline being similar for both races. That recession marked a turning point, since there has been no racial convergence of the earnings of black and white men in the last decade.

The racial gap in earnings closed much more rapidly among women. In 1960 black women had 61 percent of the hourly earnings of white women but this increased to 98 percent by 1980 and in 1985 the hourly earnings of black women exceeded those of whites. In the past, employed black women worked fewer hours than white women. Black women now report greater hours of employment and, as a result, the average annual earnings of black women are in excess of those of white women.

When the earnings of women with specific characteristics are compared, we see that black women in 1960—with the exception of college graduates—were far behind white women. By 1980 there was racial parity and, unlike the situation among men, the earnings of black women, relative to those of whites, continued to rise in the 1980s.

Trends in the earnings of employed workers provide clear evidence of racial progress. The investigation of Smith and Welch (1986) also shows that differences among men also declined in the 1940 to 1960 era. By 1980, black men—on an annual basis—earned about two-thirds as much as white men. When differences in education, residence, experience, and hours of work were taken into account, they earned about 85 percent as much (Hirschman and Wong 1984, tables 2 and 3; Farley 1984, fig. 3.5). Black women showed even greater improvements and by 1980 they earned as much as comparable white women.

Family Income and Poverty. Two indicators that are frequently cited as more descriptive measures of economic welfare are the ratio of black to white family income and the percentage of blacks below the poverty line. Since the earnings of blacks have risen more rapidly than those of whites, we might expect an improvement for blacks on these indicators. The actual trends are mixed and have been confounded by changes in family structure (Bianchi 1981).

Figure 4 records the median income of black families as a percentage of that of whites and the proportion of blacks and whites below the

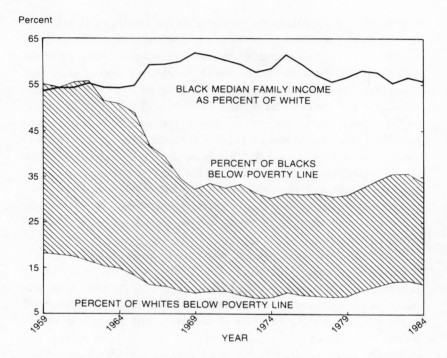

FIG. 4. Median income of black families as a percentage of that of whites and percentage of blacks and whites below the poverty line, 1959 to 1984.*

*Family income data for years prior to 1967 refer to whites and nonwhites. Poverty data for blacks for the years 1960 to 1966 are estimates.
Sources: U.S. Bureau of the Census, *Current Population Reports,* Series P-60, No. 146, table 15; No. 147, table 1; No. 149, tables 3 and 15.

poverty line since 1959, the first year for which the Census Bureau compiled such data. Throughout the 1960s, the incomes of black families rose more rapidly than those of whites so the black median as a percentage of white increased from 54 to 60 percent. The proportion of impoverished blacks fell sharply in the 1960s, reaching a minimum of 30 percent in the early 1970s. The continued urbanization of blacks and increases in earnings help account for the progress of that period.

Since the early 1970s, however, blacks have made no gains on these indicators. The proportion impoverished actually increased and the ratio of black to white family income declined. The fact that the earnings of black males are no longer rising faster than those of whites and that there is no longer a migration from southern farms to cities plays a role, but changes in family structure are also important.

At all dates, poverty rates have been high and income levels low in families headed by women. In 1984, for example, 52 percent of the black families with a woman as head of household were below the poverty line, compared to 15 percent of the black married-couple families (U. S. Bureau of the Census 1985b, tables 1 and 15). While similar trends are occurring in white families, there has been a sharper increase in the proportion of blacks living in these female-maintained families which have high poverty rates.

Table 3 summarizes changes in family living arrangements. Because of delays in age at first marriage and the increasing frequency of marital disruption, the proportion of adult women who live with husbands has fallen and by 1984 fewer than 30 percent of black women aged 15 to 44 lived with a spouse (U. S. Bureau of the Census, 1984a, table 1). Women have delayed their childbearing much less than the timing of their marriage so there has been a sharp increase in the percentage of births occurring to unmarried women. By 1983 about 6 in 10 black children and 1 in 8 white were delivered to unmarried women (U. S. National Center for Health Statistics 1985, table 17).

Delays in marriage, more frequent marital disruption, and more childbearing prior to marriage mean that a growing proportion of families with children are maintained by women who have no husband present (see table 3). As a corollary of these changes, the majority of black children under the age of 18 now live in families headed by a woman rather than by a married couple. Two-thirds of these children were in impoverished families (U. S. Bureau of the Census 1985b, tables 1 and 15).

Table 3 records that although family structure is changing among whites, blacks and whites have become increasingly different on all these indicators since 1960. These changes are certainly not the single cause and, perhaps, not the major cause of the persistently high poverty rate among blacks; they are, however, a significant factor. If all blacks and whites lived in husband-wife families, blacks would still have high poverty rates, but they would have twice, rather than three times the poverty rates of whites. The median income of black families would be about 80 percent that of white families rather than the

TABLE 3
Indicators of Racial Differences in Marital and Family Status, 1960 to Mid-
1980s

Year	White	Black	Racial difference
Percentage of women 15 to 44 living with husband			
1960*	69%	52%	17%
1970	61	42	19
1980	55	30	25
1984	55	28	27
Percentage of births delivered to unmarried women			
1960*	2	22	20
1970	6	35	29
1980	11	55	44
1983	13	58	45
Percentage of families with children under 18 maintained by a woman			
1960*	6	24	18
1970	9	33	24
1980	14	48	34
1984	15	50	35
Percentage of children under age 18 in mother-only families			
1960*	6	20	14
1970	8	29	21
1980	14	44	30
1984	15	50	35

* Data for 1960 refer to whites and nonwhites.
Source: U.S. Bureau of the Census, *Census of Population: 1960,* PC(1)-1D, table 76;
PC(2)-4A, table 2; *Census of Population: 1970,* PC(1)-D1, table 203; *Census of Population:
1980,* PB80-1-D1-A, table 264; *Current Population Reports,* Series P-20, No. 212,
table 4; No. 218, table 1; No. 365, table 4; No. 366, table 1; No. 398, table 1;
No. 399, table 4; U.S. National Center for Health Statistics, *Vital Statistics of the
United States: 1970,* Vol. 1-Natality, table 1–29, *Monthly Vital Statistics Reports,* Vol.
31, No. 8 (Supplement), November 30, 1982, table 15; Vol. 34, No. 6 (Supplement),
September 20, 1985, table 17.

actual value: 54 percent in 1984 (U. S. Bureau of the Census 1985b,
tables 1 and 15). Indicators of the economic status of black families
would not be so bleak had not the living arrangements of black adults
and children changed so rapidly (Bianchi 1980; Green and Welniak
1983, 41).

The Nature of Black Progress

The conclusions that are drawn about the changing status of blacks depend upon which indicators are stressed. Those who believe that this nation is a melting pot will place great weight upon the narrowing of black-white gaps in educational attainment, in the earnings of employed workers, and in occupational prestige. They will point to the rapid growth of a prosperous black middle class and will note that, for the first time, blacks now have real political power. A large fraction of the black population took advantage of the opportunities which, they believe, were created when the United States faced its racial dilemma (Wattenberg 1984; Wattenberg and Scammon 1973, 35).

Those who defend this model of society also recognize, however, that many other blacks are not succeeding. Increasingly the term "urban underclass" describes those ghetto residents who seem unable or unwilling to move into the economic mainstream. According to the melting-pot view, European and Asian immigrants were once in a similar position, but they escaped poverty, not by depending upon welfare and affirmative action, but rather by taking menial jobs or starting small businesses. The fact that so many blacks prosper is proof, for them, that racial discrimination is no longer a major issue.

A variety of commentators argue that the availability of governmental payments lessens incentives for the poor and makes them even more dependent (Murray 1984; Williams 1982; Gilder 1981b; Sowell 1981). In particular, it undercuts the role of black men and leads to frequent marital disruption and high rates of childbearing outside marriage, which are assumed to be the unintended effect of governmental programs rather than the result of present or past white racism. The problems of blacks will be solved, not by new civil rights laws or more welfare, but rather when blacks capitalize on the opportunities now available. This means accepting those low-income jobs that have traditionally been filled by immigrants and which are now very attractive to hundreds of thousands of Latin Americans.

Contradictory conclusions and policy recommendations will be offered by those who see this nation as fundamentally polarized by race and economic issues (Hill 1978, 1981; Pinkney 1984). While recognizing that important changes occurred in voting rights, educational attainment, and earnings, they will stress that black-white differences remain large.

Despite decades of gains, black men in 1984 earned only 65 percent as much as white men, and blacks are still much more likely than whites to be doing manual labor or operating machines. They see claims about the black middle class as inflated, since blacks—even those with high incomes—have assets that are a small fraction of those of whites with similar incomes (U. S. Bureau of the Census 1986, table 3). Other indicators are even more disturbing. In terms of unemployment rates and labor force participation, black men made no gains in the 1950s and the number of black poor increased from 7.2 to 9.5 million in the decade following 1974 (U. S. Bureau of the Census 1985b).

Rather than stressing that blacks are failing to utilize available opportunities, defenders of this model contend that the nation has not altered those basic social and economic arrangements that keep blacks at a great disadvantage. Symbolic changes may be accepted but real changes are seldom made. The *Brown* decision[1] failed to integrate schools in the metropolitan areas where most blacks live. Title VII of the Civil Rights Act of 1965 called for equal employment opportunities but the employment situation for black men has worsened since. The Fair Housing Act of 1968 was not followed by a breakdown of the "chocolate city-vanilla suburbs" pattern.

It is impossible to answer a question about black progress with a simple yes or no. It is clear that white Americans have made fundamental changes in our social institutions that extend the practices and principles of democracy to blacks, but it is also clear that neither the melting pot nor the polarization model adequately describe the racial situation in a nation of 230 million.

In his 1965 speech at Howard University's commencement, President Johnson asserted that you cannot take a man who has been hobbled by chains, liberate him, and expect him to compete fairly with all the others (Johnson 1965). Many programs of the "War on Poverty" attempted to compensate for some of the inequities in the status of blacks, but current support for such policies is lacking. Quite likely, racial differences will persist and some, such as those describing family income and poverty, will grow larger.

---

[1] *Brown vs. Board of Education of Topeka,* 347 U.S. 483 (1954).

References

Abramson, P.R., and W. Claggett. 1986. Race-related Differences in Self-reported and Validated Turnout in 1984. *Journal of Politics* 48:412–22.

Anderson, E. 1979. Some Observations on Black Youth Employment. In *Youth Employment and Public Policy,* ed. B.E. Anderson and I.V. Sawhill, 64–87. Englewood Cliffs, N.J.: Prentice-Hall.

———. 1985. The Social Context of Youth Employment Programs. In *Youth Employment and Training Programs: The YEDPA Years,* ed. C.L. Betsey, R.G. Hollister, and R. Papageorgiou, 348–66. Washington: National Academy Press.

Anderson, M. 1978. *Welfare.* Stanford: Hoover Institute.

Beller, A.H. 1984. Trends in Occupation Segregation by Sex and Race, 1960-1981. In *Sex Segregation in the Workplace,* ed. B. Reskin, 11–26. Washington: National Academy Press.

Bianchi, S.M. 1980. Racial Differences in Per Capita Income, 1960-76: The Importance of Household Size, Headship, and Labor Force Participation. *Demography* 17(2):129–43.

———. 1981. *Household Composition and Racial Inequality.* New Brunswick: Rutgers University Press.

Bianchi, S.M., and D. Spain. 1986. *American Women in Transition.* New York: Russell Sage.

Burton, N.W., and L.V. Jones. 1982. Recent Trends in Achievement Levels of Black and White Youth. *Educational Researcher* 11:10–14.

Cave, C. 1985. Youth Joblessness and Race: Evidence from the 1980 Census. In *Youth Employment and Training Programs: The YEDPA Years,* ed. C.L. Betsey, R.G. Hollister, and M.R. Papageorgiou, 367–409. Washington: National Academy Press.

Coleman, J.S., S.D. Kelly, and J.A. Moore. 1966. *Equality of Educational Opportunity.* Washington: National Center for Educational Statistics.

Datcher, L. 1980. In *Black Women in the Labor Force,* ed. P.A. Wallace, 67–76. Cambridge: MIT Press.

Farley, R. 1984. *Blacks and Whites: Narrowing the Gap?* Cambridge: Harvard University Press.

Farley, R., and W.R. Allen. 1987. *The Color Line and the Quality of Life in America.* New York: Russell Sage.

Featherman, D.L., and R.M. Hauser. 1976. Changes in the Socioeconomic Stratification of the Races. *American Journal of Sociology* 82:621–51.

———. 1978. *Opportunity and Change.* New York: Academic Press.

Freeman, R.B. 1976. *Black Elite.* New York: McGraw-Hill.

Gilder, G. 1981. *Welfare and Poverty.* New York: Basic Books.

Grant, W.V., and T.D. Snyder. 1983. *Digest of Education Statistics: 1983-84.* Washington: National Center for Education Statistics.

Green, G., and E. Welniak. 1983. Changing Families and Shifting Incomes. *American Demographics* 5(2):40–43.

Hill, R.B. 1978. *The Illusion of Black Progress.* Washington: National Urban League.

————. 1981. *Economic Policies and Black Progress.* Washington: National Urban League.

Hirschman, C., and M.G. Wong. 1984. Socioeconomic Gains of Asian Americans, Black and Hispanics: 1960-1976. *American Journal of Sociology* 90:584–607.

Hout, M. 1984. Occupational Mobility of Black Men: 1962 to 1973. *American Sociological Review* 49:308–22.

Jacob, J.E. 1986. Overview of Black America in 1985. In *The State of Black America: 1986,* ed. J.D. Williams, i–x: Washington: Urban League.

Johnson, L.B. 1965. To Fulfill These Rights. Commencement address at Howard University, June 4.

Kain, J.F. 1968. Housing Segregation, Negro Employment and Metropolitan Decentralization. *Quarterly Journal of Economics* 82:175–97.

Killingsworth, C.C. 1968. *Jobs and Income for Negroes.* Ann Arbor: Institute of Labor and Industrial Relations.

Kluger, R. 1976. *Simple Justice.* New York: Knopf.

Langberg, M., and R. Farley, 1985. Residential Segregation of Asian Americans in 1980. *Sociology and Social Research* 70:71–75.

Levitan, S.A., W.B. Johnson, and R. Taggart. 1975. *Still A Dream.* Cambridge: Harvard University Press.

Logan, J.R., and M. Schneider. 1984. Racial Segregation and Racial Change in American Suburbs: 1970-1980. *American Journal of Sociology* 89:874–88.

Mare, R.D., and C. Winship. 1984. Racial Inequality and Joblessness. *American Sociological Review* 49:39–55.

Massey, D.S. 1979. Effects of Socioeconomic Factors on the Residential Segregation of Blacks and Spanish Americans in U.S. Urbanized Areas. *American Sociological Review* 44:1015–22.

McAdam, D. 1982. *Political Process and the Development of Black Insurgency, 1930-1970.* Chicago: University of Chicago Press.

Morris, A.D. 1984. *The Origins of the Civil Rights Movement.* New York: Free Press.

Moynihan, D.P. 1986. *Family and Nation.* New York: Harcourt Brace Jovanovich.

Murray, C. 1984. *Losing Ground.* New York: Basic Books.

Orfield, G. 1983. *Public School Desegregation in the United States: 1968-1980.* Washington: Joint Center for Political Studies.

Pinkney, A. 1984. *The Myth of Black Progress.* New York: Cambridge University Press.

Schuman, H., C. Steeh, and L. Bobo. 1985. *Racial Attitudes in America.* Cambridge: Harvard University Press.

Smith, J.P., and F.R. Welch. 1977. Black-White Male Wage Ratios: 1960-1970. *American Economic Review* 67:323–38.

————. 1986. *Closing the Gap.* Santa Monica: Rand Corporation.

Sowell, T. 1981. *Markets and Minorities.* New York: Basic Books.

Spear, A.H. 1967. *Black Chicago.* Chicago: University of Chicago Press.

Swinton, D.H. 1986. In *The State of Black America: 1986.* Washington: Urban League.

Taeuber, K. E. 1968. The Effect of Income Redistribution on Racial Residential Segregation. *Urban Affairs Quarterly* 4:5–14.

————. 1983. *Racial Residential Segregation, 28 Cities, 1970-1980.* CDE working paper 83-12. Madison: Center for Demography and Ecology, University of Wisconsin-Madison.

Taeuber, K.E., and A.F. Taeuber. 1965. *Negroes in Cities.* Chicago: Aldine.

U.S. Bureau of Labor Statistics. 1976. *BLS Handbook of Methods.* Bulletin 1910. Washington.

————. 1985. *Handbook of Labor Statistics.* Bulletin no. 2217. Washington.

U.S. Bureau of the Census. 1950a. *Census of Housing: 1950,* vol. I, part 1. Washington.

————. 1950b. *Census of Population: 1950.* P-E, no. 3B. Washington.

————. 1980. *Census of Housing: 1980.* HC80-1-B1. Washington.

————. 1981a. *Current Population Reports,* series P-20, no. 360. Washington.

————. 1981b. *Current Population Reports,* series P-20, no. 362. Washington.

————. 1984. *Current Population Reports,* series P-20, no. 389, Washington.

————. 1985a. *Current Population Reports,* series P-20, no. 397. Washington.

————. 1985b. *Current Population Reports,* series P-60, no. 149. Washington.

————. 1986. *Current Population Reports,* series P-70, no. 7. Washington.

U.S. National Center for Health Statistics. 1985. *Monthly Vital Statistics Reports* 34 (6, Supplement).

Vose, C.E. 1967. *Caucasians Only.* Berkeley: University of California Press.

Wattenberg, B.J. 1984. *The Good News Is the Bad News Is Wrong.* New York: Simon and Schuster.

Wattenberg, B.J., and R.M. Scammon. 1973. Black Progress and Liberal Rhetoric. *Commentary* 55(4):35–44.

Williams, W.E. 1982. *The State against Blacks.* New York: McGraw-Hill.

Black Demographic Trends in the 1980s

WILLIAM P. O'HARE

I N THE EARLY 1980S, FOLLOWING THE RELEASE
of data from the 1980 Census of Population and Housing, several
analysts reported changes in the black population during the 1970s
(see, for example, Reid 1982; O'Hare et al. 1982; Farley 1984). These
studies revealed many important population changes experienced by
the black population in the 1970s in areas such as interregional
migration, suburbanization, family structure, and teenage childbearing.

There has been little systematic effort, however, to document post-
1980 demographic trends among blacks. This article attempts to fill
that gap and provide an important background for the other articles
in these supplements. Using a variety of demographic data sources,
the major population trends of the 1970s are examined to ascertain
which have continued during the first half of the 1980s. This demographic portrait of black Americans in the mid-1980s will provide
the context within which health status, health-related behavior, health
care delivery, and health care planning can be analyzed more effectively.

While many of the black demographic trends examined here invite
socioeconomic explanation, that is not my purpose; the focus will be
on description and documentation rather than on analysis and explanation.
Furthermore, the breadth of topics covered does not allow me to
provide much detail for the major trends identified.

Let me emphasize that the focus is on "blacks," not the broader group of nonwhites or minorities. In some sections figures for blacks are compared to the corresponding figures for whites and in other sections they are compared to the figures for the total population depending on data availability and the topic under consideration.

While the number of potential subject areas is broad, I have limited my examination to major demographic areas: population growth and distribution, age structure, fertility and mortality, and family composition. A summary section provides a sentence on each of nine major demographic trends in the black population during the first half of the 1980s identified in this study.

Black Population Growth

Throughout the 1970 to 1986 period, the black population increased more rapidly than the total population, as it had for several prior decades. This has resulted in blacks comprising an ever larger portion of the total population.

The U.S. Census Bureau estimates the size of the black population in 1986 at 29.4 million, or 12.2 percent of the total population; the 26.8 million blacks counted in the 1980 Decennial Census comprised only 11.8 percent of the total population, up from 22.5 million and 11.1 percent in 1970. The black population is likely to continue to grow more rapidly than the white population, and by the year 2050 the Census Bureau middle series projection indicates that blacks will number 52.3 million and comprise 16.9 percent of the total U.S. population (U.S. Bureau of the Census 1984).

Even though the black population was growing at a more rapid rate than the white population there was an overall slowing of population growth in recent years and the *rate* of black population growth slowed in the first half of the 1980s compared with the 1970s. Between 1970 and 1980 the black population grew at an average rate of 1.7 percent per year, but the annual average growth rate between 1980 and 1985 was 1.5 percent. This decline in the growth rate is a product of falling birth rates, which are discussed later, not quite offset by declines in mortality. Unlike other prominent minority groups such as Hispanics and Asian Americans, most of the recent increase in the black population is due to natural increase (number of births minus the number of deaths) rather than immigration.

The national rate of growth, however, masks important differences among regions. In the early 1980s, the South replaced the West as the region with the highest rate of black population growth. In the first half of the 1980s, the average annual rate of growth of the black population in the South was 2.0 percent compared with 1.7 percent during the 1970s, but the average annual rate of growth in the black population of the West fell from 3.3 percent in the 1970s to 1.4 percent in the first half of the 1980s. The rate of black population growth slowed in both the Northeast and Midwest regions between the 1970s and the early 1980s (see table 1).

Geographic Distribution of Blacks

Despite regional differences in the rate of black population growth, the distribution of blacks across the regions has changed little since 1970. Today, 54.2 percent of all blacks live in the South, with 17.7 percent in the Northeast, 19.7 percent in the Midwest, and 8.5 percent in the West. This is only slightly different from 1970 when 53.0 percent of blacks lived in the South, 19.2 percent in the Northeast, 20.2 percent in the Midwest, and 7.5 percent in the West.

Much of the regional differences in recent black population growth can be traced to patterns of black interregional migration (see table

TABLE 1

U.S. Black Population by Region: 1970, 1980, and 1985

(numbers in 1,000s)

Region	1970	1980	1985	Average annual percentage change	
				1970–80	1980–85
Northeast	4,344	4,849	5,035	1.2%	0.8%
Midwest*	4,572	5,337	5,607	1.7	1.0
South	11,970	14,041	15,428	1.7	2.0
West	1,695	2,262	2,415	3.3	1.4
Total	22,581	26,489	28,485	1.7	1.5

Sources: 1970 and 1980 data from O'Hare et al. 1982, table 2.1; 1985 data from U.S. Bureau of the Census 1986b, table 8.
* Prior to 1985 this region was referred to as the north central region.

TABLE 2
Net Migration of Blacks, by Region: 1910–1920 to 1980–1985
(numbers in 1,000s)

Period	South	Northeast	Midwest*	West
1910–1920	− 454	+ 182	+ 244	+ 28
1920–1930	− 749	+ 349	+ 364	+ 36
1930–1940	− 347	+ 171	+ 128	+ 49
1940–1950	− 1,599	+ 463	+ 618	+ 339
1950–1960	− 1,473	+ 496	+ 541	+ 293
1960–1970	− 1,380	+ 612	+ 382	+ 301
1970–1975	+ 14	− 64	− 52	+ 102
1975–1980	+ 195	− 175	− 51	+ 30
1980–1985	+ 85	− 50	− 70	+ 36

Sources: 1910–1970 data from U.S. Bureau of the Census 1979, table 8; 1970–1975 data from U.S. Bureau of the Census 1975, table 28; 1975–1980 data from U.S. Bureau of the Census 1981, table 42; unpublished 1980–1985 data from the Population Division of the U.S. Bureau of the Census.
* Formerly called the north central region.

2). For several decades prior to the 1970s, black interregional migration was dominated by the movement of blacks out of the South. Starting in the early 1970s, however, the net loss of black migrants from the South to the North stopped and blacks joined a pattern established among whites in the 1950s of net migration from the Northeast and Midwest to the South.

During the first half of the 1980s, the annual geographic mobility rates and black migration rates were lower than rates observed in the 1970s. Most of the patterns of black population movement that were evident during the 1970s, however, continued during the first part of the 1980s.

Between 1980 and 1985, the South continued to experience a net in-migration of blacks but the pace appears slower than that seen in the last half of the 1970s. Both the Northeast and the Midwest continued to experience net out-migration of blacks during the first half of the 1980s, but the rate of out-migration fell significantly in the Northeast and increased only slightly in the Midwest from what was seen in the last half of the 1970s. The West continued to have a net in-migration of blacks in the early 1980s, but at a lower rate than that of the early 1970s, and at a much lower rate than the thirty years following the end of World War II.

The Nonmetropolitan Turnaround and Black Population Change

One of the demographic trends of the 1970s that received a lot of media attention was the resurgence of population growth in non-metropolitan areas of the country. These areas grew more rapidly, in large part due to net in-migration. This trend, however, was not observed in the black population. Rather, during the 1970s there was a small net migration of blacks out of nonmetropolitan areas. Between 1970 and 1975 there was a net migration of 138,000 blacks from nonmetropolitan to metropolitan areas, and the comparable figure for the 1975 to 1980 period was 116,000 (see top panel of table 3).

During the first half of the 1980s, it appears that the yearly net movement of blacks between metropolitan and nonmetropolitan areas is so small that it is impossible to measure reliably with the Current Population Survey sample. In any case, it is clear that the movement between metropolitan and nonmetropolitan locations has not been a major factor in black population change in recent years.

Redistribution of Blacks in Central Cities and Suburbs

One of the big stories of the 1970s was the dramatic increase in black suburbanization and the corollary trend of blacks moving out of central cities. The trickle of black suburbanization of the 1960s became a steady stream during the 1970s as the black population in the suburbs grew by nearly 2.5 million, compared with an increase of just over 2 million in central cities (O'Hare et al. 1982). While the black suburban population (i.e., those living inside metropolitan areas but outside central cities) grew by 70 percent during the 1970s, blacks made up only 6 percent of the suburban population in 1980.

The net movement of blacks out of central cities, which increased from 243,000 in the first half of the 1970s to 439,000 between 1975 and 1980, appears to be sustained through 1984; the pace of this migration stream may well have increased. Data in table 3 show an annual net migration of about 200,000 blacks out of central cities for each year between 1980 and 1984.

TABLE 3

The Movement of Blacks among Nonmetropolitan Areas, Central Cities, and Suburbs: 1970–1984 (figures in 1,000s)

	1970–1975	1975–1980	1980–1981	1981–1982	1982–1983	1983–1984
NONMETROPOLITAN AREAS						
In-migrants	325	353	232	117	177	107
Out-migrants	463	469	168	135	188	144
Net-migrants	−138	−116	64	−18	−11	−37
CENTRAL CITIES						
In-migrants	737	724	344	311	395	407
Out-migrants	980	1,163	561	532	573	562
Net-migrants	−243	−439	−217	−221	−178	−155
SUBURBS						
In-migrants	827	1,123	524	539	544	561
Out-migrants	446	567	279	196	280	272
Net-migrants	381	556	245	343	264	289

Source: U.S. Bureau of the Census, *Current Population Reports* series P–20, various years.
Note: Periods refer to the period from March of the first year to March of the last year.

Although blacks were moving out of central cities, whites were moving out at a faster rate and central city populations have become increasingly black since 1970. In 1986, 22.7 percent of the aggregate population of all central cities was black, compared to 22.5 percent in 1980 and 20.6 percent in 1970.

The 1986 figures, however, reflect the populations in central cities and suburbs of many areas that have been classified as metropolitan areas only since 1980, and the 1980 figure includes standard metropolitan statistical areas (SMSAs) that were not included in the 1970 figures. In 1970 there were 243 SMSAs but by 1980 there were 318. Following the implementation of a new metropolitan classification scheme in the early 1980s, there were 280 metropolitan statistical areas (MSAs) and consolidated metropolitan statistical areas (CMSAs) in 1984 (U.S. Bureau of the Census 1987a, table 20), but these 280 areas included more territory than the 318 SMSAs of 1980. These changes in the definition of metropolitan areas confound interpretation of changes in population over time.

Not surprisingly, given these demographic trends, the number of central cities with a black population majority has climbed rapidly, from 2 in 1960, to 4 in 1970, to 13 in 1980. Nine of these 13 black majority central cities are located in the South. Unless there is a dramatic change in urban migration trends during the latter half of the 1980s, the number of black majority cities will double again by 1990.

The net migration of blacks to the suburban ring of metropolitan areas that increased during the 1970s appears to have been sustained if not accelerated during the period of 1980 to 1984. Data from the early 1980s suggest that there was a net in-migration of at least a quarter-million blacks to suburbs every year. Needless to say, most blacks moving to suburbs come from central cities and most blacks who leave central cities move to suburbs. While there is some movement of blacks from nonmetropolitan areas to the suburbs this flow is much smaller than the flow from central cities to the suburbs.

While the rate of white in-migration to suburbs has been high, the rate of out-migration has also been high, and the result is that blacks comprise a growing share of the suburban population. In the suburbs, 6.3 percent of the population was black in 1986, compared with 6.1 percent in 1980 and 4.8 percent in 1970. Interpretation of these figures, however, is also confounded by the additional metropolitan areas added since 1970.

Notably, one of the fastest-growing groups of blacks are those who are poor and live in census-defined poverty areas of central cities. Poverty areas are census tracts with poverty rates above 20 percent in 1980. While not all the people who live in a poverty area are poor, Census Bureau data show that the number of *poor blacks* living in poverty areas grew by 1.5 million or 59 percent between 1980 and 1986.

Since areas with high rates of poverty often have associated problems such as high rates of criminal activity, out-of-wedlock births, and school dropouts, the rapidly growing number of blacks in such neighborhoods has helped fuel concern about a growing black "underclass" in our major cities.

Black Age Structure

The aging of the population and the echo of the baby boom are responsible for important changes in black age structure since 1970. Over the 1970 to 1984 period, the black population aged, as reflected in a steady rise in median age from 22.4 years in 1970, to 24.9 years in 1980, to 26.3 years in 1984. The major reason for the rise in median age is the aging of the baby boom cohort born between 1946 and 1964. At each point in time, the median age for blacks was about six years lower than the median age for whites, reflecting the higher fertility and shorter life expectancy of blacks relative to whites.

Because of the differential age structure of blacks and whites, blacks comprise a relatively large share of young cohorts and a relatively small share of older cohorts. For example, blacks constitute 15 percent of the population under age 5, but only 7.6 percent of those aged 85 plus.

During the 1970s, three age groups in the black population grew dramatically: young adults (age 18 to 24) grew by 52.4 percent; young working-age persons (age 25 to 44) grew by 38.8 percent; and the elderly (age 65 plus) grew by 31.9 percent. On the other hand, the school-age population (age 5 to 17) actually declined by 1.6 percent between 1970 and 1980 (see table 4).

During the first half of the 1980s, however, a somewhat different

TABLE 4

Changes in the Numbers of Blacks in Selected Age Groups between 1970 and 1986

Age Group	Population size in 1,000s			Change 1970 to 1980		Change 1980 to 1986	
	1970	1980	1986	Number	Percentage	Number	Percentage
Preschool (0–4)	2,411	2,459	2,721	48	2.0%	262	10.7%
School age (5–17)	7,126	7,009	6,958	−117	−1.6	−51	−0.7
Young adults (18–24)	2,638	4,019	3,956	1,381	52.4	−63	−1.6
Young families (25–44)	5,061	7,023	8,852	1,962	38.8	1,829	26.0
Older families (45–64)	3,728	4,202	4,546	474	12.7	344	8.2
Elderly (65 and older)	1,586	2,092	2,394	506	31.9	302	14.4
Total	22,550	26,803	29,427	4,253	18.9	2,624	9.8

Sources: 1980 and 1986 data from U.S. Bureau of the Census 1987b; 1970 data from U.S. Bureau of the Census 1972, table 85.

set of age groups experienced growth or decline. Between 1980 and 1986, the number of blacks under age 5 began growing at a more rapid pace (10.7 percent), and the young working-age group and the elderly continued to grow at above average rates. On the other hand, school age and young adult blacks (age 5 to 24) declined in total number. Obviously, this is due to the decline in births between the mid-1960s and the early 1980s.

The number of blacks aged 85 plus (not shown in the table) grew by an astonishing 33.9 percent between 1980 and 1986 (a gain 10 percentage points higher than that for similar-aged whites) and very similar to the 35.9 percent gain observed between 1970 and 1980.

Fertility and Mortality

Since many aspects of fertility and mortality are covered in Manton, Patrick, and Johnson (1987) and Furstenberg (1987), I will be relatively brief in my treatment of those topics here.

Fertility

In the 1960s and 1970s, the fertility levels of both black and whites declined significantly and there was some convergence of black and white fertility levels. The fertility rate (number of live births per 1,000 population) of whites fell by 26 percent during the 1960s and by 23 percent during the 1970s, while the black fertility rate fell by 25 percent during the 1960s and 24 percent during the 1970s (see table 5).

Between 1980 and 1984, the fertility levels of both blacks and whites continued the decline witnessed in the 1960s and 1970s, and the gap between black and white fertility levels continued to close. In 1980 the total fertility rate (TFR) of blacks was 2.30 compared to 1.75 for whites, but by 1984 the TFR for blacks was 2.15 compared with 1.72 for whites. In other words, the black TFR was 31 percent higher than the white TFR in 1980, but only 25 percent higher in 1984. The total fertility rate measures the number of births a woman would have if she were exposed to the age-specific fertility rates observed at a given date.

The fertility differential between blacks and whites is largely due

TABLE 5

Number of Births and Total Fertility Rates by Race: 1960–1984

| Year | Registered births | | | Fertility rates* | | |
	Total	Whites	Blacks	Total	Whites	Blacks
1984	3,669,141	2,923,502	592,745	65.4	62.2	81.4
1980	3,612,258	2,898,732	589,616	68.4	64.7	88.1
1970	3,731,386	3,091,264	572,362	87.9	84.1	115.4
1960	4,257,850	3,600,744	602,264	118.0	113.2	153.5

Source: National Center for Health Statistics 1986a, 13 (table 1).
* Fertility rates reflect the number of live births per 1,000 population.

TABLE 6
Births per 1,000 Teenagers Aged 15 to 19, by Race: 1970 to 1984

	All teenagers			Unmarried teenagers		
Year	Total	White	Black	Total	White	Black
1970	68.3	57.4	147.7	22.4	10.9	96.9
1980	53.0	44.7	100.0	27.6	16.2	89.2
1984	50.9	42.5	95.7	30.2	19.0	87.1

Source: U.S. Center for Health Statistics 1986b, 17 (table 4), 32 (table 19).

to socioeconomic differences between these two groups. For example, among women of similar socioeconomic status whites are more likely than blacks to have had a child in the past year. For women in families with yearly incomes under $10,000 in 1985, there were 93.8 births per 1,000 women aged 18 to 44 among whites compared with only 87.4 for blacks (U.S. Bureau of the Census 1986a, table 4).

Even though young (aged 18 to 24) black women have had a much higher number of births to date than their white counterparts (817 per 1,000 blacks compared to 463 per 1,000 whites) young black women expect to have fewer births over their lifetime than young white women. Black women aged 18 to 24 in 1985 expect to have 1.848 lifetime births compared with 2.079 for similar-aged white women (U.S. Bureau of the Census 1986a, table 5).

Even though fertility rates fell, the number of births for blacks and whites were slightly higher in 1984 than in 1980 because the pool of potential mothers in the prime childbearing years increased due to the aging of the baby boom cohort.

Births to teenagers is another demographic topic that continues to receive a lot of attention (see Furstenberg 1987). The birthrate for black teenagers dropped significantly between 1970 and 1980, going from 147.7 births per 1,000 teenagers aged 15 to 19 in 1970 to 100.0 in 1980. This rate continued to decline between 1980 and 1984, but the rate of decrease slowed significantly. By 1984, the birthrate for black teens had dropped to 95.7 per 1,000 women (see table 6).

TABLE 7
Life Expectancy at Birth, by Race and Sex: 1970 to 1984

Year	White		Black	
	Male	Female	Male	Female
1985	71.8	78.7	65.3	73.7
1984	71.8	78.7	65.6	73.7
1983	71.7	78.7	65.4	73.6
1982	71.5	78.7	65.1	73.7
1981	71.1	78.4	64.5	73.2
1980	70.7	78.1	63.8	72.5
1970	68.0	75.6	60.0	68.3
Average annual increase in years of life expectancy at birth				
1970–1980	.27	.25	.38	.42
1980–1985	.22	.12	.30	.24

Source: National Center for Health Statistics 1986b, 12 (table 4).

Mortality

Life expectancy at birth continued to increase during the first half of the 1980s for both blacks and whites, but the pace of increase slowed. Between 1970 and 1980, the average annual increase in life expectancy at birth was .38 years for black males and .42 years for black females. Between 1980 and 1985, the average annual increase was .30 years for black males and .24 years for black females. Life expectancy at birth actually decreased between 1984 and 1985 for black males (see table 7).

Heart disease was the leading cause of death for blacks in 1984, as it has been since at least 1950. While heart disease is also the leading cause of death for whites, this cause of death is more prevalent among blacks than among whites (U.S. Department of Health and Human Services 1985).

Family Structure and Living Arrangements

Table 8 illustrates several post-1960 changes in the family status of black cohorts at various points in the life cycle. In most cases these

William P. O'Hare

TABLE 8
Marital Status of Blacks and All Races in Selected Age Groups, by Sex: 1960, 1970, 1980, and 1985

Marital Status, age, and race	Men				Women			
	1960*	1970	1980	1985	1960	1970	1980	1985
Percentage never married (age 20–24)								
Blacks	56%	57%	79%	86%	36%	43%	69%	76%
All races	53	56	69	76	29	36	50	59
Percentage separated or divorced (age 25–34)								
Blacks	8	9	13	13	17	20	28	21
All races	4	5	9	10	6	8	14	14
Percentage in intact marriages (age 35–44)								
Blacks	71	69	61	57	62	58	49	46
All races	84	84	81	76	80	79	84	72
Percentage of those aged 55 and over who are widowed								
Blacks	16	16	14	16	47	44	45	46
All races	12	11	9	9	38	38	37	36

Sources: Glick 1981; U.S. Bureau of the Census 1986c.

figures highlight differences in levels of marriage and divorce between blacks and whites, but similarities in the direction of trends continue over time.

The first horizontal panel in table 8 shows that the trend away from early marriage that was evident in the 1970s continued into the first half of the 1980s. By 1985, 86 percent of black men aged 20 to 24 had never been married, which is up from 79 percent in 1980 and 57 percent in 1970. The figures for black women are about 10 percentage points lower at each time period, reflecting their earlier mean age at first marriage. The rise in the share of young adults who are not married, of course, has enlarged the pool of women at risk of becoming pregnant and bearing a child out of wedlock.

The second panel in table 8 records that the share of black men in the group aged 25 to 34 that were divorced or separated remained constant at 13 percent between 1980 and 1985 and the figure for black women fell from 28 to 21 percent during this period. The fact that a smaller and smaller share of those aged 20 to 24 is getting married is one important reason why the share of those aged 25 to 34 who are divorced or separated is not growing. If people don't get married, they can't get divorced or separated.

One consequence of the falling marriage rates of those aged 20 to 24 and level rates of divorce and separation among those 25 to 34 years old is shown in the third panel of table 8. The share of blacks aged 35 to 44 living in intact marriages continued to fall during the first half of the 1980s. In 1980, 61 percent of black males in this age group were living in intact marriages, but that figure fell to 57 percent in 1985, and for black women the figure fell from 49 percent to 46 percent during the same time period.

The share of blacks aged 55 and over who are widowed remained fairly constant. About 15 percent of all black males in this age group reported being widowed, compared with about 45 percent of black females. These proportions have remained relatively constant since 1960 but it remains to be seen if the recent decline in the share of blacks in intact marriages at younger ages will change the share of older blacks who are widows or widowers.

Single Parent Families

One of the major trends in family demography, since at least the end of World War II, has been the increase in single parent families. The shift to single parent families has been observed among both whites and blacks, but the level is significantly higher for blacks. This trend not only continued during the first half of the 1980s, but also the rate of growth of black single parent families increased over that of the 1970s. As of 1986, over half of all black children lived in single parent families (see table 9).

Between 1970 and 1980, the number of black children living in single parent families increased by an average of 130,000 a year compared with an annual increase of 163,200 between 1980 and 1985. It should be noted that a portion of this increase in black children living in single parent families shown in census data is a product of some procedural changes made in the way the Census Bureau collects this data, which resulted in identification of single parent families that were missed in earlier surveys. This means figures prior to 1983 are likely to underestimate the number of single parent families, and therefore the changes between 1980 and 1985 are likely to be overestimated using this data series (for additional details on this change, see U.S. Bureau of the Census 1985a, 4).

This trend has a number of implications, not the least of which is the economic status of black children. The poverty rate for children in black female-headed families (66.9 percent) is three times the poverty rate for children in black male-headed families (18.8 percent), and six times that of children living in white male-headed families (10.4 percent) (U.S. Bureau of the Census 1986b, table 16). Of course, economic status has a good deal to do with health status and health resources available.

At the same time that the proportion of families headed by a woman has grown steadily, the predominant marital status of black single parents has changed. Table 9 shows that in 1960 only 10 percent of black children living in single parent households were residing with a parent who had never married, but by 1985 that figure had risen to 48 percent. The increase in the share of children living with a never-married parent was also evident in the total population where only 4.2 percent of children living in single parent families resided with a never-married parent in 1960 compared to 18.4 percent in 1985.

Racial differences in the association between childbearing and marriage are highlighted by noting that among never-married women aged 35 to 44 in 1984, 89.7 percent of whites were childless compared with only 29.4 percent of blacks (U.S. Bureau of the Census 1985b).

This shift in marital status of single parents is significant for several reasons. First, never-married single parents are much less likely to be awarded or to be receiving child support payments, which makes them more reliant on public welfare. Second, a large share of never-married parents are teenage mothers, who often cut short their education to have a child. About two-thirds of all teenage mothers eventually spend some time on welfare. Third, children who have spent at least part of their childhood in a single parent family are more likely than children who spend their entire childhood in a two parent family to become single parents themselves.

Summary

Most of the black demographic trends witnessed in the 1970s have continued during the first half of the 1980s, but the pace of demographic change has slowed in some areas and quickened in others. A short summarization of the major trends is provided below;

1. The black population is growing faster than the white population and blacks are becoming a larger share of the total population.

2. Blacks continue to move out of the North and into the South and West.

3. Blacks continue to move out of central cities into suburbs, but blacks are not moving out of central cities as fast as whites and central city populations are becoming increasingly black.

4. The growth rates of preschool-age blacks increased in the 1980s, but the growth rates of the school age and young adult populations declined.

5. The fertility rates of blacks continued to fall and to approach convergence with those of whites, although there still is a significant gap between black and white fertility rates.

6. Teen birthrates for unmarried blacks continued to fall during the first half of the 1980s.

7. Life expectancy for blacks continued to increase during the 1980s, but at a somewhat slower pace than seen during the 1970s.

8. The share of black children living in single parent families

TABLE 9

Living Arrangements of Children under the Age of 18: 1960–1985 (numbers in 1,000s).

| | All children | | | | | | | |
| | 1960 | | 1970 | | 1980 | | 1985 | |
	Number	Percentage	Number	Percentage	Number	Percentage	Number	Percentage
TOTAL	63,727	100%	69,162	100%	63,427	100%	62,475	100%
Living with:								
Two parents	55,877	87.7	58,939	85.2	48,624	76.7	46,149	73.9
One parent								
Formerly married	5,586	8.8	7,642	11.0	10,647	16.8	10,879	17.4
One parent								
Never married	243	0.4	557	0.8	1,820	2.9	3,756	6.0
(Single parent subtotal)		(9.2)		(11.8)		(19.7)		(23.4)
Other relatives	1,601	2.5	1,547	2.2	1,929	3.0	1,303	2.1
Nonrelatives	420	0.7	477	0.7	407	0.6	388	0.6

Black children

	1960		1970		1980		1985	
	Number	Percentage	Number	Percentage	Number	Percentage	Number	Percentage
Total	8,650	100%	9,422	100%	9,375	100%	9,479	100%
Living with:								
Two parents	5,795	67.0	5,508	58.5	3,956	42.2	3,741	39.5
One parent								
Formerly married	1,714	19.8	2,574	27.3	3,062	32.7	2,657	28.0
One parent								
Never married	182	2.1	423	4.5	1,235	13.2	2,456	25.9
(Single parent subtotal)		(21.9)		(31.8)		(45.9)		(53.9)
Other relatives	827	9.6	820	8.7	998	10.6	538	5.7
Nonrelatives	132	1.5	97	1.0	124	1.3	87	0.9

Source: U.S. Bureau of the Census 1986c.

continued to grow during the 1980s at a faster rate than seen during the 1970s.

9. The share of black children living with a never-married parent grew much more rapidly in the 1980s than in the 1970s.

References

Farley, R. 1984. *Blacks and Whites: Narrowing the Gap?* Cambridge: Harvard University Press.

Furstenberg, F.W., Jr. 1987. Race Differences in Teenage Sexuality, Pregnancy, and Adolescent Childbearing. *Milbank Quarterly* 65 (Suppl. 2): 381–403.

Glick, P.C. 1981. A Demographic Picture of Black Families. In *Black Families,* ed. H. P. McAdoo. Beverly Hills: Sage. 106–26.

Manton, K.G., C.H. Patrick, and K.W. Johnson. 1987. Health Differentials between Blacks and Whites: Recent Trends in Mortality and Morbidity. *Milbank Quarterly* 65 (Suppl. 1): 129–99.

O'Hare, W., J. Yu-Li, R. Chatterjee, and P. Shukur. 1982. *Blacks on the Move: A Decade of Demographic Change.* Washington: Joint Center for Political Studies.

National Center for Health Statistics. 1986a. Advance Report of Final Natality Statistics: 1984. *Monthly Vital Statistics Report* 35(4, Suppl.).

———. 1986b. Advance Report of Final Mortality Statistics: 1984. *Monthly Vital Statistics Report* 35(6, Suppl. 2).

Reid, J. 1982. Black America in the 1980s. *Population Bulletin* 37(4).

U.S. Bureau of the Census. 1972. *1970 Census of Population: General, Social, and Economic Characteristics: U.S. Summary.* Washington.

———. 1975. Mobility of the Population of the United States: March 1970 to March 1975. *Current Population Reports,* Series P–20, no. 285. Washington.

———. 1979. The Social and Economic Status of the Black Population in the United States: An Historical View, 1790–1978. *Current Population Reports,* series P–23, no. 80. Washington.

———. 1981. Geographic Mobility of the Population of the United States: March 1975 to March 1980. *Current Population Reports,* Series P–20, no. 368. Washington.

———. 1984. Projections of the Population of the United States, by Age, Sex, and Race: 1983–2080. *Current Population Reports,* series P–25, no. 952. Washington.

————. 1985a. Household and Family Characteristics: March 1984. *Current Population Reports,* series P–20, no. 154. Washington.

————. 1985b. Fertility of American Women: June 1984. *Current Population Reports,* series P–20, no. 401. Washington.

————. 1986a. Fertility of American Women: June 1985. *Current Population Reports,* series P–20, no. 406. Washington.

————. 1986b. Money, Income, and Poverty Status of Families and Persons in the United States: 1985 (Advance Data from the March 1986 Current Population Survey). *Current Population Reports,* series P–60, no. 154. Washington.

————. 1986c. Marital Status and Living Arrangements: March 1985. *Current Population Reports,* series P–20, no. 410. Washington.

————. 1987a. *The U.S. Statistical Abstract: 1986.* Washington.

————. 1987b. Estimates of the Population of the United States, by Age, Sex, and Race: 1980 to 1986. *Current Population Reports,* series P–25, no. 1000. Washington.

U.S. Department of Health and Human Services. 1985. *Health United States: 1985.* Washington.

Conceptual and Methodological Issues in the Use of Race as a Variable: Policy Implications

DORIS Y. WILKINSON and GARY KING

T HE CLASSIFICATION OF POPULATIONS INTO DISCRETE categories based on phenotypic or genotypic criteria is an accepted practice in the physical and social sciences. In attempting to explain diverse physical characteristics and sociogeographical experiences among populations, the term "race" has been employed for taxonomic purposes. In most scientific research, however, controversy and confusion have surrounded its use (Fortney 1977). For many scientists such as biologists, geneticists, and physical anthropologists, definitions have consisted primarily of biological subject matter (e.g., gene pools, blood type, skin color). Social scientists, in contrast, have used the term to refer to behavioral practices (e.g., cultural patterns, language), social factors (e.g., stratification, income status, discrimination) as well as phenotypic characteristics (e.g. hair texture, skin color, facial features). Yet, neither the biological nor sociological approach to racial classification is devoid of serious theoretical and methodological shortcomings.

Depending on the contextual application, the classification, definition, and recording of data by race have important implications for health research and health policy. The social science translation has involved considerable complexity and varied theoretical and empirical emphases. Although the concept permeates social and behavioral science as well as epidemiologic research, its meaning is rarely specific or precise with respect to its components and the possible consequences of defining it in a particular way.

Moreover, in examining human genetics and the racial proclivity for certain diseases, it is recognized that races are highly heterogeneous categories (McKusick 1969). They possess varying frequencies of the same genes, clusters of different genes, or some combination of these. Classification is thus not a simple procedure since there are many genetic similarities between the various races. Divisions may be based on blood group frequencies, prominent physical traits, geographical location, and/or admixture resulting from interracial mating. Notwithstanding, humans constitute "one species with no chromosomal differences between the various races and with free interbreeding possible" (McKusick 1969, 178–79).

Objectives

A number of prominent controversies encompassing the postulation of race as an independent or explanatory variable will be examined. Of particular interest are the diverse ways in which it is conceptualized and measured in research emphasizing health differentials and risk factors. The general objective will be to indicate some possible ramifications of particular uses for studies of disparities in health status and for policy formulation. A primary aim is to scrutinize the use of the race concept by health professionals, epidemiologists, and social and behavioral scientists who study disease prevalence and incidence, mortality, and medical care utilization among black Americans.

There are numerous methodological issues which emanate from the dependence on race as a predictive research variable. Specifically, the focus is on several of the conventional empirical and conceptual applications. These include positing race as a: (1) biological and genetic category; (2) social construct; (3) term converging with ethnic stock and ethnicity with respect to behavior, cultural beliefs and values; and (4) sociodemographic variable characterized by economic variation within race (Wilkinson 1984; Wilson 1978). Such uses have had a long history and thus are deeply embedded in the paradigms and premises of the scientific literature (Mausner and Bahn 1974, 49–50).

Various crucial dilemmas confront health researchers who study black Americans. This discussion is intended to raise questions and generate ideas rather than resolve the controversies. In addition, some comments will be made about analyses of health knowledge and awareness of symptoms; help seeking behaviors, particularly delays in seeking care; and lifestyles wherein race is postulated as an independent variable. From a public policy, theoretical, and methodological perspective, it is important to consider the basic assumptions, definitions, context, and significance of incorporating race as an explanatory factor in health research. This is especially relevant to comparative studies where the reliance on race as an analytic tool often leads to simplistic, misleading, or inappropriate conclusions. Many researchers have failed to grasp its key dimensions and broader social and political implications with respect to intergroup relations, epidemiologic studies (Cooper 1985), health services research, and clinical work (Wilkinson 1980).

Race and the Social Context: Issues for Consideration

Several interrelated questions are pertinent to this examination of the divergent meanings and interpretations of race. Among these are the following:

1. As a social concept, race cannot be interpreted apart from its environmental context. When does it refer exclusively to cultural patterns? When is it an indicator of or a covariant with socioeconomic status (see Wilkinson 1984; Wilson 1978)?

2. Is the epidemiologic use of the term consistent with the sociological model of majority-minority group status?

3. What are the socially relevant differences between race and ethnicity?

4. What are the practical implications of the misconception or misuse of the term race by epidemiologists and health researchers?

5. Given the variation in definitions, on what bases should health promotion and prevention campaigns be designed for black and other racial and ethnic populations?

The latter two questions reflect empirical and policy issues relevant to the definition of race as either a social or cultural variable.

Theoretical models and scientific inquiry that incorporate race generate debate regarding what kind of analytic tool the concept represents. Is it akin to *sex* which is a biogenetic term? Or is it more closely associated with *gender* which is a psychobehavioral and role orientation construct? Does race converge with *ethnicity* (Taylor 1978) or with *ethnic stock*? If its meaning is either *biological* or *cultural,* do the conceptual and measurement components make a difference in studies of health behaviors and in the interpretation of results? What are the probable consequences of disparate translations of race for health policy? These are among the questions that will be addressed in this discussion. The underlying assumption is that scientific axioms, federal and state policies, and the distribution of health services are contingent on the empirical explication of race. If health policies are based on one meaning over another, the outcomes could be critical.

Morbidity and Mortality Differentials

Over the past two decades there has been an increasing volume of research in areas such as chronic disease prevention and control (e.g., cancer, hypertension), the availability and utilization of health services, sociodemographic characteristics and health behaviors, and genetics. Emphases have been directed primarily toward explaining the differences in morbidity, mortality, and medical care use between blacks and whites. Many areas, such as delay in seeking treatment and differential survival, represent serious ones that require rational assessment based on sound empirical studies as well as intervention. The scientific and practical contingencies associated with the term race, however, call into question the validity and reliability of social science and health research in which its meaning is ambiguous and elusive. Much of what is written about the incidence and prevalence of disease, life expectancy, and mortality (e.g., infant, maternal), in which race is posited as an antecedent or determinant, leaves the processes of interpretation and inference to the reader.

Differential morbidity and mortality rates in the United States are assumed to be closely correlated with race as well as ethnic heritage. Rates specific for race provide a demographic context within which epidemiologists describe and explain the dynamics of the disease process. Similarly, medical sociologists and behavioral scientists seek interpretations of help-seeking behavior, health services utilization, patient satisfaction with care, and type of care dispensed in terms of the race variable. Yet, in most social science and epidemiologic research, the concepts and interpretations are not evaluated as representing fundamental sources of systematic measurement error. When ascertaining the type, distribution, incidence, or prevalence of disease, there are no concrete indicators specified of the reliability of the race concept nor of its internal and external validity. Thus, it is never precisely clear whether the variations found in health beliefs and behaviors or in disease frequency and in mortality rates are primarily the result of how race is defined or whether the findings indicate a true difference. For example, are the differences in cancer morbidity and mortality, hypertension, and in health services utilization the result of employing race as a biological variate, a component of socioeconomic status, an indicator of culture, or as a factor which interacts with social class? The health policy and planning implications of these conceptual distinctions are highly significant.

Although social scientists lack knowledge of biology and genetics, they consistently interpret correlates with race by relying on biological or genetic explanations either directly or inferentially. Analyses of racial differences in disease prevalence, infant mortality, and in life expectancy are most often based on the premise that the associations can be attributed to race as an hereditary factor. Frequently, such reductionistic assertions rule out important variables like accessibility and availability, family income status, trust in physicians, quality of care, stage in diagnosis, and the organization of and prior experience with the health care delivery system. Even when these constitute the explanations, they are used to highlight racial differentials in a biological sense.

Some Methodological Consequences

The gathering of health statistics in the United States incorporates associating race with differences in disease incidence and prevalence and in mortality. The frequency of occurrence and the severity of disease consistently show variability within as well as between racial categories. This is especially true for blacks and whites, which represent the numerically larger and physically distinct racial populations, although the dimensions of the differentiation lack clarity. Typically, epidemiologic studies indicate that while blacks have higher rates of hypertensive heart ailments and lung cancer (especially males), whites have higher rates of bladder cancer and arteriosclerotic conditions. Further, some diseases are specifically genetically linked to race or to ethnic stock such as phenylketonuria (PKU) (Centerwall and Neff 1961; Cohen, Bodonyi, and Szeinberg 1961; Saugstad 1975b); muscular dystrophy (Shokeir and Kobrinsky 1976); albinism (Nance, Jackson, and Witkop 1970); Alzheimer's disease (Heston, Lowther, and Leventhal 1966; Wheelan and Race 1959); and Tay-Sachs disease (Kaback, Rimoin, and O'Brien 1977; Yokoyama 1979).

With the aforementioned examples, race is clearly being specified as a genetic construct. This use also permeates social and behavioral science explanations of variability in health status as well as in health beliefs, values, and behaviors—especially medical services utilization. Any such interpretations are confounded by the complex and ambiguous nature of the concept and hence the lack of definitional specificity. Yet, investigators rarely, if ever, clarify what meaning of race is being conveyed, what proportion of the variance in a given dependent variable, such as hypertension or survival rates from heart disease, can be accounted for by race as a biogenetic entity, as a social phenomenon, or what proportion can be explained in terms of the interaction between race and class. The sheer process of attributing a portion of variation in a postulated dependent factor to race involves multiple dimensions. Among the salient methodological questions pertinent to these issues are the following:

1. Is it a valid analytical tool in social and behavioral science research when it is hypothesized as a biological variate or when it is ambiguously defined?

2. How can its genetic or hereditary aspects be extrapolated from the behavioral and cultural interpretations?

3. When posited in survey or health services research as an independent variable, is it possible to separate empirically its genetic or biological meaning from its sociocultural qualities and environmental context?

One basic technique for controlling unanticipated and potentially inexplicable sources of bias in research is matching. This procedure is incorporated in the study designs of cross-sectional and retrospective surveys and in controlled experiments. The variables on which groups are consistently matched are demographic or constitutional ones: sex, age, and race. An interesting and perplexing issue is whether race is construed as a genetic or biological factor when it is used for matching or when it is allowed to vary or in both instances. The different denotative and connotative meanings within a given study have significant consequences for the validity and reliability of the research results. It is never precisely clear when groups are matched in case-control, longitudinal, or cross-sectional studies whether race is a social factor, an indicator of culture, a biological variate, or a statistical construct. Thus, researchers often make sweeping generalizations about "racial differences" in disease patterns and in mortality rates without ever having offered scientifically pertinent or empirically useful operational indicators. The tacit assumption appears to exist that other researchers and all readers know how race is being used.

More important, the persistent study of biological and cultural differences among racial groups reflects an embedded ideological orientation and thus is not a value-free process nor without political and other ramifications (Deutsch 1969; Taylor 1980). A rarely posed and an unresearched question bearing on this issue was raised over twenty years ago:

> Why did the racial features of individuals take on so much importance that a new word was needed in the European language? . . . Whatever the reason for the popularity of the race idea, the fact is that Europeans began to give thought to the subject, and began to classify the peoples of the earth on a racial basis (Berry 1965, 36–37).

Definitions of Race and Their Implications

Much of the ambiguity surrounding the term and the use of racial descriptors relates to the conception of race as either a biological or social category. Although the criteria (i.e., phenotypic, genotypic, and behavioral traits) employed to classify human populations into distinct racial groups are widely recognized, there exists no universal or exact definition of what constitutes a race among either physical or social scientists. Natural scientists, including physical anthropologists, have tended to rely on genotypic descriptions in dividing people into racial categories. The two criteria most often applied are blood type and the relative frequency of genetic traits (Dobzhansky 1964). The use of genetic variation as a criterion apparently stems from the success of biologists in identifying species of plants and animals. Fortney (1977, 45) explains the fundamental dissimilarities between a biological species and race:

> Species have a discernible line of genetic demarcation from one another, whereas races do not. Consequently, races are not clearly defined biological groups. Boundaries between races are more or less blurred by the constant gene flow between human populations.

Genetic mutation, natural selection, drift, and population admixture are four of the processes that make the genetic taxonomy problematic. According to Fortney (1977), however, in the physical sciences, "current theory holds that the most valid criteria for classifying races are data on the frequencies of certain genes within populations" since the outcome differences (e.g., hair texture, eye color) are the most stable and least affected by the environment.

In theory, social scientists view race both as a phenotypic category and as a composite construct reflecting unique and historically specific experiences (e.g., cultural practices, inequality, discrimination) between groups. The significance of phenotypic distinctions is embodied in the premium placed on race as a basis for differentiation and social stratification. Given this, it would appear to have greater relevance as a social descriptor than as a biological one (Van den Berghe 1967), although the two interpretations are closely interconnected in the logic of the social sciences. Further, in the United States, blacks are not considered a minority merely because of their numbers but because they are physically distinct from the majority sector. They are also members of a racially stratified society in which they are defined and responded to as members of the same category. Thus, not only are populations arranged into groupings based on obvious physical traits such as skin color and hair texture but, more significant, behavioral characteristics are assigned to these (e.g., health knowledge and its expression). As a result, persons and populations deviating from the dominant physical norms are perceived and treated categorically. These

perceptions influence the content of social science inquiry and epidemiologic studies of "racial differences" in health status, help-seeking
behaviors, health knowledge, life expectancy, disease type and frequency,
and mortality. Apparent cultural variations are also often labeled as
racial representations and used as criteria for population group comparisons (Burkey 1978). This juxtaposition of race, behavior, and
culture further complicates and virtually inhibits objective explanation
and precision in measurement. Paradoxically, ignoring the aforementioned fundamentals contradicts the raison d'être of science.

A Prevailing Dilemma: Ethnicity versus Race

Further, in the social sciences, race and ethnicity are persistently used
interchangeably as though the qualitative distinctions were merely
semantic. For many social scientists, race, like sex, denotes physical
traits (Berreman 1985, 27). In theory, as previously indicated, it is
assumed to encompass much broader phenomena (e.g., discrimination,
social stratification, racism, and phenotypic characteristics) than ethnicity
which essentially connotes a national identity or a cultural group
(Blackwell 1985; Burkey 1978; Singer 1962; Taylor 1978; Wilkinson
1987). The historically based structural position of blacks vis-à-vis
whites refers to a hierarchical arrangement in the distribution of
societal resources and opportunities such as jobs, education, and health
care. Based on these social products of racial differentiation and the
cultural aspects of ethnic group membership, there is no inherent
association between race and ethnicity.

Of equal importance in understanding the conceptual and practical
distinction between race and ethnicity for health policy is a pervasive
belief system which, consciously or unconsciously, incorporates the
supposition and promotion of racial superiority. This ideologic system
is used to justify the structurally "advantaged" position of one group
over another (Delany 1970). Thus, in the case of black Americans,
it is their structural position and a concomitant shared societal belief
that determine and define their health status, use of medical care
resources, and differential rates of morbidity and mortality. Given
these empirical correlates with racial status and the disproportionate
concentration of black Americans in the lower socioeconomic strata,
ethnicity and race are further contrasted.

The key question with regard to race-specific health research is: What are the analytic and practical or policy implications of the view of blacks as either a racial or an ethnic group? First, the use of the term race to classify this population sector should not mean that there are no ethnic or cultural differences among them (e.g., West Indians, southern versus northern resident, lifestyle variations). The cultural diversity which does exist among blacks is, for the most part, perceived as less significant or consequential than their common phenotypic traits, shared group history, and a collective belief that gives credence to the assumed linkage between race and behavior.

If race is defined as a cultural measure or indicator of ethnicity, then researchers and policy makers are likely to make fallacious comparisons and draw unwarranted conclusions regarding the capabilities, unique experiences, and behaviors of blacks and whites. The ethnic paradigm of intergroup dynamics assumes that structural impediments and racist beliefs based on phenotypic traits are either no longer relevant or are much less so than cultural characteristics. Adherents of the ethnicity or national-cultural model postulate the notion that the status of blacks can be legitimately compared with that of all other white American ethnic groups (e.g., Jews, Italians, Irish). Yet, this view has been sharply criticized for blurring the deeply entrenched historical, political, and social distinctions between race and ethnic status in America.

> In structural terms, Blacks are qualitatively different from White ethnic groups. For White ethnic groups, there is no nationwide ideology that ranks specific groups. In contrast, racism is a pervasive ideology that ranks Blacks as a group below all others because it assumes the inherent genetic inferiority of Blacks. The stress on phenotypic differences (in this case skin color) and its expression in racist ideology determines the character of White-Black interaction in every part of the country. . . . Racism, therefore, is a fundamental factor that makes the Black situation distinctly different from that of all White ethnic groups (Barnett 1976, 13).

In health research, reliance on the ethnicity perspective of intergroup relations may lead to ignoring or placing less emphasis on the effects of social structure and racism. The underlying ideological and value dimensions of seeking and confirming racial variation in morbidity and mortality would also be overlooked. Further, the ethnicity or cultural hypotheses could result in promoting "boot-strap" theories about the health status and behaviors of all blacks and lead to victim blaming (e.g., "They lack health knowledge," "They seek care later than whites").

Defining Health Problems and Allocating Resources

In conducting race-specific health research, it is important to consider some of the salient contrasts between the biological and social definitions of race and their broader ramifications. First, biological and social explanations represent not only conceptual distinctions but are also relevant to health policy issues. Research directed toward the study of racially based genetic diseases (e.g., sickle cell anemia) may result in fundamentally disparate policy developments and services rather than socially oriented health studies which have as their focus personal responsibility and the role of behavioral intervention.

Moreover, for some diseases such as sickle cell anemia, the amount of concern and resources allocated to address these conditions is not only a product of the ideas and opinions about health and illness but also the collective ideology and structural position of blacks. In addition, those problems that are considered to be genetic in origin may be viewed and treated quite differently from those related to social forces (e.g., environmental pollutants, occupational hazards, accidents). Specifically, in the case of sickle cell anemia, more attention and support may be directed toward this disease since its etiology implies less of an individual responsibility and is unrelated to personal experiences. Therefore, it is only partially amenable to health interventions. On the other hand, such a disease could be used to encourage racial myths by groups who do not suffer from this particular genetic malady.

The issue of hypertension as a genetically based race-specific disease raises a similar set of issues. A great deal of research has shown that high blood pressure is strongly correlated with socioeconomic status, stress, lifestyles, and diet (Langford, Watson, and Douglas 1968; Howard and Holman 1970; Reed 1981; Szklo 1979; U.S. Department of Health and Human Services 1986). Some studies have suggested that hypertension may also be a product of the biological adaptation to a prior African environment and that this genetic heritage may explain the higher racial group differences (Gillum 1979; Singer 1962).

Other researchers who have studied the within-group variations for the disease among black Americans have found that hypertension varies according to skin color. That is, lighter pigmented blacks have a lower prevalence of hypertension than darker skinned ones because the former have a greater genetic admixture with whites (Boyle 1970; Harburg, Gliebermann, and Roeper 1978; Keil 1981). Depending on the interpretation, funds and services could be allocated for either social and behavioral interventions or for genetic programs involving large-scale screening, long-term counseling, and sustained monitoring. In addition, associating diseases with color among blacks might generate or intensify intraracial friction and exacerbate self concepts, especially among children.

Summary

The history, reality, and prolonged effects of racial stratification and its supportive ideology in the United States require systematic study of the impact of racial perceptions in the health sphere and in every facet of American life (Berry 1965; Berreman 1985; Blackwell 1985). In this regard, the use of race as an independent variable in social research is, in principle, similar to the presumed explanatory power of other status characteristics such as class or economic position. Depending on which meaning is intended, the potential policy, health services, and sociopolitical outcomes could be diametrically opposed to one another.

Far from being an esoteric subject among intellectuals, any definition of race has fundamental and practical extensions to cultural and political realities. Essentially, studies and discussions of racial similarities and differences in health matters, whether intended or not, go beyond statistical compilations and correlations and reflect norms, values, the country's common beliefs (Praeger 1982), and the structural positions of majority and minority groups. Presumably, these are among the reasons that racial categories are studied in social science. They are assumed to represent socially relevant and unique histories, experiences, and statuses which differentiate black and white Americans in particular. The risks in epidemiologic and in social science research involve the preoccupation with disparities in the health difficulties among them; the attribution of racial biology and genetic traits to virtually all health spheres; the assumed preponderance of disabling conditions for blacks; and the unrelenting focus on only two racial populations despite our having a multiethnic society (Wilkinson 1987).

Since health behaviors are directly associated with a group's "way of life," they should be carefully scrutinized within relevant socio-environmental contexts as part of the scientific processes of discovery, explication, and intervention. Researchers must understand and account for the underlying premises, ideological translations, and practical applications of their studies especially with respect to race-specific health research. It is likely that systematic probing beyond demographic or constitutional factors will enable social scientists and health researchers to discover that for certain behaviors (e.g., prevention), individual attributes such as race and sex—and even knowledge, roles, attitudes, and diets—may explain far less than will environmental hazards and basic structural variables such as the organization of the health care delivery system, availability of and access to care, ability to pay, provider patterns, diagnostic processes, institutional operations, and quality of care.

This discussion is not intended to suggest that genetic research should be avoided or that its findings are without merit (Heston and Mastri 1977; Saugstad 1975a; Shokeir and Kobrinsky 1976). Rather, it reiterates the fundamental point that scientific research does not take place within a social or political vacuum (Wilkinson 1974). Health researchers who employ race as an empirical variable must understand the environmental context in which this ambiguous and value-laden concept thrives. They have a responsibility to define its meaning and theoretical application with greater precision than has heretofore been the case. As scientists, they also have an obligation to assess objectively and predict the social and economic ramifications of using race in a particular way. In this respect, Tyroler and James (1978, 1172), in examining the contextual nature of research on skin color and hypertension, state:

> The danger of perpetuating or encouraging an increase in extant racism in the U.S. is real and immediate in any scientific investigation comparing black and white populations, even when the primary and explicit purpose of the investigation is to reduce the excess burden of morbidity and mortality in black populations. The dangers are particularly acute when a focal area of the investigation involves genetic studies. We regard it as a truism that all health and disease

manifestations in populations (such as high blood pressure and its sequelae) are a result of the interaction of environmental and genetic factors. The mechanisms responsible for the expression of the phenotypic manifestations of health and disease should carry no implication of either superiority or inferiority. The investigation of this subject should be value free. Obviously, this has not always been true.

References

Barnett, M.R. 1976. A Theoretical Perspective on American Racial Policy. In *Public Policy for the Black Community: Strategies and Perspectives,* ed. M.R. Barnett and J.A. Hefner, 1–54. New York: Alfred.

Berreman, G.D. 1985. Race, Caste, and Other Invidious Distinctions in Social Stratification. In *Majority and Minority: The Dynamics of Race and Ethnicity,* ed. N.R. Yetman, 21–39. Boston: Allyn and Bacon.

Berry, B. 1965. *Race and Ethnic Relations.* Boston: Houghton Mifflin.

Blackwell, J. 1985. *The Black Community: Diversity and Unity.* 2d ed. New York: Harper and Row.

Boyle, E. 1970. Biological Patterns in Hypertension by Race, Sex, Body Weight and Skin Color. *Journal of the American Medical Association* 213:1637–43.

Burkey, R.M. 1978. *Ethnic and Racial Groups: The Dynamics of Dominance.* Menlo Park, Calif.: Cummings.

Centerwall, W.R., and C.A. Neff. 1961. Phenylketonuria: A Case Report of Children of Jewish Ancestry. *Archives of Pediatrics* 78:379–84.

Cohen, B.E., E. Bodonyi, and A. Szeinberg. 1961. Phenylketonuria in Jews. *Lancet* 1:344–45.

Cooper, R. 1985. A Note on the Biological Concept of Race and Its Application in Epidemiologic Research. *American Heart Journal* 108(3):715–23.

Delany, L.T. 1970. The White American Psyche: Exploration of Racism. In *White Racism: Its History, Pathology, and Practice,* ed. B.N. Schwart and R. Disch, 155–65. New York: Dell.

Deutsch, M. 1969. Happenings on the Way Back to the Forum: Social Science, IQ, and Race Differences Revisited. *Harvard Educational Review* 39:522–57.

Dobzhansky, T. 1964. *Heredity and the Nature of Man.* New York: Harcourt, Brace and World.

Fortney, N.D. 1977. The Anthropological Concept of Race. *Journal of Black Studies* 8:35–54.

Gillum, R.F. 1979. Pathophysiology of Hypertension in Blacks and Whites: A Review of the Basis of Racial Blood Pressure Differences. *Hypertension* 1:468–75.

Harburg, E., Gleibermann, L., and Roeper, P. 1978. Skin Color, Ethnicity and Blood Pressure: Detroit, part 1, Blacks. *American Journal of Public Health* 68:1177–83.

Heston, L.L., D.L. Lowther, and C.M. Leventhal. 1966. Alzheimer's Disease: A Family Study. *Archives of Neurology* 15:225–33.

Heston, L.L., and A.R. Mastri. 1977. The Genetics of Alzheimer's Disease: Associations with Hematologic Malignancy and Down's Syndrome. *Archives of General Psychiatry* 34:976–81.

Howard, J., and B.L. Holman. 1970. The Effects of Race and Occupation on Hypertension Mortality. *Milbank Memorial Fund Quarterly/Health and Society* 43:196–263.

Kaback, M.M., D.L. Rimoin, and J.S. O'Brien. 1977. *Tay-Sachs Disease: Screening and Prevention.* New York: Alan R. Liss.

Keil, J.E. 1981. Skin Color and Education Effects on Blood Pressure. *American Journal of Public Health* 71(5):532–34.

Langford, H., R. Watson, and B. Douglas. 1968. Factors Affecting Blood Pressure in Population Groups. *Transactions of the Association of American Physicians* 81:135–45.

Mausner, J.S., and A.K. Bahn. 1974. *Epidemiology: An Introductory Text.* Philadelphia: W.B. Saunders.

McKusick, V.A. 1969. *Human Genetics.* Englewood Cliffs. N.J.: Prentice-Hall.

Nance, W.E., C.E. Jackson, and C.J. Witkop. 1970. Amish Albinism: A Distinctive Autosomal Recessive Phenotype. *American Journal of Human Genetics* 22:579–86.

Praeger, J. 1982. American Racial Ideology as Collective Representation. *Ethnic and Racial Studies* 5:99–119.

Reed, W.L. 1981. Racial Differences in Blood Pressure Levels of Adolescents. *American Journal of Public Health* 71 (10):1165–67.

Saugstad, L.F. 1975a. Anthropological Significance of Phenylketonuria. *Clinical Genetics* 7:52–61.

———. 1975b. Frequency of Phenylketonuria in Norway. *Clinical Genetics* 7:40–51.

Shokeir, M.H.K., and N. Kobrinsky. 1976. Autosomal Recessive Muscular Dystrophy in Manitoba Hutterites. *Clinical Genetics* 9:197–202.

Singer, L. 1962. Ethnogenesis and Negro Americans Today. *Social Research* 19:419–32.

Szklo, M. 1979. Epidemiologic Patterns of Blood Pressure in Children. *Epidemiologic Review* 1:143–69.

Taylor, H. 1980. *The I.Q. Game: A Methodological Inquiry into the Heredity-Environment Controversy.* New Brunswick, N.J.: Rutgers University Press.

Taylor, R. 1978. Black Ethnicity and the Persistence of Ethnogenesis. *American Journal of Sociology* 84:1401–22.

Tyroler, H.A., and James, S.A. 1978. Blood Pressure and Skin Color. *American Journal of Public Health* 68 (12):1170–72.

U.S. Department of Health and Human Services. 1986. *Cardiovascular and Cerebrovascular Disease,* part 1, vol. 4. *Report of the Secretary's Task Force on Black and Minority Health.* Washington.

Van den Bergh, P. 1967. *Race and Racism.* New York: Wiley.

Wheelan, L., and R.R. Race. 1959. Familial Alzheimer's Disease: Note on the Linkage Data. *Human Genetics* 23:300–10.

Wilkinson, D.Y. 1974. For Whose Benefit? Politics and Sickle Cell. *Black Scholar* 5:26–31.

–––––––. 1980. Minority Women: Social-Cultural Issues. In *Women and Psychotherapy: An Assessment of Research and Practice,* ed. A. Brodsky and R. Hare-Mustin, 185–203. New York: Guilford Press.

–––––––. 1984. Afro-American Women and Their Families. *Marriage and Family Review* 7:125–42.

–––––––. 1987. Ethnicity. In *Handbook of Marriage and the Family,* ed. M.B. Sussman and S.K. Steinmetz, 183–210. New York: Plenum.

Wilson, W.J. 1978. *The Declining Significance of Race.* Chicago: University of Chicago Press.

Yokoyama, S. 1979. Role of Genetic Drift in the High Frequency of Tay-Sachs Disease among Ashkenazic Jews. *Annals of Human Genetics* 43:133–36.

Black-White Differences in Health Status: Methods or Substance?

RONALD M. ANDERSEN,
ROSS M. MULLNER,
and LLEWELLYN J. CORNELIUS

THIS SUPPLEMENT TO THE *MILBANK QUARTERLY* is devoted to concerns about the effects of national health policies on the health status of the black population in the United States. Much of it necessarily addresses differences between blacks and the rest of American residents, particularly the majority white population. Our purpose is to consider how these apparent differences are influenced by issues of measurement. Do inconsistencies in the measurement process exaggerate or mask differences in health status between blacks and whites? Answers are essential to understanding how planning and resource allocation decisions based on assessed health status might be affected by methods.

The following sections will: (1) discuss problems in measuring health status and consider how various measures of health status might suggest differences between blacks and whites reflecting measurement errors and erroneous interpretation; and (2) provide empirical comparisons of health status measures for blacks and whites based largely on national data sources to explore further whether observed differences represent "methods" or "substance."

Problems in Measuring Health Status

The issues of measurement we will consider include: (1) sources of measurement error; (2) data collection methods; (3) interpretation of the measures; and (4) types of measures used to represent health status. Each issue will be defined, and related problems in comparing black and white health status will be identified.

Sources of Measurement Error

Errors in measuring health status can be separated into variable or random error and bias or systematic error (Kish 1965, 509, 519–20; Andersen et al. 1979). A common type of *variable error* arises from sampling because a sample can represent only a subset of a population. Differences between the sample estimates and the population are variable errors. These variable errors decrease as sample size increases.

Biases, on the other hand, are independent of sample size and exist in measures of the total population as well as in a sample. Important types of bias include: noncoverage or failure to include some types of individuals in reporting systems at all; nonresponse or lack of complete information on some persons; and errors of observation resulting from faulty data collection or processing. We shall consider how variable errors and biases may differentially influence health status estimates of blacks and whites.

Variable Sampling Error. The National Health Interview Survey is an annual probability sample of approximately 35,000 households with health information obtained on all household members (Moss and Parsons 1986, 132). Even this sophisticated, large survey, however, is subject to random errors which differentially have an impact on estimates for blacks and whites.

Because it is a national sample survey, the Health Interview Survey includes relatively small numbers of blacks because they are a minority of the total population. The results for blacks (especially for subgroups of blacks divided, for example, by age and sex) are subject to substantial variable errors.

The Health Interview Survey has taken steps to reduce this problem by oversampling black persons beginning with the 1985 survey (Moss and Parsons 1986, 132). Sampling rates were increased for areas known to have the highest concentrations of black persons.

Noncoverage Bias.   Other studies of the health of black populations are subject to even more substantial problems of not only variable error but also bias. Jackson (1981) documents noncoverage bias where local nonprobability samples are used to draw conclusions about more general black populations. For example, reports of black women in St. Louis who had migrated from the rural south are used in one study to generalize the health practices of all pregnant black women.

Another problem of noncoverage is the use of telephone surveys to represent the total population. When poor blacks are less likely to have phones, noncoverage bias can substantially influence comparisons of health status between blacks and whites. (In the ongoing Urban Family Life Survey being conducted for William J. Wilson in low-income segments of Chicago with largely black populations, the National Opinion Research Center (NORC) estimates that 20 percent of the households do not have telephones for personal communication [Sara Segal Loevy, NORC, Chicago].)

A final important type of noncoverage bias is the "denominator problem." Certain types of blacks (e.g., young male inner-city blacks) may be systematically excluded from population counts. In subsequent ratio comparisons such as mortality rates, the black rate might be overstated because the denominator (population count) is incomplete.

Nonresponse Bias.   Nonresponse bias can also affect black-white comparisons. The problem arises if response rates differ by race, or if nonrespondents of one race are less like respondents than is true for the other race. The evidence on participation in surveys by race is mixed. Participation tends to be higher among rural southern blacks and lower among inner-city urban blacks. Overall, Andersen et al. (1979, 135) found response rates similar in a national health survey conducted in 1970. The Health Examination Survey found blacks less likely than whites to participate in the oral glucose tolerance test to determine the presence of diabetes (Hadden and Harris 1987). Vernon, Roberts, and Lee (1984) using data from the longitudinal Alameda County Health Survey from 1965 and 1975 found blacks and Mexican-Americans less likely to be participants than whites in the follow-up survey. Some characteristics associated with black nonparticipation included younger age, unemployment, residential mobility, and depression.

Observational Bias.   Observational biases that occur in the process of reporting of illness can also influence black-white differences. An example of a possible observational bias is the interviewer effect which may arise between a white interviewer and black respondents (Shosteck 1977; Sudman and Bradburn 1980, 93–139). Another is differential reporting given the same underlying conditions. Berkanovic and Telesky (1985, 575) conclude that transitory physical sensations, however painful, are less likely to be defined as illness (by blacks) than they are by either Mexicans or whites.

Data Collection Methods

Data collection methods for measuring health status are commonly divided into: (1) direct observations of patients made by health professionals (e.g., autopsy reports and clinical examinations); (2) records originally collected for some other purpose such as treating patients (e.g., hospital records and physicians' medical charts) or compiled for administrative and legal purposes (e.g., school attendance, workers' compensation, and Social Security); and (3) self-reports provided directly by individuals (e.g., population-based health interview surveys and patient satisfaction surveys). Our concern about types of data collection is that certain collection methods may produce different results for blacks and whites not related to underlying health status.

Direct Observations. Direct observations of health status are likely to provide the most objective indicators of health for a population. Even here, however, problems in measurement can occur. Medical practices and diagnostic labeling, for example, may vary by physician and hospital as well as by geographic area. Furthermore, hospitals and physicians may unwittingly and systematically misclassify and misdiagnose patients.

Records. Records, which in many cases are completed by individuals without a medical background, provide a less objective measurement of health status. Workers' compensation records, for example, may vary by state and other political units and in the number and type of data items they contain; certain data items may routinely not be answered; and data that are reported may be inaccurate.

Self-reports. Self-reports of health status are likely to provide the least objective measurement of health status. Certain individuals and groups may refuse to participate in health surveys; or when they do participate, may not accurately report events because of lack of recall, misinterpretation of questions, or provide erroneous but socially acceptable answers.

All methods of collection have the potential to affect comparisons of health status between blacks and whites. Direct observations and records may vary because of differences in site of service by blacks or whites or may vary by race because of differences in where blacks and whites live and work. Self-reports show systematic differences between blacks and whites in reporting of conditions as well as services received and health insurance coverage (Andersen et al. 1979).

Interpretation Errors

Interpretation of measurements may lead to erroneous conclusions about differences in health status between blacks and whites. Interpretation errors can result because the meaning of a particular measure is misunderstood or the results are inappropriately generalized to another time or a more general population group.

An important way in which errors in interpretation can influence conclusions about black-white differences is failure to consider intraethnic diversity. In the past, many survey results were reported only for "nonwhites" and "whites." Jackson (1981) notes that studies need to account for potentially large differences between northern and southern blacks, urban and rural blacks, native and foreign-born blacks. Variation among blacks in other factors such as age, sex, and income should also be systematically considered in order to understand how black-white differences in health status are influenced by a myriad of other factors that determine health status.

Types of Health Status Measures

Health status is a complex concept and difficult to measure. Though various approaches to measuring health status have been suggested in the literature, we will use the five types suggested by Patrick and Elinson (1979): death, disease, disability, discomfort, and dissatisfaction. These types range from objective provider-determined measures of causes of mortality (death) to more subjective patient-oriented evaluations of how well an individual's perceived health care needs are being taken care of (dissatisfaction). Table 1 records major sources of data for each of the types of measures as well as primary methods of data collection for those sources. A central question addressed in this article is how different the health status of blacks compared with whites appears to

TABLE 1

Major Sources of Information by Type of Health Status Measure and
Method of Collection

	Primary collection method		
Health status measure	Direct observation	Record	Self-report
DEATH			
Death certificates		×	
Certificates of fetal death		×	
Autopsy reports	×		
Life insurance claim records		×	
DISEASE			
Reports of notifiable disease	×		
Hospital medical charts		×	
Private physician medical charts		×	
Prepaid group practice program records		×	
Health insurance claim records		×	
Disease registers	×		
Health interview surveys			×
Health examination surveys	×		
DISABILITY			
Employer records		×	
School attendance records		×	
Health insurance claim records		×	
Hospital medical charts		×	
Workers' Compensation records		×	
Social Security records		×	
Individual and household health surveys			×
DISCOMFORT			
Patient surveys			×
Individual and household health surveys			×
Hospital medical charts		×	
DISSATISFACTION			
Patient satisfaction surveys			×
Individual and household health surveys			×

be depending on the type of health status measure used. Consideration of sources of error, collection methods, and issues of interpretation helps to clarify this question.

Death. In obtaining and interpreting information on the number and causes of deaths for blacks and whites, a number of problems arise. The amount and quality of data on deaths depend upon such factors as: the extent to which the deceased were medically studied before death, and the degree of familiarity certifying physicians had with them. Since sources and kinds of health services differ for blacks and whites (e.g., blacks are more likely to have no regular source of care or use outpatient departments and emergency rooms and be admitted to public and large teaching hospitals [Andersen et al. 1987]) bias of largely unknown magnitude and direction may be included in comparative mortality statistics.

The diagnostic (and in some cases demographic) terms used on death certificates are revised approximately every ten years. Thus, longitudinal analyses of differences between black and white mortality may be difficult to compare over time. These changes reflect medical advances, the changing profile of health problems, and social recognition. Only in recent years, for example, have deaths been coded by race, as opposed to the color system of "white" and "nonwhite" (Cooper and Simmons 1985).

Another difficulty with death certificates is the validity of information they contain. Coding of death certificates is subject to misclassification in categories such as sudden coronary death. In many cases, demographic and occupational information is obtained by the funeral director from the available next of kin. The accuracy and completeness of this information is generally low. For example, the occupation of individuals who were employed for many years may be listed as retired, and women who have worked outside the home for many years may be described as "housewives." Such misclassifications may be correlated with race. They may be especially important in mortality studies examining race and occupation since black Americans are exposed to more occupational hazards than are whites (Kleinman, Fingerhut, and Feldman 1980, 28).

Although autopsy reports generally provide the most accurate data about the cause of death of individuals, they cannot be used to generalize about the health status of a population for they are done on a nonrandom sample of all deaths. Furthermore, because of increasing costs and perceived clinical value, the proportion of autopsies (currently about 15 percent of all deaths [Mausner and Kramer 1985, 73]) has been declining over the last decades. Also, the quality of information from autopsies may vary. Some are performed by medical examiners while others are conducted by a coroner who may not be a pathologist or even a physician. There are no current national estimates of the proportion of blacks or whites who are autopsied.

Last, comparisons of deaths for blacks versus whites reflect survivor effects as well as selection by competing cause which can lead to interpretive errors. Cooper and Simmons (1985, 344) indicate that:

> The survivor effect is best seen in the black-white crossover in old age. Thus, while few blacks live to the age of 80, those who do survive are healthier and suffer lower age-specific death rates than do whites. Since a large proportion of the white population survives into old age, they will be more likely to die of the more common diseases of old age. The phenomenon of competing cause tends to eliminate potential candidates for a specific disease through premature death from another related disease.

Disease. A common method of determining the disease status of a population is through the utilization of hospital medical charts. These charts, however, also have their deficiencies.

Data based on hospital discharges or admissions may provide a biased picture of the illnesses of a population due to noncoverage of all illnesses. For example, acute minor illnesses may be treated in a physician's office or not treated at all. In addition, serious chronic diseases that are followed on an outpatient basis may also not appear in data based on hospital inpatient records.

Nonresponse error is also a problem. Because many hospitals still do not have automated medical record systems, hospital statistics on even a primary diagnosis may be difficult to collect. Cases that should be included may be missing because records are lost or misplaced.

Bias in hospital records resulting from both noncoverage and non-response can interfere with use of these data to compare health status of blacks and whites. For example, if blacks are less likely to seek service or be admitted to the hospital for less serious conditions, hospital data would underestimate the prevalence of these conditions vis à vis whites (Kravits and Schneider 1975). Furthermore, if the kind of hospitals blacks are more likely to use (e.g., public and inner-city teaching hospitals) keep records either more or less complete than other hospitals, comparative black-white statistics could be misleading.

Disability.   Disability can be defined and measured in a variety of ways. For insurance purposes, disability is defined as the inability to engage in gainful employment. Health researchers, on the other hand, generally define disability as any temporary or long-term reduction of a person's activity as a result of an acute or chronic condition. Three measures of disability are commonly used: restricted-activity days, work-loss days, and bed-disability days.

Some of the most commonly used sources of information on the disability status of the nation's population are national household surveys such as the National Health Interview Survey (Wilder 1986). Other sources of disability data—including those from employer records, school attendance records, health insurance records, etc.—are likely to be even more subject to bias and variable error.

Using disability days to represent health status can lead to significant interpretive error. Employees who are not ill, especially single parents with a large number of children, may take sick days to stay home with a sick child. Children may not attend school for a variety of reasons. And people may falsely claim disability to collect insurance money.

Lastly, disability, in many cases, may be unrelated to disease, and may instead be a measure of morale or conformity as, for example, when workers purposely take sick days because of alienating and stressful working conditions (Patrick and Elinson 1979). Correlations between race and nonhealth-related disability days could lead to biased comparisons of black-white health status differences.

Discomfort.   Estimates of a population's level of discomfort (feelings of aches, pains, tiredness, sadness, etc.) are generally obtained through the use of individual and household surveys. Discomfort estimates are subject to considerable measurement and interpretation error.

The degree of reported discomfort of a population may vary because of a host of factors. Individuals may vary in their ability to assess various levels of discomfort and their importance. Some individuals— for example, the "worried well"—may indicate higher levels of discomfort than others. In contrast, individuals who may be experiencing great discomfort, and indeed at a high risk of death, may not report it at all. These differences as well as the perception of health status in general seems likely to vary due to learning and cultural differences in the perception of health (Linn, Hunter, and Linn 1980).

An example of apparent differences in perceived discomfort can be found in a recent study of prehospital delay of myocardial infarction among black patients conducted at Cook County Hospital in Chicago. Cooper et al. (1986) found that the delay time from onset of symptoms to arrival at the hospital for blacks was markedly prolonged compared with studies of predominantly white populations.

Another problem with measuring discomfort and other self-reported health status indicators is that few of them have been objectively evaluated and verified. Watkins (1983), for example, states that the administration of questionnaires to black Americans concerning chest pain is likely to yield overestimates of the frequency of coronary heart disease.

Dissatisfaction. Information on dissatisfaction can be used in two widely different ways. First, it can be used to measure the feelings of acceptance or rejection of health services offered by professionals. Second, it can be used to measure the degree of satisfaction with one's state of health, regardless of the medical care process.

The most common sources of information on dissatisfaction are population surveys of individuals and households and surveys of hospitalized patients. The results of these surveys generally indicate that most people are satisfied with the care they receive, while a smaller number are dissatisfied (Fleming 1979, 1981). The reasons for this dissatisfaction vary and may produce interpretive errors in any estimate of a population's health status. Individuals may be dissatisfied because they have increasing expectations which are not met; they may be treated in various ways they are not accustomed to; or they may feel, in the case of patients, that their service will be unfavorably influenced by their complaints. As reasons for expressions of dissatisfaction vary between blacks and whites, substantial potential for intepretive errors in assessing differences in dissatisfaction occur.

Empirical Comparisons of Types of Health Status Measures

In this section we will compare the health status of blacks and whites using different types of measures: death, disease, disability, discomfort, and dissatisfaction. Recent national data sources are employed for the most part. Our purpose is to show how these comparisons vary by type of measure and to explore, in some instances, how methods may influence the apparent differences between blacks and whites. Some ideas presented in the previous section concerning sources of errors, collection methods, and interpretation errors will be employed to help separate issues of "methods" from those of "substance."

Table 2 provides a summary view of black-white comparisons of health status according to a range of measures representing death, disease, disability, discomfort, and dissatisfaction. The conclusions vary greatly depending on which measures are emphasized.

For the most objective measure (death) and the most subjective measure (dissatisfaction), blacks appear to have much poorer health status. The age-adjusted death rates are 50 percent higher for blacks than for whites for both sexes. Similarly, the proportion of blacks reporting only fair or poor health is almost twice the proportion for whites, and blacks are also more likely to report little satisfaction with their health and physical condition.

In contrast, the self-reporting of acute conditions is actually higher for whites than for blacks for all age groups (especially for children). Number of disability days and symptoms of illness reported by blacks and whites varies according to age: the ratios are lower for children (whites report relatively more) and higher for adults (blacks report relatively more).

Finally, more blacks than whites report chronic conditions resulting in activity limitation but the differences (ratios) are not as great as for measures of death and dissatisfaction. We now turn to more detailed consideration of what some of these differences by types of measures may mean. We will refer back to table 2 throughout this section.

Death

The age-adjusted death rates shown in table 3 clearly reinforce the view that the health status of blacks is worse than that of whites. For both males and females the black death rate exceeds the white rate by 50 percent. The black rate is greater for all of the most common causes of death (heart disease, cancer, stroke, accidents, and homicides). Only for pulmonary disease and suicide among those listed

TABLE 2

Selected Health Status Measures According to Race: United States

Health status measure	Black	White	Ratio
DEATH (age-adjusted deaths per 100,000, 1984)[1]			
Male	1,012	690	1.5
Female	585	391	1.5
DISEASE (percentage of persons with limitations in activity due to chronic conditions, 1985)[2]			
Under 18	6%	5%	1.2
18–44	9	8	1.1
45–64	31	23	1.4
65–69	50	38	1.3
70 and over	48	39	1.2
Number of acute conditions per 100 persons per year, 1985[3]			
Under 18	183	283	0.6
18–44	130	174	0.8
45 and over	98	109	0.9
DISABILITY (number of days activity restriction per person per year, 1985)[4]			
Under 5	9	9	1.0
5–17	7	9	0.8
18 and over	22	16	1.4
DISCOMFORT (number of symptoms reported per person per year, 1982)[5]			
Under 18	0.4	0.6	0.7
18–44	1.1	1.3	0.8
45–64	1.9	1.7	1.1
65 and over	2.1	2.0	1.0
DISSATISFACTION (age-adjusted percentage of persons who report health as fair or poor, 1985)[6]			
All ages	17	9	1.9
Percentage of persons with some, little, or no satisfaction with health and physical condition, 1985)[7]			
All ages	12%	8%	1.5

[1] National Center for Health Statistics 1986a, table 20.
[2] National Center for Health Statistics 1985, table 67.
[3] National Center for Health Statistics 1985, table 3.
[4] National Center for Health Statistics 1985, table 69.
[5] Center for Health Administration Studies, University of Chicago, unpublished data. The study producing the data and the symptom measures are described in Andersen et al. 1987, chap. 6 and appendix A.
[6] National Center for Health Statistics 1986a, table 39.
[7] National Opinion Research Center 1985.

TABLE 3

Age-adjusted Death Rates for Selected Causes, According to Sex and Race,
United States, 1984, per 100,000 Resident Population

	Males			Females		
Cause	Black	White	Ratio	Black	White	Ratio
All causes	1,012	690	1.5	585	391	1.5
Heart disease	300	250	1.2	187	124	1.5
Cerebrovascular disease	63	34	1.8	52	29	1.8
Malignant neoplasms	235	159	1.5	131	110	1.2
Pulmonary disease	23	28	0.8	8	12	0.7
Pneumonia and influenza	25	16	1.6	11	9	1.2
Cirrhosis of liver	22	13	1.7	10	6	1.7
Diabetes	18	9	2.0	20	8	2.5
Accidents	65	51	1.3	20	18	1.1
Suicide	11	20	0.6	2	6	0.3
Homicide	51	8	6.4	11	3	3.7

Source: National Center for Health Statistics 1986a, table 21.

do we find the white rate higher. While measurement errors of one
sort or another might cause minor variations in the mortality ratios
shown, a general conclusion from table 3 that blacks experience poorer
health seems undeniable.

Disease

Table 2 records that blacks of all age groups in the National Health
Survey are more likely to report chronic conditions that result in
activity limitation than are whites. Chronic conditions include diseases
or impairments that are likely to be irreversible, ranging from the
major killers such as heart disease, cancer, and stroke to others less
likely to kill but which can result in considerable debilitation such
as arthritis and asthma. Chronic conditions also include all those that
have lasted two weeks or longer. The differences in reporting of chronic
conditions that limit activity by race, however, are less than the
differences in mortality rates as indicated by the ratios in table 2 (1.5
for mortality versus 1.1 to 1.4 for chronic conditions).

TABLE 4

Survival by Selected Sites of Cancer, by Race in Various Cities and States: 1973–1980*

| Site | Relative 5-year survival | | |
	Black	White	Ratio
Esophagus	3%	5%	0.6
Stomach	14	14	1.0
Colon/rectum	42	50	0.8
Larynx	57	67	0.9
Lung/bronchus	10	12	0.8
Breast	62	74	0.8
Cervix	62	68	0.9
Prostate	58	68	0.9
Bladder	48	73	0.7

* Rates are from the Surveillance, Epidemiology, and End Results Program (SEER) and include patients diagnosed through 1980 and follow-up on all patients through 1981. They are based on data from population-based registers in Connecticut, New Mexico, Utah, Iowa, Hawaii, Atlanta, Detroit, Seattle-Puget Sound, and San Francisco-Oakland.
Source: U.S. Department of Health and Human Services 1986, 38.

Acute conditions as defined by the National Health Survey include diseases or injuries lasting less than two weeks that are not included on the chronic disease list. Most commonly reported as acute conditions are respiratory problems such as "colds" and minor injuries. Table 2 records that these less serious acute conditions are actually reported more often by whites than by blacks—especially for children under 18 where the black rate is only 60 percent of the white rate.

The picture that begins to emerge is that the health status of blacks compared with whites appears worse using measures of mortality than self-reports of disease. And if we were to restrict ourselves to self-reports of acute conditions only, we might even conclude that the health status of blacks is better than for whites.

Evidence on the incidence and seriousness of disease from sources besides self-reports, however, calls the above conclusion into question. Table 4, for example, provides information on the survival rates for black and white patients diagnosed as having cancer from selected areas throughout the United States. For all sites of cancer shown except the stomach, the five-year survival rate for blacks is less than for whites. About 50 percent of all white patients registered survived five years compared to less than 40 percent of the black patients. Survival rates are influenced by the stage at which the cancer was diagnosed and the nature of follow-up treatment. The major lesson from table 4, however, is that even use of diagnosed disease prevalence for a serious condition like cancer may lead to an underestimate of the negative impact on the health status of blacks compared with whites. Once they have cancer, blacks are likely to die sooner.

In table 5 we compare national disease rates for selected conditions according to three methods of data collection: death certificates, hospital discharge records, and self-reports. Our purpose is to see if self-reports of these serious diseases suggest relatively better health status for blacks (lower ratios) than death rates would suggest (higher ratios). Hospital discharge rates differ in that they are based on treated conditions. Blacks are also, unfortunately, combined with other nonwhites in the source for hospital discharge rates. Our expectation was that black-white ratios might also be higher for hospital discharges than for self-reports. Notice that none of the rates in table 5 are age adjusted since our main purpose is to compare the ratios for different methods rather than to compare the actual black-white rates within a method.

The results in table 5 are mixed. Comparing death rate ratios to reported prevalence ratios shows death record ratios higher, as predicted, for heart disease and much higher for nephritis. The ratios, however, are the same for diabetes and the self-report ratio is actually higher than the death rate ratio for stroke.

The hospital discharge, self-report comparisons in table 5 show the black-white ratios to be higher for discharges in the case of diabetes but the same for heart disease and the self-report ratio is again higher for stroke. Thus, from a disease-specific perspective, we might conclude that blacks are in relatively better health using self-reports than if we used death or hospital discharge records for some diseases—but for other diseases this is not the case.

Table 6 records another way of examining the extent to which self-reports of disease might overestimate the health status of blacks relative to whites. It shows results from a health examination given to a national sample of the population regarding diabetes and hypertension. The diagnosed columns show the proportion of people examined who reported at the time of the examination that a physician had previously diagnosed their disease. For example, 4.5 percent of black males aged

TABLE 5

Crude Rates of Death, Hospitalization, and Self-reporting for Selected Conditions, by Race, United States, 1984

	Deaths/100,000			Hospital discharge/10,000			Reported prevalence/1,000		
	Black	White	Ratio	Nonwhite	White	Ratio	Black	White	Ratio
Heart disease	262	340	0.8	100	149	0.7	60	89	0.7
Cerebrovascular disease	64	67	1.0	31	36	0.9	15	12	1.2
Malignant neoplasms	177	198	0.9	66	84	0.8	—	—	—*
Diabetes	20	14	1.3	34	20	1.7	21	16	1.3
Nephritis and infections of the kidney	14	9	1.6	—	—	—*	15	17	0.9
Pneumonia	20	26	0.8	32	33	1.0	—	—	—**

* Not included in source.
** Not reported because of limited number of black cases.
Source: Death rates calculated from National Center for Health Statistics 1986b. Hospital discharge rates from Graves 1986. Reported prevalence rates calculated from Moss and Parsons 1986, tables 59, 64.

TABLE 6

Percentage of Persons with Diagnosed and Undiagnosed Diabetes and Hypertension, by Race, Sex, and Age, United States, 1976–1980

	Diagnosed			Undiagnosed		
	Black	White	Ratio	Black	White	Ratio
DIABETES						
Male 20–74	4.5	2.8	1.6	4.0	2.5	1.6
20–44	1.8	0.5	3.6	1.0	0.5	2.0
45–54	3.6	4.5	0.8	7.5	3.2	2.3
55–64	9.2	5.3	1.7	5.2	3.8	1.4
65–74	17.2	9.1	1.9	12.2	9.0	1.4
Female 20–74	5.9	3.6	1.6	4.6	3.4	1.4
20–44	2.6	1.4	1.9	0.9	0.8	1.1
45–54	7.5	3.9	1.9	7.0	4.6	1.5
55–64	16.3	6.6	2.5	9.1	7.9	1.2
65–74	10.8	8.8	1.2	12.3	7.3	1.7

HYPERTENSION

Male 18–74	16.1	12.5	1.3	9.9	9.8	1.0
18–24	1.4	1.7	0.8	3.3	5.2	0.6
25–34	8.2	5.7	1.4	6.2	7.2	0.9
35–44	20.2	6.7	3.0	14.5	10.5	1.4
45–54	22.6	20.2	1.1	11.0	12.2	0.9
55–64	36.7	24.6	1.5	17.2	13.4	1.3
65–74	28.4	28.6	1.0	16.8	15.0	1.1
Female 18–74	26.2	14.2	1.8	4.5	5.6	0.8
18–24	2.5	0.8	3.1	1.7	1.3	1.3
25–34	5.9	2.7	2.2	2.9	1.9	1.5
35–44	21.6	7.2	3.0	3.0	5.1	0.6
45–54	52.0	19.8	2.6	9.7	8.0	1.2
55–64	55.5	29.3	1.9	6.2	9.5	0.6
65–74	68.8	41.8	1.6	7.7	11.6	0.7

Sources: Diabetes: Hadden and Harris 1987, tables 1 and 2. Hypertension: Drizd, Dannenbury, and Engel 1986, tables 13, 15.

20 to 74 reported that they had been previously diagnosed for diabetes; 2.8 percent of the white males said the same. The undiagnosed columns show the percentages of the population found to have diabetes and hypertension at the time of the health examination survey who had *not* been previously diagnosed by a physician. For example, 4.0 percent of the black males and 2.5 percent of the white males were found to have diabetes at the time of the examination but did not know they had the disease.

The ratios in table 6 show that blacks are more likely to have previously diagnosed diabetes and hypertension. This is true for both males and females for most age groups. What is more important for our purposes is that blacks are also more likely to have undiagnosed diabetes than are whites. Blacks, however, are not more likely to have undiagnosed hypertension. The ratios show that black males have 60 percent more undiagnosed diabetes than white males and black females have 40 percent more than their white counterparts. Black and white males, however, have about the same rate of underreporting of hypertension overall, and undiagnosed hypertension is actually slightly more prevalent for white females than for black females, especially at older ages. The results from table 6, then, support our concern that self-reporting of disease in the case of diabetes may lead to conclusions that the health status of blacks compares more favorably to whites than a clinical examination would confirm. The results for hypertension, however, do not show such systematic biases.

Table 7 records another comparison of self-reporting—this time with physician and hospital records. It is based on data from a national survey of the population in which respondents were asked what physicians and hospitals they visited, what conditions they were treated for, and what surgical procedures were performed in the hospital. Physician and hospital records were then searched in an effort to match the conditions and procedures reported by the respondents. As table 7 records, less than one-half of the conditions reported by all respondents could be matched in the records while one-half to three-quarters of the surgical procedures were matched. The proportion of matches for whites exceeded that for nonwhites (over 90 percent of whom were black) for both conditions and surgical procedures. These results suggest that black self-reporting of specific conditions and procedures may be less accurate than white reporting when hospital and physician records are used as validity criteria.

TABLE 7

Percentage of Self-reports of Conditions and Procedures Matched by
Record, Race: U.S., 1970

Type of condition or procedure	Nonwhite	White	Ratio
Physician visit conditions matched by records	33%	36%	0.9%
Hospitalized conditions matched by records	35	43	0.8
Surgical procedures matched by records	54	73	0.7

Source: Daughety 1979, tables 5.1, 5.3, 5.5.

In general, the comparisons of self-reporting of disease with other data sources in this article suggest that self-reports can be misleading as measures of health status differences between blacks and whites. A similar concern is voiced by Haynes, Wolde-Tsadek, and Juarez (1985, 110), based on a study of conditions of physicians as seen in their private practices, according to the National Ambulatory Care Survey;

> If Blacks and Hispanics feel a lesser sense of medical need, then the magnitudes of the identified circulatory, digestive, and musculoskeletal problems are underestimated and there might be other problems to which they are at greater risk but whose significance is suppressed. This is of special interest since the morbidity findings are certainly not as striking as the mortality statistics would suggest.

Disability

Table 2 records the average number of days per year of people reported being unable to engage in their usual activities because of illness or injury. For preschool children, usual activity might be play; for school age children, going to school; and for adults, working, keeping house, etc. Thus, this measure is designed to capture disability that results from transitory, acute conditions rather than long-term reduction in function resulting from chronic conditions.

The number of disability days per person per year is the same for

TABLE 8

Number of Restricted Activity Days Associated with Acute Conditions per
100 Persons per Year, by Race, Age, and Type of Condition: U.S., 1985

Type of condition	Black	White	Ratio
All acute conditions			
Under 18	583	705	0.8
18–44	724	650	1.1
45 and over	862	737	1.2
Infectious and parasitic diseases			
Under 18	151	143	1.1
18–44	30	47	0.6
45 and over	20	30	0.7
Respiratory conditions			
Under 18	238	348	0.7
18–44	220	246	0.9
45 and over	317	299	1.1
Digestive system conditions			
Under 18	18	15	1.2
18–44	30	19	1.6
45 and over	70	41	1.7
Injuries			
Under 18	60	84	0.7
18–44	221	195	1.1
45 and over	193	203	0.9
All other conditions			
Under 18	114	115	1.0
18–44	144	223	0.6
45 and over	162	264	0.6

Source: National Center for Health Statistics 1985, table 18.

black and white children under 5 years of age as reported in table 2.
For children 5 to 17 the mean number of disability days reported is
actually greater for whites than for blacks. It is only for adults that
we find reported disability days higher for blacks.

Table 8 allows us to see if the general pattern of relatively more
disability days for white children and black adults holds for most
acute conditions resulting in disability days. The general pattern holds
for all acute conditions as well as for respiratory and digestive conditions
and injuries. Only for infectious and parasitic diseases and the residual
category are the relationships reversed, with the ratios higher for

children (showing relatively more disability days for black children). The data in table 8 then confirm the results from table 2 showing lower ratios for children than for adults for most acute conditions. The discrepancy for infectious disease requires further study but may reflect more serious and debilitating problems in this category for black children.

A different measure of disability is activity limitation resulting from chronic conditions, as reported in table 9. The purpose of this table is to see if blacks report relatively more serious long-term disability than the short-term type resulting from acute conditions. The data in table 9 seem to confirm this expectation. Blacks are less likely to report no activity limitation than are whites. Blacks are also less likely to report activity limitation but not in major activity for children and young adults. In contrast, blacks are much more likely than whites to report being unable to carry on major activities due to chronic conditions in all age groups.

The methodological import of these results is that disability measures based on reporting of restricted activity days in response to acute conditions or activity limitations with no specification of degree of limitation may overstate the health status of blacks compared with whites—especially for children. Measures that are limited to possibly more serious acute conditions or major activity limitation show blacks to be relatively more disadvantaged in health status compared with whites. These latter measures, in particular, suggest black children are not in better health than white children but may be in worse health.

Discomfort

Discomfort is a subjective dimension of health status, based on people's self-reports of pain, worry, or other indicators that all is not well regarding their health. The measure of discomfort used in table 2 is based on a checklist of fifteen symptoms that respondents indicate were or were not experienced in the last year. The symptoms concern various body systems and both acute and chronic problems. Some are commonly experienced (sore throat or runny nose) while others are infrequent and often associated with serious problems (loss of over ten pounds in weight). The score reported in table 2 is the mean number of these symptoms reported by samples of central city residents

TABLE 9
Percentage of Persons with Degree of Limitation Resulting from Chronic
Conditions, by Race and Age: U.S. 1985

Degree of limitation	Black	White	Ratio
No activity limitation			
Under 18	94%	95%	1.0%
18–44	91	92	1.0
45–64	69	77	0.9
65–69	50	62	0.8
70 and over	52	61	0.8
Limited but not in major activity			
Under 18	1	2	0.5
18–44	2	3	0.7
45–64	6	6	1.0
65–69	11	8	1.4
70 and over	19	20	1.0
Limited in amount or kind of major activity			
Under 18	4	3	1.3
18–44	3	4	0.8
45–64	10	9	1.1
65–69	11	15	0.7
70 and over	17	13	1.3
Unable to carry on major activity			
Under 18	1	*	1.5
18–44	4	2	2.0
45–64	15	8	1.9
65–69	28	16	1.8
70 and over	12	6	2.0

* < 0.5 percent.
Source: National Center for Health Statistics 1985, table 67.

residing in five metropolitan areas representing all sections of the
nation,

Table 2 records that black children and younger adults report fewer
symptoms than whites. The number reported among older adults is
similar according to race. These results for symptom reporting—our
measure of discomfort—parallel the findings in table 2 for reporting
of acute conditions and disability days. The ratios suggest blacks are

in relatively good health compared with whites—especially children. Further, these findings are at variance with those based on chronic disease reporting and, particularly, death rates showing blacks are in worse health.

As in the case of condition and disability day reporting, however, there is some supplementary evidence to suggest underreporting by blacks for symptoms. A national survey conducted in 1971 used the same list of fifteen symptoms described above plus an additional five. Kravits and Schneider (1975, 186) note in their analysis of this data that blacks reported fewer symptoms than did whites. But they go on to qualify these findings, observing that this evidence

> appears to contradict some of the previous findings. . . . Up until now, we have seen that blacks appear to be considerably sicker than whites when they use either medical or dental care. . . . Several interpretations . . . are possible: (1) that the black population does have fewer symptoms and that these symptoms are less severe, and (2) that there is considerable underreporting going on, particularly of more serious symptoms. This second hypothesis is strengthened slightly by the finding that, once in the system, blacks . . . with symptoms have more visits than their apparently (judging by symptoms reported) sicker white counterparts.

Dissatisfaction

The last health status dimension—dissatisfaction, like discomfort— is a very subjective one. Unlike discomfort which was measured by reporting of specific symptoms of illness, dissatisfaction is measured in table 2 by more general assessments of how people feel about their health. The results show blacks to be much more dissatisfied. They are almost twice as likely as whites to report their health as fair or poor. And they are 50 percent more likely to have only some, little, or no satisfaction with health and physical condition.

Thus, even though dissatisfaction is measured by subjective self-reports, the black-white comparisons look more like the mortality comparisons than like other comparisons based on self-reports. According to the mortality and dissatisfaction ratios, blacks are in considerable worse health than whites, while the self-reports for conditions and disability days provide a much more mixed picture of health status according to race.

One possible explanation for the apparent discrepancy between the results for dissatisfaction and those for disease, disability, and discomfort has to do with differences in measurement. The latter generally require respondents to give specifics. To show a poorer health level people must name diseases, recall particular conditions and symptoms of illness, or count days when their activity was reduced by injury or illness. If blacks indeed, for whatever reason, have a higher threshold for reporting these specifics than whites—as some of the literature and evidence cited in this article suggest—their health status would appear relatively good compared to whites. In contrast, dissatisfaction is measured by more global and less specific assessments of health and well-being. Here, the realities of death, disease, and a hostile environment may be more readily expressed by blacks, resulting in relatively poorer health status compared to whites according to dissatisfaction measures.

Summary

Apparent differences in the health status of blacks and whites vary according to methods of measurement, errors in the measurement process and interpretation of the measures, and types of measures used. This article uses the literature and secondary analysis of available data to explore the impact of methods on health status comparisons by race.

Methods to measure health status include records, direct observations, and self-reports. Blacks generally show the greatest health deficits based on observation and least on some types of self-reports.

Major types of errors in health status estimates are random errors and biases. Random errors tend to be greater for blacks because samples used to estimate their characteristics have often been smaller than white samples. Biases include noncoverage or failure to include some types of individuals in the reporting systems at all, nonresponse or lack of complete information on some persons, and use of inaccurate information due to faulty data collection or processing. Such biases tend to be greater for black persons than for whites. Their impact often is to give the illusion that blacks may be in better health than is actually the case.

The types of measures that show blacks in the poorest health status are those considered to be most objective: mortality rates and some clinical examinations and health provider records. Subjective measures of dissatisfaction with health level also show blacks to be much less healthy than whites. In contrast, self-reports of illness conditions, symptoms, and restricted-activity days show blacks, particularly children, to be relatively well off compared to whites. These self-reports may be misleading due to differential perceptions of illness and reporting biases between blacks and whites.

There is no doubt that measured differences in the health status of blacks and whites often reflect substance. There are also significant methodological problems, however, in comparing health status by race, which tend to underestimate the problems experienced by the black population.

This article and others in this volume stress the need to know much more about the sources and impact of these methodological problems. In the meantime, these problems need to be recognized and adjusted for, where possible, when health status measures are compared. It is particularly important to consider them when policy questions of equity and resource allocation are to be decided using indicators of health status.

References

Andersen, R., J. Kasper, M.R. Frankel, M.J. Banks, and V.S. Daughety. 1979. *Total Survey Error: Applications to Improve Health Surveys.* San Francisco: Jossey-Bass.

Andersen, R.M., L.A. Aday, C.S. Lyttle, L.J. Cornelius, and M.S. Chen. 1987. *Ambulatory Care and Insurance Coverage in an Era of Constraint.* Chicago: Pluribus Press.

Berkanovic, E., and C. Telesky. 1985. Mexican-American, Black-American and White-American Differences in Reporting Illnesses, Disability and Physician Visits for Illnesses. *Social Science Methods* 20 (6):567–77.

Cooper, R., and B.E. Simmons. 1985. Cigarette Smoking and Ill Health among Black Americans. *New York State Journal of Medicine* 83(7):344–49.

Cooper, R.S., B. Simmons, A. Castaner, R. Prasad, C. Franklin, and J. Ferlinz. 1986. Survival Rates and Prehospital Delay during Myocardial Infarction among Black Persons. *American Journal of Cardiology* 57:208–11.

Daughety, V.S. 1979. Illness Conditions. In *Total Survey Error,: Applications to Improve Health Surveys,* ed. R. Andersen et al., 52–74. San Francisco: Jossey-Bass.

Drizd, T., A.L. Dannenbury, and A. Engel. 1986. Blood Pressure Levels in Persons 18–74 Years of Age in 1976–80 and Trends in Blood Pressure from 1960 to 1980 in the United States. *Vital and Health Statistics,* series 11, no. 234. Washington.

Fleming, G.V. 1979. Using Consumer Evaluations of Health Care. *Hospital Progress* 60(8):54–68.

———. 1981. Hospital Structure and Consumer Satisfaction. *Health Services Research* 16(1): 43–63.

Graves, E.J. 1986. Utilization of Short Stay Hospitals, United States, 1984 Annual Summary. *Vital and Health Statistics,* series 13, no. 84. Washington.

Hadden, W.C., and M.D. Harris. 1987. Prevalence of Diagnosed Diabetes, Undiagnosed Diabetes and Impaired Glucose Tolerance in Adults 20–74 Years of Age. *Vital and Health Statistics,* series 11, no. 237. Washington.

Haynes, M.A., G. Wolde-Tsadek, and P. Juarez. 1985. Associations of Health Problems with Ethnic Groups in Ambulatory Care Visits. In *Report of the Secretary's Task Force on Black and Minority Health. Volume II: Cross Cutting Issues in Minority Health,* U.S. Department of Health and Human Services, 107–115.

Jackson, J.J. 1981. Urban Black Americans. In *Ethnicity and Medical Care,* ed. A. Harwood, 37–129. Cambridge: Harvard University Press.

Kish, L. 1965. *Survey Sampling.* New York: Wiley.

Kleinman, J.C., L.A. Fingerhut, and J.J. Feldman. 1980. Trends in Mortality. In *Health, United States, 1980,* U.S. Department of Health and Human Services, 23–28. Washington.

Kravits, J., and J. Schneider. 1975. Health Care Need and Actual Use by Age, Race and Income. In *Equity in Health Services,* ed. R. Andersen, 169–87. Cambridge, Mass.: Ballinger.

Linn, M.W., K.I. Hunter, and B.S. Linn. 1980. Self-Assessed Health, Impairment and Disability in Anglo, Black and Cuban Elderly. *Medical Care* 18(3):282.

Mausner, J.S., and S. Kramer. 1985. *Epidemiology: An Introductory Text.* Philadelphia: Saunders.

Moss, A.J., and V.L. Parsons. 1986. Current Estimates from the National Health Interview Survey, United States, 1985. *Vital and Health Statistics,* series 10, no. 160. Washington.

National Center for Health Statistics. 1985. *Current Estimates from the National Health Interview Survey, 1985,* series 10, no. 160. Hyattsville, Md.

————. 1986a. *Health United States, 1986.* DHHS pub. no. (PHS) 87–1232. Washington.

————. 1986b. *Monthly Vital Statistics Report* 35(6):Supplement 2. Washington.

National Opinion Research Center. 1985. *General Social Survey, 1985.* Chicago. (Unpublished.)

Patrick, D.L., and J. Elinson. 1979. Methods of Sociomedical Research. In *Handbook of Medical Sociology,* ed. H. Freeman, S. Levine, and L.G. Reeder, 437–59. Englewood Cliffs, N.J.: Prentice-Hall.

Shosteck, H. 1977. Respondent Militancy as a Control Variable for Interviewer Effect. *Journal of Social Issues* 33(4):36–45.

Sudman, S., and N.M. Bradburn. 1980. *Response Effects in Surveys: A Review and Synthesis.* Chicago: Aldine.

U.S. Department of Health and Human Services. 1986. *Report of the Secretary's Task Force on Black and Minority Health,* Vol. 3 (Cancer). Washington.

Vernon, S.W., R.E. Roberts, and E.S. Lee. 1984. Ethnic Status and Participation in Longitudinal Health Surveys. *American Journal of Epidemiology* 119(1):99–113.

Watkins, L.O. 1983. *Epidemiology of Coronary Heart Disease in Black Population: A Response.* (Unpublished.)

Wilder, C.S. 1986. Disability Days. *Vital and Health Statistics,* series 10, no. 158. Washington.

History of Black Mortality and Health before 1940

DOUGLAS C. EWBANK

THE LEVEL OF MORTALITY IS A BASIC MEASURE of the standard of living. Since mortality is determined by the quality of available medical care, income, nutritional status, environmental quality (including quality of water and air), and cultural habits, it incorporates many elements of the standard of living. In the United States, the study of racial differences in mortality provides one of the best approaches to measuring historical trends in the relative standards of living of blacks and whites. These studies also provide important information on the determinants of mortality rates in historic populations. Comparisons of socioeconomic differences and differences in health care practices among blacks and whites help to elucidate the factors that determined mortality levels and trends during different historical periods.

This article reviews the trends in the mortality of American blacks between 1800 and 1940 and compares those trends with the trends among American whites. It then proceeds to examine the trends in several subpopulations focusing on differences between blacks in cities and rural areas and in northern and southern states. Finally, it includes a discussion of some of the factors underlying the black-white differences and the trends in black mortality. This discussion of the determinants of black mortality is an attempt to place the history of black mortality into the context of the broader history of the mortality decline in the United States. (A few of the statistics discussed below actually refer to "nonwhites" and therefore include some American Indians, Chinese, Japanese and other minority groups. In all of these cases, however, virtually all of the persons covered by the statistic are black.)

The discussion begins with a review of estimates of mortality among blacks for various periods. This review is based on the results of recent analysis of new data on child mortality during the period of 1880 to 1930 and a reanalysis of the data on adult mortality. As a result of this research, this review presents a substantial revision of trends in mortality among blacks. In particular, it proposes much lower estimates of child mortality among blacks in the nineteenth century and much higher adult mortality during that period. It also suggests that there was little change between 1850 and 1880 and no change during the period of 1880 to 1900. This view of black mortality trends focuses attention on the first decades of the twentieth century when mortality rates of blacks began a sustained decline. The second section of the article elucidates the factors responsible for this rapid decline in child mortality with an examination of trends in New York and North and South Carolina between 1900 and 1940. These states were chosen because they reflect quite different black populations (urban and rural, northern and southern) and because they provide relatively reliable data for the whole period. This discussion includes some examination of data on cause of death for the period of 1910 to 1920.

Documenting the levels and trends in mortality among blacks and whites is only the first step in learning what we really want to know. The more interesting questions concern the reasons for racial differences in mortality and the factors that caused the decline in mortality. The final section reviews information on health practices and the effects of economic differentials on health care and mortality. This discussion includes a review of several studies of infant and child care carried out by the U.S. Children's Bureau around 1920. It also includes a discussion of trends in mortality due to typhoid fever between 1900 and 1920. Since typhoid mortality rates responded rapidly to changes in water and sanitation, it provides a useful marker of the effectiveness of basic public health services among different population groups during various periods.

Trends in Black Mortality before 1940

There are several reasons why it is difficult to document mortality trends among American blacks. First, registration of deaths did not begin in the United States until late in the nineteenth century and even then it was limited to a few states. It was not until 1933 that the whole of the continental United States was included in the national Death Registration Area (DRA). Second, the states which started registration systems first were northeastern states. The data on the white population in these states has often been used as a rough approximation of the whole country, but the blacks in these states are not representative of all blacks. In 1900 the death registration area included 26 percent of the total population, but only 4.4 percent of the black population. More than 90 percent of the blacks in the DRA lived in urban areas while only 23 percent of all blacks were urban. Third, although blacks and whites were theoretically covered by the same data collection systems after the Civil War, the data for blacks were generally less reliable than those for whites.

Despite these problems, there are several ways in which mortality can be estimated. One important source on infant and child mortality among blacks in the early nineteenth century is slave records. A second source is census data on the proportion of deceased children born to women of various ages. Estimates of adult mortality are generally derived from census age distributions by calculating the ratio of the number of persons recorded as aged x in one census to the number aged $x + 10$ at a census ten years later. By comparing all of these bits and pieces of information, it is possible to get a relatively good picture of the levels and trends of mortality for blacks and whites starting about 1850.

The following discussion examines mortality for three periods: 1800 to 1880, 1880 to 1910, and 1910 to 1940. These periods are defined in terms of the type of data that are available and therefore do not reflect standard historical eras. For each period, the estimates for blacks are compared with estimates for a comparable white population.

Because the data sources often provide estimates of only some age groups, much of the discussion is limited to either child mortality or adult mortality. The main index of child mortality is the proportion of all live births that survive to their fifth birthday. This rate is generally termed q(5). Some of the discussion is based on estimates of the infant mortality rate, which is the number of deaths under the age of one year in a given period divided by the number of live births in that period. The infant mortality rate is an approximation of the proportion of live-born children surviving to their first birthday. Both q(5) and the infant mortality rate are expressed per 1,000 live births. The index of adult mortality used here is the expectation of life at age 10, which is expressed in years. Whenever possible, the data on child and adult mortality are combined to provide an estimate of the life expectancy at birth.

Estimates of Mortality for 1800 to 1880

The best source of information on child mortality rates among blacks in rural areas before 1860 is collections of plantation records of births and deaths among slaves. Steckel (1979) has analyzed plantation lists from eleven plantations for which the reporting of mortality appears to be relatively complete. His estimates have all of the advantages and disadvantages of family reconstitution studies: on the one hand, they provide the most reliable estimates for any black population during this time period; on the other hand, there are serious questions about generalizability.

Steckel's analysis covers 1786 to 1863, although most of the recorded births were concentrated toward the end of the period. (The data cover about 200 births per decade during the period of 1786 to 1839, while there were 415 births in the 1840s and 878 between 1850 and 1863.) He estimated that q(5) was 379 for the entire period. His estimates for various decades fluctuate slightly. The estimate for the period of 1850 to 1863 is 353. He has also analyzed the data on the survival of individuals to estimate differentials. He found higher rates in rice areas and on larger plantations (those with over 100 slaves). Since large plantations and rice areas are overrepresented in this sample, the mortality rates for this population probably overstate the rates for all slaves, possibly by more than 20 percent. Reducing the estimate from Steckel's sample leads to an estimated range for q(5) of about 280 to 320 for all slaves.

A second approach to estimating mortality for this period relies on the reported census age distributions. By examining the proportion surviving between censuses, it is possible to select a life table from a set of standard model tables. These estimates provide more reliable

estimates of adult mortality than child mortality. Applications of
census survival techniques to blacks for the nineteenth century generally
produce estimates of life expectancy at age 10 of about 41 to 42 years
for black females. The estimates for black males are generally much
higher (Farley 1970, 67; Eblen 1974). It is likely that these estimates
are severely biased upward because of exaggeration of age among older
blacks. Given estimates for the end of the nineteenth century (discussed
below) and Steckel's data on child mortality, it is likely that the life
expectancy at age 10 was closer to 35 years and life expectancy at
birth was probably close to 30 years.

We do not have mortality estimates for the white populations in
the deep South before 1860, so it is not possible to compare the
mortality rates of the slaves with those of their owners or other
southern whites. Given that most blacks lived in rural areas at this
time, it is preferable to compare the rates for blacks with rates for
rural whites. Haines (1977) has analyzed child survival data for seven
counties of upstate New York from the state census of 1865 to estimate
infant and child mortality for the period of 1850 to 1865. Although
this population was in many ways quite different from the rural South,
these estimates have the advantage of providing reliable estimates of
child mortality for a rural white population. Haines estimates that
q(5) in rural areas was 192, and the rate for urban areas was 229.

Another source of mortality data for whites during this period is
the death registration data from Massachusetts. There has been extensive
discussion of the reliability of these data; Vinovskis's estimate of q(5)
for 1850, 210, however, is very similar to Haines's (1977) estimates
for New York in the period of 1850 to 1865.

Although few blacks lived in northern states, those that did probably
had higher mortality rates than southern slaves. Most northern blacks
lived in large cities and therefore suffered from the excessive mortality
rates common in cities (Davis 1973). Because of discrimination and
their poverty, blacks sometimes lived in the worst sections of many
cities and generally had poor housing; consequently, they had higher
mortality rates than urban whites. For example, Rosenberg (1962,
59–60) reports that in the cholera epidemic of 1832, blacks in Philadelphia suffered a case rate almost twice as great as that of whites,
and he suggests that this is "probably a reliable, if informal, index
to the poverty in which the North's free Negroes lived."

Despite the sparsity of data, we can conclude several things about

TABLE 1

Estimates of Child Mortality, Life Expectancy at Age 10, and Life
Expectancy at Birth, U.S. Blacks, 1850–1940

	q(5)	From e(10)	Life expectancy at age 10				Life expectancy at birth
			Census survival		DRA estimate		
			Male	Female	Male	Female	
1850	280–320	37					
1880	264	39					35.5
			36	36			
1890	264	39					35.5
			40	42			
1900	264	39					36.5
			39	39			
1910	235–255	40					
			39	39			
1920	186	45					
1930	126				44.3	45.3	48.5
1940	90				48.3	50.8	53.8

the level of mortality during this period. First, it is likely that around 1850 to 1860 about 280 to 320 black children per 1,000 died before their 5th birthday. Second, the life expectancy at age 10 among blacks was probably about 37 years in the middle quarters of the century. Third, the mortality of blacks was substantially higher than that of whites at all ages. Child mortality was probably more than 50 percent above the rate for rural whites.

Estimates for 1880 to 1910

The best source of information about adult mortality during this period is census survival methods. Table 1 presents estimates of life expectancy at age 10—e(10)—for the periods 1880 to 1890, 1890 to 1900, 1900 to 1910, and 1910 to 1920 for blacks by sex. These estimates are based on a new age pattern of mortality which is similar to the United Nations Far East pattern (United Nations 1982). The levels were selected to be consistent with the reported sizes of the cohort aged 0 to 39 at the first census and 10 to 49 at the second. These estimates show much higher mortality than most previous estimates (Farley

1970, 67; Eblen 1974) but are completely consistent with the estimates of child mortality discussed below. It appears that adult mortality was relatively constant between 1880 and 1910 with life expectancy at age 10 at about 38 to 39 years. Adult mortality probably started declining about 1910, since the estimate of e(10) for 1910 to 1920 is understated because of the large undercount in the 1920 census.

The censuses of 1900 and 1910 provide reports of women on the number of children they had ever borne and the number that are surviving. None of the child-survival data were ever tabulated by the census bureau. Recently, computerized public use samples have been produced from the original census forms which provide the first tabulations of child survival. The sample from the 1900 census is discussed in Graham (1980). The sample of 0.4 percent of the households in the 1910 census has recently been completed at the University of Pennsylvania. In addition, there is an extra sample of persons living in households headed by blacks in a large number of counties.

I have recently completed an analysis of these child-survival data from the 1900 and 1910 censuses. By comparing the child-survival reports of older and younger women, I estimate that among blacks the proportion dying by age 5 was constant at about 264 per 1,000 live births for the period of 1880 to 1900. Combining this estimate of child mortality with the estimates of adult mortality leads to an estimate of expectation of life at birth for blacks of 35 years in 1900.

This estimate of child mortality among blacks is substantially higher than Preston and Haines's (1984) estimate of 161 for whites in 1900, which is based on data from the public use sample of the 1900 census. (The data from the 1910 census on child survival among whites have not yet been analyzed.) In addition, while child mortality among blacks was generally constant during the period of 1880 to 1900, Preston and Haines's estimates suggest that among whites q(5) declined by about 28 points (14 percent) between 1885 and 1896. Data for the states in the death registration area between 1900 and 1910, which were mostly northern states with a high proportion of whites, shows a similar decline (15 percent). The child-survival data for blacks actually show some suggestion that child mortality may have increased during the 1890s in some states.

This analysis shows a very different picture of trends in childhood mortality among blacks than previously estimated. For example, in their reconstruction of demographic trends in mortality among blacks,

Coale and Rives (1973) used several estimates of mortality at the turn of the century. They relied heavily on data from the DRA states where blacks had a q(5) of 338, and their final estimates were even higher. Eblen's estimates of mortality are consistent with a q(5) of about 320 in 1880 to 1890—closer to the new estimates, but still much too high. These elevated estimates resulted from an overreliance on the DRA data and from assumed age patterns of mortality that are now seen to have greatly overstated the level of child mortality in comparison with adult mortality. (Other authors who overestimated child mortality among blacks include Demeny and Gingrich [1967], Farley [1970], and Meeker [1976].)

Analysis of the data from the 1900 and 1910 censuses also provide the first estimates of child mortality for blacks for regions. In southern states the estimates of q(5) for 1900 are generally in the range of 240 to 270 while in the North they are closer to 300. This difference is largely due to the fact that blacks in the North were far more apt to be urban and were, therefore, subjected to all of the health risks associated with urban areas.

In the nineteenth century, mortality in urban areas was generally much higher than in rural areas (Davis 1973). This urban disadvantage in mortality resulted from high mortality from infectious diseases spread through poor water and sanitation systems, and diseases such as tuberculosis and respiratory diseases which are associated with poverty and crowded, inadequate housing. Because of their low incomes and poor living conditions, urban blacks were doubly disadvantaged. The registration data in cities in 1880 reflect this situation. For example, in Baltimore, Washington, Charleston, and New Orleans the life expectancy at birth for blacks was about 25 while the values for whites averaged about 39. It is possible that about half of all black children died before their 5th birthday. These extremely high levels of mortality reflect the fact that blacks suffered more from most of the peculiarly urban ills because of their poverty. This was probably true throughout the nineteenth century.

Detailed vital statistics reports for Baltimore show that the crude death rate (total deaths per 1,000 population) for whites was basically constant with an average of 20 and 22 deaths per 1,000 population during the period of 1876 to 1895. After 1895 it began to decline at a steady pace down to 15.7 for the period of 1911 to 1915. In contrast, the rate for blacks fluctuated between 31.5 and 32.5 during the period of 1886 to 1905 before beginning a decline. It is clear from these figures that in Baltimore the decline of mortality among blacks began about 10 years after the decline among whites. Although it is not clear what was responsible for these declines, it is instructive to note that for the two races combined, 40 percent of the decline in mortality between 1891 and 1915 was due to a decline in deaths from diarrhea (among both children and adults), dysentery, cholera, and typhoid fever (Howard 1924, 235, 513).

Estimates of Black Mortality for 1910 to 1940

The establishment of the death registration area in 1900 and the start of the birth registration area in 1915 provided the first useful vital statistics for a large section of the country. It was not until 1933, however, that vital statistics were available for all 48 states and even after that date the data were affected by underreporting of births and deaths. Since most blacks lived in states that did not enter the national registration systems until the period of 1925 to 1930, we can only examine detailed trends for the period of 1910 to 1930 in a few states. In addition, the registration data for rural areas of the South and for blacks in general were especially prone to underenumeration of events throughout this period. (For a discussion of the difficulties in estimating child mortality for blacks for this period, see Farley 1970, 67–69.)

By 1940 the data on infant and child mortality were reasonably reliable. Between 1900 and 1940, q(5) declined from 264 per 1,000 to 90 in 1940, a decline of 66 percent. During this same period the rate for whites continued the decline experienced between 1880 and 1900, dropping 67 percent from 161 in 1900 to 53 in 1940 (mortality estimates for 1929 to 1931 and 1939 to 1941 from Greville 1947). Therefore, between 1900 and 1940 the child mortality rate among blacks remained about 70 percent above that of whites. Despite substantial declines in infant and child mortality, blacks did not succeed in reducing their risks relative to whites.

I have recently completed an analysis of data on the survival of the older siblings of children born in 1928, 1930, and 1933. This analysis fills the gap between the estimates for 1900 and 1940 by providing the first reliable estimates of child mortality among blacks for the period of 1915 to 1930. These data suggest that by 1915 q(5) had declined to about 218, a drop of 17 percent below the rate for 1880 to 1900. The extent of this decline suggests that the starting date of the decline must have been early in the century, perhaps about 1905. The declines in child mortality between 1900 and 1940 proceeded at a constant rate throughout the period. By 1920, q(5) had declined to about 180, and by 1930 it was down to 127. This new estimate for 1930 is substantially higher than the value of 107 used in the official life tables for 1929 to 1931 (Greville 1947, 11). These estimates suggest that child mortality fell at a rate of 3.4 percent per year between 1920 and 1940. Among whites, the rate of decline in q(5) was 2.5 percent per year between 1900 and 1930, while between 1930 and 1940 the rate of decline was 3.6 percent per year.

The trends in adult mortality during this period are not as clear. Farley (1970, 71–72) summarizes several studies that lead to conflicting conclusions. In the absence of complete registration of death until 1933, we must rely on the survival of cohorts between censuses and registration data for the few states that had reliable registration. Table 1 presents estimates of life expectancy at age 10 for various periods based on different types of data. The first set of estimates is based on the child mortality estimates and an assumed age pattern of mortality. The second set is based on the survival rates between censuses. For 1930 and 1940 the table includes the estimates from the death registration data.

It is certain that adult mortality decreased between 1900 and 1940, but it is possible that there were periods when mortality rates remained constant or even increased. The DRA life tables for 1929 to 1931 and 1939 to 1941 show that life expectancy at age 10 increased from 44.8 years to 49.5, an increase of almost 5 years in 10 years (Greville 1947, 11, 38). Life tables for North Carolina, Tennessee, and Virginia for 1920 and 1940 show an increase in life expectancy at age 10 of only about 4 years in 20 years.

One of the unusual features of black mortality during this period is that female adult mortality exceeded that of males. For example, the DRA life tables for 1919 to 1920 for areas at least 5 percent black show that life expectancy at age 12 was 43.8 for black males and only 41.4 for black females (U.S. Bureau of the Census 1923, 24–27). Data for Tennessee for the years 1917 and 1919 to 1921 (to exclude the influenza epidemic of 1918) show that this excess was limited to rural areas (Sibley 1969, 138, 150). In the rural areas of

Tennessee, life expectancy at age 10 among black males exceeded that of females by 3.2 years (44.5 for males and 41.3 for females); in urban areas, however, the situation was reversed (33.4 for males and 34.8 for females). This excessive mortality among females was generally limited to the childbearing ages.

This pattern was probably a long-standing characteristic of mortality among blacks. For example, the age-specific sex ratios of deaths reported among blacks in the censuses of 1870, 1880, and 1900 all show an excess of female deaths between ages 10 and 44 (Suliman 1983, 21). A similar situation was still found in some areas in 1939 to 1940. In Mississippi, black females had higher mortality than males during the reproductive ages. Among females who survived to age 15, 283 per 1,000 died by age 50, while among males the proportion was only 271 per 1,000 (based on life tables created using the mortality rates given in U.S. Census Bureau 1943, 56). Data are available for urban and rural areas of Texas by sex and race in the period of 1939 to 1940 (Molyneaux 1945). They show that among black females in rural areas surviving to age 15, the proportion dying by age 50 was 232 per 1,000 compared to only 221 per 1,000 for males. The situation was reversed in urban areas of Texas, where the proportion dying between ages 15 and 50 was substantially higher for males.

This excessive female mortality is very unusual. It was clearly related to problems of childbearing and probably involved complicating factors such as tuberculosis and possibly malaria. For example, in urban areas of Tennessee in the years 1917 and 1919 to 1921, there were only small sex differences in the age-standardized death rate due to pulmonary tuberculosis for both races. In contrast, in rural areas the age-standardized rate for white females was substantially higher than the rate for males (141 compared to 91), and the same was true for blacks (310 for females and 251 for males) (Sibley 1969, 40).

Mortality Trends in Three States between 1900 and 1940

Data on mortality in the states that entered the death registration area relatively early provide an opportunity to examine in more detail the trends between 1910 and 1940. In particular, the data for individual states provide an opportunity to elucidate differences between the trends in different parts of the country. The data from North Carolina,

TABLE 2

Life Expectancy at Birth by Race, New York, North and South Carolina, 1920 and 1939–1940.

	1920		1939–40	
	White	Black	White	Black
New York	53.4	38.3	64.4	54.2
N. Carolina	56.7	46.6	64.4	54.4
S. Carolina	55.5	44.4	63.6	51.2

South Carolina, and New York illustrate the trends in northern and southern states among urban and rural blacks.

North Carolina entered the death registration area in 1916 and the birth registration area in 1917. South Carolina entered the death registration area in 1916 and the birth registration area in 1919; it dropped out of the birth registration area, however, between 1925 and 1927. Although North and South Carolina cannot be considered typical of all southern states, their mortality data provide some details about what was probably happening to the majority of blacks.

New York was included in the original death registration area in 1900. Its blacks were heavily concentrated in cities: 88 percent in urban areas, 75 percent in New York City alone. Although its black population is clearly not typical of all blacks, it provides a useful comparison for the Carolinas and helps to clarify the urban-rural differences in mortality trends over the period. It is also an example of the northern industrial areas to which blacks began to move in large numbers after World War I.

Table 2 presents the life expectancies at birth for blacks and whites in these three states in 1920 and 1939 to 1940. There were substantial declines in mortality for both races in all three states; the declines were larger in New York state, however, than in the Carolinas. In 1920 blacks in New York had a life expectancy that was about 7 years below the values in the Carolinas; by 1940 the life expectancy was very similar to the value in North Carolina and slightly higher than the value in South Carolina. A similar change occurred among whites. This change was due to the virtual elimination of the excessive mortality in urban areas.

A second conclusion that can be drawn from table 2 is that, despite substantial declines in mortality, the life expectancies among blacks in 1940 were very similar to the values for whites living in the same areas 20 years earlier. Although an examination of rates for smaller areas might show smaller differences between the races, it is clear that among blacks and whites living in the same states blacks were about 20 years behind whites in terms of their mortality risks.

An examination of the reported causes of death among blacks and whites in North Carolina and New York in 1916 to 1920 shows that blacks suffered higher mortality from virtually all causes, with relative risks for most causes being in the range of 1.3 to 1.5. The few causes for which whites showed higher rates (e.g., cancer and cerebral hemorrhage) were probably underreported for blacks, since the data on cause of death among blacks were probably even less accurate than the data for whites. One cause shows unusually high rates for blacks— tuberculosis. In New York blacks had an age-standardized mortality rate from respiratory tuberculosis that was about three times as large as the rate for whites. In North Carolina, the rate for blacks was about 40 percent higher than the rate for whites. Since respiratory tuberculosis was responsible for a large proportion of all deaths (about 11 percent of the overall age-standardized crude death rate in North Carolina), this difference in respiratory tuberculosis mortality is responsible for 20 percent of the racial difference in the age-standardized crude death rate in North Carolina and 39 percent of the difference in New York.

Death registration data are available for Maryland in 1910, so it is possible to examine the trends in cause of death over the decade 1910 to 1920. Because of changes in the quality of the data on causes, these comparisons must be made carefully. Despite this caution, two changes are quite clear. First, there was a substantial drop in mortality due to respiratory tuberculosis. Between 1910 and 1920, the age-standardized death rate from this cause dropped 39 percent for whites and 26 percent for blacks. These declines were responsible for 23 percent of the total decline in mortality among whites and 50 percent of the decline for blacks. The second important change was the drop in mortality due to typhoid fever. The decline in typhoid was responsible for about 22 percent of the total decline in mortality for both races. Although the use of data from Maryland may exaggerate the importance of these two causes in urban areas, tuberculosis and typhoid were

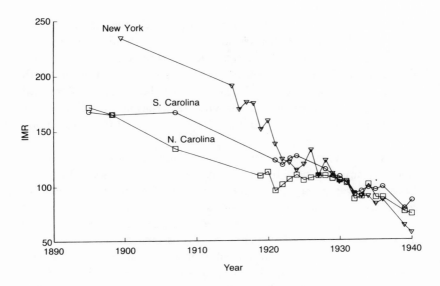

FIG. 1. Trends in infant mortality, 1895–1940 (blacks in North and South Carolina and New York)

significant overall causes of death and important to the declines of mortality during the first decades of the century.

Figure 1 shows the estimated trends in the infant mortality rate for North and South Carolina and New York for the period 1895 to 1940. The estimates for the period before 1910 are based on the child-survival data from the 1900 and 1910 censuses. The data after 1915 compare the registered infant deaths with the registered live births.

The data for blacks in New York show a rapid decline in infant mortality from a very high level in 1900 (about 235) to much more moderate levels in 1922. After 1922, the decline continues but at a slower pace. In North and South Carolina, infant mortality among blacks was about 165 in 1900, equal to the national average for blacks. In South Carolina the rate was probably constant or declining very slowly over the period of 1895 to 1910, while in North Carolina it was apparently declining. Between 1910 and 1920 the rate was dropping in both North and South Carolina. By the late 1920s the infant mortality rates in all three states were virtually identical, ranging from 102 to 107. By 1940 the blacks in New York had an infant mortality rate of only 56, well below the rates of 74 and 86 in North and South Carolina. Although the data for the Carolinas were still not based on completely accurate vital registration, the differentials were large enough to suggest the direction of the differences among these states.

In summary, although there were substantial declines in infant mortality among blacks living in these three states between 1900 and 1940, the average rate of decline in New York State (3.6 percent per year) was more than twice as fast as in South Carolina (1.6 percent per year). (Nationally, the average rate of decline in q(5) between these two dates was 2.7 percent.) As a consequence, New York went from having an infant mortality rate that was about 40 percent higher than in the other two states to having a rate 35 percent below South Carolina and 25 percent below North Carolina. This decline is even more spectacular when we note that it is likely that the infant mortality rate among blacks in New York had already declined by roughly 20 percent between 1880 and 1900.

The decline in mortality among blacks in New York reflects the elimination of the urban disadvantage in mortality. Between 1920 and 1940 a similar phenomenon occurred in North and South Carolina. Over this period the infant mortality rate among blacks in the 6 cities with populations over 100,000 (Asheville, Charlotte, Wilmington, and Winston-Salem, North Carolina and Charlotte and Columbia, South Carolina) declined by approximately the same percentage as did the rate among blacks in urban New York. This was not sufficient, however, to eliminate the urban disadvantage within North and South Carolina. From 1920 to 1923 blacks living in these 6 cities had infant mortality rates that were about 90 percent above the rate for the rural areas of those states. (In North Carolina, blacks in the large cities had a rate of 172 compared to 92 in rural areas. In South Carolina, the rates were 226 and 116, respectively.) From 1939 to 1940, the rates in these large cities were still 35 to 45 percent above the rates in rural areas. (In North Carolina, the rate in large cities was 98 compared to 67 in rural areas. In South Carolina the rates were 105 and 77, respectively. The rates for rural areas were less accurate than those for urban areas, but the comparison is probably still valid.)

Therefore, although infant mortality rates among blacks in large cities of North and South Carolina declined faster than in rural areas, they failed to eliminate completely the urban disadvantage. This is in contrast to the comparison with New York State where the urban disadvantage was turned into a northern-urban advantage.

Factors Affecting Health and Mortality

The preceding discussion documented differences by race as well as differences between blacks living in the North and the South and between urban and rural blacks. It also documented trends in mortality, especially the decline in infant and child mortality between 1900 and 1940. These differentials and trends were the result of differences in socioeconomic status, health care, and possibly environment.

Research on the causes of the general decline of mortality in the United States focuses on several diseases and several different kinds of evidence. As is true of most historical research, the list of topics that have been investigated reflects the nature of the available data as much as the relative importance of the diseases involved. For example, we know little about the factors that were responsible for the decline of tuberculosis mortality even though this was a major factor in the decline of adult mortality. The reason for this is that tuberculosis is a chronic disease the prevalence of which is closely related to the general standard of living and the general health of the population. Because of the long-term nature of the disease and the nonspecific nature of the factors related to its prevalence, it is very difficult to document the precise changes that were responsible for the substantial reduction in mortality from tuberculosis long before a cure was discovered.

The discussion that follows reviews some of the factors related to racial and regional differentials in mortality. It begins the process of examining for blacks all of the factors that have been studied more extensively for the general population. The first topic considered is evidence of the relation between income and child mortality. Despite its importance, this is a topic that is just beginning to be investigated in detail. The second topic concerns differences in child rearing and child feeding practices. The third concerns the use of health services. Although we know little about the effectiveness of health care at the turn of the century, by 1940 there were definite advantages to hospital deliveries and to treatment of many diseases by physicians. The fourth topic is the prevalence of typhoid fever. The mortality rate from typhoid is an important marker of the quality of water and sanitation. The decline of typhoid as a major cause of death was responsible for much of the decline in mortality in cities during this period. The study of the decline in typhoid is, therefore, a useful way to examine the effect of one of the major public health measures.

Economic Status and Child Mortality

It is clear that during all of the periods studied mortality rates were substantially higher for blacks than for whites. The question arises as to how much of this difference can be explained by differences in income, education, and other social and economic differences between the races. Although we cannot sort out the complex interactions among these factors, it is possible to document some differentials in infant and child mortality rates by social and economic characteristics.

In a study of differentials in infant and child mortality reported by women over the age of 65 at the time of the 1900 census, Daniel Scott Smith (1983) found that even after controlling for region and urban-rural residence, occupational status, and literacy, the single largest determinant of the proportion deceased was race. Since the children of these women were born on average about 40 years before the census date, these results apply to a period around 1860 to 1870. Black mothers reported a proportion of deceased children that was about 33 percent higher than the overall mean. Preston, Haines, and Pamuk (1981) report similar findings based on the reports of younger women in the 1900 census. After controlling for city size, husband's occupation, and a number of other indicators of economic status, they find that in the 1890s blacks still had a child mortality rate about 50 percent above whites (1981, 244–245). (The full list of control variables is as follows: city size, occupation of husband [13 categories including unknown and no husband present], husband's employment status, ownership of dwelling, wife's employment status, and migrant status.)

The occupation categories used in both studies of the 1900 census data are insufficient controls for the effect of income on child mortality. Birth registration data for 1928 on the survival of previous children show substantial differences by father's occupation within major categories. For example, I estimate that within the category of service workers, the proportion of children of servants deceased by age 5 was 158 per 1,000 (regardless of race) compared to about 120 among the children of guards, marshals, and policemen. Similarly, the children of farm laborers had a q(5) of 150 compared to 128 for farmers. Therefore, within the large occupation classifications used in the studies by Smith and by Preston, Haines, and Pamuk, there were differences of 20 to 30 percent among specific occupations. Since blacks in most industries were probably concentrated in the lower income categories, it is likely that the occupation categories used in these studies are not sufficient controls for income.

In a review of studies of infant mortality in eight cities carried out by the U.S. Children's Bureau between 1911 and 1915, Robert Woodbury (1926, 139) presented data on infant mortality rates by income of father, race, and nativity. (The cities were Johnstown, Pennsylvania; Manchester, New Hampshire; Saginaw, Michigan; Brockton and New Bedford, Massachusetts; New Waterbury, Connecticut; Akron, Ohio; and Baltimore, Maryland.) Most of the blacks in these studies lived in Baltimore. Woodbury's results lead to a different impression of the importance of economic differences between the races. The data show that in these cities there were very large differences in infant mortality by income among blacks: those with incomes under $550 had an infant mortality rate about 60 percent higher than those with an income of $650 to $849. Within income groups, blacks living in the eight cities had infant mortality rates about 10 percent higher than native whites and 5 percent higher than foreign-born whites. This excessive black infant mortality within the low-income group is apparently due to differences in the proportion of mothers who work away from home. An examination of infants of mothers not employed away from home classified by father's income shows that black infants had mortality rates slightly lower than whites (Woodbury 1926, 83). These findings suggest that a large part of the differences in infant mortality between blacks and whites in urban areas is accounted for by the relatively low incomes among blacks.

Child Rearing and Feeding Practices

Toward the end of the nineteenth century there was an increasing awareness of problems associated with infant feeding practices and contamination of milk supplies. During the first decades of this century this was reflected in increasing regulation of milk supplies in cities and in the founding of the U.S. Children's Bureau. The bureau began its work with a series of studies of infant mortality in cities and of infant and child care in rural areas. In a series of studies in eight cities, they documented the devastating effect of mixed feeding (that is, a combination of breast milk and supplementary foods) and early weaning.

The Children's Bureau study in Baltimore in 1915 found large differences in infant mortality by type of feeding. For example, during the fourth month of life, children who were completely breast-fed had a mortality rate of 2.3 per 1,000. Those who received mixed feeding at this age had a mortality rate 2.3 times as high, and those who were completely weaned had a rate 7.2 times that of the fully breast-fed. The largest part of this difference was due to gastric and intestinal diseases (Rochester 1923, 70–72).

In the Children's Bureau study of child care practices in a rural area of northern Mississippi in 1918, Dart (1921, 42) commented that "the often-repeated criticism of the feeding customs of rural mothers that they feed their babies from the table at too early an age and delay weaning too long held true in the case of the mothers included in this study." Although she found that children were breast-fed for quite long (63 percent of the black and 41 percent of the white babies were fed for at least 18 months), most were given solid foods quite early. By the fourth month 60 percent of the black and 35 percent of the white babies were receiving solid foods. In a related study in a rural lowland area of North Carolina in 1916, Bradley and Williamson (1918) documented a similar pattern. Breast feeding was long, but 35 percent of the black and 18 percent of the white babies were given supplementary foods by the fourth month. The differences in feeding practices of whites and blacks were certainly responsible for some of the differences in infant mortality in rural areas during the period around 1915.

Despite the importance of feeding practices in Baltimore, racial differences in feeding practices do not explain the differences in infant mortality rates. In terms of the proportion weaned or on mixed feeding, the feeding practices of blacks were marginally better than those of the native whites. The large difference in infant mortality between native whites and blacks (96 as compared to 159) was largely due to differences in father's income, employment of mothers, and shorter birth intervals (Rochester 1923, 81–85). It is possible, however, that some of the difference in mortality is due to the kinds of supplementary foods given to infants. For example, we do not know if the wealthier families were more apt to rely on pasteurized or certified milk.

Given the fact that there were no large differences in child feeding practices by race in Baltimore, it is difficult to explain the substantial differences in mortality under the age of 2 due to diarrhea and enteritis. In Baltimore in 1910 to 1920 the death rate from this cause was about 19 per 1,000 children under the age of 2 for whites and 28 for blacks. (These and all other rates for 1910 to 1920 are based on smoothed estimates for 1915 to adjust for year-to-year fluctuations [U.S. Bureau of the Census 1923].) Much of this is certainly due to large differences in the second year of life since the Children's Bureau documented little difference in gastric and intestinal deaths by race during the first year of life (Rochester 1923, 85).

Most of the cities in the death registration area had similar differences by race during this period and many had rapid declines in mortality due to childhood diarrhea between 1910 and 1920. Declines of about 60 to 70 percent over the decade occurred in such cities as Richmond, Virginia, New Orleans, and Atlanta for both whites and blacks. Slightly smaller declines (closer to 50 percent) were recorded in Philadelphia, New York, and Nashville. Some of these changes may have been due to improvements in milk supplies through pasteurization and related measures (Shaftel 1978). Another possible explanation is that childhood diarrhea rates were affected by the changes in sanitation and water that occurred in many cities during this period.

Sanitation and the Elimination of Typhoid Fever

In cities, the effect of improving sanitation and water supplies was often evident in rapid declines in mortality due to typhoid fever (Condran, Williams, and Cheney 1985; Sydenstricker 1933, 182–83). Figure 2 shows the decline in the age-standardized crude death rate from typhoid in five large cities between 1900 and 1920. All five experienced very rapid declines over the period. Most of the cities experienced a very sharp drop sometime during this period. For example, New Orleans experienced a sharp drop in 1908. These sharp changes were generally due to the start of new systems of water or sanitation.

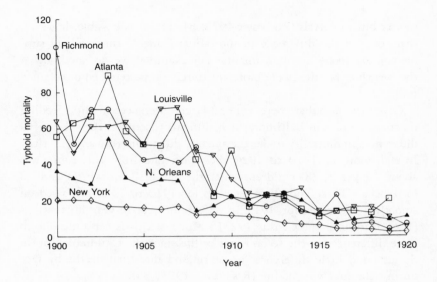

FIG. 2.   Typhoid mortality in five cities, 1900–1920 (per 100,000 population)

In a few cities the sharp decline among blacks was delayed until
several years after the decline for whites. For example, figure 3 records
that in Washington the drop in the typhoid mortality rate came about
six years later among blacks than among whites. A similar lag seems
to have occurred in Richmond, Virginia, and there appears to have
been a smaller lag in Birmingham, Alabama. These delays probably
reflect delays in receiving basic sewer or water services.

An examination of data from cities in the death registration area
in 1920 shows that southern cities were generally not as successful
in controlling typhoid. In northern cities there is no variation in the
typhoid rate by city size; the average rates are all in the range of 4
to 7 deaths per 100,000 total population. The southern cities with
populations over 200,000 have an average rate very similar to the
northern cities (7 per 100,000), but the smaller southern cities have
rates about twice as large. Even higher rates were recorded in the
DRA cities in Mississippi (34) and in the DRA cities of Louisiana
outside New Orleans (27). Although the typhoid rates were probably
declining in all cities, it is clear that the smaller southern cities lagged

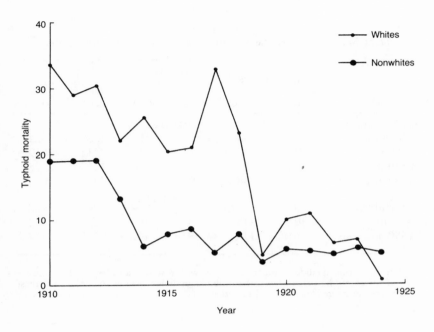

FIG. 3. Typhoid mortality in Washington, D.C., by race, 1910–1924 (per 100,000 population)

behind other urban areas in their control of water-borne diseases (Sydenstricker 1933, 65).

Although the decline in typhoid mortality explains only a small part of the overall mortality decline, changes in sanitation and water supply were probably responsible for declines in other causes of death. The Children's Bureau study in Baltimore provides evidence of the relation between infant mortality due to intestinal causes and the availability of sanitation facilities. Table 3 presents a summary of the data on infant mortality by race, father's income, and adequacy of sanitation facilities. The table excludes all children who died in the first two weeks of life for whom sanitation would not have affected survival. For the purpose of this analysis, adequate sanitation is defined as having a toilet connected to a sewer for the exclusive use of the household, and having a bathtub.

TABLE 3

Infant Mortality by Sanitary Facilities and Income, Baltimore, 1915

Sanitation:	Overall IMR		IMR to gastric and intestinal		Live births	
	Full*	Lacking	Full*	Lacking	Full*	Lacking
Father's income			WHITES			
All children	39	80	14	40	4089	5024
<$550	77	92	26	53	417	1619
$550–849	·50	70	19	31	1257	2178
$850 and over	26	58	9	26	2287	1066
			BLACKS			
All children	93	114	18	35	397	826
<$550	101	115	26	38	227	581
$550 and over	61	110	8	16	132	182

* Full sanitation includes a toilet connected with a sewer, a toilet for the exclusive use of the baby's household, and a bathtub. Households lacking one or more of these items are considered incompleted facilities.

Of the babies that survived at least two weeks, the whites were far more apt to live in houses with adequate sanitation facilities (45 percent of the whites and 32 percent of the blacks). In each race-income group, infants in households with inadequate sanitation facilities suffered elevated risks of infant death. The table shows that most of these excessive deaths were caused by gastric and intestinal diseases. In the case of blacks in the lowest income group, children in households with adequate sanitation had an infant mortality rate after the first two weeks of life of 101 per 1,000 compared to 115 for infants in other households. More than 80 percent of this excessive mortality is attributable to gastric and intestinal causes. Although this analysis does not control for differences in feeding and other child care practices, it strongly suggests that proper sanitation facilities did reduce infant mortality rates in urban areas.

Data from several southern cities in the death registration area suggest that declines in childhood diarrhea mortality rates may have been related to declines in typhoid during this period. Virginia provides one example of this. Diarrhea mortality among black children under the age of two dropped substantially in Richmond and Norfolk right after the drop in typhoid mortality, completely eliminating the urban excess mortality ascribed to childhood diarrhea. There are two likely explanations for this association between typhoid and diarrhea mortality rates. The first is that some of the diarrhea deaths under the age of two were actually due to typhoid. A second alternative is that improvements in water and sanitation might have reduced the risks or the severity of other types of childhood diarrhea.

Use of Health Services

During the first decades of this century a number of other medical and public health measures were becoming important and whites were in a better position to take advantage of these changes than blacks. For example, in the Children's Bureau study in rural Mississippi, 79 percent of the white women were delivered by a physician but the proportion among blacks was only 8 percent. Similarly, one-third of white women received some prenatal care, while the proportion among black women was only 12 percent (Dart 1921; 24, 27). A similar difference was found in the study in the lowland area of North Carolina (Bradley and Williamson 1918, 30). Most of the prenatal care documented in these studies was considered inadequate at the time, however, as improvements in medical care reached rural areas, the women treated by doctors were in a better position to benefit from these innovations.

Two factors probably affected the relative proportions of black and white women in rural areas delivered by physicians and receiving prenatal care. The first is the cost of physician-assisted deliveries. Dart mentions this as an important element in the decision to rely on a midwife rather than a physician. She noted that "the percentage of mothers, both white and colored, who were attended by a physician at confinement was much higher among those families living on farms of their own than among farm tenants, and was lowest among the half-share tenants" (Dart 1921, 27–28; see also Bradley and Williamson 1918, 30). The second possible factor was social custom. Given the shortage of black doctors and nurses and the prevailing racial attitudes, black women did not have equal access to physician care. They may also have felt more comfortable with black midwives.

These racial differences in prenatal care and delivery were not found in Baltimore where the percentage delivered by a doctor was virtually the same for native whites as for blacks (72 percent and 74 percent).

The proportions receiving prenatal care were 58 percent for native whites and 57 percent for blacks. The difference between the two rural areas and Baltimore is the presence in the city of several clinics that began providing prenatal care and infant welfare work in the period of 1914 to 1916. Most native whites received prenatal care from a private physician (53 percent) whereas only 19 percent of blacks did so. On the other hand, 38 percent of blacks but only 5.6 percent of whites went to clinics for prenatal care. Although the Baltimore study did not provide data on infant mortality by place of delivery or use of prenatal care, it is clear that the provision of welfare clinics had not yet had a substantial impact on racial differences in infant mortality.

Between 1915 and 1940 there were substantial changes in delivery practices. One reflection of these changes was the increase in the proportion of births that occurred in hospitals. In 1940, 52 percent of all babies were born in hospitals; the proportion among white births, however, 56 percent, was more than twice the proportion among black births, 22 percent. There were substantial regional variations. In the mid-Atlantic states, the proportions delivered in hospitals were quite high for both whites and blacks (74 percent and 73 percent, respectively). In the south Atlantic states, however, only 36 percent of the white and 12 percent of the black births were in hospital. The proportion of black births that occurred in hospital was lower partly because blacks were more apt to live in rural areas (55 percent of black births as compared with only 35 percent of white births) and in regions that had low proportions delivered in hospital (38 percent of black births were in the south Atlantic region as opposed to only 13 percent of white births) (U.S. Public Health Service 1954, 116–17). In most areas, however, blacks were much less likely to be delivered in a hospital than whites.

Racial differences in health care utilization were not limited to prenatal care and deliveries. The National Health Survey of 1935-1936 showed that blacks in rural counties of Georgia were far less apt to receive essential medical services when they were sick. For example, among those with an illness that disabled them for one week or more, 54 percent of the whites but only 39 percent of the blacks were treated by a physician. Similarly, 5.8 percent of the whites but only 1.0 percent of the blacks received hospitalization (Mott and Roemer 1948, 305). Mott and Roemer (1948, 306) point out that blacks had greater health care needs and conclude that "it cannot be stressed too much that the inequitable share of available rural health services received by Negroes is an expression of their greater poverty rather than their smaller need or desire for these services."

Summary and Conclusions

This article documents the history of black mortality between 1850 and 1940 and begins the process of placing that history into the context of the more general history of mortality decline in the United States. One aspect of this process has been to discuss the trends in mortality among blacks and whites living in the same general geographic areas—for example, comparing southern rural blacks with southern rural whites. A second part has been to relate black mortality to many of the factors that have been discussed as determinants of general mortality trends—such as water and sanitation, the urban disadvantage in mortality, and child care and feeding practices.

During the second half of the nineteenth century, black mortality declined only slightly or not at all. Between 1850 and 1880 there may have been some decline in child mortality, but the trends in adult mortality are indeterminate. Between 1880 and 1900 both child and adult mortality rates were constant. Sometime between 1900 and 1910 mortality rates among blacks began to decline at all ages, especially in urban areas. During the first four decades of this century mortality rates among American blacks declined substantially. Expectation of life at birth increased from about 35 years to about 54 years, which represents a significant improvement in health and living standards. The life expectancy among blacks in 1940, however, was still two years below the value for whites in the death registration area in 1920. (This may exaggerate the difference slightly since the mortality rates for 1919 and 1920 were artificially low following the pandemic of influenza in 1918. In addition, the mortality rates in the DRA may not have been representative of the whole white population.)

Throughout the period studied, blacks had substantially higher mortality rates than whites living in the same area. Although the amount of excessive mortality among blacks differed from place to place and period to period, we did not find a single area or time when black mortality rates were close to those of whites. The examination of causes of death among whites and blacks in 1920 showed that racial differences in the amount of tuberculosis explained a substantial part of the mortality differences in New York and North Carolina, but blacks probably had excessive mortality due to all causes.

Between 1920 and 1940 the mortality reductions among blacks living in northern states not only eliminated the excessive mortality of northern urban blacks, but reversed the differential. By 1940 the life expectancy of blacks in New York State was three years above the value in South Carolina. In the South, the excessive mortality rates among blacks living in cities was greatly reduced during the same period, but in the South rural blacks maintained an advantage over urban blacks. During the first decades of the century, mortality declines in cities were partly due to improvements in water and sanitation and possibly to improvements in the quality of milk supplies, both of which reduced deaths due to typhoid fever and general diarrhea. There were other factors affecting urban and rural mortality rates during this period, but like the changes that caused the reduction in tuberculosis mortality, they are even more difficult to document.

It is not possible at this point to explain all of the reasons for higher mortality rates among blacks. We have evidence that income differentials were responsible for some of the differences in infant and child mortality. We have some evidence that income levels were related to access to medical care (prenatal care and delivery by physicians), to adequate sanitation facilities, and to adequate housing. When dealing with racial differences in mortality in the United States, however, it is not sufficient to stop with income and education as ultimate determinants. Although it is difficult to document statistically the pathways through which racial discrimination affected mortality differentials, it is clear that discrimination limited the access blacks had to better incomes, better health care, better housing, and better education. It is also clear that these amenities are necessary to the achievement of modern levels of health and mortality.

References

Bradley, F.S., and M.A. Williamson. 1918. *Rural Children in Selected Counties of North Carolina*. Rural Child Welfare Series, no. 2. Children's Bureau pub. no. 33. Washington.

Coale, A., and N. Rives. 1973. A Statistical Reconstruction of the Black Population of the United States, 1880–1970: Estimates of True Numbers by Age and Sex, Birth Rates, and Total Fertility. *Population Index* 39:3–36.

Condran, G., H. Williams, and R. Cheney. 1985. The Decline in Mortality in Philadelphia from 1870 to 1930: The Role of Municipal Services. In *Sickness and Health in America,* ed. J.W. Leavitt and R.L. Numbers, 422–36. Madison: University of Wisconsin Press.

Dart, H.M. 1921. *Maternity and Child Care in Selected Rural Areas of Mississippi.* Rural Child Welfare Series no. 5. Children's Bureau pub. no. 88. Washington.

Davis, K. 1973. Cities and Mortality. In *Proceedings,* International Union for the Scientific Study of Population, 259–81. Mexico City.

Demeny, P. and P. Gingrich. 1967. A Reconsideration of Negro-White Mortality Differentials in the United States. *Demography* 4:820–37.

Eblen, J.E. 1974. New Estimates of the Vital Rates of the United States Black Population during the Nineteenth Century. *Demography* 11:301–20.

Farley, R. 1970. *Growth of the Black Population; A Study of Demographic Trends.* Chicago: Markham.

Graham, N. 1980. *1900 Public Use Sample User's Handbook.* Seattle: Center for Studies in Demography and Ecology, University of Washington.

Greville, T.N.E. 1947. *United States Life Tables and Actuarial Tables, 1939–1941.* U.S. Public Health Service, National Office of Vital Statistics. Washington.

Haines, M. 1977. Mortality in Nineteenth-century America: Estimates from New York and Pennsylvania Census Data, 1865 and 1900. *Demography* 14:311–31.

Howard, W.T. 1924. *Public Health Administration and the Natural History of Disease in Baltimore, Maryland 1797–1920.* Washington: Carnegie Institution.

Meeker, E. 1976. Mortality Trends of Southern Blacks, 1850–1910: Some Preliminary Findings. *Explorations in Economic History* 31:13–42.

Molyneaux, J.L. 1945. Differential Mortality in Texas. *American Sociological Review* 10:17–25.

Mott, F.D., and M.I. Roemer. 1948. *Rural Health and Medical Care.* New York: McGraw-Hill.

Preston, S.H., and M.R. Haines. 1984. New Estimates of Child

Mortality in the United States at the Turn of the Century. *Journal of the American Statistical Association* 79:272–81.

Preston, S.H., M.R. Haines, and E. Pamuk. 1981. Effects of Industrialization and Urbanization on Mortality in Developed Countries. In *Solicited Papers: International Population Conferences,* ed. International Union for the Scientific Study of Population, vol. 2, 233–54. Liège, Belgium.

Rochester, A. 1923. *Infant Mortality; Results of a Field Study in Baltimore, Md. Based on Births in One Year.* Children's Bureau pub. no. 119. Washington.

Rosenberg, C.E. 1962. *The Cholera Years,* Chicago: University of Chicago Press.

Shaftel, N. 1978. A History of the Purification of Milk in New York or "How Now, Brown Cow." In *Sickness and Health in America,* ed. J.W. Leavitt and R.L. Numbers, 275–92. Madison: University of Wisconsin Press.

Sibley, E. 1969. *Differential Mortality in Tennessee, 1917–1928.* New York: Negro Universities Press.

Smith, D.S. 1983. Differential Mortality in the United States before 1900. *Journal of Interdisciplinary History* 13:735–59.

Steckel, R.H. 1979. Slave Mortality: Analysis of Evidence from Plantation Records. *Social Science History* 3:86–114.

Suliman, S.E.H. 1983. *Estimation of Levels and Trends of the U.S. Adult Black Mortality during the Period 1870–1900.* University of Pennsylvania Ph.D. dissertation. (Unpublished.)

Sydenstricker, E. 1933. *Health and Environment.* New York: McGraw-Hill.

United Nations. 1982. Model Life Tables for Developing Countries. *Population Studies,* no. 77. ST/ESA/Ser.A/77. New York.

U.S. Bureau of the Census. 1923. *Mortality Rates 1910–1920.* Washington.

———. 1943. *Vital Statistics of the United States; Supplement 1939–1940,* part III. Washington.

U.S. Public Health Service. 1954. *Vital Statistics of the United States, 1950.* Vol. 1. Washington.

Woodbury, R.M. 1926. *Infant Mortality and Its Causes.* Baltimore: Williams and Wilkins.

Health Differentials between Blacks and Whites: Recent Trends in Mortality and Morbidity

KENNETH G. MANTON, CLIFFORD H. PATRICK, and KATRINA W. JOHNSON

D IFFERENCES IN THE HEALTH STATUS OF BLACKS
and whites have been documented in the United States as
long as health data have been collected. These differences
have persisted despite large increases in life expectancy and improvements
in the health status of the general population. Although some indicators
of health differentials have declined, others persist and several have
increased. Sources of these health differentials have been linked to (1)
differences in lifestyle and risk-factor exposures (e.g., alcohol, smoking,
and nutrition); (2) health consequences of low socioeconomic status
(e.g., economic barriers to access to health services and a lack of
health insurance due to chronic unemployment); (3) poorer knowledge
of health practices; (4) more hazardous occupations and environmental
exposures (e.g., exposure of children to lead); and (5) genetic factors
(e.g., sickle cell trait). Because of the interaction of these multiple
factors (e.g., the interactions of low education, smoking, and nutrition),
the exact contribution of each factor to black-white differentials in
health—or its change over time—remains unknown. Of particular
importance because of its policy implications is knowledge of how

low socioeconomic status interacts with physical risk factors to increase differentially mortality and morbidity risks for blacks and whites.

Although we do not know the precise etiology underlying health differentials between blacks and whites, the nature of those differentials and their recent changes can be documented. In this article, we discuss health differentials as they vary by sex, age, and severity of medical conditions. Many of these health differentials are related to the generally poorer economic condition of blacks relative to whites. In our analysis, however, we do not attempt to explain the etiology of health differentials—just to document them. Therefore, we will not attempt to standardize for the effect of income and other economic differentials. A complete etiological study of the wide range of conditions we examined is beyond the scope of this overview. Furthermore, because of the paucity of economic measures in mortality and other important national health data sets, it probably could not be done comprehensively.

Black-white differentials in health will be examined by sex because of well-documented differences in health between males and females. Female life expectancy, which was about 10 percent greater than that of males in 1980, has increased more rapidly than male life expectancy for both blacks and whites. In addition, differences in the prevalence of chronic conditions and disabilities between males and females (Verbrugge 1983) suggest that we need to determine whether the factors underlying sex differentials in health are the same for blacks and whites when age is accounted for.

Health differentials between blacks and whites are examined within four broad age categories. *First,* differentials in the survival and health of infants and children are important for both their immediate health consequences and their impact on physical and mental developmental processes that affect health late in life. *Second,* differences in health among teenagers and young adults are examined because differences in economic conditions, health behavior, and risk-factor exposures will affect both current health risks (e.g., homicide, morbidity from alcohol and drug use) and will have long-range implications for the prevalence of such chronic diseases as cirrhosis, lung cancer, and diabetes. *Third,* health differentials in middle and late adulthood are important because chronic diseases most often manifest themselves at those ages. *Fourth,* health differentials for the elderly are interesting because of the observed mortality "crossover" (black mortality rates are lower than those of whites at advanced ages), the role of Medicare in this phenomenon, and its economic and health care implications. The analysis also examines health conditions of varying severity.

In the following, we first consider differences in the demographic structure of the black and white populations—both now and projected into the future. We then examine mortality differentials and their effect on life expectancy. Next, we examine differentials in chronic and acute morbidity and associated disability. Finally, we discuss differentials in health care access, utilization, and risk-factor exposures that may affect future health differentials.

Methods and Data

We examine the black-white differentials in health using a number of methodologies and data sources. Among the methods used are several types of life tables, indicators of excess mortality, and measures of the relative risk of morbidity and disability. The data sources used include national vital statistics data, the National Health Interview Survey (NHIS), National Health and Nutrition Examination Survey (NHANES), National Long-term Care Survey (NLTCS), National Nursing Home Survey (NNHS), and National Health Examination Survey (NHES). We make only limited use of subnational data sources such as community epidemiological studies because very few have sufficient numbers of blacks to make valid comparisons with whites in the same environment. We also did not consider the many social surveys such as the Longitudinal Retirement History Study and the National Longitudinal Survey (or Parnes study) because health information was a secondary interest in those studies. Thus, we have relied on readily available national data sets whose major focus is some aspect of health.

We examined mortality changes over the periods of 1969 to 1971 and 1979 to 1981—periods unique in American history in terms of achieved life expectancy and the management of the health effects of chronic degenerative diseases at advanced ages. The morbidity, disability, and risk-factor analyses will be both cross-sectional (e.g., HIS survey results for 1979 to 1981; NLTCS 1982) and longitudinal (e.g., HES and HANES for 1960 to 1980).

Mortality is analyzed in several ways, each providing incremental information on the differentials between blacks and whites. Life expectancy at birth is perhaps the most common measure of the impact of mortality. We examine this figure as well as the life expectancy at age 65, an indication of the impact of mortality among the elderly. To indicate the differential impact of selected causes of death on life expectancy, we examine the change in life expectancy at birth which would occur if a given cause of death were eliminated. This has obvious policy implications for the allocation of health resources. We also analyze age-adjusted and age-specific death rates for different causes of deaths to see which segments of the population are affected by those causes, e.g., homicide among young black adult males.

To get a more comprehensive sense of cause-specific differentials, rates are used to calculate the number of "excess deaths" in the black population, indicating the number of deaths that would have been avoided had the age-specific death rates for a given cause for blacks been the same as those for whites. This excess death measure is a better indicator of the size of the disparity in health than are differences in mortality rates because the former indicator combines mortality rates with the size of the population at risk to determine the absolute number of deaths that are "excess." The absolute number of excess deaths more directly reflects the size of the public health problem and the resources required to correct it than does the differential in rates. The excess death measure has to be interpreted carefully because of two factors. First, only the rates for which blacks exceeded whites were analyzed. For some conditions like suicide, whites have higher mortality rates than blacks. Such white "excess" deaths were not subtracted from the black excess since white excesses were relatively infrequent at younger ages and black-white excesses must eventually "balance out" because both groups have a finite, and presumably similar life span. Second, white excess mortality risks should not be used as a norm or standard for blacks (i.e., we would obviously not wish to increase black mortality to the same levels of mortality for the conditions with white excess deaths).

More absolute health standards to assess the mortality status of blacks and whites are desirable. One such standard might be that of the lowest mortality rate achieved for a disease globally. Therefore, one could compare black infant mortality rates against those in certain Scandinavian countries. A more absolute standard based upon the best clinical judgment about what deaths are preventable is the Sentinel Health Events methodology (Rutstein et al. 1976). We used the

Sentinel Health Events (SHE) methodology to generate estimates of both black *and* white excess mortality based on expert judgment of the best achievable levels given current medical science. The policy implications of these measures are important for health delivery and utilization and other social issues (e.g., health insurance, gun control, drug use). We feel each measure of mortality risk differences is necessary in order to identify different aspects of health differentials existing between blacks and whites.

In the mortality analysis, two types of cause-specific mortality data prepared by the National Center for Health Statistics (NCHS) are examined: (1) underlying cause of death, and (2) multiple cause-of-death data. Underlying cause-of-death data contain only one medical condition reported for each of the two million deaths occurring yearly in the United States and are used in most official vital statistics publications (e.g., National Center for Health Statistics 1986a). Multiple cause-of-death mortality data, however, contain *all* causes of death listed on the death certificate by the physician (Manton and Stallard 1984; Israel, Rosenberg, and Curtin 1986). These data are useful to describe: (1) mortality at advanced ages where there is a high prevalence of multiple conditions, and (2) conditions such as diabetes that appear primarily in a contributory role on the death certificate.

One must exercise care in interpreting cause-specific mortality data because some black-white differentials could be affected by the quality of either the diagnoses reported on the death certificates or by the age reporting of the population data used to form the rates. Furthermore, care must be taken not to interpret the multiple cause data as direct measures of morbidity—they directly reflect only the reported prevalence of conditions at the time of death. Thus, although the differentials may be suggestive of morbidity differentials, the confirmation of multiple cause patterns requires the use of detailed epidemiological data. Nonetheless, the much greater information content of the multiple cause data makes them important in epidemiological studies (Israel, Rosenberg, and Curtin 1986).

In the underlying cause-of-death analysis, all deaths during the two three-year periods—1969–1971 and 1979–1981—were summed (roughly six million deaths for each interval) and an annual average computed. Then 1970 and 1980 population data were used with the averaged deaths to produce more stable estimates of mortality rates— especially for rarer causes of death among blacks. Conditions examined were cancer, heart disease, stroke, diabetes, cirrhosis, homicide, and infant mortality. Infant mortality as used herein includes all deaths occurring in the first year of life regardless of the cause.

In our multiple cause-of-death analysis, we examine individual deaths from 1969 to 1980, yielding data on nearly 26 million deaths and nearly 70 million reported medical conditions for the total population. Among these were about 2.5 million deaths for blacks. Since both the 8th and 9th revisions of the International Classification of Disease (ICD) (World Health Organization 1969, 1977) were employed over the study period, only comparable disease categories based upon National Center for Health Statistics comparability studies (1975, 1980) were examined.

We examined morbidity using data from major national surveys of health. For example, the NHIS—an annual survey conducted since 1957—typically covered 42,000 households and 111,000 individuals. A number of changes were made in the survey methodology and questionnaire over this period that make cross-temporal comparisons of disease prevalence with NHIS data difficult. For the single time interval of 1979 to 1981, however, we examined the ratio of black-white prevalence rates for conditions that were significant in the mortality analyses. To improve the reliability of our prevalence estimates, only reports of disease involving either health service contact or associated disability were used.

The 1982 NLTC survey reports on the characteristics of community-dwelling persons aged 65 and over who manifested chronic (over 90 days) disability according to reported limitations on activities of daily living (ADL) or instrumental activities of daily living (IADL). A telephone screen of 36,000 persons over the age of 65 drawn from the Medicare Health Insurance master file yielded 6,393 persons who reported (or anticipated) an ADL or IADL limitation lasting three months or more. An intensive household interview of the 6,393 persons (representing five million elderly persons) was conducted. Results on differences in the functional limitations of elderly blacks and whites are discussed in this article.

The NHES and NHANES (1960–1962, 1971–1974, 1976–1980) involve direct clinical measurements of certain important physiological variables. For example, these surveys provide nationally representative data on trends in blood pressure, serum cholesterol, and obesity for blacks and whites. In addition, national surveys of the utilization of acute-care hospitals (National Hospital Discharge Survey), nursing homes (NNHS for 1977 and 1973–1974, resident place surveys in 1963 and 1969), and physician visits (National Ambulatory Medical Care Survey) were employed. These were supplemented by data from select epidemiological studies and registries. For example, the mortality crossover was examined using 20-year follow-up data on total mortality from the Evans County, Georgia, study of 1,919 whites and 1,183 blacks aged 15 to 74 in 1960 (Wing, Tyroler, and Manton 1985) and in the 25-year follow-up data on total mortality for 1,388 whites and 786 blacks in the Charleston, South Carolina, heart study (Wing et al. 1987). These two closed cohort studies had extremely high rates of subject follow-up.

The primary registry source is the population-based tumor registries of the surveillance, epidemiology, and end results program of the National Cancer Institute. In 1981 the 11 registries in this program covered almost 13 percent of the entire United States population (National Cancer Institute 1984). Data in some registries have been collected since 1973. A comparison of mortality in the registry population shows good concordance with that of the American population, suggesting that the registry data are representative of national patterns.

In order to calculate rates, age-, sex-, and race-specific population estimates are needed. These estimates are subject to considerable error, especially for blacks at older ages. In forming rate estimates, we used either U.S. Bureau of the Census population figures adjusted for various race, sex, and age reporting errors (Siegel 1979) or the sum of population weights used in various surveys (e.g., the NHIS).

The Demographic Structure of the United States Black and White Population

We examined the age structure of the American white and black population by sex as estimated for 1985 and projected for the years 2000 and 2050. The age structure of the population is very different so that even if the age- and sex-specific morbidity and mortality rates were the same in the two populations, the total health needs of the two populations would be quite different. The population structure differences arise because the black population has significantly higher fertility rates than the white, resulting in the black population being much younger on average and having higher proportions of its population at younger ages. Thus, diseases of infancy and conditions affecting adolescents and young adults (e.g., homicide, accidents, drug abuse) will be proportionately more important in the black population because of the greater proportions of persons at young ages who have the highest risk of those conditions.

The difference in the age structure of the American black and white populations estimated in 1985 and projected to 2000 and 2050 is reported separately by sex in table 1.

The table contains the number of persons in each age category, the proportion that number is of the total race- and sex-specific population, the underlying fertility rate, and the mean age. The black fertility rate is 22 percent greater than that for whites in 1985. Even if there were no excess mortality risks, the relative number of infant deaths would be higher for blacks. For persons under the age of 5 and for those aged 15 to 24, the proportion of the black population is 31 and 18 percent higher than for whites. This increases for blacks the relative significance of diseases and causes of death that are more prevalent at these ages—i.e., for infants, teenagers, and young adults.

Table 1 also contains the projected population age structure of the black and white population for the years 2000 and 2050. The age structure of the black population is projected to continue to be younger than for whites, though because of the assumed convergence of the fertility rates the differentials become smaller. For example, the 10.1 year difference in the median age for females declines to 6.8 years by 2000 and 4.9 years by 2050. While the differential in median age does decrease, it remains substantial to 2050. Both black and white populations age rapidly, however, so that the aggregate health needs of both groups will become increasingly weighted toward the chronic disease risks of middle and late ages and the health differences at younger ages will become less significant—even without changes in morbidity and mortality rates. Nonetheless, significant age-related health differentials will continue to exist between blacks and whites in the coming decades.

Mortality

Life Expectancy: At Birth and in Late Life

Life expectancy has risen dramatically in the United States in recent years for both blacks and whites. In figure 1, the sex-specific increases in life expectancy at birth for blacks and whites from 1950 to 1982 are presented.

All four race-sex groups have experienced large gains, with blacks experiencing faster gains than whites. Nonetheless, significant black-white differences in life expectancy remain for both males and females. For example, in 1980, a 6.3-year difference in life expectancy (70.6 vs. 64.3 years) remained between white and black males and a 5.1-year difference (78.2 vs. 73.1 years) existed between white and black females. Both values represent substantial declines in the sex-specific differences from 1970.

Recently, both races have had significant increases in life expectancy at advanced ages. Changes in life expectancy at age 65 from 1960 to 1983 are presented in table 2.

Significant life expectancy gains at age 65 have been made for all race and sex groups, especially from 1970 to 1983. Between 1960 and 1970 the pace of change for males was slow. From 1970 to 1983 it accelerated, increasing 1.4 years for white males and 0.7 years for black males. For white females, the rapid gain from 1960 to 1970 accelerated from 1970 to 1983. The pace of improvement after 1970 for black females was slower than for white females—but a little faster than for white males. Gains after 1980 for both black males and females have been very rapid.

While life expectancy *at birth* for blacks and whites converged over time, until recently life expectancy after age 65 diverged. For males, this divergence between blacks and whites is considerable, with the differences in life expectancy increasing from 1960 to 1983. For females, the difference between blacks and whites increased from 1960 to 1980, then dropped slightly in 1983. The divergence could be explained in a number of ways. First, the divergence could be due to better recent age reporting for blacks at advanced ages, which reduced recent estimates of the elderly black population, thereby increasing estimates of mortality rates. An improvement in age-reporting accuracy could mask gains in life expectancy for blacks. Second, rapid

TABLE 1

Number of Persons (in Thousands) by Age Group, Sex, and Race; Percentage; Median Age; and Fertility Rates for Females 1985, 2000, and 2050, Middle Series

Age group	1985				2000				2050			
	White males	White females	Black males	Black females	White males	White females	Black males	Black females	White males	White females	Black males	Black females
NUMBER												
<1	1,561	1,479	319	312	1,394	1,321	312	305	1,346	1,275	331	323
1–4	6,041	5,732	1,225	1,200	5,713	5,416	1,245	1,218	5,440	5,156	1,338	1,306
5–14	14,004	13,305	2,521	2,483	15,634	14,836	3,243	3,178	13,918	13,199	3,439	3,359
15–24	16,784	16,098	2,870	2,862	14,843	14,160	2,852	2,819	14,042	13,377	3,470	3,410
25–44	31,565	31,376	4,050	4,566	33,324	32,622	5,450	5,678	29,629	28,748	6,920	6,965
45–64	18,870	20,420	1,907	2,431	25,589	26,676	2,879	3,599	28,691	28,948	5,920	6,290
65–74	6,636	8,554	579	831	6,953	8,636	615	974	11,257	12,685	1,979	2,424
75–84	3,034	5,176	271	459	4,212	6,881	334	641	7,131	10,100	1,109	1,750
85+	697	1,780	60	129	1,217	3,227	110	302	4,046	9,326	545	1,419
Total	99,192	103,920	13,802	15,273	108,879	113,775	17,040	18,714	115,500	122,814	25,051	27,246
PERCENTAGE												
<1	1.57%	1.42%	2.31%	2.04%	1.28%	1.16%	1.83%	1.63%	1.17%	1.04%	1.32%	1.19%
1–4	6.09	5.52	8.88	7.86	5.25	4.76	7.31	6.51	4.71	4.20	5.34	4.79
5–14	14.12	12.80	18.27	16.26	14.35	13.04	19.03	16.99	12.05	10.75	13.73	12.33
15–24	16.91	15.50	20.79	18.74	13.63	12.45	16.73	15.06	12.16	10.90	13.85	12.52
25–44	31.81	30.19	29.34	29.90	30.61	28.66	31.98	30.34	25.65	23.41	27.62	25.55
45–64	19.02	19.65	13.82	15.91	23.50	23.45	16.90	19.23	24.84	23.56	23.63	23.09
65–74	6.69	8.23	4.20	5.44	6.39	7.59	3.61	5.20	9.75	10.33	7.90	8.90
75–84	3.09	4.98	1.96	3.01	3.87	6.05	1.96	3.43	6.17	8.22	4.43	6.42
85+	0.70	1.71	0.43	0.84	1.12	2.84	0.65	1.61	3.50	7.59	2.18	5.21
Total	100.00	100.00	100.00	100.00	100.00	100.00	100.00	100.00	100.00	100.00	100.00	100.00
MEDIAN AGE												
	31.1	37.7	24.9	27.6	36.1	38.8	28.5	32.0	40.5	44.8	36.3	39.9

FERTILITY RATES

	1985		2000		2025	2050
	White Females	Black Females	White Females	Black Females	White Females	Black Females
10–14	0.8	4.2	0.7	3.0	0.7	1.8
15–19	45.0	98.5	44.9	85.5	44.9	65.2
20–24	109.9	145.5	112.6	140.7	114.0	128.2
25–29	115.7	113.0	120.4	118.3	121.8	120.7
30–34	65.2	68.0	74.0	76.5	71.9	73.1
35–39	19.8	26.3	23.1	28.9	22.9	25.8
40–44	3.6	6.0	3.6	5.5	3.6	4.6
45–49	0.2	0.3	0.2	0.2	0.1	0.2
Total	1,800.6	2,309.1	1,897.4	2,292.7	1,900.0	2,098.1

Source: U.S. Bureau of the Census 1984.

139

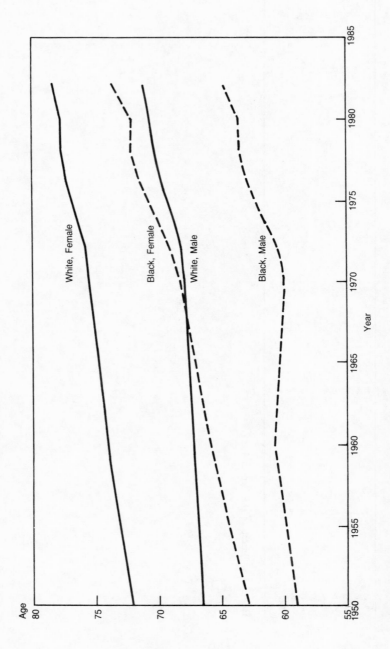

FIG. 1. Life expectancy at birth, according to race and sex: United States, 1950–1983.
Source: U.S. Department of Health and Human Services 1985, 66 (figure 2).

TABLE 2
Life Expectancy at Age 65: Changes 1960 to 1983

Year	Males		Difference between whites & blacks	Females		Difference between whites & blacks
	Whites	Blacks		Whites	Blacks	
1960	12.9	12.7	0.2	15.9	15.1	0.8
1970	13.1	12.5	0.6	17.1	15.7	1.4
1980	14.2	12.9	1.3	18.5	16.5	2.0
1983	14.5	13.2	1.3	18.9	17.2	1.7
	Number of years change between time interval					
1960–1970	0.2	−0.2		1.2	0.6	
1970–1980	1.1	0.4		1.4	0.8	
1980–1983	0.3	0.3		0.4	0.7	
1960–1983	1.6	0.5		3.0	2.1	

decreases in mortality at younger ages may have increased the number of blacks with chronic conditions surviving to advanced ages. An increase in the prevalence of chronic conditions among elderly blacks would make mortality reductions at those advanced ages more difficult to achieve. Third, special health care and nutritional programs initiated in the 1960s and 1970s may have served to improve the relative health status of black infants and mothers in some areas of the country. Less program specialization and outreach specifically for black elderly may have served to retard their improvement relative to that of whites, as suggested by large differentials in institutionalization rates above the age of 85—trends which may be accelerated by current efforts to reduce Medicaid and Medicare benefits. Identifying the contribution of each of these three factors to the slower rate of improvement in black life expectancy at later ages is a topic for further research; currently, data on black-white health differentials at later ages are insufficient to answer these questions.

A second implication of recent life expectancy gains at advanced ages is the rapid growth of the "oldest old" population (i.e., those aged 85 and over) with its attendant high per capita needs for both acute and long-term care (LTC) health services (Manton and Soldo 1985). The rapid growth of the oldest old population, shown in table 1 to occur for blacks as well as whites, is important to remember when examining black-white differentials in disability rates from the 1982 NLTCS and nursing home rates from the 1977 NNHS.

The higher disability rates of the black elderly, their rapid growth in numbers, and smaller socioeconomic resources suggest the need to develop programs to provide LTC services that are targeted to the special family and social conditions of minority elderly. Whether privately or publicly funded, paid LTC services are normally viewed as a supplement to the informal care resources of the individual (Liu, Manton, and Liu 1985). Children represent a major source of informal care for elderly females (Maonton and Liu 1984). It will be important to determine differences in the availability of such informal care resources for elderly black and white females. For example, do the generally lower socioeconomic resources of black children hinder them from performing informal care services at the same rate as for whites? On the other hand, does the more fluid, extended family structure of blacks serve to increase the availability of informal care resources?

The Trajectory of Black and White Mortality Rates at Later Ages

One issue often raised when examining black and white mortality differences at advanced ages is the so-called black-white mortality crossover (Manton 1980; Nam and Ockay 1977). U.S. national vital statistics show that black mortality rates at advanced ages converge with and then drop below white mortality rates. The reality of the crossover has been debated by a number of authors. Ryder (1985), for example, argues that such a crossover may be due to higher rates of age misstatement at later ages. The age at which the crossover occurs has increased in more current data, suggesting that the crossover may not be real and will disappear as the quality of age reporting for blacks at later ages is improved. Life expectancy among blacks at later ages, however, is also increasing; indeed, between 1980 and 1983 it increased faster for black than white females. Thus, if the crossover was due to higher rates of systematic mortality selection among blacks at early ages, then as life expectancy increases (and greater proportions of blacks survive to later ages), the effects of selection also ought to disappear and the crossover should advance to later ages.

The trajectories of mortality rates that produce the crossover are manifest even in middle age. An age-reporting explanation of the crossover would involve age misreporting in early middle age and would have to affect causes of death differently, since the crossover can be identified with disease-specific components of the total force of mortality. With higher black mortality rates at younger ages, a crossover must occur if the life span of both racial groups is the same and the maximum observed ages to which blacks and whites survive is the same. For example, Fries (1980, 1983) has argued that we are currently near a rectangularization of the survival curve in the United States and other developed countries, with deaths at very advanced ages (e.g., 85 and over) increasingly due to basic biological senescence. If the deaths of both blacks and whites at extreme ages are largely due to biological senescence, and the genetically determined life span is the same for both blacks and whites, then a crossover must eventually occur to compensate for higher black mortality rates at younger ages. Others argue that we are not currently manifesting a rectangularization of the mortality curve at advanced ages (e.g., Schneider and Guralnik 1986; Myers and Manton 1984a, 1984b; Manton 1986). In this case there would be no absolute requirement that mortality crossover must occur because of life span constraints.

Whatever arguments are made, there is probably no way to resolve whether the crossover exists using census and vital statistics data alone. An alternative approach is to examine epidemiological data where (a) one is examining a closed cohort for a lengthy period of time, and (b) one has covariate information on the risk-factor characteristics of people who die at different ages. The existence of observed risk-factor heterogeneity and its effect on mortality trajectories has been examined in a number of longitudinal studies (Manton et al. 1985). The extreme heterogeneity of risk-factor exposure within the black population could produce a crossover through systematic mortality selection. We will examine results from an analysis of the sex-specific mortality patterns for blacks and whites in two large, closed-cohort epidemiological studies (i.e., the Charleston heart study and the Evans County, Georgia, study [Wing et al. 1987]). Because these are closed-cohort designs with lengthy follow-up, it is possible to see if a crossover occurs during the course of observation. If so, then no assumption needs to be made about the quality of age reports, even though such data are probably much better in these epidemiological studies than in vital statistics.

TABLE 3

Results from a Pooled Analysis of Total Mortality in the Evans County and Charleston Heart Studies

A. One degree of freedom χ^2 associated with hypothesis that shape parameters of hazard function are equal for blacks and whites (scale parameters were separately estimated for blacks and whites to allow for different levels of risk).

	Gompertz Hazard	Weibull Hazard
Males	2.93	4.47
Females	11.90	13.87
Total (2 d.f.)	14.83	18.34

B. Value of shape parameters (value for Gompertz is multiplied by 100)

White males	7.92	6.02
Black males	6.98	5.23
White females	9.51	7.32
Black females	7.52	5.77

Cohort mortality was modeled using separate sex-specific hazard functions for blacks and whites in a pooled analysis of the two data sets. Two alternate hazard functions, the Gompertz and the Weibull, were used to see if the form of the hazard function affected the results. Separate constants were used for each subpopulation and a test made to see if the same exponential parameter, which determines the shape of the hazard function across age, could be used across race within sex. The results are presented in table 3.

The hypothesis of equal shape parameters (one-tailed directional test) is rejected for both males and females with the shape parameter for whites being higher than that for blacks. The higher value of the white shape parameter means that mortality rates rise faster with age for whites; the whites had a smaller constant parameter meaning their initial mortality is lower—hence the "crossover." Demonstrating a crossover in two tightly controlled closed-cohort studies which, because of their relative homogeneity, should probably show less of a tendency to converge and crossover than the national data is important evidence for a crossover. Preliminary examination of published tabls from other studies (e.g., Alameda County [Berkman and Breslow 1983]) also seem suggestive of a "crossover."

Cause-specific Mortality

Given the rapid improvements in life expectancy for all groups and the persistence of a relative deficit for blacks, it is important to identify factors that underlie mortality changes. One factor is the difference in infant mortality. Black rates are about twice as high as white rates. The pattern of decline in infant mortality rates for blacks and whites from 1950 to 1982, portrayed in figure 2, indicates this relatively constant difference in levels.

For both blacks and whites, the rate of decline accelerates about 1965. The rapid rate of decline persists to at least 1982. Despite the decline in infant mortality rates, black-white differentials persist. Even the United States white infant mortality rate is high relative to many other developed nations. The 1984 infant mortality rate in Japan is 6.0 (World Health Organization 1985), 40 percent lower than the 1982 United States white infant mortality rate of 10.1 per 1,000 live births (U.S. Bureau of the Census 1985). Thus, the American black infant mortality rate appears even more excessive when compared to the rate of other developed nations. Indeed, the 1982 American black infant mortality rate of 19.6 per 1,000 (U.S. Bureau of the Census 1985) does not compare favorably against less developed countries such as Cuba (infant mortality rate of 18.5 per 1,000 in 1981), Costa Rica (24.3 in 1979), or Panama (20.4 in 1983) (World Health Organization 1982, 1985), if we accept their reported rates as accurate. Indeed, infant mortality rates in certain states (e.g., Illinois and Michigan both with a black infant mortality rate of 24.6 per 1,000, or the District of Columbia with 24.1 [U.S. Bureau of the Census 1985]) begin to approach those in some African nations (e.g., 27 per 1,000 in Mauritius in 1982 [World Health Organization 1985]).

The black-white differential in infant mortality has persisted because of a number of factors. These include socioeconomic differences between black and white mothers which contribute to poorer prenatal care and nutrition, higher rates of teenage pregnancy, greater parity, and other risk factors.

Infant mortality differentials, while contributing significantly to

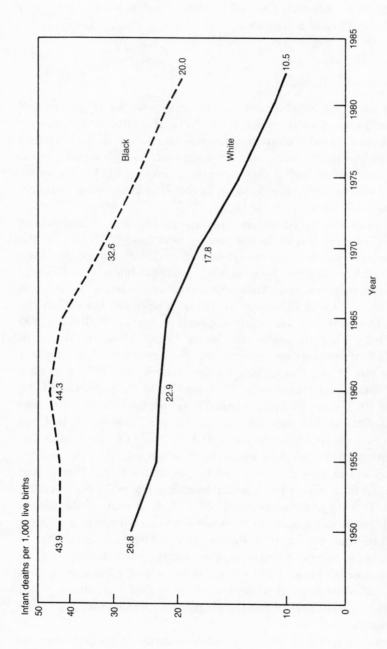

FIG. 2.   Infant mortality rates, 1950–1982.
Source: U.S. Department of Health and Human Services 1985, 172 (figure 14).

black and white life expectancy differences, are only one source. A second major source results from chronic diseases, conditions, and external events that produce mortality primarily in mid and late life. This is illustrated in the age-standardized cause-specific mortality rates in table 4.

The age-adjusted death rates for blacks are about 50 percent higher than those of whites for both males and females. The biggest black-white differential is for homicide, an external cause of death most prevalent among adolescents and young adults. Diabetes is the second most elevated cause of adult death for blacks, probably reflecting nutritional factors, including higher prevalence of obesity among black females and possible differences in the management of disease. Cirrhosis, associated with alcohol abuse, is twice as high for blacks, while stroke and heart disease, and circulatory conditions associated with hypertension and diabetes, are also higher.

We also examined mortality differentials in multiple-cause mortality data (data on all conditions reported on the death certificate). Multiple-cause data are important in describing mortality at later ages where the prevalence of multiple chronic diseases is higher and for certain diseases (e.g., diabetes, cirrhosis, pneumonia, septicemia) frequently reported as contributing to death but not being the underlying cause (Israel, Rosenberg, and Curtin 1986).

Table 5 contains the proportion of deaths for American blacks and whites in 1980 from selected causes (diabetes mellitus, stroke, pneumonia) where the condition is: (1) the underlying cause of death (UCD); and (2) mentioned anywhere on the certificate as contributing to death (TM). Table 5 also shows the ratio of the total occurrence on the death certificate of the selected causes to only their underlying cause occurrence. The proportions are estimated for life table populations so the effect of population structure has been removed. The ratio of the two proportions indicates the relative importance of the condition as a contributing cause of death. These statistics are reported for four ages (birth, 45, 65, 85).

In general, whites have a higher ratio of total mentions to underlying-cause mentions than blacks. The ratios can be quite large (e.g., for white males there are 4.5 times as many deaths where diabetes is recorded on the death certificate than there are deaths where diabetes is selected as the underlying cause). Significant reporting of conditions in a nonunderlying-cause role was observed for most major chronic

TABLE 4

Age-adjusted Death Rates by Selected Cause, Race, and Sex, 1980 (per 100,000 population)

	Black male	Ratio	White male	Ratio	Black female	White female	Ratio
Total deaths (all causes)	1,112.8	1.5	745.3	1.5	631.1	411.1	1.5
Heart disease	327.3	1.2	277.5	1.2	201.1	134.6	1.5
Stroke	77.5	1.9	41.9	1.9	61.7	35.2	1.8
Cancer	229.9	1.4	160.5	1.2	129.7	107.7	1.2
Infant mortality	2,586.7	2.1	1,230.3	2.2	2,123.7	962.5	2.2
Homicide	71.9	6.6	10.9	4.3	13.7	3.2	4.3
Accidents	82.0	1.3	62.3	1.2	25.1	21.4	1.2
Cirrhosis	30.6	2.0	15.7	2.1	14.4	7.0	2.1
Diabetes	17.7	1.9	9.5	2.5	22.1	8.7	2.5

Source: National Center for Health Statistics 1983, tables 9, 15.

TABLE 5

A Comparison of Underlying and Multiple-cause Mortality Reporting for Diabetes, Stroke, and Pneumonia: 1980

Age	White males			Black males			White females			Black females		
	UCD*	TM**	RATIO***	UCD	TM	RATIO	UCD	TM	RATIO	UCD	TM	RATIO
DIABETES												
Birth	1.3	5.8	4.5	1.7	5.5	3.2	2.0	7.8	3.9	3.4	10.2	3.0
45	1.4	6.1	4.4	1.8	6.0	3.3	2.0	8.0	4.0	3.6	10.8	3.0
65	1.4	6.3	4.5	1.8	6.1	3.4	2.0	8.1	4.1	3.4	10.4	3.1
85	1.1	4.8	4.4	1.2	4.1	3.4	1.4	5.5	3.9	2.4	6.6	2.8
STROKE												
Birth	7.3	12.5	1.7	8.4	13.4	1.6	12.2	19.7	1.6	12.6	20.1	1.6
45	7.8	13.4	1.7	9.2	14.8	1.6	12.6	20.4	1.6	13.2	21.2	1.6
65	8.9	15.4	1.7	10.6	17.2	1.6	13.6	22.0	1.6	14.3	23.1	1.6
85	11.7	19.4	1.7	11.5	18.4	1.6	15.7	25.1	1.6	15.6	24.2	1.6
INFLUENZA AND PNEUMONIA												
Birth	3.0	9.3	3.1	3.0	8.2	2.7	3.6	9.7	2.7	2.7	7.1	2.6
45	3.1	9.8	3.2	3.2	8.8	2.8	3.7	9.9	2.7	2.7	7.2	2.7
65	3.6	11.0	3.1	3.6	9.7	2.7	4.0	10.5	2.6	3.0	7.8	2.6
85	6.3	15.7	2.5	5.5	12.6	2.2	5.6	13.3	2.4	4.1	9.8	2.4

*UCD   = Underlying cause of death on the death certificate
**TM   = Total mentions of causes on the death certificate
***RATIO = TM/UCD

diseases; even for cancer there are 15 percent more deaths (or 60,000 per year) affected than are recorded in underlying-cause statistics (Manton 1986). Part of the greater multiple-cause occurrences for whites may be due to differences in death certification and medical care that leads to more complete diagnosis and treatment of conditions among whites. Another source of the higher rate of multiple-cause reporting among whites may be better survival of whites with chronic disease (because the case fatality rates for many chronic diseases such as cancer are higher for blacks than for whites). Consequently, whites may live longer with a chronic disease, thereby increasing the period of exposure for a second (or multiple) chronic disease to emerge.

In examining the individual conditions, the ratio of total to underlying-cause mentions for diabetes is lower for blacks than for whites. Females of both races have proportionally more deaths affected by diabetes, with over 10 percent of black female deaths associated with diabetes. The lower rate of multiple-cause reporting of diabetes for blacks may occur because the disease is more lethal for blacks, possibly due to later diagnosis and less access to adequate medical and personal resources for the long-term management of the disease. Alternatively, the lower rate may be due to less complete reporting of diabetes on death certificates for blacks. The latter explanation seems less likely because higher proportions of black female death certificates report diabetes overall than do those of white females. One would not expect an excess of diabetes among black females were it less completely reported.

The proportion of deaths due to diabetes in the life table population declines between ages 65 and 85, indicating that much of the mortality due to diabetes occurs in that age range. This occurs both for the underlying-cause and total occurrences of diabetes on the death certificate. thus, diabetes is less significant, either as an underlying or associated cause of death, at advanced ages for all race/sex groups. As the mortality risks for conditions associated with diabetes such as stroke decline, diabetes reported at death at advanced ages may increase (Baum and Manton 1987).

The underlying-cause-of-death rate for stroke has declined 44 percent from 1968 to 1982. Besides being an important cause of death, stroke is an important determinant of disability and nursing home use, accounting for about 7 percent of all nursing home days used in 1977 (Liu and Manton 1984). Compared to diabetes (a condition with which it is strongly associated), stroke is more important as an underlying cause of death at advanced ages—i.e., the proportion of deaths affected by stroke increases with age. After age 85 almost a quarter of both black and white female deaths are affected by stroke. Despite being a frequent underlying cause of death, stroke affects about 60 percent more deaths than is reported in the underlying-cause-of-death data. The proportion of deaths due to stroke in the life table population is similar for black and white females (even though the mortality rates are 80 percent higher for blacks) because the white female population has a higher life expectancy and stroke is predominantly a cause of death at very advanced ages. The stroke mortality rate for black males is much higher than for white males up to age 65 though we can again see the impact of greater white male survival to later ages, which increases the proportion of deaths from chronic diseases. Thus, the life table results show different aspects of the impact of the disease than the age-adjusted rates.

Influenza and pneumonia are frequent contributory factors in the deaths of debilitated, elderly persons (Besdine 1984). Within sex, blacks have smaller proportions of deaths affected by pneumonia, consistent with higher disease-specific case-fatality rates (or deaths per 100 illnesses) for blacks. This implies a shorter exposure period for the acquisition of complicating conditions like pneumonia.

The multiple-cause data can also be examined over time. Figure 3 records four plots which show the change from 1968 to 1980 in the life table proportion of deaths affected by four conditions (septicemia, cirrhosis, pneumonia, and stroke) for blacks and whites.

Septicemia is frequently a complication of chronic debilitation and has been rapidly increasing as a mortality risk in the United States— especially at advanced ages (Manton 1986). It may also reflect inadequate medical care leading to complicating infections. Septicemia has increased as a cause of death for all race/sex groups, but it affects more nonwhite deaths (e.g., nearly 5 percent of nonwhite female deaths in 1980), and increases more rapidly for nonwhites (figure 3). Table 6 contains sex and age-specific septicemia mortality life table statistics for blacks and whites.

The absolute increases in the impact of septicemia on mortality have been larger for blacks at all ages than for whites. If the increase in septicemia mortality was due to increases in the prevalence of chronic diseases at advanced ages (associated with rapid increases in

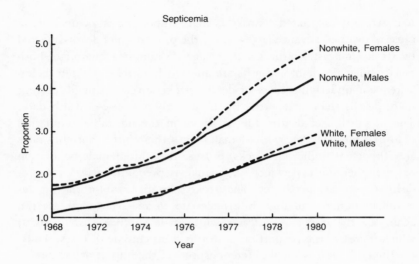

Septicemia

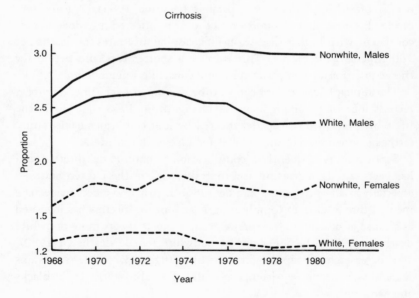

Cirrhosis

FIG. 3. Total proportion of deaths affected by four conditions, 1968 to 1980, for U.S. white and nonwhite males and females.
Source: Tabulations of national multiple cause of death files.

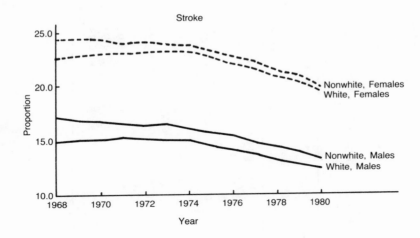

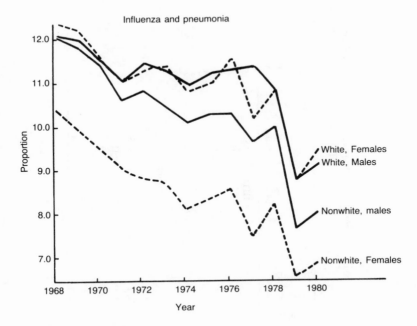

FIG. 3. Continued.

TABLE 6

Proportion of Deaths Due to Septicemia Expected after a Given Age in a Life Table Population: Underlying Cause (UC) and Total Mentions (TM), 1968 and 1980

Age	1968 Underlying cause	1968 Total mentions	1980 Underlying cause	1980 Total mentions
WHITE MALES				
At Birth	0.12	1.08	0.41	2.67
45	0.10	1.03	0.43	2.73
65	0.10	1.03	0.45	2.79
75	0.10	1.00	0.49	2.87
85	0.11	0.92	0.52	2.93
NONWHITE MALES				
At Birth	0.22	1.67	0.79	4.16
45	0.18	1.65	0.84	4.40
65	0.19	1.64	0.91	4.71
75	0.18	1.56	0.97	4.85
85	0.18	1.34	1.10	5.12
WHITE FEMALES				
At Birth	0.12	1.08	0.48	2.87
45	0.10	1.01	0.48	2.88
65	0.09	0.93	0.49	2.83
75	0.08	0.85	0.50	2.76
85	0.07	0.69	0.49	2.55
NONWHITE FEMALES				
At Birth	0.21	1.75	0.95	4.81
45	0.17	1.61	0.98	4.91
65	0.16	1.47	1.02	4.93
75	0.15	1.34	1.07	4.94
85	0.16	1.31	1.07	4.73

Source: Tabulation of U.S. mortality data.

life expectancy at later ages), one would have expected white females at very advanced ages to be at higher risk. The more rapid increase for blacks suggests that health differentials not related to age, but possibly to inappropriate or inadequate medical care, may explain recent increases.

In figure 3, cirrhosis shows little evidence of a systematic trend after rising to its 1972 levels. Males of both races have greater proportions of death affected by cirrhosis than females; within sex, blacks have more cirrhosis mortality. One major risk factor for cirrhosis is excessive alcohol consumption so that the pattern observed for cirrhosis suggests greater alcohol abuse among blacks.

Like septicemia, pneumonia and influenza are infectious diseases that affect debilitated persons. In contrast to septicemia, however, pneumonia is (1) decreasing in the proportion of deaths affected (part of the decrease from 1978 to 1979 is due to the changes in ICD revision); and (2) is less significant for blacks. This difference may result because septicemia seems to affect persons at all ages, whereas death from pneumonia is concentrated at later ages (Manton 1986). Hence, current problems with infectious diseases as contributing causes of death are becoming more related to race (increasing septicemia risks at all ages) and becoming less related to age (decreasing pneumonia risks at later ages).

Stroke is a major cause of death that has declined rapidly as an underlying cause of death. The pattern of change is also evident in figure 3 in its multiple-cause occurrences, with significant change after 1972, the year in which the national initiatives on hypertensive control began (Robins and Baum 1981). Interestingly, stroke mortality is less important for black males than for white females despite the latter's better control of hypertension (Wassertheil-Smoller et al. 1979).

How do various conditions contribute to life expectancy differentials between blacks and whites, and how do those contributions change over time? We present in table 7 two life table statistics, the mean age at death and the proportion of deaths caused by a given condition in a life table population for seven underlying causes of death. By examining the mean age at death in a life table population, differences in the mean age at death for a condition due to population structure are removed. By removing the effects of these differences, the cause-specific risk may be compared for 1970 and 1980.

The mean age at death from stroke increased for both blacks and

TABLE 7
Mean Age at Death and at Birth for Underlying Cause Occurrence of Seven
Causes of Death, and Proportion of Deaths Due to Each Cause by
Race, 1970 to 1980

Cause of death	1970	1980	1970	1980
	MEAN AGE AT DEATH			
	White males		Black males	
Stroke	76.5	78.4	70.2	72.1
Cancer	68.3	70.5	65.6	67.7
Lung cancer	66.5	68.8	62.9	65.1
Heart disease	72.1	74.3	68.7	70.3
Homicide	40.5	38.7	36.6	37.9
Diabetes	70.6	72.5	64.6	67.6
Cirrhosis	58.8	60.4	49.9	52.5
	White females		Black females	
Stroke	81.3	83.5	75.7	79.0
Cancer	69.8	71.9	66.4	69.6
Lung cancer	66.7	68.3	62.9	65.1
Heart disease	80.2	82.4	75.5	78.2
Homicide	41.9	42.0	37.3	38.7
Diabetes	75.3	77.6	69.3	73.8
Cirrhosis	59.9	62.9	49.8	54.2
	PROPORTION OF DEATHS DUE TO CONDITION			
	White males		Black males	
Stroke	9.5	7.2	10.5	8.1
Cancer	16.9	21.0	15.3	21.5
Lung cancer	4.9	6.9	4.2	6.8
Heart disease	42.2	41.0	31.3	32.5
Homicide	0.5	0.7	4.8	4.4
Diabetes	1.5	1.3	1.6	1.6
Cirrhosis	1.7	1.5	2.1	2.1
	White females		Black females	
Stroke	15.1	12.3	16.0	12.6
Cancer	16.0	18.6	13.6	17.3
Lung cancer	1.3	2.6	1.0	2.1
Heart disease	42.1	42.5	37.0	38.8
Homicide	0.2	0.2	1.0	0.9
Diabetes	2.5	2.0	3.7	3.4
Cirrhosis	0.9	0.8	1.3	1.2

Source: Tabulations of U.S. underlying cause data.

whites (e.g., 2.2 years for white females and 3.4 years for black females). The increase is evident even at age 60 for both blacks and whites. Large declines in the proportion of deaths due to stroke for both blacks and whites are also evident. Hence, improvements have occurred in both measures for stroke for blacks. The rate of improvement is more rapid for blacks than whites, though much of the *excess* risk for black males continues to 1980.

Significant race differentials are noted for cancer. The mean age at death from cancer increased for both blacks and whites, although it was lower for blacks in 1970 and 1980. The mean age at death from cancer varies by five years among the four race/sex groups. The proportion of deaths due to cancer increases for all race and sex groups, but more rapidly for blacks. The increase is largest for black males, with the proportion of cancer deaths increasing from 15.3 to 21.5 percent. This proportion is lower for black females at birth, but rises at later ages to white female levels.

The proportionate contribution of lung cancer to mortality is similar for both black and white males (4.9 and 4.2 percent, respectively), with both groups experiencing large increases. The contribution to mortality for females increased faster over the period, doubling for both races. White female lung cancer is significantly higher than black female lung cancer, in contrast to males. Because these trends can be traced to smoking patterns in different cohorts, continued increases in female lung cancer mortality rates for 20 years are likely, while white male rates may have reached their peak (Harris 1983).

Cancer trends are difficult to evaluate because they represent a large number of different diseases. For example, much of the increase in cancer mortality is due to lung cancer, which is driven by cohort patterns of smoking habits (Harris 1983). Crude breast cancer rates, especially for white females, are also increasing, possibly because of later ages at first pregnancy (MacMahon et al. 1970). In contrast, many types of cancer have declining mortality rates, such as stomach cancer and leukemia. Different types of cancer have different rates of incidence and different risk factors.

As a consequence, black-white differentials have to be examined for specific cancer types and for different types of rates. For example, there are higher age-adjusted black mortality rates for a number of cancers such as cancer of the bladder, cervix, esophagus, lung, prostate, and stomach. Among whites, there are higher crude mortality rates from cancer of the breast, leukemia, lymphoma, and pancreatic cancer (National Center for Health Statistics 1986a). The crude rates reflect the different age structure of the black and white populations, with whites having higher crude rates for cancer types that are prevalent at later ages.

Though the range of cancer types makes the study of black-white differences complex in contrast to many other chronic diseases, good race-specific data on the incidence and case fatality of specific diseases are available from the National Cancer Institute's (1984) SEER program, a system of population-based tumor registries covering 11 areas representing almost 13 percent of the American population. We examined the site-specific cancer data to identify the causes of mortality differences to determine if they are a result of differences in disease incidence, case fatality differences due to different patterns of treatment, or due to poorer general health.

The SEER data for 1978-1981 show an 11 percent higher cancer incidence rate for American blacks relative to American whites, with most of the excess occurring in black males (+25 percent). Blacks experience higher age-adjusted incidence for cancer of the cervix, esophagus, larynx, pancreas, and stomach. Of the 25 types of cancer for which SEER data are collected, blacks have poorer case fatality rates for 22. Five-year relative survival for all cancer types is 38 percent for blacks and 50 percent for whites. Cancer case fatality rates are particularly high in blacks for cancer of the bladder, breast, corpus uteri, prostate, and stomach.

Several reasons are cited for the greater incidence and poorer case fatality rates of blacks with cancer. Risk factors can be identified for increased incidence of certain cancer types. For example, the threefold mortality excess of esophageal cancer for blacks (3.5 times the incidence) may be due to higher alcohol consumption among blacks (consistent with their higher cirrhosis rates). The 45 percent higher lung cancer mortality rates for black males may be due to a combination of higher levels of smoking and higher rates of exposure in environmentally hazardous occupations. Food quality, use of smokeless tobacco, and alcohol consumption are possibly responsible for stomach cancer mortality rates being 1.5 times higher and incidence being twice as high among blacks. Black males have a 60 percent higher incidence and 100 percent higher mortality rates from prostate cancer than white males. Black females have cervical mortality and incidence 2.5 times higher than the general population. The elevation of both prostatic cancer and cervical cancer may be linked to higher rates of early sexual activity and the possibility of early infection with viral and other venereal diseases (Fraumeni 1975). Higher breast cancer mortality rates, in contrast, have been linked with later age at onset of sexual activity, lower fertility, and later age at first pregnancy (MacMahon et al. 1970).

Differences in case fatality rates (i.e., deaths as a proportion of those with the disease) can be traced to several factors. Knowledge, attitudes, and practices relating to cancer care-seeking behavior (cancer screening, detection, treatment, and rehabilitation) differ by race. National surveys suggest that blacks overestimate the fatality of cancer and underestimate its prevalence (U.S. Department of Health and Human Services 1985). Blacks are less educated about cancer signs and more pessimistic about treatment. Combining these results with possible economic constraints, blacks may delay seeking diagnosis and treatment because of their conception of cancer as a terminal disease process, thus leading to a higher relative prevalence of cancer diagnoses at advanced stages (National Cancer Institute 1984).

Other factors beyond behavior (which we presume to be partly based on knowledge and attitudes toward cancer) contribute to poorer black survival. Studies indicate that survival differences remain between blacks and whites *even* at the same stage of disease (Wilkinson et al. 1979). Socioeconomic factors explain part of the differential (Berg 1977), but even after socioeconomic factors and disease characteristics are controlled, deficits for blacks remain due to differences in treatment (Page and Kuntz 1980), immune competency, histologic type, general health status, nutrition, and other factors (Savage et al. 1981). Thus, blacks have higher cancer rates than whites because of (1) higher risk-factor exposures for many (but not all) cancer types, (2) their image of cancer as a lethal disease, which causes them not to be diagnosed early and to less aggressively pursue treatment, (3) economic and medical access variables that cause them to be less effectively treated, (4) differences in disease type, with many of the histological types affecting blacks being more aggressive, and (5) general differences in health status resulting in lower host resistance to the tumor.

The cancer life table statistics may be compared with the other diseases in table 7. There is an increase in the age at death from heart disease for both blacks and whites. The mean age at death in 1980 varies over 12 years across the four race/sex groups, indicating greater race and sex variation in heart disease risks than in cancer risks. Despite significant declines in the mortality *rates* for heart disease (e.g., 24 percent between 1968 and 1978), the life table proportion of all deaths expected from heart disease declined only slightly for white males, increased slightly at early ages for black males and females, and is nearly constant for white females. Heart disease is a less prevalent cause of death for both black males and females than for whites (due to their higher risk of death at earlier ages from other causes), though heart disease has increased for black males at younger ages.

Homicide, in absolute terms, is a frequent cause of death among black males, being nearly as likely to cause death as lung cancer. Furthermore, it is a cause of death affecting younger persons, with the mean age at death for homicide victims ranging from 37.9 years for black males to 42.0 years for white females in 1980. Between 1970 and 1980, the mean age at death from homicide increased for black males and for females of both races. In contrast, the mean age at death from homicide for white males decreased between 1970 and 1980 (from 40.5 to 38.7 years), suggesting an increase in homicide risks at early ages for white males. The proportion of all deaths due to homicide is much higher for blacks than whites, being over six times higher for black males in 1980 and nearly five times higher for black females.

The proportion of deaths due to diabetes shows a small drop for white males and no change for black males. Declines are also registered for females, although the proportion of black females affected is greater than that of white females. There has been a large increase in the mean age at death for blacks (i.e., 3.0 and 4.5 years), suggesting better control at earlier ages delaying death for blacks.

Cirrhosis is a greater mortality risk for blacks than whites starting at younger ages. For black males, excessive alcohol consumption begins early but occurs primarily after age 30, whereas for white males the prevalence is higher from ages 18 to 25 and then declines (U.S. Department of Health and Human Services 1985). Thus, it appears to be continued high alcohol consumption in adulthood that contributes most to cirrhosis in blacks. There are also both more alcohol abstainers and heavy consumers among blacks (U.S. Department of Health and Human Services 1985). Thus, exposure seems to be concentrated in certain black subpopulations.

Patterns of risk-factor exposures may be related to both geographic and sociocultural differences. For example, exposure to certain types of risks (e.g., homicide, cirrhosis, lung cancer) are probably higher in metropolitan areas than rural areas and in certain regions (e.g., Northeast and Far West) than in other regions (e.g., Southeast), although for lung cancer we see that southeastern regions are converging in risk to that in the Northeast (Manton et al. 1985). An important protective factor in rural areas and the Southeast may be sociocultural and religious norms against alcohol and drug abuse. More detailed study of such geographic differences in cause-specific mortality and risk-factor exposures could potentially produce much useful information on sociocultural and economic differences in health risks between blacks and whites.

The change in the life-table mean age at death for a disease and the proportion of deaths it causes determine the change in life expectancy anticipated if a given condition were eliminated and persons were only exposed to the risks of the remaining conditions. This statistic is important in determining the potential benefit of controlling or eliminating a condition. Two types of such "cause elimination" life expectancy gains are presented in table 8. The first, labelled "Total Population," is the usual statistic presented in the demographic literature that shows the impact (in years) of eliminating the condition on the life expectancy of the population (e.g., Chiang 1968; Keyfitz 1977). The second, labelled "Saved Population," is the effect on the life expectancy of persons who died of the disease—an alternate form of competing risk adjustment. The latter statistic allows comparison of the survival effect of common and rare causes of death and better measures the impact of the disease on the individual (Manton, Patrick, and Stallard 1980). It indicates the years of life lost by a typical decedent from the specific cause of death and is calculated by adjusting the usual-cause-elimination life-expectancy-gain figure (i.e., the "Total Population" figure) for differences in the proportion of deaths expected from the condition as reported in the bottom panel of table 7.

The cause elimination effects of the six conditions for the total population reflect the proportion of deaths caused by the disease. Hence, gain in life expectancy due to the elimination of heart disease is the largest. In contrast, the "saved population" measure describes the effect of premature mortality from a condition on the life span of the individual. Therefore, it is greatest for deaths that occur at early ages—e.g., accidental deaths and homicides.

TABLE 8

Life-Expectancy Increases (in years) Due to Elimination of Selected Causes of Death by Race and Sex, 1969–1971 and 1979–1981

Cause of death	White males		Black males		White females		Black females	
	1969–1971	1979–1981	1969–1971	1979–1981	1969–1971	1979–1981	1969–1971	1979–1981
CANCER								
Total population	2.39	2.97	2.46	3.37	2.68	3.18	2.61	3.21
Saved population	14.12	14.12	16.08	15.70	16.79	17.13	19.26	18.55
HEART DISEASE								
Total population	6.97	6.56	6.16	5.75	6.69	7.19	8.23	7.92
Saved population	16.52	15.97	19.71	17.71	15.89	16.93	22.24	20.41
DIABETES MELLITUS								
Total population	0.18	0.16	0.24	0.23	0.30	0.25	0.61	0.51
Saved population	11.87	11.74	15.02	13.81	12.17	12.43	16.42	14.90
STROKE								
Total population	0.96	0.69	1.51	1.04	1.64	1.33	2.62	1.79
Saved population	10.07	9.58	14.35	12.78	10.82	10.82	16.41	14.23
ACCIDENT								
Total population	1.74	1.60	2.20	1.59	0.80	0.70	0.94	0.69
Saved population	30.22	32.14	30.03	28.12	24.08	26.57	29.96	27.05
HOMICIDE								
Total population	0.16	0.26	1.54	1.43	0.06	0.10	0.38	0.37
Saved population	32.76	36.13	31.98	32.88	38.02	40.05	37.50	39.47

Large increases in the impact of cancer on total-population life expectancy occurred between 1969–1971 and 1979–1981, with black males having the largest increase (0.91 years). White males had the smallest saved-population gain because they had the highest mean age at death from cancer (relative to their total life expectancy). Blacks of both sexes experienced decreases, suggesting that cancer deaths occurred at older ages in 1979–1981 than in 1969–1971. White females had an increase, suggesting that cancer deaths occurred at younger ages in 1979–1981.

Heart disease shows declines in impact in both the saved and total population measures for three of the four groups, suggesting decreased population and individual impact between 1969–1971 and 1979–1981. Only white females show an increased impact over this period.

Diabetes mellitus and stroke show declines in both measures for all four groups consistent with the linkage of the two conditions. Accidental deaths show declining population impact, but increasing individual (i.e., "saved" population) impact. The impact of homicide increased on both the population and individual level for whites, but declined for blacks.

Excess Deaths

The preceding analyses showed black-white differentials in life expectancy, the underlying and multiple-cause mortality factors that produced those differentials, and recent changes in those differentials. To summarize differentials in mortality risks and the mean age at death in terms of the current impact on health, an index of "excess deaths" was calculated. Excess deaths in the black population are the number of deaths due to a particular condition above the level that would have occurred if blacks had experienced the same age-, sex-, and cause-specific mortality rates as whites. An age cutoff of 70 years was used in aggregating excess deaths. Since the maximum life span is probably not much different for blacks and whites, high early mortality among blacks must produce higher white mortality rates at later ages and negative "excesses" at advanced ages. This phenomenon would have lessened the value of the index as an indicator of disparities between blacks and whites that might be amenable to interventions at earlier ages (i.e., the age ranges where deaths are clearly premature).

TABLE 9
Excess Deaths[a] in the Black Population by Sex and Cause from Birth to
Age 69, 1969–1971 and 1979–1981

Disease	Males		Females	
	1969–1971	1979–1981	1969–1971	1979–1981
All causes	39,925	35,321	32,895	23,621
Cancer	3,674	5,782	2,175	2,268
Diabetes	696	646	1,693	1,204
Heart disease	4,258	5,633	8,898	7,235
Stroke	4,202	2,837	4,566	2,477
Accidents	3,822	2,261	1,159	559
Homicide	6,496	6,708	1,347	1,380
Cirrhosis	1,205	1,373	863	783
Infant mortality & congenital anomalies	5,145	2,155	4,260	1,847

[a] Actual deaths − expected deaths, where expected deaths = white death rates × black population (up to age 70).

The changes in the number of excess deaths between 1969–1971 and 1979–1981 are presented in table 9.

Rates of deaths changed markedly for both races during this period. As a result, the number of excess deaths drops from 73,000 to 59,000; over 65 percent of the drop occurred in black females. Large decreases are noted for stroke, accidents, and infant mortality, but large increases in excess deaths occurred for cancer (especially in males).

Observed, expected, and excess deaths by age for black males and females are presented in table 10 for the 1979–1981 period.

In table 10 the annual number of deaths expected in 1979–1981 if blacks were subjected to white mortality rates, the actual number of deaths, and the annual difference or excess are shown for six causes. For example, black males under the age of 70 would have 49,378 deaths if they had the same mortality rates as white males—84,699 black male deaths were observed. Consequently, 35,321 *excess* black male deaths occurred annually. Thus, 42 percent of black deaths in the 1979–1981 period were excess and potentially avoidable. Of the 35,321 excess deaths in males, 24 percent (8,470) were due to cardiovascular disease, 16 percent were due to cancer, and 19 percent to homicide.

The contribution of each cause to excess mortality is quite different for those aged under 45 than for persons aged 45 to 69. Under the age of 45, 15 percent of the excess male mortality is due to infant mortality (deaths occurring under one year of age). This drops to 6 percent for all excess deaths under the age of 70. Likewise, the importance of homicide drops from 37 to 19 percent. From the age of 45 to 69 the male excess due to homicide is only 6 percent. On the other hand, 58 percent of excess male mortality from the age of 45 to 69 is due to cardiovascular disease or cancer.

The excess death measure has the disadvantage that it is based upon the current level of white mortality as the "norm" or "standard." This raises the question of what our targets or goals should be when contemplating corrective actions. For example, there is excess mortality among whites for certain diseases (e.g., suicide for white males and breast cancer for white females). If there is no black excess for a cause, should we conclude that the current mortality level among blacks is acceptable? Furthermore, we know that white infant mortality is much higher in the United States than in many European countries and Japan. This means that the black infant mortality excess is less than that if compared to the lowest observed levels. Even the Japanese and European mortality levels may not represent the lowest achievable level given the current state of medical science. This suggests that we should posit an absolute health standard against which we could evaluate the health of both blacks and whites. We, therefore, calculated a second measure, the SHE index, which represents deaths due to medical conditions that were judged on the basis of known risk factors or the current level of treatment efficacy to be either preventable or curable (Rutstein et al. 1976). These measures are presented for several major age categories for the four race/sex groups in table 11.

The table confirms that there are large numbers of deaths for whites (17.6 percent for males and 12.2 percent for females) that could be prevented. Against absolute standards American whites are doing nearly as poorly as blacks in terms of the proportions of total mortality resulting from preventable or curable diseases. The age-adjusted mortality rate for the SHEs is 185.3 for black males and 177.5 for white males with 17.6 percent and 18.2 percent of all white and black male deaths being preventable.

For women the SHE mortality rate is identical (100.4). However, because a greater proportion of the black female population is at

TABLE 10

Three Measures of the Average Annual Number of Deaths by Disease Category and Sex, for U.S. Blacks, 1979–1981

	CVD[a]	Cancer	Cirrhosis	Diabetes	Homicide	Infant mortality & congenital anomalies	All others	Total
BIRTH TO AGE 44								
Males: Observed	3,236	1,587	962	202	6,486	4,832	13,789	31,094
Expected[b]	1,339	1,204	259	86	1,017	2,685	9,777	16,367
Excess	1,897	383	703	116	5,469	2,147	4,012	14,727
Percentage of total excess[c]	13%	3%	5%	1%	37%	15%	27%	100%
Observed	2,093	1,789	551	184	1,488	3,996	7,130	17,231
Expected[b]	676	1,366	131	77	344	2,150	4,278	9,022
Excess	1,417	423	420	107	1,144	1,846	2,852	8,209
Percentage of total excess	17%	5%	5%	1%	14%	22%	35%	100%
AGE 45 TO 69								
Males: Observed	21,677	14,530	1,745	989	1,448	55	13,161	53,605
Expected[b]	15,104	9,131	1,075	459	209	47	6,986	33,011
Excess	6,573	5,399	670	530	1,239	8	6,175	20,594
Percentage of total excess[c]	32%	26%	3%	3%	6%	—	30%	100%
Females: Observed	15,698	10,156	976	1,602	308	47	7,918	36,705
Expected[b]	7,403	8,311	613	505	72	46	4,343	21,293
Excess	8,295	1,845	363	1,097	236	1	3,575	15,412
Percentage of total excess[c]	54%	12%	2%	7%	2%	—	28%	100%

166

Males: Observed	24,913	16,117	2,707	1,191	7,934	4,887	26,950	84,699
Expected[b]	16,443	10,335	1,334	545	1,226	2,732	16,763	49,378
Excess	8,470	5,782	1,373	646	6,708	2,155	10,187	35,321
Percentage of total excess[c]	24%	16%	4%	2%	19%	6%	29%	100%
Females: Observed	17,791	11,945	1,527	1,786	1,796	4,043	15,048	53,936
Expected[b]	8,079	9,677	744	582	416	2,196	8,621	30,315
Excess	9,712	2,268	783	1,204	1,380	1,847	6,427	23,621
Percentage of total excess[c]	41%	10%	3%	5%	6%	8%	27%	100%

[a] CVD = cardiovascular disease and combined heart disease and stroke
[b] Calculated from the rate observed in the white population
[c] May not add to 100 due to rounding

167

TABLE 11
Annual Number of Deaths from Sentinel Health Events (SHE), Proportion
That SHE Are of All Deaths and Rate for SHE, 1979–1981

	Males			Females		
	Whites	Blacks	Ratio of rates of SHE	Whites	Blacks	Ratio of rates of SHE
Age 0–24	11,261	4,672		8,293	3,824	
Percentage	20.0%	31.9%		28.8%	41.6%	
Rate	29.7	70.6	2.38	22.7	57.1	2.52
Age 25–44	4.541	1,511		3,566	1,088	
Percentage	8.2%	9.2%		13.7%	13.6%	
Rate	17.5	47.4	2.71	13.6	29.1	2.14
Age 45–64	42,669	7,543		22,055	3,633	
Percentage	18.9%	19.3%		17.2%	14.1%	
Rate	229.6	403.1	1.76	108.9	157.4	1.45
Age 65–69	23,992	2,874		10,706	1,216	
Percentage	20.8%	19.9%		15.1%	11.1%	
Rate	689.1	866.4	1.26	247.2	273.0	1.10
Age 70 +	80,268	6,595		52,448	4,269	
Percentage	17.0%	15.5%		9.7%	9.2%	
Rate	1398.3	1280.6	0.92	558.2	537.0	0.96
All ages	162,732	23,194		97,068	14,030	
Percentage	17.6%	18.2%		12.2%	14.0%	
Rate	177.5	185.3		100.4	100.4	

younger ages, the proportion of deaths from SHEs is higher for blacks
(14.0 percent) than for whites (12.2 percent). For example, the mortality
rate from SHEs is 57.1 at ages 0 to 24 for black females and only
22.7 for white females—a ratio of 2.52 to 1.0. This ratio declines
with age until above age 70 where the risk from SHEs is higher for
white females (558.2) than for black females (537.0). This suggests
that even though white females have a higher overall life expectancy,
proportionately more preventable deaths at advanced ages occur for
white females—an observation based upon an epidemiological and
clinical evaluation of the cause of death mix at different ages that is
consistent with the crossover in the total mortality rates observed
earlier.

Similar age patterns are noted for males except that the peak age range for excess black risk is age 25 to 44 (i.e., 2.71) reflecting the effect of homicide and other external causes of death. It is also interesting to compare the mortality rates for SHEs across sex within race. For example, we see that up to age 44, white females have greater proportions of deaths due to preventable causes than white males—a pattern also found for black males and females. Past the age of 45 males of both races have considerably greater proportions of deaths from preventable causes.

Morbidity and Disability

In the preceding section we discussed mortality differences between blacks and whites. Though mortality is an excellent indicator of serious health problems, many nonlethal conditions generate considerable disability in the population. Such conditions are described in the National Health Interview Survey. Owing to methodological changes in this survey over time, it is difficult to determine how the prevalence of various conditions has changed. However, the data on disease prevalence at a given time probably accurately describe black-white differentials in the health burden of different conditions. Thus, we present the ratio of age-, sex-, and race-specific prevalence rates or relative risks for selected conditions (hypertension, circulatory disease, diabetes, arthritis, and mental and nervous disorders) in table 12.

Hypertension is a risk factor for many other conditions such as stroke, heart disease, and renal failure. Overall, blacks are two to four times as likely to report hypertension as whites. The relative risks are highest at early ages (i.e., before 45) with systematic declines in the relative risks for both sexes at later ages. The higher risk of hypertension for blacks is consistent with the greater risk of stroke mortality documented in earlier tables.

Both black males and females have a greater probability of circulatory disease than whites. The relative risk is higher for black females and is more elevated for both sexes below the age of 45 (consistent with the pattern for hypertension). Analyses of only ischemic heart disease, in contrast, showed a considerable white male excess.

Diabetes is a morbid condition which, like hypertension, is a risk

TABLE 12
Relative Risks Based on White Morbidity Rates for Blacks for Five Conditions, 1979–1981

Age	Hypertension		Diseases of circulatory system		Diabetes		Arthritis		Nervous & mental disorders	
	Males	Females	Males	Females	Males	Females	Males	Females	Males	Females
1–14	4.03	3.73	1.60	2.33	0.22	1.15	0.78	0.36	0.65	1.05
15–24	3.37	3.76	1.88	2.31	0.39	0.68	0.73	0.36	1.39	1.19
25–44	2.73	4.54	1.86	2.91	0.23	2.16	0.65	1.16	1.63	1.41
45–64	2.67	3.20	1.41	2.31	2.43	2.82	1.71	1.64	1.69	1.32
65–69	2.53	2.31	1.40	1.68	2.30	2.87	1.57	1.40	1.19	0.91
70+	2.39	2.22	1.33	1.62	1.85	2.22	1.71	1.54	1.19	1.10

Source: Tabulation of the National Health Interview Survey.

factor for many circulatory diseases. Blacks had over a twofold excess risk of diabetes past the age of 45 (table 12). Much of this risk is associated with the onset of adult diabetes related to obesity. The relative risks are higher for females and decline for both sexes at advanced ages. The decline in the relative risk may be a result of a more rapid mortality selection of black diabetics at earlier ages relative to whites. The greater prevalence of diabetes among blacks and the excess of female diabetes over the male rates within race are consistent with the previously reported mortality excesses.

A condition that causes considerable disability, especially at advanced ages, is arthritis. Past the age of 45, there is over a 50 percent greater risk of arthritis for blacks. Below the age of 25 (45 for males) arthritis is less often reported for blacks. For both races, the prevalence of arthritis is much greater for females. Arthritis has been found to be one of the most prevalent causes of activity limitation in the 1982 National Long-term Care Survey.

Mental and nervous disorders are also chronic nonlethal conditions seriously affecting quality of life—especially in middle age. Blacks report a higher prevalence of such problems between the ages of 24 to 64. At advanced ages the racial differential declines markedly.

The World Health Organization (1980) classification of impairments, disability, and handicaps describes the consequences of disease. Such consequences are particularly important for the elderly population inasmuch as the demand for long-term care services is driven by disability related to specific chronic conditions. Thus, a second important aspect of the comparison of black and white health differentials is the comparison of these disease consequences—i.e., the disability and functional impairment they produce.

Disability is often measured by the number of activities of daily living (ADL) or instrumental activities of daily living (IADL) that the person is chronically limited in performing. ADLs are assumed to be ordered according to their acquisition by a child during socio-biological development (Katz and Akpom 1976). To generate a global measure of disability we summed the number of ADLs for which a person has impairments. The sex- and age-specific disability rates are represented in table 13.

The table records that community-dwelling elderly blacks at almost all ages, disability levels, and for both sexes report higher disability rates than whites. In general, the relative risks of disability for blacks

TABLE 13

Number and Percentage of Disabled Population in 1982 at Three Age Groups and Four Disability Levels, U.S. Blacks and Whites*

Disability level	Age 65 to 74			Age 75 to 84			Age 85 and older		
	White	Black	Ratio	White	Black	Ratio	White	Black	Ratio
				MALES					
IADL only	239	44	1.88	167	26	1.66	53	8	1.76
	(4.1)	(7.7)		(6.4)	(10.6)		(8.1)	(14.3)	
1–2 ADL	200	28	1.40	172	16	0.99	82	13	1.84
	(3.5)	(4.9)		(6.6)	(6.5)		(12.6)	(23.2)	
3–4 ADL	90	18	2.00	62	6	1.00	44	4	1.07
	(1.6)	(3.2)		(2.4)	(2.4)		(6.7)	(7.1)	
5–6 ADL	132	27	2.04	112	11	1.04	41	5	1.42
	(2.3)	(4.7)		(4.3)	(4.5)		(6.3)	(8.9)	
Total disabled	661	117	1.81	513	59	1.22	220	30	1.59
	(11.4)	(20.6)		(19.8)	(24.1)		(33.7)	(53.6)	
Total population in each age group (in thousands)	5,773	569		2,590	245		652	56	

				FEMALES					
IADL only	346 (4.7)	64 (8.0)	1.71	330 (7.4)	48 (12.0)	1.62	122 (7.7)	11 (9.5)	1.23
1–2 ADL	353 (4.8)	55 (6.9)	1.44	408 (9.2)	51 (12.7)	1.38	216 (13.6)	19 (16.4)	1.20
3–4 ADL	135 (1.8)	29 (3.6)	2.02	172 (3.9)	19 (4.7)	1.21	90 (5.7)	12 (7.2)	1.27
5–6 ADL	136 (1.8)	26 (3.3)	1.81	171 (3.8)	26 (6.5)	1.71	126 (7.9)	23 (18.3)	2.31
Total disabled	970 (13.1)	174 (21.8)	1.66	1,081 (24.3)	144 (35.9)	1.48	554 (35.0)	65 (56.0)	1.60
Total population in each age group (in thousands)	7,400	797		4,448	401		1,585	116	

* Figures in parentheses are percentages

Source: Population counts are 1982 figures from U.S. Bureau of the Census, 1984, 38 (table 5). Disabled population counts are from tabulations of the National Long-term Care Survey.

seem to be higher at ages 65 to 74 than at later ages, although the ratios are higher above the age of 85—i.e., above age 85 over half of community-dwelling blacks have some disability in contrast to about a third of whites.

An important factor in studying the health status of the elderly is the interaction of morbidity, disability, and low income. We examined this factor using data from the Georgia Adult Health Services program where we had information on the health and functional status of 583 persons over the age of 65. This population represents a group of low-income elderly persons on Medicaid long-term care benefits who still resided in the community. Thus, it gives us a much more detailed look at the health and functional status of elderly blacks and whites in a high-intensity and long-term service use category. We analyzed these with a procedure called grade of membership (GOM) analysis (Woodbury and Manton 1982) that could identify subgroups among the population using a wide range of disease and functional status measures. The population could be described by five basic health and functional status profiles. These are described in table 14.

The first group or profile has chronic obstructive lung disease and digestive problems, few chronic conditions, and is relatively free of functional dependence. This group is predominantly white, relatively young, and more likely to be male than the overall study population.

The second group has diabetes and heart problems, requires few services, but tends to have four ADL limitations. This group is relatively more black, heavily female, and older than the study population in general.

The third group has circulatory and urinary tract problems and the highest frequency of dementia and psychological problems. It also has by far the largest number of behavioral problems and the greatest range of therapeutic services used. It is also disproportionately nonwhite and has a high level of ADL impairment.

The fourth group has the highest prevalence of cancer, stroke, neurological disorders, and hip fracture. It has by far the greatest number of medical treatments and is the most bedfast. It is highly functionally impaired. It is *not* distinguished by race, though it is a heavily male group and relatively young.

The final group has sensory problems and arthritis, though few impairments, and requires few services. It is female and though by far the oldest group is somewhat more likely to be black. Given its

TABLE 14

Five Health and Functional Status Profiles Determined by the Grade of Membership Technique in the Georgia Adult Health Services Program

	Frequency	1	2	3	4	5
VARIABLES USED TO DEFINE GROUPS						
I. DIAGNOSES						
1. Cancer	5.15	12.28	0.0	0.0	20.04	0.0
2. Diabetes	19.90	0.0	67.05	0.0	0.0	0.0
3. Anemia	4.97	0.0	0.0	3.82	5.02	15.49
4. Dementia	4.63	0.0	0.0	30.54	0.0	0.0
5. Psychosis, Neurosis	6.00	2.80	0.0	25.72	2.81	6.72
6. Neurological disorders	5.66	0.0	0.0	0.0	38.79	0.0
7. Eye disorders	5.15	0.0	0.0	0.0	0.0	21.34
8. Hypertension	38.77	0.0	88.12	41.90	0.0	0.0
9. Heart disease	43.91	31.72	100.00	78.06	0.0	0.0
10. Cerebrovascular disease	16.64	0.0	0.0	0.0	88.92	0.0
11. Arteriosclerosis	3.60	0.0	0.0	0.0	0.0	16.06
12. Chronic obstructive lung disease	8.58	45.64	0.0	4.08	0.0	0.0
13. Ulcers	2.74	15.71	0.0	0.0	0.0	0.0
14. Digestive disorders	3.43	18.64	0.0	1.65	0.0	0.0
15. Nephritis, Nephrosis	3.60	0.0	3.77	5.00	11.14	0.0
16. Urinary tract disorders	5.32	0.0	0.0	21.31	7.17	5.57
17. Joint problem	30.19	0.0	0.0	0.0	0.0	100.00
18. Hip fracture	2.74	5.61	0.0	0.0	11.27	0.0
19. Residual	19.90	25.87	0.0	23.62	40.62	23.04

TABLE 14—(*Continued*)

Five Health and Functional Status Profiles Determined by the Grade of Membership Technique in the Georgia Adult Health Services Program

	Frequency	1	2	3	4	5
II. CONDITIONS						
1. Decubiti	2.78	0.0	0.0	0.0	17.54	0.0
2. Bowel incontinence	22.74	0.0	0.0	76.75	100.00	0.0
3. Bladder incontinence	43.83	0.0	28.02	100.00	100.00	25.91
4. Agitation	5.20	0.0	0.0	36.34	0.0	0.0
5. Confusion	26.69	0.0	0.0	100.00	0.0	0.0
6. Cooperative	71.58	72.46	100.00	10.43	52.54	100.00
7. Depression	12.31	22.37	0.0	59.27	0.0	0.0
8. Forgetfulness	43.50	20.65	38.74	100.00	0.0	52.63
9. Alertness	46.97	72.43	69.97	0.0	31.65	48.04
10. Noisiness	1.73	1.38	0.0	10.68	0.0	0.0
11. Nonresponsiveness	0.35	0.0	0.0	0.0	0.0	0.0
12. Vacillating behavior	3.29	8.61	0.0	11.05	2.21	1.27
13. Violent behavior	0.17	0.97	0.15	0.0	0.0	0.0
14. Wandering	4.51	0.0	0.0	34.14	0.0	0.0
15. Withdrawal	2.77	0.0	0.0	18.89	0.0	0.0
16. Dependence	42.46	0.0	23.09	100.00	82.95	19.84
17. Independence	8.67	48.59	0.0	0.0	0.0	0.0
18. Anxiety	11.61	44.71	0.0	24.40	0.0	0.0
19. Disorientation	6.59	0.0	0.0	41.26	6.71	0.0
20. Inappropriateness	1.21	0.0	0.0	6.65	0.0	1.31

21. Sight impairment						
Severe	58.43	0.0	0.0	0.0	0.0	17.37
Moderate	41.57	41.32	100.00	69.14	0.0	49.65
Mild	0.0	41.24	0.0	25.89	76.78	25.44
None	0.0	17.44	0.0	4.97	23.22	7.54
22. Hearing						
Severe	32.80	0.0	6.44	0.0	0.0	8.58
Moderate	49.74	30.29	42.26	28.28	12.66	33.45
Mild	0.0	28.91	51.30	43.67	37.11	32.57
None	17.47	40.80	0.0	28.05	50.24	25.39
23. Speech						
Severe	0.0	24.16	0.0	0.0	0.0	3.68
Moderate	0.0	62.12	0.0	0.0	0.0	9.46
Mild	0.0	13.72	73.83	0.0	0.0	13.13
None	100.00	0.0	26.17	100.00	100.00	73.73
24. Limited Mobility						
Severe	0.0	100.00	0.0	0.0	0.0	20.45
Moderate	100.00	0.0	68.70	100.00	0.0	59.62
Mild	0.0	0.0	31.30	0.0	66.63	14.69
None	0.0	0.0	0.0	0.0	33.37	5.24
25. Paralysis						
Severe	0.0	26.77	0.0	0.0	0.0	3.33
Moderate	0.0	60.58	0.0	0.0	0.0	7.53
Mild	0.0	12.65	19.24	0.45	0.0	4.90
None	100.00	0.0	80.76	99.55	100.00	84.24
III. SERVICES						
1. Fluid intake	0.0	30.68	0.04	0.0	0.0	5.03
2. Fluid output	0.0	30.66	0.06	0.0	0.0	5.03

TABLE 14—*(Continued)*

Five Health and Functional Status Profiles Determined by the Grade of Membership Technique in the Georgia Adult Health Services Program

	Frequency	1	2	3	4	5
3. I.V.	0.52	0.0	0.0	0.0	3.29	0.0
4. Suction	0.52	0.0	0.0	0.0	3.32	0.0
5. Catheter	2.95	0.0	0.0	0.0	19.92	0.0
6. Sterile dressing	1.56	7.73	0.0	1.86	0.0	0.0
7. Colostomy	0.87	0.0	0.0	0.0	5.44	0.0
8. Bedfast	6.24	0.0	0.0	0.0	44.59	0.0
9. Physical therapy	19.19	0.0	0.0	100.00	31.04	0.0
10. Occupational therapy	4.93	0.0	0.0	36.77	0.0	0.0
11. Remotive therapy	5.63	0.0	0.0	45.21	0.0	0.0
12. Reality therapy	9.68	0.0	0.0	89.75	0.0	0.0
13. Speech therapy	0.88	0.0	0.0	6.37	0.0	0.0
14. Bowel & bladder training	1.76	0.0	0.0	9.68	2.98	0.0
15. Activity program	12.85	0.0	0.0	100.00	0.0	0.0
IV. FUNCTIONAL LIMITATIONS						
1. Eating	33.22	0.0	0.0	100.00	100.00	0.0
2. Confined to wheelchair	28.10	0.0	0.0	0.0	100.00	0.0
3. Transference	74.96	0.0	100.00	100.00	100.00	100.00
4. Bathing	94.08	62.87	100.00	100.00	100.00	100.00
5. Ambulatory limitations	84.67	32.95	100.00	100.00	67.62	100.00
6. Dressing	74.91	0.0	100.00	100.00	100.00	100.00

EXTERNAL VARIABLES						
V. SOCIODEMOGRAPHIC						
1. Race						
White	48.61	97.65	29.42	39.84	49.50	41.90
Nonwhite	51.39	2.35	70.58	60.16	50.50	58.10
2. Age						
65–69	15.44	41.87	14.28	0.0	29.28	0.0
70–74	16.12	49.87	14.13	2.77	23.42	0.0
75–79	18.01	0.0	29.05	17.37	2.07	26.89
80–84	24.36	8.26	23.94	39.54	29.47	23.15
85–89	15.44	0.0	18.59	31.44	0.0	22.20
90+	10.63	0.0	0.0	8.89	15.76	27.76
3. Sex						
Male	22.20	50.49	0.0	21.83	61.52	2.02
Female	77.80	49.52	100.00	78.17	38.48	97.98
4. Nursing Home Admission	10.12	19.31	3.78	11.15	13.93	8.25

extreme age but few explicit acute medical problems and no dementia (most of its difficulties appear related to musculoskeletal conditions), it is representative of relatively intact extreme elderly survivors.

In the first group of "young" elderly persons with few functional impairments and few chronic conditions, we found a disproportionate probability of being white. Groups two and three with chronic conditions and significant frailty tend to be more heavily black while the fourth group, associated with serious acute medical problems that are medically intensive, is not distinguished by race. The fifth group of extreme elderly with only moderate levels of dependency and few acute medical problems is disproportionately black. The pattern of association of race, functional limitation, and medical problems suggests that the distribution of serious acute medical problems (i.e., group 4) at advanced ages is not strongly differentiated by race, while the distribution of functional impairment over age is. This suggests that social and economic factors may be more important for low-income blacks using community-based Medicaid long-term care services than for whites. Whites may tend to use nursing homes more as a source of care for the extreme elderly, frail person than blacks who apparently are retained in the community, possibly in an extended family milieu.

Risk Factors

Up to this point black and white differentials have been described in terms of manifest morbid changes. An examination of differentials in the distribution of physical risk factors and health behavior will help to explain the pattern of health problems currently observed and suggest the patterns of health differentials that can be expected in the future. The risk factors discussed are (1) smoking, (2) obesity, (3) blood pressure, (4) serum cholesterol, (5) birth weight, and (6) health habits.

Smoking

Cigarette consumption is correlated with the risk of many different chronic conditions—e.g., lung cancer, chronic obstructive lung disease, and heart disease. Table 15 contains the percentages of blacks and whites who are current smokers for the period of 1965 to 1983.

The decline in the proportion of those who smoke is rapid for both black and white males; although black males are still more likely to be smokers, the differential has decreased. The declines in the proportion of the population who smoke are less for females, and the current differential between black and white females (2.7 percent) is less than for males (7.9 percent). For black females overall, there has been relatively little change since 1965, although there are interesting age patterns that reflect cohort-specific smoking habits by sex. For females over the age of 65, there has actually been an increase in the proportion of smokers—reduction in smoking for females has lagged 20 years behind that of males (Harris 1983). With the lengthy latency of many smoking-associated diseases, increases in the risks of those diseases can be expected for a number of years to come for females of both races.

Obesity

Being overweight is a risk factor for circulatory disease, both directly by increasing circulatory load, and indirectly by increasing the likelihood of hypertension and diabetes. Figure 4 records the percentage of those obese by age, sex, and race.

The most striking feature of figure 4 is the greater prevalence of obesity among black females compared to white females. The rate of obesity for black females is twice that of white females above the age of 55. The high prevalence of obesity explains why black females have high mortality and morbidity from diabetes. Black males also have a higher prevalence of obesity than white males. In the group aged 55 to 64, black males have a 46 percent greater likelihood of obesity. Above the age of 65, black males have a 72 percent greater chance of being obese.

Hypertension

Elevated blood pressure is an important risk factor for stroke, renal failure, and heart disease. The race-specific trends for 1960 and 1980 in hypertension are shown in table 16.

The prevalence of hypertension has declined over the interval. Consistent declines from 1960 were noted for females, but not for males. For both white and black males the hypertensive proportion increased

TABLE 15

Percentage of Persons Currently Smoking Cigarettes, 20 Years of Age and Over, According to Sex, Race, and Age: United States, 1965, 1976, 1980, and 1983 (data based on household interviews of a sample of the civilian noninstitutionalized population)

	Males				Females			
	1965	1976	1980	1983	1965	1976	1980	1983
WHITE								
Age 20 and over (age adjusted)	51.3	41.0	37.1	34.7	34.5	32.4	30.0	29.8
20–24	58.1	45.3	39.0	36.1	41.9	34.4	33.3	37.5
25–34	60.1	47.7	42.0	38.6	43.4	37.1	31.6	32.2
35–44	57.3	46.8	42.4	40.8	43.9	38.1	35.6	34.8
45–64	51.3	40.6	40.0	35.0	32.7	34.7	30.6	30.6
65 and older	27.7	22.8	16.6	20.6	9.8	13.2	17.4	13.2
BLACK								
Age 20 and over (age adjusted)	59.6	50.1	44.9	42.6	32.7	34.7	30.6	32.5
20–24	67.4	52.8	45.5	41.0	44.2	34.9	32.3	37.0
25–34	68.4	59.4	52.0	39.9	47.8	42.5	34.2	38.0
35–44	67.3	58.8	44.2	45.5	42.8	41.3	36.5	32.7
45–64	57.9	49.7	48.8	44.8	25.7	38.1	34.3	36.3
65 and older	36.4	26.4	27.9	39.0	7.1	9.2	9.4*	13.1

* Relative standard error >30%.

Note: A current smoker is a person who has smoked at least 100 cigarettes and who now smokes; includes occasional smokers. 1982 values are final estimates based on data for the last 6 months of 1980.

Source: National Center for Health Statistics 1986c.

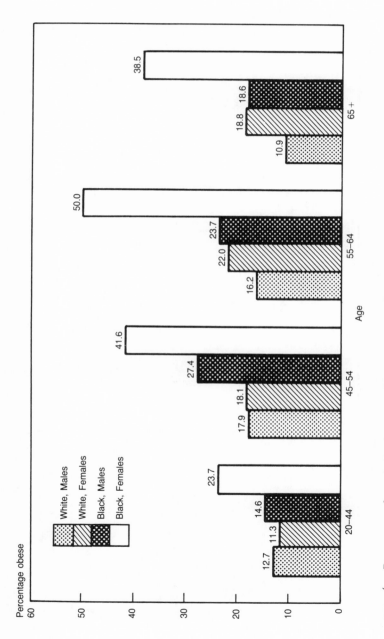

FIG. 4. Percentage of people in the most obese group, 1976.
Note: Percentage of people in the most obese group (Body Mass Index 28.49+ for males, 35.29+ for females): United States, 1976.
Source: Bonham and Brock 1985; U.S. Department of Health and Human Services 1985, 151 (figure 11).

TABLE 16

Percentage of Persons Aged 25 to 74 with Elevated Blood Pressure, According to Race, Sex, and Age: United States, 1960–1962, 1971–1975, and 1976–1980 (data based on physical examinations of a sample of the civilian noninstitutionalized population)

	Race and period					
	White			Black		
Sex and age	1960–1962	1971–1975	1976–1980	1960–1962	1971–1975	1976–1980
MALE						
All ages, 25–74 years*	14.8	18.5	16.3	32.2	36.5	23.6
25–34 years	3.8	7.5	8.4	12.5	16.4**	11.7
35–44 years	11.8	14.0	10.6	26.5	36.3***	22.3
45–54 years	17.3	22.6	21.2	30.9	36.7***	23.0
55–64 years	21.5	25.2	22.3	44.6	58.6	39.2
65–74 years	27.4	30.8	24.5	66.0	43.3*	27.5
FEMALE						
All ages, 25–74 years*	17.1	14.5	11.3	33.6	31.4	25.5
25–34 years	2.3	2.2	2.3	8.6**	12.4	4.3**
35–44 years	6.2	6.6**	6.5	25.7	23.8**	17.6
45–54 years	15.5	13.9	12.1	42.0	39.7	37.3
55–64 years	21.0	27.6	18.3	41.1	45.6	36.4
65–74 years	48.6	34.9	26.3	71.0	46.3	43.4

* Age adjusted by the direct method to the 1970 civilian noninstitutionalized population 25–74 years of age, using 5 age groups

** Figure does not meet standards of reliability or precision

Note: Elevated blood pressure includes readings of either systolic pressure of at least 160 mmHg or diastolic blood pressure of at least 95 mmHg or both. All blood pressures are the average of 3 measurements.

Source: National Center for Health Statistics 1984, 92 (table 37).

from 1960–1962 to 1971–1975, and then declined. The recent declines can be attributed to the initiation in 1972 of national hypertension control programs (Robins and Baum 1981) which have been linked to a decline of 15 percent in stroke incidence. Fully 80 percent of the hypertension control efforts have been initiated since 1972 (Baum and Manton 1987). Still, the proportion of persons with hypertension in the 1976–1980 period is 45 percent higher for black males and 126 percent higher for black females.

Serum Cholesterol

Table 17 presents trends in the prevalence of elevated serum cholesterol from 1960 to 1980.

The overall trends in the percentage of the population with elevated serum cholesterol have been downward for all groups except black males. Black males between the ages of 35 and 64 show increases occurring from 1960–1962 to 1971–1974. Large declines have been occurring for older females of both races.

Health Behavior

In the Alameda County study (Berkman and Breslow 1983) health behavior is prospectively linked to both morbidity and mortality. A summary measure of health behavior called the "health practices index" was used to present health habits for several types of health behavior (e.g., cigarette smoking, obesity, drinking, physical activity, and loss of sleep). The distribution of these scores (and associated mortality rates) are presented for blacks and whites in table 18.

Blacks generally score lower on the health behavior index than whites (e.g., over 25 percent of blacks score 0–2 versus 16 to 17 percent of whites). At most levels of the health practices index, the mortality rates for blacks are higher than for whites, suggesting differentials in other factors not represented in the index.

Infant Birth Weight

The infant mortality rate of blacks is twice that of whites. A major risk factor for infant mortality is birth weight. While only 7 percent of babies have low birth weight, they produce nearly 60 percent of all infant deaths. The proportion of low birth weight (less than 2,500

TABLE 17

Percentage of Persons Aged 25 to 74 with Elevated Serum Cholesterol Levels, According to Race, Sex, and Age: United States, 1960–1962, 1971–1974, and 1976–1980 (data based on physical examinations of a sample of the civilian noninstitutionalized population)

Sex and age	Race and period					
	White			Black		
	1960–1962	1971–1974	1976–1980	1960–1962	1971–1974	1976–1980
MALE						
All ages, 25–74 years*	20.6	17.4	16.8	14.2	20.0	19.4
25–34 years	10.8	7.8	8.4	9.0	14.0	9.3
35–44 years	21.7	16.5	15.4	8.4	20.7	23.6
45–54 years	26.4	25.0	20.8	21.1	20.4	25.3
55–64 years	24.6	19.4	22.8	13.7	23.0	24.2
65–74 years	21.5	20.7	19.1	22.9**	25.8	18.7
FEMALE						
All ages, 25–74 years*	26.7	20.7	20.0	24.1	20.7	20.0
25–34 years	6.8	5.6	5.9	12.0	5.4	6.5
35–44 years	12.9	9.4	9.9	12.1	10.7	13.3
45–54 years	28.0	24.6	23.8	31.0	27.2	25.8
55–64 years	51.9	36.2	35.8	29.1	34.7	32.0
65–74 years	51.4	41.2	35.6	50.1**	36.0	30.3

* Age adjusted by the direct method to the 1970 civilian noninstitutionalized population 25–74 years of age, using 5 age intervals
** Figure does not meet standards of reliability or precision
Note: Elevated serum cholesterol includes cholesterol levels of at least 260 mg/100 ml.
Source: National Center for Health Statistics 1984, 93 (table 28).

TABLE 18
Age-Adjusted Mortality Rates from All Causes (per 100): Health Practices*
Index and Race, Males and Females, Aged 30–69, 1965–1974

Number of low-risk health practices*	Whites	Percentage	Blacks	Percentage
	MALES			
0–2	15.9	17.2%	19.4	25.9%
	(307)**		(73)	
3	10.7	32.4	10.0	39.0
	(580)		(110)	
4–5	5.5	50.4	7.3	35.1
	(900)		(99)	
Total	9.2	100.0	11.2	100.0
	(1787)		(282)	
	FEMALES			
0–2	11.5	15.6	10.7	25.4
	(307)		(91)	
3	6.6	31.7	11.7	37.3
	(626)		(134)	
4–5	3.4	52.7	8.4	37.3
	(1040)		(134)	
Total	5.8	100.0	10.3	100.0
	(1973)		(359)	

* Cigarette abstinence, light or no alcohol use, at least moderate physical activity, sleeping 7–8 hours/night, average height and weight
** Numbers in parentheses indicate *N* values
Source: Berkman and Breslow 1983, 103 (table 3–17).

grams at birth) babies has dropped less for blacks (from 13.8 percent to 12.5 percent) than whites (from 6.8 percent to 4.7 percent) from 1969–1971 to 1979–1981. The prevalence of low birth weight babies remains over twice as high for blacks. The size of this differential is consistent with the differential in infant mortality rates.

There is significant geographic variation of the incidence of low birth weight infants, probably due to socioeconomic differences between areas. The proportion of low birth weight infants varies from 6.2 percent in the west-north central regions to 8.0 percent in the mountains for whites in the period of 1969 to 1971. For blacks the prevalence varied from 14.0 percent in the middle Atlantic to 12.4 percent in the Pacific regions. For blacks in the period of 1979 to 1981 these proportions dropped to 13 percent in the eastern-north central to 11.1 percent in the Pacific region.

In sum, blacks currently exhibit much poorer health potential than whites because of significantly elevated risk factors. The elevation of major risk factors explains, in part, the mortality differentials observed earlier and suggests that health differentials will persist. They suggest the potential among blacks for improvement by intervention in the exposure to risk factors. Differentials in three risk factors—smoking, hypertension, and obesity—can be addressed by direct prevention activities (e.g., public education programs, increased clinical screening, and better disease management and control). Low birth weight is also clearly an important risk factor linked with socioeconomic and cultural factors affecting maternal health. Serum cholesterol and obesity reflect risk factors associated with nutritional status.

Health Service Utilization

Differential rates of health service utilization represent an additional risk factor for poor health. In the past, health service utilization differed by race and constituted a major risk factor for poor health among blacks. Since nursing home utilization rates are lower for blacks, they become a special risk factor for the disabled elderly because current Medicare benefits do not include long-term care services. In this section, trends in three measures of health service utilization— nursing home use, physician use, and acute hospital visits—are discussed.

Nursing Home Use

A significant factor in the generally higher disability rates for blacks in the community are the differentials in nursing home utilization. The racial differences from 1963 to 1977 by age can be examined in table 19.

Nursing home utilization is higher for whites than blacks, although the differential declines with time. In 1963 the nursing home rates for those aged 65 and older were 160 percent higher for whites. This differential declined to 60 percent by 1977. The differentials vary by age. For persons aged 65 to 74 the rate of nursing home entry in 1977 is actually higher for nonwhites—a result of a trend that began

TABLE 19

Nursing Home and Personal Care Home Residents Aged 65 and Over and Number per 1,000 Population, According to Race: United States, 1963, 1969, 1973–1974, and 1977 (data based on a sample of nursing homes)

Year and age	White	All other	Ratio
1963			
65 years and over	26.6	10.3	2.6
65–74 years	8.1	5.9	1.4
75–84 years	41.7	13.8	3.0
85 years and over	157.7	41.8	3.8
1969			
65 years and over	38.8	17.6	2.2
65–74 years	11.7	9.6	1.2
75–84 years	54.1	22.9	2.4
85 years and over	221.9	52.4	4.2
1973–74*			
65 years and over	47.3	21.9	2.2
65–74 years	12.5	10.6	1.2
75–84 years	61.9	30.1	2.1
85 years and over	269.0	91.4	2.9
1977**			
65 years and over	49.7	30.4	1.6
65–74 years	14.2	16.8	0.8
75–84 years	70.6	38.6	1.8
85 years and over	229.0	102.0	2.2

 * Excludes residents in personal care or domiciliary care homes
 ** Includes residents in domiciliary care homes
Note: For data years 1963 and 1969, Hispanic origin was not designated; therefore, Hispanics may be included in either the white or all other category. For data years 1973–1974 and 1977, Hispanics were included in the white category.
Source: National Center for Health Statistics 1984, 116 (table 55).

in 1963. This, along with the higher disability rates at ages 65 to 74 (table 13) suggests higher disability rates for all blacks (i.e., in both the nursing home and community populations) at younger ages. Such a trend toward institutionalization among blacks at ages 65 to 74 may also suggest deficits in the provision of long-term care services which, more recently, has tended to focus on improving the delivery of long-term care to persons in the community to reduce the risk of institutionalization where possible and thereby possibly improve social autonomy and quality of life among the elderly.

Above the age of 85 whites are twice as likely to be institutionalized as nonwhites, which explains part of the higher prevalence of disability in the community for blacks over the age of 85. Even when the disabled and institutional populations are summed, however, a greater proportion of blacks (about 65 percent) are functionally dependent *or* institutionalized than whites (57 percent).

In assessing the implications of the higher black disability rates it is important to know the contribution of different medical conditions to disability. For example, cognitive impairment and dementia pose special management problems for informal care givers in the community, raising the likelihood of institutionalization. To know if black-white differences in institutionalization are appropriate requires detailed analyses of what particular medical condition produced the disability in elderly black and white populations.

Physician and Hospital Visits

Table 20 records the interval since the last physician visit and the discharge rates, days of care, and average length of stay by race for 1964, 1977, and 1982.

The table shows a large increase (from 56 to 73.3 percent) in the proportion of nonwhites who visited a physician in the last year. In 1982 the proportion of nonwhites using a physician was roughly the same as for whites. White hospitalization rates (age adjusted) dropped between 1964 and 1982, while rates for blacks increased significantly. The levels of hospitalization are higher for blacks for 1982, reflecting greater black mortality.

Though the greater morbidity of blacks causes blacks to consume greater amounts of health services (except for nursing homes) than whites, blacks still have much lower life expectancy than whites and higher mortality rates for conditions operating very early on in life (like infant mortality) which cause much premature mortality. Thus, the health services blacks receive are still failing to respond adequately to a variety of medical problems. The greater consumption of health services produces economic burdens on state and federal health programs in that a large proportion of health services provided to blacks must come from Medicaid and other government programs because of blacks' poor economic status. For example, among blacks only 49.3 percent have full-year private health insurance compared to 68.7 percent for

TABLE 20

Interval since Last Physician Visit (percent of population) and Discharges, Days of Care, and Average Length of Stay in Short-stay Hospitals (per 1,000 population) for U.S. Whites and Blacks, 1964, 1977, and 1982

	1964			1977			1982		
	Whites	Blacks	Ratio	Whites	Blacks	Ratio	Whites	Blacks	Ratio
INTERVAL SINCE LAST PHYSICIAN VISIT									
<1 year	67.3	57.0	1.2	75.3	74.5	1.0	74.9	73.3	1.0
1–2 years	13.7	14.6	0.9	11.1	12.1	0.9	10.6	12.2	0.9
2+ years	17.0	21.8	0.8	12.6	12.0	1.1	12.8	12.3	1.0
HOSPITAL USE*									
Discharges/1,000	133.8	106.3	1.3	121.4	133.0	0.9	123.2	147.3	0.8
Days of care/1,000	1053.4	1141.2	0.9	962.9	1354.9	0.7	907.0	1401.4	0.6
Average length of stay	7.9	10.7	0.7	6.9	10.0	0.7	6.5	9.3	0.7

* Excludes deliveries

Source: National Center for Health Statistics 1984, 98 (table 43), 109 (table 51).

whites. For blacks, there is a greater dependence on Medicaid insurance (22.6 percent) than for whites (3.7 percent) (U.S. Public Health Service 1985).

Conclusions

In recent years, large gains in life expectancy and improvements in health status have been noted for the American population, including gains in life expectancy at advanced ages—a historically unique phenomenon. In this article, we have examined the differences between American blacks and whites on a number of parameters of health, including life expectancy, morbidity, disability, and underlying risk factors. From that evaluation, a number of inferences can be drawn. One immediate inference is that more studies of black-white health differences are needed, especially for the elderly. Particularly limited were data from longitudinal, community-based epidemiological studies which often contain little or no data on blacks (e.g., the Framingham study). A second inference is that from a policy standpoint health resources probably are not optimally distributed in terms of closing the racial gaps in health.

Though both blacks and whites exhibited increases in life expectancy and health improvements, blacks remain significantly disadvantaged on a broad range of health measures. The health differentials could be traced to a number of different factors. Exposure to risk factors contributed to a higher incidence of certain chronic diseases. Among these risk factors were cigarette consumption, alcohol consumption, socioeconomic differentials, differences in sexual and reproductive behavior, nutritional and dietary differences, hypertension, and obesity. These factors produced excess risk for cancer, stroke, cardiovascular disease, diabetes, cirrhosis, and infant mortality. In terms of premature or excess deaths, the greatest impact is found for chronic conditions between the ages of 45 and 70.

Although the emphasis in many federal minority health programs is toward improving infant and maternal health, our analysis suggests that more attention needs to be given to reducing chronic disease risk factors for minority populations. This point received emphasis from our examination of black and white population projections which showed that, while the black population will remain significantly younger than the white population, both populations will undergo considerable "aging" and that the differences in age structures will lessen. Clearly, Medicare health benefits do not fully resolve the special health problems of black elderly—especially long-term care service needs and provision of health benefits at younger ages that could significantly affect the health of the future black elderly.

The most important factors that have an impact on the life expectancy of individuals are infant mortality, heart disease, accidents, and homicide. In the analysis of risk factors, there appeared to be specific high-risk segments of the black population with high rates of alcohol consumption, smoking, and homicide. Thus, part of the black-white differential seems to be attributed to specific groups in the black population with multiple risk-factor exposures. For example, to the extent that intravenous drug abuse is relatively higher in black young adults, deaths due to drug overdose, AIDS, and hepatitis will be growing problems in this population.

Though there are many black subpopulations with high exposure to major risk factors, black excess mortality exists despite a considerable exposure to these same risk factors in the white population. An assessment of excess mortality using an absolute health standard (i.e., SHE) shows about as much excess mortality among whites as blacks. The black excess, however, seems to be concentrated at younger ages produced in subpopulations by conditions (e.g., infant mortality, homicide, drug use) that are more sensitive to the lower socioeconomic status of blacks.

One major uncertainty, of course, in attributing this excess early disease risk to risk-factor exposures is the degree to which the early risk differentials are a product of genetic differences. There are certain well-known genetic factors (e.g., sickle cell trait) that contribute to black-white health differentials. The degree to which there are more diffuse, but highly prevalent genetic differences in the determinants of, say, hypertension or obesity (leading to increased circulatory-disease mortality risks for blacks) is currently not known, though there seems to be some cross-national evidence to support the existence of such factors; efforts to explain fully differences by purely socioeconomic factors in longitudinal studies seem not to be successful.

Furthermore, a major contributor to black excess mortality for certain diseases (e.g., cancer) is poorer quality medical care. For example, even after controlling for many individual and disease characteristics (e.g., stage of disease), there remains an elevated case fatality rate for blacks for many types of cancer. Black life expectancy continues to remain lower and mortality rates remain higher for many treatable conditions, even though the absolute volume of acute care services delivered appears to be similar in the two populations.

In addition to deficiencies in the medical services delivered to blacks, public health educational programs also are not apparently adequately reaching the black population. For example, black attitudes toward disease, treatment, screening, and outcome may significantly affect their help-seeking behavior—especially with economic constraints. Black case-fatality rates often are higher than white rates because diseases are generally presented for treatment at much later stages and because there is lower compliance with treatment. Because of higher case-fatality rates at earlier ages, there appears to be a lower prevalence of multiple chronic conditions reported at advanced ages for blacks, though black disability rates at those ages are higher.

Health service utilization data (especially on hospitalization) show the economic consequences of the poorer health of blacks. Since blacks have lower income and less private insurance coverage (U.S. Public Health Service 1985), they are more likely to utilize governmental sources of health care—especially Medicaid. Thus, the potential benefits of government intervention to improve the relative health status of blacks at multiple levels (i.e., prevention, education, improvement of acute and long-term care services) seems large. It is important to realize that while generating economic equality might require tax and other governmental policies to more equitably redistribute wealth, population health status is not a "zero-sum" game. That is, the health of the black population could be improved relative to that of the white population without in any way adversely affecting the health status of whites.

In conclusion, the differentials in health between blacks and whites are pervasive and longstanding, despite recent advances in black life expectancy. The reasons for this are numerous, and the prescriptions for change are to a large extent long term. Nonetheless, it appears clear to us that unless federal policy takes into account such factors as the relation of lower education and socioeconomic status to employment, health insurance, and access to quality medical care, as well as the detrimental impact of drugs, alcohol, and handguns on the health of young blacks, the plight of blacks relative to whites is not likely to improve. Given the direct and indirect economic consequences of allowing such health differentials to continue, a failure to reallocate federal and state resources to alleviate racial health differentials seems to be unjustified in fiscal as well as humanitarian grounds.

References

Baum, H.M., and K.G. Manton. 1987. National Trends in Stroke-related Mortality: A Comparison of Multiple Cause Mortality Data with Survey and Other Data. *Gerontologist* 27:293–300.

Berg, J.F. 1977. Economic Status and Survival of Cancer Patients. *Cancer* 39:467–77.

Berkman, L.F., and L. Breslow. 1983. *Health and Ways of Living: The Alameda County Study.* New York: Oxford University Press.

Besdine, R.W. 1984. Functional Assessment of the Elderly: Relationship between Functional Diagnoses. Paper presented at the Fifth Annual Symposium on the Elderly and Their Health—Disability in the Aged: Medical and Psychosocial Aspects, Department of Epidemiology and Preventive Medicine, University of Maryland School of Medicine, Baltimore, October 9.

Bonham, G.S., and D.W. Brock. 1985. The Relationship of Diabetes with Race, Sex and Obesity. *American Journal of Clinical Nutrition* 41:776–83.

Chiang, C.L. 1968. *Introduction to Stochastic Processes in Biostatistics.* New York: Wiley.

Fraumeni, J.F. 1975. *Persons at High Risk of Cancer.* New York: Academic Press.

Fries, J.F. 1980. Aging, Natural Death, and the Compression of Morbidity. *New England Journal of Medicine* 303:130–35.

———. 1983. The Compression of Morbidity. *Milbank Memorial Fund Quarterly/Health and Society* 61:397–419.

Harris, J.E. 1983. Cigarette Smoking among Successive Birth Cohorts of Men and Women in the United States during 1900–1980. *Journal of the National Cancer Institute* 71:474–79.

Israel, R.A., H.M. Rosenberg, and L.R. Curtin. 1986. Analytical Potential for Multiple Cause-of-Death Data. *American Journal of Epidemiology* 124:161–79.

Katz, S., and C.A. Akpom. 1976. A Measure of Primary Sociobiological Functions. *International Journal of Health Services* 6:493–508.

Keyfitz, N. 1977. What Difference Would It Make if Cancer Were Eradicated?: An Examination of the Taeuber Paradox. *Demography* 14:411–18.

Liu, K., and K.G. Manton. 1984. The Characteristics and Utilization Pattern of an Admission Cohort of Nursing Home Patients (II). *Gerontologist* 24:20–76.

Liu, K., K.G. Manton, and B. Liu. 1985. Home Health Care Expenses for the Disabled Elderly. *Health Care Financing Review* 7(2):51–58.

MacMahon, B., P. Cole, T.M. Lin, C.R. Lowe, A.P. Mirra, B. Ravnihar, E.J. Salber, V.G. Valaovas, and S. Yuasa. 1970. Age at First Birth and Breast Cancer. *Bulletin of the World Health Organization* 43:209–21.

Manton, K.G. 1980. Sex and Race-specific Mortality Differentials in Multiple Cause of Death Data. *Gerontologist* 20:480–93.

———. 1986. Past and Future Life Expectancy Increases at Later Ages: Their Implications for the Linkage of Chronic Morbidity, Disability, and Mortality. *Journal of Gerontology* 41:672–81.

Manton, K.G., and K. Liu. 1984. The Future Growth of the Long-term Care Population: Projections Based on the 1977 National Nursing Home Survey and the 1982 Long-term Care Survey. Paper presented at the Third National Leadership Conference on Long-term Care Issues, Hillhaven Foundation, Washington, March 7–9.

Manton, K.G., C.H. Patrick, and E. Stallard. 1980. Population Impact of Mortality Reduction: The Effects of Elimination of Major Causes of Death on the 'Saved' Population. *International Journal of Epidemiology* 9:111–20.

Manton, K.G., and B.J. Soldo. 1985. Dynamics of Health Changes in the Oldest Old: New Perspectives and Evidence. *Milbank Memorial Fund Quarterly/Health and Society* 63:206–85.

Manton, K.G., and E. Stallard. 1984. *Recent Trends in Mortality Analysis.* New York: Academic Press.

Manton, K.G., E. Stallard, J.P. Creason, W.B. Riggan, and M.A. Woodbury. 1985. Compartment Model Approaches for Estimating the Parameters of a Chronic Disease Process under Changing Risk Factor Exposures. *Environmental Health Perspectives* 19:151–69.

Myers, G.C., and K.G. Manton. 1984a. Compression of Mortality: Myth or Reality? *Gerontologist* 24: 346–53.

———. 1984b. Recent Changes in the U.S. Age at Death Distribution: Further Observations. *Gerontologist* 24:572–75.

Nam, C.B., and K.A. Ockay. 1977. Factors Contributing to the Mortality Crossover Pattern. Paper presented at the International Union for the Scientific Study of Population, Mexico City.

National Cancer Institute. 1984. *SEER Program: Cancer Incidence and Mortality in the United States, 1973–81.* NIH pub. no. 85–1837. Bethesda, Md.

National Center for Health Statistics. 1975. *Comparability of Mortality Statistics for the Seventh and Eighth Revisions of the International Classification of Diseases, United States.* DHEW pub. no. (HRA) 76-1340. Rockville, Md.

―――. 1980. Estimates of Selected Comparability Ratios Based on Dual Coding of 1976 Death Certificates by the Eighth and Ninth Revision of the International Classification of Diseases. *Monthly Vital Statistics Report* 28(11). DHEW pub. no. (PHS) 80–1120. Hyattsville, Md.

―――. 1983. *Health: United States, 1983.* Washington.

―――. 1984. *Health: United States, 1984.* Washington.

―――. 1986a. *Vital Statistics of the United States, 1981.* Vol. 2, Mortality, part B. DHHS pub. no. (PHS) 85–1102. Washington.

―――. 1986b. Trends in Smoking, Alcohol Consumption, and Other Health Practices Among U.S. Adults, 1977 and 1983. *Advance Data,* no. 118, Public Health Service. Washington.

―――. 1986c. *Health: United States, 1985.* Washington.

Page, W.F., and A.J. Kuntz. 1980. Racial and Socioeconomic Factors in Cancer Survival: A Comparison of Veterans Administration Results with Selected Studies. *Cancer* 45:1029–40.

Robins, M., and H.M. Baum. 1981. The National Survey of Stroke: Incidence. *Stroke* 12:45–57.

Rutstein, D.D., W. Berenberg, T.C. Chalmers, C.G. Child III, A.P. Fishman, and E.B. Perrin. 1976. Measuring the Quality of Medical Care: A Clinical Methodology. *New England Journal of Medicine* 294:582–88.

Ryder, N.B. 1985. Notes on Stationary Populations. *Population Index* 41:3–28.

Savage, D.G., J. Lindenbaum, E. Osserman, J. VanRyzin, and T. Garret. 1981. Survival of Black and White Patients with Multiple Myeloma at Two Hospitals (Abstract). *Proceedings of the American Association of Cancer Research* 22:537.

Schneider, E.L., and J.M. Guralnik. 1987. The Compression of Morbidity: A Dream Which May Come True Someday! *Gerontologica Biomedica Acta.* (Forthcoming.)

Siegel, J.S. 1979. Prospective Trends in the Size and Structure of the Elderly Population: Impact of Mortality Trends and Some

Implications. *Current Population Reports,* series P–23, no. 78. Washington.

U.S. Bureau of the Census. 1984. Projections of the Population of the United States, by Age, Sex, and Race: 1983 to 2080. *Current Population Reports,* series P–25, no. 952. Washington.

———. 1985. *Statistical Abstract of the United States: 1986.* Washington.

U.S. Department of Health and Human Services. 1985. *Report of the Secretary's Task Force on Black and Minority Health.* Vol. I. Washington.

U.S. Public Health Service. 1985. Changes in Health Status: Full-Year and Part-Year Coverage. *Data Preview* 21. DHHS pub. no. (PHS) 85-3377. Rockville, Md.

Verbrugge, L.M. 1983. The Social Roles of the Sexes and Their Relative Health and Mortality. In *Sex Differentials in Mortality: Trends, Determinants and Consequences,* ed. A. Lopez and L. Ruzicka, 221–45. Canberra: Department of Demography, Australian National University.

Wassertheil-Smoller, A., A. Apostolides, M. Miller, et al. 1979. Recent Status of Detection, Treatment, and Control of Hypertension in the Community. *Journal of Community Health* 5:82–93.

Wilkinson, G.S., F. Edgerton, H.J. Wallace, J. Reese, J. Patterson, and R. Priore. 1979. Delay, Stage of Disease and Survival from Breast Cancer. *Journal of Chronic Disorders* 32:365–73.

Wing, S., K. G. Manton, E. Stallard, J. E. Keil, H. A. Tyroler, and H. A. Hames. 1987. The Black/White Mortality Crossover in Two Community-based Studies. Chapel Hill: University of North Carolina, School of Public Health.

Wing, S., H. A. Tyroler, and K. G. Manton. 1985. The Participant Effect: Mortality in a Community-based Study Compared to Vital Statistics. *Journal of Chronic Disease* 38(2): 135–44.

Woodbury, M.A., and K.G. Manton. 1982. A New Procedure for the Analysis of Medical Classification. *Methods of Information in Medicine* 21:210–20.

World Health Organization. 1969. *International Classification of Diseases: Manual of the International Statistical Classification of Diseases, Injuries, and Causes of Death.* 8th revision. Geneva.

———. 1977. *Manual of the International Statistical Classification of Diseases, Injuries, and Causes of Death.* 9th revision. Geneva.

———. 1980. *International Classification of Impairments, Disabilities, and Handicaps: A Manual of Classification Relating to the Consequences of Disease.* Geneva.

———. 1982. *Demographic Yearbook 1980.* New York: Department of International Economic and Social Affairs, Statistical Office.

————. 1985. *World Health Statistics Annual.* Geneva.

Public versus Employment-related Health Insurance: Experience and Implications for Black and Nonblack Americans

STEPHEN H. LONG

T HE UNITED STATES DEPENDS ON A MIXTURE OF private insurance—mostly employment-related—and public programs to finance the bulk of health services for acute care. Although this system works well for the vast majority of its citizens, the number of people who remain uninsured is large and growing. Lack of health insurance is generally acknowledged to be a problem, notably because the uninsured have less access to medical care (Davis and Rowland 1983; Robert Wood Johnson Foundation 1987). Many policy options have been put forth that would deal with part or all of this uninsurance problem—including mandated employer coverage of workers and their dependents, and expansions of the federal/state Medicaid program.

The purpose of this article is to examine these issues in the specific context of differences for blacks and nonblacks in sources of insurance and the potential effectiveness of selected policy options. The article is organized in the following way. The first section examines racial differences in sources and the extent of health insurance. Next, the changes that were experienced between 1980 and 1985 are considered. Finally, the implications of some illustrative policy options are shown.

Sources of Health Insurance

There are many sources of health insurance. The majority of workers and their dependents are covered through employment-related insurance, sponsored by employers or labor unions. Premiums that support these plans may be fully paid by the employer, or they may be shared by the employer and the employee. The widespread use of this insurance source has been encouraged by the favorable tax treatment of compensation taking the form of employer-paid premiums. The other principal source of health insurance is public programs. Nearly all of the elderly, and some disabled, are insured through Medicare. In addition, some people with low incomes and assets receive Medicaid benefits, provided they meet certain categorical requirements regarding family structure, age, blindness, or disability. Finally, a small share of the population is covered only through some other insurance mechanism, which principally is private individual policies. This last mechanism is limited in use because of the very high premiums for such coverage, resulting from high administrative costs and adverse selection.

Despite these many sources, substantial numbers of people remain uninsured for their health care expenses. In some cases, individuals may be uninsured by their own choices or the choices of their parents— for example, when they choose for themselves or their dependents not to participate in an employment-related plan. In other cases, a person's employer may not offer a health plan. In yet another instance, some individuals are neither employed nor do they qualify as a dependent on a family member's plan. Provided they are not eligible for some public program, say by virtue of family structure or income, this latter group is likely to be uninsured.

Table 1 records the sources of health insurance for blacks and nonblacks in 1985, both for people of all ages and for three age groups—specifically, children, nonelderly adults, and the elderly. Because some people have more than one type of insurance, the classification in the table is based on a hierarchy. Individuals insured by an employment-related plan are classified in the first category, "employment-related," regardless of any additional public or other coverage they might have. Those with no employment-related coverage, but who had either Medicare or Medicaid, are classified in the "public" group. An individual without either employment-related or public coverage, but who had some other insurance, is placed in the "other" group. Finally, individuals who reported no source of health insurance are classified as "uninsured."

Considering people of all ages, blacks are more likely to be covered by public insurance or to be uninsured than nonblacks; and they are

TABLE 1

Sources of Health Insurance, by Race and Age, 1985

	Total	Employment-related*	Public, not employment-related**	Other, neither employment-related nor public***	Uninsured
	POPULATION (in millions)				
Black					
All ages	28.2	13.2	7.8	1.0	6.3
17 and under	9.5	4.0	2.9	0.2	2.4
18–64	16.4	9.0	2.8	0.7	3.8
65 and over	2.2	0.2	2.0	****	0.1
Nonblack					
All ages	206.0	127.7	32.3	15.2	30.8
17 and under	53.2	35.7	4.4	3.0	10.0
18–64	128.2	89.6	6.2	11.9	20.6
65 and over	24.6	2.4	21.7	0.3	0.2

PERCENTAGE

Black					
All ages	100%	47%	28%	3%	22%
17 and under	100	42	31	2	25
18–64	100	55	17	4	23
65 and over	100	8	89	1	2
Nonblack					
All ages	100	62	16	7	15
17 and under	100	67	8	6	19
18–64	100	70	5	9	16
65 and over	100	10	88	1	1

Source: Author's tabulations of the March 1985 Current Population Survey, which covers the civilian, noninstitutionalized population.

Note: Details may not add to totals because of rounding.

* This category includes respondents covered by private insurance plans sponsored by a current employer or union, and those covered by CHAMPUS (Civilian Health and Medical Program of the Uniformed Services). A small number of veterans who have no insurance, but who receive medical care from Veterans Administration facilities are included in this category because the data do not allow them to be separated from people covered by CHAMPUS. All respondents with employment-related coverage, whether or not they had public or other coverage, were classified in this category.

** This category includes respondents covered by Medicaid, Medicare, or both; provided that they did not have employment-related coverage.

*** This category includes respondents covered by individual insurance plans, provided that they were not covered by employment-related or public plans.

**** Less than 50,000.

less likely to be covered by private insurance. Lower rates of private insurance are reflected both by employment-related (47 percent versus 62 percent) and by other insurance (3 percent versus 7 percent). In contrast, 28 percent of blacks, but only 16 percent of nonblacks, have some source of public insurance. Over 6 million blacks are uninsured. They are about 1.5 times as likely as nonblacks to be uninsured (22 percent versus 15 percent).

Turning to specific age groups, black children are almost four times as likely to have only public insurance (31 percent versus 8 percent), while the corresponding multiple for nonelderly black adults is over three (17 percent versus 5 percent). Correspondingly, although about 70 percent of nonelderly nonblacks have employment-related insurance, only about one-half of blacks have this source of health insurance. The elderly, black and nonblack alike, are almost universally insured under Medicare. (Medicare is the second payer for the working elderly with employment-related insurance.) Clearly, the problem of being uninsured is almost exclusively limited to populations under 65 years of age.

These sharp differences in the sources of health insurance are in all likelihood a reflection of underlying differences in the structure and economic circumstances of black and nonblack families.

This article employs two concepts of the family to investigate this claim. The first and more common concept, used by the Bureau of the Census, defines a family as "a group of 2 persons or more, 1 of whom is a householder, residing together and related by birth, marriage, or adoption." The second concept, the "health insurance unit," is based on traditions of the private insurance industry. A health insurance unit includes a head, a spouse, all dependent children up to age 19, and older dependent children who are full-time students. In general, the family can include more people than would be included in the health insurance unit.

To illustrate, consider a husband and wife who have two children, aged 16 and 21, residing at home. The husband is employed and is covered by an employment-related policy that is fully paid by his employer. The husband, whose insurance plan allows for coverage of qualified dependents, but only at employee expense, elects not to insure the rest of the family. The 21-year-old works full-time but for an employer who provides no insurance benefits. These four people represent a single family. The 21-year-old, however, could not be covered as a dependent on the father's policy and, therefore, is a separate health insurance unit. (Tabulations in this article would show the husband as having employment-related insurance, and the other three family members as uninsured. Tabulations based on family income would consider the combined income of all four members. Tabulations on characteristics of insurance units would divide the family into two units and describe their characteristics separately.)

Table 2 records tabulations of black and nonblack people by selected characteristics of their health insurance units or of their families. Blacks are far more likely than nonblacks to live in single-headed units with children (29 percent versus 8 percent) or as single individuals (31 percent versus 24 percent). A corollary to these facts is that they

TABLE 2
Selected Characteristics of People in Health Insurance Units, by Race, 1985

	Black		Nonblack	
	In millions	Percentage	In millions	Percentage
Total*	28.2	100%	206.0	100%
DEMOGRAPHIC STRUCTURE**				
Individual adult	8.7	31	48.4	24
Couple without children	3.1	11	46.8	23
Couple with children	8.1	29	94.3	46
Single with children	8.3	29	16.5	8
NUMBER OF WORKERS***				
No worker	11.8	42	51.7	25
One worker	11.2	40	96.6	47
Two or more workers	5.2	18	57.6	28
FAMILY INCOME AS A PERCENTAGE OF THE POVERTY LEVEL****				
Under 1.00	9.6	34	24.4	12
1.00 to 1.49	4.1	15	19.1	9
1.50 and above	14.5	51	162.5	79

Source: Author's tabulations of the March 1985 Current Population Survey, which covers the civilian, noninstitutionalized population.
Note: Details may not add to totals because of rounding.
* This table shows the distribution of people by race, when they are grouped by the characteristics of either their health insurance unit or their family.
** Demographic structure describes the composition of the health insurance unit. Since health insurance units may be subsets of families, these tabulations differ from those describing the structure of families.
*** Number of workers in the health insurance unit, where a worker is defined as a person who works at least 17.5 hours per week.
**** Family income is used for this characteristic because there is no poverty measure applicable to the health insurance units.

are less likely to live as couples, either with or without children (40 percent versus 69 percent). Moreover, 42 percent of blacks are in health insurance units with no workers, but only 25 percent of nonblacks are in this situation.

Employment-related insurance generally may cover employees, spouses (if any), and dependent children (if any). The less frequent attachment to the labor force and lower likelihood of having a spouse make blacks much less likely to have health insurance coverage through an employer or a union. (The lower likelihood of employment-related insurance for blacks is much less related to the rates at which those who work are insured. Among blacks and nonblacks living in health insurance units having one or more workers, the rate of employment-related coverage is 72 percent for blacks and 77 percent for nonblacks.) In contrast, their much greater likelihood of being in single-parent families with children and their being nearly three times as likely to be poor (see table 2) make blacks far more likely to meet the categorical, income, and asset eligibility standards of Medicaid.

Experience, 1980–1985

The first half of this decade brought numerous changes for health insurance and the health care delivery system. President Reagan called for major cuts in federal spending, including Medicaid spending. Private business vowed to find ways to cut its rising costs of health care benefits. Health maintenance organizations and preferred provider organizations were springing up in many communities, promising to compete with conventional private insurance plans and their reimbursement traditions. The economy fell into and then recovered from a major recession, accompanied by high unemployment. What were the implications of these and many other changes for health insurance coverage of blacks and nonblacks?

Changes in the number of people covered by various types of health insurance between 1980 and 1985 are shown in table 3. For blacks, growth in employement-related and other insurance (6 percent) did not quite keep pace with population growth (8 percent) over the five-year period. A 9 percent growth in public insurance was not enough to offset this relative decline in private insurance, so that about 700,000 additional blacks became uninsured (a 12 percent increase, or 4 percent in excess of population growth).

TABLE 3
Change in Sources of Insurance, by Race, 1980–1985*

	1980		1985		Change**	
	In millions	Percentage	In millions	Percentage	In millions	Percentage
BLACK						
Total	26.0	100%	28.2	100%	2.1	8%
Employment-related	12.4	48	13.2	47	0.8	6
Public, but not employment-related	7.1	27	7.8	28	0.6	9
Other, neither employment-related nor public	0.9	4	1.0	3	0.1	6
Uninsured	5.6	22	6.3	22	0.7	12
NONBLACK						
Total	197.1	100	206.0	100	8.8	4
Employment-related	128.2	65	127.7	62	-0.5	0
Public, but not employment-related	27.7	14	32.3	16	4.6	17
Other, neither employment-related nor public	16.4	8	15.2	7	-1.2	-7
Uninsured	24.9	13	30.8	15	5.9	24

Source: Author's tabulations of the March 1980 and March 1985 Current Population Surveys, which covers the civilian, noninstitutionalized population.
Note: Differences may not add to totals and differences may not equal the changes shown because of rounding.
* See notes in table 1 for definitions of insurance categories.
** The change in millions is calculated as the difference between the number of people in each insurance category in 1985 and the corresponding figure for 1980. The percentage expresses this change as a percentage of the 1980 figure.

The changes for blacks were modest in comparison to those for nonblacks, however. The absolute number of nonblack people covered under employment-related insurance remained essentially unchanged over the period and those covered by other insurance declined by 7 percent, despite a 4 percent growth in total nonblack population. A much larger growth in public insurance (17 percent)—about 60 percent of which was among the elderly—was enough to yield an increase in the total number of nonblack people covered by insurance. An even larger addition to the population, however, left 5.9 million more nonblacks uninsured in 1985 than in 1980, for a 24 percent increase (or 20 percent more than could be accounted for by population growth alone). The relative decline in private insurance affected nonblacks more, both because it lagged further behind population growth and because nonblacks depend relatively more on private insurance.

The respective roles of private versus public insurance are also reflected in the effect on the number of uninsured for various age groups (see table 4). The relatively larger role of public insurance for blacks, and black children in particular, largely accounts for the fact that there was essentially no change in the number of uninsured black children between 1980 and 1985. Greater coverage by private insurance of nonblacks (and lower coverage by public insurance) is associated with the 19 percent increase in uninsured nonblack children. The 30 percent increase in the numbers of uninsured blacks and nonblacks aged 18 to 64 reflects the failure of private insurance enrollment to keep pace with population growth in this age group. (Not shown in table 4 is the fact that growth in employment-related coverage fell 4 percentage points below population growth for both black and nonblack 18 to 64 year olds during this period.)

Implications of Illustrative Policy Options

The large size of the uninsured population and its rapid increase in this decade have contributed to mounting concern. Numerous policy responses have been suggested; some would increase private coverage and others would increase public coverage. Most of the options are incremental and, even in combination with one another, would not bring about universal insurance. The purpose of this section is to suggest the implications for blacks and nonblacks of two commonly

TABLE 4

Change in the Number of Uninsured, by Race and Age, 1980–1985

	1980		1985		Change*	
	In millions	Percentage	In millions	Percentage	In millions	Percentage
BLACK						
All ages	5.6	22%	6.3	22%	0.7	12%
17 and under	2.5	26	2.4	25	−0.1	−3
18–64	3.0	20	3.8	23	0.9	29
65 and over	0.1	7	0.1	2	−0.1	−65
NONBLACK						
All ages	24.9	13	30.8	15	5.9	24
17 and under	8.4	15	10.0	19	1.6	19
18–64	15.8	13	20.6	16	4.8	30
65 and over	0.7	3	0.2	1	−0.5	−69

Source: Author's tabulations of the March 1980 and March 1985 Current Population Surveys, which covers the civilian, noninstitutionalized population.

Note: Differences between 1985 and 1980 details may not equal the changes shown because of rounding.

* The change in millions is calculated as the difference between the number of persons uninsured in 1985 and the corresponding figure for 1980. The percentage expresses this change as a percentage of the 1980 figure. The apparently large percentage changes for persons aged 65 and over is the result of calculating from a small base.

discussed options—one that would require all employers to provide a basic health insurance plan to employees and their dependents, and another that would expand Medicaid eligibility for the categorically needy to 150 percent of the poverty level.

The employer-mandate option illustrated here would require all employers to provide health insurance to all full-time employees, their spouses, and their dependent children. A full-time employee would be defined as one who works 17.5 hours or more per week. Employees would be required to accept the insurance and to cover their entire families. The self-employed would also be subject to the mandate. The implications for the uninsured of such a plan are shown in table 5. Of the roughly 37 million uninsured in 1985, about 24 million (66 percent) would gain health insurance coverage. There would be some racial differences in impact, however, since the black uninsured are considerably less likely to live in a health insurance unit with a full-time worker than are nonblacks (50 percent versus 69 percent). Therefore, just as nonblacks depend relatively more on employment-related insurance currently, so would they disproportionately benefit from policy options that would expand employment-related insurance.

Another approach to reducing the numbers of uninsured involves expansions in Medicaid eligibility. There are many ways that this could be done. One commonly discussed way, principally affecting single mothers with dependent children, would be to increase the income limits of the categorically needy to become eligible. If the Medicaid income standard were made uniform nationally so as to qualify all those units with incomes below 150 percent of the federal poverty level, about 5 million (13 percent) of the uninsured would be covered. Consistent with the overall family structure and economic characteristics discussed above, the black uninsured would be much more likely to receive insurance from this option than the nonblack uninsured (28 percent versus 10 percent). Alternative Medicaid eligibility expansions—for example, ones that would modify the categorical eligibility rules by allowing other family types, such as two-parent families, to benefit—might result in a less disproportionate outcome between blacks and nonblacks.

The bottom panel of table 5 records that the combined options would, by insuring about 27 million people, reduce the uninsured population to nearly one-quarter of its former size. This combined option would have a somewhat more balanced effect across blacks and

TABLE 5

Effects on the Number of Uninsured of Illustrative Policy Options,
by Race, 1985

	Total	Black	Nonblack
CURRENT LAW			
Uninsured			
In millions	37.1	6.3	30.8
Percentage	100%	100%	100%
ILLUSTRATIVE EMPLOYER MANDATE			
Newly insured			
In millions	24.3	3.1	21.1
Percentage	66%	50%	69%
Continuing uninsured			
In millions	12.8	3.1	9.6
Percentage	34%	50%	31%
ILLUSTRATIVE MEDICAID EXPANSION			
Newly insured			
In millions	5.0	1.8	3.2
Percentage	13%	28%	10%
Continuing uninsured			
In millions	32.1	4.5	27.6
Percentage	87%	72%	90%
BOTH ILLUSTRATIVE OPTIONS			
Newly insured			
In millions	27.2	4.2	22.9
Percentage	73%	67%	75%
Continuing uninsured			
In millions	9.9	2.1	7.8
Percentage	27%	33%	25%

Source: Author's simulations based on the March 1985 Current Population Survey, which covers the civilian, noninstitutionalized population.
Note: Details may not add to totals because of rounding.

nonblacks than would either of the options taken alone. Still, one-third of currently uninsured blacks would remain uncovered, compared to one-quarter of nonblacks. This remaining disparity might be explained, in part, by the larger proportion of adult black males who are single and who are either unemployed or are out of the labor force.

This brief discussion of policy options has been limited in two important ways. First, the analysis, which was guided by the themes of these volumes, was limited to two dimensions—the potential for reducing the number of uninsured, and proportionate effects by race. Many other dimensions—including total social costs and benefits, effects on the federal budget, and unintended negative effects on employment—are also relevant to the public policy debate.

Second, the discussion only considered options that address health insurance directly. Yet, the data presented here suggest that black/nonblack differences in health insurance may derive from more fundamental differences in family structure and labor-force attachment. Changes in these other attributes, whether or not they are stimulated by public policy, would also affect the number and characteristics of the uninsured. Finally, lines of causation in this area are somewhat blurred. Specifically, some observers argue that black family composition is as much influenced by Medicaid eligibility rules as Medicaid enrollment reflects black family composition.

References

Davis, K., and D. Rowland. 1983. Uninsured and Underserved: Inequities in Health Care in the United States. *Milbank Memorial Fund Quarterly/Health and Society* 61:149–76.

Robert Wood Johnson Foundation. 1987. *Access to Health Care in the United States: Results of a 1986 Survey*. Special Report no. 2. Princeton.

Health Care for Black Americans:
The Public Sector Role

KAREN DAVIS, MARSHA LILLIE-
BLANTON, BARBARA LYONS,
FITZHUGH MULLAN, NEIL POWE,
and DIANE ROWLAND

T HE "GREAT SOCIETY" AND THE "WAR ON POVERTY"
in the mid-1960s brought a major expansion in the federal
government's commitment to ensuring access to health care
for many of the nation's most vulnerable people—the elderly, the
poor, and minorities (Davis and Schoen 1978). Medicare and Medicaid,
enacted in 1965, pay the health bills of almost 50 million elderly,
disabled, and low-income people. Primary care programs with direct
federal government funding provide health care services through about
876 health centers to approximately 6 million people, many of whom
are members of minority racial and ethnic groups (Davis 1985).

These programs have helped many millions of Americans obtain
needed health care and have contributed to improvements in the health
and well-being of those they have touched (Davis and Schoen 1978).
Black Americans have been particularly helped, with major gains in
access to physician and other health care services.

Despite these programs and the very significant gains that have
been made since the mid-1960s, over 35 million Americans continue
to have no health insurance coverage. Cutbacks in funding for Medicare,
Medicaid, and primary health care programs in the 1980s—coupled

with the growth in poverty—threaten to reverse some of the gains that have been made in the past. It is a critical time to assess the trends in financing and delivering health care services to black Americans, identify major remaining gaps, and reflect on what the future holds.

Trends in Health and Use of Health Services

Improvements in Health

The United States has experienced major gains in health in the last twenty-five years. Minority and low-income population groups have shared in these gains. Increased access to and use of health services, which occurred with the Medicaid and Medicare programs, the development of neighborhood health centers, and the recruitment and placement of minority and other health care providers in underserved communities, are some of the factors contributing to improvements in health (Hadley 1982; Davis and Schoen 1978)

Life expectancy is one measure of health where gains by blacks are particularly noteworthy. In the period from 1960 to 1983, life expectancy at birth in the United States increased a total of 5 years—from 69.7 years to 74.7 years (U.S. Department of Health and Human Services 1985a). Blacks experienced greater gains than whites, with especially marked improvements for black females. Life expectancy of black females at birth increased almost 8 years—from 65.9 years in 1960 to 73.8 years. Although in 1983 black males continued to have the shortest life expectancy at birth (65.2 years), from 1960 to 1983 their life expectancy increased slightly more than that of white males— 4.5 years versus 4.2 years.

Longer life expectancy at birth reflects lower infant mortality and lower death rates throughout life. Gains in health status have been most notable for causes of illness and death amenable to medical care intervention. As shown in table 1, the infant mortality rate for blacks declined by more than 50 percent between 1960 and 1980, dropping from 44 deaths per 1,000 live births to 21 per 1,000 live births. Although the infant mortality rate among blacks continues to be twice that of whites, considerable progress has been achieved since 1960.

Table 1 also records declines in age-adjusted mortality rates for some of the leading causes of death in the United States. Included among these are deaths from influenza and pneumonia, which dropped by 67 percent among blacks between 1960 and 1980 and deaths from tuberculosis which dropped by 51 percent. These are causes of death that historically have been greater among the poor than among higher income individuals. Mortality rates from cerebrovascular diseases and arteriosclerosis declined by more than 50 percent. This dramatic decline

TABLE 1

Percentage Change in Death Rates from Selected Causes by Race and Years, United States, 1950-1980

	Percentage change 1950-1960	Percentage change 1960-1980
Infant deaths*		
White	− 14.6%	− 52.0%
Black	1.0	− 51.7
Influenza & pneumonia		
White	7.4	− 50.4
Black & other	− 3.0	− 67.4
Tuberculosis**		
White	N/A	− 64.4
Black & other	N/A	− 50.8
Cerebrovascular disease		
White	− 10.8	− 48.8
Black & other	− 9.4	− 53.3
Arteriosclerosis		
White	− 19.1	− 57.3
Black & other	− 12.7	− 57.2
Diseases of the heart		
White	− 6.3	− 29.8
Black & other	− 13.6	− 27.8
Diabetes		
White	− 7.9	− 28.9
Black & other	25.6	− 13.0

* Change in deaths per 1,000 live births. All others are change in deaths per 100,000 population.
** Data not available by race for 1950-1961; percentage change is for 1962-1980.
Source: Computed from death rates in U.S. Department of Health and Human Services 1985b.

in mortality represents both the lower rate of uncontrolled hypertension in the population and improved access to health services. Deaths from heart disease and diabetes dropped by 28 percent and 13 percent, respectively. Although blacks showed modest gains in reductions of deaths from diabetes, these gains represent a sharp departure from the 26 percent increase in diabetes mortality between 1950 and 1960. Deaths from cancer, suicide, homicide, and cirrhosis showed upward trends between 1960 and 1980. With the exception of cancer, however, mortality from these conditions could not be expected to be significantly affected by the availability of improved health services.

Measures of mortality are a readily available and reliable source of data used to monitor health over a long period of time. Since some improvements in health may not be reflected in mortality data for years, other indicators of improved health that show an increase in functioning capacity or reduced suffering, disability, or risk of dying are important. The monitoring of risk factors for heart disease and stroke provide evidence that hypertension prevention and treatment efforts during the last decade have been successful in motivating the public to adopt healthier patterns of living and in reducing elevated blood pressure levels of blacks. Physical exams from a nationwide sample of adults during the years 1960 to 1962 and 1976 to 1980 found a decline of 17 percent in the proportion of the United States population with elevated blood pressure. Blacks experienced the greatest gains, with a 25 percent decline. The proportion of the adult black population with elevated blood pressure levels dropped from 33 percent in 1960 to 1962 to 25 percent in 1976 to 1980 (U.S. Department of Health and Human Services 1985b).

Contrasting health status measures of blacks prior to and after 1960 provides some indication of the progress achieved in recent years. Indications of improvements are particularly significant given that many health status measures showed minimal if any change in the ten years preceding the federal government's major involvement in the financing and delivery of health services. While it is difficult to sort out the relative contribution of different factors that influence health status, increased access to and use of health services can be considered as one of the more important contributing factors. Recognition of improvements in health shows that progress can be achieved when the financial and health care resources of this country are made available to increasing numbers of Americans.

Increased Use of Health Services

Prior to 1965, the use of physician and hospital services differed dramatically by race and income. Table 2 records that between 1965 and 1980 racial differences in the use of health services narrowed considerably. These changes occurred after the introduction of Medicaid, Medicare, and other health programs for underserved areas and provide evidence of their success in improving access to care.

Primary and Preventive Care. In the early 1960s blacks, although more likely to report their health as poor or fair and to suffer from chronic conditions, saw physicians less frequently than whites. In 1964 poor blacks and other minorities saw physicians an average of 3.1 times per year compared to an average of 4.7 times for whites. By the period of 1976 to 1978 the average number of visits for poor blacks and whites, unadjusted for health status, were similar (U.S. Department of Health and Human Services 1980). Regardless of income, blacks prior to 1964 were less likely than whites to have seen a physician in two years or more. As shown in table 2, poor blacks and other minorities were the least likely to have seen a physician in two or more years. By 1976 the proportion of the population seeing a physician over a two-year period did not vary substantially by race or income (U.S. Department of Health and Human Services 1980).

More women are now getting care early in pregnancy. Studies have shown that receiving prenatal care in the first trimester is important in reducing the proportion of low birth weight infants and infant mortality. The proportion of black women receiving prenatal care in the first trimester increased from 44.4 percent in 1970 to 62.4 percent in 1981 (U.S. Department of Health and Human Services 1985a).

Although in 1980 black children were less likely than white children to receive immunizations for preventable diseases, there has been considerable improvement in the proportion of black and white children vaccinated. This has led to a marked decline in many diseases once considered major killers. Negligible cases (one case per 100,000 population or less) of diphtheria, pertussis, measles, rubella, and polio were reported in 1981—all down substantially from rates in 1960 (U.S. Department of Health and Human Services 1985a).

Routine physical examinations are important for health maintenance and for the early detection of an illness. In 1980, about two out of every five blacks (42 percent) and whites (41 percent) reported a general

TABLE 2
Use of Health Services by Selected Indices

	Poor			Nonpoor		
	White	Black & other	Ratio white:black	White	Black & other	Ratio white:black
Average no. of M.D. visits per person per year *						
1964	4.7	3.1	1.5	4.7	3.6	1.3
1976-1978	5.7	5.0	1.1	4.9	4.4	1.1
Percentage with no M.D. visits in past two years *						
1964	25.7%	33.2%	0.8%	17.1%	24.7%	0.7%
1976	15.1	14.9	1.0	12.9	13.4	1.0
Hospital discharges per 100 persons **						
1964	15.0	10.0	1.5	13.0	10.0	1.3
1979	21.0	17.0	1.2	13.0	12.0	1.1

Source: * U.S. Department of Health and Human Services, 1980.
** President's Commission for the Study of Ethical Problems in Medical and Biomedical and Behavioral Research 1983.

check-up within the past year. This reflects a major improvement from the 1970 data which showed that whites were about 20 percent more likely than blacks and other minorities to receive a general check-up (U.S. Department of Health and Human Services 1985b).

Hospital Care. Similar findings are evident in the use of inpatient hospital services. National Health Interview Survey data in table 2 show that hospital discharge rates of blacks and other minorities increased from 1964 to 1979 (President's Commission for the Study of Ethical Problems in Medicine and Biomedical and Behavioral Research 1983). In 1964 the poor were hospitalized at similar rates as higher income people; poor whites were hospitalized at a rate 50 percent greater than that of poor blacks and other minorities. By 1979 the poor were hospitalized at a higher rate than the nonpoor, reflecting their poorer health status and greater need for care.

Long-term Care. Access to long-term or extended care facilities for black Americans aged 65 years and older improved greatly with the Medicaid and Medicare programs. In 1963 whites were much more likely to receive care in a nursing home than blacks and other minorities. There were only 10 black or other minority nursing home residents in 1963 for every 1,000 blacks and other minorities aged 65 and older (U.S. Department of Health and Human Services 1985b). This was in comparison to 27 white nursing home residents for every 1,000 whites aged 65 and older. By 1977 the gap had narrowed considerably, although blacks 85 years and older were still much less likely to receive extended care services than whites.

Assessment of Overall Trends. Clear evidence exists that sizable gains in access to care have been achieved nationwide. It cannot be concluded from this data, however, that no further problems remain and that every American now has equitable access to health care. Striking differences in the use of health services persist in this country, particularly for blacks who are uninsured and who live in the South (Davis and Rowland 1983). Data on the use of health services for specific medical conditions also show differences by race that are not explained by differences in the need for care (Davis and Lillie-Blanton 1986). And finally, questions about the quality and adequacy of care obtained by blacks and other beneficiaries of government health care financing programs deserve attention in order to evaluate more fully the progress achieved.

The record of accomplishment, however, remains remarkable. Government-supported health care financing and delivery programs established in the 1960s have enabled large numbers of black Americans—along with many other poor, disabled, and elderly Americans—to share in the benefits of modern medicine.

Medicaid

The enactment of Medicaid in 1965 greatly expanded the federal government's role in financing health care for the poor. Medicaid was designed to assist states in improving access to care for the poor and to enable the poor to receive mainstream medical care. Since about one-third of the poor were black, it was assumed that Medicaid would reduce disparities in access to care by race, as well as by income.

Medicaid is a joint federal-state program administered by each state. Each state determines its own eligibility, benefits, and reimbursement policies within broad federal guidelines. As a result, the Medicaid program varies widely among states. States are required to cover individuals receiving cash assistance under the Aid to Families with Dependent Children (AFDC) program and most elderly, blind, and disabled recipients of Supplemental Security Income (SSI). At a state's discretion, similar persons whose incomes are slightly above the cash assistance level may be covered as "medically needy."

Scope of Coverage

Medicaid has provided large numbers of low-income black and white Americans with coverage for medical expenses. In 1984, 19.3 million Americans—about 8 percent of the total population—were covered by Medicaid. About one-third of Medicaid beneficiaries, or 6.6 million individuals, were black (U.S. Bureau of the Census 1985).

In the last twenty years, Medicaid has proved to be a major source of health coverage for black Americans. Table 3 records that since 1978 Medicaid has provided health coverage for nearly one out of every five blacks under the age of 65. Nearly half of black children under 6 years of age were covered by Medicaid in 1980 (O'Brien, Rodgers, and Baugh 1985). Guaranteeing health coverage for children is clearly one of the most important policies this government can

TABLE 3

Medicaid Coverage of Persons under 65 years of age, 1978, 1980, 1982

Insurance status	1978	1980	1982
Total	6.1%	5.9%	5.6%
White	4.0	3.9	3.6
Black	19.7	17.9	17.2

Source: U.S. Department of Health and Human Services 1985a.

pursue to ensure adequate access to health care and a healthy start in life for this vulnerable segment of the population.

In 1982 Medicaid provided coverage for 17 percent of blacks under the age of 65 as compared with 4 percent of whites. As is evident from this data, blacks are more likely to be covered by Medicaid than whites. The difference in Medicaid coverage largely reflects the greater concentration of blacks in poverty. Three times as many blacks as whites have incomes below the federal poverty level. Poor blacks are also more likely than poor whites to be covered by Medicaid (53 percent vs. 32 percent) (U.S. Bureau of the Census 1986). Since a greater proportion of poor black than poor white families are single-parent households, a greater proportion of blacks are thus categorically eligible for Medicaid. In addition, nearly two-thirds of poor blacks reside in urban areas where the extent of Medicaid coverage is greater.

Program Spending

Medicaid is an extremely important source of financing for health care services obtained by black Americans. Reflecting more extensive coverage of the black population, Medicaid paid on average 30 percent of the hospital expenses incurred by blacks compared to 6 percent for whites (Taylor 1983).

Analysis of 1964 and 1974 data found that Medicaid benefits were unevenly distributed by race and geographic region. Average Medicaid payments per white beneficiary were 74 percent higher than payments per black beneficiary (Davis and Schoen 1978). By 1980 the differences had narrowed, with average charges about 50 percent higher for whites than for blacks. The average per person charge for black Medicaid beneficiaries in 1980 was $598 compared with an average of $878 for white Medicaid beneficiaries (Howell, Corder, and Dobson 1985). Further investigation will be required to explain factors that may account for racial differences among Medicaid beneficiaries. Among the possible explanations are that whites differ from blacks in the quantity and mix of services used and in the use of higher cost providers.

Medicaid expenditures also vary across the major eligibility groups. Despite the common perception that Medicaid largely benefits "welfare mothers and their children," the expenditure data show that AFDC Medicaid beneficiaries incurred less than one-third (25 percent) of all costs in 1984 (Department of Health and Human Services 1985a). The aged, blind, and disabled represented less than 30 percent of total Medicaid beneficiaries, but incurred over 70 percent of the costs. Most of these costs were for nursing home services and intermediate care facilities for the mentally retarded, as well as prescription drugs. These data show that Medicaid provides an important "safety net" for elderly and disabled persons with limited financial means and high medical bills.

Accomplishments

The Medicaid program deserves much of the credit for gains in access to health care achieved by poor and ethnic minority population groups. Twenty years ago, black Americans with limited financial resources faced both economic and racial barriers to obtaining care which was timely and appropriate to their needs. The Medicaid program has been instrumental in reducing both of these barriers to care. Medicaid not only provided a source of financing for poor blacks, but also hastened the process of desegregation in health care facilities. Hospitals receiving Medicaid funds were required to be in compliance with Title VI of the 1964 Civil Rights Act. This act prohibited racial discrimination in any institution receiving federal funds. This provision helped to increase access to care for poor, as well as nonpoor, black Americans.

Differences in utilization rates for the uninsured poor and the insured poor serve as an indicator of Medicaid's impact on access to care. On average, poor blacks with health coverage make twice as many physician visits as their uninsured counterparts. Poor insured blacks made an average of 3.8 visits to physicians in 1977 compared with 1.8 for poor uninsured blacks (Wilensky and Walden 1981). The poor, excluded from Medicaid, are much less likely to use health services than their counterparts.

Data averaged for the period of 1978 to 1980 provide further evidence of Medicaid's impact on the use of ambulatory services. About one-third of uninsured blacks (33 percent) and whites (31 percent) under the age of 65 reported not seeing a physician in the past year compared with about one-fourth of blacks (24 percent) and whites (22 percent) with private coverage—and one-sixth of blacks (15 percent) and whites (15 percent) with Medicaid (Trevino and Moss 1983). Current surveys provide evidence that blacks and whites without health coverage continue to face serious problems in obtaining medical care comparable in amount to that obtained by those with coverage.

Several national studies have examined Medicaid's effectiveness by analyzing 1976 and 1980 survey data using multivariate levels of analysis adjusting for socioeconomic characteristics and health status (Link, Long, and Settle 1982; O'Brien, Rodgers, and Baugh 1985). These studies found no major racial differences in use of physician services among Medicaid beneficiaries, but significantly lower use of hospital inpatient services by blacks compared to whites. For Medicaid beneficiaries, there exists fairly conclusive evidence that racial and economic disparities in the use of health services have been substantially reduced.

Another indicator of Medicaid's impact is the dramatic decline in infant mortality. As described in the preceding section, after little change in the decade before the enactment of Medicaid, rates have plummeted since the mid-1960s.

Remaining Problems and Future Issues

Medicaid's accomplishments in improving access to care and health status are undeniable. Its shortcomings, however, should not be overlooked. Some of the issues which warrant attention are: limitations in the extent of coverage of the poor; limited participation of physicians in the program; and the quality of care received by Medicaid beneficiaries.

Extent of Coverage of the Poor.   Medicaid covered only one-half of poor blacks (53 percent) and one-third of poor whites (32 percent) in 1983 (U.S. Bureau of the Census 1986). Use of health care services for the uninsured poor lags well behind that of Medicaid beneficiaries

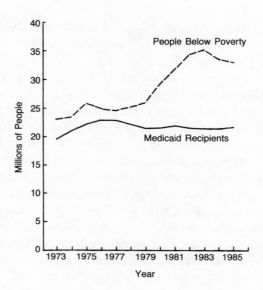

FIG. 1.   Number of Medicaid recipients
and people below poverty

Source: U.S. Bureau of the Census 1986; U.S.
House of Representatives 1987.

(Davis and Rowland 1983). Furthermore, as shown in figure 1, while
the number of individuals in poverty has been increasing, Medicaid
enrollment has been stable or declining.

Restricting Medicaid eligibility to welfare categories needs to be
reexamined. Half of the uninsured are in the work force, but are
earning marginal wages. Many of the working poor do not receive
employer-provided health coverage and cannot afford to purchase
coverage.

State income standards are also inadequate. Half of the states have
income standards below 50 percent of the federal poverty level. In
Mississippi, Alabama, and Georgia—states with large numbers of poor
blacks—there were 35 Medicaid beneficiaries for every 100 poor persons
in 1980 (Intergovernmental Health Policy Project 1981).

In 1984 and 1985 Congress required states to cover all pregnant
women and young children under state income standards regardless

of family composition. Recent action by the Congress to permit states to cover all pregnant women, children under age 6, and elderly and disabled people up to the federal poverty level is an important step. Implementation of this legislation should be carefully monitored to determine if states will expand Medicaid coverage to those poor not on welfare. Some minimum income floor on Medicaid eligibility, however, is likely to be required to assure that the poorest receive coverage. Efforts should also be pursued to encourage employers to offer coverage to all workers and their dependents.

Limited Participation of Physicians. Access to care for Medicaid beneficiaries is impeded because of limited participation in the program by physicians. While the majority of physicians nationwide report participating in the Medicaid program, almost one out of every four office-based physicians (23 percent) report that they do not accept Medicaid. Ten percent of all primary care physicians provide care to about half of Medicaid beneficiaries treated in private offices (Mitchell and Cromwell 1983).

The problem of nonparticipation is even greater within certain geographic regions and specialities. About one-third of physicians in the South (34 percent), Northeast (30 percent), and large urban areas (35 percent) report that they do not accept Medicaid patients. These findings are particularly troublesome given the concentration of poor blacks in the South and urban areas. More than one-third of obstetricians and gynecologists (37 percent), cardiologists (39 percent), and psychiatrists (40 percent) also report that they do not accept Medicaid patients. These are specialties for which there are potential benefits from improved access, given chronically high infant mortality rates among blacks and high mortality rates among black adults from diseases of the heart and violent injuries. Access to physicians with specialized knowledge and training in these disciplines could be critical for black beneficiaries who are at high risk.

Medicaid fees, by law, must be lower than fees for Medicare or private insurers. Medicaid beneficiaries, therefore, are competing with higher paying patients from the public and private sectors. Limited participation by physicians results in Medicaid beneficiaries having fewer choices and, thus, creates the conditions for a concentration of Medicaid beneficiaries with few providers. There also may be less incentive to provide high-quality care when physicians realize dissatisfied patients have a limited number of providers from which to select.

Physicians consistently cite lower reimbursement rates as the major reason for not participating in the Medicaid program. Other frequently cited important reasons were payment delays, administrative paperwork, and opposition to government's involvement in medicine. If serious attention is not given to how best to address the concerns of providers, it is conceivable that government cost-containment measures and provider fiscal constraints will further erode physicians' willingness to provide services to public program beneficiaries. The issues are complex and require careful consideration of the needs and rights of both physicians and Medicaid beneficiaries.

Quality and Adequacy of Care.   Concerns about quality of care received prominent attention in the mid-1970s following reports before the U.S. Special Committee on Aging (1976) of physicians with large Medicaid practices who were considered to provide poor quality care. Research on the quality of care received by Medicaid beneficiaries is limited. Of the studies conducted, some provide evidence of unnecessary or poor quality care; others do not (Wyszewianski and Donabedian 1981). Data do show that blacks are more likely than whites to use hospital outpatient departments and emergency rooms as their usual source of care—health care settings where the potential for some of the essential elements of good quality of care are not optimal.

The lack of data has seriously hindered the evaluation of differences in the quality and adequacy of care obtained. Although empirical evidence of inequities in quality are minimal, ample evidence exists to suggest cause for concern and to recommend an expanded focus for research on quality and continuity of care. Given the data collection mechanisms that already exist, it seems appropriate to develop and incorporate measures that can evaluate and monitor differences in the quality as well as the quantity of care obtained in the American health care system.

Medicare

Medicare, authorized under Title XVIII of the Social Security Act, finances health care for the aged and some disabled. The program has had widespread political support since its enactment in 1965 and can be credited for greatly improving access to health care services for the elderly. In 1984 almost 10 percent of the black population—2.6

million black elderly and disabled Americans—had health insurance coverage through the Medicare program (U.S. Bureau of the Census 1985).

The Medicare program was established out of desire to lessen the financial burden many of the aged faced for medical care. The 1963 Social Security survey of the aged documented that about half of the aged had no private health insurance (Merriam 1964). Insurance companies, fearful of financial losses resulting from insuring an excessive number of poor risks, were reluctant to write individual comprehensive policies for the elderly. Available policies were generally inadequate, offering limited coverage, exempting preexisting conditions, and rarely covering nursing home care in the event of infirmity or senility. Blacks particularly benefited from Medicare coverage because they tended to have lower incomes and poorer employer-related health benefits, and thus were at high risk for large uncovered medical expenses.

The Medicare program, however, went beyond relieving financial barriers to address racial barriers to health care. In part, the Medicare program worked as a vehicle for enforcement of Title VI of the Civil Rights Act of 1964. Hospitals participating in the Medicare program were required to make services available to all persons on a nondiscriminatory basis (Ball 1973). Because most hospitals chose to participate, the Medicare program helped to desegregate many hospitals, especially in the South.

Scope of Coverage

Medicare covers people aged 65 and over who receive Social Security or Railroad Retirement benefits. Beginning in 1974, benefits were also extended to disabled persons who had been receiving Social Security disability benefits and to persons with chronic renal disease. Medicare consists of two complementary parts: Part A covers hospital, nursing home, and home health services; Part B covers physician, outpatient hospital, home health and some ambulatory services.

Medicare coverage of the aged population is almost universal. Twenty-eight million aged and 3 million disabled beneficiaries were enrolled in 1986. Blacks and other minorities comprise about 10 percent of aged and 17 percent of disabled beneficiaries (U.S. Department of Health and Human Services 1984).

Part A covers all eligible persons. Those covered under Part A may voluntarily enroll in Part B by paying a premium. Nearly all beneficiaries enrolled in Part A participate in Part B. Participation in Part B has increased over time, particularly for blacks and other minorities. In 1967, 93 percent of whites were enrolled in Part B, compared to 83 percent of minorities. By 1976 this difference had narrowed considerably, with 98 percent of whites and 96 percent of minorities enrolled in Part B (Ruther and Dobson 1981).

The improvement in coverage of blacks under Part B has been attributed to the growth of the state buy-in program under the Medicaid program (Ruther and Dobson 1981). This program permits states to pay the Part B premiums, coinsurance, and deductibles for those aged and disabled on welfare. In 1967 only 27 states participated in this program; currently, all states, except Wyoming, participate in buy-in agreements (Unpublished data from the Health Care Financing Administration 1986).

Studies show that persons bought-in to Medicare by Medicaid, are older, sicker, and more likely to be minority group members than other Medicare beneficiaries. They have higher mortality rates and higher rates of hospitalization for chronic conditions, especially diabetes (McMillan et al. 1983).

About 10 percent of all Medicare enrollees are bought-in by the Medicaid program, but this varies dramatically by race and age. McMillan's study found that 9 percent of whites were bought-in to Medicare, compared to 31 percent of other races. For minorities aged 85 and over, 51 percent are covered by buy-in agreements. Recent legislation allows states the option of extending the buy-in program to Medicare enrollees with incomes up to the poverty line.

For poor elderly blacks, Medicaid is an important supplement to Medicare beyond payment of the Part B premium. Medicaid fills in the gaps in Medicare by paying the deductibles and cost-sharing requirements and providing coverage for additional services, most notably prescription drugs, dental care, and nursing home services.

Program Spending

In 1982 Medicare spent $48 billion on the elderly and disabled, of which 10 percent went toward services for minorities. As shown in table 4, two-thirds of Medicare expenditures went toward inpatient hospital care. Of the remainder, most (31 percent) went toward physician

TABLE 4

Medicare Reimbursement by Service and Race, 1982 (amount in millions)

	Hospital insurance and/or supplementary insurance	Hospital Insurance				Supplementary Medical Insurance			
		Total	Inpatient hospital services	Skilled nursing facilities	Home health services	Total	Physician and other medical services	Outpatient services	Home health services
TOTAL	$47,698	$33,092	$31,610	$402	$1,081	$14,605	$11,700	$2,900	$30
Aged	41,526	29,214	27,834	388	992	12,311	10,311	1,982	19
Disabled	6,172	3,878	3,776	14	89	2,294	1,385	909	7
WHITE									
Total	41,422	28,790	27,515	365	910	12,632	10,358	2,262	12
Aged	36,613	25,702	24,508	354	841	10,911	9,239	1,660	12
Disabled	4,809	3,088	3,007	11	69	1,721	1,119	602	—
BLACK & OTHER									
Total	5,048	3,451	3,281	26	144	1,597	1,036	556	6
Aged	3,805	2,736	2,586	24	126	1,069	797	267	6
Disabled	1,243	715	695	2	18	528	239	289	—

Source: Annual Medicare program statistics, 1982, 224, 248.
NOTE: Totals do not necessarily equal sum of rounded components.

and outpatient services. Blacks accounted for about 10 percent of these expenditures. Less than 3 percent of total expenditures were spent on home health services and skilled nursing facilities.

In the early years of the Medicare program, substantial disparity in the use and reimbursement of services among white and black aged existed but, during the past twenty years, many of these differences have narrowed (Davis 1975). As shown in table 5, Medicare reimbursement per aged person enrolled averaged $1,565 for whites in 1982 and $1,604 for blacks. In contrast, in 1968 reimbursement was 40 percent higher for whites compared to blacks. This apparent gain in equity, however, provides an incomplete picture because this measure fails to account for differences in health status. Substantial evidence indicates that blacks are sicker and, therefore, require more services (Manton, Clifford, and Johnson 1987). In addition, disparities in the use of specific services continue to persist.

For aged beneficiaries, racial differences in the use of hospital inpatient services rapidly narrowed. Among the aged in 1966, whites had 70 percent higher inpatient hospitalization rates than other races (Davis 1975). This gap closed to 25 percent in 1968, 14 percent in 1975, and by 1981 elderly blacks and whites used hospital inpatient services at similar rates (U.S. Department of Health and Human Services 1984). This is also evident in reimbursement rates for inpatient services. In 1968 whites received 28 percent higher payments per person enrolled, but by 1982 blacks were receiving reimbursement at a slightly higher level than whites—$1,142 vs. $1,061.

The Medicare program has been less successful in assuring equality of treatment in other types of medical services. Differences for physicians' services have narrowed from 65 percent higher reimbursement per white enrollee compared to blacks in 1968, to 14 percent by 1982— $406 vs. $357. The remaining differential appears to reflect minorities greater use of outpatient departments. When considering reimbursement for physician and outpatient services together, there is no differential.

The most obvious remaining inequality appears to be in the distribution of benefits for skilled nursing facility (SNF) care. In 1968 whites received more than double the extended care facility benefits received by blacks and other races. In 1982 whites continued to receive one-third more benefits (U.S. Department of Health and Human Services 1984). These differences warrant further examination to determine whether disparities reflect such factors as population group

TABLE 5

Medicare Reimbursement per Aged Person Enrolled, by Type of Service and Race, 1968 and 1982

	1968			1982		
Service	White	Black & other	Ratio white:black	White	Black & other	Ratio white:black
All Medicare services	$273	$195	1.40	$1,565	$1,604	0.98
Hospital insurance	194	147	1.32	1,112	1,208	0.92
Inpatient hospital	175	137	1.28	1,061	1,142	0.93
Skilled nursing facility	17	8	2.17	15	11	1.36
Home health	—	—	—	36	56	0.64
Supplemental medical						
insurance	83	54	1.53	480	479	1.00
Physician	79	48	1.63	406	357	1.14
Outpatient services	3	5	0.62	73	120	0.61
Home health	—	—	—	1	3	0.33

Source: Davis 1975; annual Medicare program statistics, 1982, 226.

TABLE 6
Persons Served and Medicare Reimbursements per Person Served for Aged,
by Type of Service and Race, 1982

Services	White	Black & other	Ratio white:black
PERSONS SERVED PER 1,000 ENROLLEES			
All Medicare services	648.1	585.8	1.11
Hospital insurance	253.4	229.4	1.10
Inpatient hospital	245.7	218.5	1.12
Skilled nursing facility	9.7	5.9	1.64
Home health	40.4	50.0	0.81
Supplementary medical insurance	658.7	611.2	1.08
Physician services	642.7	573.7	1.12
Outpatient services	288.9	310.4	0.93
Home health	0.5	2.2	0.23
REIMBURSEMENT PER PERSON SERVED			
All Medicare services	$2,415	$2,739	0.88
Hospital insurance	4390	5264	0.83
Inpatient hospital	4318	5224	0.83
Skilled nursing facility	1578	1804	0.87
Home health	901	1112	0.81
Supplement medical insurance	729	784	0.93
Physician services	632	623	1.01
Outpatient services	253	386	0.66
Home health	1053	1136	0.93

Source: Annual Medicare program statistics, 1982, 223, 225.

differences in age or choice of service or continuing discrimination. For home health services, blacks and other races receive a higher reimbursement than whites; reimbursement, however, for all races was small.

In 1968 most of the difference in Medicare reimbursement between the races reflected a difference in the number of persons exceeding the Medicare deductible—40 percent of whites received reimbursement, compared to 30 percent of blacks (Davis 1975). In 1982, as shown in table 6, the percentage of enrollees receiving reimbursement had increased for all aged, but a differential between whites (65 percent) and blacks (59 percent) persists. Once an aged person has exceeded the deductible, reimbursement has been fairly similar throughout the program, regardless of race.

Program Impact

The burden of heavy medical expenses on the aged and their families created the impetus behind Medicare. Medicare was created to remedy the private sector's failure to provide adequate health insurance by extending comprehensive coverage to virtually all aged. It has succeeded.

Medicare has improved access to medical care. Hospital utilization, particularly by those most in need of care—individuals living alone with low incomes, minorities, residents of the South and nonmetropolitan areas—has increased significantly. Medicare may also deserve credit for the increases in life expectancy in old age. As described in the first section, there have been notable improvements in life expectancy for blacks. In addition, gains in health since the enactment of Medicare have been especially rapid for those causes of death influenced by medical care intervention and which historically have been higher among blacks. Some of this improvement reflects advances in medical practice, but the significant improvement in access to health care services resulting from financing through the Medicare program cannot be ruled out.

Remaining Problems

Despite significant progress, gaps do remain. Under the current Medicare program, beneficiaries can be liable for substantial out-of-pocket expenses. The Medicare program covers less than half of the elderly's total health care costs, requires high levels of cost-sharing, and excludes many health care services such as prescription drugs, dental care, eyeglasses, and hearing aids (Waldo and Lazenby 1984).

The incidence of illness and the financial burden of cost sharing are not related to ability to pay. Out-of-pocket health care expenditures, excluding nursing home care, represent only 2 percent of total income in families with incomes in excess of $30,000, but 21 percent of the total in families with incomes less than $5,000 (U.S. Congressional Budget Office 1983).

Elderly blacks are particularly at risk because they are more likely to have low incomes. It is estimated that today 64 percent of aged minorities have incomes below 200 percent poverty compared to 37 percent for whites. (Commonwealth Fund Commission on Elderly People Living Alone 1987). Even routine expenses can be catastrophic for many blacks.

Fear of large out-of-pocket expenses leads many aged to purchase Medicare supplementary policies to fill the gaps resulting from Medicare deductibles, coinsurance, and some of the uncovered benefits. Many older black Americans are, however, unable to afford "Medigap." Only 39 percent of elderly blacks, compared to 58 percent of elderly whites are covered by private insurance (Rowland and Lyons 1987). Some of this difference can be attributed to income. Blacks are more likely to have lower incomes and, therefore, be unable to afford Medigap policies which cost on average $400 per year (Rice and McCall 1985). As shown in table 7, however, elderly blacks are less likely to be covered by private insurance even after adjusting for income. Lack of group health insurance among blacks may reflect their employment history. Blacks are more likely to have been employed in lower paying jobs that do not offer comprehensive retirement benefits, including health insurance.

For the aged poor, some gaps are closed by Medicaid, but the current program only covers 35 percent of this vulnerable population (U.S. Bureau of the Census 1985). Recent legislation permitting states to increase Medicaid coverage of the elderly poor may offer some relief, provided that states act. In the interim, however, many poor Americans face serious financial burdens.

In recent years improvements in Medicare have been stymied by pressure to restrain federal government spending. Today, however, there is the potential for improvement by expanding the program to include catastrophic coverage for Medicare-covered services. Improving catastrophic coverage is obviously very important for the elderly and disabled with high expenditures, but it does not offer protection for lower income aged who struggle to pay for even routine medical expenses. The future agenda for Medicare ought to include help for both groups.

Primary Care

The provision of medical care depends not only on the finances to drive the system but on the physicians and clinics that make it

TABLE 7
Health Insurance Coverage of the Elderly by Income and Race

Insurance coverage	Poverty level							
	Below poverty		100–149%		150–200%		200% +	
	White	Black & other	White	Black & other	White	Black & other	White	Black & other
Total	100%	100%	100%	100%	100%	100%	100%	100%
Medicare & Medicaid	24	50	7	14	3	17	2	15
Medicare only	28	33	24	44	17	29	13	23
Medicare & private	48	17	69	42	80	54	85	62

Source: Rowland and Lyons 1987.

function. In the 1960s a consensus emerged that the United States had a physician shortage and that major new programs would be required to get physicians to the areas of greatest need (U.S. Department of Health, Education, and Welfare 1967; Carnegie Comission Report on Higher Education 1970). Poor populations in general and ethnic minority communities, in particular, were the most underserved. Although the provision of Medicare and Medicaid benefits to elderly or poor black people made them more economically attractive to the medical community, it did them little good if there were no physicians in their communities or those that were there already were fully committed.

Programs to Expand Capacity

What was called for was a strategy that would build the "capacity" of the system to treat more people—especially blacks and others in low-income, doctor-short areas. The outcome was a series of legislative measures that, while not designed as a single strategy, resulted in a formidable array of programs to augment service delivery in poor communities that generally came to be known as the "primary care programs."

In 1965 the Office of Economic Opportunity (OEO) undertook its first health projects by funding eight demonstration health centers in poor communities. These proved to be the first of more than 100 neighborhood health centers funded by the OEO and, subsequently, by the Department of Health, Education, and Welfare between 1965 and 1971 in a program that became the centerpiece of the strategy to build medical capacity in poor communities (Zwick 1972). It should be noted that the centers were conceived as agents of community development providing opportunities for community management of health services as well as employment opportunities (Geiger 1982).

In 1963 and again in 1965 amendments were made to the Social Security Act establishing a program of Maternal and Infant Care (M&I) and Children and Youth (C&Y) centers designed to meet the comprehensive needs of mothers and children in poor communities. In 1966 the Migrant Health Act was passed providing grants to establish special clinics for migrant and seasonal workers. In 1970 the National Health Service Corps was enacted for the expressed purpose of providing physicians to staff practices in underserved areas. This was followed in 1972 by the National Health Service Corps Scholarship Program designed to link support for medical education to a period of service in a shortage area (Mullan 1982).

The 1970s saw these programs grow and stabilize. The neighborhood health centers were consolidated within the Public Health Service in 1972 where they have continued as community health centers with an increased emphasis on self-sufficiency and standard medical services. The National Health Service Corps grew rapidly through the late 1970s and into the 1980s staffed increasingly by the service-obligated graduates of the National Health Service Corps (NHSC) scholarship program. In 1986 the program had 3,127 health professionals serving in shortage areas, many of which had large black populations.

Program Impact

The Community Health Center Program has fared well in recent years, despite a restrictive federal budgetary climate. In 1986 there were 650 community and migrant health centers delivering care to 5.3 million people. About 31 percent of its users nationally are black, meaning that 1.64 million blacks receive their primary care in community health centers. The percentage of community health center users that are black in the Southeast is particularly high, with states such as Mississippi and South Carolina reporting rates in excess of 70 percent.

Numerous studies have documented the effectiveness of community health centers in improving the health of the communities they have served (Davis 1985; Grossman and Goldman 1981). Black infant mortality rates have shown particular improvement in communities served by primary health care centers.

Remaining Problems and Future Issues

Other programs have not fared as well in the restrictive budgetary climate of the 1980s. The C&Y and M&I programs we're included in the Maternal and Child Health Block Grant under the 1981 Omnibus Budget Reconciliation Act. While total Maternal and Child Health funding has increased from $374 million in 1982 to $458 million in 1986, states do not report specifically on the M&I and C&Y programs, and their continued growth and effectiveness cannot be assessed.

The National Health Service Corps was a principal target of the Reagan administration. Unable to stem the tide of scholarship recipients becoming available for service, they eliminated new scholarship awards. New placements in the NHSC will, therefore, fall from 1,000 in 1986 to 200 or less from 1987 on. Over the next several years, as a result, the numbers of National Health Service Corps physicians will drop drastically, creating manpower problems in many underserved communities. Although the physician-to-population ratio in the United States is far higher now than it was at the inception of the NHSC, the "diffusion" of physicians into endemically poor communities has not been demonstrated, and, in the absence of a new, federal physician manpower program, the staffing of community health centers and the maintenance of the current levels of access to services for poor and black populations may become problematic in the near future.

Black Physicians

Another way in which the public sector has made an impact on the health care of black Americans has been through the support of medical education and training. Over the past 20 years there have been enormous gains made in the number of black medical school enrollees and black physicians. Federal initiatives in social programs, civil rights, and affirmative action in the 1960s in part spearheaded this effort.

Since the mid-1960s, the federal government has played a direct role in influencing the supply of health care providers in terms of numbers, content, and distribution. Several factors prompted the federal government's direct involvement in the health labor market, including consistent reports and forecasts of shortages in health personnel, changing societal views about public responsibility in this regard, and the context of the civil rights movement. The federal government attempted to address problems of high unemployment and access to health care for the nation's poor and ethnic minorities concurrently.

To ensure greater access to education and job training programs, the federal government developed a number of special initiatives for underrepresented minority groups and the economically disadvantaged. Between 1963 and 1976 there were four major legislative acts designed to address problems of inequities in the supply and distribution of health professionals. They included: the 1963 Health Professionals

Education Assistance Act, the 1968 Health Manpower Act, the 1971 Comprehensive Manpower and Training Act, and the 1976 Health Professionals Education Assistance Act.

As a result of these legislative acts and their amendments, massive sums of federal dollars were infused into health education and training programs. Federal expenditures grew from $122 million in 1965 to $539 million in 1974 (Wallach 1976).

In 1970 an American Association of Medical Colleges (AAMC) task force on expanding educational opportunities in medicine for blacks and other minorities put forth the goal of increasing black medical student enrollment from 2.8 percent to 12 percent based on the model of population parity—the proportion of blacks in medical school should equal the proportion in the general population—(Shea and Fullilove 1985). Between 1968 and 1986 the percentage of black medical students in first-year classes of American 'medical schools increased over two and a half fold—from 2.8 percent to 7.0 percent. This increase was not steady during these years. Black medical student enrollment peaked in 1974 at 7.5 percent, and has ranged from 6.4 percent to 7.0 percent between 1975 and 1986. Only 3 percent of all physicians currently in practice are blacks. Although there are several forces which led to an increase in black enrollment in medical schools and an increase in the number of black physicians over the past 20 years, there is little doubt that public-sector support contributed to this increase.

Program Impact

One rationale for public-sector promotion of the education of blacks in medical careers is to increase the availability of health services to the black population. This would be the case if black physicians, having finished their medical training, diffused into geographic areas and medical specialties resulting in better access to health care for black Americans.

Several studies have indicated that this is occurring. Lloyd, Johnson, and Mann (1978) interviewed 311 physicians from the graduating classes of Howard University from 1955 to 1975 and found that black graduates had a higher percentage of black and low-income patients than all American graduates combined. A study of 1975 medical school graduates fround that 56 percent of black graduates had practices composed primarily of black patients, as opposed to 8 to 14 percent of other groups of graduates that year (Keith et al. 1985).

Black medical students are somewhat more likely to receive public-sector financial support than are other students. A higher percentage of black medical school enrollees come from low- and moderate-income families, compared to white enrollees. The Association of American Medical Colleges (1983, 1985) annual survey of seniors in medical school found that the proportion of minorities who had NHSC scholarships was higher than the proportion for nonminority students. The Health Professions Scholarship Program, the Health Professions Loan Program, the federally insured (and subsidized) student loan programs and armed forces scholarships also have helped many black physicians from low-income families support their years in training. Indirect support has also come from institutional aid to medical schools. Howard University along with Meharry Medical College, which prior to 1968 educated the majority of graduating black physicians and practicing black physicians, receives substantial federal support.

Remaining Problems and Future Issues

Despite efforts to increase the number of black physicians, the original goal was not achieved. Little progress has been made in the past decade to increase further the number of black physicians. This is particularly troubling in the current climate of forces that are shaping the health industry. Although there appears to be an overall adequate supply of physicians, there is a clear deficit in the number of black physicians (Iglehart 1986).

Career choices in medicine by talented black students may be further hindered by perceptions of the experiences of black physicians. There is a growing concern among some black leaders and medical societies that national policy goals of a health care market free of government intervention with more competition will lead to erosion of their current market share by large for-profit enterprises and that quality of care will ultimately suffer. This could potentially lead to a further displacement of black physicians and patients from the mainstream of American medicine.

There is also the concern that new payment innovations in federal programs such as prospective payment and capitation that employ fixed payments will discriminate against black physicians since their case mix is different. Patient populations of black physicians are largely Medicaid, low-income, and chronically ill patients. Some black physicians claim that their opportunities to compensate for such changes by diversifying their patient populations are limited due to discrimination by institutions, physicians, and patients.

Economic pressures may also work against the future supply of black physicians. Medical school tuitions are increasing and the NHSC scholarship program is being phased out. Although the medical profession as compared to other professions has been an excellent investment for most physicians, this is less true for black physicians since their incomes generally are less and their debt is higher. If the opportunity costs are too high, black students may not enter the medical field or once having entered the field, may choose to abandon it.

There is little likelihood that population parity of black physicians will come about under the status quo. Public-sector initiatives have helped in making great strides in the number of black physicians over the past twenty years. Private-sector support cannot be relied on alone to respond to this crisis. New directed programs to stimulate black enrollment in medical schools and continued sources of support for low-income blacks will be necessary in the current health care environment.

Implications for Future Public Policy

This article presents evidence that access to health care has improved considerably for many black Americans. Yet, on several important indicators of access, black/white differences remain. Moreover, gains achieved have not been shared evenly across subgroups of the black population. Disparities persist for blacks who are uninsured, who are under the age of 17 or over the age of 65, and who live in the South or in rural parts of the country. Some of the findings have immediate implications for public policy.

First, although the gap between blacks and whites with no health coverage has declined, the trend since 1978 has been an increase in the percentage of both black and white Americans with no health coverage. With 6.3 million black Americans estimated to be uninsured in 1984, it would mean that about one in four black Americans face a potential financial barrier in access to ambulatory and hospital care.

(Sulvetta and Swartz 1986). Efforts to expand health coverage to black Americans along with other Americans who lack coverage are therefore crucial.

Second, black Americans are still twice as likely as whites to be without a regular source of care and to identify a hospital outpatient department or emergency room as the source of physician visits. In the last twenty years, noticeable gains in reversing these patterns have been achieved. The consequences of not having a health care provider who serves as an entry point into the health care system or who monitors the care received, however, could be more serious now than ever before. It unquestionably presents a barrier in access to care. It also leaves an individual vulnerable to the more costly forms of care which could have been avoided with earlier entry into the system or better management of care. The American health care system is highly decentralized and complex with its specialties and subspecialties. For a system that seems large and impersonal, a primary provider who can facilitate the linkage with the most appropriate form of care could conceivably make a difference in when and if health services are sought. Since black Americans suffer disproportionately from chronic conditions such as hypertension, diabetes, and heart disease, continuity in management of care is as essential as access to care.

Concerns about a regular source of care are critical at this juncture in history for several reasons. In recent years, the federal government has reduced financial support for programs designed to improve the supply of physicians in underserved areas. One of the barriers to identifying a regular source of care is the physical availability of providers in a neighborhood. The findings of this study suggest that further efforts to expand the physical availability of services may be warranted. Strengthening community health centers, establishing incentives for providers to work in shortage areas, and supporting blacks entering medical school are ways of fulfilling that need.

Third, much of the data reported do not yet reflect the effects of federal changes in health financing and delivery programs in the 1980s. The federal government's retreat from the regulation and financing of health services will likely exacerbate existing differences. The changing health marketplace has advantages and disadvantages for black Americans. Those who must compete in a marketplace with limited bargaining power will be met with the greatest resistance.

Although blacks and whites have shown comparable gains in health status during the last two decades, major disparities by race remain. According to a number of other indicators, the health of black Americans continues to lag behind that of whites and contributes to suffering, disability, work-loss days, and medical expenditures. Black infants are still twice as likely as white infants to die during the first year of life and black adults are twice as likely as white adults to die of stroke, diabetes, and certain types of cancer. The gap that persists presents an agonizing dilemma for the health care system and this nation. Government health financing and delivery programs, however, have played a critical role in improvements in health and access to care which have occurred thus far.

More research is obviously needed to look at factors explaining these differentials and to form a groundwork for policy proposals to eliminate these differences. Most important, the consequences of cutbacks in major health financing and delivery programs in the last few years need to be monitored closely to detect any possible reversal of the gains that have been achieved with such difficulty over the last twenty years.

To redress remaining differences in equitable access to health care services for black Americans, the following policy actions are recommended:

1. Expand health insurance coverage under Medicaid and private employer-based health insurance plans to close the gaps in health care coverage.

2. Develop new systems of financing long-term care services, including home health and nursing home care.

3. Maintain and expand funding of primary care programs that serve disadvantaged populations and assure the availability of care in underserved communities. Renew efforts to encourage blacks to enter the medical profession.

4. Encourage physician and hospital participation in the Medicaid program by bringing reimbursement rates into line with the Medicare program.

5. Assure freedom of choice of a range of health care providers to all beneficiaries of Medicare, Medicaid, and employer health plans, including choice among managed care plans such as health maintenance organizations and among fee-for-service providers.

6. Enforce quality standards and nondiscrimination provisions on

all providers participating in public and private insurance plans, with particular attention to nursing home care and new managed-care plans.

7. Expand efforts to improve use of preventive health services and to assure ongoing continuity in the management of chronic health conditions.

8. Expand funding for data collection, monitoring, and research to further identify and understand the contributing causes of racial differences in health status and access to care.

References

Association of American Medical Colleges. 1983, 1985. *Minority Students in Medical Education: Facts and Figures.* Washington.

Ball, R.M. 1973. Unpublished talk before the Health Staff Seminar. Washington, D.C. (October).

Carnegie Commission Report on Higher Education. 1970. *Education and the Nation's Health: Policies for Medical and Dental Education.* New York: McGraw-Hill.

Commonwealth Fund Commission on Elderly People Living Alone. 1987. *Old, Alone and Poor: A Plan for Reducing Poverty among Elderly People Living Alone.* New York. Commonwealth Fund.

Davis, K. 1975. Equal Treatment and Unequal Benefits: The Medicare Program. *Milbank Memorial Fund Quarterly/Health and Society* 53(4):449–88.

———. 1985. Access to Health Care: A Matter of Fairness. In *Health Care: How to Improve It and Pay for It.* Washington: Center for National Policy.

Davis, K., and M. Lillie-Blanton. 1986. Health Care for Black Americans: Trends in Financing and Delivery. Paper prepared for the National Academy of Sciences Panel on Health Status and Demography of Black Americans, Woods Hole, Mass., July.

Davis, K., and D. Rowland. 1983. Uninsured and Underserved: Inequities in Health Care in the United States. *Milbank Memorial Fund Quarterly/Health and Society* 61(2):149–76.

Davis, K., and C. Schoen. 1978. *Health and the War on Poverty: A Ten Year Appraisal.* Washington: Brookings Institution.

Geiger, H.J. 1982. Community Health Centers: Health Care as an Instrument of Social Change. In *Reforming Medicine: Lessons of the Last Quarter Century,* ed. V.W. Sidel and R. Sidel, 11–32. New York: Pantheon.

Grossman, M., and F. Goldman. 1981. The Responsiveness and Impacts of Public Health Policy: The Case of Community Health Centers. Paper presented at the 109th annual meeting of the American Public Health Association, Los Angeles, November.

Hadley, J. 1982. *More Medical Care, Better Health?* Washington: Urban Institute.

Howell, E., L. Corder, and A. Dobson. 1985. Out-of-Pocket Health Expenses for Medicaid and Other Poor and Near Poor Persons in 1980. *National Medical Care Utilization and Expenditure Survey,* series B, descriptive report no. 4. DHHS pub. no. 85-20204. Washington: Office of Research and Demonstrations, Health Care Financing Administration.

Iglehart, J.K. 1986. The Future Supply of Physicians. *New England Journal of Medicine* 314(13):860–64.

Intergovernmental Health Policy Project. 1981. *Recent and Proposed Changes in State Medicaid Programs: A Fifty State Survey.* Washington.

Keith, S.N., R.M. Bell, A.G. Swanson, and A.P. Williams. 1985. Effects of Affirmative Action in Medical School: A Study of the Class of 1975. *New England Journal of Medicine* 313(24):1519–25.

Link, C., S. Long, and R. Settle. 1982. Access to Medical Care under Medicaid: Differentials by Race. *Journal of Health, Policy and Law* 7(2):345–65.

Lloyd, S.M., G.D. Johnson, and M. Mann. 1978. Survey of Graduates of a Traditionally Black College of Medicine. *Journal of Medical Education* 53:640–50.

Manton, K., P. Clifford, and K. Johnson. 1987. Health Differentials between Blacks and Whites: Recent Trends in Mortality and Morbidity. *Milbank Quarterly* 65. (Suppl. 2)

McMillan, A., P. Pine, M. Gornick, and R. Prihoda. 1983. A Study of the "Crossover Population": Aged Persons Entitled to Both Medicare and Medicaid. *Health Care Financing Review* 4(4):19–46.

Merriam, I.A. 1964. Testimony before the Subcommittee on Health of the Elderly of the Senate Special Committee on Aging. 88(2):1–13. Washington.

Mitchell, J., and J. Cromwell. 1983. Access to Private Physicians for Public Patients: Participation in Medicaid and Medicare. In *Securing Access to Health Care,* President's Commission for the Study of Ethical Problems in Medicine and Biomedical and Behavioral Research, 105–30. Washington.

Mullan, F. 1982. The National Health Service Corps and Health

Personnel Innovations: Beyond Poorhouse Medicine. In *Reforming Medicine: Lessons of the Last Quarter Century,* ed. V. Sidel and R. Sidel, 176–200. New York: Pantheon.

O'Brien, M.D., J. Rodgers, and D. Baugh. 1985. *Ethnic and Racial Patterns in Enrollment, Health Status, and Health Services Utilization in the Medicaid Population.* series B, descriptive report no. 8, Health Care Financing Administration, September 30.

President's Commission for the Study of Ethical Problems in Medicine and Biomedical and Behavioral Research. 1983. Securing Access to Health Care: A Report on the Ethical Implications of Differences in the Availability of Health Services. Washington.

Rice, T., and N. McCall. 1985. The Extent of Ownership and the Characteristics of Median Supplemental Policies. *Inquiry* 22:188–200.

Rowland, D., and B. Lyons, 1987. Data from the 1984 National Health Interview Survey, Prepared for the Commonwealth Fund Commission on Elderly People Living Alone. Baltimore: Johns Hopkins University. (Unpublished.)

Ruther, M., and A. Dobson. 1981. Unequal Treatment and Unequal Benefits: A Re-Examination of the Use of Medicare Services by Race, 1967–1976. *Health Care Financing Review* 2(3):55–83.

Shea, S., and M. Fullilove. 1985. Entry of Black and Other Minority Students into U.S. Medical Schools: Historical Perspective and Recent Trends. *New England Journal of Medicine* 313(15):933–40.

Sulvetta, M., and K. Swartz. 1986. *The Uninsured and Uncompensated Care.* Washington: National Health Policy Forum.

Taylor, A.K. 1983. Inpatient Hospital Services: Use, Expenditures, and Sources of Payment. DHHS pub. no. (PHS 83-3360). Rockville, Md.: National Center for Health Services Research.

Trevino, F.M., and A.J. Moss. 1983. Health Insurance Coverage and Physician Visits among Hispanic and Non-Hispanic People. In *Health, United States, 1983,* 89–94. DHSS pub. no. (PHS) 84-1232. Washington.

U.S. Bureau of the Census. 1985. Characteristics of Households and Persons Receiving Selected Noncash Benefits: 1984. *Current Population Reports,* series P-60, no. 150, Washington.

———. 1986. *Statistical Abstract of the U.S., 1986.* Washington.

U.S. Congressional Budget Office. 1983. *Changing the Structure of Medicare Benefits: Issues and Options.* Washington.

U.S. Department of Health and Human Services. 1980. *Health of the Disadvantaged, Chart Book II.* DHHS pub. no. (HRA) 80-633. Hyattsville, Md.: U.S. Health Resources Administration.

———. 1984. *Annual Medicare Program Statistics, 1982.* HCFA pub. no. 03189. Washington.

———. 1985a. *Health, United States, 1985.* DHHS pub. no. (PHS) 86-1232. Washington.

———. 1985b. *Health Status of Minorities and Low-income Groups.* DHHS pub. no. (HRSA) HRS-P-DV85-1. Washington.

U.S. Department of Health, Education, and Welfare. 1967. *Health Manpower Perspective, 1967.* DHEW pub. no. 1667. Bureau of Health Manpower. Washington.

U.S. House of Representatives. 1987. *Background Material and Data on Programs within the Jurisdiction of the Committee on Ways and Means.* Pub. no. (WMCP) 100-4. Washington.

U.S. Special Committee on Aging. 1976. Fraud and Abuse among Practitioners Participating in the Medicaid Program. Washington.

Waldo, D., and H. Lazenby. 1984. Demographic Characteristics and Health Care Use and Expenditures by the Aged in the United States: 1977–1984. *Health Care Financing Review* 6(1):1–30.

Wallach, S. 1976. Health, Budget Options for Fiscal Year 1977: A Report to the Senate and House Committees on the Budget, March. (Unpublished.)

Wilensky, G.R., and D.C. Walden. 1981. Minorities, Poverty, and the Uninsured. Paper presented at the 109th annual meeting of the American Public Health Association, Los Angeles.

Wyszewianski, L., and A. Donabedian. 1981. Equity in Distribution of Quality of Care. *Medical Care* 19 Supplement (12):29–56.

Zwick, D. 1972. Some Accomplishments and Findings of Neighborhood Health Centers. *Milbank Memorial Fund Quarterly/Health and Society* 50(4):387–420.

Constraining the Supply of Physicians: Effects on Black Physicians

RUTH S. HANFT and
CATHERINE C. WHITE

A FTER TEN YEARS OF PROGRESS, FROM THE MID-1960s to the mid-1970s, the movement to bring blacks into the mainstream of American medicine, both as providers and consumers, appears to be marking time or retrogressing. The report of the Graduate Medical Education National Advisory Committee (GMENAC) in 1982 predicted a surplus of physicians, although it noted that the "surplus" did not apply to minority, including black, physicians (see appendix note). While there is a continuing dispute about the predictions of a surplus of physicians, the theme of surplus has contributed to withdrawal of federal funds from both institutions and students, negatively affecting the socioeconomic make-up of the total medical school applicant pool, minority enrollment, and active efforts of some medical schools to attract and retain minority students. The commitment of the government and educational communities to increase the representation of minority health professionals has waned, and financial support has declined substantially.

Of particular importance is the current retrenchment in the provision of funds for financial assistance to medical and other health profession students. The change in levels and types of student assistance can be expected to erode much of the progress made thus far. There has already been a negative impact on the enrollment of low-income students in medical schools (U.S. Department of Health and Human Services 1987). The change in student aid is also affecting the proportion of black students entering college, with long-range effects on the medical school black applicant pool.

In 1985 there were an estimated 15,600 black physicians (53.7 per 100,000 black population compared to 218.5 total physicians per 100,000 total United States population) representing only 3 percent of the total physician population. It is projected that, if current trends continue, this number will increase to only 28,500 (79.7 per 100,000 black population compared to 260 total physicians per 100,000 total population) by the year 2000, at which time black physicians will represent 4.1 percent of total physicians (Department of Health and Human Services 1986a). Actual current data suggest that these estimates may be optimistic.

Historical Background

From 1920 to 1968 two medical schools, Meharry Medical College and Howard University School of Medicine, were responsible for graduating the vast majority of black physicians. All other medical schools graduated a total of 15 to 20 black physicians a year during that period (Shea and Fullilove 1985). Even as late as 1948, one-third of the existing 78 medical schools imposed a color bar, and it was not until 1966 that all medical schools were opened to blacks (Morais 1976; Shea and Fullilove 1985). Until the early 1950s there were also "quotas" that affected Jews and Catholics. These quotas, however, disappeared during the 1950s and 1960s.

As Morais notes, however, opening the doors of all medical schools to blacks did little to increase the number of blacks admitted. In 1967–1968, there were almost two applicants for every first-year place. Admission standards were high, and black applicants were at an educational and cultural disadvantage. Only 6 percent of college-age blacks were enrolled in college in 1967. More than half "were in predominantly Negro institutions, where the dropout rate averaged more than 50 percent" (Morais 1976). Recognizing this problem, the American Medical Association and the National Medical Association issued a joint statement in 1968 in which they called for "development of special college courses for promising black students, summer programs of special study and additional scholarship aid at both college and medical school levels." At that time, there were an estimated 6,000 black physicians, representing 2 percent of all practicing physicians (Morais 1976). Subsequently, the greatest *relative* gain occurred by 1975.

The impetus to increase the number of minority physicians stemmed not only from the desire to assure equal access to all levels and types of education for all population groups, but from the need for more physicians who would provide care to underserved urban and rural communities, the populations of which were disproportionately black (Keith et al. 1985; Berk, Bernstein, and Taylor 1982).

A comparison of the practice patterns of black physicians with all physicians in 1973 showed that black physicians were practicing in the inner-city and ghetto areas of urban communities in higher proportions than the general physician population, were found in higher proportions in the primary care specialties, and tended to have a patient clientele that was mostly black (Gray 1977). Other studies showed that "physicians are most likely to practice among members of their own ethnic group" (Strelnick et al. 1986). Thus, policies that would encourage the entry of black physicians into the medical profession were believed essential to the success of any program designed to bring medical care to the poor and underserved (Association of American Medical Colleges 1970). No studies exist as to whether locational and specialty patterns are matters of choice or opportunity, although some survey data show that black students indicate choice patterns differently from their white counterparts.

From the mid-1960s to the early 1970s, medical schools were also being urged and encouraged to expand first-year entering classes to meet a projected physician shortage. Federal funding of medical education began in 1963. In 1965 funds were given to schools to expand enrollment, and in 1971 legislation was enacted to pay schools on the basis of the number of students. Medical school enrollment had not kept up with population expansion or advances in medical technology and extended life expectancy. With an expansion of medical school places, an opportunity existed to increase minority enrollment substantially without displacing nonminority students.

In 1970 the Association of American Medical Colleges (AAMC) committed itself to increase the representation of blacks (and other minorities—as yet a relatively small number) in the first-year entering classes to 12 percent of the total by 1975, a goal endorsed by the American Medical Association and other leading medical organizations

(Association of American Medical Colleges 1970; Shea and Fullilove 1985). The 12 percent was based on the proportion of the black population to total population or "parity."

We will now examine the assumptions behind the one series of projections that indicated achievement of the AAMC goal was possible in the time frame of five years. In 1970 blacks comprised 6 percent of the freshman enrollment in undergraduate colleges. Approximately 6 percent of enrolled black freshmen indicated an interest in attending medical school, compared to 4 to 6 percent of white freshmen. At that time, 25 percent of those blacks who indicated interest in attending medical school actually applied (this was referred to in the AAMC report as the retention rate), compared to 35 percent of whites. According to the AAMC report, the acceptance rate for black applicants was, historically, 75 percent. The AAMC calculations showed if the black retention rate could be raised to that of whites (i.e., 35 percent), the short-term goal of raising black representation in first-year entering classes to parity could be achieved. The report does not give the basis for its projections of the increase in numbers of black college freshmen, but this point is almost moot, since, in fact, the number of black applicants to medical school for the years projected was greater than the projections (Association of American Medical Colleges 1985). What was greatly overestimated was the acceptance rate. Efforts to trace the reasons for the decline of the acceptance rate from 75 percent as stated in the 1970 report to the 43 percent reported for 1974 have been unsuccessful. In 1974 there were 2,423 black applicants to medical school. If 75 percent had been accepted, blacks would have represented about 12 percent of the entering medical school class of 1974.

Federal monies, in the form of scholarship programs and low-interest loan programs, were appropriated to support the AAMC's goal (Hall and Whybrow 1984). Additionally, affirmative action programs were introduced at all levels of higher education in an attempt to enlarge the potential pool of qualified applicants, and to overcome problems caused by lack of access to quality education resulting from years of de facto segregation. Admissions criteria were broadened, both at the undergraduate level and at professional schools, to include noncognitive measures of academic potential. Remedial programs were instituted to provide special attention to areas such as test-taking and study methods in order to improve the probability of success of the expanding minority enrollment (Keith et al. 1985). In addition, two minority schools were developed in the 1970s, Charles Drew Postgraduate Medical School, which is part of the University of California at Los Angeles, and Morehouse Medical College in Atlanta. (Schools referred to as minority schools are predominantly designed for black students.) The Charles Drew School began as a postgraduate school and now educates third- and fourth-year students. Morehouse is a private medical school.

In medicine, these actions quickly showed positive returns, though falling far short of the AAMC's stated goals. By 1975 black representation in the first-year entering classes had increased to 7.5 percent and minorities as a whole represented 10 percent of first-year medical school enrollment (Hanft, Fishman, and Evans 1983). During the next ten years, however, enrollment of nonminorities increased at a faster rate than that of minorities, so that by 1985 the 1,117 black first-year medical students represented only 6.6 percent of first-year enrollment, an actual decrease proportionately from the 1975 peak (table 1) (Hanft, White, and Fishman 1986).

Though some questioned the premise that affirmative action programs would improve access to health care for minority and low-income populations, recent studies show that blacks and other minority graduates are indeed serving or expect to serve in inner-city areas and are training in primary care specialties at greater rates than nonminorities (Keith et al. 1985; Gregory, Wells, and Leake 1986; Lloyd and Johnson 1982). A 1986 report to the Association of Minority Health Professions Schools showed that 28 percent of matriculants at Howard, Meharry, and Morehouse planned on locating their practice in inner-city areas; this compared to 12 percent of matriculants at nonminority schools. This same distribution was found for the years 1978, 1980, and 1983 (Hanft and White 1986).

Undergraduate Trends

The potential applicant pool for professional colleges and schools has been deleteriously affected by declining enrollment rates for all population groups at undergraduate institutions. The rate of increase in all enrollments declined from 8 percent for the period of 1975 to 1980 to 1.2 percent from 1980 to 1984 (American Council on Education

TABLE 1

Black Enrollment in First-year Classes in U.S. Medical Schools, Academic
Years 1969–1970 through 1985–1986*

	Total first-year enrollment	First-year black enrollment	Percentage of blacks of total first-year enrollment
1985–1986	16,963	1,117	6.6%
1984–1985	16,997	1,148	6.8
1983–1984	17,150	1,173	6.8
1982–1983	17,254	1,145	6.6
1981–1982	17,268	1,196	6.9
1980–1981	17,186	1,128	6.6
1979–1980	16,930	1,108	6.5
1978–1979	16,501	1,061	6.4
1977–1978	16,136	1,085	6.7
1976–1977	15,613	1,040	6.7
1975–1976	15,295	1,036	6.8
1974–1975	14,763	1,106	7.5
1973–1974	14,154	1,027	7.3
1972–1973	13,677	957	7.0
1971–1972	12,361	882	7.1
1970–1971	11,348	697	6.1
1969–1970	10,422	440	4.2

* Includes new entrants, repeaters, reentrants, and those continuing their initial
year. Data include three Puerto Rican medical schools, whose students are recorded
in the "total" column.
Sources: Association of American Medical Colleges, 1986b, and earlier issues; 1983.

1986). This slowing trend is partially accounted for by the downward
trend in the size of the 18- and 19-year-old population group, which
began in 1980. For blacks, there has been a 4 percent decrease in
the number of 18- and 19-year-olds since 1980; during the same
period, black enrollment at both four-year and two-year colleges declined
3.3 percent (American Council on Education 1986).

But the decline in enrollments cannot be attributed solely to declining
population figures. The cost of undergraduate tuition and fees has
risen an average of 9 percent per year at public four-year institutions
and 10 percent per year at private institutions during the past ten
years (Gutek 1985). At the same time, sources and levels of financial

assistance have declined or have been withdrawn, making it all the more difficult for lower-income students to obtain a postsecondary education (Tuckson 1984; Thomas 1986).

The decline in the college-age population group, coupled with ever-increasing costs of postsecondary education, only serves to make the task of increasing black representation in all areas of professional education more difficult. In 1984 blacks still accounted for only 8 percent of the undergraduate enrollment at four-year institutions, and received only 6.5 percent of the undergraduate degrees awarded (Baratz et al. 1985). Recent data on minority medical school enrollments and graduations are at least as discouraging. If the United States is to keep its commitment to provide access to quality medical care to all segments of its population, it must also fulfill its promise to supply the means by which the less fortunate may share in the wealth of quality education available in this country.

Applicants/Acceptances

During the early 1970s, the acceptance rates for blacks were higher than those for nonminority students; as noted earlier, the Association of American Medical Colleges reported acceptance rates for blacks at 75 percent prior to 1970, when the rate for whites was reported to be about 45 percent. By 1974, however, the rate of acceptance for blacks had declined to 43 percent and continued to decline to 41 percent by 1985. It dipped to a low of 39 percent in 1981. During the same period, acceptance rates for all students rose from 35 percent to 52 percent (table 2) (Hanft, White, and Fishman 1986).

In 1981 there were 2,644 black applicants to medical school, comprising 7.2 percent of the total applicant pool; 1,037 or 39.2 percent of these were accepted. In 1985 the number of applicants decreased by 8.2 percent to 2,428. Because of a steeper decline in the total applicant pool to medical schools, the proportion of applicants who were black actually rose slightly to 7.4 percent (table 2). Forty-one percent (993 individuals) of the black applicants in 1985 were accepted, and 38 percent (923) actually enrolled. This compares to the enrollment of 49 percent of all applicants (Association of American Medical Colleges 1986b).

TABLE 2

Total Applicants and Percentage of Acceptances to U.S. Medical Schools, 1974 to 1985

		Total	Non-minority	Total minority*	Blacks	Blacks as percentage of applicants
1985–1986	Total number	32,893	29,572	3,321	2,428	7.4%
	percentage	52	53	45	41	
1981–1982	Total number	36,727	33,186	3,541	2,644	7.2
	percentage	47	48	42	39	
1977–1978	Total number	40,557	37,258	3,299	2,487	6.1
	percentage	39	39	40	39	
1974–1975	Total number	42,624	39,450	3,174	2,423	5.7
	percentage	35	35	44	43	

* Includes blacks, Mexican-Americans, mainland Puerto Ricans, native Americans, Asian/Pacific Islanders.
Source: Association of American Medical Colleges 1985, 1986b.

Enrollment

In 1967, 83 percent of all black first-year students were enrolled at the two minority medical schools, Howard and Meharry. The remaining 34 blacks represented 0.4 percent of first-year students at nonminority medical schools (Shea and Fullilove 1985). Following federal initiatives in the late 1960s and the announced commitment of the medical community leadership to increasing the number and percentage of black and minority physicians, the number of blacks in all first-year classes increased. By 1974 there were 1,106 blacks enrolled in first-year classes, 17.6 percent at the two minority schools, with the remainder representing 6.3 percent of all first-year students at the nonminority schools (Epps 1986; Shea and Fullilove 1985).

Since 1974, as the total first-year medical school class continued to increase in size, blacks as a proportion of the total first-year class have lost ground, although continuing to make absolute gains in numbers until the last several years. Following the opening of Morehouse College of Medicine in 1978, the proportion of first-year black medical students at the three minority medical schools rose to 24.9 percent, but by 1985 this had once again declined to 17.5 percent (table 3). (Charles Drew Postgraduate School of Medicine also opened in the late 1970s. Data on student enrollment at Charles Drew are included in the data for the University of California at Los Angeles and are not separately identifiable.) In part, this decline reflected the reduction in first-year places at Meharry Medical School by 40 students, a result of recommendations from the Liaison Committee on Medical Education to reduce enrollment (Tuckson 1984). In addition, Morehouse has not yet been able to increase its enrollment from 32 students per year to the planned 64. The number of black first-year students (including students repeating the first year) peaked at 1,196 in 1981, but since 1983 has been declining and was at 1,117 in 1985, below the figure for 1980 (Hanft, White, and Fishman 1986).

While concerns about a surplus of physicians are not the reason for reduction in enrollment at Meharry or the problem of increasing enrollment at Morehouse, a number of individuals and organizations have called for a cutback in enrollment. In addition, a number of medical schools, primarily the lower-cost public schools, have reduced enrollment in the last several years.

The reasons for reductions are complex and include a decline in

TABLE 3

Black Enrollment in First-year Classes by Majority/Minority Medical Schools, Academic Years 1977–1978 through
1985–1986

	Total black first-year enrollment	Blacks at majority schools	Percentage of total black enrollment	Blacks at minority schools*	Percentage of total black enrollment
1985–1986	1,117	922	82.5%	195	17.5%
1984–1985	1,148	952	82.9	196	17.1
1983–1984	1,173	955	81.4	218	18.6
1982–1983	1,145	934	81.6	211	18.4
1981–1982	1,196	912	76.3	284	23.7
1980–1981	1,128	856	75.9	272	24.1
1979–1980	1,108	832	75.1	276	24.9
1978–1979	1,061	802	75.6	259	24.4
1977–1978	1,085	865	79.7	220	20.3

* Includes Howard University, Morehouse School of Medicine, and Meharry Medical College.
Source: Association of American Medical Colleges, 1986b, and earlier issues.

the number of applicants, state fiscal constraints, and national pressure to reduce enrollment because of concerns with surplus. The decline in first-year places, however, combined with the change in acceptance rates for whites and blacks, bodes ill for increasing black participation in medicine.

In 1985, ten years beyond the target date set by the Association of American Medical Colleges, only five of the 122 medical schools (excluding Howard, Meharry, and Morehouse) could report that blacks comprised 12 percent of total enrollment, the proportion of blacks to total population. These were the University of Illinois, the College of Medicine and Dentistry of New Jersey (CMDNJ), Michigan State University, Southern Illinois University, and East Carolina University. Another four nonminority schools reported black enrollment of 10 to 12 percent. These nine schools, representing 8 percent of nonminority schools, had a total of 577 black students enrolled—18 percent of the total black medical student enrollment at all nonminority schools. Forty of the 122 nonminority medical schools in 1985 had 3 percent or less black enrollment, and more than half of the nonminority schools had the same or a smaller percentage of blacks in 1985 than in 1978. These discrepancies cannot be accounted for solely on the basis of population distribution (Baratz et al. 1985; Hanft, Fishman, and Evans 1983). The data suggest that the majority of medical schools are not actively pursuing the stated goals of increasing black participation in medicine. Certainly, the enrollment trends of the last five to ten years do not presage an expanded role for blacks in the medical education process, either as students or faculty.

Retention

The plateau in the enrollment of blacks is all the more discouraging when one examines data relating to successful graduation of this minority group. Data published by the Association of American Medical Colleges (1985) for the entering classes of 1978, 1979, and 1980 show attrition rates between 10 and 12 percent for black students actually entering the fourth year of medical school. In 1985, 17 percent of blacks repeated the first year—an increase from 14 percent in 1978—and 6 percent repeated one or more of the remaining three years. For all other students, the comparable figures were 3 percent attrition, with 3.3 percent repeating the first year and 1.1 percent repeating one or more years two through four (Association of American Medical Colleges 1985; Hanft, White, and Fishman 1986).

Attrition rates vary widely, but studies show that an institution committed to ensuring that qualified individuals are given every opportunity to complete their studies can achieve positive results in enhanced graduation rates and overall retention. For example, at the University of Illinois, only 55 percent of minorities in the classes from 1969 to 1978 graduated on time, with total attrition amounting to 18.75 percent. The introduction of an enhanced support program aimed at assisting minorities in the areas of test-taking, study skills, and stress reduction, resulted in an increase in the percentage graduating on time (to 72.5 percent), and a reduction in total attrition to 6.7 percent (Payne et al. 1986).

A similar intervention program introduced at the University of North Carolina, Chapel Hill, resulted in significantly improved performance by minority students on the National Boards Part I (Frierson 1984). Since passing this examination is required for advancement to the third year of medical school, successful programs such as this tend to reduce the time required for graduation. Other intervention programs described in applications for Health Careers Opportunity grants emphasize the low or zero attrition rates for students who have participated (U.S. Department of Health and Human Services 1987). Unfortunately, the enrollment and graduation data for blacks and other minorities suggest that relatively few schools are making a serious effort either to increase the proportion of minorities enrolled, or to ensure the successful completion of studies for those that are enrolled.

Costs of Medical Education

The fact remains, though, that retention and intervention programs cannot directly overcome a major obstacle to obtaining a medical education—cost. In 1985 a student entering medical school faced, on average, a minimum four-year cost of about $46,000 at public schools and $89,000 at a private school (Hanft, White, and Fishman 1986). Senior medical school students in 1985 graduated with average debts of $30,256, an increase of 12.5 percent over the previous year (Association of American Medical Colleges 1986a; U.S. Department of Health and

Human Services 1986b). Repayment of loans with interest can be daunting for all but the most affluent and those willing to assume high debt. For individuals from lower-income groups, the costs of medical education, with the attendant burden on themselves and their families, are overwhelming. In addition, census data indicate that the mean income of black health professionals is considerably less than that of the majority health professionals, making it more difficult to repay debt. In 1980 there was a $10,000 annual difference in the mean income between black and white health professionals (U.S. Bureau of the Census 1984).

Family resources to meet these financial burdens are limited, especially so for minority students. A comparison of family income reported by matriculants at medical schools shows a lower percentage from lower-income families in 1985 than in 1978. In 1978, 49 percent of minority school matriculants reported parental income below the median range for all students, compared to 37 percent of nonminority school matriculants. By 1985 these figures had changed to show 34 percent of minority school matriculants and 27 percent of nonminority school matriculants with parental income below the median for all matriculants (Hanft and White 1986). A recent report to Congress cites data showing that a "disproportionate share of recent applicants are coming from more affluent families" (U.S. Department of Health and Human Services 1986b).

The Hanft and White (1986) report also shows that students entered medical school with substantially more education debt in 1985 than in 1978. Whereas, in 1978, 54 percent of minority school matriculants and 70 percent of nonminority school matriculants reported no educational debt on entry into medical school, less than one-half of matriculants in both groups reported no educational debt in 1985. Nine percent of minority and 5 percent of nonminority school matriculants reported debts in excess of $6,000 in 1978. Those reporting debts over $6,000 had increased to 18 percent of minority and 24 percent of nonminority school matriculants by 1985. One recent study of medical student indebtedness notes that greater access to low-interest loans and scholarships for students from low socioeconomic backgrounds may account for the lower debt amounts reported by minority students (Bazzoli, Adams, and Thran 1986). But continued access appears to be in jeopardy.

Concomitant changes occurred from 1978 to 1985 in the percentages of students requiring large amounts of financial assistance. For minority school matriculants, those requiring $20,000 or more increased from 25 to 52 percent and for nonminority school matriculants the change was from 19 to 48 percent (Hanft and White 1986).

The availability of scholarships and low-cost government loans until recently has made it possible for individuals from all socioeconomic levels to enter even the most prestigious medical schools during the last decade and a half (Bazzoli, Adams, and Thran 1986). Most of the funds have been provided by the federal government. Funds under the Health Professions Student Loan Program, the Scholarship Program for First-year Students of Exceptional Financial Need, and the National Direct Student Loan Program are provided directly to the medical schools for disbursement to qualifying students. The National Health Service Corps scholarship program, which required service payback, was drawn on extensively by minority and low-income students. Under the Health Education Assistance Loan Program (unsubsidized) and the Guaranteed Student Loan Program (subsidized), students may obtain loans from banks or other lending institutions. Some programs provide for repayment through required service in designated shortage areas; some pay only tuition and fees; others include a stipend to cover living expenses (Bazzoli, Adams, and Thran 1986; Association of American Medical Colleges 1986a).

The relatively low-cost Guaranteed Student Loan Program is still the primary source of financial assistance sought by medical students (Association of American Medical Colleges 1986a). Funds to support this program have, however, been cut back in the last two years, and it is becoming increasingly necessary for students to turn to the much higher-cost loans provided under the Health Education Assistance Loan program (HEAL). It has been estimated that for a student borrowing under the HEAL program, at an interest rate of 15 percent compounded semiannually, the total repayment of a $40,000 loan over a period of 25 years will amount to $400,000. As other sources of financial assistance continue to decrease, it is projected that within a few years the HEAL program will constitute 20 percent or more of the financial assistance available to students, up from its present level of 7 percent (Sandson 1983).

The Health Resources and Services Administration recently reviewed the literature to determine the effects of high rates of debt on an individual's choice of career in the health professions. While they conclude that there is no hard evidence to support the theory that high rates of debt discourage individuals from choosing the health field, they also note that only in recent years has the amount of indebtedness risen to its present levels. This report also points out that "applications and enrollment of persons from disadvantaged and minority backgrounds were greatest during the period of readily available scholarships and low-interest loans, suggesting that participation of these groups in health professions training programs may be sensitive to the availability of programs that reduce out-of-pocket student costs." In addition, the report cites anecdotal evidence that increasing numbers of minority students are choosing engineering, business, and computer careers, which take less time to compete and are less expensive (U.S. Department of Health and Human Services 1986b).

Faced with ever-increasing medical school tuition and expenses and falling levels of financial assistance, it is likely that medical education will once again become the province of those individuals with substantial family resources available to them. The pool of qualified applicants from lower socioeconomic backgrounds, already dwindling, is likely to become smaller as individuals look to other professions with shorter training periods and lower costs to fulfill their ambitions.

The Minority Schools

There are four minority medical schools in the United States: Meharry Medical College, Morehouse School of Medicine, Charles Drew Post-graduate Medical School, and Howard University School of Medicine.

The rationale for the development of the first two minority schools was clearly related to the issue of segregation and the denial of opportunity in state and private professional schools, similar to the rationale for development of historically black colleges. This is not a unique phenomenon. The development of Albert Einstein and Mt. Sinai medical schools was in response to the long-standing quotas limiting Jewish participation in medical education. Separate Catholic schools are a long-standing national phenomenon. None of the racial or ethnic or religious schools, however, limits enrollment to its group.

The rationale for the development of the two newer minority medical schools, Drew and Morehouse, was in part a response to the slower than anticipated progress toward increasing black enrollment at majority schools and the decline in acceptance rates. There is continuing evidence that acceptance rates for blacks in majority schools remain a problem. Furthermore, a number of groups in our pluralistic nation believe that some students benefit and achievement is enhanced when the minority students are a "majority" at an institution.

Drew is part of the University of California system, and Howard University receives a special federal appropriation. The financial base of Meharry and Morehouse differs significantly from the financial base of virtually all other medical schools. They do not receive substantial amounts of support from biomedical research, which constitutes on average 23 percent of medical school revenues. Though they do receive some indirect assistance from those states that contribute to the tuition of their students, they do not receive direct underwriting from any state.

Because the patient population served as part of the education function is a low-income group, Meharry and Morehouse do not generate a high proportion of faculty salaries from patient care services as do the nonminority schools. Their economic foundation is fragile, limiting their ability to provide the support services and developmental capability that most schools take for granted (Hanft, Fishman, and Evans 1983). In the current era of cutbacks in federal financial assistance programs, the economic base of these two schools becomes even more fragile, as medical schools are increasingly required to draw upon their own resources to provide scholarship and loan funds (Association of American Medical Colleges 1986a).

In 1981 Meharry was required to reduce its enrollment, and Morehouse has been unable to expand its first-year class from the current 32 students to its goal of 64. Part of the problem is the lack of financial resources to recruit faculty and obtain access to clinical facilities and support services. These schools also take "higher risk" students, students that score below-standard grade point averages and MCAT scores. More investment in remediation and individual tutorials is necessary. In spite of these setbacks, these two schools, together with Howard University, continue to enroll 17.5 percent of all black first-year students, and, in 1984, 20 percent of black graduates were from these three schools (Association of American Medical Colleges 1985).

The minority schools clearly have made a major contribution to the education and production of black physicians. Some mechanism for providing stable funding and developmental funds is needed to ensure their continued contributions. Relatively modest funding would be needed to sustain and enhance these few institutions that contribute disproportionately to the education of black physicians.

Clashing Goals: Reducing Oversupply and Increasing Minorities in Medicine

Recent federal cutbacks in support of medical education and student aid are not merely a function of the federal deficit and a shift in federal priorities between defense and domestic sectors of the economy, but a response to a perceived but controversial "surplus" of physicians. Evidence of the service that minority physicians provide to low-income, inner-city and rural areas marries goals of improved access to care and equal education opportunities as critical components of improved minority health status. Furthermore, the public policy goal has been to increase the proportion of primary care physicians. The distribution of blacks between primary care and all other specialties already achieves the recommendation in the 1980 GMENAC report. In 1985 almost 60 percent of black residents were concentrated in the areas of internal medicine, family practice, pediatrics, and obstetrics-gynecology, compared with 46 percent of nonblack residents. Blacks were twice as likely to be training in obstetrics-gynecology and pediatrics as were their nonblack counterparts. They were underrepresented in almost all other specialties, especially surgery and its subspecialties. In 1985, however, blacks still constituted only 4.5 percent of all residents— barely higher than their 4.4 percent representation in 1978 (Hanft and White 1986). Clearly, the generic issue of surplus should be disaggregated in public policy discussions to assure that the goal of increased participation of minorities in medicine is not undermined.

Conclusions

While health policy analysts argue whether there is a real surplus of physician manpower and the degree of the surplus, the shortage of minority physicians continues, and progress made to date to increase the number of minority physicians is being reversed. Numerous studies and national data show continued disparities in the health status of minorities (U.S. Department of Health and Human Services 1985). Studies also show that minority physicians fill critical needs of access to care in low-income inner-city and rural areas. Society bears the cost of lack of access to health care through premature death and disability, high infant mortality, and lowered productivity, in addition to the high costs of health care incurred when prevention, early diagnosis, and treatment are forgone. Access to care is directly dependent on the availability of manpower and the sensitivity of that manpower to the problems of the population they serve. There are still underserved areas and underserved populations in these United States. As access to health care has become an increasing problem, despite several prior decades of progress, equal education opportunity is again emerging as a problem, particularly for lower-income people, a disproportionate number of whom are minorities.

An increase in opportunities for minorities to become physicians is dependent on a number of factors. These factors include: the commitment of majority schools to increase acceptance rates and retention rates for minority students; improved high school and college preparation for minority students; a stable financial base for the minority medical schools; and—critical to the ability of minorities to enter the protracted education process—affordable student financing. We are in grave danger of slipping backward to the era before affirmative action when there was an acute scarcity of minority health professionals and continuing disparities in health status between the majority population and minorities.

References

American Council on Education. 1986. *Fifth Annual Status Report: Minorities in Higher Education.* Washington: Office of Minority Concerns.

Association of American Medical Colleges. 1970. *Report of the Association of American Medical Colleges Task Force to the Inter-Association Committee on Expanding Educational Opportunities in Medicine for Blacks and Other Minority Students.* Washington.

———. 1983. *U.S. Medical Students, 1950–2000: A Comparison Factbook for Physicians in the Making.* Washington.

———. 1985. *Minority Students in Medical Education: Facts and Figures II.* Washington.

————. 1986a. Datagram: Financial Assistance for Medical Students, 1984–85. *Journal of Medical Education* 61:695–97.

————. 1986b. *Medical School Admission Requirements 1987–88.*. Washington.

Baratz, J.C., M.S. Ficklen, B. King, and P. Rosenbaum. 1985. *Who Is Going to Medical School? A Look at the 1984–85 Underrepresented Minority Medical School Applicant Pool.* Princeton: Educational Testing Service.

Bazzoli, G.J., E. K. Adams, and S.L. Thran. 1986. Race and Socio-economic Status in Medical School Choice and Indebtedness. *Journal of Medical Education* 61:285–92.

Berk, M.L., A.B. Bernstein, and A.K. Taylor. 1982. *Use and Availability of Medical Care in Federally Designated Health Manpower Shortage Areas.* U.S. Department of Health and Human Services, National Center for Health Services Research. Washington.

Epps, C.H. 1986. The Black Practitioner: Challenges of the Future. *Journal of the National Medical Association* 78(5):365–70.

Frierson, H.T. 1984. Impact of an Intervention Program on Minority Medical Students' National Board Part I Performance. *Journal of the National Medical Association* 76(12):1185–90.

Gray, L.C. 1977. The Geographic and Functional Distribution of Black Physicians: Some Research and Policy Considerations. *American Journal of Public Health* 67(6):519–26.

Gregory, K., K.B. Wells, and B. Leake. 1986. Which First Year Medical Students Expect to Practice in an Inner-City or Ghetto Setting. *Journal of the National Medical Association* 78(6):501–4.

Gutek, G.L. 1985. Estimated Undergraduate Tuition and Fees and Room and Board Rates in Institutions of Higher Education, by Type and Control of Institution: United States. 1974–75 to 1983–84. In *Standard Education Almanac, 1984–85*, 328–29. 17th ed. Chicago: Professional Publications.

Hall, F.R., and P.C. Whybrow. 1984. Financial Aid for Medical Students: A Review and a Proposal. *Journal of Medical Education* 59:380–85.

Hanft, R.S., L.E. Fishman, and W.J. Evans. 1983. *Blacks and the Health Professions in the 80's: A National Crisis and a Time for Action.* Washington: Association of Minority Health Professions Schools.

Hanft, R.S., and C.C. White. 1986. *Changing Characteristics of Minority School Matriculants.* Washington: Association of Minority Health Professions Schools.

Hanft, R.S., C.C. White, and L.E. Fishman. 1986. *Minorities in the Health Professions: Continuing Crises.* Washington: Association of Minority Health Professions Schools.

Keith, S.N., R.M. Bell, A.G. Swanson, and A.P. Williams. 1985. Effects of Affirmative Action in Medical Schools: A Study of the Class of 1975. *New England Journal of Medicine* 313(24):1519–25.

Lloyd, S.M., and D.G. Johnson. 1982. Practice Patterns of Black Physicians: Results of a Survey of Howard University College of Medicine Alumni. *Journal of the National Medical Association* 74(2):129–44.

Morais, H.M. 1976. *The History of the Afro-American in Medicine.* Cornwell Heights, Pa.: Publishers Agency.

Payne, J.L., C.M. Nowacki, J.A. Girotti, J. Townsel, J.C. Plagge, and T.W. Beckham. 1986. Increasing the Graduation Rates of Minority Medical Students. *Journal of Medical Education* 61:353–58.

Sandson, J.I. 1983. A Crisis in Medical Education: The High Cost of Student Financial Assistance. *New England Journal of Medicine* 308(21):1286–89.

Shea, S., and M.T. Fullilove. 1985. Entry of Black and Minority Students into U.S. Medical Schools: Historical Perspective and Recent Trends. *New England Journal of Medicine* 313(15):933–40.

Strelnick, A.H., R.J. Massad, W.B. Bateman, and S.D. Shepherd. 1986. Minority Students in U.S. Medical Schools. *New England Journal of Medicine* 315(1):67–68.

Thomas, G. 1986. *The Access and Success of Blacks and Hispanics in U.S. Graduate and Professional Education.* Washington: National Academy Press.

Tuckson, R. 1984. Health Care Problems in the 1980s: Part II. The Black Physician and the Challenges of the 1980s. *Journal of the National Medical Association* 76(10):977–80.

U.S. Bureau of the Census. 1984. *Earnings by Occupation and Education.* Washington.

———. 1986. *Statistical Abstract of the United States: 1986.* Washington.

U.S. Department of Health and Human Services. 1985. *Health Status of Minorities and Low-income Groups.* Health Resources and Services Administration. DHHS pub. no. HRS-P-DV 85-1. Washington.

———. 1986a. *Estimates and Projections of Black and Hispanic Physicians, Dentists, and Pharmacists to 2010.* Health Resources and Services Administration. DHHS pub. no. HRS-P-DV 86-1. Washington.

———. 1986b. *Report to Congress on an Analysis of Financial Disincentives to Career Choices in Health Professions.* Health Resources and Services Administration, Bureau of Health Professions. Washington.

———. 1987. *Summary Descriptions of Retention Programs from Medical and Dental Schools Applying for Continuation of Health Career Opportunity Program (HCOP) Grants Provided by the Health Resources and Services Administration, Division of Disadvantaged Assistance.* Washington.

Appendix Note

The term minority in the context of this report refers to those racial and ethnic groups whose representation in the physician population is less than their representation in the general population. The term as used in the majority of statistics cited includes blacks, who are 11.7 percent of the United States population but only 3 percent of physicians; Mexican-Americans and mainland Puerto Ricans who are 6.5 percent of the population and 4 percent of physicians; and native Americans (American Indians, Eskimos, Aleuts) who are .6 percent of the population but .1 percent of physicians. Asian/Pacific Islanders are 1.6 percent of the population but 10 percent of physicians—thus, they are not included in the minority counts (Association of American Medical Colleges 1985).

The minority schools referred to in this report are Howard University, Meharry Medical College, and Morehouse College of Medicine, each of which has a student population that is predominantly but not exclusively black. Although the Charles R. Drew Postgraduate Medical School is also a minority school (predominantly black), published student statistics for this school are included with those of the University of California, Los Angeles, and cannot be separately identified. The program at Charles R. Drew is designed to attract individuals committed to caring for disadvantaged and underserved populations regardless of the race of the applicant.

Paying the Price: Medical Care, Minorities, and the Newly Competitive Health Care System

MARK SCHLESINGER

> I took one Draught of Life —
> I'll tell you what I paid —
> Precisely an existence —
> The market price, they say.
>
> Emily Dickinson, poem no. 1725

T HERE HAS LONG BEEN A TENSION IN AMERICAN policy making between reliance on government and reliance on the market to allocate socially valued services such as health care, education, and social services. Nowhere has this tension been more pronounced than for those services used by racial and ethnic minorities.

The market has been portrayed by its advocates as preserving free choice, safeguarding minorities from the oft-times insensitive will of the majority (Friedman 1962). But these safeguards clearly have their limits. Minorities who lack financial resources will have little voice in the market. With a poverty rate for black families that is three times that of white households, much of the black community is economically disenfranchised (Jones and Rice 1987). Nor are all choices in the market freely made. Those who face discrimination lose much of their free choice. Under some circumstances, discrimination based on race is not only possible, but virtually inevitable in a market system (Spence 1974).

If the market only imperfectly reflects minority interests, the same is certainly true for government. When a representative government inadequately represents blacks, it will not be fully responsive to their concerns. And despite two decades of voting-rights legislation and registration campaigns, blacks continue to be underrepresented, particularly in Congress and most state legislatures (Persons 1987).

For those who would promote minority interests, there are, therefore, no obvious choices between public and private sectors, between markets and the political process. Equally thoughtful observers reach diametrically opposed conclusions, some favoring the market (Sowell 1981), others government action (Winn 1987).

American medicine of the 1980s, though, has seemingly neared a concensus favoring a greater role for market forces and private enterprise (Goldsmith 1984; Schlesinger et al. 1987). These views have strongly shaped the health policies pursued by the Reagan administration (Dobson et al. 1986). They have been encouraged by large employers and other private purchasers of health services. Virtually all observers agree that the United States health care system of the 1990s will be far more "competitive" than at any period in recent history (Arthur Anderson & Co. 1984).

But those who advocate these changes often do so on the basis of very broad generalizations, arguing that the "average" purchaser of health care services is almost certain to benefit (Kindig, Sidel, and Birnbaum 1977). Relatively little attention has been paid to the fate of individuals and groups that are in some manner not "typical," either because of their health care needs or the options open to them as consumers of health care (Anderson and Fox 1987; Schlesinger 1986, 1987). Receiving perhaps the least attention are the racial minorities of this country, who are likely to face some important disadvantages in the newly competitive markets for health services (Winn 1987).

This article assesses the effects of competition on the health care of black Americans. Because there has been relatively little empirical research on this topic, the evidence presented below is often fragmented and incomplete, drawn in large part from research intended for other purposes. In some instances, no data are available at all, and it becomes necessary to reason by analogy. Though the inadequacy of this data makes clear the need for additional research, it does not in my assessment undermine the basic conclusions of the article—that while some black Americans will benefit from a more competitive health care system, the least advantaged will likely be made even worse off.

The article is divided into four sections. The first describes in detail the various changes in American medicine that are often grouped together under the label of "increasing competition." The second identifies subsets of the black population that may fare more or less well under competition. The third section reviews recent evidence on the actual costs and benefits of competition to black communities, evidence used in the final section to discuss the appropriate future role of public policy in this area.

Competition in the Health Care System

American medicine, like the rest of our society, has always contained a strong element of competition (Vladeck 1985). Labeling ongoing changes in the health care system as "increased competition" is thus to some degree a misnomer. What is changing is the nature, as well as the extent, of competition among health care providers.

Historically, health care providers competed to attract patients— in particular, to attract patients with the resources or insurance to pay for their health care. Following the post-World War II expansion of hospital facilities, the most aggressive competition occurred in the market for hospital services. To attract patients, hospital administrators believed that they had to attract physicians. Hospitals could do this by offering physicians more supportive environments for their practices, with a larger nursing staff as well as more elaborate and accessible technologies. Consequently, competition during this period tended to increase costs. Studies of hospital markets during the 1970s found that the more competitive the local market for hospital services, the higher the hospitals' operating costs (Noether 1987; Robinson and Luft 1985; D. Farley 1985). Increased competition and higher costs were associated with more full-time-equivalent staff per bed and a broader range of diagnostic and therapeutic services (Noether 1987; D. Farley 1985).

Sharp declines in hospital use over the past few years—occupancy rates fell from 76 percent in 1981 to 65 percent in 1985—have increased pressures for hospitals to find additional patients. Their methods for doing this, though, have changed from the strategies of the 1970s.

The nature of the relation between hospitals and physicians has changed. The expansion of medical schools in the 1960s and 1970s has led to what many perceive to be a "glut" of physicians (Harris 1986). Consequently, hospitals have become less concerned with attracting medical staff, and have increasingly sought to market directly to potential patients (Seay et al. 1986). At the same time, private practitioners have become more entrepreneurial, establishing a host of free-standing facilities such as ambulatory surgery centers and emergency medical centers (Ermann and Gabel 1985). These directly compete with hospitals, and many observers believe that this competition will intensify in the future (Seay et al. 1986; Arthur Anderson & Co. 1984).

In addition, purchasers of health care have become far more sensitive to the price of services. Faced with the rapidly rising costs of health care benefits, private employers and public agencies have developed purchasing systems that encourage or require enrollees to seek lower-cost providers. In the private sector, these have most often taken the form of "preferred provider arrangements" (PPAs). In a PPA, enrollees pay lower copayments if they obtain health care from providers who have established reduced-price contracts with the employer or insurer (Lissovoy et al. 1986). In the public sector, these innovative arrangements are generally termed "competitive bidding" systems. In a number of Medicaid programs, for example, providers bid for the right to treat Medicaid enrollees, and the state selects the low-cost bidder or bidders in each region (Anderson and Fox 1987; Freund and Neuschler 1986).

These changes in the market for health services can significantly alter the behavior of providers, and thus the accessibility and quality of health care. How these changes will affect blacks is discussed in some detail below. But changes in market conditions are not the only potentially important consequences of the new competitiveness in health care. Market conditions are to some extent a reflection of, and to some extent reflected by, what could be termed a new "competitive ethos," a shift in popular perceptions about the appropriate roles of health providers in the community and public policy in the health care system.

For hospitals and other institutional providers, this ethos represents a change in expectations. Increasingly, health care facilities are being perceived and portrayed as commercial enterprises, rather than as institutions with a fiduciary responsibility to the community in which they are located. This changes the expectations of and incentives for the administrators of the facility.

> Any hospital administrator who doesn't do all he can to fend off as many general assistance patients as he can . . . just isn't being "businesslike" and will be so judged by his board of trustees. The word "businesslike" poses the problem in a larger context. The chorus of criticism of the not-for-profit hospital now coming from business leaders and government alike and much abetted by the present editorial content of many hospital journals is that they need to be "better managed." Not surprisingly, many CEOs are taking this to mean that you shouldn't treat many patients who represent bad debts, free care, or oversized "contractual allowances" (Kinzer 1984, 8).

These changes undoubtedly go beyond admissions policies. The more health care facilities are viewed as commercial operations, the more their governing structure is likely to become like that of any other business. One would thus expect the board of directors to include fewer "members of the community" and more representatives of the professionals with which the facility does business—physicians, large employers, and officers of local financial institutions.

The growing competitive ethos in health care is also shaping public policy. Most evident have been policies promoting "deregulation," allowing market forces to work unfettered (Winn 1987; Davis and Millman 1983). A dozen states, for example, have discontinued their certificate-of-need programs to encourage the entry of new health care facilities (Polchow 1986). Less obvious, but potentially more significant, have been changes in public subsidies to health care agencies. Proponents of competition typically call for "a level playing field," that is, for the elimination of subsidies that are available only to some providers. Their rationale is that "fair play" in the market requires that all competitors begin on an even footing.

Whatever the merits of this argument on ethical grounds, it can have important consequences for the delivery of health services. Preferential subsidies, including tax exemption, are made available primarily to public and private nonprofit agencies (Clark 1980). But with subsidies there comes an expectation of community service. The Hill-Burton program, for instance, subsidized the construction of a number of public and nonprofit hospitals (Lave and Lave 1974). In return, hospitals receiving funds were required to make services available to the medically indigent.

Not all subsidies explicitly require community service, and those that do may not be effectively enforced (Silver 1974). Nonetheless, subsidies have provided both a legal and, to some extent, a moral basis for encouraging private providers to take actions in the public interest (Blumstein 1986). Eliminating subsidies would inhibit the extent to which policy makers and public advocates can influence the delivery system in this manner. Making subsidies available to all providers would diffuse their effectiveness, since it is the' public and larger private nonprofit facilities that are disproportionately located in the most disadvantaged communities of our country (Vladeck 1985; Davis and Millman 1983).

As this discussion suggests, the changes wrought by competition will be reflected in both the market and public policy. Competition will alter access to care, but it will also change the nature and extent of public influence on private health care providers. The consequences for blacks, and other groups, will thus involve their role as members of the community as well as consumers of health care. Before assessing whether these changes will be for good or ill, it is useful to review briefly some of the important factors that have historically affected blacks' use of health services.

Black Americans as Consumers of Health Care Services

The benefits of competitive health care markets depend to a large extent on the potential for patients to purchase treatment suited to their health needs, choosing among alternative sources of care. Two important hindrances exist for many black Americans.

First, many lack the purchasing power to voice effectively their preferences in the market. A disproportionate number of blacks live in low-income households. A third of all black households have incomes below the poverty line, and almost half of all black children live in these families (Jones and Rice 1987; U.S. Congressional Budget Office 1985). With such limited resources, many blacks cannot afford to purchase private health insurance. Only 58 percent of all black respondents under the age of 65 reported on the 1984 National Health Interview Survey that they had private insurance coverage (Andersen et al. 1987). Respondents without private coverage were divided evenly between those enrolled in Medicaid and those with no insurance coverage. Blacks are thus 50 percent more likely than whites to have no health insurance and 5 times as likely to be covered by Medicaid.

These financial factors have a number of important consequences for use of health care. Blacks will be disproportionately affected by experiments that introduce competitive bidding to the Medicaid program—40 percent of all Medicaid enrollees are black. Many other black Americans face significant financial barriers when seeking needed health care. Nine percent reported in 1986 that they did not receive health care for "economic reasons" (Freeman et al. 1987). Blacks who reported themselves to be in "poor or fair health" had one-third fewer visits to a doctor than did whites with comparable health status; a quarter of all blacks with chronic illnesses did not see a physician at all in the previous year (Freeman et al. 1987).

Black Americans thus are often less "connected" than are whites to the health care system. Twenty percent reported that they had no "regular source of care" in 1986; for many of the others, their regular source of care was a hospital emergency room or outpatient department, where they had only limited continuity of contact with a particular provider (Leon 1987; Okada and Sparer 1976). This limited contact affects the options and choices available to blacks as patients.

The second important consideration for blacks as consumers of health services is that, apart from differences in income, they have fewer alternative sources of health care. This is true for several reasons. Black communities are much more likely to have a limited number of health care providers. This includes both inner cities and rural areas in relatively poor states (Foley and Johnson 1987; Ruiz and Herbert 1984). As of 1985, for example, one-third of the 750 American counties with the highest proportion of black population had been designated by the federal government as "critical shortage areas" for primary care physicians; this is half again as common as for all other counties in the country. Consequently, a disproportionate number of blacks rely on hospitals and community health centers to provide primary care (Davis et al. 1987; Hanft 1977). Black overall health care utilization in these communities is lower than that of whites with comparable incomes (Okada and Sparer 1976).

Even when services are geographically accessible, blacks may face racial discrimination that makes it difficult for them to obtain care or limits their choices among health care providers (Jones and Rice 1987; Holliman 1983; Windle 1980). This discrimination may simply be the result of irrational racial prejudice, but may also reflect a more calculated judgment that black patients will be more difficult or expensive to treat. The origins of this expectation are discussed in detail later in this article.

Lack of information prevents many blacks from becoming effective consumers of health care. Surveys have shown that minority Americans are less informed than are whites about both the services available in their community and the provisions of their health insurance policies (Holmes, Teresi, and Holmes 1983; Marquis 1983). There are several possible explanations for these differences. As noted above, blacks tend to be less closely tied to a particular health care provider and thus are less likely to have a physician who fully understands their health needs and can adequately advise them. And communication between provider and patient may be further impeded by barriers of culture and language (Foley and Johnson 1987). The episodic employment history of many black workers makes it less likely that they will have contact with benefits managers at the companies that employ them (Jones and Rice 1987). All these problems are compounded by lack of education—minority Americans are three times as likely to have less than five years of formal education (Rudov and Santangelo 1979).

For many blacks the changes in competition among health care providers discussed above will have much the same costs and benefits as they do for the rest of the country. Assessing the consequences of competition for this broader population is an important task, but it is one that has been discussed extensively elsewhere (Meyer 1983; Luft 1985; Willis 1986). The remainder of this article will focus instead on those black communities—urban and rural—that in the past have lacked the financial and medical resources for adequate access to health care. The critical question is thus whether the changing nature of health care competition will ameliorate or exacerbate these problems.

Disadvantaged Minorities and Competition in American Medicine

As discussed above, a number of shifts in health care and health policy are often associated with increasing health care competition. For simplicity, these will be combined here into three general categories. The first set of changes are reflected in the private market for health care, affecting blacks in their role as consumers. The second involves reforms designed to introduce competitive bidding to the Medicaid program, affecting the 5 million blacks enrolled in that program. The third involves the set of changes in public expectations and public policy associated with the growth of a competitive ethos in health care, affecting blacks by reducing the influence that they, and the general body politic, have over the delivery of health care.

Competition in Private Markets for Health Services

Two ongoing trends have altered competition among health providers: first, the apparently growing excess supply of both hospital beds and physicians; and second, the increased price sensitivity of private insurers and employers. One would expect that these trends would work in offsetting directions, the first enhancing, the second reducing, the accessibility of health care in low-income black communities.

The more empty hospital beds and physicians' waiting rooms, the greater the financial incentive for health care providers to treat patients they would previously have viewed as undesirable (Vladeck 1985). These conditions may induce providers to overlook racial prejudice. It may encourage them to locate practices in areas that they would otherwise have considered unsuitable (Lewis 1976).

The effects of increased price competition are likely to be more problematic. On the positive side, if price-based competition causes providers to become more efficient, they will profitably be able to treat more patients with limited insurance or financial resources. Disadvantaged black communities would clearly benefit (P. Farley 1985). On the other hand, competitive pressures are likely to lead to larger reductions in prices than in operating costs (Schlesinger, Blumenthal, and Schlesinger 1986). This reduces the profits generated by treating privately insured patients, and providers become less able to cross-subsidize care of the uninsured or provide services that do not yield sufficient revenues to cover costs (Schlesinger et al. 1987; Shortell et al. 1986). Low-income communities, which have disproportionately black populations, will bear the brunt of these cutbacks.

The net effect on access depends on the relative magnitudes of these various changes. Unfortunately, there has been too little research in this area to identify conclusively the effects of competition on access in general, let alone for specific racial groups. The expanding supply of physicians does appear to have had some positive effects. In 1980, 41 percent of the counties in the highest quartile for the proportion of inhabitants who were black had been designated critical shortage areas for primary care physicians. By 1985 this had declined to 34 percent.

This greater availability of providers, however, seems to have been offset by other changes. Prior to 1980 racial differences in health care use had been steadily declining over time (Leon 1987). Since 1980, as competitive pressures in health care have been building, black overall access to health care has clearly declined. Studies have found that financially motivated transfers of patients from private to public hospitals—up to 90 percent involving minority patients in some cities—increased significantly during this period (Schiff et al. 1986). Between 1982 and 1986 the gap in physician use between blacks and whites in poor or fair health grew by more than a quarter (Freeman et al. 1987). The proportion of blacks without a regular source of care rose from 13 to 20 percent (Leon 1987).

Competition alone did not cause these outcomes. Other important changes in the health care system have occurred during this period that also may have hindered black access to care, including state cutbacks in Medicaid eligibility and benefits as well as changes in the coverage and practices of private insurers (Goldsmith 1984; Munnell 1985). Without further research, it is impossible to identify the separate effects of competition. It seems very likely, however, that the blacks who benefit from increasing competition are those with at least limited insurance coverage, making them marginally profitable to treat. Those lacking any insurance are likely to find it increasingly difficult to find private health providers who are willing or able to provide them with care.

Competition in Public Programs: Competitive
Bidding in Medicaid

Corresponding to the growing emphasis on competition for the privately insured, there has been greater interest in competitive reforms for public programs like Medicare and Medicaid (Willis 1986). This interest has been embodied in a series of demonstration projects and several more permanent program changes. As noted above, because one in five black Americans is enrolled in Medicaid, representing 40 percent of the program's recipients, changes in Medicaid have a particularly pronounced effect on low-income black communities.

The specific nature of these Medicaid experiments varies from state to state. Some have focused on reducing charges paid to hospitals, others on enhancing the role of primary care physicians (Anderson and Fox 1987; Freund and Neuschler 1986). Because many of these programs involve a fixed annual payment to an HMO or other prepaid health provider, I will focus here on this approach.

Most of these programs have several common features. Providers wishing to treat Medicaid enrollees must submit a "bid," stating the price at which they are willing to provide services. State officials (or an organization acting at their behest) select one or more of the bidders to be the designated Medicaid provider in each community. These are typically chosen on the basis of cost, though other criteria may also affect the selection (Christianson et al. 1983). If there are several designated providers in an area, Medicaid recipients are generally given the option of selecting their preferred provider—those who do not make a choice within a specified period are assigned to a provider. Most programs periodically permit beneficiaries who are dissatisfied with a provider to switch to another in the area.

The potential advantages and disadvantages of these competitive models reflect in part the competitive bidding process, in part the requirement that providers be prepaid for the care they provide. Competitive bidding arrangements reduce program costs, at least in the short run (Christianson et al. 1983; Freund and Neuschler 1987). They do so by restricting enrollee choices to a limited number of lower-cost providers. This would seem to reduce access to care and potentially to threaten quality, since it restricts the alternatives for enrollees if they are dissatisfied with the care that they receive.

In practice, however, these may be small liabilities. Historically, many states have had difficulty convincing providers, particularly physicians, to participate in their traditional Medicaid programs, because they are paid relatively little for medical services (Sloan, Mitchell, and Cromwell 1978; Davidson et al. 1983). As a result, Medicaid recipients often had few real choices for obtaining treatment, so that being limited in the future to choosing among a small number of participating HMOs may not seriously restrict their options, though it may reduce somewhat their access to minority physicians (Foley and Johnson 1987; Kindig et al. 1977; McDaniel 1985). In fact, accessibility and quality of care may be enhanced because patients are formally linked to a particular provider or group of providers. If significant numbers of enrollees go without needed treatment, it becomes easier to assign responsibility to those providers.

It is often argued that this sense of responsibility is augmented when providers are prepaid for the care that they provide. To the extent that prepayment places providers at financial risk for illness, it creates an inducement for them to identify illness at an early stage when it is less expensive to treat. This is thought to be a particularly important consideration for minorities from low-income communities, who often lack a regular source of care and may thus require outreach to bring them into the health care system (Wolfe 1977).

Not all the consequences of competitive bidding, however, are likely to be favorable. Although competitive bidding systems increase the probability that Medicaid recipients will be formally tied to a particular provider, they do not guarantee that the recipients will actually receive treatment. Prepaid plans must operate within a fixed budget. The more effective the competitive bidding system is in cutting costs, the smaller this budget will be. To keep within budget, prepaid plans have adopted a variety of administrative procedures for rationing care (Luft 1982).

It remains a matter of considerable debate whether enrollees with lower incomes and less education are able to negotiate effectively these administrative requirements and obtain needed health care (Foley and Johnson 1987; Luft 1981). Studies of HMOs operating in predominantly black, low-income communities have also reached somewhat mixed results, but generally suggest that access and quality of care in prepaid plans is at least as high as, and often higher than, that for solo practitioners (Dutton and Silber 1980; Gaus, Cooper, and Hirschman 1976).

Less recognized, however, is the extent to which operating under limited budgets may encourage a form of economic discrimination against black enrollees. HMOs participating in competitive bidding programs receive a fixed payment for each member. Plans that enroll relatively healthy Medicaid recipients will prosper under this system; those with unusually sick and therefore expensive enrollees will face financial difficulties. Race serves as an effective predictor of future health care costs. In part as a legacy of past restrictions on access, blacks are 50 percent more likely than whites to be in fair and poor health (Freeman et al. 1987). As a result, when given greater access to care, they tend to have longer stays in the hospital and higher overall health care costs (Andersen et al. 1987; Heyssel 1981). Providers concerned with limiting their expenditures can thus be expected to discourage enrollment by black Medicaid recipients and perhaps to focus their cost-containment efforts on this group.

Because Medicaid competitive bidding programs are new, we have relatively little hard evidence to determine the consequences for black participants. Preliminary evidence suggests that in urban areas, at least, the programs have been reasonably successful at attracting a number of participating plans and satisfying Medicaid recipients (Anderson and Fox 1987). In Arizona, for example, 79 percent of black enrollees reported that they found health care more accessible under the competitive bidding program than under previous arrangements (Flinn Foundation 1986). Over two-thirds preferred the care they received under the program to that available previously (Flinn Foundation 1986). (It should be remembered, however, that prior to adopting the competitive bidding system Arizona was the only state without a Medicaid program and thus represented a rather low standard of comparison.)

Several caveats, however, should be added to this basically positive assessment. First, competitive bidding systems are likely to be less effective in rural areas, in which the number of bidders is fewer and geographic barriers to access greater (Turner 1985; Christianson, Hillman, and Smith 1983; Martin 1977). It is, therefore, not surprising that the native American population in Arizona was significantly less satisfied with the competitive bidding program than was the more urban black population (Flinn Foundation 1986). Second, these programs generally offer less choice than is initially apparent. Even in areas in which there are a significant number of participating providers, the most popular typically reach their enrollment capacity fairly quickly, leaving few attractive options for many Medicaid recipients (Rowland and Lyons 1987). Third, few if any of the existing competitive bidding programs have developed the administrative capacity to monitor effectively provision of services, and thus to hold providers responsible if health needs are going unmet (Anderson and Fox 1987). This is perhaps natural in new programs, but it is unclear how long it will take for their administrative capabilities to improve.

Finally, whatever the impact of competitive bidding on Medicaid recipients, it is likely to have a decidedly adverse effect on health care for the uninsured living in the same community. Providers who treat substantial numbers of Medicaid recipients also often have many uninsured patients. Consequently, as competitive bidding cuts payments for Medicaid enrollees, it further reduces provider ability to cross-subsidize unprofitable patients. Under these conditions, providers become less willing to treat the uninsured (Schlesinger et al. 1987). In addition, competitive bidding programs induce providers to join HMOs, few of which encourage their medical staff to treat uninsured patients (Anderson and Fox 1987).

Evidence from Arizona documents the loss of access for the non-Medicaid poor after a competitive bidding program has been established. The proportion of low-income blacks who did not have a regular source of care increased by over 60 percent (Flinn Foundation 1986). The proportion of low-income families not in Medicaid who were refused care for financial reasons also increased; the proportion unable to obtain care for a sick child more than doubled (Kirkman-Liff 1986).

The Competitive Ethos and Control over the Health Care System

Although most discussions of competition focus on the market for health care, more significant consequences for black communities may lie outside the direct delivery of services. With the growth of a competitive ethos, and the corresponding perception of health facilities as commercial enterprises, have come changes in popular expectations of providers and the extent of public influence over their performance. These changes can be seen in both the internal governance of health care organizations and the public policies that shape their behavior.

Competition and the Governance of Health Care Facilities. One potentially important influence on the services provided at a health care facility is its sense of commitment to the local community and the influence of community members on its governance (Dorwart and Meyers 1981). Although nonprofit organizations are generally expected to encourage community participation, actual practices have been highly variable (Middleton 1987). In general, representation of minority interests appears to be weakest in larger institutions, such as general hospitals, in which boards of directors tend to be dominated by community elites (Kindig et al. 1977; McDaniel 1985). Minorities seem to have greater influence in facilities such as community health and mental health centers, which operate under more explicit federal guidelines governing participation on boards of directors (Dorwart and Meyers 1981). As one review of these organizations observed:

> The ability of some minority community groups to build leadership and power via the federally funded community health center program served to defuse conflict over health services as well as to bring services into congruence with community perceptions of need (Davis and Millman 1983, 75).

To the extent that health facilities are seen as commercial enterprises, however, they are less likely to be required or pressured to maintain this community participation in governance. There are, as yet, no studies of this outgrowth of competition. Comparisons between for-profit and nonprofit hospitals, however, seem analogous, since the public generally perceives the former as more commercially oriented than their private nonprofit counterparts (Jackson and Jensen 1984). Surveys of hospital boards of directors indicate that there is less potential for broad community representation on the boards of for-profit facilities. In part, this is simply because these boards are significantly smaller than those of comparable-sized nonprofit hospitals (Sloan 1980). The composition of the boards is also rather different. In the average private nonprofit hospital, just over half of the board is composed of physicians and representatives of the business community. In the average for-profit hospital, these groups represent between 80 and 85 percent of the board (Sloan 1980). It is, therefore, likely that the governance of these more commercial facilities is shaped to a greater extent by professional concerns (Alexander, Morrisey, and Shortell 1986). Broader community interests may be given less attention.

Competition and Community Influence over Health Care Facilities. The practices of health care providers are also shaped by political pressures and government regulation. These can work to the benefit of otherwise disadvantaged communities, particularly in those public programs that explicitly require participation by members of the community. Provider behavior may be changed by either formal regulatory requirements or more informal moral suasion.

The certificate-of-need (CON) program represents a good example of these benefits. In many states, health care institutions intent on substantial new capital acquisitions or construction projects are required to seek approval from a local health systems agency (HSA). In 27 of the 39 states with CON programs, approval of a CON request is contingent on the willingness of the facility to provide care to the medically indigent. In 22 of these states this is required by law or administrative regulation, in 5 states it has emerged as a practice of the committees reviewing CON applications (Polchow 1986).

To the extent that a competitive ethos is associated with deregulation of the health care system, this source of leverage over facility behavior will be lost. The consequences of this loss for disadvantaged black communities are difficult to assess accurately. On one hand, blacks have been well represented in the health planning and regulatory system (Altman, Greene, and Sapolsky 1981). Nationwide, 15 percent of the board members of local HSAs have been black (Institute of Medicine 1981).

On the other hand, many observers have questioned whether participants in these public programs actually represent the interests of the less advantaged members of their communities (Morone 1981; Lewis 1976). Those on HSA boards were rarely from low-income households. In communities in which blacks were most likely to face racial discrimination when seeking health care, they were also least likely to participate in the CON program (Checkoway 1981). Even these critics acknowledge, however, that HSAs have often provided effective political leverage to encourage providers to treat more low-income patients (Checkoway 1981).

It therefore seems likely that the growing competitive ethos in American medicine will be associated with a decline in black influence over the performance of health care facilities. More generally, it will reduce public pressures for private facilities to act in the interests of disadvantaged communities. The consequences of these changes, being indirect, are more difficult to quantify and document than are some of the market-based changes discussed earlier. It would be a mistake, however, to equate quantifiability with importance. It seems very likely that the long-term responsiveness of the health care system to the needs of black communities will depend at least as much on the ability of community members to participate and influence the governance of medical institutions as on the willingness of providers to see black patients as profitable customers.

Conclusion: Competitive Markets and Competing Health Policies

Owing to the recency of competitive pressures in health and the dearth of research on their implications for minorities, much of the foregoing discussion was necessarily speculative. Nonetheless, it seems clear that a more competitive health care system will have mixed, but predominantly negative, effects on less-advantaged black Americans. Competition does offer some benefits to the partially insured who should gain in access because a larger number of providers become willing to offer them care. Since somewhere between 18 and 25 percent of the black population can be classified in this group, this is not an insignificant benefit (P. Farley 1985). But it is likely to be overshadowed by questions about the care of blacks enrolled in competitive bidding programs under Medicaid and by the almost certainly large losses of access for the 5 million blacks who have no health insurance. Perhaps more important in the long term will be the accompanying reduction in influence over the governance and performance of health facilities located in black communities.

This assessment assumes a continued incremental expansion of price-based competition and a competitive ethos in American medicine. Were policy makers to adopt some of the more comprehensive proposals for competitive reform, though, the implications for minorities might be quite different. Proponents of these competitive plans generally acknowledge most of the problems discussed above. To overcome these liabilities, they propose large-scale redistributions of income to increase the ability of low-income households to purchase adequate health care. For example, Enthoven's proposed "Consumer Choice Health Plan" (CCHP) would provide low-income families with a voucher worth

$1,350 in 1978 dollars ($2,250 in 1985 dollars) toward the purchase of prepaid health care:

> One of the goals of any national health insurance proposal is to redistribute resources so that the poor will have access to good care. The most effective way to redistribute income is to do it directly, i.e., to take the money from the well-to-do and pay it in cash or vouchers to the poor. . . . Purchasing power is the most effective way to command resources. A low-income family with a voucher worth $1350 to shop around in a competitive market is much more likely to receive good quality services willingly provided than in any other system (Enthoven 1977, 5).

Faced by discrimination and limited geographic access to health care providers, disadvantaged black families may not fare as well as the average low-income household. Nonetheless, these concerns should be addressable, and a proposal such as Enthoven's clearly holds appeal for many black families with limited financial resources. Of course, so would any proposal that redistributes income to this extent—in 1985 dollars, CCHP would entail a payment of well over $15 billion annually to low-income black families. The advantages and disadvantages of competition, relative to other resource allocation systems, are trivial compared to the consequences of payments this size.

Unfortunately, the redistributive aspects of the program are likely to be the weak political link in the proposal. Historical experience with policy making in this country suggests that the redistributive provisions of public policies tend to be lost somewhere between the initial program conception and its eventual implementation (Ripley and Franklin 1982). The risk seems particularly great in this case. Not only would many blacks receive large vouchers as a result of their limited incomes, but their vouchers would have to be additionally augmented to compensate providers for agreeing to treat a population with below-average health status (and thus above-average future health care expenses) (Winn 1987). A second rather bitter lesson of history is that programs or provisions targeted explicitly to blacks in this manner rarely have the political support to assure their continued survival (Jones and Rice 1987; Kieser 1987). Realistically then, the rather ambiguous benefits of procompetition provisions are far more likely to survive to become law than are the certainly beneficial redistributive aspects of the proposal.

But if a comprehensive plan that promotes competition and redistributes income is beyond the reach of contemporary policy makers, how then should they respond to concerns about the consequences of competition for disadvantaged black communities? To address this question, it is helpful to introduce a simple conceptual framework for considering policy interventions of this type.

Generally speaking, policy makers have available three strategies for addressing the needs of groups who are adversely affected by broad societal changes: separation, adaptation, or compensation. Under the first approach, policies could be designed to isolate, or shield, disadvantaged communities from competitive pressures. Under the second strategy, competitive models could be adapted to meet the special needs of black participants. Finally, competitive influences could be allowed to fully evolve in the health care system, but compensation would be provided to those made worse off by competition.

A complete and detailed assessment of these strategies is beyond the scope of this article. Political circumstances and historical experience suggest, however, that some of these strategies can be more fruitfully pursued than can others. First, the history of racial tensions and segregation in this country makes it difficult to initiate and maintain a program that differentiates, even in a positive sense, one racial group from another. This limits the extent to which compensatory programs can be explicitly targeted to black families. For example, a recent review of programs designed to reduce the disparity between black and white infant mortality questioned the value of racially targeted programs on the grounds that they would be perceived as either "labelling the beneficiaries as different in a negative sense" or would polarize other racial groups who "might perceive their needs to be just as great" (Howze 1987, 131–2). For similar reasons, it may prove difficult, or even impossible, to shield minority groups from society-wide competitive pressures that policy makers wish to encourage in order to limit the growth of health care costs.

> Anyone who believes that rich white people are prepared to absorb increased costs of medicine for black people is living in a fool's paradise. . . . It is necessary, therefore, for blacks to be in the forefront of alternative methods for managing medicine. . . . They must recognize the inevitable fact that medical expenditures will be managed and must seek strategies that minimize the impact on the black community (McDaniel 1985, 110).

Whether or not racial polarization in policy making is in fact this extreme, concerns of this sort will certainly limit the range of politically feasible responses to the adverse by-products of competition. These considerations suggest that a conversion or adaptation strategy may be more effective than separation or compensation strategies, which carry greater overtones of racial discrimination.

This approach could take several forms. Several seemingly promising reforms involve better adapting competitive bidding systems to fit the needs of black communities. For example, these programs could be made more suitable for potentially high-cost patients by incorporating health status adjustments into provider payments or by offering publicly funded reinsurance to providers to pay for very high-cost cases. Modifications of this type would reduce the incentive for participating plans to discriminate against black patients on economic grounds. Competitive bidding systems could also adopt provisions to mitigate the adverse effects for the uninsured of expanding the role of HMOs in low-income communities. Participating plans could, for example, be required to provide a minimum amount of care to the medically indigent living in the area.

It may not, however, prove necessary to abandon completely the compensation strategy. Although it may prove politically difficult to tie compensatory programs to particular racial groups, it may be feasible to link these programs to geographic areas or communities in which there are a disproportionate number of disadvantaged black residents. Congressional precedents exist for this approach. Programs that "forgive" medical school loans for physicians who practice in medically underserved areas work on this principle. More recently, to cope with some of the consequences of Medicare's shift to prospective payment for hospital care, Congress authorized the Health Care Financing Administration to develop more generous provisions for so-called "disproportionate share" hospitals. These are facilities located in areas with an unusually large number of low-income patients. Indirectly, such provisions disproportionately benefit disadvantaged minority groups.

The two greatest problems created by increased competition in many black communities are the reduced ability of providers to treat the uninsured and the reduced influence of the community over facility performance. These could be simultaneously addressed with a single compensating program. By authorizing a program that provided a pool of funds to pay for uncompensated care in particularly disadvantaged communities, policy makers could reduce the incentive to avoid treating the uninsured (Lewin and Lewin 1987; Rice and Payne 1981). By channeling these funds through a local board composed of community representatives, the program could restore some of the community's leverage over the health care institutions located within their boundaries.

These proposed strategies for public policy are simply meant to be suggestive. Defining effective and politically resilient reforms clearly requires far more detailed analysis. The overall strategy or particular proposals offered here can be further refined as we gain a better understanding of how system-wide changes in competition among health care providers affect particular groups of patients and communities. But it is important that policy makers begin to consider these issues. They must develop ways of constructively addressing the growing variations in health system performance that are related to race. Political action and public policy in this area will obviously raise some sensitive questions. But continued inaction will only guarantee that groups that have in the past lacked adequate access to health care will in the future face even greater barriers and threats to their well-being.

References

Alexander, J., M. Morrisey, and S. Shortell. 1986. Physician Participation in the Administration and Governance of System and Freestanding Hospitals: A Comparison by Type of Ownership. In *For-Profit Enterprise in Health Care,* ed. B.H. Gray, 402–21. Washington: National Academy Press.

Altman, D., R. Greene, and H. Sapolsky. 1981. *Health Planning and Regulation: The Decision-Making Process.* Washington: AUPHA Press.

Andersen, R., M. Chen, L. Aday, and L. Cornelius. 1987. Health Status and Medical Care Utilization. *Health Affairs* 6(1):136–56.

Anderson, M., and Fox, P. 1987. Lessons Learned from Medicaid Managed Care Approaches. *Health Affairs* 6(1):71–86.

Arthur Anderson & Co. 1984. *Health Care in the 1990s: Trends and Strategies.* Chicago.

Blumstein, J. 1986. Providing Hospital Care to Indigent Patients: Hill-Burton as a Case Study and a Paradigm. In *Uncompensated Hospital Care, Rights and Responsibilities,* ed. F. Sloan, J. Blumstein, and J. Perrin, 94–107. Baltimore: Johns Hopkins Press.

Checkoway, B. 1981. Consumer Movements in Health Planning. In *Health Planning in the United States: Selected Policy Issues,* ed. Committee on Health Planning Goals and Standards, Institute of Medicine, vol. 1, 184–203. Washington: National Academy Press.

Christianson, J., D. Hillman, and K. Smith. 1983. The Arizona Experiment: Competitive Bidding for Indigent Medical Care. *Health Affairs* 2(3):88–102.

Clark, R. 1980. Does the Nonprofit Form Fit the Hospital Industry? *Harvard Law Review* 93:1416–89.

Davidson, S., J. Perloff, P. Kletke, D. Schiff, and J. Connelly. 1983. Full and Limited Medicaid Participation among Pediatricians. *Pediatrics* 72(4):552–59.

Davis, K., M. Lillie–Blanton, B. Lyons, F. Mullan, N. Powe, and D. Rowland. 1987. Health Care for Black Americans: The Public Sector Role. *Milbank Quarterly* 65(Suppl. 1):213–47.

Davis, E., and M. Millman. 1983. *Health Care for the Urban Poor: Directions for Policy,* Totowa, N.J.: Rowman and Allanheld.

Dobson, A., J. Langenbrunner, S. Pelovitz, and J. Willis. 1986. The Future of Medicare Policy Reform: Priorities for Research and Demonstrations. *Health Care Financing Review* 1986 annual supplement: 1–7.

Dorwart, R., and W. Meyers. 1981. *Citizen Participation in Mental Health*. Springfield, Ill.: Charles C. Thomas.

Dutton, D., and R. Silber. 1980. Children's Health Outcomes in Six Different Ambulatory Care Delivery Systems. *Medical Care* 18:693–714.

Enthoven, A. 1977. The Consumer Choice Approach to National Health Insurance: Equity, the Market Place, and the Legitimacy of the Decision-making Process. In *Effects of the Payment Mechanism on the Health Care Delivery System,* ed. W. Roy, 4–10. DHEW pub. no. (PHS) 78–3227. Washington.

Ermann, D., and J. Gabel. 1985. The Changing Face of American Health Care: Multihospital Systems, Emergency Centers, and Surgery Centers. *Medical Care* 23(5):401–20.

Farley, D. 1985. *Competition among Hospitals: Market Structure and Its Relation to Utilization, Costs and Financial Position*. DHHS pub. no. (PHS) 85–3353. Washington.

Farley, P. 1985. Who are the Uninsured? *Milbank Memorial Fund Quarterly/Health and Society* 63(3):476–503.

Flinn Foundation. 1986. *Health Care for Arizona's Poor, 1982–1984*. Phoenix.

Foley, M., and G. Johnson. 1987. Health Care of Blacks in American Inner Cities. In *Health Care Issues in Black America,* ed. W. Jones, Jr., and M.F. Rice, 211–32. New York: Greenwood Press.

Freeman, H., R. Blendon, L. Aiken, S. Sudman, C. Mullinix, and

C. Corey. 1987. Americans Report Their Access to Health Care. *Health Affairs* 6(1):6–18.

Freund, D., and E. Neuschler. 1986. Overview of Medicaid Capitation and Case-management Initiatives. *Health Care Financing Review* annual supplement:21–30.

Friedman, M. 1962. *Capitalism and Freedom,* Chicago: University of Chicago Press.

Gaus, C., B. Cooper, and C. Hirschman. 1976. Contrasts in HMO and Fee-For-Service Performance. *Social Security Bulletin* 39(5):3–14.

Goldsmith, J. 1984. Death of a Paradigm: The Challenge of Competition. *Health Affairs* 3:5–19.

Hanft, R. 1977. Problems and Issues in the Financing of Health Care. Paper presented at a National Conference on Health Policy, Planning, and Financing the Future of Health Care for Blacks in America, Washington, October 28–29.

Harris, J. 1986. How Many Doctors Are Enough? *Health Affairs* 5(4):73–83.

Heyssel, R. 1981. Competition and the Marketplace for Health Care— It Won't Be Problem Free. *Hospitals* 55(22):107–14.

Holliman, J. 1983. Access to Health Care. In *Securing Access to Health Care: Ethical Implications of Differences in the Availability of Health Services,* President's Commission for the Study of Ethical Problems in Medicine, 79–106. Washington.

Holmes, D., J. Teresi, and M. Holmes. 1983. Differences among Black, Hispanic and White People in Knowledge about Long-term Care Services. *Health Care Financing Review* 5:51–65.

Howze, D. 1987. Closing the Gap between Black and White Infant Mortality Rates: An Analysis of Policy Options. In *Health Care Issues in Black America,* ed. W. Jones, Jr., and M.F. Rice, 119–39. New York: Greenwood Press.

Institute of Medicine. 1981. *Health Planning in the United States: Selected Policy Issues.* Vol. 1. Washington: National Academy Press.

Jackson, B., and Jensen, J. 1984. Consumers See Chain Ownership as Minus for Hospitals: Survey. *Modern Healthcare* 14:176–78.

Johns, L. 1983. Selective Contracting in California: Early Effects and Policy Implications. *Inquiry* 22:24–32.

Jones, W., and M. Rice. 1987. Black Health Care: An Overview. In *Health Care Issues in Black America,* ed. W. Jones, Jr., and M.F. Rice, 1–20. New York: Greenwood Press.

Kieser, K. 1987. Congress and Black Health: Dynamics and Strategies. In *Health Care Issues in Black America,* ed. W. Jones, Jr., and M.F. Rice, 59–77. New York: Greenwood Press.

Kindig, D., V. Sidel, and I. Birnbaum. 1977. National Health

Insurance for Inner City Underserved Areas: General Criteria and Analysis of a Proposed Administrative Mechanism. In *Effects of the Payment Mechanism on the Health Care Delivery System,* ed. W. Roy, 60–75. DHEW pub. no. (PHS) 78–3227. Washington.

Kinzer, D. 1984. Care of the Poor Revisited. *Inquiry* 21:5–16.

Kirkmann-Liff, B. 1986. Refusal of Care: Evidence from Arizona. *Health Affairs* 5(4):15–24.

Lave, J., and L. Lave. 1974. *The Hospital Construction Act.* Washington: American Enterprise Institute.

Leon, M. 1987. *Access to Health Care in the United States: Results of a 1986 Survey.* Robert Wood Johnson Foundation Special Report no. 2. Princeton: Robert Wood Johnson Foundation.

Lewin, L., and Lewin, M. 1987. Financing Charity Care in an Era of Competition. *Health Affairs* (6)1:47–60.

Lewis, C. 1976. Efforts to Increase the Number of Physicians: Impact on Access to Medical Care. In *A Right to Health: The Problem of Access to Primary Medical Care,* ed. C. Lewis, R. Fein, and D. Mechanic, 92–110. New York: John Wiley.

Lissovoy, G., T. Rice, D. Ermann, and J. Gabel. 1986. Preferred Provider Organizations: Today's Models and Tomorrow's Prospects. *Inquiry* 23(1):7–15.

Luft, H. 1981. *Health Maintenance Organizations: Dimensions of Performance.* New York: John Wiley.

———. 1982. Health Maintenance Organizations and the Rationing of Medical Care. *Milbank Memorial Fund Quarterly/Health and Society* 60:268–306.

———. 1985. Competition and Regulation. *Medical Care* 23(5):383–400.

Marquis, M. 1983. Consumers' Knowledge about Their Health Insurance Coverage. *Health Care Financing Review* 5(1):65–80.

Martin, E. 1977. Consumer Choice Health Plan Impact on Rural America. In *Effects of the Payment Mechanism on the Health Care Delivery System,* ed. W. Roy, 45–50. DHEW pub. no. (PHS) 78–3227. Washington.

McDaniel, R. 1985. Management and Medicine, Never the Twain Shall Meet. *Journal of the National Medical Association* 77(2):107–12.

Meyer, J.A. 1983. Introduction. In *Market Reforms in Health Care,* ed. J. Meyer, 1–11. Washington: Enterprise Institute for Public Policy Research.

Middleton, M. 1987. Nonprofit Board of Directors: Beyond the Governance Function. In *The Nonprofit Sector,* ed. W. Powell, 141–53. New Haven: Yale University Press.

Morone, J. 1981. The Real World of Representation and the HSAs.

In *Health Planning in the United States: Selected Policy Issues,* ed. Committee on Health Planning Goals and Standards, Institute of Medicine, vol. 2, 257–89. Washington: National Academy Press.

Munnell, A. 1985. Ensuring Entitlement to Health Care Services. *New England Economic Review* November/December:30–40.

Noether, M. 1987. *Competition among Hospitals.* Staff Report of the Bureau of Economics, Federal Trade Commission. Washington.

Okada, L., and G. Sparer. 1976. Access to Usual Source of Care by Race and Income in Ten Urban Areas. *Journal of Community Health* 1(3):163–75.

Persons, G. 1987. Blacks in State and Local Government: Progress and Constraints. In *The State of Black America,* ed. Janet Dewart, 167–92. New York: National Urban League.

Polchow, M. 1986. *State Efforts at Health Cost Containment: 1986 Update.* Washington: National Conference of State Legislatures.

Rice, H., and L. Payne. 1981. Health Issues for the Eighties. In *The State of Black America,* ed. National Urban League, 119–51. New York: National Urban League.

Ripley, R., and G. Franklin. 1982. *Bureaucracy and Policy Implementation.* Homewood, Ill.: Dorsey.

Robinson, J., and Luft, H. 1985. The Impact of Hospital Market Structure on Patient Volume, Average Length of Stay, and the Cost of Care. *Journal of Health Economics* 4:333–56.

Rowland, D., and B. Lyons. 1987. Mandatory HMO Care for Milwaukee's Poor. *Health Affairs* 6(1):87–100.

Rudov, M., and N. Santangelo. 1979. Health Status of Minorities and Low-income Groups. DHEW pub. no. (HRA) 79–627. Washington.

Ruiz, D., and Herbert, T. 1984. The Economics of Health Care for Elderly Blacks. *Journal of the National Medical Association* 76(9):849–53.

Schiff, R., D. Ansell, J. Schlosser, A. Idris, A. Morrison, and S. Whitman. 1986. Transfers to a Public Hospital: A Prospective of 467 Patients. *New England Journal of Medicine* 314(9):552–57.

Schlesinger, M. 1986. On the Limits of Expanding Health Care Reform: Chronic Care in Prepaid Settings. *Milbank Quarterly* 64(2):189–215.

———. 1987. Children's Health Services and the Changing Organization of the Health Care System. In *Children in a Changing Health Care System: Prospects and Proposals for Reform,* ed. M. Schlesinger and L. Eisenberg. Baltimore: Johns Hopkins University Press. (Forthcoming.)

Schlesinger, M., J. Bentkover, D. Blumenthal, R. Musacchio, and

J. Willer. 1987. The Privatization of Health Care and Physicians' Perceptions of Access to Hospital Services. *Milbank Quarterly* 65(2):1–33.

Schlesinger, M., D. Blumenthal, and E. Schlesinger. 1986. Profits under Pressure: The Economic Performance of Investor-owned and Nonprofit Health Maintenance Organizations. *Medical Care* 24(7):615–27.

Seay, J., B. Vladeck, P. Kramer, D. Gould, and J. McCormack. 1986. Holding Fast to the Good: The Future of the Voluntary Hospital. *Inquiry* 23(3):253–60.

Shortell, S., E. Morrison, S. Hughes, B. Friedman, J. Coverdill, and L. Berg. 1986. The Effects of Hospital Ownership on Nontraditional Services. *Health Affairs* 5(4):97–111.

Silver, L. 1974. The Legal Accountability of Nonprofit Hospitals. In *Regulating Health Facilities Construction,* ed. C. Havighurst, 76–89. Washington: American Enterprise Institute.

Sloan, F. 1980. The Internal Organization of Hospitals: A Descriptive Study. *Health Services Research* 15(3):203–30.

Sloan, F., J. Mitchell, and J. Cromwell. 1978. Physician Participation in State Medicaid Programs. *Journal of Human Resources* 13:211–45.

Sloan, F., J. Valvano, and R. Mullner. 1986. Identifying the Issues: A Statistical Profile. In *Uncompensated Hospital Care, Rights and Responsibilities,* ed. F. Sloan, J. Blumstein, and J. Perrin. Baltimore: Johns Hopkins Press.

Sowell, T. 1981. *Markets and Minorities.* New York: Basic Books.

Spence, A.M. 1974. *Market Signaling: Informational Transfer in Hiring and Related Screening Processes.* Cambridge: Harvard University Press.

Turner, T. 1985. Health Care Issues in Southern Rural Black America. *Urban League Review* 9(2):47–51.

U.S. Congressional Budget Office. 1985. *Reducing Poverty among Children.* Washington.

Vladeck, B. 1985. The Dilemma between Competition and Community Service. *Inquiry* 22:115–21.

Willis, J. 1986. Preface. *Health Care Financing Review* 1986 annual supplement. 1–2.

Windle, C. 1980. Correlates of Community Mental Health Centers' Underservice to Non-Whites. *Journal of Community Psychology* 8:140–46,

Winn, M. 1987. Competitive Health Care: Assessing an Alternative Solution for Health Care Problems. In *Health Care Issues in America,* ed. W. Jones, Jr., and M.F. Rice, 233–44. New York: Greenwood Press.

Wolfe, S. 1977. Problems and Issues in the Financing of Health Care. Paper presented at the National Conference on Health Policy, Planning and Financing the Future of Health Care for Blacks in America, Washington, October 28–29.

Reduction of Hypertension-associated Heart Disease and Stroke among Black Americans: Past Experience and New Perspectives on Targeting Resources

DANIEL D. SAVAGE, DANIEL L. McGEE, and GERRY OSTER

P AST STRATEGIES AND THE RESULTS OF THOSE
strategies for prevention of hypertension-associated morbidity
and mortality help to guide assessment of future needs and
may serve as prototypes for the development of more efficient efforts
for primary and secondary prevention of other chronic diseases. Choices
among competing needs and interests and finite resources are becoming
increasingly difficult to make: What new efforts are needed and which
ones are to be emphasized? What data need to be acquired, and in
what ways can these data be used to promote and evaluate preventive
programs? Mathematical modeling provides one tool for orderly assessment of such information and for use as an aid in sound decision
making. Quantitative information from such modeling does not substitute for the social, ethical, and political dynamics of policy making
but helps to clarify the potential impact and cost of specific decisions.
It can add precision to the assumptions that are part of policy decisions.
It can direct attention to opportunities for more effective use of
resources. It can point out subgroups that may need specific strategies
that would not be of substantial benefit relative to the cost and other
competing needs for the entire population.

The continuing critical role of hypertension in black-white disparities in morbidity and mortality (Kumanyika and Savage 1985) makes such analyses particularly important in the assessment of national hypertension-control policies to insure the adequacy of the policy for blacks. Past analyses (Drizd, Dannenberg, and Engel 1986; Joint National Committee on Detection, Evaluation, and Treatment of High Blood Pressure 1985) have suggested that, in general, the national hypertension-control policies have had as great, if not a greater, positive impact on the black population than on the white population. These analyses appropriately used blood-pressure level as a key indicator of the impact of the policy. Other intermediate measures of the impact of national hypertension-control policies included the percentage of hypertensive persons: (1) aware of their hypertension, (2) taking antihypertensive medications, and (3) having their hypertension under control (i.e., below an agreed-on cut-point). The ultimate measure of success of hypertension-control policies is the degree of reduction in hypertension-associated disease and death. Some evidence (U.S. Public Health Service 1986) points to a similar impact of the national policy on hypertension-associated disease and death (i.e., stroke and death from heart disease) in the black and white populations. Future policy analyses will increasingly focus on strategies to reduce the risk associated with mild elevations of blood pressure, partially because of past successes in reducing the prevalence of moderate and severe hypertension. The greater heterogeneity of risk in black and white populations with mild elevations in blood pressure suggests that, for future gains in efficiency and equity in outcome, past approaches for achieving (and assessing) hypertension control will need to be updated. Blood pressure levels alone may no longer be adequate indicators for such purposes. Tarazi (1985) signaled the potential importance of other factors in hypertension when he stated that the definition of hypertension solely in terms of arterial pressure levels has obscured the other biologic dimensions of the disease. One biologic dimension of hypertension that will become increasingly important in future policy analyses is target organ damage secondary to hypertension. The heart, the brain, the kidneys, and blood vessels throughout the body are major target organs in hypertension. Recently, the use of sound waves (echocardiography) to identify heart changes (such as increased left-ventricular mass) (see appendix) has allowed early identification of target organ damage in the heart before damage is apparent elsewhere (Savage et al. 1979a). There is increasing evidence that such measures may identify individuals at substantially increased risk of subsequent morbidity and mortality (independent of other standard risk factors, including blood pressure level) (Savage et al. 1985; Casale et al. 1986; Levy et al. 1987a). Framingham data (Savage et al. 1983; Savage et al. 1987; Levy et al. 1987b) suggest that the echocardiographic left-ventricular mass helps to integrate the overall blood pressure experience. This assessment of target organ damage may reflect the risk associated with the overall blood pressure experience better than two or three blood pressure tests taken on one or two occasions (the usual approach for evaluating blood pressure level and risk). The finding by Hammond et al. (1986) and Dunn et al. (1983) of greater echocardiographic evidence of target organ damage in black individuals with mild hypertension—matched by apparent blood pressure level, age, sex, and treatment status to white hypertensive individuals—suggests that analyses of hypertension control and policy decisions based on blood pressure level alone may not have the same meaning in black and white populations and may lead to faulty conclusions on the relative impact of efforts to reduce hypertension-associated morbidity and mortality in black and white populations. The future data requirements for both assessing and planning hypertension-control strategies need to be reexamined.

This article describes the apparently similar impact of national policy on hypertension control in the black and white populations as measured by currently available national indicators. The elements of a type of mathematical modeling previously applied to hypertension-control policy (cost-effectiveness analysis) are briefly described. The suggestion is made that future strategies would be improved by an updating of such analyses, with improved data on stratification of risk in race-specific analyses.

Finally, the article briefly describes a mathematical analysis (based on published Framingham data) that predicts that the stratification of risk associated with echocardiographic assessment of left-ventricular mass as a continuous variable may represent a breakthrough. This stratification of risk in the population could, along with several other benefits, allow much more precise assessment of the adequacy of hypertension control and aid in more efficient targeting of resources to reduce the continuing excess cardiovascular morbidity and mortality in the black as compared to the white population. Future incorporation of such information into assessments of national progress and cost-effectiveness modeling would be severely limited without population-based data similar to the Framingham data (an almost exclusively white population sample) for the black population. An important step in efficient allocation of resources to reduce the apparent excessive hypertension-associated morbidity and mortality in the black population is a more accurate and sensitive approach to monitoring of target organ damage associated with hypertension. Data presented here suggest that echocardiographic assessment of left-ventricular mass may provide a much-improved assessment of hypertension status. The best data for planning national policy with such profound health and economic implications are national data from representative samples of the black and white populations, because of potential differences between and within racial groups in various areas of the country (Savage et al. 1979b; Gazes et al. 1986; Savage et al. 1987).

Profile of Reduction of Heart Disease and Stroke and Control of Hypertension: Magnitude of the Problem and Progress

Cost-effectiveness modeling in hypertension policy analysis is important partly because of the magnitude of the problem and its associated morbidity and mortality. Small changes in policy could have enormous impact on public health and health care costs. Despite substantial progress in disease prevention and health promotion, as well as the emergence of new important public health concerns, heart disease and stroke remain the number-one cause of death for black and white men and women in the United States. Heart-disease death rates from 1979 to 1981 were 319.4 deaths per 100,000 population for black men, and 274.4 deaths per 100,000 for white men. Heart-disease death rates during this period for black women were 194.4 deaths per 100,000, and for white women were 131.9 deaths per 100,000. Stroke death rates during this period were 76 and 41.2 per 100,000 for black and white men, respectively. Stroke rates during this two-year period were 60.2 and 34.7 for black and white women, respectively (U.S. Department of Health and Human Services 1985, vol. 4, pt. 1; see also Manton, Patrick, and Johnson 1987).

Hypertension-associated cardiovascular disease is a major contributor to this mortality. Based on projections made in the early 1980s from national survey data, 58 million Americans are estimated to be at increased risk of morbidity and premature mortality because of high blood pressure, warranting some type of systematic monitoring (Joint National Committee on Detection, Evaluation, and Treatment of High Blood Pressure 1985). This includes 38 percent of the adult black population and 29 percent of the adult white population.

The annual cost of treating cardiovascular disease in the United States (most of which is associated with hypertension) has recently been estimated to be 78.6 billion dollars (Stason 1986). Harlan (1987), citing data from the National Medical Care Utilization Survey indicated that hypertension is the most common chronic disease treated in the medical care system. He has indicated that the per capita cost was about $120 per year in 1980. His analyses indicated that if hypertension is complicated by overt evidence of atherosclerotic disease or associated with other conditions (e.g., renal disease, diabetes, etc.) the per capita costs increased about tenfold. Stason (1986) estimates that nearly eight billion dollars is being spent directly each year on the treatment of hypertension in the United States. The number of individuals with elevated blood pressure taking antihypertensive medications has increased rapidly since the modern era of hypertensive therapy began in the early 1960s.

In one population-based sample of adult men followed for the past 27 years, zero (black men) and 3 percent (white men) of the entire sample of black and white men were taking antihypertensive medications in 1960, whereas 59 percent (black men) and 41 percent (white men) of these subjects were taking such medications two and one-half decades later (Gazes et al. 1986). The estimated prevalence of hypertension in the 1960 sample would have led to an expected finding of roughly 30 percent of the sample taking antihypertensive medications rather than the near-zero percent who actually were. The National Examination Survey of the 1960s and the two National Health and Nutrition Examination Surveys of the 1970s (NHANES I and II) documented the national progress in getting the groups with highest blood pressures on antihypertensive treatment. For example, in the 1970s the definition for "definite hypertension" indicating a need for treatment was a systolic blood pressure equal to or greater than 160 mm Hg and/or a diastolic blood pressure equal to or greater than 95 mm Hg. The 1976 to 1980 national survey data indicated that 73.6 percent of definite hypertensive individuals (i.e., with blood pressures at or above these cut-points or on antihypertensive medications) had been diagnosed (i.e., had previously been told by a doctor that they had high blood pressure or were hypertensive) (Drizd, Dannenberg, and Engel 1986). Black adult hypertensives found to have definite hypertension during this survey were more likely than their white counterparts to have been previously diagnosed (80.9 percent versus 72.3 percent, respectively). This finding was consistent in the sex-specific comparisons but only reached statistical significance in women. Some 69.1 percent of the black hypertensive men were previously diagnosed, compared to 65.9 percent of the white hypertensive men. Overall, 87.6 percent of black women with definite hypertension had been previously diagnosed, compared to 79.3 percent of their white counterparts. Nearly 90 percent of black women aged 35 years and older with definite hypertension were previously diagnosed as hypertensive (Drizd, Dannenberg, and Engel 1986). This is an extraordinary example of the apparently successful relative impact of preventive action in the black compared to the white population.

Over three-fourths of the diagnosed definite hypertensives reported taking antihypertensive medication "always," "often," or "sometimes" (Drizd, Dannenberg, and Engel 1986). Among hypertensive individuals, the younger groups were less likely than the older age group to be taking medications—40.9 percent for those 18 to 24 years of age versus 85.4 percent of those 65 to 74 years of age. Adult women hypertensives were more likely than hypertensive men to be taking antihypertensive medications (79.3 percent versus 68.9 percent, age-adjusted to the combined population) (Drizd, Dannenberg, and Engel 1986). Among the male hypertensive subjects the percentage taking antihypertensive medications ranged from 37.6 percent for those aged 18 to 24 to 81.8 percent for those aged 65 to 74. For hypertensive women the percentage taking antihypertensive medications ranged from 44 percent for those aged 18 to 24 to 87.2 percent for those aged 65 to 74.

Current data suggest that younger hypertensives with the same level of blood pressure as older hypertensives benefit from treatment with antihypertensive medications as much if not more than the older hypertensives. Of course, older as well as younger hypertensive patients are recommended to have a trial of nonpharmacological therapy when appropriate (e.g., weight reduction if they are overweight, salt reduction if they are salt sensitive, and reduced alcohol intake). If such non-pharmacological therapy is successful in controlling blood pressure after a few weeks, it may suffice. If not, pharmacological therapy is recommended in addition to the continued attempts at nonpharmacological intervention.

Once diagnosed, black hypertensives were as likely as white hypertensives to be taking antihypertensive medications (72.7 percent versus 75.1 percent, respectively). Women who were previously diagnosed as hypertensive were more likely to be taking medications than men. This was consistent in race-specific comparisons. Thus, 75.9 percent and 66 percent of black diagnosed hypertensive women and men, respectively, and 81 percent and 68.8 percent of white diagnosed hypertensive women and men, respectively, were taking antihypertensive medications. Some 88.9 percent of black women hypertensives aged 65 to 74 were taking antihypertensive medications—the highest rate of all age/sex groups. Thus, 58 percent of all black women aged 65 to 74 in the United States were taking antihypertensive medications (Drizd, Dannenberg, and Engel 1986). The question should be raised as to whether the efforts at nonpharmacologic management in black hypertensive patients are as great as in white hypertensive patients, given the relatively greater prevalence of overweight and possibly salt sensitivity in the black population.

From the early 1960s to the late 1970s the systolic blood pressure declined more in black adults than in white adults. The mean age-adjusted systolic blood pressure declined 4 mm Hg in white men, 6 mm Hg in white women, 8 mm Hg in black men, and 12 mm Hg in black women (Drizd, Dannenberg, and Engel 1986). During this period the decline in mean systolic blood pressure was greatest in the older individuals. For example, the systolic blood pressure declined 12 mm Hg in white men and women aged 65 to 74 compared to a 1 mm drop in those aged 18 to 24.

Repeated cross-sectional blood pressure surveys in several areas—Minnesota (Folsom et al. 1983; Luepker et al. 1984), Baltimore (Apostolides et al. 1978), Chicago (Berkson et al. 1980), Charleston (McClure et al. 1982), Maryland (Entwisle et al. 1983), and Connecticut (Freeman et al. 1985)—have consistently shown the improvement in blood pressure control, supporting the earlier findings of the national surveys (Drizd, Dannenberg, and Engel 1986). Evidence from physician visits (figure 1) continues to show that "large segments of the population are undertaking appropriate measures to control their blood pressure" (Lenfant and Moskowitz 1983). From 1982 to 1985, visits to physicians

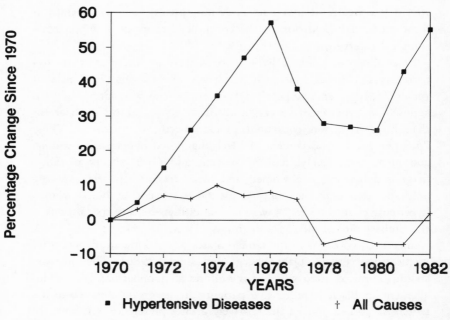

FIG. 1.   Percentage change since 1970 in number of physician visits for all causes and for hypertensive disease (hypertensive and hypertensive heart disease). *Source*: National Disease and Therapeutic Index, IMS America (Lenfant and Moskowitz 1983, ref. 13).

for high blood pressure increased 52.7 percent while visits for other reasons increased 4.8 percent (U.S. Public Health Service 1986). The increased visits provide an opportunity for more effective use of non-pharmacological adjunct or primary therapy for elevated blood pressure, which has in some ways lagged behind pharmacological management. For example, the percentage of adult individuals who are overweight (roughly 40 to 45 percent of black women and 20 percent of white men, white women, and black men) has not changed from the early 1960s to the late 1970s (Kumanyika and Helitzer 1985).

Nevertheless, the blood-pressure changes are believed to have made an important contribution to the documented decline in mortality from heart disease and stroke since the 1960s. From 1972 to 1984 the death rate from heart disease, in general, fell 33.9 percent (U.S. Public Health Service 1986). From 1980 to 1986 this death rate fell at least another 9 percent. Between 1968 and 1976 the annual age-adjusted coronary-heart-disease death rate in all race/sex groups except white women declined by 60 to 70 per 100,000 (U.S. Department of Health and Human Services 1985). For white women the decline was 34 per 100,000. Stroke mortality declined 47.8 percent between 1972 and 1984 and has fallen at least another 17 percent since 1980 (U.S. Public Health Service 1986). Between 1970 and 1980 stroke mortality has shown the greatest decline in black women, falling by 46 to 56 percent in various age decades between 35 and 74 years (U.S. Department of Health and Human Services 1985). The declines in stroke death rates during this time period in the other three race/sex groups were in a similar range, varying from 39 to 48 percent for various age decades between 35 and 74 years.

Public and private efforts have contributed to the progress in hypertension control. In 1972 the National Institutes of Health established the National High Blood Pressure Education Program to bring national attention to hypertension as a major public health problem. A cornerstone of the program, the National High Blood Pressure Education Program Coordinating Committee, was established at that time as well. This committee currently comprises over 30 volunteer health, professional, and public agencies and organizations, and serves as a forum for consensus and action for these groups. It provides direction as well as a national network for the program's education effort. An example of the committee's efforts is the consensus on lowering the level of blood pressure at which pharmacological treatment should begin if nonpharmacological management was not successful from 95 to 90 mm Hg. These recommendations were widely and rapidly disseminated using the network of the coordinating committee. The success of this process is believed to have contributed to the above-noted acceleration in physician visits for hypertension in the early 1980s (figure 1). State and local hypertension control programs have also been an integral part of the program's network. To enhance the effectiveness of the program in minority communities, the Ad Hoc Committee on Hypertension in Minority Populations was formed in 1975. This committee was comprised of Hispanic, Asian, Native American and black health professionals, selected for their strong ties to minority communities throughout the United States. This committee aided in two-way communication between the program and the minority communities. The ad hoc committee continues this function with an expanded role of aiding in reduction of all of the risk factors for cardiopulmonary disease.

The overall profile of past high blood pressure control efforts and reduction of heart disease morbidity and stroke in the black and white United States populations is positive and suggests a beneficial relative impact on the black population. There are, however, a number of considerations that suggest that these efforts need reassessment and refinement:

1. Despite the overall reduction in heart disease and stroke mortality in all race/sex groups, a five to six year life-expectancy gap (at birth) remains between black women and men compared to white women and men. Expressed in other terms, this gap is responsible for 59,000 deaths annually in black men and women that would not occur if blacks had the same death rates as whites (Manton, Patrick, and Johnson 1987). Forty-one percent of these excess deaths in black women and 24 percent of the excess deaths in black men are attributable to heart disease and stroke (U.S. Department of Health and Human Services 1985). A detailed review of the risk factors for this excess cardiovascular disease identified hypertension as a key contributor (Kumanyika and Savage 1985).

2. Some evidence from the mid-1970s suggests that cardiovascular disease mortality may show a decreased rate of decline in black men and women and white women in contrast to the unchanged rate of decline in white men (Sempos et al. 1986).

3. Clinical trial information suggests that the reduction in heart disease deaths associated with reducing blood pressure with medications is less ("fraction of benefit" equals 40 to 60 percent) than that predicted from observational epidemiologic studies (Russell 1987; Kuller et al. 1986). This is in contrast to the fraction of benefit (nearly 100 percent) in reduction of stroke. Subgroups of subjects with resting electro-cardiographic abnormalities (including changes suggesting left-ventricular hypertrophy) at baseline who were treated with diuretics had a significantly greater heart disease mortality than those that had no such resting abnormalities or that were less vigorously treated with diuretics (Kuller et al. 1986).

4. Hypertensive patients with some forms of left-ventricular hypertrophy may be made worse when treated with some classes of

antihypertensive agents (Topol, Traill, and Fortuin 1985; Savage 1987a). Some evidence suggests that black patients may be more likely to have such conditions (Topol, Traill, and Fortuin 1985; Savage 1987b).

5. Some classes of antihypertensive agents (diuretics and beta blockers) have been associated with modest unwanted changes in blood lipid profiles (Wright 1987).

6. New classes of antihypertensive agents are increasingly being used instead of diuretics as first-step therapy for hypertension. These agents are substantially more expensive than diuretics (Gallup and Cotugno 1986; Saunders 1986).

As noted above, policy changes in hypertensive management should be carefully considered because of their potentially large health and economic impact. Groundwork for quantitative considerations of such policy was laid in the mid-1970s by Weinstein and Stason (1976).

Cost-effectiveness Modeling in Hypertension

In 1976 Milton C. Weinstein and William B. Stason published a classic study: *Hypertension: A Policy Perspective*. They examined the cost-effectiveness of the treatment of hypertension. They used data from the long-term prospective epidemiologic study at Framingham to estimate the morbidity and mortality benefits of blood pressure control. They took the social perspective and counted all costs, regardless of who paid them, and all health effects, no matter who experienced them. The cost per year of life gained was calculated using the following formula: cost per year = net costs/net health effects.

As summarized by Russell (1987), net costs are the total costs of treatment, minus the savings in medical costs secondary to heart attacks and strokes prevented, plus the costs of treating side effects of the medications, plus ordinary medical costs during the years of life added by the treatment. The net health effects included years of life added by drug therapy, plus improvements in health because of treatment (valued in an equivalent number of years of life), minus the side effects of drugs (also calculated in an equivalent number of years of life). As noted, the Framingham data gave the risk of heart disease, stroke, and death as a function of blood pressure level. These data fit a logistic curve (i.e., risk of death or disease rose more rapidly

at higher levels of blood pressure). For example, a ten-point rise in
blood pressure from 115 mm Hg to 125 mm Hg is associated with
a greater increment in risk of disease or death than an increase from
95 mm Hg to 105 mm Hg (Russell 1987). Data were available for
white men and women but not for black subjects.

Weinstein and Stason derived their information on effectiveness of
treatment from the Veterans Administration clinical trials. Statistical
information was not totally adequate for all ages and different lengths
of treatment, so they used expert opinions for filling in such gaps in
information not available from the trials. They expressed the benefits
of antihypertensive therapy in terms of the gain in "quality-adjusted
life years." This adjustment allows one to equate a number of years
with poor health (e.g., with side effects of medicines) that people
would give up in order to have a year of good health (e.g., with no
heart disease). They used a number of simplifying assumptions and
used national death rates to estimate the remaining parameters. Thus,
they estimated that the cost of treatment of hypertension was $4,850
per year of life gained for people with moderate or severe hypertension
(Russell 1987). This rose to $7,000 if the cost of screening to identify
the individual was included. Age at identification, sex, and initial
blood pressure were variables that affected these costs. Adherence to
therapy had an important effect since lack of adherence could increase
the cost 30 percent to as much as four-fold more (Russell 1987). In
a recent update, the cost of screening and treatment for persons with
a diastolic pressure of 105 mm Hg was $12,000 per quality-adjusted
year of life gained in 1984 dollars (assuming incomplete adherence)
(Stason 1986). This increased to more than $60,000 per person per
quality-adjusted year of life gained for those with diastolic blood
pressure of 90–94 mm Hg.

Hypertensive patients with mild elevations of blood pressure are a
heterogeneous group with a lower benefit relative to the cost of pharmacologic treatment. This has increased interest in both nonpharmacologic treatment and in further stratification of this group into
high- and low-risk individuals. This could mean that perhaps millions
of individuals with mild hypertension could be identified as being at
such low risk that they need only be managed with nonpharmacologic
therapy. A smaller subgroup (that also had apparently mild hypertension
on the basis of their blood pressure level) might be identified who
were at much higher risk and might need both pharmacologic and

nonpharmacologic treatment. This could lead to a much more efficient program of reduction in cardiovascular morbidity and mortality. For this reason, interest in assessing cardiac target-organ damage (especially echocardiographically detected increases in left-ventricular mass) for such stratification of risk in individuals with mild to moderate hypertension has grown.

A mathematical model of cardiovascular mortality risk associated with such target-organ damage helps to quantify the potential of the echocardiographic measurements in risk assessment. Such a model is shown in figure 2, in which the gradient of risk associated with increasing echocardiographic left-ventricular mass (from the 50th to 99th percentile) is compared with the gradient of risk between similar percentiles of serum cholesterol or diastolic blood pressure. Details of the construction of this risk model are given in the appendix. The model predicts that a strikingly greater risk of cardiovascular mortality will be associated with increments in left-ventricular mass compared to increments of diastolic blood pressure or total cholesterol. This greater risk is not only striking at very high levels of the risk factors (e.g., the 99th percentile) but, more importantly for potential impact in cost-effectiveness analyses, is also striking at lower percentiles of risk factors. Data derived from our mathematical model predict that echocardiographic left-ventricular mass as a continuous variable may give a much more powerful stratification of risk than the level of blood pressure and, in particular, might help in stratification of risk among mild hypertensive patients.

Data are already available that are consistent with this model. For example, figure 3 records the progressive increase in cardiovascular events in white middle-aged men with mild hypertension associated with an increased left-ventricular mass index. The gradient of risk ranged from 0.8 cardiovascular events per 100 person-years for an echocardiographic left-ventricular mass index of 95 grams/meter squared to 4.3 events per 100 person-years for those with a left-ventricular mass index of 125 grams/meter squared or greater (Casale et al. 1986).

Echocardiograms performed in the Framingham study sample will allow the model to be tested directly in a population-based sample of white adults. As noted earlier, preliminary follow-up data from Framingham have already shown the echocardiographic left-ventricular mass to be a powerful risk marker for two-year all-cause mortality in men and women from the original cohort, independent of the standard

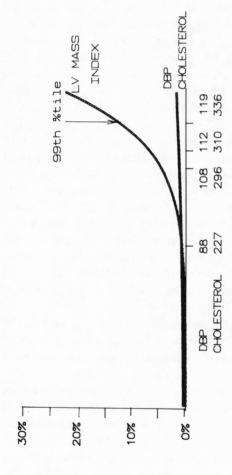

FIG. 2. Incidence of cardiovascular death for two years associated with percentile of echocardiographically determined left-ventricular mass (index), diastolic blood pressure, and total serum cholesterol in men aged 45 to 54. The risk-function curves are derived from interpolation between mean risk for the upper 99th percentile of the distribution of a risk factor and the mean risk for the remainder of the population using published Framingham data. The occurrence of electrocardiographic left-ventricular hypertrophy was conservatively considered the equivalent of the 99th percentile of echocardiographic left-ventricular mass (or mass index). LV = left ventricular, DBP = diastolic blood pressure in mm Hg. Cholesterol in mg/dl. See appendix for details.

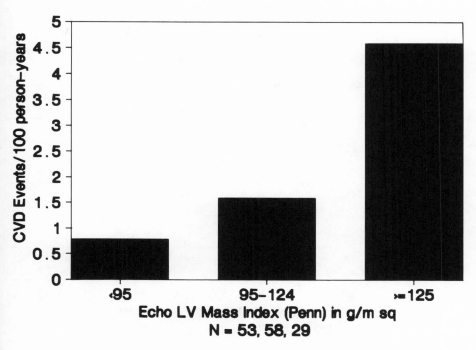

FIG. 3. Risk of development of cardiovascular (CVD) morbid events in middle-aged white men (mean age 48 years) with mild hypertension (and free of overt cardiovascular disease at baseline) as a function of range of echocardiographic left-ventricular mass index. "Penn" criteria LV mass indexed to body surface area was used. *Source:* Savage 1987a (adapted from Casale et al. 1986).

cardiovascular risk factors (Savage et al. 1985). Further analyses will allow more precise coefficients to be developed for the relation of cardiovascular morbidity and mortality to the level of echocardiographic left-ventricular mass. The utility of echocardiographic left-ventricular mass as a tool for stratification of risk will depend partially on the precision of these coefficients. No such data are available for blacks.

Figure 4 records the distribution of left-ventricular mass for a general population sample of Framingham (white) men (Savage et al. 1987) and for a small general population sample of black men aged 60 to 69 (Gazes et al. 1986). The relative shift in left-ventricular mass in black men to higher left-ventricular mass remained after various age-group- and blood-pressure-specific comparisons.

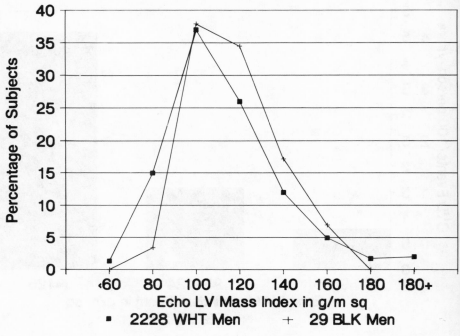

FIG. 4.   Distribution of echocardiographic left-ventricular mass index in 2,228 Framingham white (WHT) men and in 29 elderly black (BLK) men. "Penn" criteria LV mass indexed to body surface area was used. *Source:* Savage 1987b.

Conclusions and Implications

These data are of importance for policy decisions regarding hypertensive patients in general but have particular significance for black hypertensive patients. If the above-cited two-fold greater prevalence of echocardiographic left-ventricular hypertrophy in blacks with mild hypertension, as compared with white hypertensives, has generality to the nation, the model would suggest significant differences in the meaning of mild hypertension in black and white hypertensives. This would suggest potentially different strategies for reducing hypertension-associated morbidity and mortality in black and white mild hypertensives. This would be especially important if reversing the increased left-ventricular mass is shown to be an important independent goal of antihypertension management. More information is needed on the distribution of left-ventricular mass and its prognostic significance in various demographic groups of men and women. Such information may come from the third National Health and Nutrition Examination Survey, which may include echocardiography in the second of two national examination samples. This survey will have long-term follow-up and could be a valuable source of information for investigating the relation of left-ventricular mass to outcome in various demographic groups. Information on the degree of reduction of risk conferred by reducing left-ventricular mass independent of blood pressure reduction in various smaller demographic groups would be needed to complement the national observational data for precise cost-effectiveness analyses.

There are already data that suggest the differing importance of various potential determinants of increased left-ventricular mass in various groups of individuals, such as white and black men (Gazes et al. 1986). Thus, left-ventricular mass increases in one demographic group may have strikingly different implications than those in another group. This suggests that measurement of echocardiographic left-ventricular mass should be a part of clinical trials of antihypertensive agents and surveys assessing cardiovascular risk factors in various demographic groups of subjects. This is important even if the main purpose of a given survey and subsequent analyses is to investigate other risk factors for cardiovascular disease and death, because of the confounding effect that such an apparently important risk factor as left-ventricular mass might have on such analyses (Oster and Epstein 1986). If the prediction of the model developed above is confirmed, these data may have a profound impact on the choice of treatment as well as the therapeutic goal of treatment. The World Health Organization–International Society for Hypertension (1986) joint 1986 memorandum on treatment guidelines has already recommended that echocardiographic left-ventricular hypertrophy, in the absence of another explanation, is an indication for drug therapy in an individual with mild hypertension.

Echocardiographic information from race- sex- age-specific population-based observational studies and clinical trials could be used in refining analyses of the cost-effectiveness of alternative strategies for managing hypertension. Such analyses could lead to a more efficient reduction of cardiovascular morbidity and mortality for all racial groups, but especially for blacks who appear to be overrepresented in the higher percentiles of echocardiographic left-ventricular mass even after controlling for blood pressure level.

If the assumptions in the model of cardiovascular mortality risk associated with echocardiographic left-ventricular mass prove correct, and the reduction of left-ventricular mass reverses the markedly elevated risk, such reduction of mass may be an essential component of the strategy for reducing the excess cardiovascular mortality in blacks as compared to whites.

Appendix

Mathematical Model Predicting the Prognostic Power of Echocardiographically Determined Left-ventricular Mass (figure 2)

Echocardiography, the use of sound waves to assess the structure and function of the heart, is widely accepted as the most sensitive and specific tool widely available for detecting left-ventricular hypertrophy—increased mass or weight of the left ventricle (Liebson, Devereux, and Horan 1987). The electrocardiogram (EKG) and the chest x ray were used in the past to assess left-ventricular hypertrophy or heart enlargement associated with hypertension. The EKG is still recommended for assessment of cardiac target-organ damage as part of the assessment of all hypertensive patients. It is a highly specific tool for detection of left-ventricular hypertrophy but is not very sensitive. Echocardiography maintains the high specificity of electrocardiography for this diagnosis (Savage et al. 1987, 1979a) while achieving a high sensitivity (correlations with autopsy left-ventricular mass exceed 0.9) (Devereux and Reichek 1977). Thus, only about 10 percent of subjects with echocardiographic left-ventricular hypertrophy are detected by the EKG, while almost all of the subjects with electrocardiographic left-venticular hypertrophy are detected by the echocardiogram (Savage et al. 1987, 1979a). The chest x ray does even less well than the other two tests (Savage et al. 1979a, 1983). Knowledge of the relation between echocardiographic left-ventricular mass and left-ventricular hypertrophy allows exploration of the prognostic significance of increased left-ventricular mass detected by the echocardiogram.

Two things are now accepted about left-ventricular hypertrophy: first, that it can be treated—that is, it is reversible (Liebson and Savage 1987)—and second, that the simple dichotomization of populations into those with and without left-ventricular hypertrophy is a gross oversimplification of a more complex continuous process (increased left-ventricular mass). Data are beginning to accumulate on many emerging medical technologies including those used to assess left-ventricular hypertrophy. These procedures are often not only technologically complex, but may be expensive to perform. It is important to be able to make rational decisions as to which technologies show the most promise in terms of preventing disease.

One option is "modeling" to compare the impact of numerous risk factors and hypothesize what the decrease in occurrence of disease would be if certain population characteristics were changed. In the current context, the possible relation between a continuous measure of left-ventricular mass and cardiovascular mortality was modelled, based on published data from the Framingham Heart Study and three simple assumptions:

1. Left-ventricular hypertrophy on the electrocardiogram is a marker for a continuous measure of left-ventricular mass.

2. The distribution of this continuous measure may be approximated by a normal distribution.

3. The relation between this continuous measure and disease outcomes can be described by a logistic model.

The assumption that there is a continuous underlying process is reasonable and is supported by most of the recent literature (Savage et al. 1987). The second assumption, that the process has a normal distribution, is made for mathematical simplicity. This assumption is not crucial to the derivation but simplifies the mathematics involved. This assumption could be varied in future analyses. The third assumption, that the relation between the continuous measure and outcome can be described by a logistic equation, is also made for mathematical convenience but the logistic model is the model most generally used in epidemiology to describe the relation between characteristics associated with risk ("risk factors") and outcome variables. In addition, since the model has two parameters, a two-point estimation procedure can be used.

Having assumed a normal distribution for the underlying characteristic, it was reasoned that the comparison of the upper 2.5 percent of the population with the lower 97.5 percent of the population is approximately equivalent to comparing a person at the mean with a person at the 99th percentile. This assumption was verified by running simulations that indicated that this reasoning was approximately correct, but somewhat conservative. That is, it led to a smaller coefficient than the true one. Nonetheless, this conservative result was used since it was desirable to explore possible relationships and to avoid overestimating the size of these relationships. As indicated, the logistic function involves two parameters. Knowing the value at two points on the X scale, one can derive estimates of the unknown parameters. The simulations involved taking the known relation between a continuous variable, for example diastolic blood pressure, and an outcome— cardiovascular death—and generating populations such that blood pressure was normally distributed and such that the probability of cardiovascular death was described by a logistic function. The diastolic blood pressure in the population was then dichotomized at the 99th percentile and the rate of disease compared in the two groups. The logistic parameters were estimated using the procedure subsequently used for LV mass and these were compared to the known parameters (available from previously published Framingham data, Shurtleff 1974). The results were reasonably close to the underlying logistic function. The simulations were done for populations of several sizes, and were repeated several times for each population of fixed size.

To simplify the problem of parameter estimation and to focus efforts on exploring the relation between left-ventricular mass and cardiovascular sequelae, all analyses, except one, were restricted to males in a ten-year age group, 45 to 54 years. The same procedure was carried out for total cholesterol for comparison. Finally, using the conservative assumption that electrocardiographic left-ventricular hypertrophy represented the 99th percentile of echocardiographic left-ventricular mass (indexed to body size), the relation of echocardiographic left-ventricular mass could be plotted between the 99th percentile and the mean risk of cardiovascular death for men without electrocardiographic left-ventricular hypertrophy using the logistic function. This resulted in the predicted relation between the percentiles of echocardiographic left-ventricular mass and cardiovascular death shown in figure 2. The relation of diastolic blood pressure and total cholesterol to cardiovascular death is also shown in figure 2.

References

Apostolides, A.Y., G. Entwisle, R. Ouellet, and J.R. Hebel. 1978. Improving Trend in Hypertension Control in a Black Inner-city Community. *American Journal of Epidemiology* 107:113–19.

Berkson, D.M., M.C. Brown, H. Stanton, J. Masterson, L. Shireman, D.K. Ausbrook, O. Mikes, I.T. Whipple, and H.H. Moriel. 1980. Changing Trends in Hypertension Detection and Control: The Chicago Experience. *American Journal of Public Health* 70:389–93.

Casale, P.N., R.B. Devereux, M. Milner, G. Zullo, G.A. Harshfield, T.G. Pickering, and J.H. Laragh. 1986. Value of Echocardiographic Measurement of Left Ventricular Mass in Predicting Cardiovascular Morbid Events in Hypertensive Men. *Annals of Internal Medicine* 105:173–8.

Devereux, R.B., and N. Reichek. 1977. Echocardiographic Determination of Left Ventricular Mass in Man: Anatomic Validation of the Method. *Circulation* 55:613–18.

Drizd, T., A.L. Dannenberg, and A. Engel. 1986. Blood Pressure Levels in Persons 18–74 Years of Age in 1976–80, and Trends in Blood Pressure from 1960 to 1980 in the United States. *Vital and Health Statistics,* series 11, no. 234. DHHS pub no. (PHS)86-1684. Washington.

Dunn, F.G., W. Oigman, K. Sungaard-Riise, F.H. Messerli, H. Ventura, E. Reisin, and E.D. Frohlich. 1983. Racial Differences in Cardiac Adaptation to Essential Hypertension Determined by Echocardiographic Indexes. *Journal of the American College of Cardiology* 5:1348–51.

Entwisle, G.E., J.C. Scott, A.Y. Apostolides, S. Su, J. Southard, B. Brandon, and S. Shapiro. 1983. A Survey of Blood Pressure. *Preventive Medicine* 12:695–708.

Folsom, A.R., R.V. Leupker, R.F. Gillum, D.R. Jacobs, R.J. Prinens, H.C. Taylor, and H. Blackburn. 1983. Improvement in Hypertension Detection and Control from 1973–1974 to 1980–1981:

The Minnesota Heart Survey Experience. *Journal of the American Medical Association* 250:916–21.

Freeman, D.H., A.M. Ostfeld, K. Hellenbrand, V.A. Richards, and R. Tracy. 1985. Changes in the Prevalence Distribution of Hypertension: Connecticut Adults 1978–79 to 1982. *Journal of Chronic Disease* 38:157–64.

Gallup, G., and H.E. Cotugno. 1986. Preferences and Practices of Americans and Their Physicians in Antihypertensive Therapy. *American Journal of Medicine* 81(Suppl. 6C):20–24.

Gazes, P.C., J.E. Keil, D.D. Savage, P.F. Rust, S.J. Anderson, and S.E. Sutherland. 1986. Left Ventricular Mass by Echo in White and Black Men: Correlation with Blood Pressure, Obesity and Physical Activity (abstract). *Circulation* 74 (Suppl. 2):76.

Hammond, I.W., R.B. Devereux, M.H. Alderman, E.M. Lutas, M.C. Spitzer, J.S. Crowley, and J.H. Laragh. 1986. The Prevalence and Correlates of Echocardiographic Left Ventricular Hypertrophy among Employed Patients with Uncomplicated Hypertension. *Journal of the American College of Cardiology* 7:639–50.

Harlan, W.R. 1987. Economic Implications for Policy and Research in Hypertension (abstr.) National Heart, Lung and Blood Institute Workshop: Antihypertensive Drug Treatment: the Benefits, Costs and Choices. Washington.

Joint National Committee on Detection, Evaluation, and Treatment of High Blood Pressure. 1985. Hypertension Prevalence and the Status of Awareness, Treatment, and Control in the United States: Final Report of the Subcommittee on Definition and Prevalence of the 1984 Joint National Committee on Detection, Evaluation, and Treatment of High Blood Pressure. *Hypertension* 7(3):457–68.

Kuller, L.H., S.B. Hulley, J.D. Cohen, and J. Neaton. 1986. Unexpected Effects of Treating Hypertension in Men with Electrocardiographic Abnormalities: A Critical Analysis. *Circulation* 73:114–22.

Kumanyika, S.K., and D.L. Helitzer. 1985. Nutritional Status and Dietary Patterns of Racial Minorities in the United States. In *Report of the Secretary's Task Force on Black and Minority Health*, U.S. Department of Health and Human Services, vol. 2, 118–90. Washington.

Kumanyika, S.K., and D.D. Savage. 1985. Ischemic Heart Disease Risk Factors in Black Americans. In *Report of the Secretary's Task Force on Black and Minority Health*, U.S. Department of Health and Human Services, vol. 4, pt. 2, 229–82. Washington.

Lenfant, C., and J. Moskowitz. 1983. The National Heart, Lung and

Blood Institute: A Plan for the Eighties. *Circulation* 68:1141–44.

Levy, D., R.J. Garrison, D.D. Savage, W.B. Kannel, and W.P. Castelli. 1987a. Left Ventricular Mass Predicts Coronary Disease Events Independent of the Standard Risk Factors. *Circulation* 76 (Suppl. 4):434.

Levy, D., K. Anderson, D.D. Savage, W. B. Kannel, and W.P. Castelli. 1987b. Influence of 30-Year Mean Blood Pressure Levels on LV Mass: The Framingham Heart Study. *Journal of the American College of Cardiology* 9 (suppl A):115a.

Liebson, P.R., R.B. Devereux, and M.J. Horan. 1987. Hypertension Research: Echocardiography in the Measurement of Left Ventricular Wall Mass. *Hypertension* 9(Suppl., pt. 2).

Liebson, P.R., and D.D. Savage. 1987. Echocardiography in Hypertension: A review. Part II: Echocardiographic Studies of the Effects of Antihypertensive Agents on Left-ventricular Wall Mass and Function. *Echocardiography* 4:215–49.

Luepker, R.V., D.R. Jacobs, J.W. Brown, J.L. Sobel, and R. Prineas. 1984. Hypertension Control in Two Rural Communities. *Minnesota Medicine* 67:341–44.

Manton, K.G., C.H. Patrick, and K.W. Johnson. 1987. Health Differentials between Blacks and Whites: Recent Trends in Mortality and Morbidity. *Milbank Quarterly* 65 (Suppl. 1):129–99.

McClure, G.V., J.E. Keil, and M.C. Weinrich. 1982. Hypertension, Education, Quetelet, and Treatment: Changes in Prevalence 1960–79 in Charleston, S.C. and Their Association with CVD Decline (abstract). *American Heart Association Council on Cardiovascular Epidemiology Newsletter* 31:32.

Oster, G., and A.M. Epstein. 1986. Primary Prevention and Coronary Heart Disease: The Economic Benefits of Lowering Serum Cholesterol. *American Journal of Public Health* 76:647–56.

Russell, L.B. 1987. *Evaluating Preventive Care.* Washington: Brookings Institution.

Saunders, E. 1986. Stepped Care and Profiled Care in the Treatment of Hypertension: Considerations for Black Americans. *American Journal of Medicine* 81(Suppl. 6C):39–44.

Savage, D.D. 1987a. Left Ventricular Hypertrophy and Diastolic Functional Abnormalities in Black and White Hypertensive Patients. *Journal of the National Medical Association* 79 (Suppl.):13–16.

———. 1987b. Overall Risk of Left Ventricular Hypertrophy. *American Journal of Cardiology* 60 (Suppl.):8–12:.

Savage, D.D., R.D. Abbott, S.J. Padgett, S.J. Anderson, and R.J. Garrison. 1983. Epidemiologic Aspects of Left Ventricular Hypertrophy in Normotensive and Hypertensive Subjects. In *Cardiac Left Ventricular Hypertrophy*, ed. H.E.D.J. teur Keurs and J.J. Schipperheyn, 2–15. The Hague: Martinus-Nijhoff.

Savage, D.D., J.M. Drayer, W.L. Henry, E.C. Mathews, Jr., J.H. Ware, J.M. Gardin, E.R. Cohen, S.E. Epstein, and J.H. Laragh. 1979a. Echocardiographic Assessment of Cardiac Anatomy and Function in Hypertensive Patients. *Circulation* 59:623–32.

Savage, D.D., W.L. Henry, J.R. Mitchell, A.A. Taylor, J.M. Gardin, J. M. Drayer, and J. H. Laragh. 1979b. Echocardiographic Comparison of Black and White Hypertensive Subjects. *Journal of the American Medical Association* 71:709–12.

Savage, D.D., R.J. Garrison, W.P. Castelli, W.B. Kannel, S.J. Anderson, and M. Feinleib. 1985. Echocardiographic Left Ventricular Hypertrophy in the General Population Is Associated with Increased 2-Year Mortality, Independent of Standard Coronary Risk Factors—The Framingham Study. *American Heart Association Council on Cardiovascular Epidemiology Newsletter* 37:33.

Savage, D.D., R.J. Garrison, W.B. Kannel, D. Levy, S.J. Anderson, J. Stokes III, M. Feinleib, and W.P. Castelli. 1987. The Spectrum of Left Ventricular Hypertrophy in a General Population Sample— The Framingham Study. *Circulation* 75 (suppl.):I-26–I-33.

Sempos, C.T., R.S. Cooper, M.M. McMillen, and M.G. Kovar. 1986. Trends in Cardiovascular Mortality in the United States (abstract). *Circulation* 74(Suppl. 2):75.

Shurtleff, D. 1974. Some Characteristics Related to the Incidence of Cardiovascular Disease and Death: Framingham Study, 18-year Follow-up. In *The Framingham Study: An Epidemiological Investigation of Cardiovascular Disease*, ed. W.B. Kannel and T. Gordon, 1–4. DHEW pub. no. (NIH) 74-559. Washington.

Stason, W.B. 1986. Opportunities for Improving the Cost-Effectiveness of Antihypertension Treatment. *American Journal of Medicine* 81(Suppl. 6C):45–49.

Tarazi, R.C. 1985. The Heart in Hypertension. *New England Journal of Medicine* 312:308–9.

Topol, E.J., T.A. Traill, and N.J. Fortuin. 1985. Hypertensive Hypertrophy Cardiomyopathy of the Elderly. *New England Journal of Medicine* 312:277–83.

U.S. Department of Health and Human Services. 1985. *Report of the Secretary's Task Force on Black and Minority Health*. Washington.

U.S. Public Health Service. 1986. *The 1990 Health Objectives for the Nation: A Midcourse Review*. Washington.

Weinstein, M.C., and W.B. Stason. 1976. *Hypertension: A Policy Perspective.* Cambridge: Harvard University Press.

World Health Organization–International Society for Health. 1986. 1986 Guidelines for the Treatment of Mild Hypertension: Memorandum from the WHO/ISH. *Hypertension* 8:957–61.

Wright, J.T. 1987. Risk Factors in the Management of the Unique Hypertensive Patient. *Journal of the National Medical Association* 79(Suppl.):13–16.

Health Policy: Gaps in Access, Delivery, and Utilization of the Pap Smear in the United States

CLAUDIA BAQUET and KNUT RINGEN

CONCERN REGARDING CERVICAL CANCER MORTALITY has a long history which is tied closely to gynecology and maternal health. The fact that this is an accessible cancer site and that tumor formations are visible to the naked eye at advanced stages has contributed to its early recognition (Sand 1952).

Cervical cancer has been a significant cause of death among women and has been recognized as a contributor to mortality in mid-life. Much like maternal mortality, this disease has struck strong emotional chords in the population, and public demand for prevention and control has been frequent (Galdston 1937; Ringen and Kean 1986).

Emergence of cervical cancer as a public health problem is largely a twentieth-century phenomenon. Only 50 years ago little was known about cancer (Shryock 1979), and there was great pessimism about the potential for cervical cancer control measures (Ellwein 1978). Yet, in those 50 years, the death rate for white women has declined from greater than 10 per 100,000 females (Ellwein 1978) to less than 4 (Baquet et al. 1986), and the rate for all cancers of the uterus for white women has declined from about 30 (Ellwein 1978) to less than 7 (Baquet et al. 1986). While great progress has been made, however, major differences continue to exist between whites and blacks for both incidence and mortality. The rates for blacks are 2 to 3 times higher than for whites. The gap between these two groups has not narrowed (Baquet et al. 1986) as will shortly be described in more detail.

The recognition that cancers are linked in many cases to social and economic disparities parallels the epidemic emergence of these diseases. In 1935 Brunet classified cancer together with alcoholism as being social diseases in the same way that infectious diseases like syphilis, tuberculosis, and leprosy were considered social.

Cancers of the uterus, by the nature of the differential patterns of incidence and mortality associated with race, ethnicity, and socioeconomic status clearly exhibit a sociological pattern. Thus, a policy review of cervical cancer control has to consider social welfare as much as individual behavior. The distribution of cervical cancer in the population also reflects the distribution of resources and needs—medical and otherwise—in our society, with regard to both causality and the degree to which diagnosed cancers are successfully treated.

Today, there are roughly 16,000 newly diagnosed cases and 4,000 deaths from cervical cancer in the United States per year (Sondik et al. 1987). In the overall scheme of health and disease in the population, this number of deaths is not high; it represents only about 1 percent of all cancer deaths. In some ways, it represents a great success. The decline of cervical cancer mortality is one of the most encouraging examples of cancer control (Ellwein 1978). Yet, much emphasis is given to this disease; it is included as one of the five specific objectives for cancer control in the United States for the period of 1985 to 2000 (Greenwald and Sondik 1986). Surely part of this emphasis stems from the fact that an effective control technology exists in the form of Pap smears for early detection. And just as surely, part of this emphasis stems from the largely unstated but intuitively accepted knowledge that today's deaths from cervical cancer represent a social inequity for which the public health professions share a sense of responsibility and a desire to overcome.

The fundamental policy questions that must be addressed with regard to cervical cancer are:

- How far toward eradication *can* society move? Iceland, with a homogeneous, very small, and extremely literate population (about 270,000), has been able to eradicate cervical cancer mortality for all practical purposes (Johannesson, Geirsson, and Day 1978). Thus, eradication can be theoretically achieved. In another long-term public health effort in British Columbia, however, the results have been impressive but not as encouraging. After actively screening

TABLE 1

Age-standardized Cervix Uteri (ICD-8: 180), Incidence Rates per 100,000
for Selected International Cancer Registries

Algeria (1966–1975)	24.1
Nigeria (1970–1976)	36.9
Swaziland (1979–1983)	28.2
United Republic of Tanzania (1975–1979)	9.4
Argentina (1980)	20.1
Bolivia (1978–1979)	57.8
Martinique (1981–1982)	34.6
Panama (1974–1980)	39.5
Fiji (November 1979–May 1982)	29.2

Source: Parkin 1986.
Note: U.S. age-standardized incidence rates per 100,000 for 1978-1981 were: 8.8
for whites and 20.2 for blacks (SEER program).

since 1949, the age-adjusted mortality rate has dropped from
11.5 in 1955 to 4.8 in 1974 per 100,000 women over 20 years
of age (Boyes et al. 1977). According to a leader of this effort,
this may be the best that can be accomplished (Boyes 1984). In
practical terms, what then should we expect as a minimum level
of feasible control in the United States, with its large size, heterogeneous population, and cumbersome medical care system?

• How far toward eradication is society *willing* to move? This political
  question is outside the realm of this article and is resolved only
  though the equitable allocation of resources. The willingness to
  spend on cervical cancer control ultimately is indicative of the
  extent to which society is willing to spend resources on the needs
  of the disadvantaged.

Indeed, cervical cancer is a mirror of—or represents in microcosm—
social development. It is a sentinel event for a broader public health
problem (Howard 1987). Today, it increasingly mirrors the inequity
in resource distribution between rich and poor countries, between
north and south. More and more, cervical cancer is emerging as a
major cause of death in major female population segments in developing
countries, where incidence rates may be 3 to 5 times the rates for
white American women (table 1) (Waterhouse 1982). This reflects,
in part, the ability to control infectious diseases, the ability to diagnose

and register cervical cancer (which is inexpensive), and the inability to treat (which is expensive). Thus, the gap between black and white—poor and nonpoor—in the United States—and what to do about it—and the gap between poor and rich nations have many parallel features. Therefore, while this article is about the United States, its broader extension and relevance should be obvious.

A Conceptual Model for Cancer Control

The paths to prevention are traditionally conceptualized as either primary or secondary. Primary prevention activities address risk factors that predispose the individual to cancer development. Reduction in these risk factors should result in a reduction in cancer incidence.

Secondary prevention activities address risk factors that predispose to mortality without affecting incidence directly. Thus, the focus is on enhancing the duration of survival after a cancer diagnosis through improved detection, diagnosis, and treatment. Mortality rates are influenced by both changes in incidence rates associated with primary prevention strategies and in survival rates associated with secondary prevention methods.

This article does not deal with primary prevention of cervical cancer for the following reasons:

- Etiologic data on cervical cancer are not consistent and the excess risks identified for any particular risk factor are relatively low (Hulka 1982).
- The major risk factors that have been suggested—notably sexual practices, poor hygiene, and viral infections—are not readily addressed by categorical prevention programs. At least, to date, no categorical cervical cancer prevention programs exist to be drawn on as examples.
- The reductions in incidence rates in Western nations that have taken place in the last four decades cannot be accounted for by any specific public health effort. Rather, they are probably associated with general socioeconomic development which has afforded better health practices in general, such as nutrition and hygiene as affected by both social change and greater citizen awareness (Devesa 1984).

Secondary prevention efforts will be dealt with extensively. The main model that is used draws on the tradition of health services research (Myers 1965). The major risk factors for cancer mortality that are addressed by secondary prevention can be categorized as: access, availability quality, continuity, and compliance with regard to the delivery and use of health and medical care services.

The paths to cancer prevention and control may be general and population-wide or they may be targeted at special population segments where risk is great. These are trade-off considerations that are made— often implicitly—in policy. A relatively small level of change in either incidence or mortality distributed over a broad population base may have a greater effect in terms of absolute numbers than a large level of change in a small population segment. Cervical cancer control clearly falls into the category where targeted approaches directed at high-risk populations are required.

Cervical Cancer in the United States

Epidemiological Classification Problem

There are inconsistencies in the classification of cervical cancer data, which may affect some of the analysis of this problem:

Numerator Problems. Although microscopic confirmation of all diagnoses now exceeds 98 percent for both whites and blacks in the United States, 7 to 9 percent of all histologic classifications are unspecified carcinoma (Baquet et al. 1986). A more significant problem may be the classification of premalignant (dysplasia) and noninvasive malignant diseases (e.g., cervical intraepithelial neoplasia [CIN]) as early stages or carcinomas in situ, or vice versa. It is not probable that late stage cancers are affected significantly by pathologic classification problems.

Denominator Problems. The use of different population denominators may affect incidence and mortality rates greatly. There are at least three broad approaches to defining the denominator:

1. All females regardless of age. (This dilutes the denominator by including children and adolescents.)

2. Mature females. Typically, this definition will include all females above an arbitrary age cut-off, usually either age 16 or age 20.

3. One of the two above with the additional qualification of "having an intact uterus." With rates for total hysterectomies in the United States approaching 30 percent or more of mature females, this has become an important consideration. For instance, one study in Los Angeles has suggested that 25 percent of the decline in cervical cancer mortality may be attributed to the increased performance of total hysterectomies (Stern et al. 1977).

The basis for defining the denominator is rarely discussed when cervical cancer rates are presented. This could be a very serious confounder in comparative studies of incidence and mortality rates domestically as well as internationally.

Adjustment and Standardization Problems. Cancer rates are typically reported as age-adjusted or standardized to some reference population at a particular time period. While this is convenient for the summary of large data sets to indicate time trends, the simplification can result in reduced accuracy. Two problems are especially noteworthy with regard to the population selection on which standardization is based:

1. Lack of sex differentiation. Often, age standardization may be based on the entire population (as the denominator), male and female. This presents clear problems when the cancer site studied is limited to one sex, such as for cervical cancer.

2. Lack of race differentiation. Given that life expectancies vary between races (U.S. Department of Health and Human Services 1985), it would seem worthwhile to standardize or adjust rates by race. Rarely is this done, however.

Age-specific and race-specific rates are, therefore, preferred to standardized or adjusted rates when attempting to understand, particularly for policy purposes, patterns of cancer in the population. Figure 1 presents age-specific incidence and mortality rates for cervical cancer in whites and blacks in the United States. While the age-specific rates are lower for whites than for blacks in all age categories, there are very dramatic increases in both incidence and mortality rates in older-

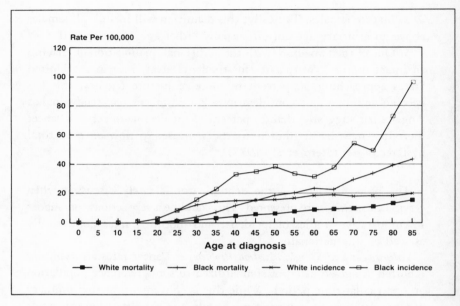

FIG. 1.   Cervix uteri incidence and mortality by race, 1980–84.

aged blacks, while the rates remain more stable for whites after age 30. Given the latency periods associated with cervical cancer, sequential age-specific cohort analysis may be important to monitor changes in social and behavioral patterns (related to policy initiatives or otherwise) and how these might affect rates in different age groups in the future. The use of age-standardized or adjusted rates would not provide a clear understanding of these nuances.

Descriptive Cervical Cancer Statistics

The following data are derived from the National Cancer Institute SEER (Surveillance Epidemiology and End Results) program, a population-based cancer incidence and survival reporting program which involves eleven population-based tumor registries. This program is described in detail elsewhere (Sondik et al. 1987; Baquet et al. 1986). The following data refer only to invasive cervical cancer. They do not include in situ cases.

Age-adjusted Incidence Rates, 1975 to 1984

Black females have higher age-adjusted incidence rates when compared to their white counterparts (table 2). Age-adjusted cervical cancer incidence has decreased in black and white females during the period of 1975 to 1984. Although decreases have occurred for both groups— and more so among black women than white women—black women continue to have higher incidence rates. During this period incidence rates decreased by 41.4 percent (6.1 percent annually) in blacks and 25.8 percent in whites (a 4.0 percent annual decrease). In 1975 age-adjusted incidence was 27.6 per 100,000 population in black females compared to 11.0 in whites. In 1984 incidence was 16.0 and 8.1 in black and white females respectively.

Age-specific Incidence

Age-specific incidence rates have decreased also during 1975 to 1984 for most age groups for both blacks and whites. The age-specific rates for invasive cervical cancer, however, increases more for blacks as age advances. Black women have over 200 percent higher incidence than whites in the 70-plus age category.

Age-adjusted Mortality, 1975 to 1984

Cervical cancer mortality is also higher in blacks. In 1975 the age-adjusted mortality rate was 11.0 per 100,000 in blacks and 3.9 in whites. Although decreases have occurred during the referenced time period, differences in mortality persist. In 1984 the mortality rate for blacks was 7.5 per 100,000 compared to 2.8 in females. During the period of 1975 to 1984, the age-adjusted mortality rates for both blacks and whites declined by roughly the same proportion, that is, 27.8 percent and 28.1 percent respectively (table 3).

Five-year Relative Survival

The five-year relative survival rate for the time period of 1974 to 1982 was 61.2 percent for blacks and 68 percent for whites (table 4). Survival differences also exist within stage (extent of disease) for blacks and whites. Caution is advisable when interpreting these rates

TABLE 2

Cervical Cancer Age-adjusted Cancer Incidence Rates, 10-year Trends, 1975-1984 (per 100,000 population)

	Year of diagnosis										Average annual percentage change	Percentage change
	1975	1976	1977	1978	1979	1980	1981	1982	1983	1984		
Black	27.6	24.2	22.4	19.2	23.5	18.9	18.4	18.0	14.3	16.0	−6.1%	−41.4%
White	11.0	10.7	9.6	9.3	9.1	8.9	7.9	7.7	8.0	8.1	−3.9	−25.8

Source: National Cancer Institute. Surveillance, Epidemiology and End Results (SEER)

TABLE 3

Cervical Cancer Age-Adjusted Cancer Mortality Rates, 10-year Trends, 1975-1984 (per 100,000 population)

					Year of diagnosis						Average annual percentage change	Percentage change
	1975	1976	1977	1978	1979	1980	1981	1982	1983	1984		
Black	11.0	10.6	10.0	9.5	8.8	8.9	8.1	8.0	8.0	7.5	-4.2%	-27.8%
White	3.9	3.9	3.5	3.4	3.3	3.1	3.1	2.9	2.8	2.8	-4.0	-28.1

Source: National Cancer Institute. Surveillance, Epidemiology and End Results (SEER)

TABLE 4
Percentage of Cervical Cancer Five-Year Relative Survival Rates, by
Historical Stage, 1974-1982

	All stages	Localized	Regional	Distant	Unstaged
Black	61%	84%	44%	17%	59%
White	68%	88%	50%	12%	68%

Source: National Cancer Institute. Surveillance, Epidemiology and End Results (SEER)

since they are based on small samples of cancer patients (1,840 blacks, 8,857 whites), a problem which is even more severe when the cases are disaggregated by stage.

Risk Factors for Secondary Prevention

It is possible to identify some factors associated with the adequacy (or inadequacy) of secondary prevention strategies as practiced today. For example, in 1970 a national survey of women under the age of 45 who had ever been married found that approximately 10 percent had never had a Pap test. The rate of those never having had a Pap test was twice as high in the black population as in the white population. Having had a Pap test was significantly related to education and family income (Rochat 1976). Based on data from the 1973 National Health Interview Survey, Kleinman and Kopstein (1981) concluded that among all women the group least likely to report having had a Pap test was that of poor black women living in nonmetropolitan areas. Among the women in this group, 25 percent of those aged 25 to 44 reported never having had a Pap test, 50 percent of those aged 45 to 64 reported never having had a Pap test, and 68 percent for those aged 65 and over. In two retrospective studies of women diagnosed with cervical cancer in the 1970s, screening history and patterns of health care were examined. Fruchter, Boyce, and Hunt (1980) reported that 52 percent of the women in a Brooklyn, New York, study had no previous Pap test and that 62 percent had no Pap test in the previous 5 years. Walton and Kernodle (1979) reported in their study of Eastern North Carolina that only 12 percent of women diagnosed with cervical cancer had previously received a Pap test. Even though 62 percent of the women had been exposed to the health care system for some medical care service in the recent past, they had not received a Pap test. Another study reported reasons given to outreach workers regarding why high-risk women in California mass-screening programs refuse to participate. Most of the replies related to lack of convenience, indicating that the women probably did not feel that cervical cancer was a great risk or that cervical screening was worthwhile (Misczynski and Stern 1979). Alternatively, a report on work-site cervical cancer found that convenience of screening is a significant factor that influenced participation rates, and that (at least in Australia) the workplace may be a good place to conduct screening because of its convenience for working women (Raphael 1977).

The Potential for Cervical Cancer Control

As the previous section indicates, cervical cancer incidence and mortality rates have declined steadily during the past 30 years (Devesa 1984). Nevertheless, disparities continue to exist between whites and blacks for both incidence and mortality rates. The differences for incidence are approximately two-fold, while the differences for mortality are about three-fold. The magnitude of the differentials has not declined appreciably during this period. Nor can the difference in mortality rates be accounted for by the differences in incidence rates alone; among incident cases blacks clearly experience poorer survival rates than whites. There are no apparent host or biological explanations for why the cervical cancer survival differences persist. Consequently, a substantial reason appears to be the inequitable distribution of health and medical resources (i.e., quality treatment) between blacks and whites.

The Value of Earlier Detection

About one-third of cervical cancer cases detected are at stage II or higher. Given the significantly reduced survival associated with the more advanced stages, there clearly is room for improvement. The significantly poorer rates that blacks experience further suggest that targeted approaches to early detection and follow-up could produce improved survival.

Programs of screening and early detection can have a significant impact even where the baseline of cervical cancer incidence and mortality are low. The Scandinavian countries exemplify this. These homogeneous, socioeconomically advanced populations are served by national health systems that have significantly eliminated the problem of access to and availability of health care services. Nevertheless, within Sweden there has been a marked decline in advanced-stage disease associated with cervical cancer screening (Stenkvist et al. 1984). Among the Scandinavian nations, cervical cancer mortality rates in Norway have not declined as rapidly as in the other Scandinavian nations. Norway was alone in not instituting vigorous programs of cervical cancer screening (Day 1984). This suggests that it should be possible to accelerate the decline in advanced-stage disease for both whites and blacks in the United States through targeted aggressive promotion of cervical cancer screening.

Critical Factors in Secondary Prevention

Analysis of factors that have contributed to avoidable mortality from cervical cancer is fairly complete. The main risk factors for poor survival include the following:

Lack of Pap Smears.   The Pap smear has been well established by scientific concensus and extensive research to be an effective and efficacious detection tool with a high degree of predictive value (National Institutes of Health 1980). The strongest predictor for cervical cancer being diagnosed at a late stage is the lack of a Pap smear being offered in the last five years before diagnosis. In a case control study in Baltimore, a three-fold odds ratio was identified for this factor (Celentano et al. 1985). Much of this problem relates to access to care, for there is a clear association between having had a Pap smear and having a regular source of care and health insurance coverage. Even among those with complete access, however, such as members of prepaid group practices, there have been differentials in the reported use of Pap smears. Minorities seem to have received fewer Pap smears (Breslow and Hochstim 1964; Warneke and Graham 1976; Graham et al. 1972). To what extent that is accounted for by patients' behavior, and to what extent provider behavior is responsible, remains undetermined.

Source of Care. Several studies have found source of care to be another critical factor. Two concerns are noted. In terms of diagnosis, never having seen an obstetrician/gynecologist has been associated with advanced-state cancer diagnosis with an odds ratio of 3.4 in Baltimore (Celentano et al. 1985). For treatment following diagnosis, in one study in Buffalo, N.Y., survival was better for patients treated by gynecologists and surgeons and by doctors who had treated many cervical cancer cases. Expertise and experience also seemed to be an important characteristic of the hospital/institution providing the treatment (Graham et al. 1972). This problem can be related to the needs of high-risk women, based on a recent study of emergency rooms and sexually transmitted disease (STD) clinics. In either case, availability of gynecologic services was an exception. As a consequence, Pap smears are not routinely offered as part of the pelvic examination in STD clinics (Marcus et al. 1986).

Lack of Continuity. Because risk of advanced stage cervical cancer is associated with low income and lack of health insurance coverage, the highest-risk individual often must rely on emergency rooms, public health clinics, and outpatient departments for care. This pattern of care raises obvious concerns about continuity of care. This problem is being studied in Los Angeles. Preliminary data on follow-up of 419 abnormal Pap smears taken in hospital clinics or emergency rooms between December 1984 and July 1985 are now available (A.C. Marcus, University of California, Los Angeles, Jonsson Comprehensive Cancer Center, personal communication). Only 54 percent of the women with abnormal Pap smears received adequate follow-up. In interviews with the patients not receiving follow-up, the reasons given for this failure in medical care delivery were: financial reasons (28 percent); not informed about need for follow-up (18 percent); patient was told she was O.K. (13 percent); too busy to participate/comply (13 percent). The two strongest predictors of nonfollow-up were severity of Pap test results (the worse the result the lower the follow-up likelihood) and the nature of the clinic. The rate of nonfollow-up ranged from 30 percent to 66 percent depending on the clinic. This study is now testing an intervention strategy to improve follow-up, which suggests that with relatively minor efforts aimed at improving administrative procedures in clinics, personalized communication with the patient and transportation, major improvements can be made. These interventions, however, are not a substitute for identifying means to overcome the financial barriers that now exist for needed medical care services.

Quality of Laboratory Practices. The Pap smear is a detection tool, not a diagnostic procedure. Increasingly, the laboratory reading of slides is being conducted in specialized cytopathology laboratories, often on a mail-order basis. In the 1970s the Centers for Disease Control conducted a laboratory proficiency study to establish the quality of these laboratories (Yobs, Swanson, and Lamotte 1985). This study found significant variations among laboratories including: (a) lack of standardized criteria and classification systems for reading slides and reporting results; (b) inadequate smears being taken and prepared; and (c) cytopathologic reading error. For these reasons, it is likely that error rates may exceed 10 percent.

Policy Considerations

When considering strategies to reduce cervical cancer mortality, two distinctions need to be made: (a) strategies to reduce cervical cancer mortality in general in the population, and (b) strategies to reduce the gap in mortality rates between whites and minorities. In this article we are concerned mainly with reducing cervical cancer mortality in the black population.

Race or Economic Disadvantage

There is no known inherent host or biological reason that would explain the excessive cervical cancer rates experienced by blacks. Articles elsewhere in these volumes document both the demographic structure of the black population—including its disadvantage relative to the white population for a variety of socioeconomic factors—and the problems that blacks face in seeking access to the health care system. Recently, the American Cancer Society (1986) issued a report which assigned preeminence to economic disadvantage as a major factor explaining the differentials in cancer incidence and mortality rates between blacks and whites. Economic disadvantage certainly can be related to some of the differentials. It does not, however, explain all of the differentials in cervical cancer rates between blacks and whites. In fact, a major study of 3,802 invasive cervical cancer cases among white women and

954 cases in black women found that income and education could account for two-thirds of the incidence difference (Devesa and Diamond 1980). Likewise, as we have noted earlier, receiving routine Pap smears is not dependent on access to care alone; even in prepaid clinics black women have had lower Pap smear rates in the past (Breslow and Hochstim 1964) and probably still do today. Clearly, factors other than socioeconomic status are related to cervical cancer incidence and mortality and have yet to be identified by well-designed analytic (rather than descriptive) studies. Additionally, the exact nature of the relation of income or socioeconomic status to cancer has not been characterized.

Maternal Mortality—A Useful Model

The application of the history of maternal mortality control as a model for secondary prevention of cancer has been set forth elsewhere (Ringen and Kean 1986). In the 1930s, responding to the alarming rate of deaths during childbirth, particularly in the immigrant tenements, public health and preventive medicine activists initiated through their professional organizations measures to define the causes and propose interventions to reduce them (Galdston 1937). The first of these studies was conducted in the five boroughs of New York City under the auspices of the New York Academy of Medicine. Every case of maternal death was tracked down and analyzed by an expert committee in accordance with established standards of maternity (and perinatal) practice. The committee found that 66 percent of the deaths could have been avoided, and that, of these, 61 percent could be ascribed to provider error and the remaining 39 percent to patient error. A maternal mortality committee was established to review each case in the future and to recommend corrective actions (New York Academy of Medicine 1933). Soon similar committees were established in other communities, and before long maternal death rates began a dramatic decline toward eradication.

Although it would be naive to suggest that this model has direct application to the complexities entailed in cancer control, it provides many useful guidelines, especially related to the control of cervical cancer. First, by conducting the studies in defined populations, the scientific *and* demonstration impacts were maximized, and, as an example, strongly influenced the inclusion of Title V in the Social

Security Act of 1935 for support to perinatal hospital care and other remedies for maternal and infant mortality. Second, the use of the in-depth retrospective case analysis proved useful to the analysis of relatively rare events in communities. Third, the use of the expert committees to establish standards of care and review case material proved to be a powerful vehicle to bridge the gap between scientific and research expertise, on the one hand, and, on the other hand, public health action responsibility. This is not a perfect model. The science was somewhat crude. And in the long run it is unclear whether the continued presence of permanent maternal committees serves a useful purpose. But there can be no doubt that their initial value was great in terms of documenting the problem, setting standards of practice, and demonstrating that improvements could be made, and that this model is useful in the context of control of cervical cancer (and other cancers) today (Breslow 1984).

Some Principles for Cervical Cancer Control

There are some basic principles that apply to cervical cancer control:

- Cervical cancer is a relatively rare event in the population, including among black women. For that reason, a case-finding/management approach seems an essential tool, and it is for this reason the maternal mortality model holds great appeal as an example.
- Cervical cancer is a "non-contagious" disease. Consequently, there is no constitutional basis for applying the police powers of the state for public health purposes, and there is no basis for compulsory approaches to controlling the disease. This clearly complicates the use of the case-finding/management approach.
- In the absence of compulsory authority, as well as in light of the limitations on financing and access to medical care, there is no basis on which to propose population-based screening in the formal sense of the word "screening," that is, the ability to achieve complete case ascertainment.
- Early detection, as implied in screening, is not the only issue involved in reducing avoidable cervical cancer mortality. A broad range of activities directed at early detection, continuity, improved quality, and compliance are required. This means that a strategy

aimed broadly at secondary prevention is more useful than a strategy simply based on screening for early detection.

- To the extent that cervical cancer mortality is avoidable, it must be recognized that both providers and individuals at risk have responsibilities. Recognition that cervical cancer is symptomatic of long-standing and deep-rooted problems in the relation between medical care provider and medical care consumer is essential.

Recommendations

Within the framework suggested above, a number of recommendations can be made which should help reduce the rates of cervical cancer mortality. These recommendations exclude approaches to medical care financing and improvements in access to care since others in these volumes cover these subjects extensively. Our concern is with improving the delivery and use of detection and follow-up services.

Service Delivery. The following changes could be made immediately without changes in financing:

- Pap test recommendations. Table 5 records the major sets of recommendations that now exist with regard to Pap testing. None of these sets is identical, and there is a great deal of confusion about the best recommendations. Of particular concern is the widespread belief that Pap testing should not apply to elderly women or women over the age of 60. The age-standardized data on cancer in figure 1 clearly indicate that this is not an appropriate recommendation. Black women, in particular, experience high rates of both incidence and mortality after the age of 60, and should continue to receive Pap smears regularly, even after menopause. The respective professional societies should achieve agreement on this subject immediately.
- Laboratory standardization and quality control. After more than 30 years of cervical cancer detection with the Papanicolaou smear, it should be possible to reach agreement on standardized nomenclatures for classification, cytopathology proficiency testing, and general laboratory quality control. As there is a great deal of concentration in the number of active cytopathology laboratories processing Pap smears, this task should have been made less complicated technically (although perhaps not politically). There

TABLE 5
Current Pap-Testing Recommendations

	National Cancer Institute 1983[a]	American Cancer Society 1980[b]	American College of Obstetricians and Gynecologists 1980[c]	NIH Consensus Development Conference 1980[d]	Canadian Task Force 1982[e]
Age to begin Pap tests	Onset of sexual activity	20 or at onset of sexual activity if earlier	18 or at onset of sexual activity if earlier	Onset of sexual activity	18 if sexually active
Age to discontinue Pap Tests	None specified	65	None specified	After 2 negative smears after age 60	60 (unless never specified)
Frequency	After 2 annual negative smears, every 1 to 3 years	After 2 annual negative smears, every 3 years	Annual	After 2 annual negative smears, every 1 to 3 years	Annual for ages 18–35, then every 5 years

Sources: Adapted from Weisman et al. 1986.
[a] National Cancer Institute 1983.
[b] American Cancer Society 1980.
[c] American College of Obstetricians and Gynecologists 1980.
[d] National Institutes of Health 1980.
[e] Walton, R.J. 1982.

can be little doubt that the laboratory error rates could be reduced significantly, and this again is within the purview of the professional societies.

- Improve outpatient detection. Adoption of Pap smear practices in emergency rooms, outpatient clinics, and public health clinics is more an administrative problem than an economic problem. By assigning one person the responsibility for oversight of Pap smear practices and follow-up of nonnegative cases, a great deal of improvement can be made in individual clinics. And there is no justification for sexually transmitted disease clinics not performing a Pap smear when performing a routine pelvic exam (Marcus et al. 1986).
- Improved inpatient detection. A large proportion of women who are diagnosed with cervical cancer have been hospitalized for other reasons in the immediate years preceding diagnosis without receiving a Pap smear. This presents a special opportunity for improved detection, especially in older women who no longer have regular gynecologic care, or who are uncomfortable about having outpatient pelvic examinations. It also provides the opportunity to assure better rates of follow-up than may be the case in the outpatient setting, where contact with individual patients—especially those at highest risk—may be hard to maintain. One estimate from New York State suggests that 53 percent of the deaths from cervical cancer for the years 1967 to 1969 might have been prevented had it been assured that hospitalized women received "routine" cytologic testing (Greenwald, Nasca, and Gordon 1972).

Data Needs. Extensive data exist to describe the cervical cancer patterns in the United States. Nevertheless, data needs exist, especially in the following areas:

- Uniform definitions of numerators and denominators. For numerators, agreement on how to classify and include early lesions is especially important; this relates to the pathology classification systems above. For denominators, the age groups—especially the lower age cut-off needs to be standardized. Also, denominators should control for varying rates of total hysterectomies, which has emerged as a major secular trend in the last thirty years.
- Analysis by stage of disease. Rather than reporting overall rates,

rates by stage of disease would be more useful for policy purposes. Because advanced-stage disease is associated with the poorest survival, this is a major concern to policy formulations that seek to reduce mortality. At the same time, however, analysis of data by stage reduces the number of cases and, thereby, the statistical power significantly, which suggests the need for innovative ways of aggregating data geographically or over time.

• Age-specific reporting. Age-specific rates may be more useful to policy development than age-adjusted or age-standardized rates, since these methods tend to dilute age-related variations. For instance, we have noted that recommendations for Pap testing have "cut-offs" at ages 60 to 65 in many cases. Clearly, the age-specific rates for black women, in particular, indicate the need to eliminate this cut-off, something that age-adjusted or age-standardized rates would not indicate.

Basic Research Needs.   There is a critical need to conduct studies on the contribution of transmittable viral agents and viral titers in relation to cancer prevention and control. Human papilloma virus studies would be useful. Of concern is carrier status and transmission for *both* men and women, and the potential for vaccine development to control this risk factor. A major area in need of both laboratory and analytic epidemiology study is the identification and control of precursors to advanced disease.

Research in Prevention and Control—Applied Epidemiology.   Rigorous studies are needed to test intervention strategies in controlled settings. Although a large number of studies have been conducted to test various aspects of cervical cancer control measures, there is a serious lack of well-controlled, population-based studies in the United States. The Centers for Disease Control (Center for Environmental Health) and the National Cancer Institute (Division of Cancer Prevention and Control) both support a number of studies, mainly directed at urban black populations. Ultimately, there is a need to develop rigorous studies to document the level of mortality reduction that can be achieved realistically in the United States. Areas in need of special emphasis include:

• Adherence. Testing of different recommendations to determine

which achieve optimal provider and patient adherence. Of special
concern is the frequency of Pap testing.

- Follow-up and continuity. Ways to assure follow-up of suspicious
and positive test results in patients seen in outpatient or clinic
settings need study. Another area in critical need of continuity
research is the change in the pattern of medical care delivery that
women experience in mid-life, and how this affects Pap testing
practices.

- Special population segments. Populations in need of special emphasis
in terms of cancer control interventions include, in addition to
blacks, the following: native Americans, whose rates approximate
those experienced by blacks; older women who stop using gyne-
cological services; and rural populations, for whom little research
has taken place.

- Alternative delivery modes. The significance attached to convenience
in effective detection programs and the problems of maintaining
continuity in follow-up and over time suggest the need to explore
alternative approaches to delivering detection services. The possibility
of offering Pap testing as part of occupational medical services
needs to be studied at a time when participation by women in
the work force is growing. Organizing programs within the auspices
of social service agencies, child care centers, churches, etc. have
been suggested as means to providing, promoting, or offering
referral to detection and treatment services. The need to determine
the potential coverage by such programs is critical. It is just as
important to know who such programs will reach effectively as
who they will not reach.

Conclusions

Although a relatively rare event, cervical cancer demonstrates a clear
social inequity between blacks and whites. While a significant proportion
of this inequity can be attributed to blacks being overrepresented in
the low socioeconomic categories compared with whites, low socioeconomic status cannot explain the entire disparity. There does not
appear to be any inherent biological reason for the differences in
cervical cancer rates between blacks and whites. Consequently, race
as a sociological factor must be implicated.

For incidence rates the difference is about two-fold. For mortality rates, the difference is about three-fold. While these rates for both blacks and whites have declined over time, the differentials have not changed much. This suggests that both the socioeconomic and racial discrimination factors that may account for these differences have persisted over time.

The need for special efforts aimed at cervical cancer control should remain a public health priority. A broad range of measures need to be implemented, including changes in classification systems for pathology, improved laboratory standardization, proficiency testing and quality control, and delivery of services. It is apparent that many changes that would improve detection and follow-up care could be implemented at little additional cost, such as changing procedures in outpatient clinics and inpatient settings and providing Pap smears in sexually transmitted disease clinics. Such efforts would be likely to benefit black women especially because of their lower frequency of Pap smears and greater reliance on outpatient clinics and emergency rooms.

It is not possible to predict the impact of an effective public health program of cervical cancer in the United States today. By one estimate in New York State based on data from the late 1960s, however, the simple practice of assuring that all hospitalized women received Pap smears (and were followed up) could reduce deaths from cervical cancer by 50 percent (Greenwald, Nasca, and Gordon 1972). Thus, a benchmark of reducing cervical cancer death rates by 50 percent is conservative in the overall population, and very conservative in the black population where the base-line of avoidable mortality is highest.

References

American Cancer Society. 1980. Guidelines for the Cancer-related Check-up: Recommendations and Rationale. *CA: Cancer Journal for Clinicians* 30:193–240.

———. 1986. *Cancer in the Economically Disadvantaged: A Special Report.*

American College of Obstetricians and Gynecologists. 1980. Periodic Cancer Screening for Women: Policy Statement (June). (Unpublished.)

Baquet, C., K. Ringen, E. Pollack, J.L. Young, J.W. Horm, L.A.G.

Ries, and N.K. Simpson. 1986. *Cancer among Blacks and Other Minorities: Statistical Profiles.* NIH pub. no. 86-2785. Bethesda, Md.: National Cancer Institute.

Boyes, D.A. 1984. Statement at Workshop on Cervical Cancer Detection, National Cancer Institute, Bethesda, Md., July 26–27. (Unpublished.)

Boyes, D.A., T.M. Nichols, A.M. Millner, and A.J. Worth. 1977. Recent Results from the British Columbia Screening Program for Cervical Cancer. *American Journal of Obstetrics and Gynecology* 128(6):692–93.

Breslow, L. 1984. Statement in transcript of meeting of the Board of Scientific Counselors, Division of Cancer Prevention and Control, National Cancer Institute, Bethesda, Md., Jan. 22–23, pp. 376–78.

Breslow, L., and J.R. Hochstim. 1964. Socioeconomic Aspects of Cervical Cytology in Alameda, California. *Public Health Reports* 79(2):107–12.

Brunet, E. 1935. Médicine expérimentale et médicine sociale. *Revue hygiene et de médicine préventive* 57(5):321–42.

Celentano, D. 1985. *Case Control Study of Risk Factors for Cervical Cancer.* Baltimore: Johns Hopkins University, School of Hygiene and Public Health, Department of Behavioral Sciences and Health Education.

Day, N.E. 1984. The Effect of Cervical Cancer Screening in Scandinavia. *Obstetrics and Gynecology* 63:714–18.

Devesa, S.S. 1984. Descriptive Epidemiology of Cancer of the Cervix. *Obstetrics and Gynecology* 63:605–12.

Devesa, S.S., and E.L. Diamond. 1980. Association of Breast Cancer and Cervical Cancer Incidences with Income and Education among Whites and Blacks. *Journal of the National Cancer Institute* 65:515–28.

Ellwein, L.B. 1978. Detection of Uterine Cervical Cancer. In *A History of Cancer Control in the United States,* ed. L. Breslow, DHEW pub. no. (NIH) 79-1518. Bethesda, Md.: National Cancer Institute.

Fruchter, R.G., J. Boyce, and M. Hunt. 1980. Missed Opportunities for Early Diagnosis of Cancer of the Cervix. *American Journal of Public Health* 70:418–20.

Galdston, I. 1937. *Maternal Deaths: The Way to Prevention.* New York: Commonwealth Fund.

Graham, S., R.L. Priore, E.F. Schueller, and W. Burnett. 1972. Epidemiology of Survival from Cancer of the Cervix. *Journal of the National Cancer Institute* 49:639–47.

Greenwald, P., P.C. Nasca, and E.D. Gordon. 1972. Prevention of

Cervix Deaths through Hospital Screening. *New York State Journal of Medicine* 72:742–45.

Greenwald, P., and E. Sondik. 1986. *Cancer Control Objectives for the Nation 1985–2000.* NIH pub. no. 86–2880. National Cancer Institute Monographs no. 2,3–74. Washington.

Howard, J. 1987. Avoidable Mortality from Cervical Cancer: Exploring the Concept. *Social Science and Medicine* 24:507–14.

Hulka, B. 1982. Risk Factors for Cervical Cancer. *Journal of Chronic Diseases* 35:3–11.

Johannesson, G., G. Geirsson, and N.E. Day. 1978. The Effect of Mass Screening in Iceland, 1965–74, on the Incidence and Mortality of Cervical Carcinoma. *International Journal of Cancer* 21:418–25.

Kleinman, J.C., and A. Kopstein. 1981. Who Is Being Screened for Cervical Cancer? *American Journal of Public Health* 71:73–76.

Marcus, A.C., L.A. Crane, C.P. Kaplan, K.J. Goodman, and E. Savage. 1986. *Improving the Effectiveness of Screening for Cervical Cancer: A Recommendation to Mobilize Emergency Centers and STD Clinics for Cancer Control.* Los Angeles: University of California, Los Angeles, Jonsson Comprehensive Cancer Center.

Misczynski, M., and E. Stern. 1979. Detection of Cervical and Breast Cancer: A Community-Based Pilot Study. *Medical Care* 17:304–13.

Myers, B.Z. 1965. *A Guide to Medical Care Administration.* Vol. 1: *Concepts and Principles.* Washington: American Public Health Association.

National Cancer Institute. 1983. *Cancer of the Uterus.* Pub. no. (NIH) 83–171. Bethesda, Md.

National Institutes of Health. 1980. *Cervical Cancer Screening: The Pap Smear.* Consensus Development Conference Summary 3(4). Bethesda, Md.

New York Academy of Medicine. 1933. *Maternal Mortality in New York City: A Study of All Puerperal Deaths 1930–32.* New York: Commonwealth Fund.

Parkin, D.M. 1986. *Cancer Occurrence in Developing Countries.* Lyon, France: International Agency for Research on Cancer.

Raphael, M. 1977. Cancer Detection in Working Women: A Report on 7450 Subjects. *Medical Journal of Australia* 2:557–60.

Ringen, K., and T. Kean. 1986. Reductions of Avoidable Mortality from Cancers through Secondary Prevention. In *Advances in Cancer Control: Health Care Financing and Research,* ed. P. Engstrom, 23–35. New York: Alan R. Liss.

Rochat, R.W. 1976. The Prevalence of Cervical Cancer Screening in the United States in 1970. *American Journal of Obstetrics and Gynecology* 125:478–83.

Sand, R. 1952. *The Advance to Social Medicine.* London: Staples Press.

Shryock, R.H. 1979. *The Development of Modern Medicine.* Madison: University of Wisconsin Press.

Sondik, E., J.L. Young, J.W. Horm, and L.A.G. Ries. 1987. *Annual Cancer Statistics Review.* Bethesda, Md.: NIH pub. no. 87-2789. National Cancer Institute.

Stenkvist, B., R. Bergstrom, G. Ecklund, and C.H. Fox. 1984. Papanicolaou Smear Screening and Cervical Cancer: What Can You Expect? *Journal of the American Medical Association* 252:1423–26.

Stern, E., M. Misczynski, S. Greenland, K. Damus, and A. Coulson. 1977. Pap Testing and Hysterectomy Prevalence: A Survey of Communities with High and Low Cervical Cancer Rates. *American Journal of Epidemiology* 106:296–305.

U.S. Department of Health and Human Services. 1985. *Report of the Secretary's Task Force on Black and Minority Health,* Washington.

Walton, R.J. 1982. Cervical Cancer Screening Programs: Summary of the 1982 Canadian Task Force Report. *Canadian Medical Association Journal* 127:581–89.

Walton, L.A., and W. Kernodle. 1979. Profiles and Perspectives in Patients with Advanced Carcinoma of the Cervix in Eastern and Piedmont North Carolina. *North Carolina Medical Journal* 40:751–54.

Warneke, R.B., and S. Graham. 1976. Characteristics of Blacks Obtaining Papanicolaou Smears. *Cancer* 37:2015–25.

Waterhouse, J., ed. 1982. *Cancer Incidence in Five Continents.* Vol. 4. Lyons, France: International Agency for Research on Cancer.

Weisman, C.S., D.D. Celentano, M.N. Hill, and M.P.H. Teitelbaum. 1986. Pap-testing: Opinion and Practice among Young Obstetricians. *Preventive Medicine* 15:342–51.

Yobs, A.R., R.A. Swanson, and L.C. Lamotte. 1985. Laboratory Reliability and the Pap Smear. *Obstetrics and Gynecology* 65:235–44.

Improving the Mental Health of Black Americans: Lessons from the Community Mental Health Movement

HAROLD W. NEIGHBORS

T HIS ARTICLE OUTLINES A RESEARCH STRATEGY FOR the primary prevention of psychopathology among black Americans. It argues that the basic philosophical tenets of the community mental health movement should be embraced as an integral part of this prevention research strategy. The article also argues that mental health prevention programs must be informed by sound epidemiologic research. More important, this epidemiologic research must be linked with empirical findings from social psychological and sociological research on black Americans. This research, while not specifically focused upon prevention of mental health problems, does contain valuable information concerning potentially modifiable risk factors appropriate for understanding the development of mental health problems among blacks. As such, this literature has important implications for the design of programs and policies aimed at preventing psychopathology among black Americans. Furthermore, because of the social psychological and sociological emphasis of this literature, the research strategy outlined below provides an opportunity to improve other, nonmedical aspects of black American life.

Community Mental Health and Civil Rights

In the early 1960s President John F. Kennedy called for a "bold new approach" for dealing with mental health problems in the nation. At the same time, black Americans were demonstrating and protesting for civil rights. Among the many demands of the civil rights movement was the emphasis on adequate health care as a right previously denied many black Americans. The Community Mental Health Centers Act, passed in 1963, was characterized by an emphasis on accessibility, responsiveness, and comprehensiveness for previously disfranchised groups (Wagenfeld and Jacobs 1982; Snowden 1982). Because of the growing influence of the civil rights movement, the community mental health initiative focused on blacks in particular. Drawing on public health concepts taken from social and community psychiatry, the community mental health ideology placed heavy emphasis on prevention as a means of improving minority mental health (Caplan 1964; Sarason 1974). Findings showing that social structural variables were correlated with mental health measures led to the etiologic hypothesis that stressful social conditions increase the prevalence of mental disorder (Leighton et al. 1963; Srole et al. 1962; Faris and Dunham 1939; Hollingshead and Redlich 1958). The logic of this preventive strategy seemed simple enough. Social engineering through environmental change (i.e., to reduce racism or eliminate poverty) would result in mental health improvements. Community mental health's emphasis on primary prevention via social structural interventions was very compatible with the civil rights movement's emphasis on social change for the betterment of life quality among blacks. Many of the mechanisms to be attacked to accomplish this prevention goal were the very same social ills (poverty, racism, discrimination, prejudice, etc.) that were the targets of the civil rights movement and the "War on Poverty."

History and many failed attempts at prevention have taught us that it is just not that simple. The relations among variables such as race, social class, stress, and racism are complex. Attempts to measure these concepts and model their developmental course have proven so complicated that many prevention programs turned out to be nothing more than poorly conceptualized consultation and education services (Ketterer 1981). As these preventive promises were broken and as mental health providers and consumers became cynical, community mental health's prevention initiative came to be seen as a failure (Goldstein 1987). As mental health and public health pulled away from each other, black Americans were left to battle the stresses of racism and poverty with the help of a mental health care delivery system that was not equipped to take a proactive, primary preventive stance toward the social problems that were seen as important antecedents of black psychopathology.

The community mental health movement has been criticized for unfulfilled promises and fuzzy theoretical thinking (Dunham 1965; Dinitz and Beran 1971). As a result, there has been a retrenchment from many of the "lofty" ideals of the 1960s and early 1970s. Yet, there are components of the community mental health movement that must continue to be addressed in the 1990s as we continue to struggle with the dilemma of how to improve the mental health status of black Americans. With a careful, critical eye on conceptual clarity, theoretical specification, and rigorous research methodology, we can move toward the prevention goals espoused by the community mental health movement.

Community mental health, while increasing access to professional services among previously disfranchised minorities, also stimulated a large amount of research concerned with black mental health. As a result, substantial progress was made in our understanding of the factors impinging upon the state of black mental health. But as the following literature review will demonstrate, much work remains to be done, especially in the areas of risk-factor specification and intervention demonstrations.

In summary, powerful social forces stemming from the civil rights and community mental health movements came together to focus economic and intellectual resources on the notion that psychological problems among black Americans could be prevented if mental health policy moved away from an individual-oriented clinical delivery model to one that focused on social/structural change. This new model would use a social stress conceptualization of psychopathology as the guiding framework for action and intervention (Cannon and Locke 1977). Unfortunately, many now reject this notion, feeling that community mental health overstepped its bounds and made promises that it could not deliver (Feldman 1978). While in many respects this is true, it does not necessarily follow that we must retreat from the philosophy and goals of the community mental health movement—especially with respect to the mental health of black Americans. On the contrary, we should apply a public health approach to understanding the mental health of blacks. Furthermore, we can and must pursue the idea of prevention of psychopathology in black Americans. But we cannot afford to pursue these notions in the same manner that they were pursued by the early community mental health practitioners. The climate of the 1990s will call for a different strategy. We can arrive at the point of seriously addressing the idea of psychopathology prevention in black Americans by conducting more and better epidemiologic research. Thus, this review will begin by evaluating issues relevant to the epidemiology of black mental health.

Epidemiologic Research on Race

Stimulated by the philosophy and energy of the community mental health movement and in an effort to understand better the issues relevant to black mental health, a number of epidemiologic researchers focused their efforts specifically on black Americans (Pasamanick 1963; Fischer 1969; Jaco 1960). If it were not for the work of these researchers, the epidemiologic knowledge based on black Americans, while still limited, would not be where it is today (Neighbors 1984). As a result of these early writings, a number of epidemiologic studies were conducted during the 1970s. These studies have produced a battery of findings concerning racial differences in mental health status that have accumulated over the last 15 years. The vast majority of these community surveys focusing on race relied on the symptom-checklist method of estimating mental illness prevalence. These short screening scales measure mild, global distress rather than discrete mental disorders. Despite regional and methodological differences across these studies, the following general conclusions can be drawn. First, blacks tend to have higher mean levels of distress than whites. Second, when socioeconomic status is controlled, blacks either exhibit lower levels of psychological distress (Antunes et al. 1974; Dohrenwend and Dohrenwend 1969; Gaitz and Scott 1972; Yancey, Rigsby, and McCarthy 1972) or there are no racial differences (Bell et al. 1981; Mirowsky and Ross 1980; Warheit, Holzer, and Schwab 1973, 1975; Neff and Husaini 1980; Roberts, Stevenson, and Breslow 1981; Eaton and Kessler 1981; Frerichs, Aneshensel, and Clark 1981; Neff 1985b).

In short, these data indicated that blacks were no more likely than whites to have higher rates of distress. These findings are intriguing because blacks are known to be disproportionately exposed to social conditions generally considered to be antecedents of psychiatric disorder

(Farley 1984; U.S. Health Resources and Services Administration 1987). Such results completely contradict the assumptions underlying the theory of social causation which was so fundamental to the thinking behind the community mental health movement. Such results also contradict the minority status argument which predicts a direct effect of race on mental health, regardless of socioeconomic status (Mirowsky and Ross 1980). The minority-status argument predicts higher morbidity among blacks because of the added stress of racism—that is, the stress due to blocked opportunities which whites do not experience. As a result, one would expect blacks to exhibit higher rates of distress than whites at *all* levels of socioeconomic status. In other words, the minority-status argument provides good reason to believe that socioeconomic status alone does not fully capture the unique stress to which blacks are more exposed than whites. Recent evidence suggests, however, that we may not be able to discount completely the minority-status argument. An analysis of eight different epidemiologic surveys found that there *were* race differences in psychological distress, but only among people of the lower classes, a result that is consistent with the view that racial discrimination exacerbates the damage to mental health of poverty status among blacks (Kessler and Neighbors 1986).

How can we explain the reluctance of psychiatric epidemiologic researchers to push past a simple additive model of race, class, and distress to explore the interaction just described? The answer lies in the pejorative manner in which mental illness statistics historically have been used to support racist theories of black inferiority (Neighbors 1985; Fischer 1969; Pasamanick 1963; Kramer, Rosen, and Willis 1973). This reluctance was also heavily influenced by the political ideology that prevailed in the aftermath of the Moynihan report and the subsequent black reaction which sought to describe the plight of low-income black Americans in a more positive light. At the time these race-comparative epidemiologic surveys were being conducted, it was not very popular to say negative things about black America. A finding that showed blacks to be suffering from higher rates of mental illness than whites most likely would have been interpreted as a racial slight on the survival strengths of black families. Within such a climate, there was no real purpose to be served by challenging the notion that socioeconomic status eliminated the main effect of race on psychological distress.

But as the analysis by Kessler and Neighbors (1986) shows, race is an important determinant of mental health status, particularly among the poor. Faced with such results, one cannot help but wonder why high-income blacks are not any worse off than their white upper-class counterparts. Are we really to believe that upper-class blacks suffer no stress due to racism and discrimination? Perhaps they are exposed to racism and discrimination but it is not as serious as that experienced by the black poor. On the other hand, racism could be equally stressful for low- and high-income blacks, but upper-income blacks may have access to the kinds of social resources (money, power) that allow them to deal with that stress more effectively. Or, it could be that overcoming adversity by moving up the socioeconomic ladder could create especially competent copers among the black middle and upper classes—individuals who possess the internal resources needed to meet almost any crisis effectively (Kessler and Cleary 1980).

In summary, epidemiologic research on race raises a number of stress-coping scenarios which need to be addressed. There is a large "black box" situated between demographic variables like race and class on one side, and mental health outcomes on the other. To begin to open this box, epidemiologic research on blacks must first focus on the stress due to racism, and then move beyond the stress-exposure hypothesis. How blacks respond to or cope with the stress they are exposed to must also be taken into account. If it is true that blacks lead more stressful lives than whites, then we need to know more about the cultural strengths and coping resources that may account for the comparable or lower rates of psychological morbidity among blacks in comparison to whites.

Most of the stress research that takes this more complex approach to understanding mental health has focused on social class and sex (Wheaton 1980; Eaton 1978). With a few notable exceptions, stress research on black mental health has not moved in this direction (Kessler 1979; Neff 1985a; Dressler 1985; Husaini 1983). On the other hand, the applicability and appropriateness of a stress-adaptation approach to understanding black mental health issues has been the frequent topic of *discussion* (Cannon and Locke 1977; Hilliard 1981; Brooks 1974; Carter 1981; Myers 1982). On the whole, research on black mental health has yet to apply the sophisticated multivariate statistical techniques and panel designs that are generally characteristic of the stress and mental health research on nonminority populations. It is imperative that we move the field in that direction. We will never acquire an adequate knowledge base for preventive interventions in black mental health if researchers continue to ignore the issues outlined above.

We need to evaluate critically the assumptions underlying our various theories about why being black is or is not a risk factor for mental disorder. By focusing more specifically on these theoretical assumptions, we should be able to answer long-standing questions of whether or not psychopathology is differentially distributed *across race* as well as how it is differentially distributed *within* the black community. One very good source of information on risk factors that link race to psychopathology is sociological and social psychological research on blacks. Drawing on this research, we can generate a number of hypotheses about why low-income blacks exhibit the highest rates of distress. In this way we can begin to fulfill the promises once held out as reachable by the community mental health movement.

Sociological and Social Psychological Risk Factors

With respect to the field of race and mental health, there are a number of ways to take the unique stress of being black into account. For example, we could focus on the use of the life events methodology and look for differences in stress across race. This has been done to some extent (Uhlenhuth et al. 1974; Mellinger et al. 1978; Dohrenwend 1973; Husaini 1983). We also need to focus on the actual meaning of racism and discrimination. Parker and Kleiner (1966, 43–44), for example, examined the unique impact of racism by using a diagrammatic representation of the "best" and "worst" possible way of life to measure discrepancies between aspiration and achievement in various areas of goal striving (e.g., education, occupation, income, self-image, racial context of social situations, and hypothetical offspring). This is an approach that needs to be replicated and refined for use in future epidemiologic studies. We need to focus more of our attention on the stress of trying to "make it" as a black in this country. What is the mental health impact of successfully or unsuccessfully negotiating an opportunity structure that is not colorblind?

If we look beneath what is typically meant by the assumption that race exposes blacks to unique stresses, we can see a number of interesting but useful hypotheses about the effect that striving for upward social mobility might have on emotional health. For example, the racism argument implies that it is more difficult for hard-working, talented lower-class blacks to "move up" than it is for similar whites; and that is is more difficult for recently upwardly mobile middle-class blacks to remain in their newly acquired status positions. The manner in which the members of black subgroups adjust to the failure to rise or the inability to maintain an elevated socioeconomic status will have important implications for mental health.

It is also likely that internal and external stress-mediating factors are influenced by the social histories of upward and downward mobility that blacks experience. Given the fact of racism, what impact might these factors have on the emotional health of black Americans and what are the implications for preventive interventions? We can begin to formulate answers to these questions by reviewing certain aspects of social science research focused on the black experience. It will become clear from this review that while much research has been conducted on black Americans, the epidemiologic implications have yet to be adequately specified. These studies often claim that they are concerned with black mental health, but rarely do they include the kinds of mental health outcomes psychiatric epidemiology is concerned with. They do, however, measure many variables that can be viewed as mechanisms intervening between race and mental health. As such, they begin to construct a "socio-pathogenesis" of mental disorder for blacks, thus providing causal hypotheses which can be tested later using experimental or quasi-experimental research designs (Kessler 1987; Hough 1985; Price and Smith 1985). Epidemiologic risk-factor research focused on the mental health implications of racism (prejudice, discrimination) should have important implications for the types of interventions we might design in order to prevent the psychic pain of downward mobility and blocked opportunities.

There are three basic assumptions that underlie research in the areas of race, class, and mental illness. First, everyone in the United States shares the value of striving to be upwardly mobile (Merton 1957). Second, lower-class individuals feel like failures because they have been unsuccessful in their attempts at upward social mobility (Wheaton 1980). Third, being poor is stressful, not only because poverty per se exposes one to more stress but also because there is stress involved in trying to advance but not being able to do so (Silberman 1964). Blacks especially are victims of aspirations they cannot achieve (Pettigrew

1964). The specific mental health consequences of this situation for blacks are unclear. For example, we are only at the early stages of understanding how personal histories of success and failure are related to important risk factors like locus of control, self-esteem, and a sense of fatalism. Furthermore, there is still much to be learned about how these latter constructs are related to mental health measures like psychological distress and discrete disorders (e.g., DSM-III). Some researchers argue that it is more adaptive to *reduce* mobility striving in order to bring subjective aspirations more in line with the objective realities of a racist opportunity structure (Parker and Kleiner 1966). Others feel that the most mentally healthy response is to work collectively with other, socioeconomically similar blacks to change the system and open more opportunities for advancement (Gurin et al. 1969; Gurin, Gurin, and Morrison 1978).

Most researchers argue that having an internal sense of control has positive mental health benefits and that being external (or "fatalistic") does not. Wheaton (1980) defines fatalism as a learned, persistent attributional tendency that emphasizes environmental rather than personal causation of behavior. It increases vulnerability to stress because it undermines coping persistence and effort (i.e., reduces motivation) via long-term personal histories of failure. Wheaton (1980, 107) also states that avoiding self-blame for failure through external attributions may be ego-protective but will inevitably undermine personal feelings of efficacy even when those external explanations are plausible (as they most certainly are for blacks). Unfortunately, psychiatric epidemiologists have not explored how these ideas relate specifically to the situations of black Americans.

Research using Rotter's internal/external locus-of-control scale has shown that blacks are more externally oriented than whites (Porter and Washington 1979). Gurin et al. (1969) were the first to show that, for blacks, Rotter's scale consisted of two dimensions—one factor made up of items phrased in the first person (personal control) and the other referring to people in general (control ideology). Comparing blacks and whites on control ideology showed that blacks were just as likely as whites to subscribe to the typical American values of the importance of work, effort, skill, and ability in striving to get ahead. Thus, the greater externality of blacks on the locus-of-control measure was actually due to a reduced sense of *personal* control only, not an endorsement of different cultural values (Gurin, Gurin, and Morrison

1978). Racism, then, while reducing personal control among blacks, does not erode belief in the work ethic.

The Gurins went on to argue that the reduced sense of personal control among blacks reflected a realistic perception of restricted opportunities. Thus, while blacks were more externally oriented than whites, this was due to an accurate assessment of a racist environment and such externality among an oppressed group was not necessarily a bad thing. In other words, the Gurins would disagree (for blacks at least) with Wheaton's argument that an external orientation is detrimental, no matter how plausible the explanation. In fact, when the Gurins assessed this realistic and accurate external orientation via the concept of "system blame," they found the more external blacks to have higher aspirations and to engage in more innovative coping efforts.

Others have speculated on the positive mental health benefits of system blame for blacks but, in actuality, this hypothesis has never really been tested (McCarthy and Yancey 1971; Neff 1985b; Veroff, Douvan, and Kulka 1981). Thus, there is no way to resolve the apparent disagreement between Wheaton (1980) and the Gurins (Gurin et al. 1969; Gurin, Gurin, and Morrison 1978). For example, while the Gurins discuss the relation between system blame and mental health, what actually gets measured is motivation, efficacy, and coping. These are not mental health outcomes but important risk factors. The system-blame concept has become closely linked with the idea of mental health through Merton's (1957) statement that it is healthy for a subordinate group to react against the system, which is actually a political statement cloaked in a medical analogy. Nevertheless, the fact that the research of the Gurins shows that externality via the system-blame concept does not result in reduced motivation, persistence, and effort (as Wheaton predicts) suggests that this is an important area for further research.

The work by Parker and Kleiner (1966) comes close to empirically testing this notion. Their results suggest that it is not mentally healthy to react continually against the system. It may be more adaptive to know when *not* to strive—especially when probabilities of success are low. Specifically, Parker and Kleiner (1966) found that low-status blacks had low goal-striving stress but high rates of psychological distress. They also found that downwardly mobile lower-class blacks had higher levels of goal-striving than their more stable lower-class counterparts. Further analysis revealed that: (1) downwardly mobile lower-class blacks who would not or could not reduce the aspirations associated with past status affiliations showed the highest rate of symptomatology; and (2) stable lower-class blacks with low goal striving showed a lower rate of symptomatology. These findings led Parker and Kleiner (1966) to conclude that it was the downwardly mobile at the lowest end of the socioeconomic scale with high goal striving who showed the lowest self-esteem and, consequently, the highest rate of psychological distress.

Feelings of power and efficacy are related to the perception of the world as controllable and predictable. The feeling that one is able to manipulate and influence important events in one's life can be significantly influenced by personal success/failure experiences. Such experiences can, in turn, lead to increased or decreased efforts at coping during times of crisis. Research shows that blacks and whites do differ on a number of important concepts like self-esteem, efficacy, and control. Although many of these variables can be seen as modifiable risk factors causally related to the development of psychopathology, there is still much speculation. More research is needed to specify the relations among these variables and mental health.

In summary, the literature on race and locus of control and the literature on social psychiatric epidemiology have not been brought together despite much speculation about the relations among race, internal/external attributions, and mental health. The former has studied the locus-of-control concept without an explicit concern for empirically demonstrating the relation of these variables to mental illness. The latter has focused on fatalism and mental illness without much regard for the special or unique issues related to race. System blame has been related to collective action but not to measures of psychological distress.

Expectancy Theory as a Framework for Intervention

The stress-research paradigm does not overemphasize social causation to the neglect of personal factors. Rather, it is transactional, taking into account the environment and the person. As such, the stress model of mental health is completely consistent with an expectancy approach to clarifying issues of race and poverty. The controversy surrounding the relative importance of environmental and personal factors in explaining the behavior of blacks and the poor is not a new one (Caplan and Nelson 1973). Over 15 years ago, social psychologists working to understand problems of motivation and unemployment among the black poor saw the need for a more balanced approach. Gurin and Gurin (1970, 83–84), advocating an expectancy approach to understanding the problems of poor blacks, put it most eloquently:

> One approach focuses on the institutional aspects of the problem— on the current realities that the poor must deal with. The other focuses on the problems "in" the poor—on pathologies that are the residue of past disadvantage. For psychologists who have been interested in problems of poverty, this bifurcation has also had some negative consequences, although for converse reasons: the distinction between these two approaches has often been too sharply drawn. Psychological and situational approaches are sometimes considered antithetical and even mutually contradictory. Approaches that have focused on reality problems have often assumed that motivational and psychological problems would disappear if basic changes in our institutions and opportunity structures were effected. In parallel fashion, those concerned with psychological and motivational issues have also separated "psychology" and "reality." They have conceptualized the psychological problems of the poor in terms of "basic" personality dispositions that are the product of early socialization— motives, values and behavior patterns that have become self-perpetuating and do not necessarily reflect current realities.

Expectancy theory is based on the notion that one's belief that actions will be rewarded enhances motivation and affective behaviors. Expectancy models emphasize conscious actions on the environment to attain positive outcomes and to avoid negative results. Expectancies are not reducible to traits nor situations but represent both characterological *and* situational forces. Because of racism, expectancy research on blacks must be particularly concerned with the implications of situational assessments (Bowman 1987). For poor blacks, expectancy problems (low and external expectancies) result from the feeling that there is little chance of attaining a particular goal. As the research of Parker and Kleiner (1966) suggests, blacks may have lower expectations in the face of objective difficulties and discouraging odds (i.e., blocked opportunities or an unfair opportunity structure) and point to the distinct possibility that such negative expectancies operate as psychological risk factors.

Expectancy research has the potential to guide researchers interested in understanding how blacks cope when faced with systematic obstacles to striving. Specifically, we need to document the mental health effects of strategies aimed at the elimination of barriers to opportunity that may produce negative expectancies in blacks. That mobility patterns are important for mental health was demonstrated by Kessler and Cleary (1980), who found that the upwardly mobile were less influenced by stress than the nonmobile. They argued that the experience of success associated with upward mobility created assertive coping skills needed to avoid psychological damage which results from undesirable events. Since expectancies are formed as a result of social histories of success and failure, Kessler and Cleary's data support the assumption that success experiences in the opportunity structure increase competence, thus decreasing vulnerability to stress. Isaacs (1984), using data from the National Survey of Black Americans, compared the father's main job while the son was growing up to the son's current job and found that 47 percent were upwardly mobile, 25 percent were nonmobile, and 28 percent were downwardly mobile. Isaacs (1984) also found that the upwardly mobile showed a significantly higher sense of self-esteem, personal efficacy, and general happiness.

Thus, it appears that programs designed to facilitate upward mobility among the black poor could improve mental health status by changing expectancies. But research from "War on Poverty" programs shows that expectancies do not automatically change to conform with changes in objective conditions (Gurin and Gurin 1970). If we argue for policy changes that emphasize the creation of structural opportunities *only*, we might be missing the point. Adequate care must be taken to prepare people for these new roles, which means training programs that focus on skills and assessment of psychological concepts such as low or external expectancies. To quote Gurin and Gurin (1970, 101–2):

Learning new expectancies is no longer a matter of changing from external to internal but poor people are presented with a more difficult problem of making complex judgements as to when internal and external interpretations are realistic, when an internal orientation reflects intrapunitiveness rather than a sense of efficacy and when an external orientation becomes defensive rather than a realistic blaming of the social system. These judgements must be made when objective opportunities are in flux, making an accurate picture of reality even more difficult to determine.

If expectancies can be changed over time, these changes would hopefully be stable and generalize to other aspects of the person's life. Below, two areas that are particularly relevant for intervention research focusing on changing the expectancies of black Americans are reviewed.

Targets and Settings for Preventive Interventions

From a public health perspective, the ultimate goal of epidemiologic research is the application of intervention programs designed to reduce the incidence of disease, thereby reducing prevalence. A further goal of epidemiologic research is to uncover the modifiable risk factors that can form a rational basis for preventive action. Identification of black strengths and weaknesses through careful epidemiologic risk-factor research can contribute to the design of programs aimed at upgrading those weaknesses and taking advantage of those strengths to reduce the occurrence and impact of stressful social situations. By intervening in black population subgroups known to be at risk of developing low self-esteem or low/external expectancies, prevention programs could have a positive impact on black mental health outcomes. The important factor, however, will be to develop programs for such groups *before* they begin to display evidence of the types of serious mental disabilities that can result from potentially pathogenic social circumstances. There are a number of specific areas where we should intervene. If done carefully and in the right settings, we do not need to mention explicitly mental health, mental illness, psychopathology, or any other potentially stigmatizing terms.

Children in Schools

Whenever the topic of prevention is discussed, the issue of children inevitably arises. Because of various developmental theories, many argue that the best way to ensure competent adults is to strengthen coping skills in children. This was a fundamental premise of the "Child Guidance" movement. This idea was also an integral part of the philosophy of the Head Start program. In the last few years, results from a number of studies focusing on preschool and elementary school interventions with black children have raised the distinct possibility that this is a fruitful mental health prevention strategy. More relevant for this review are studies that have attempted to intervene with low-income black youth. Head Start had a legitimate role in helping to facilitate the normal unfolding of self-esteem and social competence, defined as "the ability to master formal concepts, to perform well in school, to stay out of trouble with the law and to relate well to adults and other children" (Palmer and Andersen 1979, 3). Head Start's philosophy was heavily influenced by community mental health ideology, with child mental health professionals stressing prevention, early detection, and the social determinants of emotional problems. The clinicians who worked in the Head Start classrooms estimated that 10 to 25 percent of the children were suffering from serious disturbances, although systematic epidemiologic studies were never conducted (Cohen, Solnit, and Wohlford 1979).

In the 1960s, a group of preschool intervention studies were begun and, in 1975, ten of these investigators pooled efforts, relocated the children, and compared them to matched groups. For all programs, the children were predominantly poor and black. The results of these studies indicated that preschool children were significantly less likely to be set back one grade or more in school. Four out of the five studies for which data were available showed that fewer preschool children were in special education (learning disabled) classes. Five studies reported significantly higher reading scores in the preschool group; two found higher scores but the differences were not significant and one study showed no difference. Seven studies had data on arithmetic scores. Two showed significantly higher scores for the preschool group, two showed significantly higher scores on some subtests, two showed higher scores for girls but not boys, and one showed higher but insignificant scores. Thus, while no study affected all variables associated with elementary school performance, all studies affected one or another variable and some affected several. Palmer and Andersen (1979, 447) concluded that these results "have implications not only for the academic performance of children, but for socio-emotional and cost aspects as well."

Glazer (1985) reported on a study by Darlington and Lazar (1984). This study followed up 1,599 of 2,700 children in 1976 and 1977 who had been in 11 preschool programs in the early 1960s (all had comparisons to a control group). There were differences in the degree to which those who attended preschool were held back or were assigned to special education classes. The median rates of failing a grade or being assigned to special education were 45 percent to 24 percent. Glazer (1985) also reported on the Sustaining Effects Study of Compensatory and Elementary Education funded by the Department of Education. This research followed up 120,000 students in a sample of 300 schools over a three-year period. The results showed gains for Title I students relative to needy students (who qualified but did not receive the intervention) for grades 1 through 6 for mathematics and grades 1 through 3 for reading. By the time these children reached junior high school, however, there was no evidence of sustained effects.

In the Yale-New Haven Prevention Project, an elementary school that was 99 percent black and had 50 percent of the families on AFDC received an intervention (Comer 1985). Educators and mental health personnel collaborated to create a desirable social climate in the school to effect coordinated management, curriculum and staff development, teaching, and the learning process. They did not focus on the children and their families as "patients" but, rather, the intervention was targeted toward the organization and management system of the school in order to provide students with adequate educational skills and support. The project had four elements: (1) a representative governance and management group; (2) a parent-participation program; (3) a mental health program and team; and (4) an academic program. As part of a larger study, 16 girls and 8 boys who had been part of this elementary school intervention were contacted 3 years later. They were randomly matched on age and sex with the same number of students who attended another elementary program. The intervention group did significantly better on achievement test scores, including doing better on 9 different subscales. They also did better in language, mathematics, and school grades.

Shure and Spivack (1982) used a variety of games, discussions, and group interaction techniques to focus children's attention on listening to and observing others, and on learning that others have thoughts, feelings, and motives in problem situations. In this particular study, 113 black inner-city children (47 boys, 66 girls) were trained in the nursery school year, while 106 served as a control group. The 131 who were available in kindergarten were divided into 4 groups: (1) twice-trained; (2) once-trained in nursery; (3) once-trained in kindergarten; and (4) a never-trained control group. Results showed that the impact of the training program lasted a full year and that the training was as effective in kindergarten as in nursery school. Children trained in nursery school were less likely than controls to begin showing behavioral difficulties over a two-year period.

Recent information from the Perry Preschool Project in Ypsilanti, Michigan, deserves attention (Berrueta-Clement et al. 1984). The Perry study (123 black youth) saw preschool as an intervention to prevent negative effects of poverty on school performance, creating a foundation for life success. Students were randomly assigned to attend or not to attend the preschool program and followed through age 19. Results revealed that 2 out of 3 of the preschool group vs. only 1 out of 2 of the controls graduated from high school. Persons attending preschool did better on measures of skill competence. Preschool led to more employment, less unemployment, and higher earnings. The preschool group was also more likely to be supporting themselves (45 percent vs. 25 percent) and Department of Social Services records showed less public assistance use by the preschool group. Finally, the preschool group had fewer contacts with the criminal justice system and fewer arrests. These results suggest that the initial effects of intellectual performance can have a long-term impact upon the scholastic achievement, commitment to schooling, and scholastic placement of black children.

The Poor in Job-training Programs

Successful interventions at the pre- and elementary school level would have positive payoffs in another area that receives much attention for black Americans—job-training programs for the black unemployed. Better school performance among the black high-risk children should result in staying in school longer, increased likelihood of obtaining a diploma, and increased employment. To the extent that the early interventions with young children are successful, there should not be as many black teens or young adults in need of job-skills training later in their lives. Inevitably, however, many black youth will wind up unskilled and unemployed. For this group, job-training programs provide an opportunity to change expectancies.

Job-training programs are relevant to the concerns of this article because they should be able to teach us something about how to have an impact upon employability and thus the upward mobility of low-income blacks. Glazer (1985), citing Taggart's (1981) review of job-training programs, concluded that the most intensive programs have done best, and cites Job Corps, the Youth Employment and Demonstration Act and the Youth Incentive Entitlement Pilot Project as examples. Two studies of Job Corps found significant program effects in terms of increased employment, earnings, reduced welfare dependence, unemployment insurance usage, criminal activity, and out-of-wedlock births. Weinberg (1985) argued that the perceived role of work experience within a welfare program should be studied. He asks the very timely question, "Can the concept of reciprocity (establishment of a quid pro quo in exchange for welfare benefits—"workfare") lead to increased exit from welfare by imbuing an increased sense of self-worth to the recipients?" (Weinberg 1985, 5). In 1985 a preliminary report by the Manpower Demonstration Research Corp., evaluating new welfare approaches in 11 states, focused on workfare in West Virginia and found that 80 percent of the participants thought that a requirement to work for checks was "satisfactory" or "very satisfactory."

It seems clear that "workfare" will be a major movement within the welfare policy area. Workfare experiments are being conducted in Michigan, Pennsylvania, California, and New York. In Ohio, workfare programs are being extended into 40 of the state's 88 counties. As another example, in March of 1987, a report from the American Enterprise Institute recommended that welfare recipients be *required* to participate in education, training, and work programs in order to reduce poverty, *increase* self-esteem, and decrease behavioral dependence. It is interesting to note that the report is reminiscent of the expectancy approach to poverty in that it advocates a two-pronged approach to helping the poor. Specifically, the report said that economic improvements must be combined with an effort to change thinking and behavior among the "underclass." This is similar to the ideas psychologists were trying to promote in the early days of the "War on Poverty":

> For although their motivational problems are affected by the immediate reality situation, there is more to the motivational problem than that. I have commented that those who have stressed the motivational and psychological issues presented by these trainees have tended to neglect the reality and institutional problems. In a similar vein, those who have approached the problem of poverty with suggestions for changes in social institutions and opportunity structure have

tended to ignore the fact that motivational problems will not automatically disappear with these structural changes. Just as a concern with motivational issues does not necessarily imply a neglect of reality, a concern with reality does not mean that motivational and personality issues are irrelevant (Gurin 1970, 286).

One workfare program that will be worth monitoring is Project Self-Sufficiency. Fifty households in Ann Arbor and another 50 in Grand Rapids, Michigan, headed by single parents were among 5,000 families nationwide selected for a federal demonstration program designed to help them become self-sufficient within 5 years. The U.S. Department of Housing and Urban Development is spending $25 million for rent subsidies, counseling, job training, and child care aid. Another workfare program in Michigan, Project Self-Reliance, reported that 37 percent of the 7,000 people who took part moved off the welfare rolls and into jobs, another 24 percent moved into a position to find employment within 6 months to a year, while 39 percent went back on welfare. California launched a program that requires able-bodied welfare recipients to work or risk losing benefits. This program also makes provisions for job training and child care, while exempting parents with children under age 7. Those who are not required to join the program can volunteer. The program provides job counseling, supervised job searches, job training, educational classes, and a guarantee of public service jobs for those who cannot find work elsewhere.

While the "new" workfare policy initiatives sound promising, the issues are the same complex ones we have been struggling with since the early days of the "Great Society." Years of research on poverty, race, and achievement show that manipulating the attitudes, motives, and expectations of the black poor in a manner that will be beneficial and long-lasting is very difficult. It is clear that there is still much we do not know. For example, Bassi and Ashenfelter (1985, 32) conclude: "Unfortunately, despite nearly twenty years of continuous federal involvement to assist this group, we still have to do a good deal of guess work about what will work and for whom." Glazer (1985, 38) stated: "It is understandable that it should be very hard to come to conclusions, and if we could say nothing in 1974, we can say little more in 1984 despite a great expansion in the scale and sophistication of evaluations of work-training programs."

As far back as the late 1960s Gurin and Gurin (1970, 98) outlined four essential issues that researchers will need to resolve: (1) "Under what conditions will success experiences and opportunity changes increase personal expectancies and under what conditions will they lead to denial and avoidance responses? (2) How can success experiences in an intervention program be used to affect long-range stable expectancy changes that carry into the world beyond the program? (3) How can the effects of a series of specific positive experiences be made to affect an individual's general self-confidence and trust in the environment? (4) Under what conditions can positive effects on psychological expectancies also have positive implications for behavior?"

The workfare programs represent an important opportunity for researchers to investigate many age-old issues and theories about the poor. One of the reasons that we do not know enough about the impact of job-training programs is that very few of the training programs were run on an experimental basis (Glazer 1985; Bassi and Ashenfelter 1985). In this regard it is interesting to note that a recent White House policy team recommended that communities be permitted to use welfare funds to finance experimental programs (U.S. Domestic Policy Council 1986). The report states that the purpose of the experiments should be to move more welfare recipients into paying jobs. This is consistent with the position taken by Bowman and Gurin (1984, 126–27) who state,

We should stress that we feel that the next steps in motivational research on issues of poverty could be most effectively studied around policy and program interventions—not that they have not been. There have been countless evaluations of policy and program interventions. When they have shown any concern with measuring attitudes and motivations they have generally followed a dispositional model, looking at attitudes as predictors of greater or lesser success following the intervention experience or using the attitudes as controls in estimating economic impact. There has been little or no specific conceptualization of the relevance of the interventions to the literature on how attitudes change and how these changes relate to behavior.

As mentioned earlier, welfare policy analysts have had two opposing views on the problems of the poor. One viewpoint emphasizes the flawed character of low-income people (sometimes referred to as the "culture of poverty," or the "underclass"), while the other stresses restricted opportunities (Hill et al. 1985). Within the second perspective, the barrier most frequently cited with respect to the black poor is, of course, racial discrimination. While neither perspective denies that attitudinal or motivational factors exist, they differ with regard to the basic origin and permanence of the attitudinal problems (Bowman and Gurin 1984). The underclass approaches assume that the problems of the black poor are deep-seated and self-perpetuating. Thus, they are not expected to be very amenable to social interventions. The restricted-opportunity perspective, on the other hand, suggests that these problems are due to situational barriers and, as such, can be influenced or changed or alleviated by educational, training, and job-creation interventions.

Recent results from the Panel Study of Income Dynamics of the Survey Research Center, Institute for Social Research, University of Michigan, are relevant here. Analyses revealed modest and usually insignificant effects of basic motives on economic outcomes. Changes in expectancy measures were, however, significantly predicted by economic and noneconomic events. Thus, expectancies appeared to be related to economic outcomes, but causation ran from the outcomes to the expectancies rather than in the reverse direction (Hill et al. 1985). The most dramatic findings were of the variability of economic status for the poor. Many highly motivated people did succeed in pulling themselves out of poverty, but almost as many of the unmotivated did as well. "Opportunities provided by more schooling or by living in areas of high employment growth were more consistently significant in producing higher than average short-run improvement than were attitudes" (Hill et al. 1985, 9).

In another study focusing specifically on the labor market problems of black youth, Bowman and Gurin (1984) found that personal efficacy failed to emerge as a significant predictor of increases in education or employment. These results were consistent with those from the Panel Study of Income Dynamics: motivation as measured by personal efficacy did not have a direct causal effect on subsequent changes in employment or occupational status. Increases in education and employment did, however, boost motivation for males (but not females). Specifically, young black males who completed additional schooling increased their personal efficacy. Bowman and Gurin (1984, 113) concluded that "cross-sectional correlations between personal efficacy and status attainments can best be interpreted as evidence that motivation is largely the result rather than the cause of mobility outcomes."

The crucial point is that low-income blacks may not be victims of poor motivation as a result of inadequate predispositions (e.g., lack of a need for achievement, or a poor work ethic) but rather, suffer from negative expectancies that have resulted from a history of poor success due to slim chances. Given that this appears to be a problem of expectancies, there is hope for change. If it were purely a problem of deep-seated dispositions, then there would be no point to social programs. The new social programs mounted under the "workfare" label are in many cases motivated by a conservative ideology that views welfare as fostering dependency and leading to a culture of poverty or a permanent underclass. Nevertheless, they could have a positive impact on black expectations to the extent that they provide opportunities for successful work experiences and career paths. The positive potential of these programs is that they are not concentrating on attitudes and motivational problems only. They are also structural in focus in that they are providing jobs. If the ambition is there (and the PSID analyses as well as preliminary results from some of the workfare programs seem to show that it is) but the expectations are low, then it makes sense to create opportunities in order to increase expectations of success. It remains to be seen, however, whether the new round of workfare programs will be able to accomplish this goal.

It is also crucial that we not forget that if expectancy theory is correct, providing structural opportunities will not solve motivational problems for *all* of the black poor. Note the percentages from Michigan's Project Self-Reliance. While 61 percent eventually had successful work experiences, 39 percent went back on welfare. As the following quote indicates, the project director saw poor motivation as a critical factor for this latter group:

> They were not able to translate the opportunity into a step forward. In some cases, even with help, they just couldn't build a work record. They quit, or their record was spotty. They're just not prospects to be marketed for permanent private-sector jobs. Most of them, quite frankly, weren't willing to work hard" (*Detroit Free Press* 1985).

Obviously, there is no way of knowing if the project director is correct in his assessment. The point is, however, that motivational problems among some of the urban poor is not an unreasonable hypothesis, especially in light of what an expectancy approach would suggest. It could very well be that some of this 39 percent represent a subgroup of the poor who will need the benefit of interventions that do more than merely offer an employment opportunity. Perhaps this group will need an intervention that includes an educational or training component that will focus more intensely on how to increase the likelihood that expectancies *will* change to coincide with new, objective realities and the opportunities provided by workfare initiatives.

Discussion

This article has argued that the community mental health ideology still has much to offer to the field of black mental health. If epidemiologic risk-factor research based upon social psychological and sociological theory can empirically demonstrate the manner in which black Americans adjust to social mobility and expectancy problems, those findings can be used as a knowledge base upon which to design preventive interventions. Within this viewpoint, it has tried to point out some of the linkages between mental health, stress, and expectancies. Furthermore, this article has argued that there is a reservoir of useful knowledge to be drawn from the social experiments started in the 1960s under the auspices of the "Great Society" and the "War on Poverty." Specifically, the greatest potential lies in the areas of preschool programs, early elementary education, and job-training.

It should be noted that this article is not arguing that *all* poor black children will eventually require mental health care if they do not have access to special preschool and elementary school programs. It is important that we think in terms of probabilities of events occurring in *groups* rather than individuals. Herein lies the strength of the public health approach. Many ask how one can show that something was "prevented" when it never even occurred. The answer is through the employment of carefully designed experimental or quasi-experimental research designs that employ comparison or control groups. It is only in this manner that we can demonstrate the impact of a preventive program by showing significant differences in outcome between those who received the intervention and those who did not.

Another strength of the prevention approach outlined here is that there could be positive by-products of targeting mental disorder for prevention based on changing expectancies using a social-educational model of psychopathogenesis. Because this approach and the risk factors targeted for modification (e.g., educational achievement, labor market participation) are important outcomes for other fields, a prevention strategy that views these variables as risk factors for mental illness has the potential for reaching humanitarian, educational, criminal justice, and economic goals. If our interventions are powerful, and if the theory is correct, we not only improve self-esteem and decrease distress and discrete mental disorders, we also reduce delinquent behavior, unemployment, school truancy, and drop-out rates.

In discussing prevention in mental health, one cannot overlook the problem of the stigma of early identification. Consider for a moment what the concept of early identification really means within the context of mental health. It means that someone will have to tell a black person that they or one of their significant others are at risk of becoming mentally ill. This will not be welcome news to many blacks. We know that there is a tremendous amount of stigma attached to labeling someone with a psychiatric condition, and most blacks simply will not appreciate being told they need psychological help because, statistically speaking, they possess a number of social characteristics that indicate an increased probability of psychological problems. Attacking mental health problems within the contexts discussed in this article (e.g., schools, anti-poverty programs) will help alleviate this problem.

In short, an educational approach to prevention is preferable because it is nonmedical. Thus, we are not talking about early detection or case-finding for mental illness only. Rather, we are talking about using a social theory of psychopathology to target interventions toward suspected antecedents of psychological distress. If our theory is correct, it should have an impact on the prevalence of mental disorder and other social problems. To document this, however, will mean broadening our outcome measures (especially in long-term follow-up) to include assessment of psychological morbidity, including discrete mental disorders and the use of rigorous research designs.

Another important issue that needs more discussion is the notion of victim-blaming. In this regard, we must be careful to distinguish between two important points. One is the attribution of blame for the unjust social situations that blacks have been subjected to. This, clearly, is the fault of an oppressive social system set up by whites. The second is the notion that blacks can, however, in the face of oppressive conditions, take responsibility for changing those social conditions that were not necessarily the fault of blacks or the poor (Committee on Policy for Racial Justice 1987). Related to this second point is the notion that blacks and the poor should take personal responsibility for changing individual behaviors known to be deleterious to mental health. This is not victim-blaming, although some would have us think so (Crawford 1977). Victim-blaming is a one-sided attitude, that *all* of the problems of the poor are indeed *their fault* and due to deficits "within the person," with no appreciation whatsoever of the role played by social stress and oppressive environmental conditions (Gurin and Gurin 1970; Gurin 1970; Ladner 1973; Ryan 1971; Yette 1971). The notion of individual responsibility for health behavior is completely consistent with the current trend in public health toward health promotion. The health-promotion view is based on research that shows that many of the health problems of individuals are made worse by poor health behaviors (e.g., smoking, drinking, no seat belts, poor nutrition, etc.). Thus, it follows that improvements in health can be made by targeting interventions toward changing those risky behaviors. It would be a mistake not to take advantage of this promotional approach while social-change agents are advocating environmental reform.

There is a need to join black researchers with black practitioners, especially clinicians and health educators, in joint research endeavors in community settings (Price 1982; Goldston 1986). It is clear that the action-research strategy outlined in this article cannot be carried out by university-based researchers alone. It needs the input of blacks who are skilled and knowledgeable in how to deliver human services to target groups in a manner that takes the unique cultural experiences into account (Lefley 1975; Miranda and Kitano 1986). Often researchers are hesitant to intervene until they are certain that the intervention will have an impact on the dependent variable. Action research requires researchers who are willing to put aside some of this scientific skepticism in order to "get going." The research community can gain important ideas about issues for intervention research from programs already in progress. Researchers can take advantage of the things that practitioners are already doing in piloting intervention research projects designed to manipulate variables shown to have an impact on black mental health. Practitioners, on the other hand, must be willing to subject programs they "know" are effective to research designed to evaluate their actual impact on black clients. For example, many health education programs are based on a number of assumptions, many of which go untested. They attempt to impart cognitive information on the assumption that this will change health attitudes, which will in turn have an impact on health and illness behavior. Not only do we need to test the assumption that health attitudes directly affect health behavior; we also need to document attitude change, not just class attendance.

In many ways, community mental health is synonymous with public health. And as such, the community mental health ideology still has much to offer in developing a sensible, feasible strategy of mental health promotion for black Americans. That strategy must be based on sound epidemiologic knowledge. This will mean continued research, focusing on descriptions of the distribution and course of psychological morbidity in cross-sectional and longitudinal samples of blacks. It will also mean intense investigation of methodologic issues in the measurement of psychopathology across race. Among those committed to a psychosocial theory of pathogenesis, it will mean precise specification of the risk factors assumed to link marker variables to morbidity outcomes. Finally, this strategy will necessitate the development of collaborative efforts among groups who, while interested in the goal of black mental health promotion, rarely have the opportunity to work together.

Conclusions

In closing, the following points should be highlighted. First, it has been shown that the highest rates of psychopathology reside in the lowest socioeconomic groups, and this is especially the case for black Americans (Neighbors 1986). Research on social mobility shows that the benefits for blacks of moving up the social ladder outweigh the costs (Kessler and Cleary 1980; Isaacs 1984); and that moving down in socioeconomic standing can be detrimental to black mental health (Parker and Kleiner 1966). As a result, policies and programs designed to influence the mobility patterns of blacks can be viewed as having implications for mental health. Two settings, in particular, should command the interest of epidemiologic researchers: (1) preschool and elementary schools; and (2) job-training programs ("workfare"). Using experimental research designs along with appropriate measures of mental health outcomes (e.g., self-esteem, psychological distress, discrete DSM-III disorders), a preventive effect can be demonstrated. Finally, even if significant reductions in psychopathology cannot be demonstrated, the risk-factor model put forth in this article contains potential for a positive impact in other important areas of black American life.

In arguing this position, I am asking that we not forget the tenets originally put forth within the rubric of the community mental health movement. The data reviewed here demonstrate convincingly that sociological and social psychological factors are important determinants of psychological morbidity. Furthermore, the idea of linking epidemiologic research with the notion of prevention in mental health is a reasonable, feasible goal to pursue. But this task can only be accomplished by clearly specifying what it is we want to prevent, the particular factors that contribute to those outcomes, the settings and targets for preventive interventions, and the use of an evaluation strategy that will allow clear statements about significant reductions in incidence and prevalence.

References

Antunes, G., C. Gordon, C. Gaitz, and J. Scott. 1974. Ethnicity, Socioeconomic Status and the Etiology of Psychological Distress. *Sociology and Social Research* 58:361–68.

Bassi, L., and O. Ashenfelter. 1985. The Effect of Direct Job Creation and Training Programs on Low-skilled Workers. Paper delivered at a conference, "Poverty and Policy: Retrospect and Prospects," Madison, Wis., Institute for Research on Poverty.

Bell, R., J. Leroy, E. Lin, and J. Schwab. 1981. Change and Psychopathology: Epidemiologic Considerations. *Community Mental Health Journal* 17:203–13.

Berrueta-Clement, J., and colleagues. 1984. *Changed Lives: The Effects of the Perry Preschool Program on Youths through Age 19*. Ypsilanti, Mich.: High/Scope Press.

Bowman, P. 1987. Psychological Expectancy: Theory and Measurement in Black Populations. In *Handbook of Tests and Measurements for Black Populations*, ed. R. Jones (Forthcoming.)

Bowman, P., and G. Gurin. 1984. *A Longitudinal Study of Black Youth: Issues, Scope and Findings.* Final Report, Motivation and Economic Mobility of the Poor. Ann Arbor: Institute for Social Research.

Brooks, C. 1974. New Mental Health Perspectives in the Black Community. *Social Casework* 55:489–96.

Cannon, M., and B. Locke. 1977. Being Black is Detrimental to Your Mental Health: Myth or Reality? *Phylon* 38:408–28.

Caplan, G. 1964. *Principles of Preventive Psychiatry.* New York: Basic Books.

Caplan, N., and S. Nelson. 1973. On Being Useful: The Nature and Consequences of Psychological Research on Social Problems. *American Psychologist* 28:199–211.

Carter, J. 1981. Treating the Black Patient: The Risks of Ignoring Critical Social Issues. *Hospital and Community Psychiatry* 32:281–82.

Cohen, D., A. Solnit, and P. Wohlford. 1979. Mental Health Services in Head Start. In *Project Head Start: A Legacy of the War on Poverty,* ed. E. Zigler and J. Valentine, 259–82. New York: Free Press.

Comer, J. 1985. The Yale-New Haven Primary Prevention Project: A Follow-up Study. *Journal of the American Academy of Child Psychiatry* 24:154–60.

Committee on Policy for Racial Justice. 1987. *Black Initiatives and Governmental Responsibility.* Washington: Joint Center for Political Studies.

Crawford, R. 1977. You Are Dangerous to Your Health: The Ideology and Politics of Victim Blaming. *International Journal of Health Services* 7:663–80.

Darlington, R., and I. Lazar. 1984. Letter. *Phi Delta Kappa* 66:231–32.

Detroit Free Press. 1985. Workfare Ends Test Phase with Encouraging Results. February 4.

Dinitz, S., and N. Beran. 1971. Community Mental Health as a Boundaryless and Boundary-busting System. *Journal of Health and Social Behavior* 12:99–108.

Dohrenwend, B.S. 1973. Social Status and Stressful Life Events. *Journal of Personality and Social Psychology* 28:225–35.

Dohrenwend, B.P., and B.S. Dohrenwend. 1969. *Social Status and Psychological Disorder: A Causal Inquiry.* New York: Wiley-Interscience.

Dressler, W. 1985. Extended Family Relationships, Social Support and Mental Health in a Southern Black Community. *Journal of Health and Social Behavior* 26:39–48.

Dunham, H.W. 1965. *Community and Schizophrenia.* Detroit: Wayne State University Press.

Eaton, W. 1978. Life Events, Social Supports and Psychiatric Symptoms: A Re-analysis of the New Haven Data. *Journal of Health and Social Behavior* 19:230–34.

Eaton, W., and L. Kessler. 1981. Rates of Symptoms of Depression in a National Sample. *American Journal of Epidemiology* 113:528–38.

Faris, R., and H. Dunham. 1939. *Mental Disorders in Urban Areas.* Chicago: University of Chicago Press.

Farley, R. 1984. *Blacks and Whites: Narrowing the Gap?* Cambridge: Harvard University Press.

Feldman, S. 1978. Promises, Promises or Community Mental Health Services and Training: Ships That Pass in the Night. *Community Mental Health Journal* 14:83–91.

Fischer, J. 1969. Negroes and Whites and Rates of Mental Illness: Reconsideration of a Myth. *Psychiatry* 32:428–46.

Frerichs, R., C. Aneshensel, and V. Clark. 1981. Prevalence of Depression in Los Angeles County. *American Journal of Epidemiology* 113:691–99.

Gaitz, C., and J. Scott. 1972. Age and the Measurement of Mental Health. *Journal of Health and Social Behavior* 13:55–67.

Glazer, N. 1985. Education and Training Programs and Poverty; or, Opening the Black Box. Paper delivered at a conference, "Poverty and Policy: Retrospect and Prospects," Madison, Wis., Institute for Research on Poverty.

Goldstein, M. 1987. Mental Health and Public Health: Issues to be Considered in Strengthening a Working Relationship. Unpublished manuscript submitted in fulfillment of the U.S. Department of Health and Human Services contract no. 427303010.

Goldston, S. 1986. Primary Prevention: Historical Perspectives and a Blueprint for Action. *American Psychologist* 41:453–60.

Gurin, G. 1970. An Expectancy Approach to Job Training Programs. In *Psychological Factors in Poverty,* ed. V. Allen, 277–99. Chicago: Markham.

Gurin, G., and P. Gurin. 1970. Expectancy Theory in the Study of Poverty. *Journal of Social Issues* 26:83–104.

Gurin, P., G. Gurin, R. Lao, and M. Beattie. 1969. Internal-External Control in the Motivational Dynamics of Negro Youth. *Journal of Social Issues* 25:29–53.

Gurin, P., G. Gurin, and B. Morrison. 1978. Personal and Ideological Aspects of Internal and External Control. *Social Psychology* 41:275–96.

Hill, M., S. Augustyniak, G. Duncan, G. Gurin, P. Gurin, J.K.

Liker, J.N. Morgan, and M. Ponza. 1985. *Motivation and Economic Mobility*. Research Report Series. Ann Arbor: Institute for Social Research.

Hilliard, T. 1981. Political and Social Action in the Prevention of Psychopathology of Blacks: A Mental Health Strategy for Oppressed People. In *Primary Prevention of Psychopathology*. Vol. 5: *Prevention through Political Action and Social Change,* ed. J. Joffe and G. Albee, 135–52. Hanover, N.H.: University Press of New England.

Hollingshead, A., and F. Redlich. 1958. *Social Class and Mental Illness: A Community Study*. New York: John Wiley.

Hough, R. 1985. Psychiatric Epidemiology and Prevention: An Overview of the Possibilities. In *Psychiatric Epidemiology and Prevention: The Possibilities*, ed. R. Hough, P. Gongla, V. Brown, and S. Goldston, 1–28. Los Angeles: Neuropsychiatric Institute of the University of California, Los Angeles.

Husaini, B. 1983. *Mental Health of Rural Blacks in West Tennessee*. Final Report to the U.S. Department of Agriculture by the Cooperative Agricultural Research Program, Tennessee State University, Nashville. (Unpublished.)

Isaacs, M. 1984. The Determinants and Consequences of Intergenerational Mobility among Black American Males. University Microfilms International no. 8422728. Waltham, Mass.: Heller School for Advanced Studies in Social Welfare, Brandeis University. (Unpublished Ph.D. diss.)

Jaco, E.G. 1960. *The Social Epidemiology of Mental Disorders: A Psychiatric Survey of Texas*. New York: Russell Sage.

Kessler, R. 1979. Stress, Social Status and Psychological Distress. *Journal of Health and Social Behavior* 20:259–72.

———. 1987. The Interplay of Research Design Strategies and Data Analysis Procedures in Evaluating the Effects of Stress on Health. In *Stress and Health: Issues in Research Methodology*, ed. S. Kasl and C. Cooper, 113–40. New York: Wiley & Sons.

Kessler, R., and P. Cleary. 1980. Social Class and Psychological Distress. *American Sociological Review* 45:463–78.

Kessler, R., and H. Neighbors. 1986. A New Perspective on the Relationships among Race, Social Class and Psychological Distress. *Journal of Health and Social Behavior* 27:107–15.

Ketterer, R. 1981. *Consultation and Education in Mental Health: Problems and Prospects*. Beverly Hills: Sage.

Kramer, M., B. Rosen, and E. Willis. 1973. Definitions and Distributions of Mental Disorders in a Racist Society. In *Racism and Mental Health*, ed. C. Willie, M. Kramer, and B. Brown, 353–459. Pittsburgh: University of Pittsburgh Press.

Ladner, J. 1973. *The Death of White Sociology*. New York: Vintage Books.

Lefley, H. 1975. Approaches to Community Mental Health: The Miami Model. *Psychiatric Annals* 5:26–32.

Leighton, D., J. Harding, A. MacMillan, and A. Leighton. 1963. *The Character of Danger: Psychiatric Symptoms in Selected Communities*. New York: Basic Books.

McCarthy, J., and W. Yancey. 1971. Uncle Tom and Mr. Charlie: Metaphysical Pathos in the Study of Racism and Personal Disorganization. *American Journal of Sociology* 77:648–72.

Mellinger, G., M. Balter, D.I. Manheimer, I.H. Cisin, and H.J. Parry. 1978. Psychic Distress, Life Crisis and Use of Psychotherapeutic Medications. *Archives of General Psychiatry* 35:1045–52.

Merton, R. 1957. *Social Theory and Social Structure*. Glencoe, Ill.: Free Press.

Miranda, M., and H. Kitano. 1986. Mental Health Research and Practice in Minority Communities: Development of Culturally Sensitive Training Programs. Rockville, Md.: National Institute of Mental Health.

Mirowsky, J., and C. Ross. 1980. Minority Status, Ethnic Culture and Distress: A Comparison of Blacks, Whites, Mexicans and Mexican Americans. *American Journal of Sociology* 86:479–95.

Myers, H. 1982. Stress, Ethnicity and Social Class: A Model for Research with Black Populations. In *Minority Mental Health*, ed. E. Jones and S. Korchin, 118–48. New York: Praeger.

Neff, J. 1985a. Race and Vulnerability to Stress: An Examination of Differential Vulnerability. *Journal of Personality and Social Psychology* 49:481–91.

———. 1985b. Race Differences in Psychological Distress: The Effect of SES, Urbanicity and Measurement Strategy. *American Journal of Community Psychology* 12:337–51.

Neff, J., and B. Husaini. 1980. Race, Socio-economic Status and Psychiatric Impairment: A Research Note. *Journal of Community Psychology* 8:16–19.

Neighbors, H. 1984. The Distribution of Psychiatric Morbidity: A Review and Suggestions for Research. *Community Mental Health Journal* 20:5–18.

———. 1985. Comparing the Mental Health of Blacks and Whites: An Analysis of the Race Differences Tradition in Psychiatric Epidemiologic Research. Paper presented at the First Conference on Racial and Comparative Research, Institute for Urban Affairs and Research, Howard University, Washington, October 17.

————. 1986. Socioeconomic Status and Psychological Distress in Black Americans. *American Journal of Epidemiology* 124:779–93.

Palmer, F., and L. Andersen. 1979. Long-term Gains from Early Intervention: Findings from Longitudinal Studies. In *Project Head Start: A Legacy of the War on Poverty*, ed. E. Zigler and J. Valentine, 433–65. New York: Free Press.

Parker, R., and S. Kleiner. 1966. *Mental Illness in the Urban Negro Community*. New York: Free Press.

Pasamanick, B. 1963. Some Misconceptions Concerning Differences in the Racial Prevalence of Mental Disease. *American Journal of Orthopsychiatry* 33:72–86.

Pettigrew, T. 1964. *A Profile of the Negro American*. Princeton: Van Nostrand.

Porter, J., and R. Washington. 1979. Black Identity and Self-Esteem: A Review of Studies of Black Self-concept. *Annual Review of Sociology* 5:53–74.

Price, R. 1982. Priorities in Prevention Research: Linking Risk Factor and Intervention Research. Washington: National Institute of Mental Health, Prevention Research Branch. (Unpublished.)

Price, R., and S. Smith. 1985. *A Guide to Evaluating Prevention Programs in Mental Health*. Rockville, Md.: National Institute of Mental Health.

Roberts, R., J. Stevenson, and L. Breslow. 1981. Symptoms of Depression among Blacks and Whites in an Urban Community. *Journal of Nervous and Mental Disease* 169:774–79.

Ryan, W. 1971. *Blaming the Victim*. New York: Vintage Books.

Sarason, S. 1974. *The Psychological Sense of Community: Prospects for a Community Psychology*. San Francisco: Jossey-Bass.

Shure, M., and G. Spivack. 1982. Interpersonal Problem-solving in Young Children: A Cognitive Approach to Prevention. *American Journal of Community Psychology* 10:341–56.

Silberman, C. 1964. *Crisis in Black and White*. New York: Random House.

Snowden, L. 1982. *Reaching the Underserved*. Beverly Hills: Sage.

Srole, L., T. Langner, S. Michael, M. Opler, and T. Rennie. 1962. *Mental Health in the Metropolis: The Midtown Manhattan Study*. Vol. 1. New York: McGraw-Hill.

Taggart, R. 1981. *A Fisherman's Guide: An Assessment of Training and Remediation Strategies*. Kalamazoo: W.E. Upjohn Institute for Employment Research.

Uhlenhuth, E., R. Lipman, M.B. Balter, and M. Stern. 1974. Symptom Intensity and Life Stress in the City. *Archives of General Psychiatry* 31:759–64.

U.S. Domestic Policy Council. 1986. Up from Dependency: A New National Public Assistance Strategy. U.S. Domestic Policy Council Low-income Opportunity Working Group pub. no. 1987-170-753-814/51126.

U.S. Health Resources and Services Administration. 1987. *Health Status of the Disadvantaged Chartbook, 1986.* DHHS pub. no. (HRSA) HRS-P-DV86-2. Washington.

Veroff, J., E. Douvan, and R. Kulka. 1981. *The Inner American: A Self-portrait from 1957–1976.* New York: Basic Books.

Wagenfeld, M., and J. Jacobs. 1982. The Community Mental Health Movement: Its Origins and Growth. In *Public Mental Health,* ed. M. Wagenfeld, P. Lemkau, and B. Justice, 46–88. Beverly Hills: Sage.

Warheit, G., C. Holzer, and J. Schwab. 1973. An Analysis of Social Class and Racial Differences in Depressive Symptomatology. *Journal of Health and Social Behavior* 14:291–99.

———. 1975. Race and Mental Illness: An Epidemiologic Update. *Journal of Health and Social Behavior* 16:243–56.

Weinberg, D. 1985. A Poverty Research Agenda for the Next Decade. Paper delivered at a conference, "Poverty and Policy: Retrospect and Prospects," Madison, Institute for Research on Poverty.

Wheaton, B. 1980. The Sociogenesis of Psychological Disorder: An Attributional Theory. *Journal of Health and Social Behavior* 21:100–24.

Yancey, W., L. Rigsby, and J. McCarthy. 1972. Social Position and Self-evaluation: The Relative Importance of Race. *American Journal of Sociology* 78:338–59.

Yette, S. 1971. *The Choice: The Issue of Black Survival in America.* New York: Berkely Medallion Books.

Race Differences in Teenage Sexuality, Pregnancy, and Adolescent Childbearing

FRANK F. FURSTENBERG, Jr.

L ATE IN 1986 THE NATIONAL ACADEMY OF Sciences (NAS) released the report of a special scientific panel established to review and evaluate existing research on the causes and consequences of adolescent pregnancy and childbearing (Hayes 1987). The panel, consisting of social scientists and health professionals, had been given the charge of drawing lessons for public policy from the massive research literature on teenage fertility. One of the issues discussed by the panel was the extent to which teenage parenthood is perceived and defined as largely a problem among blacks.

The panel's report was exceedingly cautious in addressing the question of whether and how early childbearing is linked to racial status. In the executive summary, which provides a digest of the major findings and recommendations, no mention is made of race whatsoever. In the body of the report, racial differences in patterns of sex, pregnancy, and childbearing among adolescents are frequently documented, but the panel refrains, as is evident in the passage cited below, from interpreting the meaning of black/white differences.

Race differences in patterns of early sexual activity and fertility are dramatic, yet disagreement exists over the source of these differences: some attribute the disparity wholly or in large part to socioeconomic differences among blacks and whites; others maintain that differences in the acceptability of early nonmarital sexual activity, pregnancy, and parenthood account for the difference. Research has yet to resolve the debate, for in many cases it has failed to ask the right questions.

In the face of limited evidence, the NAS panel was reluctant to draw any conclusions about the complex causal chain between race, socioeconomic status, perceived life options, and strategies of family formation. Instead, they made an urgent plea for additional research on the question of whether racial differences in teenage fertility reflect "deep-seated subgroup values or more transient attitudinal adjustments to external circumstances."

The wariness of the experts sharply contrasts with opinions often voiced by social commentators, journalists, policy makers, and some politicians who portray teen pregnancy and childbearing as a black problem. In the year or so preceding the publication of *Risking the Future,* the NAS report, a large number of articles and stories appeared that clearly implied that teenage childbearing principally afflicts blacks and must be solved by reducing the susceptibility of black youth to sexual activity, pregnancy, and childbearing.

Just after the NAS report was released an editorial in the *Wall Street Journal* (1986) declared:

> After spending $600,000 given by five foundations, the National Academy of Sciences has concluded that virtually no known public policy can contain the surge in *black* teenage pregnancy. . . . None-theless this study of sex and pregnancy among *black* teenagers by a prominent group of U.S. social scientists deserves attention and discussion.

In a reply to this comment, the chair of the panel, Daniel Federman, in noting the *Journal's* assertion that teen pregnancy was a black problem, pointed out that the panel did not subscribe to this view. But this mismatch in communication shows how deeply imprinted in the public mind is the notion that teenage parenthood is largely confined to blacks.

This article reconsiders the evidence on the link between race and teen childbearing in hopes of resolving the seeming wide discrepancy between scholarly and popular perception. The data presented here mostly come from secondary sources, though I will occasionally introduce evidence from several studies that I have conducted. (For an excellent summary of the research evidence and an intelligent discussion of racial differences in teen childbearing, see Moore, Simms, and Betsey 1986.) My main objective will be in interpreting, in some instances reinterpreting, available data that address the origins of racial differences in rates of pregnancy and childbearing and provide possible explanations of these differences. As one of the members of the NAS panel, I am obviously sympathetic with the caution exercised in *Risking the Future.* In this article, however, I am prepared to be more speculative about the sources of racial differences and the implications for public policy.

The first part of the article discusses demographic and survey data on black/white differences in patterns of intercourse, contraceptive use, pregnancy and resolution of pregnancy, and marital and nonmarital childbearing. The following section reviews the varying consequences of pregnancy and childbearing for whites and blacks. The final part takes up interventions and their potential effect on diminishing racial differences in premature parenthood.

Race Differences in Sexuality, Pregnancy, and Childbearing

It has often been noted that rates of teenage childbearing are the product of the rates of sexual activity, the risk of conception, and different strategies used for resolving a pregnancy (Cutright 1972). Consequently, racial differences can be produced by any or all of these components. In fact, differences occur among blacks and whites at each stage of the process, complicating our task of explaining racial disparities in the rate of teenage parenthood.

Overall, as is recorded in table 1, sizable differences exist in the rate of both marital and nonmarital childbearing between black and white teenagers. In the group aged 15 to 19, the total birthrate of blacks is somewhat more than twice as high as the rate for whites— a ratio that has been reasonably constant over the past several decades during which teenage fertility has dropped by more than 40 percent. The more revealing statistic, also displayed in table 1, is the rate of nonmarital fertility which has risen by 100 percent since 1955. For white teens, out-of-wedlock rates have more than tripled while for blacks they have climbed only 12 percent. Black nonmarital fertility among teens in 1984 is still 4.6 times higher than for whites—a steep decline from the 12.9 : 1 ratio that existed in 1955, but a sizable

TABLE 1
Adolescent Fertility by Race, 1955–1984

Age/Race	1955	1960	1970	1980	1983	1984
	Number of births (in thousands)					
15–19						
Total**	484	587	645	552	489	470
White	373	459	464	388	338	321
Black	111*	129*	172	150	137	134
18–19						
Total	334	405	421	354	317	303
White	269	329	320	260	229	216
Black	65*	76*	95	84	79	77
15–17						
Total	150	182	224	198	173	167
White	104	130	144	128	110	105
Black	46*	53*	77	66	58	57
<15						
Total	6	7	12	10	10	10
White	2	3	4	4	4	4
Black	4*	4*	7	6	5	6
	Birthrates (per thousand women)					
15–19						
Total	90.3	89.1	68.3	53.0	51.7	50.9
White	79.1	79.4	57.4	44.7	43.6	42.5
Black	167.2*	156.1*	147.7	100.0	95.5	95.7
18–19						
Total	—	—	114.7	82.1	78.1	78.3
White	—	—	101.5	72.1	68.3	68.1
Black	—	—	204.9	138.8	130.4	132.0
15–17						
Total	—	—	38.8	32.5	32.0	31.1
White	—	—	29.2	25.2	24.8	23.9
Black	—	—	101.4	73.6	70.1	69.7
10–14						
Total	0.9	0.8	1.2	1.1	1.1	1.2
White	0.3	0.4	0.5	0.6	0.6	.6
Black	4.8*	4.3*	5.2	4.3	4.1	4.3

TABLE 1—Continued

Age/Race	1955	1960	1970	1980	1983	1984
Rates of out-of-wedlock births (per thousand unmarried women)						
15–19						
Total	15.1	15.3	22.4	27.6	29.8	30.2
White	6.0	6.6	10.9	16.2	18.5	19.0
Black	77.6*	76.5*	96.9	89.2	86.4	87.1
Ratios of out-of-wedlock births (per thousand births)						
15–19						
Total	143	148	295	476	534	556
White	64	72	171	330	391	415
Black	407*	421*	628	851	883	891
18–19						
Total	102	107	224	398	457	481
White	49	54	135	270	323	349
Black	324*	337*	521	792	835	848
15–17						
Total	232	240	430	615	676	692
White	102	116	252	452	527	552
Black	524*	543*	760	928	948	950
<15						
Total	663	679	808	887	904	910
White	421	475	579	754	799	807
Black	801*	822*	935	985	984	985

* Includes all nonwhites, not only blacks
** All totals include all nonwhites, which is somewhat more than the sum of whites plus blacks.

Sources: Moore, Simms, and Betsey 1986; National Institute of Child and Human Development 1984; U.S. Bureau of the Census 1984; National Center for Health Statistics 1985, 1986.

differential nonetheless (National Center for Health Statistics 1986). Were we to confine these comparisons to the group of teens under age 18, who are the greatest source of public concern, the trends described above of diminishing racial differences over time would stand, but the persisting racial differences would be somewhat greater— close to 5 times as high for young unmarried blacks as young unmarried whites.

Thus, the complexion of teen childbearing has changed dramatically in the past thirty years. A growing proportion of teen mothers are unmarried. Whites increasingly, especially those under the age of 18, are having out-of-wedlock births, following what was at midcentury predominantly a black pattern. Childbearing was almost an exclusive problem for unmarried black youth a generation ago; today, it has become a problem for whites as well. In 1955, 71 percent of all unmarried mothers below the age of 18 were black; in 1984, their proportion had dropped to 45 percent.

Dramatic as these changes are, unmarried blacks are still five times as likely to become mothers before age 18 than whites. Or, to put it in more comprehensible terms, approximately a quarter of all unmarried blacks will have a child by age 18 compared to about one in twenty whites. Thus, teenage childbearing still remains a far more serious problem for blacks than whites.

Patterns of Sexual Activity

A closer look at the process of unwed parenthood is instructive for revealing why these racial differences persist. A series of studies in the 1970s carried out by Zelnik and Kantner (Zelnik, Kantner, and Ford 1981; Zelnik and Kantner 1980; Zelnik and Shah 1983) uncovered sharp differences in the timing and prevalence of intercourse among blacks and whites. In 1971 unmarried black females living in metropolitan areas were almost three times as likely to engage in intercourse by age 15 as whites (31 percent vs. 11 percent); by 1979 this ratio had dropped to about 2 to 1 (41 percent vs. 18 percent). Several surveys carried out in the early 1980s reveal similar race differences (Hofferth and Hayes 1987). Apparently, the incidence of sexual activity at early ages has leveled off or even slightly declined, but black females continue to initiate intercourse earlier than whites.

Many social scientists believe that these racial patterns are spurious and actually represent socioeconomic differences. The few efforts testing this interpretation suggest that it is only partially supported by empirical evidence. The NAS panel commissioned a series of special analyses of data on sexual activity collected in the National Longitudinal Survey, a representative survey of youth conducted in 1983. Their report shows that when socioeconomic differences are taken into account, racial differences are diminished only modestly (Hofferth and Hayes

1987). Similar findings emerge from a separate examination of data from the National Survey of Children, another nationwide sample of adolescents. Controlling for social class, black females initiate sexual activity earlier in adolescence and attain higher levels of nonvirginity by age 16. Differences are even sharper for males (Furstenberg et al. 1987). Several other studies reveal that substantial proportions of black males engage in sex prior to puberty (Clark, Zabin, and Hardy 1984). Thus, the best available evidence suggests that race differences in the timing and incidence of sexual intercourse among teens are not entirely a correlate of high rates of economic disadvantage among blacks.

If this is true, what could account for distinctive patterns of early intercourse among blacks and whites? Several ethnographic studies indicate the possibility of normative differences in attitudes toward nonmarital sex and childbearing (Staples 1971; Schultz 1969; Hannerz 1969; Levy and Grinker 1982). Qualitative research indicates that many young black males, especially in urban ghettos, are encouraged, even provoked, into having sex at a very early age by peers. This peer group pressure for sexual engagement extends to females as well where sexual activity, and sometimes motherhood, is regarded as a marker of adulthood. While similar patterns are evident among white working and lower-class youth, the peer pressure for early sex may not be as strong and may still be moderated by fears of the consequences of pregnancy.

One study based on survey data revealed strong ecological variations in rates of early intercourse (Furstenberg, Gunn, and Morgan 1987). Blacks in racially isolated school settings were much more likely to engage in early intercourse than those in racially mixed schools, even controlling for social class. Possibly racial segregation in neighborhoods or schools creates or intensifies differences in normative climates that can result in distinctive sexual patterns (see also Hogan and Kitagawa 1985).

Use of Contraception

None of the exisiting evidence suggests sharp racial differences in contraceptive use among teenagers. Modest black/white differences, however, emerge in birth control practices, which put blacks at somewhat greater risk of conception. Sexually active blacks are somewhat less likely than whites to use birth control at first intercourse, slightly less likely to use contraception regularly, and more likely to have never used contraceptives. On the other hand, blacks are somewhat more likely to have used prescriptive methods of contraception. These seemingly anomalous and contradictory trends probably result from the fact that blacks are disproportionately more likely to use family planning clinics (and less likely to receive services from private physicians). Overall, access to contraceptive services remains a problem for black and white teens alike, and they are equally likely to delay a visit to a contraceptive provider.

The racial differences in the consistency of contraceptive practice mentioned above probably are due, at least in part, to the earlier timing of intercourse among blacks. Intercourse in the early teens is less likely to be planned, reducing the likelihood of contraception. Younger teens, even when provided with contraception, are probably less able to use contraception regularly. For these reasons, it seems likely that blacks, who generally initiate intercourse earlier than whites, will encounter more difficulty using contraception (Moore, Simms, and Betsey 1986). These empirical findings have important policy implications which will be discussed later in this article.

Abortion

Black/white differences in patterns of abortion are complicated by the higher incidence of pregnancy among blacks. Their greater risk of pregnancy increases their odds of abortion during their teen years. In any given year, blacks are about twice as likely as whites to obtain an abortion, which is roughly proportional to their chances of becoming pregnant (Moore, Simms, and Betsey 1986). Given a pregnancy, black teens are slightly less likely to end it in abortion (41 percent) than white teens (47 percent). Whether this difference is due to preference or access to services is not known (Hayes 1987).

A small proportion (about 13 percent) of teen pregnancies are terminated by miscarriage. This figure does not seem to vary greatly by race and consequently does not have important implications for race differences in childbearing rates (Henshaw 1987).

Nonmarital Births

It is well known that white teens are much more likely to marry in the event of a pregnancy than are blacks. In 1984 42 percent of births to white teens occurred out of wedlock compared to 89 percent of births to black teens. As large as this difference is, it should be noted that the racial differential in the proportion of nonmarital births has been declining. In 1955 only 6 percent of white births to teenagers were nonmarital compared to 41 percent of black births (Furstenberg, Lincoln, and Menken 1981). In other words, the pattern of nonmarital teen childbearing that was prevalent only among blacks a generation ago has now extended to whites; fewer and fewer whites are electing to marry when a premarital conception occurs.

The declining appeal of marriage among pregnant whites was fore-shadowed by black attitudes toward marriage several decades ago (Cherlin 1981). Marriage was an attractive solution when and only when the father of the child was in a position to provide economic support. During the 1950s and 1960s a diminishing number of black males were "marriageable," and accordingly the stigma attached to out-of-wedlock parenthood faded. This is precisely what is happening among pregnant whites today, especially those under the age of 18 for whom over half of all births occur out of wedlock today. As more white teens see marriage as an undesirable way of resolving a premarital pregnancy, public concern over teenage parenthood grows.

To summarize, the sources of race differences in rates of nonmarital childbearing are diverse. Blacks are more likely to be at risk of becoming pregnant because they are sexually active at an earlier age, they are slightly less likely to use contraception effectively, a little less likely to obtain an abortion, and much less likely to marry. We have not presented data on patterns of adoption, as accurate statistics by age and race are unavailable. All evidence indicates that adoption, while relatively common among whites several decades ago, is relatively rare today and does not importantly affect the racial differential in rates of nonmarital childbearing.

As I have noted throughout, racial differences in teen sexual activity, pregnancy, and childbearing have been declining in recent decades. In the 1970s, the proportion of whites engaging in sex during their teen years grew rapidly. While there is little prospect that white teens will match the incidence of sexual behavior among blacks in the near future, racial differences are not nearly so large as they once were. The same is true among marriage patterns—the other major source of the racial disparity. Fewer white teens are resorting to marriage to resolve a teen pregnancy, resulting in a sharp rise in the rate of nonmarital births. This pattern is likely to continue for the foreseeable future. Thus, there is reason to expect further declines in the patterns of race differences that were so prominent in the middle of the twentieth century.

Consequences of Early Childbearing

Over the past decade an extensive amount of research has been conducted on the consequences of early childbearing for young mothers and their children (Chilman 1983; McAnarney and Schreider 1984; Hayes 1987). Some investigations have also been undertaken on the impact of early childbearing on the life chances of young fathers (Park and Neville 1987). This work is inconclusive in part because it is difficult to obtain reliable information on male fertility patterns and to devise effective research designs to study males who become fathers. Finally, some studies have been carried out on the effect of early childbearing on the families of teen mothers, though this area of research remains relatively unexplored and will not be discussed in this article (Ooms 1981).

I shall not attempt to summarize this literature as it has been fully described in several recent articles and monographs and was extensively reviewed in the report of the NAS panel. It is sufficient to say that little disagreement exists that early childbearing adversely affects the life chances of young mothers to complete school and attain economic self-sufficiency. Premature parenthood clearly reduces the prospects of marital stability and increases the odds of having more children than desired. The effects of early childbearing on the offspring of teen mothers are less clearcut. Though many researchers are convinced that the children of young mothers are at a developmental disadvantage, the extent and sources of this disadvantage have not been clearly delineated (Hayes 1987; Brooks-Gunn and Furstenberg 1986). At the very least, the educational and economic handicaps that early childbearing impose on young mothers creates a family environment for their offspring that is not strongly conducive to success. Added to that the immaturity of the parents, the strain of managing motherhood while still in school or at work, the limited assistance provided by fathers, and the instability of child care figures further complicate and perhaps compromise the child's cognitive and emotional development.

Less can be said about how parenthood in adolescence affects young men. Perhaps family commitments early in life could constrain educational attainment and economic achievement in later life for males as they appear to for females. But the supporting evidence for this proposition is scanty (Card and Wise 1978). As we have already seen, an increasing proportion of males eschew marriage and many, if not most, eschew paternal support as well (Weitzman 1985). Thus, it is entirely possible that the effects of early childbearing on men are relatively small, except for the males who marry or undertake to support their children.

Even for females, the magnitude of the differences in life chances attributable to early childbearing may be somewhat exaggerated. Moreover, the question of whether racial differences exist in the consequences of teen childbearing has not really been explored. Given the substantial variations in sexual patterns among blacks and whites and racial differences in the response to teen pregnancy described earlier in this article, there is some reason to expect that teenage whites and blacks may respond to early parenthood differently as well.

Early parenthood is far more common among blacks and consequently there may be less selectivity in the population of individuals who become young parents than among white teens for whom parenthood, at least out-of-wedlock parenthood, is still a relatively rare event. Both evidence from qualitative and quantitative studies indicates a strong commitment among black parents to provide assistance to pregnant teens in order to discourage them from leaving school (Furstenberg 1976). It is less clear whether white teens receive the same level of family support. White teens are, on the other hand, more likely to marry and, consequently, may receive greater support from the biological father. Thus, evidence exists that blacks and whites manage early parenthood somewhat differently and have access to different types of resources. Do the long-term effects of early parenthood differ by racial status accordingly?

Evidence from a longitudinal study of a predominantly black sample of teen mothers and their children in Baltimore, which I and my colleagues, J. Brooks Gunn and Philip Morgan, have conducted reveals that many black teen mothers manage to deal surprisingly well with the potential handicaps imposed by premature parenthood (Furstenberg, Gunn, and Morgan 1987). A substantial majority of the 300 teen parents followed over nearly a twenty-year period were able to complete school, become economically self-sufficient, and limit their family size.

When we compared these findings to the educational, occupational, and family histories collected from black teenage mothers in several national surveys, there was a good deal of consistency across studies. In no sense were the Baltimore data atypical of the experience of most black teenage mothers, at least those aged now in their early thirties. And it would appear that teen mothers do not entirely live up to the conventional sterotype of the adolescent mother. They are generally not high school dropouts, the majority are not receiving public assistance, and most do not end up with a large number of children (see table 2).

Lest we paint too rosy a picture of the situations of the teen mothers, most women in Baltimore were struggling economically. Two-thirds were single mothers and had family incomes of under $15,000. Even when they were fully employed, most were unable to rise much above the poverty level. Again, these findings were replicated when the national surveys were consulted, though a somewhat higher proportion of black teen mothers nationwide were currently married than was true for the Baltimore women (table 2).

Black teen mothers in both the Baltimore study and the national surveys were clearly not making out as well as black women who delayed childbearing until their twenties. Consistent with the evidence cited earlier, older childbearers were noticeably more likely to complete high school, attain economic self-sufficiency, be currently married, and limit their family size than teen mothers (table 2).

The analysis of the Baltimore data was confined to black women as there were too few whites in the study to provide reliable comparisons with the national data. But the national data sets do contain information on the situations of white women as well, permitting us to see whether the impact of birth timing differs among blacks and whites. Table 3 summarizes that information.

The contrast between white early and later childbearers reveals the same patterns observed among blacks, showing greater disadvantage when the first birth occurred before age 20. Some interesting racial differences, however, appear in the configuration of disadvantage. Schooling is somewhat more likely to be curtailed among whites than blacks. Whites who delayed childbearing almost always completed

TABLE 2

Socioeconomic Variables among Black Females Aged 29–36 with at Least One Biological Child

| Data set: | Baltimore* 1984 | CPS** 1983 | | NLS** 1982 | | NSFG** 1982 | |
| Year: | | | | | | | |
Age at first birth:	14–19	14–19	20+	14–19	20+	14–19	20+
Age (mean)	32.7	32.3	32.7	32.1	32.2	32.3	32.4
Education							
High school graduates (%)	70.5	73.4	86.3	59.0	86.2	69.9	87.9
Years completed (mean)	12.0	12.3	13.1	11.4	12.8	12.0	13.3
Marital Status							
Currently married (%)	30.2	35.1	47.9	37.5	57.2	32.2	56.9
First marriage (%)	80.8	—	—	82.0	91.0	73.7	88.3
Remarriage (%)	19.2	—	—	18.0	9.0	26.3	11.7
Previously married (%)	45.7	41.5	32.9	45.4	23.3	43.3	26.1
Never married (%)	24.0	23.5	19.3	17.1	19.5	24.5	17.0
Biological Children (mean)	2.3	2.7	2.0	2.9	1.9	2.9	2.0
Occupational Status							
Currently employed (%)	67.8	56.1	65.6	61.5	71.8	63.7	70.3
Welfare Received in Past Year (%)	29.1	—	—	29.7	14.3	27.5	20.0
Family Income							
Less than $15,000	52.8	61.7	51.2	61.9	41.1	54.6	35.0
$15,000 — $24,999	23.6	19.4	20.4	18.6	19.3	20.9	22.6
$25,000 or more	23.6	18.9	28.4	19.4	39.6	24.5	42.4
N (unweighted)	(258)	(242)	(233)	(252)	(231)	(289)	(310)

* A few white respondents (30) excluded from analysis.
** Respondents residing in SMSAs only. Figures weighted to represent national population.
— Data not available.

TABLE 3

Socioeconomic Variables among White Females Aged 29–36 with at Least One Biological Child

Data set: Year: Age at first birth:	CPS* 1983		NLS* 1982		NSFG* 1982	
	14–19	20+	14–19	20+	14–19	20+
Age (mean)	32.5	32.7	32.2	32.5	32.4	32.6
Education						
High school graduates (%)	72.1	89.8	61.1	94.0	61.1	94.8
Years completed (mean)	11.9	13.3	11.5	13.5	11.3	13.7
Marital Status						
Currently married (%)	65.4	82.4	74.5	86.4	67.5	84.2
First marriage (%)	—	—	64.5	86.3	63.0	85.3
Remarriage (%)	—	—	35.6	13.6	37.0	14.7
Previously married (%)	32.1	15.3	24.1	12.4	28.9	14.0
Never married (%)	2.5	2.3	1.5	1.2	3.6	1.8
Biological Children (mean)	2.6	1.9	2.5	2.0	2.7	2.0
Occupational Status						
Currently employed (%)	59.7	51.2	65.7	59.9	53.7	54.7
Welfare Received in Past Year (%)	—	—	8.0	3.9	10.8	3.2
Family Income						
Less than $15,000	33.4	19.1	28.4	13.9	31.4	14.8
$15,000 - $24,999	27.1	22.8	25.8	24.2	25.4	24.7
$25,000 or more	39.4	58.1	45.7	61.9	43.1	60.5
N (unweighted)	(490)	(1632)	(238)	(824)	(169)	(530)

* Respondents residing in SMSAs only. Figures weighted to represent national population.
— Data not available.

school whereas those who became mothers in their teens had a quite high probability of not completing high school. Educational attainment differences are less sharp among blacks, if only because blacks are more likely to drop out *even* if they delay childbearing.

The most distinctive racial differences occur in marriage patterns. Regardless of the timing of childbearing, whites are much more likely to enter marriage and remain wed than blacks. Younger and older black mothers alike are far less likely to marry than whites. Early parenthood seems to reduce slightly the chances of blacks entering marriage by their early thirties; for whites, the effect of early childbearing is the reverse: it slightly increases the odds of marriage among women in their early thirties.

Both blacks and whites who become teen mothers and marry are more likely to divorce eventually. The great majority of black teen mothers who married ultimately separated and rather few made their way back into marriage. Only about a quarter of the black teen mothers are currently in a first marriage as compared to roughly half of the blacks who delayed childbearing. The impact of early childbearing on white teen mothers is almost as large. More than half the teen mothers divorce, though a much higher proportion of white divorcees eventually remarry. So by comparison to blacks, white teen mothers are significantly more likely to be currently married. Of course, compared to white women who postponed childbearing, white teenage mothers are notably less likely to be currently married or in their first marriages. Still, white *teen* mothers are much more likely to be currently married and almost as likely to be in a first marriage than black *older* mothers.

These differences in marriage patterns have important implications for the economic situation of black and white mothers. Black *older* mothers have lower family incomes than white *teen* mothers, partly owing to the fact that they are much more likely to be living with a spouse. White teen mothers are about equally likely to be working as black teen mothers, but because they are much more likely to be married they typically have the benefit of two incomes. Note that white teen mothers are actually more likely to be employed than white older childbearers. Among blacks the opposite is true. It appears that white early childbearers can obtain and afford to hold secondary jobs which supplement their family incomes. Accordingly, fewer white teen mothers are receiving public assistance than blacks who postponed parenthood.

Still, large differences exist in the family income distributions of white women depending on their age at first birth. Older childbearers are half as likely to be living near or below the poverty level (under $15,000). Presumably, the husbands of older childbearers are earning more as also may the women themselves.

The distribution of income among black mothers is sharply skewed downward regardless of the timing of her first birth. Blacks who postpone parenthood are much less well off than white early childbearers, despite the fact that white adolescent mothers are less often employed. Presumably, their poor prospects of marriage adversely affect the family incomes of blacks, even if they wait to have children. Blacks who entered parenthood as teenagers are even worse off, but delaying only helps their situation modestly.

The single area in which the consequences for black and white women appear to be identical is family size. The magnitude of birth timing is the same regardless of race; early childbearers averaged between .5 and 1.0 more children than later childbearers. In the Baltimore study, however, many women had become sterilized by their early thirties, suggesting the possibility that these differences could diminish over time. Early childbearers may be at a different stage in their family development than later childbearers.

Are the consequences of early childbearing, then, better or worse for blacks than whites? Readers may draw their own conclusions from tables 2 and 3. I would argue that they are neither better nor worse—they are different. For both races, the costs of premature parenthood are evident. Yet, the majority of teenage mothers—black and white—manage to stage a recovery, attaining economic self-sufficiency by their early thirties. Most young mothers regardless of race also manage to limit subsequent childbearing. The racial differences lie in the strategies of recovery from the handicaps of premature parenthood and the success of those strategies.

Black teen mothers are less likely to marry, remain married, and to remarry when divorce occurs. Single parenthood, although not an inevitable consequence of teen pregnancy, is a likely one. For whites, marriage operates as a major recovery route, offering an alternative or, at least, an important supplement to their own earning ability. Low education and restricted job opportunities, therefore, are not quite as costly as they are for black young mothers.

On the other hand, the advantages of delaying parenthood are not so great for blacks as well. As we discovered, blacks who postponed motherhood are less likely to do well economically than whites who enter parenthood in adolescence. The cruel fact is that for blacks delaying childbearing has a relatively low payoff. They are damned if they do and damned if they don't. These data lend credence to observations voiced by leaders in the black community that a major source of early childbearing among blacks is a despair of future opportunities. This perception has important implications for policies and programs designed to prevent early childbearing, the final topic of concern in this article.

The Prevention of Teen Pregnancy

No review of current programs and policies aimed at preventing teen pregnancy or ameliorating its effects has provided a very reassuring picture of the possibilities for effective intervention (Moore, Simms, and Betsey 1986; Furstenberg and Brooks-Gunn 1986; Hayes 1987). The NAS panel on adolescent pregnancy and childbearing summarized the burgeoning literature on intervention and strategies in some detail. It did not directly address the question of whether the special needs of racial or ethnic subgroups might require different types of programs or services than those offered to the general population of adolescents. Nevertheless, the NAS review of alternative interventions and the panel's priorities for social action provide a framework for thinking about how different types of programs and policies may have an impact on persistent racial differences in rates of teen pregnancy and childbearing.

The NAS panel identified several different strategies for preventing teen pregnancy. Some observers had viewed these measures as competing but the NAS report clearly regarded them as complementary.

Lowering the Barriers to Sex Education and Contraception

The NAS panel reviewed a number of seemingly attractive ideas for reducing early and unprotected sexual experience. Among the most popular of these have been a wide variety of sex education and life education programs to equip youth with contraceptive information or provide decision-making skills associated with birth control use. Newer programs promoted by conservatives have placed more emphasis on teaching teens to postpone sexual experience, encouraging them to "say no to sex." More recently, educational efforts have been directed at expanding adolescents' knowledge about their life options and the problems associated with premature parenthood.

The NAS report strongly recommended a variety of measures to increase access to contraceptives for teens. Since the 1970s, considerable efforts have been made to recruit sexually active teens to publicly funded family planning programs by modifying these services to fit the special needs of teenagers. In the 1980s, attention shifted to bringing family planning services closer to the adolescent population by establishing health clinics on or near the school premises. While none of these approaches has met with great success, the panel urged continued efforts to experiment with making birth control more available to sexually active adolescents. It also called for aggressive promotion of condom use for males and experimenting with ways to make pill distribution easier.

Another direction recommended by the panel was to alter social environments which promote adolescent sexual experience and inhibit the use of contraception. Media content has been a principal target of reformers who believe that teens are directly and indirectly taught to engage in unplanned and unprotected sex. In addition, the panel noted the important efforts being made by advocacy groups like the Children's Defense Fund and the Urban League to increase community awareness of the costs of premature parenthood.

Finally, the NAS report, recognizing the widespread perception that early parenthood is a symptom of blocked social opportunities, have advocated programs and services that reduce social disadvantage. A new wave of programs has been recently instituted that attempts to provide incentives for teens to defer parenthood. Remedial education, job training, summer employment, and guarantees of postsecondary education have all been discussed as possible strategies for discouraging youth from entering parenthood prematurely.

The panel discovered that very little evaluation has been conducted on the impact of any of these intervention strategies. Accordingly, it is extremely difficult to assess whether or how they might affect black and white youth differently.

Earlier I identified two major sources accounting for higher rates of early childbearing among blacks—a much greater likelihood of early inception of intercourse and a much lower probability of marriage in the event of pregnancy. To a lesser extent, sexually active black teens appear to be less likely to use contraception effectively, in part because they initiate intercourse at a younger age.

Will programs aimed at postponing sexual activity and decreasing unprotected sex reduce the racial disparity in rates of pregnancy and childbearing? If they were successful, they could have this impact. Assuming a program were able to delay the onset of intercourse by a year or so, we might expect that blacks would benefit disproportionately for reasons mentioned above. Existing programs, however, do not seem to be achieving results of this magnitude. The most ambitious program designed to delay early sex has been carried out in the Atlanta public schools. It is too early to tell with any certainty how effective this program is, but preliminary estimates suggest that it is having a modest impact. Similarly, the community education programs appear to have small effects, at best, in reducing early sexual activity or decreasing unprotected intercourse.

More aggressive and effective contraceptive services would probably also reduce the racial differential, especially if they reached younger teens. Yet, the existing repertoire of techniques for promoting contraceptive practice do not show any immediate prospect of producing dramatic increases in use of birth control among younger teens. Data on school-based programs, the most innovative program for reaching younger teens, are still lacking. Preliminary indications from ongoing evaluations, however, are not sufficiently encouraging to suggest large changes in the incidence of early childbearing.

The NAS panel placed a strong emphasis on increasing contraceptive availability and use among sexually active young people as a major means of pregnancy prevention. The figures on racial patterns in contraceptive use suggest that greater access to birth control would probably diminish black/white differences somewhat, especially if very young males were encouraged to use condoms.

Differences in marriage rates following premarital conception remain large between blacks and whites. No programs adequately address the underlying causes of the low, and still declining, incidence of marriage among younger blacks. Clearly, rising rates of unemployment among young black males and poor economic prospects for poorly educated men have affected the pool of marriage eligibles for black females. In addition, and probably linked to their declining economic position, large numbers of young black men are afflicted with a variety of social ills—drug use, alcoholism, delinquency and crime, mental disabilities, and so on. Rough estimates of the proportion of marriageable males suggest that the rise of single parenthood can be traced, at least in part, to the economically marginal position of black men (Wilson and Neckerman 1986).

While it is difficult to demonstrate empirically the direct association between racial differences in social opportunity and teen pregnancy, the NAS panel recognized the plausibility of this explanation.

> Chronic unemployment and poor job prospects among some subgroups of the population have had serious adverse effects on many young people's perceptions of opportunity. The lack of meaningful employment options may diminish the motivation to delay parenthood. As with educational reform, the development of a comprehensive plan for youth employment is beyond the mandate and expertise of the panel, yet we emphasize the need to enhance the employability of high-risk youth (Hayes 1987, 268).

We suspect that if all the measures proposed by the NAS panel were adopted, some further decline would occur in the racial differential in early intercourse, use of contraception, and resolution of premarital pregnancy. More likely than not, the difference will continue to decline, if only because the situation of young whites is becoming more like that of young blacks. More white teens have been engaging in early intercourse, using contraception only casually, and showing great reluctance to marry in the event of a premarital conception.

Summary

This article has examined the origin and consequences of racial differences in teen sexuality, pregnancy, and childbearing. Black/white differences in rates of early and out-of-wedlock childbearing have been declining in the past several decades though the incidence of nonmartial fertility among younger teens is still about five times as high for blacks as for whites.

Early sexual behavior, irregular use of contraception, and a much lower probability of marrying prior to having a birth all contribute to the racial differential. Evidence suggests that both normative and socioeconomic differences may account for these demographic patterns.

Black teens show markedly higher tolerance for childbearing before marriage. They also express much greater reservations about the viability of marriage, especially at an early age, than do whites. These views may affect their willingness to risk early pregnancy and initiate intercourse at an early age.

Several types of interventions that might reduce black/white differences in teen childbearing were reviewed. The most promising of these involved simultaneously strengthening the community sanctions that discourage early parenthood while expanding social opportunities. Presently, poor, especially poor minority youth, may feel that they have little to lose by entering parenthood prematurely. Unless we are able to persuade these youth that they have a larger stake in the future, we are unlikely to see a dramatic decline in the incidence of early childbearing among blacks. This does not necessarily mean that racial differences are destined to persist. Increasingly, white youth are subject to many of the same conditions that have produced high rates of early and out-of-wedlock childbearing among blacks. Thus, racial differences may decline not because the situation of blacks is improving but because white youth are less willing to defer sexual activity or less able to marry when pregnancy occurs. This may at least change the perception of early childbearing as a "black" problem. Whatever else it is, teenage childbearing represents the inability of our society to manage the transition to adulthood effectively. This ineptitude appears to be, to a growing extent, colorblind.

References

Brooks-Gunn, J., and F.F. Furstenberg, Jr. 1986. Children of Adolescent Mothers: Physical, Academic, and Psychological Outcomes. *Developmental Review* 6:224–51.

Card, J.J., and L.L. Wise. 1978. Teenage Mothers and Teenage Fathers: The Impact of Early Childbearing on the Parents' Personal and Professional Lives. *Family Planning Perspectives* 10(4):199–205.

Cherlin, A.J. 1981. *Marriage, Divorce, Remarriage.* Cambridge: Harvard University Press.

Chilman, C.S. 1983. *Adolescent Sexuality in a Changing American Society: Social and Psychological Perspectives for the Human Services Professions.* 2nd ed. New York: Wiley.

Clark, S.D., L.S. Zabin, and J.B. Hardy. 1984. Sex, Contraception and Parenthood: Experience and Attitudes among Urban Black Young Men. *Family Planning Perspectives* 16:77–82.

Cutright, P. 1972. Illegitimacy in the United States, 1920–1968. In *Demographic and Social Aspects of Population Growth,* ed. C. Westoff and R. Parks, 375–438. Washington.

Furstenberg, F.F., Jr. 1976. *Unplanned Parenthood: The Social Consequences of Teenage Childbearing.* New York: Free Press.

Furstenberg, F.F., Jr., and J. Brooks-Gunn. 1986. Teenage Child-bearing: Causes, Consequences and Remedies. In *Applications of Social Science to Clinical Health,* ed. L.H. Aiken and D. Mechanic. New Brunswick, N. J.: Rutgers University Press.

Furstenberg, F.F., Jr., J. Brooks-Gunn, and S.P. Morgan. 1987. *Adolescent Mothers in Later Life.* New York: Cambridge University Press.

Furstenberg, F.F., Jr., R. Lincoln, and J. Menken, eds. 1981. *Teenage Sexuality, Pregnancy and Childbearing.* Philadelphia: University of Pennsylvania Press.

Furstenberg, F.F., Jr., S.P. Morgan, K.A. Moore, and J.L. Peterson. 1987. Race Differences in the Timing of Adolescent Intercourse. *American Sociological Review* 52(8):511–18.

Hannerz, U. 1969. *Soulside: Inquiries into Ghetto Culture and Community.* New York: Columbia University Press.

Hayes, C.D., ed. 1987. *Risking the Future.* Vol. 1. Washington: National Academy Press.

Henshaw, S.K. 1987. Characteristics of U.S. Women Having Abortions, 1982–1983. *Family Planning Perspectives* 19(1):5–9.

Hofferth, S., and C.D. Hayes. 1987. *Risking the Future.* Vol. 2. Washington: National Academy Press.

Hogan, D., and E. Kitagawa. 1985. The Impact of Social Status, Family Structure, and Neighborhood on the Fertility of Black Adolescents. *American Journal of Sociology* 90:825–55.

Levy, S.S., and W.J. Grinker. 1982. Project Redirection: An Eth-nographic Study. Manpower Demonstration Research Corporation.

McAnarney, E.R., and C. Schreider. 1984. *Identifying Social and Psychological Antecedents of Adolescent Pregnancy: The Contribution of Research to Concepts of Prevention.* New York: William T. Grant Foundation.

Moore, K.A., M. Simms, and C.L. Betsey. 1986. *Choice & Circumstance Racial Differences: Adolescent Sexuality and Fertility.* New Brunswick: Transaction Books.

National Center for Health Statistics. 1985. Advance Report of Final Natality Statistics, 1983. *Monthly Vital Statistics Report,* 34:6 (suppl.). Hyattsville, Md.

———. 1986. Advance Report of Final Natality Statistics, 1984. *Monthly Vital Statistics Report* 35:4. Hyattsville, Md.

National Institute of Child and Human Development. 1984. *Adolescent Pregnancy and Childbearing: Rates, Trends, and Research Findings.* Washington.

Ooms, T., ed. 1981. *Teenage Pregnancy in a Family Context: Implications for Policy.* Philadelphia: Temple University.

Park, R.D., and B. Neville. 1987. Teenage Fatherhood. In *Risking the Future,* ed. C.D. Hayes, 145–73. Vol. 2. Washington: National Academy Press.

Schultz, D.A. 1969. *Coming Up Black: Patterns of Ghetto Socialization.* Englewood Cliffs, N.J.: Prentice-Hall.

Staples, R., ed. 1971. *The Black Family: Essays and Studies.* Belmont, Calif.: Wadsworth.

U.S. Bureau of the Census. 1984. Childspacing among Birth Cohorts of American Women: 1905 to 1959. *Current Population Reports,* series P–20, no. 385. Washington.

Wall Street Journal. 1986. Editorial. December 15.

Weitzman, L.J. 1985. *The Divorce Revolution: The Unexpected Social and Economic Consequences for Women and Children in America.* New York: Free Press.

Wilson, W.J., and K.M. Neckerman. 1986. Poverty and Family Structure: The Widening Gap between Evidence and Public Policy Issues. In *Fighting Poverty: What Works and What Doesn't,* ed. S.H. Danziger and D.H. Weinberg. Cambridge: Harvard University Press.

Zelnick, M., and J.F. Kantner. 1980. Sexual Activity, Contraceptive Use and Pregnancy among Metropolitan-area Teenagers: 1971–1979. *Family Planning Perspectives* 12:230–37.

Zelnick, M., J.F. Kantner, and K. Ford. 1981. *Sex and Pregnancy in Adolescence.* Sage Library of Social Research, vol. 133. Beverly Hills: Sage.

Zelnick, M., and F. Shah. 1983. First Intercourse among Young Americans. *Family Planning Perspectives* 15:64–69.

Trends in Racial Inequality and Exposure to Work-related Hazards, 1968–1986

JAMES C. ROBINSON

THE ISSUE OF RACIAL DIFFERENCES IN EXPOSURE to risk of work-related injury and illness lies at the juncture of two important areas of public policy: equal employment opportunity and occupational health. While emanating from the same general spirit of social reform, public programs in the areas of equal opportunity and occupational health have evolved independently of each other. The goal of affirmative action and equal opportunity programs since the 1960s has been to increase employment and occupational advancement of minorities and women, with occupational advancement measured largely in terms of wages received rather than working conditions faced. The target of occupational health policy since 1970 has been improvement in working conditions, without undue concern for the demographic mix of workers employed in particular jobs. The potential gains for both sets of objectives from collaboration among equal opportunity and occupational health programs were evident from the beginning: racial differences in risk of injury and illness were at least as great as racial differences in earnings. Improved working conditions in the riskiest occupations would thus lead to a narrowing of overall racial differences in job market opportunity.

This article examines trends in the risk of work-related injury and acute illness of blacks relative to whites from the late 1960s to the mid-1980s. Large files on individual workers from the U.S. Census Bureau's Current Population Survey are used to calculate ratios of black to white injury risks, both in absolute terms and after controlling for racial differences in education and potential work experience. A single cohort of approximately 4,000 workers was tracked over the 1971 to 1984 period to obtain insights into the experiences faced by particular black and white workers over the course of their working lives. The findings are quite mixed, with a convergence being observed in injury rates for black and white men but a slight divergence being observed for black and white women. Since injury rates as a whole were rising over most of this period, these various trends in racial risk ratios were accompanied by an absolute increase in risk of injury for both blacks and whites. The article concludes with a discussion of the implications of these findings for policy initiatives in equal opportunity and occupational health.

Equal Opportunity and Occupational Health

Trends in racial inequality with respect to work-related injuries and illness can be expected to reflect the influence of policy initiatives in the areas of equal opportunity and occupational health. They will also reflect the underlying dynamics in the economy, particularly changes in technology and changes in labor force participation. Before discussing the available evidence on the effects of these factors on employment and working conditions in general, it will be useful to examine the point of departure: relative hazard exposure levels for blacks and whites in the 1960s.

There exists one published study that examines the distribution of black and white workers across jobs with different types of working conditions in the 1960s. Using data on 28,135 workers from the 1967 Survey of Economic Opportunity, Lucas (1974) computed proportions of sampled black and white men and women who were employed in occupations containing safety or health hazards. The measures of working conditions were derived from the *Dictionary of Occupational Titles*, which is based on job-site reviews by job evaluators (who generally lack formal training in safety engineering and industrial hygiene). Among men, blacks were found to face a 29 percent greater chance than whites of facing safety hazards and a 64 percent greater chance of facing health hazards. Among women, blacks were found to face a 106 percent greater chance than whites of facing safety hazards and a 91 percent greater chance of facing health hazards. These figures exceed the race-related differences in earnings levels during this period (Freeman 1973).

Given the complex mixture of events influencing the labor market in the 20 years since Lucas's data were collected, it still is not possible to postulate the magnitude or even direction of change in relative exposure levels. Equal opportunity and affirmative action programs aimed at increasing employment of minorities and women in firms with federal contracts, and also at improving their chances for promotion and occupational advancement. The criterion for judging occupational advancement was generally improvements in wages; the relation between this job characteristic and the risk the job poses to worker safety and health is not obvious. Economists tend to argue that jobs with hazardous working conditions pay extra high wages (Thaler and Rosen 1975; Viscusi 1978); to the extent hazard pay is an important factor in the labor market, improvements in wage rates might signify a deterioration in working conditions. The bulk of the statistical evidence, however, indicates that hazardous occupations are generally low- rather than high-wage positions, due mainly to the low levels of education and on-the-job training they require (Robinson 1986). If equal opportunity and affirmative action programs were, in fact, successful in narrowing racial differences in wage rates, they would probably exert an indirect salutary impact on relative levels of exposure to injury and illness.

The impact of equal opportunity and affirmative action on the distribution of employment and wages has been the subject of a large number of studies. This literature indicates that, after a weak initial period in the late 1960s, governmental programs have been remarkably successful in achieving their stated goals. Employment of minorities and women has increased substantially faster at firms subject to federal regulations than in unregulated firms (Brown 1982; Leonard 1985). Within-firm occupational advancement has also been more rapid in regulated than in comparable unregulated firms (Leonard 1984). The magnitude of these effects appears generally to have been stronger for minorities than for women. The relatively poor performance of these programs in improving the job prospects for white women relative to white men is probably due to the substantial increase in labor force participation among women during this period.

The evidence on the effectiveness of governmental efforts to reduce occupational injuries and illnesses is substantially weaker. Studies using data from the early years of the Occupational Safety and Health Administration's programs find either no effect or only small effects (Smith 1979; Viscusi 1979; Mendeloff 1979). The most recent study, which uses data from the late 1970s and early 1980s, finds OSHA to have exerted a statistically significant though modest-sized reduction in disabling injury rates in the manufacturing sector (Viscusi 1986). Any tendency for OSHA's efforts to reduce injury rates in the firms inspected for standards violations over the past 15 years has been swamped, however, by long-standing and powerful trends toward increasing injury rates. Injury rates in manufacturing rose rapidly during the 1960s (thereby contributing to the enactment of federal policy initiatives) and continued to do so throughout most of the 1970s. Injury rates dropped precipitously during the first years of the 1980s, when the recession of 1981–1982 reduced employment in hazardous industries. They began rising again in 1984 (Robinson 1988). No studies have examined OSHA's impact on rates of chronic disease related to work-place exposures.

The impact of OSHA on the racial mix of employment in hazardous jobs is not predictable. To the extent that blacks are disproportionately employed in the most hazardous occupations and to the extent that OSHA targets its efforts at these occupations, one would expect a narrowing of racial differences in injury and illness rates. The indirect effect of OSHA enforcement could work in the opposite direction, however. One main effect of OSHA's efforts has been an increasing awareness on the part of workers and members of management of the extent of health and safety hazards in particular jobs. As previously unrecognized or unappreciated hazards come to be a focus of attention, the status of jobs containing those hazards declines relative to the status of jobs not containing them. This decline will, over time, lead to a flight from those jobs on the part of workers with other good employment opportunities. In the absence of conscious efforts by equal opportunity programs to counteract this process, hazardous jobs will over time become increasingly filled with the least advantaged members of the working population.

Data and Methods

The primary source of statistical data used in this study is the Current Population Survey (CPS), an ongoing household survey conducted by the U.S. Bureau of the Census which serves as the source of employment and unemployment figures published by the government. The CPS does not contain information on working conditions, but it does code the occupation and industry in which each respondent works, whereby working condition data from other sources can be matched to individual workers. The CPS provides basic demographic information, including race, sex, years of education, and age. This article uses the March 1968 file, the first CPS file available on computer-accessible tapes, plus the March 1986 file, the most recent available. The May 1977 file is used in order to examine relative hazards at the midpoint of the period under consideration. The main advantage of the CPS for the purposes of this article is the large sample size: 35,564 usable records for 1968, 32,860 for 1977, and 65,266 for 1986. Approximately 9 percent of each year's sample is black. Recent years of the CPS code Hispanics separately from non-Hispanic whites. Hispanics cannot, however, be distinguished from other whites in the 1968 CPS; this article thus focuses on differences between working conditions faced by blacks on the one hand and both Hispanic and non-Hispanic whites on the other.

The CPS samples are chosen to be representative of the entire United States population and, with their large sample sizes, permit valid estimates to be made of risks faced by blacks and whites across all occupations and industries. Independent "snapshots" of risks for the entire population at successive points in time do not, however, allow inferences to be drawn concerning the experiences over time of a particular cohort of individuals. The experiences of a particular cohort would be expected to differ from that of the population as a whole, since the cohort members accumulate education and on-the-job experience over time in a manner that the general population does not. Wage rates earned by individual workers tend to rise with their levels of education and experience, producing the well-documented positively sloped "age-earnings profile." The wage rates earned by blacks have been found to rise much less quickly with increases in education and experience than those of whites, however.

The one published study of education and experience effects on the probability of facing risks of injury and illness at work found that more educated and experienced workers were employed in substantially safer jobs on average than less educated and less experienced workers (Robinson 1984). That study was based on data from one point in time and thus could not examine racial differences in age-hazard profiles.

In order to obtain insights into the relative hazard levels faced over the course of their working lives by blacks and whites during the period since the enactment of the equal opportunity and occupational health legislation, this study uses data from the Panel Study of Income Dynamics (PSID). The PSID is a longitudinal study of approximately 6,000 individuals interviewed yearly since 1968 by the Institute for Social Research at the University of Michigan. Of these 6,000 individuals, approximately two-thirds are employed at the time of any given interview. Blacks are systematically oversampled by the PSID, and constitute approximately one-third of the cohort. While interviewing of the PSID cohort began in 1968, respondents were not asked their field of employment until the 1971 interview. As industry information is crucial for the matching of information on working conditions, this study starts with the 1971 PSID interview year. While PSID interviewing continues, the production of publicly available data tapes lags considerably. The most recent PSID interview tape is from 1984. As in the case of the CPS, this article examines the 1977 PSID tape as constituting a midpoint for the time period under consideration.

Results obtained using the PSID must be interpreted with caution due to the nonrandom manner with which cohort members move in and out of the labor force over time. This movement in and out of the labor force will tend to make the PSID results nonrepresentative of the working population as a whole. The direction of the bias with respect to risk of work-related injury or illness is not clear. Economic theories of labor force participation argue that participation rates will be lower and more irregular for workers who, if employed, would be at the bottom end of the wage scale. These "marginal" workers find the value of time spent at work low relative to the value of time spent doing other things (including work at home). Although workers in hazardous jobs may receive some compensation for the extra risks they face, they are generally less skilled and hence lower paid than the rest of the working population. This train of thought would imply that examination of the PSID cohort over time would yield an overly optimistic estimate of the population "age-hazard profile," since those workers experiencing the fewest improvements would be those most likely to leave the sample. Workers in particularly hazardous jobs are also, by definition, most likely to leave the work force due to work-related injury or illness. On the other hand, the probability of retirement increases strongly with age, other things being equal, and older workers have generally been able over time to move to safer occupations than those in which they started their working careers.

Data on working conditions was derived from two sources: the annual establishment surveys conducted by the Bureau of Labor Statistics (BLS), which yield injury and acute illness rates by detailed industry, and state Workers' Compensation claims records, which yield information on probability of injury or illness by occupation. BLS injury rates are matched with individual workers in the CPS and PSID surveys via the industry codes included in those surveys. Data from 1972 are used with the 1971 PSID survey; 1971 injury rate data are unreliable since the BLS was reorganizing its statistical data system during that year. Injury rates for 1986 were not available at the time this study was conducted; 1985 injury rates were thus used with the 1986 CPS. In all cases the figures used were from the BLS data on injuries that result in at least one day lost from work. The figures from 1968 are not directly comparable with those from later years due to the changes in reporting methods imposed as part of the 1970 Occupational Safety and Health Act. These changes do not affect inferences concerning relative injury rates for blacks and whites in any one year.

There are two major problems besetting any study that employs the BLS figures. First, these data reflect only experiences with injuries and acute occupational illnesses and do not count work-related chronic diseases such as cancer. Second, these data are tabulated at the industry level and provide no insights into differences in risk levels faced by workers in different occupations within the same industry.

There is, unfortunately, no way around the first limitation to the BLS data; it is impossible to obtain from any source historical data on exposure to risk of chronic occupational disease for the working population as a whole. The BLS data do provide a consistent historical source of information on rates of injuries. The lack of occupation-specific information, however, constitutes a very serious limitation to the BLS data even as a source of information on risks of work-related injury. This study adjusted the industry figures using occupation data from state Workers' Compensation records. The BLS has published indexes of relative risks of injury by broad occupational classification for each of the major industrial sectors. The indexes were calculated using 1978 data from the 25 state Workers' Compensation programs participating in the Supplementary Data System of the BLS (Root and Sebastian 1981). Occupations accounting for the same fraction of total injuries as of total employment were assigned an index of 1. Occupations accounting for proportionately more injuries than employment were assigned indexes greater than 1; occupations accounting for proportionately fewer injuries than those for total employment, conversely, were assigned indexes lower than 1. For purposes of this study, therefore, the risk of work-related injury faced by each individual CPS and PSID worker was calculated as the injury rate prevailing in his or her detailed industry and year, weighted by the hazard index for his or her major occupational classification (i.e., craft worker, operative, laborer), with occupational weights varying by major industrial sector.

Each of the three CPS and PSID files were first sorted into black and white subfiles, and mean injury rates were calculated for each ethnic group. Rates for men and women were analyzed separately. Adjusted injury rates by ethnic and gender group were then calculated controlling for individual differences in age and educational attainment. Educational attainment was measured in terms of three possible levels: no high school diploma, high school diploma but no further education, education beyond high school. The differentiation of workers according to high school record was judged to be more relevant for purposes of predicting differences in exposure to work-related injury than differentiation of those workers who continued past high school into groups according to extent of college education. It was not possible to measure directly the extent of on-the-job experience held by individual CPS and PSID workers. Following the standard approach taken by studies of earnings (Mincer 1970), this study included years of age and the square of years of age. Economic studies of age-earnings profiles typically find that earnings increase with age, due either to accrual of skills or seniority rights, but that the rate of increase declines over time. This nonlinear relationship can be captured using the quadratic form of the age variable.

Changes in risk of occupational injury were calculated for each member of the PSID cohort for the periods of 1971–1977, 1977–

TABLE 1
Rates of Disabling Injuries per 100 Workers: The Current Population
Survey, 1968–1986

	Men	Women
1968		
Blacks	5.7 (N = 2,039)	2.3 (N = 1,247)
Whites	3.2 (N = 21,306)	1.4 (N = 10,972)
1977		
Blacks	8.3 (N = 1,510)	3.0 (N = 1,428)
Whites	5.2 (N = 18,071)	2.3 (N = 11,851)
1986		
Blacks	6.5 (N = 2,822)	4.5 (N = 3,030)
Whites	4.6 (N = 31,676)	2.3 (N = 27,739)

1984, and the entire period of 1971–1984. This second set of calculations
was restricted to those members of the cohort employed in each pair
of years, and thus the sample size varied for each time period. Workers
employed in 1971 and 1984 were included in the calculations for the
1971–1984 period even if they were not in the labor force in 1977.
These year to year changes in injury risk by definition control for the
effects of increasing age on job opportunities, since all workers age
at the same rate. To control for differences among workers in extension
of education over this time period, changes in injury risks were also
calculated controlling for changes in total years of educational attainment.

Results

Table 1 presents rates of work-related injuries resulting in at least
one day lost from work for black and white CPS workers in 1968,
1977, and 1986, plus the sample sizes upon which the rates were
estimated. Risks of injury on the job are higher for blacks than for
whites for both genders for all three time periods. In each year and
gender group, blacks faced risks of on-the-job injury approximately
one and one half times those faced by whites.

The most interesting feature of the data in table 1 concerns trends
over time in the risks faced by blacks relative to the risks faced by
whites. The racial risk differential has narrowed substantially among

men, from a ratio of 1.78 in 1968 to 1.60 in 1977 and then to 1.41 in 1986. This 50 percent reduction in the excess risk faced by black men is a remarkable and important fact, and a considerable tribute to the success of society's general efforts to reduce racial inequality over the years since the Great Society programs in the 1960s. The record with respect to racial differences among women is substantially less encouraging, however. After narrowing from 1.64 to 1.30 between 1968 and 1977, the ratio of black to white female injury rates increased to 1.96 in 1986. This divergence was due to the rise in injury rates in the industries and occupations where black women are concentrated; injury rates for white women stayed constant over the 1977–1986 period.

It is indeed tempting to focus on the trends in injury rates themselves over time, in addition to the trends in black-white injury ratios. This should be done only with caution, however. Comparison of the 1968 rates with those from 1977 and 1986 pick up the effects in the change from voluntary to mandatory injury reporting effected as part of the Occupational Safety and Health Act of 1970. Comparison of figures from 1986 with those from 1977 (and interpretation of the apparent decline in injury rates between those two years) is rendered problematic by the serious questions raised concerning increased underreporting of injuries by employers. In recent years the Occupational Safety and Health Administration has used employer injury reporting as the basis for establishing the priority of inspections, giving strong incentives for firms to minimize the number of injuries they report. Several cases of systematic underreporting have come to light, and the Bureau of Labor Statistics is currently conducting a major review of reporting procedures (U.S. Department of Labor 1986).

Table 2 presents adjusted rates of disabling injuries for black and white CPS men and women after controlling for individual-specific differences in age and education. To the extent that age and education differences capture differences among workers in skill level, these adjusted injury rates reflect the residual impact of racial discrimination per se. Needless to say, years of age and education constitute only crude measures of worker skill, missing the effects of differences in quality of education and number of job changes over the course of a working career. Controlling for years of education produces under-estimates of the true impact of racial discrimination, on the other hand, if educational achievement (generally higher among whites than

TABLE 2

Adjusted Rates of Disabling Injuries per 100 Workers, Controlling for
Differences in Education and Age: The Current Population Survey,
1968–1986

	Men	Women
1968		
Blacks	4.9	2.1
Whites	3.3	1.5
1977		
Blacks	7.3	2.6
Whites	5.3	2.3
1986		
Blacks	5.9	3.3
Whites	4.6	2.2

Note: These rates were calculated based on least squares regressions that controlled
for educational attainment, age, and the square of age. Full regression results are
presented in appendix tables 1 and 2.

blacks) is used as a rationale for racial differentiation in job assignments
to an extent not justified by skill requirements.

The racial differences in injury rates are narrower in table 2 than
in the unadjusted figures in table 1, but the trends over time are
similar. The ratio of black to white injury rates among male workers
has declined steadily since 1968; among female workers, on the other
hand, the ratio increased between 1977 and 1986 and currently exceeds
the 1968 ratio. The overall similarity between tables 1 and 2 implies
that the trends reported in the first table are not due merely to racial
differences in the accumulation of education and experience in the
period since 1968.

Table 3 presents relative injury rates over time for black and white
members of the PSID cohort. The figures in this table are not adjusted
for age and education and thus are comparable to the CPS figures in
table 1. They differ from the CPS figures, however, in representing
the experiences of one group of workers over a 13-year period rather
than three independent snapshots of the working population as a
whole. These figures permit inferences concerning racial differences
in occupational mobility over the course of the life cycle. The risk
ratio among PSID women is very similar over time to that reported

TABLE 3
Rates of Disabling Injuries per 100 Workers for One Cohort: The Panel
Study of Income Dynamics, 1971–1984

	Men	Women
1971		
Blacks	5.8 (*N* = 920)	3.8 (*N* = 468)
Whites	3.3 (*N* = 2,444)	2.5 (*N* = 377)
1977		
Blacks	6.8 (*N* = 886)	4.3 (*N* = 492)
Whites	3.8 (*N* = 2,405)	3.5 (*N* = 392)
1984		
Blacks	7.0 (*N* = 739)	5.8 (*N* = 418)
Whites	4.2 (*N* = 2,160)	3.6 (*N* = 302)

for the much larger CPS samples in table 1: a marked convergence
of injury rates between 1971 and 1977 followed by an equally marked
divergence between 1977 and 1984, with consequentially no substantial
trend over the 1971–1984 period as a whole. The male PSID cohort
experienced a considerably different trend in relative injury rates than
did the CPS population, however. The ratio of work-related injury
rates for black and white PSID workers stayed almost constant, rising
slightly from 1.67 in 1971 to 1.79 in 1977 and then settling back
to 1.67 in 1984. This suggests that the trend observed in the CPS
data was due to the narrowing of injury risks faced by new entrants
to the labor force rather than to the experiences of those blacks and
whites already in the labor force at the beginning of the period.

The experiences of individual members of the PSID cohort are
portrayed more precisely in table 4. These figures portray the changes
in injury rates for individual PSID workers, controlling for changes
in educational attainment. Owing to movement in and out of the
labor force on the part of particular individuals, these figures are not
simply the differences in adjusted injury rates between pairs of years,
equivalent to those that could be calculated from the CPS figures in
table 2. In this instance, the mean of the differences is not equivalent
to the difference of the means. This distinction is, however, of more
theoretical than practical import, since most members of the PSID
cohort did remain in the labor force over the time period under
consideration.

TABLE 4

Changes in the Rate of Disabling Occupational Injury per 100 Workers in
One Cohort, Controlling for Changes in Education: The Panel Study
of Income Dynamics, 1971–1984

	Men	Women
1971–77		
Blacks	1.00 (*N* = 677)	0.16 (*N* = 328)
Whites	0.47 (*N* = 1,939)	0.74 (*N* = 277)
1977–84		
Blacks	0.48 (*N* = 550)	1.33 (*N* = 266)
Whites	0.06 (*N* = 1,672)	0.22 (*N* = 248)
1971–84		
Blacks	1.69 (*N* = 523)	1.48 (*N* = 214)
Whites	0.65 (*N* = 1,580)	0.81 (*N* = 204)

Industrial injury rates were generally rising over the 1971–1984 period; the figures in table 4 permit insights into how an individual's race influenced the fraction of that general increased risk he or she would have to bear, controlling for changes in the amount of education he or she gained over those years. Comparison of injury rates across time periods is acceptable with these data in a manner not possible with the CPS data in tables 1 and 2 since these PSID data relate to the period after the change in injury reporting in 1970 and before the major concerns about systematic underreporting were raised with respect to the injury rate data for 1985 and 1986.

While injury rates increased for all race and sex groups for each of the time periods under consideration, the pattern varied extensively. Among PSID men, injury rates increased among blacks much faster than among whites: twice as fast between 1971 and 1977 and eight times as fast between 1977 and 1984. Among PSID women, on the other hand, injury rates increased substantially faster among whites than among blacks between 1971 and 1977; the opposite occurred between 1977 and 1984. For the 1971–1984 period as a whole, the risk of work-related injury increased 160 percent faster for black men than for white men and 83 percent faster for black women than for white women, controlling for changes in education level.

Discussion

The data presented in this article provide new insight into a heretofore neglected area of overlap between two important topics of social concern: racial inequality and occupational health. While too crude to permit the detailed evaluation of any one policy initiative, they do permit a measurement of society's overall movement in the direction of its stated goals.

The most important numbers are the simplest: between 1968 and 1986 the excess risk of disabling occupational injury faced by blacks relative to whites declined by 50 percent among men but increased by 20 percent among women. Given the exceptionally high overall risk faced by black men, the decline in their excess risk is especially important. Black men continue, however, to face the highest risk of any major group; in 1986, 6.5 percent of black male workers suffered a work-related injury resulting in at least one day lost from work. The increase in injury risks of black compared to white women reflects a different and disturbing trend. In 1986, black women faced nearly the same injury risk as white men.

The statistical evidence from the PSID cohort is similar to that for the larger CPS files in the case of women, but considerably less encouraging in the case of men. Black male workers followed by the PSID experienced an increase in injury risks two and one half times greater over the 1971–1984 period than did white male workers, controlling for changes in educational attainment. This finding is analogous to those wage studies where blacks are found to experience a considerably "flatter" age-earnings profile than whites.

The overall record for social concern and public policy in this area of overlap between equal opportunity and occupational health appears to be positive, with important qualifications. The excess risks faced by those at highest initial risk have been substantially reduced. No equivalent statement may be made in the case of female workers, but here the public policy emphasis has been on gaining entry for women into previously all-male jobs in manufacturing, mining, and construction. Many of these jobs present substantial risks to worker health and safety.

The least encouraging dimension of these data is the absolute increase in occupational injury rates for both blacks and whites. The overall trends have been examined in detail elsewhere (Robinson 1988) but are reflected in these figures as well. Rates of work-related injuries are high and are not falling. Occupational safety appears to be the neglected stepchild of an occupational health policy focused primarily on chronic disease and of injury prevention policies focused primarily on the home and the highway.

References

Brown, C. 1982. The Federal Attack on Labor Market Discrimination: The Mouse-that Roared? In *Research in Labor Economics* 5:33–68. Greenwich, Conn: JAI Press.

Freeman, R. 1973. Changes in the Labor Market for Black Americans 1948–72. *Brookings Papers on Economic Activity* 1:67–120.

Leonard, J. 1984. Employment and Occupational Advance under Affirmative Action. *Review of Economics and Statistics* 66(3):377–85.

————. 1985. What Promises are Worth: The Impact of Affirmative Action Goals. *Journal of Human Resources* 20(1):3–20.

Lucas, R. 1974. The Distribution of Job Characteristics. *Review of Economics and Statistics* 56(4):530–40.

Mendeloff, J. 1979. *Regulating Safety*. Cambridge: MIT Press.

Mincer, J. 1970. The Distribution of Labor Incomes: A Survey. *Journal of Economic Literature* 8(1):1–26.

Robinson, J.C. 1984. Racial Inequality and the Probability of Occupation-Related Injury or Illness. *Milbank Memorial Fund Quarterly/Health and Society* 62(4):567–90.

————. 1986. Hazard Pay in Unsafe Jobs: Theory, Evidence, and Policy Implications. *The Milbank Quarterly* 64(4):650–77.

————. 1988. The Rising Long-term Trend in Industrial Injury Rates. *American Journal of Public Health*. (In press.)

Root, N., and D. Sebastian. 1981. BLS Develops Measure of Job Risk by Occupation. *Monthly Labor Review* 104(10):26–30.

Smith, R.S. 1979. The Impact of OSHA Inspections on Manufacturing Injury Rates. *Journal of Human Resources* 14(2):145–70.

Thaler, R. and R. Rosen. 1975. The Value of Saving a Life: Evidence from the Labor Market. In *Household Production and Consumption*, ed. N. Terleckyj, 265–98. New York: National Bureau of Economic Research.

U.S. Department of Labor. 1986. Bureau of Labor Statistics Reports on Survey of Occupational Injuries and Illness in 1985. (Press release, November 13).

Viscusi, W.K. 1978. Wealth Effects and Earnings Premiums for Job Hazards. *Review of Economics and Statistics* 60(3):408–16.

――――. 1979. The Impact of Occupational Safety and Health Regulations. *Bell Journal of Economics* 10(1):117–40.

――――. 1986. The Impact of Occupational Safety and Health Regulation 1973–1983. *Rand Journal of Economics* 17(4):567–80.

APPENDIX TABLE 1

Demographic Determinants of Employment in High-risk Positions for Male Workers: The 1968–1986 Current Population Surveys (Dependent Variable: Occupation-adjusted Industry Injury Rate)

	1968	1977	1986
Worker is black	16.08	20.02	12.09
	(0.91)	(1.67)	(1.01)
No high school	37.84	56.44	47.91
diploma	(0.65)	(1.18)	(0.79)
High school diploma	19.13	34.13	32.22
but no college	(0.64)	(1.02)	(0.62)
Years of age	−0.748	−2.618	−0.445
	(0.136)	(0.204)	(0.115)
Years of age squared	0.0059	0.0234	−0.0002
	(0.0017)	(0.0025)	(0.0014)
Intercept	31.27	87.79	42.70
	(2.63)	(3.95)	(2.25)
Adjusted R^2	0.15	0.14	0.14
N	23,345	19,581	34,498

APPENDIX TABLE 2
Demographic Determinants of Employment in High-risk Positions for
Female Workers: The 1968–1986 Current Population Surveys
(Dependent Variable: Occupation-adjusted Industry Injury Rate)

	1968	1977	1986
Worker is black	6.83	3.41	10.28
	(0.52)	(0.84)	(0.59)
No high school	18.62	33.73	29.66
diploma	(0.43)	(0.76)	(0.56)
High school diploma	5.08	11.85	11.76
but no college	(0.38)	(0.57)	(0.38)
Years of age	0.294	−0.349	0.141
	(0.078)	(0.118)	(0.074)
Years of age squared	−0.0036	−0.0028	−0.0027
	(0.0010)	(0.0015)	(0.0009)
Intercept	1.55	20.53	13.05
	(1.42)	(2.23)	(1.42)
Adjusted R^2	0.17	0.13	0.10
N	12,219	13,279	30,768

The Health, Physical Functioning, and Informal Supports of the Black Elderly

ROSE C. GIBSON and JAMES S. JACKSON

T HE OLDER POPULATION'S SHARE OF THE TOTAL population has been rising steadily. The black elderly population—those aged 65 and over—is growing more rapidly than the white elderly population (Siegel and Taeuber 1986). The disproportionate growth of the older black population is of social policy significance for several reasons. Larger numbers of older blacks with chronic, physically limiting illnesses will further complicate payment of the health care bills of an aging population (Davis 1986; Rice and Estes 1984); extraordinary strains will be placed on already burdened black families; and long-term care policies in the United States will be significantly affected (Rice and Feldman 1983). Despite a growing recognition that long-term care policies for an aging society need careful development (Soldo and Manton 1985), the debate, thus far, has not considered the interplay among the special life circumstances of blacks and other ethnic minorities, their levels of physical functioning, their traditional and current patterns of informal support, and their health care needs (Suzman and Riley 1985). The quality and quantity of informal support available to the black elderly will have profound effects on their need for long-term care. A small but growing body of literature, in fact, suggests that the informal support of older blacks—help from friends, family, and church members—is important to their physical health and effective functioning, and that exchanges within the social networks of older blacks have some special insulating qualities (Cantor 1979; Chatters, Taylor, and Jackson 1985; Taylor 1985, 1986).

The social epidemiological literature also emphasizes the importance of informal support in health and functioning. Social ties affect the etiology and course of disease, physical functioning, and mortality (Rowe and Kahn 1987; Berkman 1983; House and Kahn 1985; Kasl and Berkman 1981; Satariano and Syme 1981; House, Robbins, and Metzner 1982; Blazer 1982). Informal support has different effects on health and functioning depending upon its type, quality, amount, and frequency (Antonucci and Jackson 1987; Minkler, Satariano, and Langhauser 1983; Stoller 1984). Findings from social epidemiological and social networks research may be used to reveal the ways in which older blacks use their informal networks to improve their physical functioning.

The purpose of this article is to examine the relation between physical functioning and informal support in the present cohort of black elderly (individuals aged 65 and over), and to explore the findings with a view to new research that will inform health policy. First, we describe the physical health, functioning, and informal support of older blacks. Next, we identify the determinants of effective functioning; then we proceed to analyze the relation between informal support and physical functioning. The article concludes with recommendations for new health research on the black elderly.

The data are drawn from two national probability samples of blacks: the National Survey of Black Americans (NSBA) (1980) and the Three-generation Black Family Study (TGBFS) (1981). These datasets provide culturally relevant, and carefully collected sources of information on the adult black population. We focus on the subsample of 734 non-institutionalized black men and women aged 65 to 101. The findings are representative of blacks aged 65 and over from the high rises of New York City to the most rural areas of the South. The technical appendix contains descriptions of the NSBA and the TGBFS. Subsample characteristics are set forth in table 1.

Physical Health and Physical Functioning

As indicated in table 2, physical health status and physical functioning generally decline in successively older age groups. The oldest group

TABLE 1
The Black Elderly Study Sample: Percentages Comparing the Young,
Middle, and Very Old (*n* = 734)

	65–74 (*n* = 462)	75–79 (*n* = 142)	80 and over (*n* = 130)
Gender			
Men	33.1%	36.6%	35.4%
Women	66.9	63.4	64.6
Family income in dollars per year			
Less than 5,000	44.6	43.4	40.9
5,000–9,999	18.6	18.0	15.9
10,000–19,999	10.6	7.5	6.8
20,000 or more	5.2	2.6	9.1
Not ascertained	20.9	28.5	27.3
Education (number of grades completed)			
0–8	68.6	72.3	79.8
9–11	16.4	11.3	10.1
12	8.6	7.8	8.5
More than 12	6.4	8.5	1.6
Lifetime occupation			
Professional, managerial, sales, clerical	5.4	3.5	6.2
Craftspersons, operatives	11.5	4.2	6.9
Laborers, farmers, farm workers	5.8	7.7	7.7
Service	21.6	23.2	9.2
Not asked	55.6	61.3	70.0
Region			
Northeast	12.3	12.7	6.2
North central	15.8	19.0	17.7
South	68.2	63.4	73.1
West	3.7	4.9	3.1
Area of residence[a]			
Large urban	37.8	50.0	36.0
Small urban	35.2	24.2	22.0
Rural	27.0	25.8	42.0
Marital status			
Married	42.2	31.2	20.8
Never married, divorced, separated	13.2	10.6	5.4
Widowed	44.6	58.2	73.8
Number of children living			
None	16.3	17.3	17.2
One	13.9	14.4	11.7
Two or more	69.8	68.3	71.1

TABLE 1—*Continued.*

	65–74 (n = 462)	75–79 (n = 142)	80 and over (n = 130)
Where children live[b]			
In respondent's house	27.8	18.1	34.1
Outside respondent's house	72.2	81.8	64.9
Residents in respondent's house by relationship[b]			
Respondent alone	29.1	38.5	28.2
Respondent and spouse	22.2	25.6	14.1
Respondent and other nuclear family combinations[c]	15.7	14.1	24.4
Respondent and extended family combinations[d]	29.6	19.2	29.5
Respondent and augmented family combinations[e]	3.5	2.6	3.8

Note: Totals may not equal 100% due to rounding.
[a] Three-generation study respondents were not asked the question.
[b] Cross-section study respondents were not asked the question.
[c] For example, respondent spouse, and children; or respondent, no spouse, and children.
[d] For example, respondent and other relatives.
[e] For example, respondent and nonrelatives.

(aged 80 and over) is more likely to have three or more health problems, say they have "very serious health problems," have difficulty with three or more activities of daily living—housework, shopping, cooking, climbing stairs; and be limited "a great deal" in the amount of work or activities they can perform. Three facts are notable here, however. First, the oldest age group is as likely as the younger groups to be without health problems—13 percent of each age group. Second, the mean scores on an overall health status index (OHSI) for the three groups were about the same—5.2 for the oldest, and 5.0 for each of the younger groups (high scores denote good health). Third, fully 40 percent of those aged 80 and over reported not being limited at all or limited very little in their activities.

It is interesting to note here some race differences in the likelihood of functional limitation in age groups. Preliminary findings from the Americans' Changing Lives dataset, a new study at the University of Michigan's Institute for Social Research (House 1984), indicate that among those aged 65 to 74, blacks are about twice as likely to be extremely limited; and among those aged 80 and over, blacks are about one and one-half times as likely to be so limited. Among those aged 75 to 79, however, blacks and whites are about equally likely to be very limited. This means that blacks and whites aged 65 to 74 differ more than other age groups in the likelihood of extreme functional limitation. These findings also identify a young, disabled and an older, more able group of black elderly. It is intriguing that Manton and Soldo (1985) also identified in their data a young, predominantly black, morbid and an older, predominantly black, more robust group.

Taken together, the findings indicate that blacks aged 65 and over are a heterogeneous group in regard to health and physical functioning, and age may not be a strong predictor of functioning. The relation between age and physical functioning warrants closer examination.

Age as a Determinant of Physical Functioning

Multiple classification analysis, a procedure appropriate for the regression of an intervally scaled variable on categorical variables (Andrews, Morgan, and Sonquist 1967), was used to determine the relative and collective effects of age, informal support, and demographic, physical, social, and mental health factors on the functional limitation of blacks aged 65 and over. We wished to contrast the effects on functioning of the more disabled group (aged 65 to 74), the more robust group (aged 75 to 79), and the very old group (aged 80 and over). The findings in this analysis, even after controlling for factors that also affect functional limitation, add to the argument that age is not a strong determinant of physical functioning among older blacks and reinforce the idea that the group aged 75 to 79 is the most able of older blacks. We present only a summary of the study since details of the measures, methods, analyses, and findings appear elsewhere (Gibson 1986a).

The significant predictors of functional limitation in order of importance were: physical health status (eta-squared = .16); recent levels of stress-distress (.06); and income (.04) (table 3). Age was a poor predictor of functioning (.01). The adjusted coefficients for the age

TABLE 2

Physical Health and Functioning of the Black Elderly: Percentages Comparing the Young, Middle, and Very Old ($n = 734$)

	65–74 (n = 472)	75–79 (n = 142)	80 and over (n = 130)
PHYSICAL HEALTH			
Number of health problems			
0	13.4%	14.1%	13.1%
1	23.4	20.4	14.6
2–3	44.4	50.1	47.7
3 or more	18.8	15.5	24.6
Satisfaction with health[a]			
Very satisfied	52.6	53.6	62.0
Somewhat satisfied	32.4	27.9	26.4
Somewhat dissatisfied	12.6	17.7	10.1
Very dissatisfied	2.4	1.4	1.6
Self-rated health[a]			
Very serious health problems	15.6	20.6	26.4
Health problems, but not very serious	38.1	29.4	37.5
Very best of health	46.3	50.0	36.1

Overall Health Status Index [OHSI][a]			
Good	28.6	24.1	24.5
Fair	49.9	50.0	46.2
Poor	25.5	25.9	29.2
OHSI mean scores[b]	5.0	5.0	5.2
PHYSICAL FUNCTIONING			
Number of activities of daily living (ADL) problems[c]			
None	42.2	38.8	23.8
1–2	36.6	35.0	40.0
3–7	21.1	26.3	36.3
Extent of physical functional limitation			
Not limited at all or limited very little	50.9	53.5	40.8
Limited some	23.2	21.8	24.6
Limited "a great deal"	26.0	24.6	34.6

[a] Three-generation telephone respondents excluded from percentage base.
[b] Scores on the OHSI ranged from 1–13 (high scores = the worst health).
[c] Cross-section respondents excluded from percentage base.

categories in table 3 indicate that even after controlling for the effects of other variables, functional limitation still did not increase in a clear manner in successively older age groups. Although being aged 80 and over increased functional limitation scores the most (.17), being 75 to 79 decreased these scores more than did being age 65 to 74 (coefficients are − .09 and − .02, respectively). This finding supports the previous bivariate findings and means that the group aged 75 to 79 is less likely than those aged 65 to 74 to be functionally limited, even when the effects of class, social, and psychological functioning are removed. This adds considerably to the argument that a more debilitated younger group and a more robust older group of black elderly exist. It is interesting that in the Americans' Changing Lives data reported earlier, age and functional limitation are related in the white, but not the black, elderly sample. Statistics for blacks and whites, respectively, are: chi-square with 6 degrees of freedom = 3.2 and 33.2; p = .79 and .00; Cramer's V = .16 and .25). This suggests that age and disability are related linearly among older whites, but not among older blacks. In fact, there may be a race/disability/age interaction effect.

Although not a focus of this article, it is interesting to note that older black men and women were alike in the factors that explained their physical functioning. This is in contrast to the findings on majority populations that identify gender differences. The similarity between black men and women in the correlates of functional limitation fits patterns observable in other life domains and circumstances (Gibson 1986a). There may be a certain androgyny of blacks at very old ages (Bengston 1986).

Surprisingly, the informal support measures were not related significantly to functional limitation. The counterintuitive effects of large and moderate amounts of emotional support, however, are of interest. The unadjusted deviation scores in table 3 indicate that receiving moderate amounts of emotional support has a larger decremental effect on functional limitation (− .13) than receiving large amounts (− .01). This was especially true among the very old; emotional support in moderation appeared more beneficial to functioning than emotional support in excess. Before we focus more specifically on this role of informal support in the physical functioning of the very old, we describe the informal support of blacks aged 65 and over.

TABLE 3

Multiple Classification Analysis (MCA) Predicting Physical Functional Limitation from Demographic, Physical, Social, and Mental Health and Informal Support Factors, for Older Black Americans, Aged 65 and Over. $n = 370$[a]

Predictors	Eta^2	Beta^2	Deviation	Coefficient
DEMOGRAPHIC FACTORS				
Region	.00	.00		
Non-South			−.08	−.05
South			.03	.02
Family income per year	.04*	.03		
Less than $5,000			.13	.10
More than $5,000			−.22	−.18
Age	.01	.01		
65–74			−.02	−.02
75–79			−.11	−.09
80 and over			.16	.17
Gender	.01	.00		
Men			−.13	−.05
Women			.07	.02
PHYSICAL HEALTH				
Overall health status index	.16*	.20		
Excellent			−.44	−.39
Good			.17	.14
Fair			.35	.33
Poor			.49	.43
SOCIAL HEALTH				
Social activities/integration index	.00	.01		
Low			.01	.06
High			−.02	−.11
INFORMAL SUPPORT				
Number of available helpers	.00	.00		
Few			−.00	−.02
Many			.01	.10
Amount of emotional support	.00	.00		
None			.03	−.00
Small			.01	.03
Moderate			−.13	−.06
Large			−.01	−.05
Frequency of contact/help	.00	.00		
Low			−.04	−.01
High			.06	.02

TABLE 3—Continued

Predictors	Eta^2	Beta^2	Deviation	Coefficient
MENTAL HEALTH				
Recent stress-distress	.06*	.03		
Low			−.08	−.06
High			.48	.31
Indefinite period of stress-				
distress	.01	.00		
Low			−.04	−.01
High			.30	.07
R^2 adjusted	.26			
unadjusted	.29			

Note: Estimates are from the final equation. Etas^2 are adjusted. Deviations are unadjusted coefficients and coefficients refer to adjusted coefficients. Asterisks indicate significance at $p \leqslant 05$.
[a] Respondents with valid data on all study variables and with one or more health problems.

The Informal Supports of the Black Elderly and Exchanges With Adult Children

The findings of this analysis indicate that the family and friend support of the black elderly is rich and satisfying, and that differences in support among the age groups are more qualitative than quantitative.

Available Helpers

About one-third of each age group of blacks has immediate family members nearby—in the same household, neighborhood, or city; and a large proportion of each group has neighbors they know well enough to visit (table 4). The very old (aged 80 and over) are more likely than the middle-old group (aged 75 to 79) to have greater numbers of these neighbors (a function, no doubt, of the rural southern areas in which the oldest group live). Large numbers in each age group report having friends with whom to discuss problems, as well as a close or best friend. Summing the total number of helpers available—neighbors, friends, and family members—the mean number of helpers

TABLE 4

Informal Support of the Black Elderly and Exchanges with Adult Children: Percentages Comparing the Young, Middle, and Very Old (*n* = 734)

	65–74 (*n* = 272)	75–79 (*n* = 142)	80 and over (*n* = 130)
AVAILABILITY OF HELPERS			
Geographical proximity of most immediate family members			
No immediate family	16.1%	24.8%	18.3%
In same household, neighborhood, city	36.8	29.9	34.9
In same county or state	21.4	12.4	23.0
Outside of state	25.8	32.8	23.8
Number neighbors know well enough to visit			
Have no neighbors, or know none well	3.9	14.5	8.0
Many, some	47.8	41.9	52.0
A few	48.3	43.5	40.0
Number friends with whom to discuss problems			
Many, some	27.5	20.7	27.3
A few	56.7	64.9	49.1
None	15.8	14.4	23.6
Have best or close friend?			
Have best friend	58.5	60.4	58.6
No best friend, but someone close	28.1	23.7	24.2
No best friend, no one close	13.4	15.8	17.2
Who on this list would give help if ill?			
Nuclear family member	64.0	54.0	62.0
Other family member	14.0	13.0	10.0
Nonrelative	4.0	6.0	8.0

TABLE 4—*Continued*

	65–74 (n = 272)	75–79 (n = 142)	80 and over (n = 130)
Rely more on family or friends?			
Relatives	48.0	41.1	44.5
Friends	18.0	24.8	18.8
Both	33.3	34.0	35.9
Neither, no one	.7	.0	.8
Mean scores on number of available helpers index [NAHI][a]	4.2	3.8	3.6
FREQUENCY OF CONTACT/HELP			
Family help[b]			
Very often	70.7	70.8	74.5
Never	29.3	29.2	25.5
Church member help[c]			
Often	27.8	18.9	31.0
Sometimes	27.2	33.6	33.3
Hardly ever, never	44.8	47.3	35.6
Family contact			
At least once/week	60.6	61.3	55.5
At least once/month	26.2	25.2	25.5
Few times/year; hardly ever; never	13.2	13.5	19.1
Friend contact			
At least once/week	70.1	62.5	55.5
At least once/month	16.5	20.5	20.0
Few times/year; hardly ever; never	13.5	16.9	24.6
Mean scores on the frequency of contact/help index [FCHI][d]	2.9	2.7	2.8

ADEQUACY OF HELP			
From family[e]			
A lot or a great deal	63.8	64.1	64.8
Only a little	36.2	35.9	35.2
From church members[f]			
Some or a lot of help	82.5	78.3	78.0
Only a little help	17.5	21.7	22.0
Mean scores on adequacy of help index [AHI][g]	.75	.62	.75
TYPE OF HELP			
From family[e]			
Emotional	33.9	35.8	27.9
Instrumental	66.1	64.2	72.1
From church members[f]			
Emotional	26.0	30.0	25.4
Instrumental	16.1	10.0	7.2
Prayer	57.8	60.0	67.2
From close friend[h]			
Emotional	63.7	70.9	64.6
Instrumental	36.3	29.1	35.4
Total amount of emotional support			
None	41.1	34.0	43.3
Mid-level	41.7	50.0	43.3
High level	17.2	16.0	13.5
EXCHANGES WITH ADULT CHILDREN			
Helps children[i]			
Very often	37.1	28.6	31.0
Fairly often	13.3	10.7	13.1
Not too often	31.8	36.9	31.0
Never	17.8	23.8	25.0

TABLE 4—*Continued*

	65–74 (n = 272)	75–79 (n = 142)	80 and over (n = 130)
Type of help given children[j]			
Emotional	29.2	32.2	29.0
Instrumental (goods/services)	11.7	20.3	17.7
Financial	29.6	27.1	33.8
Other (such as care of adult child's family members)	29.2	20.3	19.3
Helps children more or less often, or the same as in the past[k]			
More	10.1	8.1	8.7
Less	43.2	39.4	52.2
Same	46.4	52.5	39.1
Children help more or less often, or the same as in the past[k]			
More	22.0	30.6	37.6
Less	21.3	17.3	11.8
Same	57.7	52.0	50.5
Type of help children give that is most helpful to respondent[j]			
Emotional	32.4	30.5	21.1
Instrumental (goods/services)	24.9	28.2	29.4
Financial	15.8	20.0	15.2
Other (such as care of family members)	26.7	21.2	34.1

[a] Scores ranged on the NAHI from 1 to 7 helpers. No one had zero helpers.

[b] Excluded from percentage base: Those whose families never help; respondents who never needed help.

[c] Excluded from percentage base: Those who never needed help; those who have not attended church since age 18.

[d] Scores on the FCHI ranged from 0 to 2, 2 = high frequencies.

[e] Excluded from percentage base: Family never helped; never needed help.

[f] Excluded from percentage base: Have not attended church since age 18; attended less than once a year; hardly ever or never receive help; never needed help.

[g] Scores on the AHI ranged from 0 = inadequate to 2 = a great deal of help.

[h] Excluded from percentage base: No close friends; friend does nothing; telephone respondents.

[i] Excluded from percentage base: Those without children; cross-section respondents.

[j] Excluded from percentage base: Those without children; cross-section respondents.

[k] Excluded: Those without children; those whose children never give help; cross-section respondents.
   Excluded: Those without children; cross-section respondents

was not all that different for the three age groups—3.6, 4.2, and 3.8 for the very old, young old, and middle old, respectively. Asked who would give them help if they were ill, the oldest age group named a larger and more varied pool of helpers; they were not as bound to family members. As table 4 records, the very old were slightly more likely to say they rely on *both* family and friends (Chatters, Taylor, and Jackson 1985). These findings, although cross-sectional, parallel longitudinal findings indicating that individuals, as they age, do not limit help-seeking to single family members. Rather, there is a kind of virtuosity in substituting one type of informal helper for another as spouses and children are lost (Gibson 1982; Cantor 1979; Litwak 1986; Taylor and Chatters 1986). In sum, the friend and kin networks of blacks expand rather than contract in successively older age groups; the oldest-old's helpers are more varied; and regardless of age, virtually no respondent is without someone on whom to rely in times of illness.

Frequency and Perceived Adequacy of Help

A large majority of the black elderly receive help very often from family, and are in contact with family and friends at least once a week. The very old are more likely than younger groups to receive frequent help from church members, again demonstrating a more varied source of help and a greater tendency on the part of very old blacks to reach beyond family members for support. Summing the frequencies of family, church member, and friend contact and help and calculating mean scores, there is little difference in mean frequencies among the age groups (2.9, 2.7 and 2.8 for the young old, middle old, and very old, respectively). As table 4 further records, perceptions of the adequacy of support are strong among older blacks and do not diminish in successively older age groups.

Type of Help

A majority of the black elderly receive instrumental help (goods and services) from family members; emotional support (advice, counsel, encouragement, moral support, validation of attitudes and perceptions) from friends; and prayer from church members. The very old are more likely than the middle old to receive instrumental support from family and friends; while the middle old are more likely to receive emotional support. Emotional support decreases as instrumental support increases in successively older age groups. On a measure of the total amount of emotional support (the amount of emotional support from each helper multiplied by the number of helpers), the very old were, in fact, the most likely to have received none and the least likely to have received high "doses." This suggests that the informal network is responding to the younger group's poorer mental health and morale and the oldest group's declining physical abilities (see Gibson 1986c for an analysis of mental health in age groups of black Americans). These findings indicate a tailoring of the help to fit the need best (Litwak 1986; Cantor 1979).

Exchanges with Adult Children

Large proportions of older blacks in all age groups are still helping their adult children. The very old, however, were less likely than others to provide services and care of family members; and more likely to say they had decreased help to children from past levels (while their children had increased help to them). Even so, the very old were likely to provide financial aid. Help from adult children to aged parents seems responsive to the changing needs of the parents—less emotional and more instrumental aid; help from very old parents to their adult children, on the other hand, seems to be of the type the parent is physically capable of giving—more emotional and financial and less instrumental. These patterns of reciprocity between the black elderly and their adult children support the idea that blacks accumulate "social credits" earlier in life and "cash them in" as needed later in life (Antonucci 1985; Antonucci and Jackson 1987). On balance, there seems to be a special relation between functional health and social support in the oldest age group. We turn now to specific ways in which informal support is related to the physical functioning of the very old.

Informal Support and Physical Functioning

The findings of this analysis suggest that perceptions of numbers of available helpers, frequency of contact and help, and type of help affect the physical functioning of very old blacks indirectly rather than directly, and reinforce the idea that age is a poor predictor of effective functioning. Since the methods, measures, analysis procedures, and findings of the study are detailed elsewhere (Gibson 1986a), only the highlights are presented here.

The measures for this analysis were based on more than thirty years of social epidemiological and informal support literature that suggests specific ways in which informal support affects health and functioning (Rowe and Kahn 1987; Minkler, Satariano, and Langhauser 1983; Stoller 1984; Cassel 1976; House 1983; Kaplan, Cassel, and Gore 1977; Nuckolls, Cassel, and Kaplan 1972; House 1980; House et al. 1979; House, Robbins, and Metzner 1982; George 1988). Functional limitation was conceptualized as the absence or presence of extreme physical limitation; therefore, logit regression was selected as the method of analysis (see Hanushek and Jackson 1977 for the regression of a dichotomous dependent variable). Using this procedure, the logarithm of the odds of functional limitation was regressed on physical, mental, and social health and three measures of informal support. The three social-support indices were: perceptions of numbers of helpers in the network—neighbors, friends, and church and family members (see George 1988 for a discussion of subjective measures of social support); the actual frequency of contact and help from network members; and the total amount of emotional support received from all network members. The mental health measures included recent stressful life events and the frequency and magnitude of reactions to these events. Those aged 75 to 79 were again included to observe the contrasting effects on functioning of the three age groups of interest: the younger, more able group (aged 75 to 79), the group aged 80 to 84, and those aged 85 and over.

The probability of being extremely limited was significantly increased by living in the South and being in overall poor physical health (logit estimates are recorded in table 5). Consistent with findings in the earlier analyses, age in the present analysis is a poor predictor of the probability of disability. Once again, the group aged 75 to 79 is associated with the lowest probability of limitation. And also in support of earlier findings, the group aged 80 to 84, rather than the group aged 85 and over, is associated with the highest probability of limitation (logits = −.18, .31, and −.10, respectively). These are compelling findings because they support the ideas that the group aged 75 to 79 is the least disabled of the black elderly; and the probability of disability does not increase in a straightforward way in successively older age groups of the black very old.

Although the three social-support indices had no significant direct effects on the probability of functional limitation, high numbers of helpers ($-.13$) and high frequencies of contact and help ($-.35$) were associated with decreased probabilities of limitation. In contrast, large amounts of emotional support from family, church members, and friends were associated with an increased probability of limitation (.13), while small and moderate levels were associated with a decreased probability.

The frequency of actual contact and help seemed to operate more in a mediating capacity on the relation between stress and the probability of disability, whereas infrequent contact and help increased the probability of limitation more among individuals under high than low stress. Since perceptions of the number of available helpers in the total network did not have mediating effects, actual help may be a more effective stress-buffer than perceived help. Although interaction effects were weak in the present analysis, new research should investigate a possible interaction among frequency of actual support, stress, and physical functioning. In brief, actual help seems to moderate the impact of stress; too much emotional support, perceptions of too few helpers, and too infrequent contact and help have increasing effects on the probability of poor physical functioning.

Several investigators report synergistic effects of informal support (see, for example, House, Robbins, and Metzner 1982). In the present analysis, however, the total amount of emotional support received from all sources, the total number of helpers perceived in the network, and the total frequencies of actual contact and help had no more significant relation with the probability of disability than did their component parts; the whole of social support was not larger than the sum of its parts in this study.

It should be noted that these findings on the informal support and functional limitation of very old blacks are strikingly different from a comparable analysis of blacks at mid-life (Gibson 1986a). Differences in the two sets of findings suggest an age, informal support, and functional limitation interaction among older black adults.

It is instructive to note that by calculating probabilities from the logarithmic function, the individual most likely to be extremely func-

TABLE 5

The Probability of Physical Functional Limitation, Black Men and Women
Aged 75 and Over (logit estimates)

Predictive Power (adj.)	.55
Constant	−.22(.19)
VARIABLES	
Gender	
Men	−.19(.24)
Women	.12(.15)
Region	
Non-South	−.70(.34)*
South	.25(.12)*
Age	
75–79	−.18(.20)
80–84	.31(.26)
85 and over	−.10(.40)
Social activities/integration	
Low	.21(.15)
High	−.37(.27)
Recent stress-distress	
Low	−.01(.07)
High	.10(.52)
Health status index	
Good	−1.43(.42)*
Fair	−.26(.20)
Poor	1.46(.31)*
Number of available helpers	
Low	.02(.08)
High	−.13(.53)
Amount of emotional support	
Small	−.04(.26)
Moderate	−.01(.19)
Large	.13(.45)
Frequency of contact/help	
Low	.32(.20)
High	−.35(.22)

Note: The first figure is the estimated coefficient. The asymptotic standard errors are
reported in parentheses. Asterisks are used to indicate significance at $p \leq .05$. Minus
signs indicate decreased probabilities of functional limitation.

TABLE 6
Estimated Probabilities[a] of Extreme Physical Functional Limitation,
Selected Cases of Black Men and Women Aged 75 and Over

Case	Probability of extreme limitation	Age	Region	Overall health status	Amount of emotional support
1	.87	80–84	South	poor	large
2	.85	80–84	South	poor	small
3	.80	75–79	South	poor	large
4	.07	75–79	non-South	good	small
5	.09	85 or older	non-South	good	large
6	.08	85 or older	non-South	good	small

Note: Probabilities were calculated using the estimated coefficients reported in table 5.
[a] Considering only the variables included in the calculations.

tionally limited lived in the South, was between 80 and 84 years old, and was receiving large amounts of emotional support from family, friends, and church members (probability of limitation = .87 [case 1 in table 6]). An individual less likely to be limited was, conversely, living in a nonsouthern state, aged 85 or older, had overall good health status, and was receiving small amounts of emotional support from family, friends, and church members (probability of limitation = .08 [case 6]). It is interesting that cases 4, 5, and 6 show that, even with excellent health, there is still about a .08 chance of functional limitation. This is evidence that factors other than actual physical health are reflected in the self-reported functional limitation of very old blacks. Selected other cases appear in table 6. Such probability calculations could be used with an eye to more effective health policy, planning, and programming.

Discussion

The major goal of this article was to examine in a preliminary way the health, physical functioning, and social networks of the black elderly, and raise issues for further study. Toward this end, data were analyzed from the largest probability samples of older black Americans to date. Several trends dominated the data and have implications for new health research and policy. First, the black elderly are a heterogeneous group in regard to health, functioning, and social support. Their physical functioning ranged from extremely able to extremely disabled. Our findings indicate that caution must be taken in examining older blacks as a monolithic group; not to do so would obscure important countervailing trends among the subgroups. Heterogeneity among the old is apparently not specific to blacks because Rowe and Kahn (1987) identify the variability of older individuals in other samples. Our findings also mean that certain subgroups of the black elderly will need more extensive and intensive health care than others. For policy and planning purposes, new research should identify more precisely the contrasting social, psychological, and informal support characteristics of these functional health subgroups of the black elderly. In addition to these within-group differences, recent research is identifying ways in which the life experiences of minority and majority elderly diverge (Markides 1983; Jackson 1987b; Jackson 1981; Jackson and Gibson 1985; Taylor and Chatters 1986). These new findings urge a consideration of race and ethnic group differences in designing health policies.

The relation between age and certain measures of physical and functional health is possibly nonlinear among the black elderly. Percentages of the very healthy did not decrease in older age groups, and age did not predict functional limitation in the regression analyses, even after controlling for relevant factors. The reason was that individuals aged 65 to 74 were more disabled than were those aged 75 to 79; and individuals aged 80 to 84 were more disabled than those aged 85 and over. New research should determine for which dimensions of health the relation with age is linear and for which it is not. These are important issues in anticipating differences in the health care needs of different age groups of the black elderly.

Two distinct groups of black elderly were identified: a disabled younger group aged 65 to 74, and a more able older group aged 75 to 79. This finding parallels that of Manton and Soldo (1985) who found a more robust predominantly black older group in their elderly sample and a younger more morbid group, also predominantly black. Manton and Soldo suggest that identification of a robust older and a morbid younger group is consistent with an "adverse mortality selection of a disadvantaged group" explanation of the racial mortality crossover

(Manton 1982; Wing et al. 1985). Manton and Soldo also predict that their morbid group will be less likely than the robust group to survive. We are beginning to examine the differential mortality of our more and less disabled groups in a new follow-up study of individuals in the present study (Jackson 1988a, 1988b).

Because individuals aged 85 and over in our sample were less likely than those aged 80 to 84 to be disabled, there is some limited support for increasing selectivity in successively older age groups after age 75. Much more research is needed which focuses on race differences in the peak ages for morbidity and disability, and the phenomenon of increasing selectivity with age.

The present research supports previous work on the social networks of older blacks. The findings indicate a rich, fluid, and plastic kind of network that is highly responsive to the changing needs and abilities of successively older age groups of blacks on into extreme old age (Litwak 1986; Cantor 1979; Taylor and Chatters 1986). Also consonant with past work, informal support was found related to effective functioning, having differential effects depending upon its type, amount, frequency, and perceived availability (Antonucci and Jackson 1987; Minkler, Satariano, and Langhauser 1983; Stoller 1984). Generally, adequate support was associated with better physical functioning.

There was a certain malleability of informal networks; help was tailored to meet particular needs, especially among the very old. The type, amount, and frequency of help seemed to be on a sliding scale: the more the disability, the larger the number of helpers; the higher the frequencies of contact and help, the more proximate the family members, and the more likely were increases in aid from adult children. Instrumental help increased as emotional help decreased in successively older age groups, seeming to mold to the physical needs of the very old and to the emotional needs of the younger old. Very old blacks had a greater variety of available helpers and were more versatile than younger groups in substituting these helpers one for another. New research should focus more specifically on the roles of the resiliency of social networks, and the strategy of versatility in combining and substituting helpers in the adaptation of blacks to very old age. Our findings reveal the current operation of the social networks of older blacks. If changes in the structure and economic stability of the black family continue (Gibson 1986b), the very nature of this support could be altered. The rich, varied, responsive, and satisfying help from family, friends, and church members under more adverse conditions would not be guaranteed. This could seriously undermine the in-home care of older blacks and have profound effects on their long-term health care needs (Soldo and Manton 1985). Careful monitoring of the interplay between the informal support systems of older disabled blacks and the formal health care system will be necessary. Public funds to increase the effectiveness of informal support systems could reduce the strain on formal health care systems. Because older blacks are more likely than others to be solely dependent upon Medicaid and Medicare, these sources of health insurance will gain in importance as black family and black community resources dwindle. The structure and operation of Medicare will be of paramount importance as the number of black elderly grows. Increasing copayment requirements and placing Medicare under greater local control will have adverse effects on the health care of older blacks.

As mentioned earlier, the relation between informal support and functional limitation was complex. Social support moderated, ameliorated, or exacerbated physical functioning, depending upon the type, amount, frequency, and source. Large, in contrast to moderate amounts of emotional support seemed to decrease functioning. Extreme levels of emotional support from multiple helpers may constitute a kind of psychological immersion (Antonucci 1985), which acts to the detriment of older individuals. These detrimental effects can be interpreted within self-efficacy theory—where the efforts of the individual are stultified and personal coping capacities are seriously undermined (Rowe and Kahn 1987; Shupe 1985; Langer and Rodin 1976; Avorn and Langer 1982; Antonucci and Jackson 1987; Langer 1981; Rodin 1986); exchange theory—where older blacks may now find themselves in an unbalanced and therefore stressful exchange relationship in which the receiving exceeds the giving (Dowd 1975); or sick role theory—where significant others are encouraging an adoption of the sick role (Parsons 1951). As Rowe and Kahn (1987) urge, new research should establish a causal sequence that includes the individual's need for support, the type of support required (material, information, emotional), and the effect of that support on their autonomy and control. These findings on the interfaces of stress, informal support, and functional limitation raise some major issues for future conceptual models, and for policy developments in regard to the black elderly's needs for health and long-term care. Figure 1 presents a preliminary model of the factors that affect the functional limitation of the black elderly.

Although not explicitly examined in this article, some characteristics of very old blacks are consistent with an adverse-mortality-selection explanation of the racial mortality crossover. A fairly large proportion of those aged 80 and over bore certain of the health characteristics of younger blacks; functioning was not related linearly to age; and individuals aged 65 to 74 were more disabled than were those aged 75 to 79. The very old also function better in regard to stress, distress, and morale than younger groups of elderly (Gibson and Jackson 1988). In addition, the very old were characterized by factors associated with longevity, and by psychosocial factors speculated to explain the crossover. There were, in fact, notable similarities between the long-lived in other countries (Mapleton 1973) and very old blacks in our sample. Interestingly, these common factors of stress and social support have been found related to the onset and course of disease and mortality (see Rowe and Kahn 1987 for a review of these studies; see also Jackson, Bacon, and Peterson 1978). Moreover, both the identification of a disabled younger and more able older group, and the better functioning of the 85 and over group than the group aged 80 to 84 support the adverse-mortality explanation of the racial-mortality crossover. It seems premature to discount the idea that very old blacks constitute a group with "extra-special hardiness"—the physical and psychological survivors. New research should examine whether mortality differences between blacks and whites after age 80 are accounted for in part by race differences in social and psychological characteristics at those ages (Manton 1982; Nam, Weatherby, and Ockay 1978). As Rowe and Kahn (1987) point out, research has not focused on the modifying effects of social and psychological factors on health, functioning, and longevity. Biomedical, social, and psychological data should be examined in tandem to investigate the racial-mortality crossover effect. More prospective studies of the correlates of the mortality of blacks and whites are called for.

If we were to identify some organizing themes for future research on the health and functioning of older blacks, the first would be that their present circumstances must be examined within the context of their unique lifetime experiences, underscoring the importance of the interface of social and institutional factors with their idiosyncratic

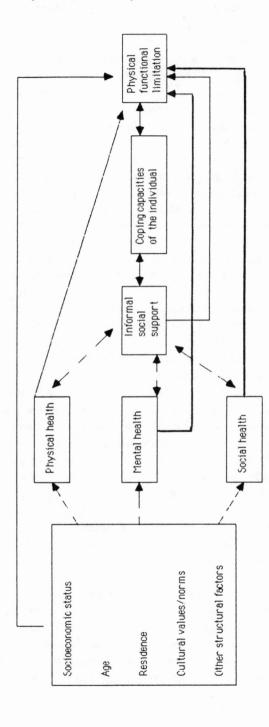

FIG. 1. A model of the physical functional limitation of the black elderly.
Note. Bold lines indicate the effects estimated in this research. The double-headed arrows indicate possibly reciprocal effects.

experiences. Such a comprehensive framework will spawn increasingly complex tiers of substantive and methodological issues with respect to research on this group. The first layer of issues that would stem from such a framework would have to do with using a lifespan approach. An intriguing question, for example, is whether blacks age more rapidly socially than whites. If true, then the "elderly" label should be moved back to age 55 or so. Certainly, earlier aging among blacks is evident in several physical and social areas. Blacks, for example, experience earlier sexual maturity, onset of certain diseases, functional limitation, and mortality than whites. And socially, the timing of certain critical life events is accelerated: the birth and loss of first child, the loss of spouse, and the earlier ending of work lives (Gibson 1986c, 1986d; Jackson 1987b). A question research must ask is whether the physical and social characteristics of the black elderly are similar to those of whites who are several years their seniors. If yes, it is impractical to compare the black and white elderly age for age. This accelerated aging of blacks may be evident in other life domains. Race-comparison research on longitudinal datasets is needed to identify these areas. The issue of unequal aging involves the inappropriateness of age-based health policies and programs (Jackson and Gibson 1985).

But to the extent that individual life courses are affected by social change, major societal trends will have very much to do with shaping the needs of the black elderly. Issues in the second tier involve ways in which successive cohorts of older blacks will be different. Recent research suggests that the masses in future cohorts of older blacks (despite higher levels of education) will be less, not more advantaged in regard to family and economic stability (Gibson 1986b).

This brings us to a final tier of issues. The aging experience of blacks is most effectively studied by attention to the fact that social processes, the individual's experience of them, and the meanings attributed to these processes often have contrasts and parallels. Insight might be gained into the role of family systems in physical functioning by looking across cultures. In brief, research on the black old should be conducted within a framework of their lifetime experiences and major social change, overlaying differential experiences within subgroups of the black old and across cultures. This approach necessitates interdisciplinary, international, and longitudinal studies.

The limitations of cross-sectional data and small sample size make our findings preliminary and our conclusions tentative. Because of the inadequacies of cross-sectional data in isolating effects, age group differences found here cannot be construed to mean differences due to aging. We, in fact, do not know whether these relations found among physical health, age, and informal support are unique to the present cohort of the black elderly because they shared the same life experiences, are peculiar to this group because they became old in a certain period, or are characteristic of a particular life stage of blacks— the penultimate transition. Longitudinal studies are needed to isolate each of these sets of effects.

Some of our findings parallel, while others are in contrast with, findings on the white population. New research should precisely identify similarities and differences between the black and white elderly. Furthermore, we do not know which of our findings are due to race and which to class, because a majority of the black elderly are poor, poorly educated, and worked over a lifetime in low-level occupations. Investigations are needed that make class-by-race comparisons of the health, functioning, and informal support of the elderly (Haan and Kaplan 1985). We are beginning to examine issues of class and race among the elderly in the Americans' Changing Lives dataset (House 1984).

Our study population was the noninstitutionalized black elderly. Undoubtedly, the sample was biased toward better physical, social, and psychological functioning and informal support. These factors may vary among older blacks who are institutionalized, or who were "weeded out" by selective survival. As is typical of survey research data, the responses in this study were filtered through the eyes of the respondents. These findings could be different if more objective appraisals of physical health and informal support were used.

Methodologies used to examine the health and functioning of the black elderly should not only have as a goal the identification of major effects of variables, but also the objective of examining structural linkages among constructs that underlie these variables. It is also important to examine the validity of the measures currently being used to measure the social class, physical health and functioning, and informal support of older blacks. Health, functioning, and social support disparities between the black and white elderly could be due, in part, to differences in the underlying structures of these factors, and/or to differences in the measurement error of the items and indices used to measure the constructs. Increasingly, sophisticated types of methodologies will be needed for race comparisons of the health, functioning, and informal support of the elderly.

Physical functioning in the present research was treated as a consequence of informal support in a recursive model. It is possible that the functionally limited are more likely than others to mobilize their social networks, and that functioning and support affect each other. There is a need to estimate nonrecursive models of functioning and support on longitudinal data to identify such causal ordering and reciprocal effects.

The findings presented here add substantially to our knowledge about the health, functioning, and informal support of older blacks, but they are only the beginning. We hope the issues raised in this article will stimulate thought and provide an initial framework for future research on the interplay of these factors and the health care needs of black adults as they age in American society.

Technical Appendix: The Health, Physical Functioning, and Informal Supports of the Black Elderly

The National Survey of Black Americans (NSBA)

The NSBA cross-section sample is a multistage probability sample of the black population consisting of 2,107 respondents aged 18 to 101. The sampling design was based on the 1970 census and each black American residing in an individual household within the continental United States had an equal chance of being selected. The sample design is similar to that of most national surveys but has unique features of primary area selection and stratification to make it responsive to the distribution of the black population. Eligibility for selection into this household sample was based on citizenship and noninstitutionalized living quarters within the continental United States. Reflecting the nature of the distribution of the black population, more than half (44) of the 76 primary areas used for final selection of households were located in the South. Two methods of screening were developed to guarantee inclusion of blacks—meeting selection criteria— in both high- and low-density areas. The sample had a 69 percent response rate and all face-to-face interviewing was conducted from 1979 to 1980 by black interviewers trained through the Survey Research Center of the University of Michigan's Institute for Social Research.

The questionnaire used in the NSBA was developed especially for use with the black population. Two years of pretesting and refinement preceded actual use in the field. The instrument contained both open- and closed-ended items and took approximately 2 hours and 20 minutes to administer. Although our present concern lies in the physical health and functioning, neighborhood life, family, social support, mental health, and demographic sections, the questionnaire also includes the broad areas of work, retirement, racial and self-identity, and political participation. Jackson (1987a) provides a detailed description of the NSBA methods.

The Three-generation Black Family Study

The cross-section NSBA served as the parent study for the Three-generation Black Family Study. When respondents in the cross-section survey had living family members from at least two other generations, interviews were attempted with one randomly selected representative from each of those two generations. The cross-section respondent was reinterviewed with a form of the three-generation instrument. Multiplicity sampling was adapted to generate the new national probability samples from the original national cross-section sample. (For descriptions of multiplicity sampling see, for example, Frankel and Frankel 1977 and Sirkin 1970; for adaptations of multiplicity sampling for use in generating a supplemental sample of black elderly see Gibson and Herzog 1984.) Having a defined set of inclusion-exclusion rules and establishing specific probabilities of selection for each of the three-generation respondents, the Family Network Sampling Procedure generated a nationally distributed sample of three-generation families; Jackson and Hatchett (1986) contains a detailed description of these methods. Data on the adult children of the black elderly were drawn from this three-generation sample.

References

Andrews, F.M., J.N. Morgan, and J.A. Sonquist. 1967. *Multiple Classification Analysis*. Ann Arbor: Survey Research Center, Institute for Social Research, University of Michigan.

Antonucci, T.C. 1985. Personal Characteristics, Social Networks, and

Social Behavior. In *Handbook of Aging and the Social Sciences,* ed. R.H. Binstock and E. Shanas, 94–128. 2d ed. New York: Van Nostrand Rheinhold.

Antonucci, T.C., and J.S. Jackson. 1987. Social Support, Interpersonal Efficacy, and Health. In *Handbook of Clinical Gerontology,* ed. L. Carstensen and B.A. Edelstein, 291–311. New York: Pergamon Press.

Avorn, J., and E.J. Langer. 1982. Induced Disability in Nursing Home Patients: A Controlled Trial. *Journal of the American Geriatric Society* 30(6):397–400.

Bengston, V. 1986. Sociological Perspectives on Aging Families and the Future. In *Dimensions in Aging: The 1986 Sandoz Lectures in Gerontology,* 237–62. London: Academic Press.

Berkman, L. 1983. *Health and Ways of Living: Findings from the Alameda County Study.* New York: Oxford University Press.

Blazer, D.G. 1982. Social Support and Mortality in an Elderly Community Population. *American Journal of Epidemiology* 115(5):684–94.

Cantor, M.H. 1979. Neighbors and Friends: An Overlooked Resource in the Informal Support System. *Research on Aging* 1:434–63.

Cassel, J. 1976. The Contribution of the Social Environment to Host Resistance. *American Journal of Epidemiology* 104(2):107–23.

Chatters, L.M., R.J. Taylor, and J.S. Jackson. 1985. Size and Composition of the Informal Helper Networks of Elderly Blacks. *Journal of Gerontology* 40(2):605–14.

Davis, K. 1986. Aging and the Health-care System: Economic and Structural Issues. *Daedalus* 115:227–46.

Dowd, J. 1975. Aging as Exchange: A Preface to Theory. *Journal of Gerontology* 30:584–94.

Frankel, M.R., and L.R. Frankel. 1977. Some Recent Developments in Sample Survey Design. *Journal of Marketing Research* 14:280–93.

George, L.K. 1988. Easing Caregiver Burden: The Role of Informal and Formal Supports. In *Health in Aging: Sociological Issues and Policy Directions,* ed. R.A. Ward and S.S. Tobin. (In press.)

Gibson, R.C. 1982. Blacks at Middle and Late Life: Resources and Coping. *Annals of the American Academy of Political and Social Science* 464:79–90.

———. 1986a. *The Physical Disability of Older Blacks.* Final report to the National Institute of Aging, grant no. AGO3553. (Unpublished.)

———. 1986b. *Blacks in an Aging Society.* New York: Carnegie Corporation.

————. 1986c. Blacks in an Aging Society. *Daedalus* 115(1):349–71.

————. 1986d. Outlook for the Black Family. In *Our Aging Society: Paradox or Promise?*, ed. A. Pifer and L. Bronte, 181–97. New York: W.W. Norton.

Gibson, R.C., and A.R. Herzog. 1984. Rare Element Telephone Screening (RETS): A Procedure for Augmenting the Number of Black Elderly in National Samples. *Gerontologist* 24:477–82.

Gibson, R.C., and J.S. Jackson. 1988. Health, Effective Functioning, and Informal Support among the Black Oldest Old. In *The Oldest Old*, ed. R. Suzman and D. Willis. New York: Oxford University Press. (In press.)

Haan, M.N., and G.A. Kaplan. 1985. The Contribution of Socioeconomic Position to Minority Health. In *Report of the Secretary's Task Force on Black and Minority Health*. Vol. 2: *Crosscutting Issues in Minority Health*. Washington: U.S. Department of Health and Human Services.

Hanushek, E., and J.S. Jackson. 1977. *Statistical Methods for Social Scientists*. New York: Academic Press.

House, J.S. 1980. Occupational Stress and the Physical and Mental Health of Factory Workers. NIMH grant no. 1RO2MH28902. Research Report Series. Ann Arbor: Institute for Social Research, University of Michigan.

————. 1983. Social Support and the Quality and Quantity of Life. Paper presented at the Fourth Annual Institute for Social Research Founders Symposium, The University of Michigan, Ann Arbor, February 18.

————. 1984. Productivity, Stress, and Health in Middle and Late Life: Program Project Grant Application to the National Institute on Aging. Ann Arbor: Institute for Social Research, University of Michigan. (Unpublished.)

House, J.S., and R.L. Kahn. 1985. In *Social Support and Health*, ed. S. Cohen and S.L. Syme, 83–108. Orlando, Fla.: Academic Press.

House, J.S., A.J. McMichael, J.A. Wells, B.N. Kaplan, and L.R. Landerman. 1979. Occupational Stress and Health among Factory Workers. *Journal of Health and Social Behavior* 20:139–60.

House, J.S., C. Robbins, and H.L. Metzner. 1982. The Association of Social Relationships and Activities with Mortality: Prospective Evidence from the Tecumseh Community Health Study. *American Journal of Epidemiology* 116(1):123–40.

Jackson, J.J. 1981. Urban Black Americans. In *Ethnicity and Medical Care*, ed. A. Harwood, 37–129. Cambridge: Harvard University Press.

Jackson, J.S. 1988a. The Program for Research on Black Americans. In *Advances in Black Psychology,* ed. R. Jones, Richmond, Calif.: Cobb and Henry. (Forthcoming.)

————. 1988b. The Graying of Black America: Research on Aging Black Populations. In *Research on Aging Black Populations,* ed. J.S. Jackson. New York: Springer. (Forthcoming.)

Jackson, J.S., J.D. Bacon, and J. Peterson. 1978. Life Satisfaction among Black Urban Elderly. *Aging and Human Development* 8:169–79.

Jackson, J.S., and R.C. Gibson. 1985. Work and Retirement among the Black Elderly. In *Current Perspectives on Aging and the Life Cycle,* ed. Z.S. Blau, vol. 1, 193–222. Greenwich, Conn.: JAI Press.

Jackson, J.S., and S.J. Hatchett. 1986. Intergenerational Research: Methodological Considerations. In *Intergenerational Relations,* ed. N. Datan and H.W. Reese, 51–76. Hillsdale, N.Y.: Earlbauer Associates.

Kaplan, B.H., J.C. Cassel, and S. Gore. 1977. Social Support and Health. *Medical Care* 15(5):47–58.

Kasl, S.V., and L.F. Berkman. 1981. Some Psychosocial Influences on the Health Status of the Elderly: The Perspective of Social Epidemiology. In *Aging, Biology and Behavior,* ed. J.L. McGaugh and S.B. Kiesler, 345–85. New York: Academic Press.

Langer, E.J. 1981. Old Age: An Artifact? In *Aging, Biology and Behavior,* ed. J.L. McGaugh and S.B. Kiesler, 255–81. New York: Academic Press.

Langer, E.J., and J. Rodin. 1976. The Effects of Choice and Enhanced Personal Responsibility for the Aged. *Journal of Personality and Social Psychology* 34:191–98.

Litwak, E. 1986. *Helping the Elderly.* New York: Guilford Press.

Manton, K.G. 1982. Temporal and Age Variation of United States Black/White Cause-specific Mortality Differentials: A Study of the Recent Changes in the Relative Health Status of the United States Black Population. *Gerontologist* 22(2):170–79.

Manton, K.G., and B.J. Soldo. 1985. Dynamics of Health Changes in the Oldest Old: New Perspectives and Evidence. *Milbank Memorial Fund Quarterly/Health and Society* 63(2):206–85.

Mapleton, A.J. 1973. Factors of Human Longevity: Mystery, Myth or Truth? A Critical Review of Empirical and Experimental Findings. Ann Arbor: University of Michigan. (Unpublished.)

Markides, K.S. 1983. Minority Aging. In *Aging in Society: Selected Review of Recent Research,* ed. M.W. Riley, B.B. Hess, and K. Bond, 115–37. Hillsdale, N.J.: Lawrence Erlbaum.

Minkler, M.A., W.A. Satariano, and C. Langhauser. 1983. Supportive Exchange: An Exploration of the Relationship between Social Contacts and Perceived Health Status in the Elderly. *Archives of Gerontological Geriatrics* 2:211–20.

Nam, C.B., N.L. Weatherby, and K.A. Ockay. 1978. Causes of Death Which Contribute to the Mortality Crossover Effect. *Social Biology* 25(4):306–14.

Nuckolls, K.B., J. Cassel, and B.H. Kaplan. 1972. Psychosocial Assets, Life Crisis and the Prognosis of Pregnancy. *American Journal of Epidemiology* 95:431–41.

Parsons, T. 1951. *The Social System.* New York: Free Press.

Rice, D.P. 1986. Living Longer in the United States: Health, Social, and Economic Implications. *Journal of Medical Practice Management* 1:162–69.

Rice, D.P., and C.L. Estes. 1984. Health of the Elderly: Policy Issues and Challenges. *Health Affairs* 3:25–49.

Rice, D.P., and J.J. Feldman. 1983. Living Longer in the United States: Demographic Changes and Health Needs of the Elderly. *Milbank Memorial Fund Quarterly/Health and Society* 61:362–96.

Rodin, J. 1986. Aging and Health: Effects of the Sense of Control. *Science* 233:1271–76.

Rowe, J.W., and R.L. Kahn. 1987. Human Aging: Usual and Successful. *Science* 237:143–49.

Satariano, W.A., and S.L. Syme. 1981. Life Changes and Disease in Elderly Populations: Coping with Change. In *Aging, Biology and Behavior,* ed. J.I. McGaugh and S.B. Kiesler, 311–37. New York: Academic Press.

Shupe, D.R. 1985. *Deaf and dying; A life span approach.* In *Cognition, Stress, and Aging,* ed. J.E. Birren, and J. Livingston, 174–97. Englewood Cliffs, N.J.: Prentice-Hall.

Siegel, J.S., and C.M. Taeuber. 1986. Demographic Perspectives on the Long-lived Society. *Daedalus* 115:77–118.

Sirken, M.G. 1970. Household Surveys with Multiplicity. *Journal of the American Statistical Association* 65:257–66.

Soldo, B.J., and K.G. Manton. 1985. Changes in the Health Status and Service Needs of the Oldest Old: Current Patterns and Future Trends. *Milbank Memorial Fund Quarterly/Health and Society* 63(2):286–319.

Stoller, E.P. 1984. Self-assessments of Health by the Elderly: The Impact of Informal Assistance. *Journal of Health and Social Behavior* 25:260–70.

Suzman, R., and M.W. Riley. 1985. Introducing the Oldest Old.

Milbank Memorial Fund Quarterly/Health and Society 63(2):177–86.

Taylor, R.J. 1985. The Extended Family as a Source of Support to Elderly Blacks. *Gerontologist* 25(5):488–95.

———. 1986. Receipt of Support from Family among Black Americans: Demographic and Familial Differences. *Journal of Marriage and the Family* 48:67–77.

Taylor, R.J., and L.M. Chatters. 1986. Patterns of Informal Support to Elderly Black Adults: Family, Friends, and Church Members. *Social Work* 31:432–38.

Wing, S., K.G. Manton, E. Stallard, C.G. Hames, and H.A. Tyroler. 1985. The Black/White Mortality Crossover: Investigation in a Community-based Cohort. *Journal of Gerontology* 40:78–84.

The AIDS Epidemic among Blacks
and Hispanics

SAMUEL R. FRIEDMAN, JO L.
SOTHERAN, ABU ABDUL-QUADER,
BENY J. PRIMM, DON C. DES JARLAIS,
PAULA KLEINMAN, CONRAD MAUGÉ,
DOUGLAS S. GOLDSMITH, WAFAA
EL-SADR, and ROBERT MASLANSKY

A DISPROPORTIONATE NUMBER OF PERSONS WITH AIDS have been blacks and Hispanics. Members of minority groups survive for a shorter period after having been diagnosed as having AIDS than do whites with the disease (Centers for Disease Control 1986b; Weston 1986). In spite of these facts, studies of race and AIDS have been few, although this is beginning to change (Bakeman et al. 1988; Bakeman, Lumb, and Smith 1986; Centers for Disease Control 1986b; Rogers and Williams 1987). The dominant image of the disease has been that it primarily affects (white) gays (Rogers and Williams 1987); secondary images have been of transmission among individuals of unspecified race by sharing drug-injection equipment or by heterosexual intercourse. One consequence of the neglect of the differential racial impact of AIDS has been a lack of programs to allocate extra resources to AIDS-related efforts of medical institutions, health education, or community groups in minority communities (Nickens 1986). In addition, there has been little mobilization by minority communities or organizations to come to grips with AIDS (Nickens 1986). This lack of minority mobilization has undoubtedly been furthered by the fact that black and Hispanic gays were more stigmatized and less organized than white gays before the advent of the epidemic (Craig Harris, National Coalition of Black Lesbians and Gays, as quoted in Weston 1986), and by the hostility of many minority institutions and leaders to intravenous (IV) drug users.

In order to understand the individual, community, and group reactions to AIDS among members of different races, it is helpful to develop a model of race and its dynamics. In spite of the useful argument by Wilkinson and King (1986) in these volumes, neither our data nor the extent of our understanding of race and AIDS allows us to present a precise definition of what we mean by "race." On the other hand, as we develop our description and analysis, a partial model of what race means as a process *does* emerge. This model goes beyond the common view of minorities as deprived and subordinated, and, thus, as less able than whites to protect themselves against the epidemic, while recognizing that blacks and Hispanics are indeed subjected to relations of dominance and inequality that leave them with lower levels of material resources and of formal education than whites. It also goes beyond the "social pathology" model that holds that, in reaction to deprivation and subordination (and perhaps for other reasons as well), many minority race members take up behaviors or lifestyles (such as IV drug use) that are ultimately harmful both to these individuals and to their communities. In addition to deprivation, subordination, and pathology, however, minorities are constantly developing resources and dynamics of their own that aid their individual and collective struggles for survival, dignity, and happiness. These involve developing grapevines to carry information, networks to help each other out, and even formal organizations to formulate and achieve specific goals. In the context of AIDS, these contradictory aspects of racial relationships lead to contradictory and somewhat confusing findings. For example, rather than simply finding that black and Hispanic IV drug users are more likely than white ones to engage in behaviors that transmit the virus that causes AIDS, or that they are less likely to know enough to protect themselves (see Rogers and Williams 1987), we find that minorities know more about issues that depend upon knowledge carried by street grapevines, but are less likely to know about subjects recently promulgated in professional channels. Likewise, although blacks or Hispanics are more likely to engage in some risky behaviors, they are less likely to engage in others.

In sum, then, this article has three themes and one additional goal: (1) AIDS has disproportionately affected minorities; (2) There is a great need for minority community mobilization to deal with the epidemic and its effects, and for financial and other assistance of these mobilizing efforts by national institutions; (3) Blacks and Hispanics are not just dominated and subordinated, but have developed resources and relationships that offer many benefits in fighting AIDS. As an additional goal, this article presents considerable data about different aspects of AIDS and race. These data are by no means complete. The inadequacy of the general research effort on this topic cannot be compensated for in one article, and the fact that the authors have worked primarily in the field of IV drug users and AIDS means that there are undoubted weaknesses in what we cover about race and AIDS among gay men. What we do attempt to accomplish, however, is to demonstrate the existence of important racial dimensions to AIDS and to provoke appropriate research, debate, and action.

AIDS: A Brief Overview of the Disease

AIDS, the acquired immunodeficiency syndrome, is an infectious disease caused by the human immunodeficiency virus (HIV). This virus disables the immune system and enables infections that normally are controllable to overcome control and, ultimately, kill the patient. HIV can also infect cells in the brain and cause a severe dementia. As of this writing (in February 1987) approximately 30,000 AIDS cases have been diagnosed in the United States. More than half of these persons have died from the disease.

Many thousands of people are believed to have AIDS related complex (ARC), in which serious immunosuppression caused by HIV leads to other medical conditions or diseases, such as lymphadenopathy, which are not per se diagnostic of AIDS. ARC itself is sometimes fatal. In addition, there is growing evidence that the rapid increases in tuberculosis, pneumonia, and endocarditis cases among IV drug users may be due to HIV infection (Stoneburner, Guigli, and Kristal 1986;

Des Jarlais, Friedman, and Hopkins 1985). Although there are, as yet, no conclusive studies of the prevalence of HIV in the population, estimates of the number of Americans infected by HIV range up to 2 million.

No one knows what proportion of those infected will ultimately develop AIDS. Estimates range from 25 to 50 percent within 10 years, and the mean latency period between infection and development of AIDS is estimated as approximately 5 years (Institute of Medicine 1986). So far, in the United States over 90 percent of adults with diagnosed AIDS have been gay men, intravenous (IV) drug users, or the sex partners of IV drug users (Centers for Disease Control 1986a), and 61 percent of pediatric cases have been children of bisexual men or IV drug users. In central Africa, where statistics are limited but where HIV infection and AIDS have probably claimed many thousands of lives, there is strong evidence that the major mechanism of spread has been heterosexual activity.

In discussing the issue of AIDS among minorities, it is important to stress that, so far, there is no evidence that race per se is a biological risk factor for vulnerability to AIDS. That is, in spite of the fact that greatly disproportionate numbers of blacks and Hispanics have developed AIDS, we have no reason to believe that there is any genetic reason why HIV is more likely to survive in, thrive in, or lead to disease in blacks or Hispanics rather than non-Hispanic whites. Thus, in trying to understand racial differences in HIV seroprevalence, in AIDS diagnoses, or in the time from diagnosis to death, we have to look at the social meanings of race and their implications for the probability and mechanisms of exposure to the virus, for exposure to other infectious agents such as tuberculosis (TB), for the preexisting vulnerability of the body to these diseases, for the patterns of seeking medical care, and for the medical care and personal assistance a person receives when ill. The social dynamics of race have also affected the way in which AIDS is perceived—as a disease of gay white men—and the response of the public and of major institutions to the epidemic.

Additional Notes on the Relative Lack of Research on Race and AIDS

Social researchers and epidemiologists have been slow to address racial aspects of the AIDS epidemic. In part, this may be due to the "medical model" of most AIDS research. A medical approach has much to recommend it as a way to determine the nature of the disease and how it is transmitted. Standard scientific practice has enabled us to determine that AIDS is caused by a virus transmitted in blood and semen, and has let us discover that HIV is particularly likely to be transmitted by behaviors such as receptive anal intercourse or going to shooting galleries to inject one's drugs. The medical model can limit insights, however, about how to mobilize, whether for behavior change, support services for the sick, or political pressure to increase AIDS funding. Here, the medical model tends to focus attention on individually motivated risk reduction (as in educational models that assume that filling minds with knowledge about risks suffices to produce protective behavioral change) rather than on changing the values, world views, or interests of threatened groups. It also tends to focus attention on activity by members of risk groups rather than political or outreach activity by broader groups (such as minority communities), which include many of the individuals (and subcultures) at risk. In the case of IV drug use, the medical model has been valuable as an alternative to theories that "blame the victim," but even here it might be useful to consider the deep structures of society that underlie some IV drug use in trying to develop long-term strategies against AIDS.

Finally, in dealing with a subject like AIDS and race, it is important to heed the central message of the sociology of knowledge, i.e., that the social position of the observer affects what is observed and how it is interpreted. The first author of this article is a white American. He was asked to write this paper because he has a degree of experience in the study of AIDS among IV drug users—and most IV drug users with AIDS have been black or Hispanic—and some experience in writing about other aspects of AIDS. He agreed, in spite of his previous inexperience with research specifically about race and AIDS, for several reasons. Very little other research on this topic has been published, in spite of its importance. The image that many minority (and other) persons have, that AIDS is a white gay-related disease, may retard community efforts at educating and organizing for self-protection. Also, more attention to AIDS and race may encourage more government and foundation resources to be devoted to this issue. Friedman also had a strong belief that he should do whatever he could to bring the issue forward in a helpful way. In writing this article, he has had it brought strongly to his attention that he is reliving a common pattern of social and medical research—where whites are brought in to study the problems of minorities. In no instance has anyone who made this point urged that he not write the article. The relatively small number of black and Hispanic researchers in this field undoubtedly restricts the kinds of insights that are brought to bear on these issues, as does the relative lack of AIDS researchers with serious social ties to the lower reaches of the working class, where so many drug-user AIDS cases originate.

The Impact of AIDS on Different Races

Epidemiology

National Surveillance Data. In trying to understand race and AIDS in the United States, a good starting point is the racial distribution of AIDS cases and of HIV infection. Tables 1 through 3 record national data for risk behavior categories by race.

As table 3 shows, blacks and Hispanics are overrepresented among persons with AIDS. Three-fifths have been white, one-quarter non-Hispanic black, 14 percent Hispanic, and 1 percent have been either in other racial categories or did not have their race determined. The racial disproportion is even more striking among children. Among the 422 AIDS cases in children under the age of 13 at the time of diagnosis, 80 percent have been nonwhite (57 percent have been black, 23 percent Hispanic, and only 20 percent white (Centers for Disease Control, personal communication, January 19, 1987).

Table 2 records the percentage in each transmission category within the racial categories the Centers for Disease Control (CDC) uses; in table 3 the same data is presented, but as percentages of each race within transmission categories. The fact that 88 percent of white cases have been homosexual/bisexual males (including those who are also IV drug users), and that 74 percent of the homosexual/bisexual male category has been white—together with the initial discovery of AIDS as a disease afflicting gays—is probably one reason for the common public impression of AIDS as a white gay-related disease. The fact that 14,995 (52 percent of the total cases) (table 1) do not fall into the category of white men with no risk factor other than homosexual activity often gets lost to view.

TABLE 1

Adult and Adolescent AIDS Cases, United States: Transmission Categories by Racial/Ethnic Group, January 19, 1987

Transmission category	White, not Hispanic	Black, not Hispanic	Hispanic	Other/ Unknown	Total
Homosexual/bisexual male	14,119	2,785	1,993	182	19,079
IV drug user	907	2,525	1,486	33	4,951
Homosexual male & IV drug user	1,456	502	287	15	2,260
Hemophilia/coagulation disorder	215	14	17	6	252
Heterosexual cases*	133	832	140	5	1,110
Transfusion, blood/components**	419	84	30	11	544
Undetermined***	321	393	186	18	918
TOTAL	17,570	7,135	4,139	270	29,114

* This category is composed of 521 persons (91 men, 430 women) who have had heterosexual contact with a person with AIDS or at risk for AIDS and 589 persons (474 men, 115 women) without other identified risks who were born in countries in which heterosexual transmission is believed to play a major role although precise means of transmission have not yet been fully defined. The latter set of persons is overwhelmingly Haitian.

** Owing to the long latency period between infection and the development of AIDS, the number of cases based on blood transfusions continues to increase as a result of infections that occurred prior to the use of antibody testing to screen donated blood.

*** Many of the cases listed in the "undetermined" transmission category died before they could be interviewed about risk behaviors.

Source: Centers for Disease Control, personal communication, 1987.

TABLE 2

Adult and Adolescent AIDS Cases, United States: Percentage in Each Transmission Category by Racial/Ethnic Group, January 19, 1987

Transmission category	White, not Hispanic	Black, not Hispanic	Hispanic	Other/ Unknown	Total
Homosexual/bisexual male	80%	39%	48%	67%	66%
IV drug user	5	35	36	12	17
Homosexual male & IV drug user	8	7	7	6	8
Hemophilia/coagulation disorder	1	0	0	2	1
Heterosexual cases	1	12	3	2	4
Transfusion, blood/components	2	1	1	4	2
Undetermined	2	6	4	7	3
TOTAL	99	100	99	100	101

TABLE 3

Adult and Adolescent AIDS Cases, United States: Percentage in Each Racial/Ethnic Group by Transmission Category, January 19, 1987

Transmission category	White, not Hispanic	Black, not Hispanic	Hispanic	Other/ Unknown
Homosexual/bisexual male	74%	15%	10%	1%
IV drug user	18	51	30	1
Homosexual male & IV drug user	64	22	13	1
Hemophilia/coagulation disorder	85	6	7	2
Heterosexual cases	12	75	13	0
Transfusion, blood/components	77	15	6	2
Undetermined	35	43	20	2
TOTAL	60	25	14	1
For reference: U.S. population ≥ 15 years old*	81	11	6	2

* From Centers for Disease Control 1986b, table 2.

Table 2 also records that different racial groups vary in the way in which they have been exposed to the virus. Among blacks and Hispanics, heterosexual IV drug users comprise over one-third of the cases. Among blacks, an additional 12 percent of the cases were exposed to the virus by heterosexual activity with someone in another transmission category; among non-Haitian blacks, these heterosexual partners were primarily IV drug users.

Table 3 records that over 50 percent of the IV drug user cases have been black, and 30 percent have been Hispanic. Men who have engaged in both homosexual sex and IV drug use are more likely than non-IV drug using gay AIDS cases to be black. The heterosexual transmission category as reported is overwhelmingly black, which is partially a result of the somewhat controversial inclusion of a large number of Haitian blacks in this category and partially due to the relatively large proportion of IV drug users who are black. (In addition, there may be a tendency for black and Hispanic women to be more vulnerable than white women to heterosexual transmission through sex with bisexual men. A larger proportion of black and Hispanic gay males with AIDS report having sex with both men and women than do whites; the proportions are 30 percent for blacks, 20 percent for Hispanics, and 13 percent for whites [Rogers and Williams 1987]. It has been argued that minority gay men are more likely than white ones to put women at risk due to being "closet gays" who maintain sexual relations with women [S. Ports, Minority AIDS Task Force, National Council of Churches, personal communication, February 1987].)

Another way to look at the racial distribution of AIDS cases is to look at statistics for cumulative incidence (CI)—the number of cases in a subgroup per million population of that subgroup. This was done by Bakeman et al. (1988). They report CIs as of October 6, 1986, as being 593 for black men, 560 for Hispanic men, 224 for white men, 79 for black women, 58 for Hispanic women, and 6 for white women. The greater CIs for minorities are evident. Black and Hispanic men were about 2.5 times as likely to get AIDS as white men, black women 12 times as likely as white women; and Hispanic women 9 times as likely as white women. Bakeman et al. (1988) further report that minority CIs are higher than white CIs even if they remove the IV drug user cases (who, in their data, were 82 percent minority among men, and 77 percent minority among women). Thus, the

number of adult non-IV drug using homosexual and bisexual black
male AIDS cases per million black adult males was 289; for Hispanics
this rate was 297; but for whites it was only 186. This means that
non-IV drug using gay minority men were about 1.6 times as likely
to get AIDS as similar white men. Non-IV using black women were
8.0 times, and non-IV using Hispanic women 6.8 times, as likely
to get AIDS as non-IV using white women.

AIDS among Children. Data on pediatric cases by transmission
category and race are presented in table 4 (reprinted from Centers for
Disease Control 1986b). Of the 350 children under the age of 15
with AIDS, 58.3 percent were black and 22.0 percent were Hispanic.
The cumulative incidences of pediatric cases are that blacks were
overrepresented by a factor of 15 and Hispanics by a factor of 9.
Blacks were a majority of the cases in the largest transmission category—
children with IV drug using mothers. They also were a majority in
several of the smaller transmission categories: children whose mothers
had a bisexual sex partner; whose mother was infected with HIV but
had no identified risk factor; and those children with an undetermined
risk factor. Blacks and Hispanics comprised almost all of the 38 cases
of children with mothers who had an IV drug using sex partner, with
17 such cases in each group. Hispanics were also highly overrepresented
among pediatric AIDS cases with mothers who are IV drug users.
Whites were a majority in only two groups—those with hemophilia
or other clotting factor disorders, and blood transfusion recipients
(categories which have received a wildly disproportionate share of
media attention, considering that only 67, or 19 percent, of the 350
pediatric cases were in these transmission categories).

AIDS in New York City. Surveillance data for New York City as
of January 19, 1987, are presented in tables 5–8. New York City
reported 8,887 adult cases (30 percent of the national total). Of these,
the New York percentage of the national figures by race were 23
percent for whites, 38 percent for blacks, 50 percent for Hispanics,
and 24 percent for others/unknown. Since much of our other data is
based on studies in New York, and since (primarily minority) IV
drug use cases are concentrated in New York, these figures are worth
our consideration. They show a pattern that may become increasingly
common as the epidemic spreads among IV drug users in cities like
San Francisco, where HIV infection rates among IV drug users have

TABLE 4

Percentage Distribution of AIDS Cases among Children (age < 15 years), by Race/Ethnic Group, by Selected Transmission Category, as of September 8, 1986

Transmission category**	Total number	White*	Black*	Hispanic	Other*
U.S. population < 15 years	51,290,339	73.3%	14.6%	9.1%	3.0%
Children with hemophilia or other clotting factor disorder	18	66.7	27.8	5.6	0.0
Children whose mother:					
Was an IV drug user	162	8.6	63.0	28.4	0.0
Had a bisexual male sex partner	13	30.8	53.8	15.4	0.0
Had a male sex partner who was an IV drug user	38	10.5	44.7	44.7	0.0
Was infected with HIV but had no identified risk factor	11	9.1	81.8	9.1	0.0
Blood transfusion recipients	49	55.1	30.6	14.3	0.0
Undetermined risk factor	10	30.0	60.0	10.0	0.0
TOTAL***	350	19.4	58.3	22.0	0.3

* Non-Hispanic.
** Patients with more than one risk factor are shown only in the first applicable category listed.
*** The total includes 5 children whose mothers' only identified risk was a blood transfusion, one child whose mother's male sex partner had received a transfusion, and 43 children whose mothers were born in countries in which heterosexual transmission is believed to play a major role (virtually all of whom are black, non-Hispanic). The total excludes 2 children of unknown race/ethnic group.
Source: Centers for Disease Control 1986b, 665, with minor modifications.

TABLE 5

United States AIDS Cases by Transmission Category and Race, for New York City and Non-New York City, January 19, 1987

Transmission category	White, not Hispanic	Black, not Hispanic	Hispanic	Total*
Homosexual or bisexual male				
N.Y.C.	3,330	929	766	5,033
Not N.Y.C.	10,789	1,856	1,227	14,046
% N.Y.C.	23.6%	33.4%	38.4%	26.4%
IV drug user				
N.Y.C.	383	1,227	1,013	2,628
Not N.Y.C.	524	1,298	473	2,323
% N.Y.C.	42.2%	48.6%	68.2%	53.1%
Homosexual male & IV drug user				
N.Y.C.	183	157	121	462
Not N.Y.C.	1,273	345	166	1,798
% N.Y.C.	12.6%	31.3%	42.2%	20.4%
Hemophilia/coagulation disorder				
N.Y.C.	15	2	1	18
Not N.Y.C.	200	12	16	234
% N.Y.C.	7.0%	14.3%	5.9%	7.1%

TABLE 5—Continued

Transmission category	White, not Hispanic	Black, not Hispanic	Hispanic	Total*
Heterosexual cases**				
N.Y.C.	32	277	88	398
Not N.Y.C.	101	555	52	712
% N.Y.C.	24.1%	33.3%	62.9%	35.9%
Transfusion, blood/components				
N.Y.C.	49	14	4	68
Not N.Y.C.	370	70	26	476
% N.Y.C.	11.7%	16.7%	13.3%	12.5%
Undetermined, other				
N.Y.C.	46	113	73	280
Not N.Y.C.	275	280	113	638
% N.Y.C.	14.3%	28.8%	39.2%	30.5%
TOTAL				
N.Y.C.	4,038	2,719	2,066	8,887
Not N.Y.C.	13,532	4,416	2,073	20,227
% N.Y.C.	23.0%	38.1%	49.9%	30.5%

* Total includes persons of other races and of undetermined race.
** This category is composed of 521 persons (91 men, 430 women) who have had heterosexual contact with a person with AIDS or at risk for AIDS and 589 persons (474 men, 115 women) without other identified risks who were born in countries in which heterosexual transmission is believed to play a major role although precise means of transmission have not yet been fully defined. The latter set of persons is overwhelmingly Haitian.

TABLE 6

AIDS Cases: Risk by Race and Sex, New York City, January 19, 1987

Risk	Males				Females			
	White	Black	Hispanic	Other* Unknown	White	Black	Hispanic	Other* Unknown
Homo/bisexual	3,332	929	767	42	0	0	0	0
IV drug user	300	970	834	2	83	262	180	2
Homo/bisexual & IV drug user	181	148	114	1		9		
Persons from countries where risks are unclear	0	155	0	0	3	39	7	0
Sex partners of at risk group	1	1	1	0	31	82	87	1
Transfusion	29	6	2	1	20	8	2	0
Hemophiliac	14	1	1	0	1	1	0	0
No identified risk	8	15	17	3	4	14	4	0
Other	27	49	36	2	7	35	16	0
TOTAL	3,892	2,274	1,772	51	149	450	296	3

* Includes 34 Asians and 7 American Indians. Because of small numbers and concern for confidentiality, risk group information is not provided for them.

Source: New York City Department of Health 1987.

TABLE 7

AIDS Cases: Percentage in Each Racial/Ethnic Group by Risk and Sex, New York City, January 19, 1987*

Risk	Males				Females			
	White**	Black**	Hispanic	Total*** (3 races)	White**	Black**	Hispanic	Total*** (3 races)
Homo/bisexual	66%	18%	15%	99%	0%	0%	0%	0%
IV drug user	14	46	40	100	16	50	34	100
Homo/bisexual & IV drug user	41	33	26	100	—	—	—	—
Persons from countries where risks are unclear	0	100	0	100	0	100	0	100
Sex partners of at-risk group	—	—	—	—	15	41	43	99
Transfusion	76	16	5	97	67	27	7	101
Hemophiliac	—	—	—	—	—	—	—	—
No identified risk	19	35	40	94	—	—	—	—
Other	24	43	32	99	12	60	28	100
TOTAL	49	28	22	99	17	50	33	100

* Where a percentage would be calculated with a denominator less than 30, figures are not given.
** Non-Hispanic.
*** Percentage of total who are white, black, or Hispanic.

TABLE 8

AIDS Cases: Percentage in Each Risk Group, by Racial/Ethnic Group, by Sex, New York City, January 19, 1987*

	Males			Females		
Risk	White**	Black**	Hispanic	White**	Black**	Hispanic
Homo/bisexual	86%	41%	43%	0%	0%	0%
IV drug user	8	43	47	56	58	61
Homo/bisexual & IV drug user	5	7	6	2	2	2
Persons from countries where risks are unclear***	0	7	0	0	9	0
Sex partners of at-risk group	0	0	0	21	18	29
Transfusion	1	0	0	13	2	1
Hemophiliac	0	0	0	1	0	0
No identified risk	0	1	1	3	3	1
Other	1	2	2	5	8	5
TOTAL	101	101	99	101	100	99

* Where a percentage would be calculated with a denominator less than 30, figures are not given.
** Non-Hispanic.
*** All are Haitians.

recently begun to climb (R. Chaisson, University of California, San Francisco, personal communication, 1986; J. Watters, Haight-Ashbury Free Medical Clinics, personal communication, 1987).

The racial breakdown of total AIDS cases in New York City is 45 percent white, 31 percent black, 23 percent Hispanic, and 1 percent others (of whom 34 were Asian and 7 were native American) or unknown. This compares with 1980 U.S. census figures that give a New York City population distribution of 52 percent white, 24 percent black, 20 percent Hispanic, and 4 percent other. AIDS seems to have hit blacks and even Hispanics at a higher rate than whites. One way of expressing this is that the cumulative incidence of AIDS cases per million population is 1,100 for whites, 1,600 for blacks, and 1,500 for Hispanics. (Since AIDS case data are not given for other races, CIs cannot be estimated for them.) These different CIs should be interpreted with the realization not only that census data have been criticized for undercounting minorities, and that migration to New York may have been racially disproportionate since then, but also that AIDS surveillance reports may also be subject to racially imbalanced reporting or that whites may obtain medical care earlier.

Within the 2,628 IV drug use cases, 47 percent are black, 39 percent are Hispanic, and 15 percent are white. Although the exact racial distribution of the city's IV drug users is not known, our best estimate (based on admissions data, supplied by the New York State Division of Substance Abuse Services, of heroin users to drug treatment programs for 1980 and 1986) is about 38 percent for blacks, 38 percent for Hispanics, 23 percent for whites, and 2 percent for other races. It appears that blacks may be overrepresented, and whites underrepresented, among IV drug using AIDS cases in New York City.

As can be seen from the bottom row in table 7, the racial distribution of cases differs considerably by gender. Male cases are 49 percent white, which reflects the fact that 66 percent of the gay male cases occur among whites. Female cases are 50 percent black, a result of the greater relative weights of the IV drug user and heterosexual partner groups among female AIDS cases. From table 8, we can see that over 90 percent of New York City white male cases are gay, whereas for blacks and Hispanics about half the cases are not gay (mostly being IV drug users). For women, IV drug users comprise almost 60 percent of the cases in each racial group. Heterosexual partner cases are most prevalent among Hispanic women.

Racial distributions in New York AIDS cases have changed over time. Comparing the cases diagnosed prior to 1985 with those diagnosed in 1985, the percentage of white cases decreased from 52 percent of the total to 44 percent, blacks increased from 27 percent to 32 percent, and Hispanics increased from 21 percent to 24 percent (table 9). When we examine the ratios of 1985 cases to pre-1985 cases by race, we find that these ratios are .65 for whites, .90 for blacks, and .86 for Hispanics. This probably implies that the epidemic is further along the epidemic curve for whites than for minorities, and, thus, that the proportion of cases that is black and Hispanic will continue to increase. From table 10, we see that the percentages of cases among drug users and heterosexual partners increased, and those among gays decreased. Interestingly, the percentage of white cases who were gays

TABLE 9
Percentage of AIDS Cases of Each Transmission Category That Is in Each Racial Group, pre-1985 and 1985, New York City*

Risk	White, not Hispanic		Black, not Hispanic		Hispanic		Other/ don't know		Total
Homo/bisexual									
pre-1985	1,381	68.8%	359	17.9%	261	13.0%	7	0.3%	2,008
1985	915	64.8	256	18.1	230	16.3	12	0.8	1,413
IV drug user									
pre-1985	148	17.0	397	45.5	327	37.5	1	0.1	873
1985	104	13.3	382	48.7	296	37.8	2	0.3	784
Homo/bisexual & IV drug user									
pre-1985	56	32.6	59	34.3	56	32.6	1	0.6	172
1985	50	38.2	57	43.5	24	18.3	0	0.0	131
Heterosexual partner									
pre-1985	8	15.1	21	39.6	24	45.3	0	0.0	53
1985	8	13.3	27	45.0	25	41.7	0	0.0	60
Other									
pre-1985	123	61.2	50	24.9	25	12.4	3	1.5	201
1985	30	23.4	72	56.2	22	17.2	4	3.1	128

* Haitians who fall into a listed risk group are included as blacks. AIDS cases who give homosexual activity as a risk but whose drug use status is unknown are included as gays; and cases who have injected drugs but whose sexual orientation is unknown are included as IV drug users. There are only 167 of these cases in which either drug injection or sexual orientation is unknown before 1985, and 41 in 1985. The decline in these numbers of cases for whom only one of these categories is determined is a product of improved interviewing techniques.

TABLE 10
Percentage of Each Racial Group That Is in Each Transmission Category, pre-1985 and 1985, New York City*

	White, not Hispanic		Black, not Hispanic		Hispanic		Other/ don't know		Total	
Homo/bisexual										
pre-1985	1,381	80.5%	359	40.5%	261	37.7%	7	58.3%	2,008	60.7%
1985	915	82.7	256.	32.2	230	38.5	12	66.7	1,413	56.2
IV drug user										
pre-1985	148	8.6	397	44.8	327	47.2	1	8.3	873	26.4
1985	104	9.4	382	48.1	296	49.6	2	11.1	784	31.2
Homo/bisexual & IV drug user										
pre-1985	56	3.3	59	6.7	56	8.1	1	8.3	172	5.2
1985	50	4.5	57	7.2	24	4.0	0	0.0	131	5.2
Heterosexual partner										
pre-1985	8	0.5	21	2.4	24	3.5	0	0.0	53	1.6
1985	8	0.7	27	3.4	25	4.2	0	0.0	60	2.4
Other										
pre-1985	123	7.2	50	5.6	25	3.6	3	25.0	201	6.1
1985	30	2.7	72	9.1	22	3.7	4	22.2	128	5.1
TOTAL										
pre-1985	1,716		886		693		12		3,307	
1985	1,107		794		597		18		2,516	

* See note for table 9.

increased, while the percentage of blacks who were gays decreased considerably. From table 9, it appears that black IV drug using cases have been increasing more rapidly than white.

Survival after AIDS Diagnosis

In a disease in which most of the patients die within two years of diagnosis, one possible effect of race may be to create differences in survival times after diagnosis—whether due to differences in seeking medical care, differences in the medical treatment that is available, differences in preexisting health, genetic differences, or other reasons. The mean survival time for blacks after diagnosis is eight months, while that for whites is 18 to 24 months (Weston 1986). In New York City, of all persons who have been diagnosed as having AIDS as of March 1987, 38.4 percent of non-Haitian blacks, 41.1 percent of Hispanics, and 45.5 percent of whites are still alive (M.A. Chiasson, New York City Department of Health, personal communication, April 1987). The meaning and analysis of survival time in AIDS cases is complicated by the fact that post-diagnosis mortality rates are affected by the initial diagnosis of the patient (Kaposi's sarcoma or opportunistic infection), patient's risk group, date of diagnosis, age, and sex. Richard B. Rothenberg, Centers for Disease Control (personal communication, February 1987), has been conducting a detailed study of factors that affect survival time. He reports that patients who are first diagnosed as having AIDS due to their developing Kaposi's sarcoma (KS) have longer mean survival times than patients with opportunistic infections such as pneumocystis carinii pneumonia; IV drug users tend to die sooner after diagnosis than gays; and there is a cohort effect in that patients who developed AIDS later in the epidemic were likely to benefit from newly developed knowledge about how to treat KS and opportunistic infections and thus to survive longer. These relationships, however, are univariate ones, and they do not take into account the interrelations among the variables listed or the effects of other variables (such as prior health status). In his multivariate analyses, Rothenberg finds that blacks and Hispanics with AIDS survive for a shorter period than do whites even when initial diagnosis, date of diagnosis, risk group, and sex are controlled.

The Social Meaning of Race for Persons with AIDS

Although we have collected no data on this topic, it has been suggested that the experience of having AIDS may be quite different for whites than for minorities, and for members of different social classes. Such differences would parallel differences in many other aspects of life. Thus, Suki Ports (personal communication, February 1987) of the Minority Task Force on AIDS of the New York Council of Churches suggests that "for lower-income people, and most minorities, it's a different disease from what it is for whites with education, employment, and therefore links through the job. For middle-class whites, AIDS leads to losses in these, and thus to a fight for what is being lost. For minorities, they've never had these advantages, so they tend to accept their AIDS problems without fighting, they lack the same drive (from losing) to fight, and lack educational tools to fight."

Similarly, there may be racial differences in the probability and timing of seeking medical care, and as Richard B. Rothenberg (personal communication, February 1987) speculated, the differences in post-diagnosis survival times may be due in part to minority patients being slower to seek medical care. Such racial differences may be due to many minority persons with ARC and AIDS being IV drug users, or to their being unemployed or in jobs that lack adequate health insurance (New York City Commission on Human Rights 1986). In the future, racial differences may occur in the probability of getting antiviral medication for either of two reasons. First, IV drug users are a difficult group upon whom to conduct controlled experiments, so they are less likely to be included in experimental protocols. Second, when medications get approved for prescription use, their cost may be prohibitive for many black and Hispanic patients. Black and Hispanic people with AIDS may also be affected by the lower quantity and quality of medical facilities in minority communities.

Finally, many persons with AIDS have benefited from the network of service and support organizations that have developed, starting with the Gay Men's Health Crisis in New York City. These organizations have performed a vital and heroic role, but have been more effective in serving persons with ties to the primarily white gay subculture than in serving those blacks and Hispanics with weaker ties to this subculture. This is often true in spite of determined efforts to prevent it. Thus, to the extent that volunteers have primarily been white,

TABLE 11

Seroprevalence among Gay Men in Four Cities: Percentage Seropositive

Race	Baltimore/ Washington	Los Angeles	Pittsburgh/ tristate area	Chicago (MACS)	Chicago
Whites	30%	51%	20%	42%	38%
Blacks	47	52	35	60	49
Others	46	41	27	50	41

Source: For the first four columns, Kaslow and Ostrow 1988; for the fifth column, Chmiel et al. 1986.

there are often cultural or other problems in offering assistance to gay blacks or Hispanics. These difficulties have been magnified for minority drug users with AIDS or ARC.

Seroepidemiology

Seroprevalence in General Populations.　Since AIDS attack rates seem to vary by race and gender, we would expect exposure to HIV also to vary by race and gender. In one study, seroprevalence data were collected for 300,000 military recruits (Centers for Disease Control 1986a). For whites, they found a seroprevalence rate of 9/10,000; for blacks, 39/10,000; and for members of other racial groups, 2.6/10,000. Although this study has an extremely large number of subjects, it is clear that military recruits are not a representative sample of the population as a whole or even of their age groups. The researchers who conducted this study report that they have not determined the ways in which this sample differs from the population as a whole or from particular subgroups (D. Burke and R. Redfield, Walter Reed Army Institute of Research, personal communication to S.R. Friedman, October 21, 1986).

Blood donors also have been studied. Ward et al. (1986) report that in one city black potential donors were 5.6 times more likely to be seropositive than white potential donors. Blood donors, however, may also not be representative of the population as a whole.

Seroprevalence among Gays.　Seroprevalence studies have also occurred for gay men (table 11). Chmiel et al. (1986) found that, among a sample of Chicago gays, 49 percent of blacks, 38 percent of whites, and 41 percent of others were seropositive. The Multicenter AIDS Cohort Study (MACS) collected sera from gay men in the Baltimore/Washington area, Chicago, Los Angeles, and the Pittsburgh/tristate area (Kaslow and Ostrow 1988). Using the Dupont ELISA test, without confirmation by Western blot or other assay, MACS found that blacks were more likely to be seropositive than whites in all of these cities except Los Angeles. Samuel and Winkelstein (1987) report that in an area-probability sample of 1,034 single men aged 25 through 34 in a heavily gay neighborhood of San Francisco, 800 classified themselves as homosexual/bisexual; of these, 100 were of minority race. Seroprevalence rates were 48.7 percent (341/700) for non-Hispanic whites; 50 percent (22/44) for Hispanic whites; 66 percent (19/29) for non-Hispanic blacks; 30 percent (3/11) for Asians; and 40 percent (6/16) for other (3 Hispanic blacks, 2 native Americans, and 11 who stated "other"). The rate for non-Hispanic blacks was significantly greater than for non-Hispanic whites at the .05 level, and multivariate analysis confirmed that the white/black difference was not explained by differences in major risk factors (needle sharing, multiple sexual partners, or frequent receptive anal/genital contact with ejaculation). Summarizing these data on seroprevalence among gays by race, it appears likely that black gay men may be more likely to have been infected than whites. The small numbers of non-whites in all of these studies, and the difficulties in determining the sampling biases in convenience samples or the residential selectivity bias in the area sample, however, indicate that this conclusion must be interpreted as preliminary. Further research on this issue is clearly needed.

Seroprevalence among IV Drug Users. Tables 12 and 13 present data on HIV seropositivity by race and gender from two groups of drug-treatment patients we have studied. Antibody to HIV was measured by Abbott ELISA and Western blot. In the 1984 sample, Hispanic men were significantly more likely to be seropositive than white or black men. Three-fifths of both black and Hispanic women were seropositive, as compared to 44 percent of white women, but the small sample size meant that this difference was not statistically significant. In the smaller 1986 sample, almost three-fifths of black and Hispanic men were seropositive, as compared to 34 percent of white men (chi-squared $= 5.59$, $p < .025$). (The number of women subjects in this sample is too small to detect significant racial differences in seroprevalence among them.)

TABLE 12

Antibody to HIV, by Race and Gender, among Former Intravenous-drug-using Methadone and Drug Detoxification Patients in Manhattan, 1984: Percentage Positive

Race	Men	Women	Total
White	39%	44%	40%
N	71	18	89
Black	41%	60%	45%
N	75	20	95
Hispanic	58%	64%	60%
N	84	36	120
p (chi squared)	.031	.386	.012

Other studies have also been performed of seroprevalence by race among IV drug users. Most of them also find that minority users are more likely to be seropositive. In the Bronx, 42 percent of both Hispanic and black subjects were seropositive, as compared to 14 percent of whites. In logistic regression analyses of risk factors for seropositivity, race remained a significant predictor, but wide variation among clinics in different areas of the Bronx makes it likely that the observed racial relation to seropositivity is primarily a result of geo-

TABLE 13

Antibody to HIV, by Race and Gender, among Former Intravenous-drug-using Methadone Patients in Manhattan, 1986: Percentage Positive*

Race	Men	Women	Total
White	34%	41%	37%
N	38	22	60
Black	58%	57%	57%
N	33	14	47
Hispanic	59%	48%	54%
N	34	21	56
p (chi squared)	.061	.636	.066

* These patients were recruited in 1986 at a different drug treatment program from those attended by the subjects in table 12. The treatment programs are in the same area of Manhattan.

graphical clustering of the infection (Schoenbaum et al. 1986; P. Selwyn, Montefiore Medical Center/Albert Einstein College of Medicine, personal communication, 1987). Weiss (1986) reports that in New Jersey, black IV drug users, at 45 percent, were significantly more likely to be seropositive than whites (30 percent) or Hispanics (33 percent). In San Francisco, two studies have been conducted, with somewhat different results (Chaisson et al. 1986, 1987; Watters, Newmeyer, and Cheng 1986). Chaisson found a statistically significant difference by race: 6 percent for white subjects, and 14 percent for "black, Latino, and other" subjects. Analysis controlling for needle sharing (which was also related to seropositivity) showed that race remained a significant predictor of seropositivity. Watters, on the other hand, did not find significant racial differences: seropositivity rates were 9 percent for whites, 8 percent for blacks, 11 percent for Latinos, and 2 percent for others. Watters (personal communication, February 1987) reports that they have not determined why these two studies show different results.

Summary on Seroprevalence. The studies of HIV antibody seroprevalence give a picture similar to that given by AIDS case-surveillance data. Minorities are more likely to be seropositive than are whites. The evidence is quite strong that blacks are more likely to be seropositive than whites among IV drug users, gays, and the general population, although a few studies do find equal exposure rates. Data for Hispanics are scarce, but indicate that they are at least more likely to be seropositive among New York City IV drug users.

It has not been determined why these differences in infection rates exist. Some studies find that racial behavioral differences explain the racial seroprevalence differences in their samples; other studies find that racial seroprevalence differences remain after behavioral differences are accounted for. In those geographical areas and risk groups for which behavioral differences do not explain seroprevalence, this implies that there may be a higher risk of exposure to HIV per risky act. We would speculate that these higher risks may be a result of higher probabilities that one's sex or needle-sharing partner has been infected.

Susceptibility and Race: Preexisting Conditions and
Behaviors, and Individual Knowledge and Risk Reduction

Racial Differences in Health among Seronegative IV Drug Users

Black and Hispanic risk-group members may be more likely to be
in worse health conditions before exposure to HIV, and to have more
frequent infection by other agents, than white risk-group members.
On the other hand, among IV drug users, racial differences might
be submerged by their poor health conditions. We were able to
perform a limited and incomplete investigation of this question using
data from our 1984 and 1986 samples of patients in detoxification
and methadone treatment. We analyzed selected aspects of subjects'
medical history: whether they had had hepatitis, gonorrhea, syphilis,
herpes, pneumonia, tuberculosis, skin abscesses, night sweats of more
than four-weeks duration, diarrhea of more than one-week duration,
unexplained fever of more than four-weeks duration, or unexplained
weight loss of 10 percent of their body weight or more. In order to
avoid the effects of HIV infection, we restricted the analysis to seronegative subjects, and pooled the 1984 and 1986 data so that there
would be enough cases of each of these diseases or conditions to
analyze. The limited number of such cases made it impossible to
control for other variables (such as the duration of stay in their drug
treatment program, or age) that might also affect having had these
diseases or conditions. Only one of these eleven variables was significantly
related to race. Fifteen percent of seronegative whites reported having
had diarrhea of one or more weeks duration, as compared to 2 percent
of blacks and 7 percent of Hispanics (chi-square $= 8.6$, $p < .014$).

Thus, among the subjects studied and for the diseases and conditions
investigated, there is no evidence that black or Hispanic IV drug
users have been more subject to health problems than whites. We
urge against generalizing from this conclusion to other drug users,
and we suggest that further research about preexisting conditions may
be useful in understanding racial patterns of response to HIV infection.

Racial Differences in Behaviors That May Affect Viral Transmission

Given the higher rate of AIDS cases in minority communities, and the scattered evidence for higher rates of seropositivity among minorities, it is worth considering why these differences exist. Research has not yet answered this question; indeed, relatively little attention has been paid to it in the literature. Many studies of risk behavior and/or seroprevalence among gay males, for example, have used convenience samples recruited in gay bars, hospitals, or physicians' offices that have resulted in numbers of minority subjects that are too small to analyze (Karolynn Siegel, Memorial-Sloan-Kettering Cancer Center, personal communication, February 1987).

In this section of the article, we will review some evidence about racial differences in risk behavior and in behaviors that reduce risk, including data from our studies of New York City drug users.

IV Drug Use Behaviors That Risk Transmission. A number of studies have found that drug-injection frequency is associated with seropositivity in New York (Cohen et al. 1985; Marmor et al. 1987; Schoenbaum et al. 1986) and New Jersey (Weiss et al. 1985). In our studies based on a 1984 sample of 307 methadone and detoxification patients, we found that the single variable that best predicts seropositivity among IV drug users is drug-injection frequency (Cohen et al. 1985; Marmor et al. 1987). In these 1984 data, drug-injection frequency varies significantly by race. Mean monthly drug-injection frequencies for the two years prior to the interview were 136 for Hispanics, 76 for blacks, and 46 for whites ($F_{2, 304} = 19.23$, $p < .0001$; difference between Hispanics and whites significant by Duncan multiple-range test). In our smaller 1986 sample of methadone patients, racial differences in mean monthly drug-injection frequencies during 1985 and 1986 were consistent with those found in 1984, but did not reach statistical significance. Hispanics averaged 31 injections, blacks 19, and whites 15 ($F_{2, 180} = 2.02$, $p < .14$). Sample differences make it unwise to infer anything from the lower mean injection frequencies for the 1986 group as compared to the 1984 sample.

Our analysis of risk factors for seropositivity (Cohen et al. 1985; Marmor et al. 1987) indicated that the proportion of injections that one took in shooting galleries (clandestine commercial establishments whose "owners" rent space, syringes, and needles to IV drug users to use in shooting up) was a risk factor in addition to drug-injection frequency. Similar findings have been reported by later studies (Schoenbaum et al. 1986; R. Chaisson, University of California, San Francisco, personal communication, 1986). In the 1984 sample, the proportion of injections that took place in shooting galleries varies significantly by race. Hispanic subjects used shooting galleries 31 percent of the time, which was significantly more by the Duncan multiple-range test than the 18 percent for blacks or the 16 percent for whites ($F_{2, 284} = 8.18$; $p < .0004$).

On the other hand, in the smaller 1986 sample there was no racial difference in shooting gallery use. This may be because these respondents reported much lower levels of attendance at shooting galleries, since only 10 percent of their injections took place in these establishments.

We found one relationship in the 1986 data that indicates that white IV drug users may take certain risks more often than do nonwhites. In particular, whites are significantly more likely to inject with works which they had previously let others use: they did so 18 percent of the time, as compared to 7 percent for Hispanics, and 6 percent for blacks ($F_{2, 97} = 4.2$; $p < .02$).

Thus, among the IV drug users we studied in 1984, it appears that Hispanics were significantly more likely than whites or blacks to engage in two behaviors that have been tied to seropositivity: high drug-injection frequency and use of shooting galleries. Furthermore, although the data in the 1986 sample indicate similar racial variations in drug-injection frequency, they seem to show a somewhat different pattern of racial variation in specific injection practices.

Knowledge and Risk Reduction among IV Drug Users. In our 1986 study all subjects were asked about their deliberate attempts to reduce the risk of getting AIDS. Almost two-thirds (65 percent) report having made some behavioral change (in drug or sexual behavior, or both) in order to reduce their risk of getting AIDS. Relatively few of the subjects, 34 of 184 (18 percent), had attempted to reduce their sexual risk of infection by sexual transmission, and no racial differences in sexual risk reduction were discovered. A majority of the subjects (58 percent) had tried to reduce their drug-injection frequency or sharing works, or had tried to use new or clean needles more consistently. Seventy percent of blacks had done so, as compared to 57 percent of whites, and 49 percent of Hispanics (chi-squared $= 5.045$; df $= 2$; $p < .08$; if blacks are compared to whites and Hispanics, chi-squared

= 4.32; df = 1; $p < .05$). Blacks were significantly more likely, in particular, to report reductions in sharing works; 48 percent of blacks did so, as compared with 26 percent of whites and 23 percent of Hispanics (chi-squared = 9.4; df = 2; $p < .009$.)

One particularly revealing racial difference in knowledge was found among the drug users in the 1986 sample. Whites were significantly more likely than nonwhites to have heard of those techniques for cleaning works that are believed to kill HIV—i.e., bleach, hydrogen peroxide, alcohol, and boiling. Among those who had heard of at least one of these four techniques, whites were significantly more likely to have heard of bleach as a sterilizer. These differences suggest that scientific innovations concerning AIDS may diffuse more rapidly to white drug users than to black or Hispanic users.

In late 1986 the Street Studies Unit of the New York State Division of Substance Abuse Services interviewed 136 drug users in the streets of Brooklyn, the Bronx, and Queens. The interviewers were former drug users who conducted informal interviews about what respondents knew about AIDS and how they had tried to protect themselves. An attempt was made to keep the interview unobtrusive. Interviews were conducted in the form of informal street conversations, respondents were not informed that they were being interviewed, and data were not recorded at the scene of the interview but were instead written down after the interviewer left the scene. Thus, these data are an attempt to get information about IV drug users who are *not* in drug treatment in as natural a setting as possible; of course, street conversations are subject to biases of their own. In particular, it can be harder to ask neutral probes, and the memory of the interviewer may fail. Thus, these findings must be taken as minimal estimates of knowledge and behavior change. Finally, analysis of these data is still in the early stages, so the findings reported below must be regarded as preliminary.

With these caveats, the findings of the unobtrusive street survey are as follows. Of the 136 subjects, 21 were white, 63 black, and 52 Hispanic. When asked what they knew about how AIDS was transmitted, 60 percent of Hispanics, 73 percent of blacks, and 90 percent of whites mentioned IV-drug-related means of transmission (chi squared = 7.195; df = 2; $p < .03$). Knowledge about sexual transmission and reported attempts to reduce exposure by risk reduction involving drug use were reported less often by blacks and Hispanics than by whites, but neither of these relationships was statistically significant. Blacks were more likely to report sexual risk reduction (44 percent) than whites (14 percent) or Hispanics (23 percent) (chi squared = 9.47; df = 2; $p < .0088$).

In summary, the data on racial differences in knowledge and risk reduction among New York City IV drug users present a somewhat unclear picture (rather than simply a picture of minorities with less knowledge and higher risks). In spite of this, we would offer some tentative generalizations in the hope that they may stimulate further research. White IV drug users seem more likely to learn about scientific innovations—in this case, the use of bleach as a sterilizing agent for injection equipment. On the other hand, the social organization of black drug users may make them more likely to act upon information about risk reduction.

Gay Behaviors That Risk Transmission. In spite of the fact that many studies of gays and AIDS have used sampling techniques that have resulted in too few interviews with blacks or Hispanics to analyze racial differences in risk behavior, we know of two studies in which these differences could be studied. In the Chicago portion of the MACS study, 584 whites and 46 nonwhites were interviewed in the first wave of the project in 1984. There were no significant differences between these racial groups in terms of such risk behaviors as the number of sex partners in the preceding month, number of anonymous sex partners, or number of occasions in which the subject had anally receptive sex. White gays were significantly more likely to be involved in the gay community network and marginally ($p < .053$) more likely to report that their gay peers had norms which encouraged safer sex (Jill Joseph, University of Michigan, Ann Arbor, personal communication, March 16, 1987). Samuel and Winkelstein (1987) report no significant racial differences in risk behaviors among San Francisco gay men interviewed in their area probability sample; they do, however, report a trend for a higher percentage of white than of black subjects to have had ten or more sexual partners in the previous two years ($p < .1$).

Another data source gives another way to approach the issues of how gay sexual practices changed after AIDS became known and of racial differences in risk-reduction attempts. Rectal gonorrhea is a disease that is transmitted through anal sex and that develops more rapidly than AIDS. Thus, statistics on rectal gonorrhea reflect safer sex practices or reductions in homosexual sexual frequency fairly rapidly.

The San Francisco Department of Public Health Bureau of Communicable Disease Control (1986) studied changes in rectal gonorrhea from October 1984 through September 1986. They found that male rectal gonorrhea declined every month during this period, with an exponential rate of decline of 5.7 percent per month that did not vary by race. Since data for the period before October 1984 have not yet been computerized, they have been unable to study whether there were any racial differences in when the declines began (G. Bolan, Department of Public Health, San Francisco, personal communication, February 1987.)

Heterosexual Behaviors That Risk Transmission. Sexual abstinence and condom use are believed to reduce the risk of heterosexual transmission of HIV. Mosher and Bachrach (1986, percentages from table 8) studied these behaviors among 8,000 women in 1982, before AIDS became a matter of public knowledge. They found that both were rare among women aged 15 to 44 years, and that white women are more likely to avoid heterosexual transmission due to celibacy or to contraceptive use, but two caveats have to be made to this conclusion. First, these differences in protection are relatively small—27.1 percent of white women, 19.3 percent of black women, and 24.2 percent of Hispanic women report one of the forms of lessened probability of exposure. The black/white difference is largest, but is less than 8 percent. Second, there is a methodological problem in that Mosher and Bachrach used a hierarchical definition of "current contraceptive method" so that women who reported using sterilization, the pill, the IUD, or the diaphragm as well as condoms would not be included as condom users. The most important implication, however, is that the pre-AIDS sexual practices of American heterosexual women provided little protection against HIV transmission if one's partner was infectious.

In our 1986 sample of drug users, we examined (for males and females separately, and separately for sexual activity with members of the same and the opposite gender, since the biological consequences may vary by gender) the frequency of sexual intercourse, the number of sexual partners, the number of regular sexual partners, the number of regular sexual partners who are IV drug users, and the number of regular sexual partners who are not IV drug users. We also examined data on prostitution and on sexual intercourse with persons who then or later were diagnosed as having AIDS. There were no significant racial differences in any of these behaviors.

Racial Variation in AIDS-related Knowledge, Beliefs, and Protective Behavior among the General Public

The beliefs that people hold about AIDS are extremely important. They affect what individuals do to protect themselves against it, and they can affect what groups do as well. Differences in beliefs among races can affect the ways in which they respond on both the individual and collective levels. Inasmuch as there is neither a vaccine to prevent HIV infection nor a treatment for it, and inasmuch as individual and group self-protection is the major way in which we can influence the course of the epidemic, racial differences in beliefs can lead to racial differences in the response to and development of AIDS.

As awareness has increased of the racial differences in AIDS incidence rates, concern has been expressed that minorities may be less able to protect themselves than whites because of the ways in which the epidemic is depicted in the media or because of lower educational levels (Nickens 1986). The New York City Commission on Human Rights (1986), for example, has suggested that "since many heterosexual minorities do not realize they are at risk for AIDS, they are not greatly affected by efforts to educate the public about modes of AIDS transmission. The little information that does arrive in the daily media implies that one is safe if one is not a white gay male or intravenous drug user." Since the data on AIDS incidence and seroprevalence indicate that minorities are probably at greater risk of exposure to HIV than are whites, any such failure to understand the epidemic and the ways in which one can protect oneself could lead to tragedy.

Not much is known, however, about racial variations in AIDS knowledge, beliefs, or protective behaviors among the general public. Although the generally higher educational levels of whites certainly lead to concern that blacks and Hispanics may learn about AIDS belatedly, it is neither good science nor good public health policy simply to assume that such a racial difference exists. After all, there are other sources of knowledge besides formal ones, and minorities have often benefited from these in the past. Thus, it is worth investigating what has been determined about racial differences in knowledge and beliefs.

One source of such information is opinion polls. One poll, conducted for *Newsday* in January 1987, found relatively little racial variation in knowledge, although it did find that Hispanic New Yorkers were more likely to believe that AIDS could be transmitted by dirty toilet seats (Holmberg 1987). Bausell et al. (1986) report on a national telephone poll of 1,256 adults aged 18 and over that seems to challenge the view that minorities are less aware of AIDS and, therefore, less likely to protect themselves. They found that 41 percent of the total sample reported having taken special steps or precautions to avoid AIDS. Only 37 percent of whites (calculated by the authors of this article from tables in Bausell et al. 1986), as compared to approximately 60 percent of blacks and Hispanics, had tried to protect themselves. The article did not, unfortunately, indicate the nature of these protective steps, so we do not know whether there are racial differences in the efficacy of attempted risk reduction. They also report that blacks and Hispanics were more likely than whites to support government spending "as much money as it takes to find a cure or vaccine," and strongly to support government restrictions of gay behavior in gay bath houses and bars until AIDS is under control.

The Illinois Department of Public Health sponsored a January 1987 telephone survey of 800 Illinois adults (Linda Haase, Illinois Department of Health, personal communication, February 1987). Of the respondents, 79 percent were white, 14 percent black, and 6 percent Hispanic or other. Hispanics were more likely to have a personal fear of AIDS: 59 percent of them said they were afraid they might get it, as opposed to about one-sixth of blacks and of whites; and 41 percent of Hispanics, as opposed to about one-third each of blacks and whites, said they were afraid someone they knew personally would get AIDS. When asked whether AIDS can be gotten by using a needle, all Hispanics, 97 percent of whites, but only 90 percent of blacks responded affirmatively. All the Hispanics, 95 percent of whites, and 91 percent of blacks said that unprotected sex with a person who has the AIDS virus can cause AIDS. A number of questions were asked to determine false beliefs about transmission; by and large, Hispanics tended to be most likely to have such erroneous beliefs. Nonwhite Illinois respondents were more likely than whites to say that government has "a lot" of responsibility for AIDS care, research, and education. Blacks and Hispanics also believe that government should spend more on AIDS treatment. When it comes to government spending for AIDS research and for AIDS education, on the other hand, although blacks remained most supportive, Hispanics were less so than whites.

In summary, the Illinois data indicate that Hispanics there accept more untruths about AIDS, and that Hispanics have more concern about AIDS—but also that all Hispanics interviewed recognize the possibility of sexual and intravenous transmission. Indeed, the over-whelming majority of all races respond correctly when asked whether sex or needles can transmit AIDS, although approximately 10 percent of blacks reply "no" on each of these questions. The form of the questions, however, leaves it open whether such a large proportion have enough of an awareness of these risks for it to cross their minds when they have the opportunity to take drugs or have sex. The Illinois data also indicate substantial minority support for government action against AIDS. This support may imply that fears expressed by some AIDS activists about minority distaste for AIDS prevention programs may underestimate what can be done.

DiClemente and Boyer (1987) discuss a May 1985 survey of San Francisco public high school students' knowledge, attitudes, and beliefs about AIDS. Adolescents are sometimes viewed as particularly at risk of HIV infection due to the sexual and drug experimentation many youths engage in. San Francisco youths, with a major and well-publicized AIDS epidemic among gays, and a high gay seroprevalence rate (49 percent, according to Samuel and Winkelstein 1987), would be expected both to be aware of AIDS as a sexually transmitted disease and to be at risk for HIV sexual infection. Given the fact that only 33 cases of AIDS had been reported among heterosexual IV drug users as of the end of 1986, and that estimates of seroprevalence among IV drug users in the city were between 9 percent and 16 percent in a sample tested in 1985 and 1986 (Watters, Newmeyer, and Cheng 1986), we might expect considerably less knowledge about intravenous transmission among these youth.

The findings from the survey are somewhat encouraging about the extent of AIDS-related knowledge among high school students, and present a mixed picture of racial variations in this knowledge. Almost all of the subjects knew that AIDS could be transmitted by having sex with someone with AIDS or by sharing needles; if we look at the racial breakdowns, we find that 5 percent of the white as compared with only 1 percent of the black and 3 percent of the Hispanic students did *not* know about sexual transmission, and that 15 percent of the whites, 8 percent of the blacks, and 17 percent of the Hispanics were unaware of the risks of sharing works. These data indicate that black high school students may be less likely to be ignorant of these basic transmission facts (unfortunately, neither here nor elsewhere do the authors report either statistical significance data or sufficient data to let us calculate them). On the other hand, 72 percent of the whites know that condoms lower the risk of sexual transmission, as compared to 60 percent of the blacks and 58 percent of the Hispanics.

DiClemente and Boyer also report on the misconceptions these adolescents hold. Black and Hispanic students are approximately twice as likely as whites to believe that AIDS can be contracted by touching, kissing, or being near someone with AIDS, and about 20 percent of black and Hispanic as compared with 9 percent of white students, believe that "all gay men have AIDS."

Collective Responses to AIDS

No systematic studies have been conducted about how different groups, institutions, communities, and races have responded to the AIDS epidemic. As a result, this section of the article is based upon impressionistic data, personal experience, and interviews with persons involved in AIDS-related projects. We raise more questions than we answer here, but do so in part with the hope that we will provoke others to conduct the research needed to analyze these issues more adequately.

Although the data presented above about the impact of AIDS show that the epidemic has affected thousands of blacks and Hispanics, there has been little organized black or Hispanic response as of this writing. The major black and Hispanic institutions have done little or nothing, and there has been no grass-roots flowering of new AIDS-related organizations in minority communities. In the last year or two, indeed, something new has occurred, such as the New York Council of Churches' Minority AIDS Task Force; the Minority AIDS Project in Los Angeles; the Kupuna Network in Chicago; and the Third World AIDS Advisory Task Force, Black Coalition on AIDS, and Latino Coalition on AIDS/SIDA Education and Action in San Francisco. In addition, the Southern Christian Leadership Conference has begun to get involved. These efforts are welcome, but they are, as yet, totally inadequate as compared to the need for minority mobilization around AIDS.

Why has there been such a limited response? It should be noted that black and Hispanic organizations have few resources, so it is hard to mount new campaigns to deal with a new disease—particularly since many of the strongest minority organizations deal with issues of racism that seem far removed from AIDS. This explanation, however, is far from the whole story. Two additional factors seem to us to be of extreme importance. First, the epidemic has a public image as a white gay disease. As such, it does not seem to most blacks or Hispanics to be an issue for their special attention and mobilization. (Here, we should be careful not to misconstrue this lack of particular concern as heartlessness; as noted in our discussion of public opinion surveys, black and, to a lesser extent, Hispanic respondents are more likely than white to support government spending on AIDS research, education, and treatment.) Second, there are deep fissures in minority populations and leaderships about how to deal with the homosexuality and IV drug use aspects of AIDS. Overt homosexuality became somewhat more accepted among urban whites as a result of the gay activism of the last generation. Among blacks and Hispanics, gay activism was much more muted, and minority cultures remain homophobic (C. Harris and G. Nene, personal communication, Montefiore Medical Center, March 1986; Harris 1986). Thus, to many black and Hispanic persons, raising the idea of helping people with AIDS seems to be giving support to sexual behaviors they cannot accept. This can lead to phenomena such as the following example given by Suki Ports (personal communication, February 1987): "Sometimes minority churches are reticent to be public on AIDS—as in being open about AIDS as the cause of death at a funeral—because the churches are poor. They might need the money to get their boiler fixed, so they can't afford to lose economic support from the congregation. It's safer to talk about South Africa than AIDS in these churches."

The disagreements are even stronger in relation to IV drug use. Minority communities bear a disproportionate burden of crime by drug users seeking money for drugs, and a disproportionate loss of access to neighborhood facilities that are taken over by drug users. Thus, many blacks and Hispanics are unfriendly to drug users or to any proposals that seem to offer aid to drug users. One indicator of this attitude is a poster that was plastered on many lamp posts in Harlem in 1986. It says: "When will all the junkies die so the rest of us can go on living?"; on many occasions, we have seen approving graffiti added to these posters. This attitude has taken a more visible form in some discussions of the appropriate policy to take toward AIDS among IV drug users. One proposal that has been raised— including by some authors of this article—is that experiments should be conducted about making sterile works available to IV drug users so they will not face legal or economic pressure to share works. Several black men in responsible positions in the New York area—including Benjamin Ward, the Police Commissioner, and James Curtis, head of Psychiatry at Harlem Hospital—have opposed this proposal as either not being effective (because IV drug users will not change their behaviors) or as being likely to increase IV drug use. It has also been opposed as being racist, as being directed against minorities, since the proposal ignores the effects of increased IV drug use on minority communities and on the minority individuals who may become IV drug users as a result of the greater availability of works. On the other hand, other blacks in responsible positions have supported the proposal. Thus, Beny Primm, Director of the Addiction Research and Treatment Center (and one of the authors of this article), has argued that "you may call people racist now if they adopt this policy; but if they do not do it, in five years you will accuse them of racist genocide." The point here is not to discuss the merits of the proposal, but rather to show that the disagreements can paralyze action.

One final collective response should be mentioned. It involves organization among drug users—a group that is important for this article because of its high proportion of blacks and Hispanics and because IV drug users are the major source of in utero transmission of HIV and of transmission to heterosexual partners. Two white ex-drug users who worked for the New York State Division of Substance Abuse Services initiated an organization to deal with AIDS among IV drug users, with gay AIDS groups as an underlying model. Since then, this group, called ADAPT, has been quite successful. It has scores of active members; engages in street education of drug users and their sexual partners; negotiates with shooting gallery owners to have sterile works, bleach, and other materials useful for relatively safe injection at hand; and assists AIDS patients in the New York jail at Rikers Island. ADAPT went through a number of leadership changes in its early days. Currently, its president is a Hispanic woman, and its leading members are composed of all races. In all of its intervention efforts, it is careful to develop an understanding of the implications of racial differences, and of cultural differences among persons of the same race, for what it should do. (For additional discussion of collective self-organization among drug users, see Friedman et al. 1987.)

Conclusions and Recommendations

Findings: A Brief Recapitulation

Blacks and Hispanics are more likely than whites to get AIDS. This is true among gays, among IV drug users, among heterosexual partners, and among children.

Although the findings on risk behaviors and risk reduction are not conclusive, there is considerable evidence that blacks have been at least as likely as whites to attempt to reduce their risk. In particular, in spite of all the difficulties they face, many IV drug users have cut back on behaviors that put them and others at risk. As has been argued elsewhere, however, the demands of addiction and the social relationships that exist among IV drug users make continuous, complete risk avoidance extremely difficult; and deliberate attempts by drug users and exdrug users to organize themselves to reduce their risks are both possible and essential (Friedman et al. 1987; Friedman, Des Jarlais, and Goldsmith 1988).

Recommendations

Target Education at Minority Groups. One implication of the heavy impact of AIDS on minorities is that education campaigns should be conducted to build awareness of this fact. This will be a difficult and potentially dangerous process, and one that will require efforts by leaders and researchers of all races. If the data are presented only by white spokespersons, many blacks and Hispanics will reject them as just another white attempt to blame minorities for the nation's troubles. If white spokespersons do not get involved, this could lead to charges that minority leaders are just engaging in special pleading and to minority criticisms of whites as not caring about AIDS among other races. In addition, there is a serious risk that whites will come to see blacks and Hispanics as AIDS carriers. This would further burden minority individuals seeking jobs, promotions, or housing. Indeed, given recent racial tension and incidents of racial violence, of AIDS-related harassment, and of incidents of violence against gays, it is possible that stigmatization of minorities as AIDS carriers might lead to physical attacks against them. In spite of these risks, however, public awareness of the minority dimension to AIDS is needed so that support for the other recommendations in this article will be forthcoming from persons and policy makers of all races.

A related dimension of the health education campaign concerns the need for education about safer sex. There appears to be a relative lack of knowledge about sexual transmission and safer sex among IV drug users (many of whom are black or Hispanic). Culturally sensitive education about these issues will be needed (Worth and Rodriguez 1987). (It is possible that the wide public education campaign about heterosexual transmission and condoms that is getting under way as this is being written in early 1987 may lead to greater awareness and sexual risk reduction among IV drug users and/or among the sexual partners of IV drug users and bisexual men. It should be remembered that discussion in the general media was sufficient to bring about considerable knowledge about AIDS among IV drug users long before any focused efforts to educate them about AIDS took place [Friedman, Des Jarlais, and Sotheran 1986; Selwyn et al. 1985].)

Strengthen and Increase the Medical Care Available to Minorities. In many parts of the country, black and Hispanic communities have inadequate medical resources available to them. The AIDS epidemic mandates that adequate resources be provided. Furthermore, hospitals that care for minority patients with HIV infections need to have staff who are capable of relating to the cultures of these patients. This is particularly obvious in the case of teaching ways to avoid transmitting HIV to other people, which involves discussions of sexual practices that can be hindered either by cultural insensitivity (or ignorance) on the part of medical personnel or by feelings of racially or professionally induced deference on the part of the patient.

Further Research Is Needed. There is need for more research about race and AIDS. This article is an effort to provoke such research, and the process of writing it has shown the authors how much is unknown. We need better information about racial variations in many aspects of the epidemic: HIV seroprevalence; survival time after diagnosis; AIDS-related knowledge and risk-reduction among gays, IV drug users, and heterosexuals; medical, public health, and social service responses, including access to experimental trials of medications; organization by risk groups in response to the epidemic; and barriers to effective responses by individuals and collectivities.

Encourage Minority Community Reach-out and Support Groups. Efforts to combat AIDS have been greatly helped by gay organizations that were established to meet the epidemic. These groups have offered assistance to the sick, conducted education campaigns, debated proposed changes in gay lifestyles and values (and thus made individual risk reduction more socially acceptable to other gays), and monitored AIDS research and AIDS policy to make sure that they have taken adequate account of the realities and needs of gay life. We believe that community efforts by blacks and Hispanics can help their communities to deal with this epidemic, too. AIDS makes it necessary to reduce any stigma that prevents homosexual or bisexual individuals from making their sexual orientation public so that they and others can engage in sexual risk reduction; similarly, it means that condom use must be seen as a medically necessary form of self-protection. In many parts of the black and Hispanic communities, such changes will not be easy. Sunny Rumsey, who has conducted many AIDS education sessions in minority communities for the New York City Health Department, argues that many minority cultures have tremendous resistance to homosexuality, so gays remain in the closet and many gay men get married, or have sex with women who do not know they are gay (presentation at an ADAPT meeting, March 5, 1987). AIDS-related organizations can help raise these issues and can help develop ways in which gays can come out of the closet safely. Their efforts, of course, will be helped immeasurably to the extent to which minority churches and other groups support them.

Similarly, AIDS-oriented black and Hispanic groups can reach out to IV drug users and help them in their efforts to reduce their risks. In most cases, this will require community groups to adopt a non-judgmental style. The point will not, in most cases, be to reproach drug users for immorality or even with their self-destructiveness, but rather to develop ways to help them minimize their risk of AIDS. In some instances, drug users will want help in stopping drug use, but in many others they will seek help only for preventing injection, or for discontinuing the sharing of works, or for learning how to sterilize works more effectively and consistently. Minority drug users will be more likely to accept education and assistance from supportive local groups than from white-dominated institutions.

Cooperate with and Support Drug Users' Own Reach-out and Support Efforts. Beyond this, minority community groups need to cooperate with drug users' and ex-drug users' own efforts to organize to deal with AIDS. In New York, as mentioned above, ex-drug users and others (including some current users) have formed ADAPT to reach out to IV drug users and others about AIDS. The formation of such organizations should be encouraged, and minority community groups can help them by making office space or other facilities available.

Aid by Government and Private Institutions. Finally, government and private institutions should offer financial and other assistance to black and Hispanic groups that try to deal with AIDS. Economic realities dictate that minority organizations often cannot get adequate funding through minority donations, so this outside support is extremely important. Given the cultural differences between whites, blacks, and Hispanics, and the long history of white or official actions that have hurt minorities, it will be important for assistance to be offered without putting conditions on their use that are derived from official or white conceptions of morality or proper language. Among many minority audiences, for instance, street language is the most appropriate way to get messages across; in others, discussion about sex must be much more guarded (at least to begin with) than for middle-class white audiences.

References

Bakeman, R., J.R. Lumb, E. McCray, R.E. Jackson, and P.N. Whitley. 1988. The Incidence of AIDS among Blacks and Hispanics. *Journal of the National Medical Association.* (Forthcoming.)

Bakeman, R., J.R. Lumb, and W.S. Smith. 1986. AIDS Statistics and the Risk for Minorities. *AIDS Research* 2(3):249–52.

Bausell, R.B., S. Damrosch, P. Parks, and K. Soeken. 1986. Public Perceptions Regarding the AIDS Epidemic: Selected Results from a National Poll. *AIDS Research* 2(3):253–58.

Centers for Disease Control. 1986a. Human T-lymphotropic Virus Type III/Lymphadenopathy-associated Virus Antibody Prevalence in U.S. Military Recruit Applicants. *Mortality Morbidity Weekly Reports* 35:421–24.

———. 1986b. Acquired Immunodeficiency Syndrome (AIDS) among Blacks and Hispanics—United States. *Mortality Morbidity Weekly Reports* 35:655–66.

Chaisson, R., A. Moss, R. Onishi, et al. 1987. Human Immuno-deficiency Virus Infection in Heterosexual Intravenous Drug Users in San Francisco. *American Journal of Public Health* (77):169–72.

Chaisson, R., R. Onishi, A. Moss, et al. 1986. Risk of HTLV-III/LAV Infection in Heterosexual Intravenous (IV) Drug Abusers (IVDAs) in San Francisco (SF). Paper presented at the International Conference on AIDS, Paris, June.

Chmiel, J., R. Detels, M. van Raden, R. Brookmeyer, L. Kingsley, and R. Kaslow. 1986. Prevention of LAV/HTLV-III Infection through Modification of Sexual Practices. Paper presented at the International Conference on AIDS, Paris, June 23–25.

Cohen, H., M. Marmor, D.C. Des Jarlais, T. Spira, S.R. Friedman, and S. Yancovitz. 1985. Risk Factors for HTLV-III/LAV Sero-positivity among Intravenous Drug Users. Paper presented at the International Conference on the Acquired Immune Deficiency Syndrome (AIDS), Atlanta, April 14–17.

Des Jarlais, D.C., S.R. Friedman, and W. Hopkins. 1985. Risk Reduction for the Acquired Immunodeficiency Syndrome among Intravenous Drug Users. *Annals of Internal Medicine* 103:755–59.

DiClemente, R.J., and C.B. Boyer. 1987. Ethnic and Racial Mis-conceptions about AIDS. *Focus: A Review of AIDS Research* 2(3):3.

Friedman, S.R., D.C. Des Jarlais, and D.S. Goldsmith. 1988. An Overview of Current AIDS Prevention Efforts Aimed at Intravenous Drug Users. *Journal of Drug Issues.* (Forthcoming.)

Friedman, S.R., D.C. Des Jarlais, and J.L. Sotheran. 1986. AIDS Health Education for Intravenous Drug Users. *Health Education Quarterly* 13(4):383–93.

Friedman, S.R., D.C. Des Jarlais, J.L. Sotheran, J. Garber, H. Cohen, and D. Smith. 1987. AIDS and Self-organization among Intravenous Drug Users. *International Journal of the Addictions* 22:201–20

Harris, C.G. 1986. NCBLG's National Conference to Address AIDS among Blacks. *Black/Out* 1(1):4.

Holmberg, D. 1987. Poll: 28% Say Keep AIDS Kids at Home. *Newsday.* February 3.

Institute of Medicine. 1986. *Confronting AIDS: Directions for Public Health, Health Care, and Research.* Washington: National Academy Press.

Kaslow, R.A., and D.G. Ostrow. 1988. The Multicenter AIDS Cohort Study: Rationale, Organization and Selected Characteristics of the Participants. *American Journal of Epidemiology.* (Forthcoming.)

Marmor, M., D.C. Des Jarlais, H. Cohen, S.R. Friedman, S. Beatrice, N. Dubin, W. El-Sadr, D. Mildvan, S. Yancovitz, U. Mathur, and R. Holzman. 1987. Risk Factors for Infection with Human Immunodeficiency Virus among Intravenous Drug Abusers in New York City. *AIDS: An International Bimonthly* 1:39–44.

Mosher, W.D., and C.A. Bachrach. 1986. *Contraceptive Use: United States 1982.* Washington: United States Public Health Service.

New York City Commission on Human Rights. 1986. AIDS and People of Color: The Discriminatory Impact. Report of the AIDS Discrimination Unit of the New York City Commission on Human Rights. November 13. (Unpublished.)

New York City Department of Health. 1987. AIDS Surveillance Update January 28, 1987: Preliminary Data. (Unpublished.)

Nickens, N. 1986. National Minority AIDS Council Report on AIDS and Ethnic Minorities. (Unpublished.)

Rogers, M.F., and W.W. Williams. 1987. AIDS in Blacks and Hispanics: Implications for Prevention. *Issues in Science and Technology* (Spring): 89–94.

Samuel, M., and W. Winkelstein. 1987. Prevalence of Human Immunodeficiency Virus Infection in Ethnic Minority Homosexual/Bisexual Men. *Journal of the American Medical Association* 257:1901–2.

San Francisco Department of Public Health Bureau of Communicable Disease Control. 1986. Rectal Gonorrhea in San Francisco, October 1984–September 1986. *San Francisco Epidemiologic Bulletin* 2(12): 1–3.

Schoenbaum, E.E., P.A. Selwyn, R.S. Klein, M.F. Rogers, K. Freeman, and G.H. Friedland. 1986. Prevalence of and Risk Factors Associated with HTLV-III/LAV Antibodies among Intravenous Drug Abusers in a Methadone Program in New York City. Paper presented at the International Conference on AIDS, Paris, June 23–25.

Selwyn, P.A., C.P. Cox, C. Feiner, C. Lipschutz, and R. Cohen. 1985. Knowledge about AIDS and High-risk Behavior among Intravenous Drug Abusers in New York City. Paper presented at the annual meeting of the American Public Health Association, Washington, November 18.

Stoneburner, R., P. Guigli, and A. Kristal. 1986. Increasing Mortality in Intravenous Drug Users in New York City and Its Relationship to the AIDS Epidemic: Is There an Unrecognized Spectrum of HTLV-III/LAV-related Disease? Paper presented at the International Conference on AIDS, Paris, June 23–25.

Ward, J.W., A.J. Grindon, P.M. Feorino, C.A. Schable, and J.R. Allen. 1986. Epidemiologic Evaluation of Blood Donors Positive on the Anti-HTLV-III Enzyme Immunoassay (EIA). Paper presented at the International Conference on AIDS, Paris, June 23–25.

Watters, J.K., J.A. Newmeyer, and Y-T. Cheng. 1986. Human Immunodeficiency Virus Infection and Risk Factors among Intravenous Drug Users in San Francisco. Paper presented at the American Public Health Association Conference, Las Vegas, October.

Weiss, S.H. 1986. Rates of Seropositivity among I.V. Drug Abusers. Paper presented at a conference on AIDS in the Drug Abuse Community and Heterosexual Transmission, Newark, March 31.

Weiss, S.H., H.M. Ginzburg, J.J. Goedert et al. 1985. Risk for HTLV-III Exposure and AIDS among Parenteral Drug Abusers in New Jersey. Paper presented at the International Conference on the Acquired Immune Deficiency Syndrome (AIDS), Atlanta, April.

Weston, G. 1986. AIDS in the Black Community. *Black/Out* 1(2):13–15.

Wilkinson, D.Y., and G. King. 1987. Conceptual and Methodological Issues in the Use of Race as a Variable: Policy Implications. *Milbank Quarterly* 65 (Suppl. 1):56–71.

Worth, D., and R. Rodriguez. 1987. Latina Women and AIDS. *SIECUS Report* (January-February):5–7.

Race in the Health
of America

S. M. MILLER

A T THE BEGINNING OF THIS CENTURY W.E.B. DuBois prophetically declared that "the problem of the twentieth century is the problem of the color line—the relation of the darker to the lighter races of men in Asia and Africa, in America and the islands of the sea" (DuBois 1961 [1903], 23). Much has happened since DuBois first published his stirring, brilliant essays but the color line continues to be a disturbing force in the United States as well as in South Africa. Certainly, the issue of race is different today in America from what it is in South Africa, but progress in the United States has not erased racial divisiveness.

What to do—if anything—becomes the uncertain next question after reading the articles on health in these volumes, which document the heart-rending lives of many blacks as they relate to poverty, deprivation, and social exclusion. This article provides a review of some of these findings on race, economic and social conditions, and health, discusses interpretations of continuing black and white differences, and concludes by offering ways of thinking about and acting on policy issues that have a bearing on these issues.

Patterns

Health cannot be understood simply as a biological phenomenon. Consequently, the health of black America is first discussed in terms of economic and social conditions and racial attitudes, and, then, in terms of the differential data between blacks and whites.

Economic Conditions

Poverty, as it is now understood in the United States, is defined by a simple measurement: a poverty line is determined by 30-year-old food expenditure data; those with incomes below that line are officially designated as poor. The result is that the poor are probably worse off relative to the rest of society today than they were in 1960.

Racial inequality is measured by comparing blacks and whites on a variety of conditions. Some view the last 20 years as a movement toward a "melting pot" that has narrowed economic and social differences between the races, so that blacks are now experiencing the pattern of various ethnic groups who began as poor immigrants and achieved sizable economic gains over time. In this view, race is becoming less important; class-linked factors like schooling are pointed to to explain income differences among blacks. Others see increasing "polarization"; for them, the differences between blacks and whites are widening rather than declining. Farley sees both of these perspectives as misleading (Farley 1987). My own view is that evolving and revolving sets of relationships form "jagged changes," with some reductions in inequalities, small changes, and some widening inequalities all occurring at the same time.

Poverty and unemployment are two economic areas in which wide racial differences are disturbingly apparent. The white poverty rate in 1986 was 11 percent while the black rate was 31 percent. Between 1985 and 1986, the poverty rate declined slightly for both blacks and whites but was higher than it was in 1978. The percentage of the black population below the poverty line was higher in 1986 than in 1969. The most dismal statistic is that 45.6 percent of black children were living in households with incomes below the poverty line in 1986; this compares with a figure of 17.7 percent for white children (Pear 1987). A broader measure of the poor is the near-poverty line, which refers to all those whose household incomes are below 125 percent of the poverty line; in 1984, more than two-fifths of blacks lived below this standard compared to somewhat more than one of six whites (U.S. Bureau of the Census 1985, 458). While black and white rates are closer than they were in 1959, the percentage of blacks living in poverty or near poverty today does not support a melting-pot interpretation.

The median family income of black households is a smaller percentage of white household income today than it was in 1969, 1974, or 1979. The continuing difference is partially due to the growth of single-parent households among blacks but, controlling for this factor, black household incomes are still only 80 percent of those of whites (Farley 1987).

An illustration of the improvement in the black economic picture accompanied at the same time by widening racial inequalities is provided by data on the percentage of blacks and whites in the top income groups (above $35,000 in constant dollars) in 1984 compared to 1967. In 1967, 20.1 percent of whites and 6.6 percent of blacks were in this high-income category, a difference of 13.5 percentage points; in 1984, 31.7 percent of whites and 13.6 percent of blacks were receiving high incomes. Blacks had definitely improved their chances of moving into higher income positions but the gap in percentage points between blacks and whites was now 18.1 percent (U.S. Bureau of the Census 1985, 445). In addition, a higher percentage of high-income black households had two earners and, of course, high black poverty rates continued despite the growth of a sizable number of better-off blacks.

The greatest relative gain for blacks is in the occupational earnings distribution for women. The differences have declined to close to zero; in some comparisons, employed black women do better than employed white women. Two limitations should be noted, however. Women, both black and white, still substantially lag behind white men who have a big income advantage even when differences in education are controlled. When attention shifts to one-parent families, black female heads of households have smaller incomes than do their white counterparts.

Unemployment continues to plague black communities. The black unemployment rate is twice that of whites and has remained at that multiple for 30 years. The unemployment rate among young black males is staggering: over 30 percent of those in the labor force. Perhaps of greater damage is the high percentage of young black males who are not considered to be looking for employment, those "out of the labor force." "Indeed, all indicators report that the employment situation of young blacks vis-a-vis that of whites has deteriorated since 1960" (Farley 1987).

The widely heralded advent of a sizable black middle class does not mean that many blacks do not suffer from great deprivation. Nor does improvement in black economic conditions mean that the differences between blacks and whites have evaporated. Jagged rather than smooth upward change is occurring; gains, continuing inequalities, and some retrogression coexist.

Social Conditions

Black fertility rates have declined very dramatically and are much closer to those of whites than in 1960 (O'Hare 1987). While the number of black teenage births has not increased, they are a larger percentage of all black births (O'Hare 1987; Furstenberg 1987). In part, the importance of these teenage births is due to what sociologist Cheryl Townsend Gilkes terms the "constrained fertility" of older and/or middle-class black women, who do not have children or have only one (Wilson 1985, 157). The concern about black teenaged mothers is not misplaced but has narrowed the analysis of what is occurring. Some analysts (Wilson 1987) partially attribute the large number of unmarried black mothers to a shortage of suitable males— men who are not in jail and are employed at a decent wage.

Housing has decidedly improved, partly because fewer blacks live in the rural South, but even there black housing has advanced. This overall gain may mask the deterioration of housing in many center-city areas and ignores the fact that blacks spend a higher proportion of their incomes for housing than whites (U.S. Bureau of the Census 1985, 732). The general housing gain has been accompanied by continuing and perhaps increasing residential segregation (Farley 1987).

Differences between blacks and whites in years of schooling have decreased markedly, especially for women (Farley 1987). A warning sign is that the percentage of blacks in colleges and universities has declined in recent years, possibly due to the contraction of funds available to minority students. The overall improvement in years of schooling of blacks is not as positive as it appears, for the gap between blacks and whites in school skills has not diminished and may have increased (Farley 1987). School segregation has been reduced in the South but not in the North.

What is to be made of these changes in economic and social conditions? A sizable slice of the black population has improved its economic position, but a large, perhaps larger, group of blacks is living under very inadequate conditions. American society is less occupationally segregated than in the past, but it is still residentially and (especially in the North) school segregated.

The Kerner commission on urban unrest, created by President Johnson in 1967, foresaw two societies, separate and unequal. While many newspaper editorials declared on the 20th anniversary of its final report that the prediction proved inaccurate, the inequalities experienced today by many blacks are very great. Indeed, it has recently become common to employ the term "underclass," introduced by the Swedish social scientist Gunnar Myrdal in the early 1960s, to refer unclearly and ambiguously to a center-city, largely minority population that is unemployed or out of the labor force, largely dependent on public assistance and/or crime for its wherewithal. The size of the underclass varies with every politician or social analyst; sometimes it comprises everyone on welfare, sometimes only those who have been persistently on welfare, and sometimes it refers only to those young black males who have no visible means of economic livelihood. While I believe that the size of the underclass is usually exaggerated, the existence of an uprooted, economically unattached, center-city population is a reflection of the failure of American society fully to integrate blacks into the new economy. To "integrate" does not mean only to overcome barriers of segregation but also to build processes for active inclusion of those who are excluded and marginal.

Racial Attitudes

If some of the markers and effects of discrimination have been reduced, that does not mean that discrimination and prejudice—barriers against full inclusion and participation—are down. The terrible episode of Howard Beach in New York City, the surprising recognition of the continuing existence of old-time segregation in Forsythe County, Georgia, and civilian and police violence against blacks as blacks, force the realization that the old virulent racism has not been eradicated. While certainly less widespread and evident than before, it still exists. Despite public opinion polls that show that most Americans do not favor it, prejudice and discrimination against blacks still persist in small and personal ways (in what historian Joseph Boskin terms "genteel" or covert racism) and in the large and institutionalized ways that operate to limit opportunities for blacks and other minorities.

The continuation of residential segregation, especially in the North, indicates that discrimination and prejudice are still alive. The gentrification of city neighborhoods, which pushes out low-income blacks, is an illustration of institutional racism in that its results are not due to prejudice but to the operation of economic processes. Gentrification drives up housing prices, forcing blacks to lose their communities and to face higher rents in the neighborhoods still available to them.

A new form of racial denigration has appeared in recent years. It is not racist in the sense that the term has been used. Rather than regarding blacks (or other minorities or women) as inferior, the charge is that they receive preference in hiring, promotion, and admission to universities and professional schools on the basis of their race (or gender). The feeling that is conveyed is that of resentment at the "unfair advantage" that they are presumably accorded because of affirmative action pressure. In some cases there is an intellectual tone to the resentment, in the argument that presumably meritocratic rules that formerly prevailed are now undermined; in others, there is a more direct condemnation or rejection of the new competition for access to scarce places. How damaging this attitude is to blacks is uncertain, but clearly it does not contribute to their sense of inclusion in mainstream America.

A process of exclusion underlies the inequalities that blacks experience, which is likely to bear heavily on them—economically, socially, and physically.

Health Differences

Health is a key indicator of well-being, and health statistics a measure of both progress and continuing inequalities. The health of blacks has improved considerably but inequalities between blacks and whites are still significant.

Mortality Differences. Black longevity has certainly increased, but a 50 percent difference remains in adjusted death rates for blacks and whites (Manton, Patrick, and Johnson 1987). If blacks had the same death rates as whites, 59,000 black deaths a year would not occur (Savage, McGee, and Oster 1987). Infant mortality in 1984 was almost twice as frequent among blacks as whites (*New York Times* 1987); this difference is not completely attributable to more young black mothers. Except for stomach cancer, the cancer survival rate of blacks is lower than that of whites (Andersen, Mullner, and Cornelius 1987).

That considerable progress has been made (and presumably could be made) is revealed in the relative change in mortality rates in the Carolinas between 1900 and 1940. In the earlier year, black mortality rates were 40 percent higher in the more urban northern state; by 1940, the New York State black mortality rate was at least 25 percent lower than that of the more rural Carolinas (Ewbank 1987). Various influences were involved, but improved housing, water supply, and other public measures in New York undoubtedly contributed to the absolute and relative decline in mortality rates.

Morbidity Differences. Blacks have more undetected diseases than whites, and black children may be in worse health than white children (Andersen, Mullner, and Cornelius 1987). The incidence of low-weight births (and their attendant difficulties) are almost twice as frequent among blacks as whites. This difference, as with infant mortality, is not completely attributable to more young black mothers (*New York Times* 1987). Older blacks suffer from more functional limitations than older whites, a situation of "accelerated" or "unequal" aging, which is associated with poverty, low education, and low-level occupations (Gibson and Jackson 1987). At the young end of the age ladder, black children seem in worse health than whites (Andersen, Mullner, and Cornelius 1987).

Self-report data indicate that 50 percent more blacks than whites are likely to regard themselves as only in fair or poor health (Schlesinger 1987). Blacks report more frequently that they feel "little" satisfaction with their health and physical conditions. Yet, there is more undetected disease among blacks than whites (Andersen, Mullner, and Cornelius 1987). While whites report more acute conditions, blacks report more chronic conditions (Manton, Patrick, and Johnson 1987). The statement that "differentials in health between blacks and whites are pervasive and long-standing, despite recent advances in black life expectancy" (Manton, Patrick, and Johnson 1987) summarizes what the morbidity and mortality data record.

To be poor *and* black is to run the risk of ill health; those who are black alone share the same health risks.

Use of Facilities. Medicaid has made a difference in access to and use of physicians and hospitals. Differences in utilization (as measured by visits to physicians) between blacks and whites has been eliminated. A further indication of the importance of financing mechanisms to provide access to and use of medical care is that poor blacks with health coverage make twice as many visits to physicians as do poor uncovered blacks (Davis et al. 1987).

Nonetheless, some important differences persist. Whites receive more skilled nursing home care than blacks, although the differences are decreasing (Davis et al. 1987). Blacks have a lower cancer survival rate than whites, except for stomach cancer (Andersen, Mullner, and Cornelius 1987).

Despite Medicaid, 22 percent of blacks are without any medical insurance coverage, compared to 15 percent of whites (Long 1987). Furthermore, in terms of physician contact, the factors of emergency room and hospital treatment are almost twice as important among blacks as whites (U.S. Bureau of the Census 1985, 105).

While the number of black physicians has increased, the rate of increase is diminishing. The fear is that the number of black physicians will not expand as a percentage of all physicians as market pressures become more significant (Schlesinger 1987) and financial aid to black student physicians does not expand. Since black physicians are more likely to serve black patients than do white physicians, this limitation could prove important (Hanft and White 1987).

The utilization issue has three important components: (1) Does medical care make a difference? An influential survey (Levine, Feldman, and Elinson 1982) argues the importance of medical attention. The improvement in the survival rates of low-weight babies is attributed to advances in hospital care, not to other conditions (Starr 1986). (2) Will blacks, and especially the black poor, take advantage of opportunities for care? Again, surveys show that when poor individuals are provided services that are accessible and appear to them to be useful they will be used, undermining the notion of underutilization of services by the uneducated or resistant poor (Riessman 1974). (3) Do finance and delivery systems affect utilization? A strong conclusion is that they "have played a critical role in improvements in health and access to care" (Davis et al. 1987).

The clear inference is that health conditions of blacks and the poor can be influenced by governmental actions. The distribution of medical resources relative to need affects causality and successful treatment (Baquet and Ringen 1987; Savage, McGee, and Oster 1987). General

economic gains, the reduction of barriers to blacks, and governmental
programs including occupational health regulations (Robinson 1987)
have improved the health situation of blacks. Some important differences
still persist. Black mortality and morbidity could be reduced by further
government-sponsored economic and health programs.

Interpretations

Studies reported in this volume show that racial differences in health
exist; numerous investigations report that class or income level influence
health conditions. Surprisingly few analyses try to discern whether
race is related to health conditions when differences in income levels
are controlled. Studies that have made this type of cross-tabulation
point to the significance for health of being black, even at higher
income levels.

In Oakland, California, a comparison of age-specific mortality rates
in poverty and nonpoverty areas shows that differences between blacks
are much less than between whites. Improved housing, a lower concentration of poor people, and more income seem to have less effect
on blacks than on whites (Haan, Kaplan, and Camacho 1987, 994).

A study of stress found its severity highest in lower-class blacks
and lowest in middle-class whites. This result would confirm the
importance of class factors, but an additional comparison points to
the significance of racial experience: middle-class blacks and lower-
class whites had similar levels of stress (Dohrenwend and Dohrenwend
1970, 132ff.). For a contrary interpretation, see Neighbors (1987).

We turn from the limited data on the important question of whether
race as well as class is important in health conditions to interpretations
of why black and white health differences persist despite distinct
improvements in black health. Five sets of explanations are examined:
biological, cultural, economic, social, and service.

Biology

Sickle cell anemia is often cited as a genetic factor among blacks.
But such genetic influences would by themselves not explain higher
mortality and morbidity rates for particular disease conditions (Wilkinson
and King 1987). A somewhat more compelling argument is that

certain black genetic characteristics conduce toward disease. But if such biological influences were important, they would interact with economic, social, or psychological situations to produce effects (Manton, Patrick, and Johnson 1987).

It is difficult to explain black women's pronounced gains in health without introducing nonbiological influences. Nor would it be easy to contend that black health could not be further improved because it has met the limits placed by genetic factors. For example, "there does not appear to be any inherent biological reason for the differences in cervical cancer rates between blacks and whites" (Baquet and Ringen 1987). Extending this point to other diseases and afflictions, we need to rethink health policy in broader than strictly medical terms. The cloudiness of the concept of race and the many genetic strains among American blacks make purely biological explanations questionable (Wilkinson and King 1987).

Culture

Cultural explanations of health problems have even reached the extreme concept of "health criminals." Blacks and others, because they do not take proper care of themselves (e.g., poor diet, lack of exercise, homicide) are indicted as the producers of their sad fate, driving up medical expenditures and exacting tribute from the careful healthy. Certainly, a healthy life is in large measure produced by what people do for themselves, but not completely. It is too easy to blame a group's behavior rather than to look for broader or deeper causes and outcomes. For example, the higher incidence of low-weight births among blacks is sometimes attributed to the greater number of black births to teenage mothers; examination of the data shows that older black women still have a greater percentage of low-weight births than older white women (Pear 1987). Although possible biological differences have not been studied sufficiently to be ruled out categorically, cultural influences are more likely to be important, but not in the simplistic way implied in the teenage mother explanation.

Where cultural influences might be significant, the questions become: Why the pattern? What maintains it? Since not all practices of one generation are exhibited in the next, continuity has to be explained rather than taken for granted (Wilkinson and King 1987). In the case of black and white health differences, the implication is that blacks do not behave in ways that are as conducive to health as do whites. The further implication is that conditions for blacks and whites are the same and that health differences are due to malperformance on the part of blacks (Miller, Riessman, and Seagull, 1988.) Take the greater percentage of teenage births among blacks that receives so much attention. Furstenberg (1987) explains that delaying parenthood has little payoff for blacks who suffer from "a despair of future opportunity." Circumstance as well as a presumed cultural implanting have to be considered.

A cultural explanation does not adequately reveal the dynamics of at least one health hazard, particularly important for blacks, which seems particularly suited for such an explanation—the high incidence of obesity. The continuation of eating habits of a poor childhood that relied on cheap, fattening food; work and family tensions that make planned, diet-conscious eating difficult; inadequate incomes that reduce possibilities and choices; a low sense of destiny control; and limited knowledge are all implicated in obesity. Even in this most personal of behavior, simply relying on an explanation in terms of habit and attitudes may be inadequate. Nor does the cultural approach lead to a comprehensive strategy for dealing with the issue (Susser, Watson, and Hopper 1985, 255).

Economic Factors

"To be a poor man is hard, but to be a poor race in a land of dollars is the very bottom of hardships" (DuBois 1961 [1903], 20). Black and white disparities in economic conditions contribute to health differentials despite black gains. Since a much larger and very sizable slice of blacks are poor, economic conditions and their ramifications undoubtedly adversely affect black health. Inadequate incomes affect many aspects of daily life that impinge on health. These range from housing problems (e.g., rat-infested neighborhoods and overcrowding, which quicken the spread of communicable diseases), malnutrition, the stress of struggling to make ends meet, and dangerous jobs. Jobs and housing conditions may expose blacks to certain cancers to a much greater extent than whites (Manton, Patrick, and Johnson 1987; Robinson 1987).

The emphasis on improvements in economic gains for blacks ignores the possibility that early deprivation can affect later health states.

Nutritional deprivation of children during World War I affected their health, especially of women, in later life (Titmuss 1951). Recent advances in material circumstances of blacks may not overcome the effect of earlier life experiences. With perhaps one-half of black children under the age of 6 living in poverty, this current deprivation may maintain later health differences, even if many of these children later improve their economic conditions.

Social Explanations

The problem is not only that of poverty but of economic and social inequalities associated with race. A British study provides a suggestive line of thought: A pronounced difference in mortality risk exists between high- and low-level members of the white-collar civil service. Both groups had secure tenure, relatively good pay, and fringe benefits. The author's point is that hierarchy produces tensions and stresses even where individuals seem somewhat similarly situated (Hart 1986). For blacks in the United States the sense of economic inequality, social distance, discrimination and hierarchy—of not being accorded full equality—is undoubtedly strong and persisting (Williams 1987). Racial discrimination probably "exacerbates the mental health-damaging effects of poverty status among blacks" (Neighbors 1987).

An older observation is still relevant: almost any encounter, at whatever level, with "the machinery for administering justice is a confrontation (for blacks) with a hostile environment and represents a potential stress situation above and beyond that which normally exists for whites" (Teele 1970, 237). This contention is probably still relevant and for a larger sphere than the justice system (Schlesinger 1987; Manton, Patrick, and Johnson 1987).

The concept of "endemic stress" (Fried 1982) is useful in thinking about the experience of blacks. This term emphasizes the long-run, continuing burdens, such as prolonged unemployment, and their consequences for those who have to cope with them. "Economic hardships, frustrated aspirations, chronic insecurity about jobs, frequent disruption of social ties are all features of the lives of the working class and the poor" (Susser, Watson, and Hopper 1985, 254). The experiences of poverty and inequality and uncertainty about how one is perceived because of one's race is certainly a type of continuing, prolonged stress. Such stress not only makes its victims susceptible to acute illnesses but also harms them socially. They suffer "role contraction," a limitation of the range of roles that they are able to carry out in daily life. For example, the constrained fertility of middle-class black women shows the pressures on black women and implicitly on black men as well. Since many blacks suffer the endemic stress that is produced by low income as well as overt and covert racism, motivational problems and narrowed social roles are likely to be exhibited.

In the health area, then, the call for individuals to change to more positive health practices may not be effective among blacks because the shift requires exploration of new roles, norms, and practices, as well as access to facilities, information, and support: "Maladaptive patterns of coping . . . and hazardous forms of consumption . . . can be seen to reflect the molding of social and cultural life by contemporary economic (and race) relations" (Susser, Watson, and Hopper 1985, 255–56).

A more specific influence on blacks may be widespread and disturbing uprooting and resettlement. Although the black population of center-city areas is declining, it may be that new blacks are moving in as long-time residents move out. The data on this point are uncertain and O'Hare's (1987) data cannot be utilized for testing this hypothesis. If true, the new residents may experience heavy pressures in accommodating to a difficult set of center-city circumstances and lack the social supports that would be helpful.

What is clear is that black neighborhoods suffer disruption resulting from urban renewal, abandonment, and arson. People are forced to move, severing networks of relationships, which are important for social well-being and which impinge on health, especially of the aged (Gibson and Jackson 1987).

Some investigators believe that racial discrimination is almost inevitable in a market economy (Schlesinger 1987; Manton, Patrick, and Johnson 1987), and infer that the stress resulting from discrimination continues to affect health. Many successful blacks point not only to limitations on their occupational progress but to stressful encounters around the job.

Medical Services

Despite noticeable improvements in health care for the poor and blacks resulting from Medicare and Medicaid, there is still less adequate medical attention for blacks than whites. The quality of health care is likely to be better in white areas, especially in access to physicians and hospitals. At every income level, blacks have substantially higher reliance on emergency room and outpatient departments for contacts with physicians than do whites. Indeed, racial differences are greater above the $10,000 annual income level than below it. Since 1980 blacks have experienced decreased medical attention as a result of federal cutbacks (Schlesinger 1987). If such patterns continue, black and white differences in health services will not be reduced.

While these influences offer substantial reasons why racial health differences have not disappeared despite substantial black gains, they do not satisfactorily explain the relative improvements in health and occupational conditions of black women. Black women do as well as white women in the labor market (Farley 1987). These gains are surprising in light of the high incidence of female-headed families, widespread obesity, teenage mothers, and other patterns that presumably do not contribute to a state of good health.

The general implications of this array of influences are that race is still an important factor in affecting health in the United States, and that the connection between race and health is not completely due to more frequent poverty conditions among blacks. Nor are black men and women moving in completely parallel ways.

Advancing the incomes of blacks is important in improving their health condition. But economic gain would not eliminate the black-white differential. The position of blacks as blacks would also have to improve. Further, to reduce the sizable number of black poor requires dealing with issues of race and inequality.

Policy

The burdens of knowledge are heavy. Knowing that health care can be improved and health inequalities reduced, it is immoral as well as economically wasteful to refuse to pursue these goals. For in the realm of health, rights to equal consideration and conditions are much less controversial than in the realm of employment. In the 1960s a president of the American Medical Association declared that health care was a privilege, not a right. Today, few would agree. There is now a consensus that blacks should have mortality and morbidity

rates much closer to those of whites. Much less agreement exists about
what to do to close the gaps.

Policy Criteria

In this section, we deal with three policy issues: creaming; universality
vs. targeting; and poverty or inequality reduction.

Creaming. The jagged progress characteristic of blacks can be partly
considered a result of creaming. Creaming is a policy, intentional or
unintended, of concentrating on the "easiest cases." Where the poor
or disadvantaged are involved, it improves the situation of the better-
off of the badly-off population—those least disadvantaged of a disadvantaged group. The expectation is that as each layer moves up,
those worse off gradually become the recipients of attention and will
then improve their situation.

Two assumptions are usually made: The methods which led to the
improvement among the better-off of the badly-off will be equally
useful for the worse-off who were left behind; the departure of the
better-off will not adversely affect the worst-off who remain. Both
assumptions are frequently, perhaps usually, wrong. The "last mile"
of social improvement—dealing with the worse-off of the disadvantaged—is more difficult than the earlier run and may require different
(and more extensive and expensive) interventions than those that helped
the better-off. The departure of the better-off changes the communities
that they leave, by concentrating problems, depriving them of some
leaders, weakening established institutions like churches, encouraging
sterotyping, caricaturing, and stigmatizing those left behind (e.g.,
"blaming the victim").

A creaming approach is individualistic; the imagery is of plucking
individuals from the arms of slothful poverty and "reducing poverty"
by decreasing the numbers who suffer from it but not changing the
conditions of those who remain poor nor challenging the forces that
structure poverty.

The experience of creaming helps to explain the dual feelings of
improvement and impoverishment among blacks; more of them now
enjoy a middle-class economic status and leave low-income center-
city neighborhoods, while conditions in the center-city locations
deteriorate.

Creaming has its merits and role but in today's circumstances it is inadequate if large numbers of poor blacks are to improve their condition. A broader collective effort is needed.

Poverty Reduction or Equality. Is the objective only to reduce poverty or unemployment among blacks because of the damage inflicted by that economic condition? Or is it to reduce economic inequalities between blacks and whites? In the latter case it would be unsatisfactory if black poverty rates were reduced while white household income increased and widened the gap between blacks and whites. Despite strong disagreements about the goal of economic equality, the dismay when economic inequality between blacks and whites is increasing indicates widespread agreement that these inequalities should be decreasing, even if complete equality is not the objective.

The consensus seems to be that poverty and inequality should not be disproportionately concentrated in an ascriptive group (i.e., one characterized by unchangeable characteristics like race, ethnicity, or gender), and should be dwindling rather than expanding. While this outlook is not as demanding as the right to equal health and health care, it demands reductions in inequalities as well as in poverty.

The underlying issue from the perspective of health policy is the strong likelihood that the persistence of economic, social, and political inequalities, even if black poverty is reduced, is injurious to the health of black Americans. This outlook treats equality as instrumental to health; the deeper question is, of course, the moral one of the nature of our obligations to one another.

Black and white equality may be insufficient in some health respects. The concept of "excess deaths" points to American mortality rates for certain diseases that exceed those of other nations. More effective interventions would be likely to lower American rates. If black rates were the same as white rates, that achievement would be unsatisfactory. The case of "excess deaths" illustrates a general point about equality: incorporating the excluded or disadvantaged into existing structures and improving their situation may be inadequate; the general situation for all may have to be improved. American medical care may have to face that challenge.

Universality or Targeting. The specific policy questions of how to improve the situation of blacks is part of the general policy debate about the competing principles of, on one hand, universality or comprehensiveness and, on the other, targeting, selectivity, or means-testing (Miller and Rein 1988). The first set of terms refers to programs available to (almost) all; by virtue of being a citizen, resident, or wage earner, one receives benefits from a program. In practice, no program is available to everybody, but Social Security and Medicare come closest to it. Age and past contributions of the former and age alone for the latter make one eligible for benefits. The targeted principle sets out conditions, usually of income inadequacy, that must be met in order to receive benefits. Eligibility is not on the basis of a noneconomic characteristic like age or sickness alone; rather, one must show need, the inability to provide for one's household, or to seek the needed service in the marketplace. Targeted programs like Medicaid are aimed at "needy" persons; untargeted or universal programs do not require that the individual or household demonstrate a lack of means to cover needs.

The advantage of universal-type programs available to (almost) all is that it builds support for a program because so many, especially politically potent nonpoor persons, benefit from it. Other gains are that it avoids stigmatization of beneficiaries, may promote social solidarity by establishing institutions and activities in which all are involved (at least at some point in their lives), and is likely to promote higher quality service because of the threat of widespread political discontent if quality is low or deteriorating.

The negative side, emphasized by economists in their benefit-cost calculations, is "leakage," diffusion of program resources, which reduces the "target efficiency" of a program because it aids those not in need. By providing to all rather than to only those with insufficient resources, less is available to low-income people who need more substantial aid. Public resources are "wasted" or "leaked" to those who could handle the burden of the costs that they face. By eliminating this diffusion and concentrating the public program on those with real resource needs, more funds would be available to those who need them.

The assumption is that cost savings resulting from targeting and removal of benefits from those who do not lack resources would lead to a practice where greater resources are expended on those who lack means. No iron law of policy or politics dictates that result.

Indeed, the argument against selectivity or targeting goes further and contends that participants in means-tested programs tend to be or feel stigmatized, so that some of the benefits to them of the program may be lost because of the burden of the disgrace. (The spread of the doctrine of "rights" or "entitlements" to even means-tested services may have reduced the dangers of self-feelings of stigma.) Determining eligibility and eliminating "abuses" by the ineligibles become a prime operation of targeted programs, leading to heavy and intrusive bureaucracy. Programs exclusively for the poor frequently become poor programs—hastily formulated or modified, inadequately funded, plagued by conflicting objectives of aiding the poor and regulating them as well, oversold as panaceas, incompetently and/or under-staffed, over-investigated and overevaluated, and political whipping objects. They tend to become politically unattractive programs, subject to easy abuse by politicians courting support by denigrating program participants and operations. Swift, deep progress is expected from targeted programs; beneficiaries are expected to "shape up" so that they soon do not need the aid that is provided. If not, programs are curtailed, punitive sanctions are imposed on those who do not seem to respond to what are regarded as incentives, or the should-be beneficiaries are bitterly critized. Poor people, accused of the inability to defer gratification (Miller, Riessman, and Seagull 1988), suffer from the short attention span and the low ability of legislators to live with delayed payoffs.

Programs that are seen as for the poor, the underclass, welfare cheats, and blacks in general face political, financial, and operational obstacles. The contrast between a universal program like Social Security and a targeted program like Aid to Families with Dependent Children (AFDC) is instructive: in the 1970s and 1980s Social Security payments more than kept up with inflation while AFDC suffered real income losses as many states did not increase benefits at all despite the high rise in prices.

An "on the other hand" exists. Special needs programs that are targeted for low-income persons can garner support that is unlikely to occur without attention to specific targets. A prominent example is the anachronism of food stamps. An East European policy expert told me of her amazement at the importance of food stamps for low-income people in the United States. Programs of that type, generalized from the venerable charitable food basket to national programs limiting how people could use public resources made available to them, had long been deemed undesirable and a target of elimination in her and other nations. They were seen as demeaning and controlling; their termination was regarded as great progress. In the United States, the food stamp program is regarded by many liberal policy makers as a way of getting Congress to augment funds for low-income people that would not be forthcoming if a plea for general increases in benefits for the poor were requested. Targeting needs can have a payoff.

The Reagan administration's objectives of drastic reductions in the levels of and eligibility for means-tested programs were largely unsuccessful. That is not to say that they achieved no significant reductions but they could not institute the depth of cuts that were initially believed could be attained. Considerable public and political pressure for maintenance of these programs blocked many Reagan efforts. While many people are critical of something called "the welfare state," they often recognize the usefulness of specific programs. This outlook can be explained in terms of the wide variety of participants in means-tested programs (Duncan et al. 1984). One-quarter of American households in a 10-year period used at least one of three means-tested programs (AFDC, food stamps, or Medicaid). Assuming that most of them felt that they benefited from the program and that each had at least one relative or friend who regarded the means-tested programs as having been of use in this instance, then over one-half of the population had a direct or near-direct positive contact with a program. A lot of people in different means-tested programs can become a political constituency of note.

This recital has moved back and forth in terms of arguments about universality and targeting. One complication is that considerations of both good policy and good politics are involved. Another is that a number of criteria for positive performance (e.g., level of resources, stigma, low bureaucracy, quality) are important. The result is that no simple rule can be induced, but I will offer a set of guidelines toward a policy of dealing with dilemmas rather than resting with the dilemmas of policy.

The first line of defense or improvement should be universal programs; they are likely to be better programs and to have strong political constituencies. The general principle is to make the needs of the black low-income population part of efforts to improve the situation of all or most Americans. Where that principle is inadequate, then targeting within the universal program can be a desirable and effective instrument. The outstanding example of the merger of these approaches is the Social Security program, which favors low-income participants. Their benefits are greater relative to their contributions than are those with higher income. Differences in preretirement wage incomes are narrowed in postretirement Social Security benefits. Elderly blacks who suffered from low wages during their working lives are somewhat improved relative to those who were in a better situation in the preretirement period. Yet, elderly blacks are not singled out for this gain, a situation which makes that advance more politically secure.

In practice, both universality and targeting have to be utilized. When and how are the issues. Universality is the policy of first resort, but such programs often cream, are more effectively utilized by those with more education and resources, provide inadequate resources for those in greatest need, and have only a limited effect on reducing economic inequalities. Universality reduces the likelihood of two Americas or two sets of institutions—one for the "disadvantaged," the other for those who are better off. It improves the political chances of maintaining and improving funding for programs and enhancing their quality. Nonetheless, universality has to be supplemented and sometimes supplanted by targeting on those who are disadvantaged and discriminated against.

Economic and Social Policies

Employment is a prime area for improvement of the situation of blacks—more and better jobs and a more effective upgrading of existing jobs are all needed. Following the approach just discussed, the first step is an expanding economy that produces more jobs and good jobs at that. Blacks do better in an expanding than in a contracting economy. An effective macroeconomic policy that stimulates the economy is an important first step. At issue within job growth is the quality of jobs produced. Many of the new jobs of the 1970s and 1980s have been low-paying, part-time, and devoid of fringe benefits; many of the good blue-collar jobs in mass-production industries have disappeared.

An increase in jobs, especially good jobs, does not assure that blacks will get them. Affirmative action, to which we shall return, is one route. Encouraging black entrepreneurship is another. But education, training, improved transportation, and child care are of greater importance in helping blacks to move into good jobs in greater numbers.

The current emphasis on higher standards in public education may worsen the schooling of many poor and black children if particular effort is not put into improving their learning. Federal aid to education has diminished; the downward cycle should be reversed. The Elementary and Secondary Education Act, which provides funding to school districts

with many low-income children, should be better funded and strengthened to insure that the funds are spent in ways that benefit low-
income students.

A difficulty within the dual pressures on schools today—pressures
toward "excellence" as well as on general learning and vocational
preparation—is that schools for the poor, especially the black poor,
may become so heavily vocationalized that students learn little of the
world around them. If the vocational training does not lead to a good
job and provides few adaptable skills, then poor blacks will be doubly
handicapped—ill-prepared for employment and uninformed about significant matters. And, if they fail to measure up to "excellence," they
will drop out or be pushed out of school.

The United States lacks a comprehensive, accessible, well-funded
system of worker training and development like the permanent or
recurrent education schemes of France and Sweden. We have community
colleges, adult education programs, and nationally funded and state
and locally operated job training programs. They do not add up to
a national program with priorities and direction. A comprehensive
national program is needed with specific targeting to improve the
employment prospects of those who are more difficult to place. At
the same time, access to higher education should be facilitated by
expanding aid and loan programs for low-income students. Where
higher education is concerned, targeted financial help is not stigmatizing
nor politically unattractive.

Affirmative action has a definite role to play, but it is certainly
not the most important item on the economic agenda for blacks.
Without affirmative action, many educated and trained blacks would
not have attained middle-class positions. Indeed, they might not have
been willing to seek further education and training if they did not
believe that affirmative action would open up positions that had been
closed to their parents. Despite the grievances that they are still not
making it to the upper echelons of business and professional life,
there is little doubt that without affirmative action some blacks would
not be in the outer reaches of executive suites. Affirmative action has
also been important in opening many blue-collar and white-collar jobs
which had previously been barred to blacks. It has stimulated some
upgrading of positions for blacks.

A charge against it is that it has not improved the situation much
for those blacks with limited schooling and training and low initial

job motivation and capacity. To benefit the black poor, not only does affirmative action need to be strengthened but programs going beyond it need to be devised. For example, low unemployment rates can increase the demand for workers—including black workers—reduce entry qualifications, and promote on-the-job training. Or, the promotion of local economic development in poor black neighborhoods can improve the accessibility of jobs and improve community life.

"Workfare" and "welfare reform" are current buzzwords for efforts to improve jobs and job training among those poor who are on AFDC. While about one-half of the AFDC households are white, AFDC is politically regarded as a program dealing with black mothers and their children. The theme of many of these proposals is to turn welfare into a selective employment and training program. It will not be possible to move everyone into decent jobs that pay more than AFDC and provide medical insurance: some mothers should not or cannot work; enough jobs are not available; it is very expensive to provide the support systems of child care and transportation; good training and effective induction into work settings require quality supervision. Proposals are frequently made more attractive by grossly underestimating these costs. Creating jobs is not an easy or a cheap task. The result is that many programs produce results that fall far below expectations and the women receiving AFDC are blamed for the failures.

There is certainly a role for such programs; many women on AFDC are searching for ways into the labor market. Quality programs are needed, and mandatory requirements are not likely to lead to quality programs. Removing the threat of losing Medicaid benefits if one moves to a job would be of great help. Overcoming the appalling bureaucratic nightmare that is the daily experience of poor people who have to seek aid from diverse public programs would be an enormous boon. Furthermore, public programs should be conducted so as to promote, not thwart, self-help and community development. But self-help should not be seen as an alternative to government aid; the aid itself is needed. How it is provided is the issue.

Even with a successful welfare-type program, direct aid or transfers to low-income people would still be necessary. Again, if universal programs reduced the need for targeted transfers, the poor would benefit. Improving Social Security benefits for low-wage earners would benefit the aged black poor without invoking a special system for them. If unemployment insurance payments were weighted so that not only previous wage income but the number of members in the household influenced the benefit, some large unemployed white and black families would gain. Or, if all families with children received a family or child allowance, that would be of aid to single-parent and low-income families without singling them out. If it were coupled with elimination or reduction of the income tax deduction for children, income inequalities would be reduced. Or, a modified version of the child allowance would provide (taxable) benefits to all single-parent households; the state or federal government would exact a payment from the absent parent but would not reduce aid to the single-parent family if it failed to get the payment from the absent parent. The aim of these proposals is to eliminate the bureaucracy of means-testing and the operation of separate systems that segregate a particular population. Instead, it aims to have one system that benefits all households with children.

Health Services

Unfortunately, only two approaches to extend medical insurance coverage are on the current congressional agenda (Long 1987). Both are limited. One would nationally mandate that employers provide a minimum package of medical insurance for their employees. A difficulty with this approach is that those who are unemployed or out of the labor force would not benefit nor would those sporadically employed if mandatory coverage applied only to those who have been with an employer for some period. A second consideration is whether all firms would be covered or only those with a minimum number of employees. It is quite likely that poorer blacks work in very small enterprises and would not be covered by the minimum-worker requirement. A third issue is the content of that mandated package and to what extent it meets the needs of blacks. A fourth point is that larger, better-off firms that are likely to be unionized have sizable medical benefits. While a mandatory program will reduce the gaps in medical coverage resulting from employment in differently situated firms, inequalities in access to health care will continue.

The alternative proposal is to extend Medicaid to more people by raising income eligibility limits (and continuing for some time Medicaid coverage for those who were on AFDC and left the rolls for a job). This approach makes sense because Medicaid in the 1980s has been serving a smaller percentage of the poor than in the early 1970s (Starr 1986). The negative side is that by extending Medicaid we maintain a dual system of medical insurance coverage, which provides lower-quality service for the non-aged poor compared to older persons covered by Medicare and those at all ages with private insurance. Further, state variations in Medicaid provisioning would continue, so that access to health care by the poor would still depend on where they lived. Expenditure patterns are important as well. Two-thirds of Medicaid spending goes for the medical needs of the aged and disabled (Starr 1986); the more ordinary medical needs of lower-income people, especially blacks, may not be met by extension of Medicaid, particularly if the extension of coverage to more people leads to limits on the services available.

Each proposal does take an important step toward increasing medical access for lower-income citizens. Neither meets the objective of a universally based system especially targeted to aid the poor. Neither assures that hospitals and physicians would be easily available to blacks in center-city areas. Neither deals with primary and preventive health care.

Since national health insurance appears remote, the highest, somewhat realistic, hope in the next years would be to move to mandatory employer provision of a medical insurance package, to extended Medicaid eligibility, and to expanded Medicaid services. In addition, the accessibility issue could be partially met by increasing the number of black physicians through scholarships and start-up loans and by expanding incentives for physicians to locate in low-income areas.

The community health centers (CHCs) established by the Office of Economic Opportunity in the 1960s should be increased to the grand scale originally envisaged (1,000 centers serving 25 million persons), and become key health providers and educators in lower-income areas. Although they never received the acclaim accorded health maintenance organizations, they had "a decidedly positive impact" (Starr 1986). The CHCs could become the primary and preventive health care providers in black low-income communities and be closely related to community life and to school health education programs. With the extension of health insurance coverage, the targeted element is less likely to experience diminished quality.

The attention to improving financial access to medical personnel and hospital care draws concern away from the advancement of public health measures (e.g., reduction of air and water pollution, improved regulation of food and drugs, reduction of work injuries and diseases, elimination of dangerous dumps). Public health measures are particularly important for lower-income citizens. Good health is not only a result of what physicians and hospitals do for us, or what we do for ourselves; our environments, broadly viewed, are implicated in our health status.

A final, difficult-to-resolve issue is how much should be spent on health measures to improve health and how much on improving economic and social conditions that affect health. Class and race data point inevitably to the conclusion that improving incomes and social conditions would enhance the health of blacks, especially low-income blacks. Even those who espouse the importance of personal health practices (e.g., quitting smoking, good nutrition, exercise) have to question whether improved incomes or social conditions will do more for health outcomes than medical interventions or health education. It is difficult to change practices without changing circumstances. Is the way to improve the health of blacks through the economy and society rather than through the clinic, hospital, or health maintenance organization? Reducing economic and social inequalities may be the road to the achievement of individual health and a healthy society.

Class Perspectives

Constructing policies to deal with the situation of blacks in contemporary America is complicated by the tension between opposing sensibilities: Many whites contend that much, perhaps too much, has been done to aid blacks; many blacks believe that white America has refused to produce equality and end racism. That division is not easily reconciliable.

A basic step, though only a step, is greater clarity about what America is like. In recent years, the confusion about race and class has grown and makes policy difficult to construct and implement. In this section we discuss the stunted nature of the class structure of the United States and some of its implications for blacks.

In the 1980s a new version of American social stratification was enunciated by politicians and media pundits: there was "the poor," living below the official poverty line, and then there was everyone else, "the middle class." Although this two-class view is something of an improvement over the 1950s perspective that "everyone is now middle class," it blocks understanding of the nation.

It may be unclear what a "middle-class standard of living" is in terms of income, assets, economic security, future social mobility, and social standing, but there can be little doubt that a family of four with an income below the national median family income, relying upon two wage earners, is not living a middle-class American life. Such families are scraping by and likely to be exceedingly fearful of what a layoff or illness could do to their level of living. At best, they slide in and out of middle-class conditions. Economic insecurity is not restricted to a few and middle-class life is changing dramatically if fear of the future becomes a dominating motif for many who are regarded as in this privileged sector. At the upper end of the "middle class" are those who make better than four times the median income, in professional, entrepreneurial, and managerial occupations, or through speculation, are they to be regarded as in the same economic and social circumstances as those at or just above the median family income level? Quantity thus becomes quality and produces a profound difference in everyday life and outlook.

The two-class approach also provides a misleading aura of general equality. We all share basically similar economic and social perches and outlooks—that of the middle class—except for those unfortunates, some of whom are lamentably authors of their fate, labeled "the poor" by official statistical measurements. This view obscures the economic and social processes that sort people, underestimates the divisions— economic, social, and political—in American life and constrains the ways in which we think of people and policy. For if we are all pretty much the same, except for that small but disturbing group of misfits or unfortunates, then national policies will benefit those in the one middle-class boat as it is swept along by the rising tide of economic growth. But if the United States is not a simple two-class society in which only a relatively few are classed as poor, then rising tides unequally or even adversely affect people.

The sharp split in economic conditions and social outlook conveyed by the two-class approach affects blacks. First, it portrays low-income blacks as different from the rest of us, needing the whip to push and keep them in work. Some writers loosely include all those officially poor or on welfare as members of "the underclass," a category that connotes a reluctance to do "honest" work, an individual pathology, and social disorganization. The effect is to focus attention on what is wrong with those so labeled rather than on broader economic and social processes that foster what is thought of as "antisocial behavior." Certainly, such behavior exists, but the way to deal with it is not simply through a moral uplift motif, though that has an important role. Circumstances are implicated and have to be changed.

Second, it encourages divisiveness within black life. The enlarged "talented tenth" of educated middle-class blacks whom DuBois envisioned as providing leadership is encouraged to separate itself from the black poor, while it is castigated for being alone in benefiting from the civil rights legislation of the 1960s. The role of the so-called "black bourgeoisie" has long been questioned; the development of good employment for educated blacks outside black communities changes many things; but the curious misunderstanding of class changes in America makes it even more difficult for nonpoor blacks to play a constructive part in the current scene. The turning of many black organizations toward major concern for the black poor and to a rethinking of national and organizational policies may overcome some of these difficulties.

Race Questions

The issue of race does more than linger in the experience of America. True, profound changes have occurred in the four decades since Myrdal published *An American Dilemma* (Myrdal 1944), a two-volume account of how blacks were segregated, impoverished, and deprived of civil rights, and that this was widely acceptable despite the American creed of equality and freedom. At the attitudinal level, most whites do not express support for a separate, segregated world for blacks. But many are unwilling to change their own lives and outlooks so that blacks could enter a truly open, colorblind society. Today's "white American dilemma" is that to create a more equal society requires at least disturbing some ongoing behavior and important institutions. The hope of the early 1960s that the United States could be transformed dramatically on the cheap and without white dislocation cannot be resurrected today. Often, whites do not accept the changes that would make life different for blacks. We are often unwilling to inconvenience or burden ourselves to facilitate the entrance of blacks into the mainstream. Partly, it is because of the fear of job competition or increased taxes; partly, it is because we do not enter into full intellectual and social acceptance of blacks. Sometimes, the belief is that enough has been done or blacks should do more for themselves. The result is a reluctance to become involved with the major problem of the twentieth century. Another problem is the false belief that all of the American poor are black and all blacks are of the underclass, a misconception that angers blacks and confuses our understanding of poverty and race issues.

There is the "black American dilemma" which was not the focus of Myrdal's book. Characteristically, it concerns the issues of integration or separatism. In the immediate post-World War I years with the widespread appeal of Garveyism, the choice seemed to be either to return to Africa or to remain in the segregated, discriminatory United States, hoping for a day of deliverance. More recently, the form the issue took was whether to build black communities and institutions and gain a high degree of self-sovereignty—what some thought of as "black power"—or to fight for desegregation and integration. These two sets of aims do not always diverge in practice but in ideology they appear as polar opposites.

While the choice may pose a dilemma for blacks, they do not have full control over what happens. In practice, they have achieved some desegregation but not full elimination of barriers, some increased influence over their local institutions but with grossly inadequate resources and very limited power.

The desegregation-separatism issue remains, though less forcefully than in the 1960s and 1970s, as a new-old controversy emerges over the question of the relative importance of class and race. Is race much less a barrier to progress? Is the lower-class status of many blacks the challenge? Or is race a persistent obstacle for blacks and still *the* problem for American society?

The class versus race issue is frequently debated as if it were a proposition about economic and social mobility. But it is essentially a political-value issue. The way that the class perspective usually plays out—it need not be used this way but largely has had this cast—is that it *is* possible to make big changes in black conditions without deep changes in American structures and life. In this view, inserting blacks into the American mainstream through education and training does not require great shifts in the way that things are done in the United States.

The race approach explicitly declares the issues are deeper. Bringing blacks into the economic and social mainstreams is not a simple process of education and training. At the level of means, the task is complicated by race, its history, and its present impact on both whites and blacks. Changes in American life—significant changes—are needed to bring about the full equality that is part of the American Dream. Such a transformation can only occur if American institutions are transformed. In the near term, the issues are about overt, covert, and institutional racist practices. In the never-ending quest, the challenge is how to construct an equal society that does not require the submergence of a group's life and consciousness into the dominant group's way of life.

These are issues that seem far removed from the issue of differences in health and health care between blacks and whites. But health cannot be considered apart from other dimensions of life, especially in areas where public policy plays a large role.

DuBois (1961[1903], 139) saw many of the issues that we have discussed, and I conclude with a passage that ends his essay "Of the Sons of Master and Man":

> It is not enough for the Negroes to declare that color prejudice is the sole cause of their social condition, nor for the white South to reply that their social condition is the main cause of prejudice. They both act as reciprocal cause and effect, and a change in neither alone will bring the desired effect. Both must change, or neither can improve to any great extent. The Negro cannot stand the present reactionary tendencies and unreasoning drawing of the color-line indefinitely without discouragement and retrogression. And the condition of the Negro is ever the excuse for further discrimination. Only by a union of intelligence and sympathy across the color-line in this critical period of the Republic shall justice and right triumph,

> "That mind and soul according well,
> May make one music as before,
> But vaster."

References

Andersen, R.M., R.M. Mullner, and L. Cornelius. 1987. Black-White Differences in Health Status: Methods or Substance? *Milbank Quarterly* 65 (Suppl. 1):72–99.
Baquet, C., and K. Ringen. 1987. Health Policy: Gaps in Access, Delivery, and Utilization of the Pap Smear in the United States. *Milbank Quarterly* 65 (Suppl. 2):322–47.

Davis, K., M. Lillie-Blanton, B. Lyons, F. Mullan, N. Powe, and D. Rowland. 1987. Health Care for Black Americans: The Public Sector Role. *Milbank Quarterly* 65 (Suppl. 1):213–48.

Dohrenwend, B.S., and B.P. Dohrenwend. 1970. Class and Race as Status-related Sources of Stress. In *Social Stress,* ed. S. Levine and N.A. Scotch. Chicago: Aldine.

DuBois, W.E.B. 1961 [1903]. *The Souls of Black Folk.* Greenwich, Conn.: Fawcett.

Duncan, G., et al. 1984. *Years of Poverty, Years of Plenty: The Changing Economic Future of American Workers and Families.* Ann Arbor: Institute for Social Research, The University of Michigan.

Ewbank, D.C. 1987. History of Black Mortality and Health before 1940. *Milbank Quarterly* 65 (Suppl. 1):100–28.

Farley, R. 1987. The Quality of Life for Black Americans Twenty Years after the Civil Rights Revolution. *Milbank Quarterly* 65 (Suppl. 1):9–34.

Fried, M. 1982. Endemic Stress: The Psychology of Resignation and the Politics of Scarcity. *American Journal of Orthopsychiatry* 4–19.

Furstenberg, F.F., Jr. 1987. Race Differences in Teenage Sexuality, Pregnancy, and Adolescent Childbearing. *Milbank Quarterly* 65 (Suppl. 2):381–403.

Gibson, R.C., and J.S. Jackson. 1987. The Health, Physical Functioning, and Informal Supports of the Black Elderly. *Milbank Quarterly* 65 (Suppl. 2):421–54.

Haan, M., G.A. Kaplan, and T. Camacho. 1987. Poverty and Health: Prospective Evidence from the Alameda County Study. *American Journal of Epidemiology* 1925, 6:989–98.

Hanft, R.S., and C.C. White. 1987. Constraining the Supply of Physicians: Effects on Black Physicians. *Milbank Quarterly* 65 (Suppl. 2):249–69.

Hart, N. 1986. Inequalities in Health: The Individual versus the Environment. *Journal of the Royal Statistical Society* 149(3):228–46

Levine, S., J. Feldman, and J. Elinson. 1982. Does Medical Care Do Any Good? In *The Handbook of Health Care and the Health Profession,* ed. D. Mechanic. New York: Free Press.

Long, S. 1987. Public versus Employment-related Health Insurance: Experience and Implications for Black and Nonblack Americans. *Milbank Quarterly* 65 (Suppl. 1):200–12.

Manton, K.G., C.H. Patrick, and K.W. Johnson. 1987. Health Differentials between Blacks and Whites: Recent Trends in Mortality and Morbidity. *Milbank Quarterly* 65 (Suppl. 1):129–99.

Miller, S.M., and M. Rein. 1988. Policy Dichotomies in Poverty

Programs. In *Poverty in America,* ed. L. Ferman, A. Haber, and J. Kornbluh. 3rd. ed. Ann Arbor: University of Michigan Press.

Miller, S.M., F. Riessman, and A. Seagull. 1988. Poverty and Self-Indulgence. In *Poverty in America,* ed. L. Ferman, A. Haber, and J. Kornbluh. 3rd. ed. Ann Arbor: University of Michigan Press.

Myrdal, G. 1944. *An American Dilemma.* New York: Harper Bros.

————. 1963. *Challenge to Affluence.* New York: Random House.

Neighbors, H.W. 1987. Improving the Mental Health of Black Americans: Lessons from the Community Mental Health Movement. *Milbank Quarterly* 65 (Suppl. 2):348–80.

New York Times. 1987. Birth in America: A Fact Sheet. June 26.

O'Hare, W.P. 1987. Black Demographic Trends in the 1980s. *Milbank Quarterly* 65 (Suppl. 1):35–55.

Pear, R. 1987. Poverty Rate Dips as the Median Family Income Rises. *New York Times,* July 31.

Riessman, C.K. 1974. The Use of Health Services by the Poor. *Social Policy* May/June: 41–49.

Robinson, J.C. 1987. Trends in Racial Inequality and in Exposure to Work-related Hazards, 1968–1986. *Milbank Quarterly* 65 (Suppl. 2):404–20.

Savage, D.D., D.L. McGee, and G. Oster. 1987. Reduction of Hypertension-associated Heart Disease and Stroke among Black Americans: Past Experience and New Perspectives on Targeting Resources. *Milbank Quarterly* 65 (Suppl. 2):297–321.

Schlesinger, M. 1987. Paying the Price: Medical Care, Minorities, and the Newly Competitive Health Care System. *Milbank Quarterly* 65 (Suppl. 2):270–96.

Starr, P. 1986. Health Care for the Poor: The Past Twenty Years. In *Fighting Poverty: What Works and What Doesn't,* ed. S.H. Danziger and D. H. Weinberg, 106–32. Cambridge: Harvard University Press.

Susser, M., W. Watson, and K. Hopper. 1985. *Sociology in Health.* New York: Oxford University Press.

Teele, J.E. 1970. Social Pathology and Stress. In *Social Stress,* ed. S. Levine and N.A. Scotch. Chicago: Aldine.

Titmuss, R. 1951. *Problems of Social Policy.* London: Her Majesty's Stationery Office.

U.S. Bureau of the Census. 1985. *Statistical Abstract of the United States: 1986.* 106th ed. Washington.

Wilkinson, D.Y., and G. King. 1987. Conceptual and Methodological Issues in the Use of Race as a Variable: Policy Implications. *Milbank Quarterly* 65 (Suppl. 1):56–71.

Williams, L. 1987. For the Black Professional, the Obstacles Remain. *New York Times,* July 14.

Wilson, W.J. 1985. The Urban Underclass in Advanced Industrial Society. In *The New Urban Reality,* ed. P. Peterson, 129–60. Washington: Brookings Institution.

———. 1987. *The Truly Disadvantaged: The Inner City, the Underclass and Public Policy.* Chicago: University of Chicago Press.